THE NEW
ENCYCLOPEDIA
OF FLOWER REMEDIES

By the Same Author

The Enclyclopaedia of Flower Remedies (with Amanda Cochrane)
The Principles of Vibrational Healing
The Healing Spirit of Plants
The Compendium of Flower Essences
Live Better: Flower Essences

Clare G Harvey is an internationally recognized authority on flower essences. She was trained by her grandmother, who was herself taught by Dr Edward Bach, creator of the famous Bach Flower Remedies. She helped her parents found one of the first truly holistic residential natural healing centres in the UK, winning the Daily Express Oscars for the best team of therapists.

Since her early years Clare was highly trained in healing, flower essences, yoga (teaching from the age of 18) and numerous other healing techniques including Chinese medicine. She was a consultant at The Hale Clinic and is currently consulting at the Centre for Complementary and Integrated Medicine in Upper Harley St., London. A teacher and lecturer, Clare started the first International Professional Flower Essence Training school in 1988.

Her *Encyclopaedia of Flower Remedies*, written with Amanda Cochrane, was the first authoritative work on the subject. Clare has her own range of flower essences, derived from the exotic flowers from the Far East, 'The Flowers of the Orient' specially designed for women to feel good about themselves, and has just launched an innovative range of skincare products ('Spirit of Beauty') incorporating essences from the Amazonian jungle. She is managing director of FlowerSense which is dedicated to integrating education within the retail market and has an educational website designed to inform and educate: www.flowersense.co.uk

To my wonderful son Alex, the Harveys, Bijal, Lynn, Deborah, Tiny, Jane, Margaret and Hetti for their patience and love. To Harsh and Anu for their invaluable help. To the late J Krishnamurti and Dr David Bohm for their friendship and influence in my life. To all the flower girls and boys that have shared the journey with me when being taught by the Flowers. To my Grandmother, who taught me the wonders of the remedies when I was young and continues to encourage me to explore further!

THE NEW
ENCYCLOPEDIA
OF FLOWER REMEDIES

The definitive practical guide to all flower remedies,
their making and uses

CLARE G. HARVEY

WATKINS PUBLISHING

LONDON

Distributed in the USA and Canada by Sterling Publishing Co., Inc.
387 Park Avenue South, New York, NY 10016

This edition first published in the UK and USA 2007 by
Watkins Publishing, Sixth Floor, Castle House,
75–76 Wells Street, London W1T 3QH

**The Author and Editor wish to thank Amanda Cochrane for her invaluable work
and contribution to *The Encyclopaedia of Flower Remedies* originally published by
Thorsons (an imprint of HarperCollins) in 1996, substantial passages of which have
been included in this current edition**

1 3 5 7 9 10 8 6 4 2

Designed by Jerry Goldie
Typeset by Dorchester Typesetting Group
Printed and bound in Great Britain

Library of Congress Cataloging-in-Publication Data Available

ISBN 13: 978-1-84293-178-3
ISBN 10: 1-84293-178-4

www.watkinspublishing.com

For information about custom editions, special sales, premium and
corporate purchases, please contact Sterling Special Sales
Department at 800-805-5489 or specialsales@sterlingpub.com

CONTENTS

LIST OF PLATES

ACKNOWLEDGMENTS

A big thank-you to all those in the world of flower essences for their generosity of spirit and support throughout this venture.

We would particularly like to thank the following for their continued support: Ian White (Australian Bush & White Light); Andreas Korte (Amazon, African, Cactus); Julian Barnard (Healing Herbs, Bach); Shabd-sangeet Khalsa (Dancing Light); Fred Rubenfeld (Pegasus); Tanmaya (Himalayan Enhancers); Philippe Deroide (Deva); Steve Johnson (Alaskan); Patricia Kaminski and Richard Katz (Flower Essence Society); Machaelle Small Wright (Perelandra); Vasudeva and Kadambii Barnao (Living Essences of Australia); Judy Griffin (Petite Fleur); Sabina Pettitt (Pacific); Drs Rupa and Atul Shah (Himalayan Aditi); Simon Lilly and Sue Griffin (Green Man); Cynthia Athina Kemp Scherer (Desert Alchemy); Arthur Bailey (Bailey); Lila Devi Stone (Masters); Marion Stoker (Findhorn); Ellie Webb (Harebell); Rose Titchner (Light Heart); Shelly Shiston & Debbie Sellwood (Purely Essences); Vivien Williamson and Jane Stevenson (Sun, Animal Essences); Laurence Harry (Aurora Borealis photo); Peter Aziz (Habundia Essences); Bram and Miep Zaalbergís (Bloesem Essences); Star Riparetti and Roger Valencia (Peruvian Essences); Colette Prideaux-Brune (Soundwave Essences) and Cathie Welchman (Hawaiian Essences).

Thanks also to Dr Masuaro Emoto (Messages from Water); Harry Oldfield and Erik Pelham for their invaluable input; to Gregory Valmis and Marion Bielby for their insight and input on Bach; to Zhi-xing Wang (Qigong Master); Burgs (Meditation Teacher); Peter Tadd (Clairvoyant Adviser); Vladimir Raipolov (Russian herbalist) for their words of wisdom; Maura McClean for her invaluable insights (spiritual advisor); to Michael Mann at Watkins publishing, and Susan Mears, our agent, for their faith and encouragement.

Special thanks to Dr Richard Gerber and Dr George Lewith for giving their valuable time to write the Foreword and the Preface.

Finally, to Dr Edward Bach, for being the father of the flower remedies, our inspiration, and for rekindling awareness of the healing powers of flowers.

Clare G Harvey

PREFACE

I am delighted to be asked to provide an updated preface to the second edition of Clare G Harvey's *Encyclopedia of Flower Remedies*. She has diligently updated this comprehensive text and it provides an up-to-date, thorough, exceptionally well researched resource for those patients and practitioners who are interested in flower essences.

In spite of their long history, flower essences began to be used by homoeopaths in the West in the 1920s. This was largely due to the excellent effective range of flower remedies initially developed by Edward Bach in the early part of this century. His painstaking research based on a combination of intuition and detailed case observation, has resulted in a now-rapidly expanding body of knowledge which will allow the practitioner to treat both physical and mental problems through the unique approaches offered by flower essences. These remedies provide a whole new dimension for medicine – in particular homeopathic medicine. They allow for the treatment of both mental and physical problems in a safe and well-judged manner.

The Encyclopedia represents a compilation of various flower remedies available throughout the world, their indications and the clinical experiences that have been used to define their use and support their prescription.

It is my hope that over the coming years more people will use these powerful treatments and more detailed evaluation will become available. At present our knowledge is largely empirical, based exclusively on the clinical observation of individual patients. I believe that it is possible to translate this body of knowledge into approaches that will allow its evaluation in more exacting scientific terms. From my own clinical experience I believe the flower essences offer a powerful approach to the treatment of illness, particularly mental symptoms. If this could be further established in a more scientific context then we may begin to see a real revolution in medical care.

Dr George Lewith, MA, DM, FRCP, MRCGP
The Centre for Complementary & Integrated Medicine
2006

FOREWORD

We are living during a unique period in human history. Over the past 50 years, science has discovered many ways of looking at the world and, in the process, has redefined the very nature of what it means to be human. Revolutionary discoveries in medical science have given us an understanding of the way in which the body works and how intricately linked the body and mind truly are. But a new breed of spiritual scientists has begun to explore the links between the body, the mind and the spiritual nature of human beings. Vibrational medicine is the evolving field of healing research that focuses on these links. Although the principles behind vibrational medicine are quite ancient, the development of modern technologies which can visualize and quantify the energetic nature of the links between body, mind and our spiritual anatomy are very new.

The concept that human beings are multidimensional energy systems is an idea that stems, in part, from the Einsteinian realization that matter and energy are dual expressions of the same universal substrate that makes up all things. Quantum physicists have begun to awaken to the concept that the subatomic particles that make up the entire universe, including people, are actually patterns of frozen energy and light. Many other scientists have begun to see the world in a similar light, having been led there by science instead of pure spirituality and intuition. We are literally beings of light and energy assembled in a way that is fundamentally hidden from our limited physical senses. The vibrational medicine perspective ascribes to this light/energy link by viewing humans as multi-dimensional beings consisting of far more than a physical brain and body. The new field of vibrational medicine is actually a fusion of science and spirituality which has defined the energy networks linking the physical body and its energetic substrates to the more rarefied world of spirit. Vibrational medicine views the world from the perspective of vibration and energy with an eye towards how this understanding of our energetic natures can lead to many new and wonderful forms of diagnosis and healing.

Our physical bodies are controlled by many biochemical cellular systems which are, in turn, finely tuned by subtle energy systems including the acupuncture meridian system and the chakra system. While our physical body is nurtured by physical nutrients and oxygen, it is also fed by subtle environmental energies such as *chi* and *prana* which we absorb through the meridian and chakra networks. These subtle energetic forms of nutrition, understood by the ancients of China and India, are just as important as food and water to sustaining life. The subtle energy networks also connect the physical body to another type of energy system – the etheric body – which is a holographic energy template that invisibly guides human growth and development. Scientific evidence for the existence of subtle energy systems is growing. Modern technology has begun to validate ancient wisdom in a marriage of science and spirituality the like of which has not been seen on this planet for thousands of years.

It is only through a fuller appreciation of a multidimensional model of human functioning that subtle energy therapies, such as flower essences, can be truly understood. Modern medicine has become rigid and locked into a mechanistic model of the body, and the model does not explain how subtle life energies can affect cellular machinery. It is only when one takes into account the larger picture of human beings from a newly evolving multidimensional perspective that flower essences as a healing modality begin to make sense. Flower essences do not work like drugs in which molecular patterns often bind to specialized receptors throughout the cells of the body. Instead they work by influencing the subtle energy structures that feed life energy into the body/mind. Flower essences modify energy flow through the acupuncture meridians, the chakras and the subtle bodies with the end result of affecting the very energetic patterns that influence consciousness.

The essences of flowers have been used in healing for hundreds (and possibly thousands) of years. Dr Edward Bach was one of the first modern pioneers of healing with flower essences. Bach was a medical practitioner as well as a psychic who experienced disturbing emotional patterns within himself when he was near a particular flower. Bach came to learn that taking an essence of the nearby flower would neutralize his psychically induced emotional disturbance. He discovered that the same flower essence would heal similar emotional patterns in others. Bach was among the first vibrational healers of the 20th century to realize how healing the emotions would contribute to the healing of any physical illness, regardless of the cause. It is in this regard, the energetic healing and repatterning of emotional energies, that flower essences have a wide spectrum of applications.

Since Dr Bach's pioneering work in the first half of the 20th century, flower essence usage has undergone a veritable explosion of interest. Working groups that study the effects of local flower essences have sprung up all over the world, from England and North America to the outbacks of Australia. The merging of healing traditions has also begun to occur as practitioners have learned to apply principles of acupuncture to healing with flower essences by applying them to specific acupoints on the body. The wide variety of flower essence applications in healing has become an entire subspecialty within vibrational medicine.

It is because of this renaissance of interest in flower essences that *The New Encyclopedia of Flower Remedies* is of great importance. Clare Harvey has performed an invaluable service by compiling the knowledge and wisdom of healing with flowers from around the world. It has been said that the answers to curing all of humanity's ills lie within nature. This book is an important step towards revealing the incredible healing wisdom within nature that we have only begun to discover. After all, modern medicine does not have all the answers to healing the afflictions of our techno-industrialized society. Perhaps the real answers to curing modern ailments exist within an exploration of our ancient past in order to synthesize a healing science of the 21st century.

I encourage you to read this book and experiment with the healing and transforming life energy of flower essences. The study and usage of flower essences and flower remedies will allow us to rediscover new ways of healing and remember our true inner spiritual nature as evolving beings of light. Those who take this journey will be richly rewarded for their efforts.

Richard Gerber, MD
Author of *Vibrational Medicine: New Choices for Healing Ourselves*

Introduction

I am delighted to present the revised and greatly expanded *New Encyclopedia of Flower Remedies* which reflects the exciting growth, development and usage of flower remedies over the last ten years.

Have you ever felt happier for surrounding yourself with fresh flowers, been especially attracted to certain kinds of blooms, or found solace strolling among fields or gardens filled with flowering plants? If so, you have already experienced the therapeutic power of flowers.

Since the dawn of time we have instinctively known that flowers can lift our spirits and make us feel well again. Flowers and their remedies feature in the traditional healing practices of many cultures around the world. They play an important role in restoring or evoking a sense of harmony in mind, body and spirit. This concept of wholeness is a recurring theme in many ancient philosophies, and we are now rediscovering its relevance to us. We are at last emerging from a time when good health is interpreted as the absence of disease. True wellbeing is something that lies beyond this limited concept, encompassing contentment and security, peace of mind and an abundance of vitality that is essential if our lives are to be enjoyable and fulfilling.

Many ancient and native cultures believe that everything in nature is infused with a vital energy, the spark of life. Wise men living several thousands of years ago proposed that when mind, body and spirit are perfectly integrated, this life force abounds, bringing with it a real sense of health and happiness. The way to attain such inner harmony, they claimed, is to respect nature and her ways.

Symbolizing love and friendship, flowers have always been a source of pleasure and happiness – of healing in its quintessential form. From the sensuous rose to the humble daisy, the delicate blooms adorning gardens, fields, hedgerows, mountainsides, woodlands and jungles throughout the world possess special qualities that can ease emotional distress, boost self-confidence, lift energy levels, increase resilience to all kinds of illness and even enrich our relationships. Most importantly, they offer the perfect antidote to stress in its many different guises.

Our existence is becoming increasingly artificial. Cocooned in towns and cities, it is easy to feel isolated from the natural environment. We no longer rely on the flowering of different plants to tell us what time of year it is as our distant ancestors once did. In severing the bond with nature, we risk losing our sense of wholeness. When this happens we become increasingly vulnerable to stress.

Stress is recognized as a major source of unhappiness and ill health. Too many people feel completely at its mercy, powerless either to avoid or conquer its disruptive effects. Orthodox medicine offers little in the way to relieve stress-induced turbulence. Drugs such as tranquillizers may ease the discomfort by dulling our perceptions and reactions, but they do not really help us to stay afloat in this sea of turmoil. This is where flower remedies come to our rescue.

Flower essences are not like other medicines. They do not contain active chemicals or possess pharmaceutical properties. They are best described as a sort of liquid energy, a vibrational medicine that brings about benefits by influencing each person's own life force. Taking these remedies can be likened to surrounding yourself with exquisite flowers which never fade or die.

The state of the world has altered dramatically in the last 50 years and many new sources of stress have arrived on the scene. Horrific events such as wars, famines, tragic accidents, violent incidents and natural disasters may not be new, but thanks to television, radio and newspapers we are now bombarded with their details on a regular basis. We may try not to think about them, but still they often shake us to the core.

Overpopulation in many areas creates competition for vital resources and work, leading to widespread greed and insecurity. Meanwhile the breakdown of close-knit communities leaves many people feeling lonely and isolated.

Stress tends to be infectious: if you work in an office full of anxious, frazzled people, it will be difficult to keep calm. Add the pressures of feeling hemmed in due to overcrowding, the constant noise of traffic and the almost stifling levels of pollution in some cities and it is hardly surprising that stress has become the twentieth-century ailment. It not only plays havoc with our nervous systems, but also weakens our immunity, leaving us easy prey to the new so-called 'super bugs' that keep appearing on the scene. Flower remedies are needed now more than ever.

Responding to this cry for help, certain people have set out to research and rediscover the therapeutic properties of indigenous flowers growing in countries all over the world. The new flower essences are made from an extraordinarily diverse variety of flora, ranging from the modest hedgerow and alpine flowers to romantic roses, exotic orchids and the blossoms of fruits like the banana and avocado. Some flowers, especially those from the Australian Bush and Himalayan mountains, have a long tradition of being used in natural healing. The beneficial properties of others are only just being discovered.

While some flower essences free us from negative moods and emotions, others go further, helping us to recognize and let go of behaviour patterns that generate negative feelings.

When we feel confused about a situation or relationship in our lives, flower essences help us to see things from an entirely different perspective – just as escaping to a place of stunning natural beauty leaves you feeling that your problems and worries are less daunting than you had imagined. Some essences act at the physical level, strengthening and rebalancing various areas of the body such as the immune system. Others offer protection against new sources of environmental stress. Many aspire to more spiritual realms, helping us to find our true direction and purpose in life.

Although I have been a professional flower remedy consultant for more than 20 years, I actually grew up with this form of healing. As a child I would watch my grandmother working with the Bach Flower Remedies and I have always been amazed by the profound ways in which people respond to this gentle form of treatment. I have witnessed the emergence of the newer flower essences and steadily added them to my own repertoire of remedies. Using specially chosen combinations of essences from around the world, I have helped people who were suffering from all kinds of illnesses back to health. Typical conditions I have treated include infertility, premenstrual tension, hay fever, arthritis and nervous exhaustion. I firmly believe that what sets flower essences apart from other forms of remedies and therapies is their ability to address physical, mental, emotional and spiritual aspects of ourselves simultaneously, bringing about complete healing.

The beauty of flower remedies is that they are relatively inexpensive, easy to use and totally free from any unpleasant side-effects. Furthermore, you can prescribe them for yourself and now that there are ready-made combinations addressing common problems they are very accessible. We all have different needs, and the flowers that may benefit one person will differ from those that can help another. You may notice that you are instinctively attracted or drawn to certain flowers such as roses, just as you may choose to use certain herbs when cooking. These are very often the flowers that you probably need.

As you begin to use the flower essences you will embark on a journey of self-discovery. You will become aware of your strengths and weaknesses as well as any stress patterns you have acquired over the years. These are reactions and responses to situations and people that, if left unchecked, consistently undermine your health and happiness.

The remedies will give you the strength and support you need to cope with change in your life, as well as with the more far-reaching upheavals occurring on this earth. There is no doubt that anything that calls for a shift in our lives and thinking will generate stress and the more we resist the challenges and transitions we have to face, the more painful the experience of change tends to be. Flower essences can help us to go with the flow, to be more flexible and enable us to respond appropriately to the increasing demands made upon us.

In these testing times, let flower essences help you regain control of your life and destiny, to find the vitality you need to pursue your dreams and goals, and above all, to rediscover the true joy of living.

How to use this book

This book is for anyone who wishes to explore the benefits of using flower remedies.

Part One tells you what flower remedies are and how they work. You will discover how to choose remedies that can help you and others.

Part Two is made up of an Encyclopedia of 32 families of flower essences from around the world, giving a brief description of the properties and benefits of over 2,000 remedies, combinations, mists and creams.

Part Three contains an Ailment Chart for easy reference, covering a range of typical physical, emotional/psychological, and spiritual problems with suggested remedies that can help to relieve them. It also includes recipes you can make up for your own use (such as my Stress Buster and Infection Fighter combinations), a chapter of case histories for which I have used remedies successfully to combat a variety of conditions, and further advice for flower essence practitioners.

PART ONE

The History of Healing Flowers

The idea that flowers possess healing powers may seem new and revolutionary. It is, however, a very ancient concept the origins of which can be traced back into the mists of time.

For at least 40,000 years the Aborigines of Australia have been using flowers as part of their natural healing system. In other parts of the world where folk medicine is still alive, the tradition of utilizing flowering plants and their essences to restore wellbeing to body, mind and spirit has continued down the centuries to the present day.

Many of us instinctively turn to flowers to lift our spirits and make us feel better. It is second nature to bring bouquets to those who are sick or ailing. Without floral decorations, festive occasions or religious ceremonies would seem soulless and incomplete.

The task before us is to uncover and rediscover knowledge about the natural world that has existed for aeons.

Tales of a Golden Age

Lemuria and Atlantis

Legend has it that flower essences were first used for healing some 500,000 years ago in a mythical place called Lemuria or Mu. Located in an area now covered by the Pacific Ocean, Lemuria was reputedly a veritable 'garden of Eden'. The land was lush and, thanks to a near-perfect climate, all kinds of exquisite flowering plants flourished.

It is said the inhabitants of this civilization were gentle, sensitive souls who truly appreciated the beauty of their environment and were content to live close to the earth. They were also aware of the natural empathy that exists between human and plant life. To them, every plant was special and had its own personality, and some believe these people were ethereal beings who could sense the energy or vibration of all living things. It has been suggested that, to them, all living things including plants appeared as luminous or shimmering objects.

These people realized that the highest concentration of life force in a plant is found in its flowers. Just by being close to a delicate bloom they became aware of its particular healing qualities. The Lemurians were not, however, troubled by physical disease – indeed it is said they lived for around 2,000 years. Instead they used flower essences to evolve spiritually, to attain enlightenment.

According to the myth, Lemuria gave way to Atlantis. Those who believe or suspect there was a civilization known as Atlantis think it probably existed between 12,000 and 150,000 years ago. Unlike the Lemurians, the Atlanteans were reputedly not content to live in harmony with nature. They wanted to dominate and manage it to their advantage. As their society became increasingly technologically advanced, stress seeped into their lives bringing with it all kinds of new physical, emotional and mental diseases. At this time, so the legend goes, flower essences were first used as a complete system of medicine.

Ancient Egypt, Crete and India

The ancient Egyptians certainly harnessed the healing powers of flowers; they did, after all, perfect the art of aromatherapy. Within magnificent temples high priests built laboratories where they distilled flowers to obtain aromatic essential oils. These were then blended to create medicinal formulations for treating a wide variety of illnesses. It should be stressed that essential oils are not the same as flower essences, although the Egyptians recognized the therapeutic benefits of both, for they also collected the dew from flowers and exposed it to sunlight to increase its potency.

The lotus flower, which grew in abundance along the banks of the Nile, was sacred to the Egyptians. In their mythology it was the first living thing to appear on earth. When its petals unfurled the supreme god representing intellectual rulership was revealed to them. Its flower essence was used in rituals, as were those of other indigenous plants such as bamboo and papyrus. It has been suggested that the Egyptians imparted thoughts to certain plants, knowing they would reach and help us today.

The Minoans of Crete were another highly cultured people who recognized the healing potential of flowers. They are said to have held rituals devoted to the quest for spiritual understanding during which they would place a splendid flowering plant such as a wild rose in the centre of the ceremonial chamber, and place flowers or sprigs of plants floating in bowls of water around the room. Participants would sip the water or eat the petals to cleanse themselves of any disturbing thoughts or feelings during the ceremony.

At about this time, many miles away in the remote Himalayan mountains, flowers were playing their part in Ayurveda ('science of life'), an ancient system of natural medicine dating back at least 5,000 years. We know of it because the Ayurvedic principles have been handed down from generation to generation and are still alive today. Flowers with spiritual significance such as the lotus continue to be used in Ayurvedic healing ceremonies. The petals were traditionally sprinkled into bowls of water, which were then drunk and used to anoint various parts of the body.

Flowers and Folk Medicine

If we look at the folk medicines practised by native peoples around the world, most make use of the flowers and plants growing in each region.

The Australian Aborigines

The Aborigines have always turned to their exotic flora for help in healing mind, body and spirit. They collect the dew that settles on petals at dawn, believing it to enhance emotional wellbeing and help them enter into the 'dream time'. In some instances they may also eat the flowers themselves.

The Aboriginal story of how flowers were born and came by their healing powers was handed down from generation to generation and is told here by Ken Colbung of the Bibulmun people:

The Aborigines living in the southwest of Western Australia are known as the Bibulmun people. Their legends were given to them by the *Demmagoomba* – the spirits of the old people who lived here previously. According to the *Demmagoomba*, the creator (also known as the *Gujub*, God, Supreme Being or senior spirit) sent the Rainbow Snake, *Waugal*, down to earth as a life-giving element. It landed at a place in the southwest of Bibulmun country known as Broiungarup.

Rainbow colours of the Rainbow Snake gave the flowers their colour at the time of creation. At Broiungarup you will always see beautiful rainbows. Some of the smallest and rarest flowers are only found in this one area.

The *Broiunga* is a clan. It is where you get your spirituality and your mortal being. You can be clan to birds, to a tree or to flowers. Your *Broiunga* is a special being for which you are responsible. If your *Broiunga* is a flower, then you must maintain this flower. It also has a responsibility to you. It gives you a beautiful feeling of colour, of its essence, which is the link to the Rainbow Snake.

The flowers of the earth have different link-ups for different people's needs. There are a lot of occasions when the body needs to be associated with the different types of flowers. The essences are important for our own spirit, or *Djugubra*. So we have what is known as *Kaba nij nyoong* (*Kaba* is the flower essences, *nij* is the 'I', and *nyoong* is the understanding of the person). We must be aware that when we first see a flower it will bring us happiness; when we have the essence from that flower it will bring us health and with health and happiness we have wealth – the wealth of the spirit *Djugubra*.

The flower sauna is a unique feature of traditional Aboriginal healing and is arguably one of the earliest forms of flower essence therapy, dating back around 10,000 years. The ceremony, still performed the same way today, is conducted by the Maban, a man or woman who is healer and Keeper of the Law. The sauna is prepared by lining a shallow pit with hot coals which are then covered with a layer of earth. Steam is created by sprinkling water over the hot earth. Clay blended with crushed flowers (specially chosen for the occasion) is then smeared onto the body of the person being healed – this helps the flower essence penetrate the skin.

The Maban takes charge of the patient, who enters the pit and is then covered with an animal skin to seal in the warmth. The patient remains there until sunrise the next day when he or she emerges, renewed with the spirit of the flowers.

Another ritual sees people sent to sit among a clump of flowers so that their souls may be purified and they become 'spiritually reborn'.

Native Americans
In ancient times, the native peoples of North America were blessed with the ability to draw energy from flowers and plants. When they lost this gift they turned to imbibing the therapeutic properties of flowers in the form of teas and extractions. Some spiritual medicine people can still utilize this energy, but always request the flower's permission first. The Native Americans match the energy of the flower to the particular part of the body that is out of balance and needs healing. Indeed, in their version of the creation story, when humans came into being much of their physical body was derived from the plants, rocks and waters of Mother Earth, while their spirit or soul came from the heavens or sky. To them this explains why certain plants have a special affinity for certain areas of the body. This idea is echoed in the legends relating to Lemurian times and in the creation myths of other indigenous peoples.

Russian Medicine Men
Across the Atlantic in Russia, medicine men or shamans also practise a natural form of healing handed down to them by their forefathers. All knowledge is passed on by word of mouth; nothing is committed to print. The medicine people living in the richest floral area of the Caucasus Mountains are called the Koldum. Nearly half the flowers growing here are unique to this area. These indigenous flowers are taken in the form of essences and tinctures. So famous are these remedies that people have been known to travel for miles to this region –

even the infamous Genghis Khan, who made his pilgrimage from Mongolia. He reputedly prescribed them to his men to give them strength for battle.

The Mystical Paracelsus

Healing with flowers was introduced into Europe during the fifteenth century by the renowned physician and mystic Philippus Aureolus Theophrastus Bombast von Hohenheim, better known as Paracelsus.

While still in his early twenties Paracelsus left his home in Austria to embark on a ten-year adventure which took him to Russia, England and North Africa, where he encountered different kinds of folk medicines.

It is said that he would collect the early morning dew from flowers which he took himself and prescribed to treat emotional disturbance in others. Paracelsus was also responsible for reviving the old 'Doctrine of Signatures', a system of equating certain features of a flower or plant – its shape, colour, scent, taste or natural habitat – to its healing properties. For example, Eyebright, a blue flower with a yellow centre, looks like an eye and is said to help treat eye problems. Similarly the Skullcap flower, resembling the shape of a human skull, may be used to treat headaches and insomnia, while the bark of Willow, a tree that grows in wet places, eases rheumatism and other conditions that are worse for damp weather. We now know that Willow bark contains an anti-inflammatory substance called salicin which eases the pain of rheumatism as well as headaches. Its synthetic form is taken by millions each day as aspirin.

Paracelsus also believed that plants tend to grow where they are needed most; dock leaves, which can be used to treat nettle rash, always grow near nettles, while plants for easing fevers can often be found close to swamps.

The Language of Flowers

With the birth of modern medicine, belief in the healing power of flowers appeared to die out. But this was not so; it simply became channelled into the popular notion that certain qualities or virtues are associated with flowers. From the earliest times the Rose has been a symbol of love. Cleopatra placed such faith in its romantic charm that she reputedly carpeted her bedroom with millions of fresh rose petals to help her seduction of Marc Anthony. Today, the Rose is still a symbol of love and romance, which is why lovers give each other red roses on St Valentine's Day.

Centuries before the slogan 'Say it with flowers', people knew intuitively the special meanings of different blooms. In ancient Egypt the Iris was seen as an emblem of power. It adorned the brow of the Sphinx of Giza and the sceptres of kings. To the Egyptians flowers also represented certain thoughts and feelings; just as we might send telegrams or cards to wish someone good health during an illness or to show our affection or love, they would send an appropriate flower.

Flowers had their own language and meaning to the ancient Greeks and Romans too, and it should come as no surprise that the Rose is associated with Aphrodite/Venus, the goddess of love. But the Rose is by no means the only flower linked to love. Others include the Iris, which is named after the goddess of the rainbow who guided the souls of women to their final resting place. Carnations also express pure love and constancy, while the Tulip denotes a declaration of love.

Many of the classical gods, goddesses and nymphs such as Hyacinthus, Narcissus and Iris are remembered today because they gave their name to flowers. Narcissus owes its name to the young man who, it was prophesied, would have a long and happy life unless he caught sight of his reflection and fell in love with his own beauty. To his cost he did indeed become enraptured by himself. Thus in most books about the language of flowers the Narcissus represents egotism. In the Middle East, however, it is traditionally linked with love, the beginning of new relationships and the enhancement of existing ones.

Flower symbolism occurs throughout the world. In India flowers are associated with various deities and ceremonies, *pujas*, prayers and certain festive occasions. A sprig of the magical Mimosa is often suspended above the bed to ward off ill fortune. Its yellow flowers give a sweet aroma which is also said to evoke psychic dreams. To the Chinese, Jasmine represents feminine sweetness, while in India it is considered sacred. The flower of sensuousness and physical attraction, the Jasmine is believed to enhance self-esteem and is always used in traditional bridal wreaths.

Flowers often have religious significance. The Lotus flower is recognized as a symbol of spirituality all over the world. It is not only sacred to the Ancient Egyptians, but throughout Asia, and the Far East especially, it is associated with Buddhism and the state of enlightenment. The figure of Buddha is often depicted sitting on a Lotus flower.

Good fortune, protection and strength have also traditionally been associated with flowers. For this reason they have often been adopted by kings and leaders. The Sunflower became the symbol of Atahualpa, King God of the Incas, for it was believed to hold great magical properties. Like the sun itself it has a strong life force, encouraging action and strengthening willpower.

The English Plantagenets derived their name from *planta genista* (Latin for Broom) after Geoffrey Count of Anjou wore it as an emblem on his helmet when he went into battle in 1140. The sweet scent of its fresh flowers is said to purify thoughts and feelings. Inhaling the aroma also instils a sense of peace and tranquillity. And the people of Shakespeare's day were well acquainted with the ancient meanings associated with plants and flowers, as demonstrated by Ophelia in *Hamlet* as she cries, 'There's rosemary, that's for remembrance'.

However, it was not until more than 200 years later that the language of flowers really took shape. In 1817 the first real flower dictionary, *Le Langage des*

Fleurs by Madame Charlotte de la Tour, was published in Paris. It proved so popular and sparked off such great interest that other versions followed. With the help of these flower dictionaries, shy Victorians found ways to express what they would not say in words. They sent each other bouquets in which every blossom, leaf and stem was fraught with significance. The language of flowers flourished, and was even given the special name florigraphy.

At the beginning of that century, 'flower fairies' epitomizing the personality or character of various blossoms and buds also became fashionable. These tiny ethereal beings with gossamer wings reputedly lived among the flowers at the bottom of the garden. They captured the imagination of writers like J M Barrie, who conjured up Peter Pan's rather wayward guardian angel, Tinkerbell. Sherlock Holmes' creator, Arthur Conan Doyle, was also fascinated by these nature spirits – as his book *The Coming of the Fairies* reveals. Legend has it that these nature spirits, or devas, first made their appearance in Lemurian times. Each fairy was entrusted with a different flower, and together they were said to be responsible for teaching us how to live in harmony with nature.

Folklore tells us that if we wish to see the fairy kingdom we should make a concoction of Rose water, Marigold water and wild Thyme. Leave this lotion in the sunlight for three days, apply it to the eyes and the windows of the fairy world will magically open!

Flowers and Signs of the Zodiac

When astrology became fashionable, flowers, like gem stones, were also attributed to the signs of the zodiac, as follows:

Aries: Geranium, Honeysuckle
Taurus: Rose, Violet
Gemini: Forsythia, Morning Glory
Cancer: Acanthus, Jasmine
Leo: Marigold, Sunflower
Virgo: Anemone, Melissa
Libra: Columbine, Orchid
Scorpio: Gentian, Hyacinth
Sagittarius: Pinks, Dandelion
Capricorn: Pansy, Tulip
Aquarius: Orchid, Primrose
Pisces: Clematis, Hydrangea

Rediscovering the Healing Power of Flowers

In the 1930s, healing with flowers was rediscovered by a remarkable man called Dr Edward Bach. Thanks to his pioneering work, flower essences have come to the rescue of millions of people throughout the world.

Bach was born near Birmingham, England in 1886. Even at an early age he was fascinated by nature and loved going for walks in the countryside. He pursued a career in medicine specializing in pathology and bacteriology. In 1920 he established a successful practice in Harley Street, London.

During the next few years he became increasingly disenchanted with the orthodox medical approach, which he felt focused on relieving the symptoms of disease rather than its true cause. At the same time he felt increasingly drawn towards the homeopathic principle of treating the whole person.

He began to carry out his own research. He isolated certain bacteria from the intestinal tract with which he prepared vaccines according to homeopathic principles. These vaccines proved remarkably helpful to people suffering from chronic diseases, and could be taken orally instead of injected (a method Bach particularly disliked). Remedies prepared from toxins such as viruses became known as the Bach nosodes, and are still used by many homeopaths today.

During his work Bach noticed that his patients tended to fall into distinct personality types, and those in a particular group frequently responded to the same treatment. Ahead of his time, he also recognized the link between stress, emotions and illness. Bach believed that the disturbing moods or feelings different people experienced were a key cause of ill health. In *Heal Thyself*, a small booklet he wrote which sums up his philosophy of healing and the problems of orthodox medicine, Bach proposed that:

> The real primary diseases of man are such defects as pride, cruelty, hate, self-love, ignorance, instability and greed. Each of these defects... will produce a conflict which must of necessity be reflected in the physical body, producing its own specific type of malady.

Correcting emotional factors, he reasoned, would go a long way towards increasing physical and mental vitality, which in turn would help to resolve any physical disease.

At the same time, Bach became interested in the idea of replacing vaccines based on bacteria, themselves the instigators of disease, with more wholesome remedies. He discovered these in the flowers growing in the fields and hedgerows. Bach was a sensitive soul who relied on his intuition for guidance. During a visit to Wales, he was drawn to two particular wild flowers, Impatiens and Mimulus. These flowers, he felt, emitted a special kind of energy or vibration which could exert a positive influence on certain negative states of mind.

In 1930 Bach decided to give up his lucrative London practice, and he spent the next six years living in several parts of rural England in the quest for a new floral healing system. Aware that personality affects the way we react to stress, the first remedies Bach looked for related to what he perceived to be the 12 key personality types (*see* Chapter Four). To him flowers had their own little personalities reminiscent of certain characteristics in us. The wistful Clematis reminded him of quiet, dreamy people who are wrapped up in their thoughts and fantasies, who as a result are prone to drowsiness, indifference, sensitivity to noise, poor concentration and difficulty recuperating from illness. As a remedy Clematis would lend support to people with these characteristics, reducing their susceptibility to such tendencies.

The colour, texture, flowering patterns and growth patterns of flowers told Bach something of their healing qualities. The sturdy Oak, for instance, suggested to him the type of strong, reliable, patient, dependable people who shoulder their burdens without complaining.

The next 26 flower remedies he looked for were intended to bring relief from different kinds of emotional discomfort and distress. Bach felt that they could deal with negative mind-states like fear, apathy, loneliness and despair, which he believed were not truly a part of our nature but which we only succumbed to in difficult and trying times.

The flowers, Bach has said, have a particular quality which is an exact equivalent to the human emotion. For example, Wild Rose, a remedy for apathy and resignation, is a positive representation of this state. In other words, it replaces these negative feelings with dynamism and optimism.

For Bach the colours of flowers were also indicative of their remedial qualities. Blue flowers such as Cerato express receptive feelings, the red or yellow flowers are more dynamic, while green flowers such as Scleranthus are associated with balance. Remedies for fear have a dynamic colour reflecting their vibrant strength. Bach confirmed the effects of the various flowers by observing how each one affected his own emotional state. It is said that he would think himself into feeling a particular way, then search for remedies to help restore a sense of calm and contentment.

With a few exceptions such as Vine, Olive, Honeysuckle and Cerato, Bach's healing flowers can still be found growing wild in the fields and hedgerows of Oxfordshire. Almost half of them come from trees, while others (such as Gorse and Cerato) are from shrubs.

In 1936 Bach passed away, satisfied that his work was complete. His close friend and companion Nora Weeks was largely responsible for safeguarding and keeping his work alive. Until recently the flowers continued to be gathered from the Oxfordshire countryside, and prepared and bottled at Mount Vernon, as Bach himself had done, and each year hundreds of people from all corners of the world make their pilgrimage to Mount Vernon, to witness the place where Bach performed much of his pioneering work.

For many years Bach's Flower Remedies stood alone. Then in the mid-1970s interest in the healing power of flowers was rekindled. Richard Katz was one of a few people in the forefront of this revitalization, establishing the Flower Essence Society in California. His aims were to research new flower essences and gather together those working with the essences so they could exchange ideas and information.

Others, too, have been inspired to research the healing qualities of locally growing flowers. From Alaska to Australia, the Mediterranean to Thailand, and Hawaii to the Himalayas, distinct remedies have been rediscovered in the flowers that are indigenous to each particular country or region. The Orchids of the Amazon, for instance, come from the exotic flowers that grow 100ft up on the branches and treetops of the rainforests of Colombia.

These new essences come at a time when they are most needed, for the world has changed considerably in the last 50 years and is continuing to do so at an alarming rate. Many of the flowers address not only emotional problems but also aspire to more spiritual healing, as well as acting at the fundamental physical level, treating the whole person – mind, body and spirit.

Energy Fields

To understand how flower essences work, we have to become familiar with the idea that all living things are infused with energy, or life force. We cannot see or touch this energy but, like the air we breathe, it is essential to life. Most people living in the West find it hard to believe that there may be more to us than meets the eye. In other regions of the world, especially the Far East and Asia, this view is commonplace.

Over 5,000 years ago, Indian holy men spoke of a universal energy. Known as *prana*, this energy is still seen as the basic constituent and source of all life. Prana, the breath of life, moves through all things and brings vitality to them. The same idea forms the basis of Taoism, the ancient Chinese philosophy which also emerged during the third millennium BC. It holds that the universe is a living organism infused and permeated with a rhythmic, vibrational energy called *chi* or *qi*. The concept of an energy pervading all things is not as mystical as it may seem. Modern physics is beginning to lend credence to what the ancient wise men supposed all those years ago. In the last century it has become outmoded to think of things as solid objects, as Newton and his colleagues in the late 17th and early 18th centuries suspected.

With the discovery of the atom, physicists felt they had found the fundamental building blocks of the universe. Yet as they delved deeper, they found that atoms are composed of even tinier particles which seem to be constantly on the move. Furthermore, the behaviour of things on this very tiny scale is very different to what one might expect. In 1905 Albert Einstein shattered the principles of the old Newtonian worldview when he published his theory of relativity. With this hypothesis came the idea that matter and energy are interchangeable. All particles can be created from energy, and matter is simply slowed-down or 'crystallized' energy.

A few years later another important discovery was made by Max Planck. He found that light and other forms of electromagnetic radiation are emitted in the form of energy packets which he called quanta. These light quanta, or energy packets, have been accepted as bona fide particles. Oddly, though, they also behave as if they were waves rather than individual particles.

The latest 'super-string' theories, which first came to light during the 1960s, now propose that these fundamental particles are not really particles at all. They are more like snippets of infinitely thin string. In 'string theories', what were previously thought of as pinpoints of light are now pictured as waves travelling down the string, like waves on a vibrating kite-string. This means that at the most basic level everything would appear to be shimmering, or moving in light waves all the time. What all this suggests is that our world of seemingly solid objects is composed of wave-like patterns and energy fields that constantly interact with one another. Indeed, some scientists view the universe as rather like a vast web of inseparable energy patterns.

In 1964 the physicist John S Bell came up with the now well-known mathematical formula called Bell's Theorem. This supports the idea that subatomic particles are connected in some way, so that everything that happens to one particle affects all the others. The late David Bohm, Professor of Theoretical Physics at Birkbeck College, London, also came to the conclusion that the universe is an interconnected whole, after devoting 40 years of research into physics and philosophy. He would have received a Nobel Prize for his work had he not died unexpectedly in 1993.

In his book *Wholeness and the Implicate Order*, Bohm discusses the idea that, in reality, things are not separate and independent of each other, they only exist this way in our minds. We split things up and file them away in neat compartments to make the world around us more manageable. Seeing everything as being separate is purely an illusion which leads to endless conflict and confusion within ourselves and society as a whole. Not realizing this fragmentation is of our own making, humanity has always been driven by a quest for wholeness. Indeed the word 'health' derives from the word 'hale', originally an Anglo-Saxon word meaning whole.

This lends credibility to ancient philosophies which tell us that we cannot enjoy a sense of total wellbeing unless all facets of us – mind, body and spirit – are in balance. This in turn will come from living in harmony with nature. Should we slip out of this balanced state, nature possesses the remedies to make us whole again.

The Essence of a Flower

Evidence to suggest that these energy fields do indeed exist came to light back in the 1940s. While investigating electrical phenomena, Harold Saxton Burr (Professor of Anatomy at Yale University Medical School) accidentally discovered energy fields around living plants and animals. He called these fields bioelectrical or electrodynamic L-fields – the fields of life. After discovering that the electrical fields around tiny seedlings resemble those of the adult plant, not of the original seed, he suggested that the organization of a living thing, its pattern, is established by its electrodynamic field. Like a fingerprint, this electrical field is characteristic of a particular living thing and has a shaping influence on it, maintaining its established energetic 'status quo', or blueprint. Today, certain techniques can be used to reveal these fields. The most well-known is Kirlian photography, a form of high-frequency, high-voltage electro-photography which was developed by the Russian researcher Semyon Kirlian. In very simple terms, Kirlian's photography captures the interference pattern which is set up when a high-frequency electrical charge interacts with the energy field of a living object. The pattern usually appears as streaks of light surrounding the outline of the object, be it a leaf or a hand.

Erik Pelham is pioneering the use of Kirlian photography to show that flower essences do indeed possess energy fields. Furthermore, he has discovered that the energetic patterns produced by different flower essences vary, often quite dramatically – lending support to the idea that each flower has its own personality or character. The first photograph Erik takes is of a cleansed quartz crystal. Having obtained his 'control', Erik then places a few drops of flower essence onto the crystal and makes a series of exposures. The individual energy pattern of the essence emerges, reflecting the unique qualities of that particular flower.

Capturing a Flower's Energy

Flower essences are best described as a kind of 'liquid energy'. They literally encapsulate the energy pattern or vibration of the flower they come from. Since early times it has been believed that the early morning dew which settles on petals becomes infused with a flower's energy. The art of capturing this energy pattern so that it could be used therapeutically was perfected by Dr Bach (*see* Chapter One). In the beginning Bach would collect morning dew from flowers, just as the peoples of ancient cultures did. He then noticed that the droplets taken from flowers that had been exposed to sunlight were more beneficial than those which formed on shaded flowers. Sunlight, he concluded, seemed to bring potency to the remedy. To his delight, Bach also discovered that by floating flowers in a bowl of pure spring water for several hours in the sunlight he could obtain powerful vibrational tinctures. The method he devised is remarkably simple and is still used by many people making flower essences today.

The Sun Method

Flowers for making essences are ideally picked very soon after they come into bloom. Freshly picked and undamaged flowers are floated in a glass bowl filled with spring water so that they cover the surface. The bowl is then left out in the sunlight on a clear, cloudless day for three to four hours (or less if the petals show signs of fading). Bach believed that during this process a flower's energies were transferred to the water. Sunlight plays a role in charging the water with an energetic imprint of the flower's vibrational signature. The blooms are then lifted out with a twig and discarded. The energized liquid or 'essence' is then poured into bottles with an equal volume of brandy to form the flower stock. The brandy acts as a preservative which stabilizes and anchors the flower's energy.

The Boiling Method

A clean enamel saucepan is three-quarters filled with newly picked flowers and stems. These are covered with spring water and brought to the boil, uncovered. After simmering for 30 minutes the liquid is left to cool; when cold the essence is filtered. Again this liquid is bottled half-and-half with brandy. (For those who wish to try making their own remedies, these methods are described in greater detail in *The Healing Herbs of Edward Bach* by Julian and Martine Barnard – *see* Further Reading.) If possible, flowers destined for healing should be growing wild in places that are not often visited and are free from pollution. If they are taken from cultivated plants it is important they are tended with loving care and without the use of chemical pesticides or fertilizers.

New environmentally-friendly ways of capturing a flower's energy are also coming to light. In India, Drs Atul and Pupa Shah have devised a technique which means they do not have to cut the flowers to make their Aditi Flower Essences (*see* pages 146–7). And Andreas Korte has invented a crystal method which he uses to make his Amazonian Orchid, Rose, and Cactus essences (*see* page 64). Ever conscious that increasing demand for some of the rarer flowers may actually jeopardize their existence, many are turning to these and other alternative forms of extraction.

Water Holds the Memory

Water plays a vital role in making flower essences, for the energy is believed to imprint itself on the liquid. Do not expect to find any dissolved chemicals from the petals in the essence. All it contains is the flower's energy or signature. It may seem remarkable that energized water alone can possess healing properties, yet evidence to suggest this emerged in 1987 when a French immunobiologist called Dr Jacques Benveniste, working in laboratories just outside Paris, found that certain highly diluted substances can be as potent as vastly greater quantities of the same substance. Using a constant called the Avagadro number, Benveniste confirmed mathematically that it was impossible for water to retain a single molecule of the active antibody, immunoglobulin E. Despite this, the water set off a powerful reaction in the test tube. Somehow the water had retained the 'memory' or 'vibration' of the molecule.

The remarkable research conducted by Dr Masaru Emoto from Japan has also discovered that water is a mirror reflecting our mind; words, thoughts and emotions have a powerful effect on water which reacts by picking up and revealing, through water in its crystalline form, the different vibrational patterns to which it is exposed. When the imprinted water is frozen it is then possible to see and record the effect of the spoken word in the formation of beautiful crystals. (*See* plate section for water crystal experiments by Dr Emoto as illustrated in his book *Messages from Water*). This supports the efficacy of flower remedies as the water in which the flower is placed becomes imprinted with the vibrational qualities of that flower, and then has an easy entrance and absorption by the body, which is itself composed of a high proportion of water. So flower remedies have the power to erase negative disease or mental emotional patterns within the human organism, flooding the system with positive vibrations.

Gem or crystal essences are worth mentioning here, as they work in a similar 'vibrational' way to flower remedies and are prepared in much the same way. Flower and gem essences tend to complement each other and work well in combination. Like all living entities, we are also infused with energy; it permeates every part of our being and its abundance goes hand in hand with good health and vitality. This energy flows freely in newborn babies, but as we proceed on our journey through life it begins to wane for all kinds of reasons which we will discuss in Chapter Three.

The traditional medical systems of the Chinese, Japanese, Tibetans, Native Americans and Australian Aborigines all regard this energy as something tangible. As science has yet to validate this energy's existence, no one knows for sure what form it takes within us, yet for centuries healers have being working with energy systems described by ancient medical and esoteric teachings. As flower essences are believed to have a restorative effect on this energy, it is a good idea to know a little more about these different systems.

The Meridian System

Traditional Chinese medicine views all matter as being infused with a subtle energy known as *chi* or *qi*, which manifests itself through vibration, circulation and waves of movement. This *chi* flows along a network of channels called meridians, which spreads like an intricate web through the body. It may be likened to a second nervous system which forms a connection between the physical body and the subtler energy system surrounding it. It may also be perceived as an aura of light that may at times be colourful. According to the Chinese model, there are 12 pairs of meridians, each pair associated with a different organ system or function. The first reference to this energy network is found in the *Nei Ching*, or *Yellow Emperor's Classic of Internal Medicine*, written during the reign of the Emperor Huang Ti between 2697 and 2596 BC.

The concept of *chi* continues to be very much alive today, and millions of people believe that good health and peace of mind rely on ensuring that this energy flows smoothly and evenly. Traditional Chinese medicine offers various ways to promote the movement of energy to preserve wellbeing and encourage spiritual development. The flowing movements of *QiGong* (pronounced cheegung) and T'ai Chi, and the techniques of acupuncture and acupressure all use knowledge of the meridians to clear energy blockages and heal illness. All QiGong masters have the ability to diagnose illness at a distance by reading the subtle anatomy. According to QiGong master Zhi-xing Wang, any illness can be explained as an energy blockage in the body. Circulation and movements of the subtle energy can clear this blockage and, therefore, heal the illness.

But is there any scientific proof that such energy channels or meridians exist? Over 20 years ago Dr Hiroshi Motoyama, a researcher in Japan, devised a system of measuring the electrical characteristics of the 12 major meridians by attaching 28 electrodes to the 'entry points' on the skin for each of the meridians. It is known as the AMI machine (apparatus for measuring the functions of the meridians and corresponding internal organs). Uing the AMI machine, Dr Motoyama studied over 5,000 subjects and found strong correlations between meridians that are electrically out of balance and the presence of underlying disease in the associated organ.

A more recent study was carried out at the UCLA School of Medicine. It looked at the electrical conductivity of the distal lung acupuncture (meridian) point in 30 patients. X-ray examination had already shown that four members of the group had lung cancer, but the tester did not know which of the 30 these were. On the basis of the reading of the distal lung acupuncture point, the four patients were identified correctly.

The Chakras

Common to Eastern medical and mystical traditions is the idea that special centres known as 'chakras' play a vital role in moving energy around the body. There are seven major chakras which are inextricably linked to the meridian system.

The chakras may be regarded as 'transformers', simultaneously receiving, assimilating and transmitting energy. They are capable of gathering and holding various types of energy, and can also alter their vibration so this energy can be used for different purposes – for example, by bringing higher vibrations down to the physical plane. You could visualize the chakras as many-petalled, vibrantly coloured flowers which are attached by invisible threads to the spine. These 'petals', known as *nadis*, are woven into the nervous system and distribute the energy of each chakra into the physical body. The chakras are continuously opening to receive information about the state of the subtle bodies (*see* 'Fields of Energy' below) and closing again, rather like a periwinkle which unfurls its petals when the sun shines.

The seven chakra centres govern the major glands of the endocrine system and influence both our physical and psychological health. The chakra associations differ slightly from East to West, which may help to explain why people from one culture can find it difficult to feel totally at ease in another. It should be noted that the definitions given below are based primarily on the Western chakra tradition.

Each chakra has its own 'pulse rate'. Some vibrate very quickly, others are more slow, depending largely on the ways in which we use and regard our bodies. Indeed, it is said that each chakra has its own 'note'. If one chakra is not functioning properly it will affect those above and below it. Ideally the top centres should vibrate faster and more subtly than the lower ones, but this is not always the case and heavy vibrations can appear in all the centres.

First or Root Chakra
Situated at the base of the spine and associated with basic raw energy.

- Colour: red.
- Physical connections: large intestine, legs, feet, skeletal structure. Imbalance is linked to problems like obesity, constipation, haemorrhoids, sciatica, arthritis, knee problems and poor circulation in the legs and extremities.
- Psychological influences: connecting with the earth (grounding), survival, letting go of emotional tension. Imbalance is linked to accident proneness, dependency, identity crisis and weak ego.

Second or Hara Chakra
Situated at the centre of the abdomen, just below the navel, and thought of as the seat of power and vitality.

- Colour: orange.
- Physical connections: ovaries, testicles, uterus, bladder, circulation. Imbalance is linked to low back trouble, infertility, reproductive problems, premenstrual syndrome, urinary problems and arthritis.
- Psychological influences: sexuality, creativity. Imbalance is linked to a weak personality, depression, hysteria and an inability to be sexually intimate.

Third or Solar Plexus Chakra
Situated above the navel, this is the seat of the emotions.

- Colour: yellow.
- Physical connections: adrenal glands, solar plexus, spleen, pancreas and stomach. Imbalance is linked to nervous stomach, anorexia, diabetes and blood glucose problems, anaemia, allergies, and obesity as well as

liver, adrenal and spleen problems.

- Psychological influences: feeling empowered and being in control. Imbalance is linked to addictive and compulsive behaviour, excessive anger or fear, manic depression, sleep problems and all kinds of psychosomatic conditions.

Fourth or Heart Chakra

Situated in the centre of the chest, this chakra is concerned with self-love and universal goodwill.

- Colour: green.
- Physical connections: heart, thymus gland, immune system, circulatory system, lungs and respiratory system. Imbalance is linked to heart and circulatory as well as lung and respiratory problems, high blood-pressure, upper back troubles and childhood diseases.
- Psychological influences: understanding, compassion, unconditional love. Imbalance is linked to inner conflict, self-destructive tendencies, relationship problems and feelings of alienation and loneliness.

Fifth or Throat Chakra

Situated in the throat, this is the centre of trust.

- Colour: turquoise.
- Physical connections: thyroid, parathyroid, lymphatic system, immune system, neurological system. Imbalance is linked to teeth, ear, neck and shoulder problems as well as to sore throats, bronchial problems and hearing and speech difficulties.
- Psychological influences: trust, expression, creativity and communication. Imbalance is linked to an inability to express oneself in words, poor memory, stuttering and doubt as to the sincerity of others.

Sixth or Third Eye Chakra

Situated in the centre of the forehead and associated with perception, discernment and clairvoyance.

- Colour: indigo.
- Physical connections: the pituitary gland, left-brain hemisphere, central nervous system. Imbalance is linked to nervous upsets, eye and vision problems, headaches and sinusitis.

- Psychological influences: clarity and insight, interest in spiritual issues. Imbalance is linked to confusion, poor memory, inability to focus, paranoia, detachment from reality and, in severe cases, schizophrenia.

Seventh or Crown Chakra

Situated at the crown of the head, this is the seat of consciousness.

- Colour: white.
- Physical connections: pineal gland, right-brain hemisphere and the ancient mammalian brain. Imbalance is linked to migraine headaches, pituitary problems, epilepsy.
- Psychological influences: intuition, to be open and have faith; connection to higher energies or realms. Imbalance is linked to being gullible, having nightmares, having multiple personalities, being spiritually closed off.

For centuries mystics have talked about an ethereal body surrounding the physical one, which they refer to as the aura. It was first recorded by the Pythagoreans (circa 500 BC) as a luminous body. They believed that its light could produce a variety of effects in human organisms, including the cure of disease.

In the early 12th century two well-known scholars, Boirac and Liebeault, suggested that humans have an energy that can cause an interaction between two individuals even when they are some distance apart.

Count Wilhelm von Reichenbach spent 30 years during the 1800s experimenting with a field he named the 'odic' force, but it was not until 1911 that knowledge of the human energy field started to take shape. Using coloured screens and filters, Dr William Kilner, a medical doctor, described the aura as a glowing mist around the body which had three distinct zones. He found it differed considerably from person to person depending on age, sex, mental ability and health. Certain diseases showed as irregularities in the aura, which led Kilner to develop a system of diagnosis based on the colour, texture, volume and general appearance of this ethereal body. At around the same time Dr Wilhelm Reich, a humanist psychologist and pupil of Sigmund Freud, became interested in a universal energy he called 'orgone'. He studied the relationship between disturbances in the orgone flow within the human body and psychological and physical illness. He suggested that when strong feelings like anger, frustration, sadness and even pleasure are not expressed, the energy that should have been released became locked in the body, thus sapping vitality.

During the mid-1900s Dr George de la Warr and Dr Ruth Drown invented new instruments to detect the subtle radiation being emitted from human tissues.

Dr de la Warr was also responsible for developing Radionics, a system of detection, diagnosis and healing from a distance utilizing the human biological energy field.

Medical science now recognizes that the body does have a weak electromagnetic field which is generated by the activity of brain waves and nervous impulses. A group of scientists from the A S Popov Bioinformation Institute recently reported the finding that living organisms emit energy vibrations at a frequency of 300 to 2,000 nanometers (nms). They called this energy field the bio-field or bioplasma.

No one knows for sure whether the aura, electromagnetic field and other forms of radiation emitted by the body are one and the same thing. It is more than likely that the human energy field is composed of many different vibrations. Based on their observations and other findings, researchers have created theoretical models of the aura and subtle bodies.

The Aura

This is an invisible yet luminous kind of radiation which looks like a halo surrounding the physical body. From ancient times artists and mystics have 'seen' auras. Ancient Indian sculptures, aboriginal rock paintings in Australia and Native American totem poles all show figures surrounded by light or with lines emanating from their bodies. Highly sensitive or 'psychic' people who claim they can see auras describe them as softly shimmering lights forming a misty outline around people, animals, plants and other objects.

Despite its mystical connotations, the aura has distinct parallels with the body's electromagnetic force-field. All life forms possess an aura. In humans it varies widely in size, density and colour. Its vibrancy and hue is said to depend upon the spiritual evolution of that person as well as his or her general health. Personality and emotions can also be glimpsed in the aura. Those whose auras have soft-fringed edges are susceptible to the influence of others, while a hard, distinct outline may indicate a person with a defensive and hostile attitude resulting from deep insecurity.

The aura differs remarkably from the other energy fields known as the subtle bodies (*see* below) in that it is a general field of energy emanating from the physical form whereas the subtle bodies are fixed bands of energy at set distances from the body. The aura surrounds the person with an overall field of bio-magnetic energy which acts rather like a barometer of the body's physiological processes. Although we are not usually aware of it, the aura determines our first responses to people and situations. That sense of unease we feel when close to certain people may be the result of your aura literally clashing with theirs. It is a quicker and more accurate gauge than our more rational faculties. The aura affects overall balance in the system and is the direct result of the physical body's activities, whereas the function of the subtle bodies is much more specific.

The Subtle Bodies

The seven subtle bodies are specialized bands of different types of energy at fixed distances from the physical body, rather like the rings of Saturn, creating a multi-halo impression. They are said to relate to the soul and its coordination on the physical level.

Each of these specific layers of energy emanating from the physical body via the chakras vibrates at a slightly different frequency and has its own specialized function. The layers differ in density, colour and appearance, and each is connected to a different chakra through which it exerts an influence over various psychological and physiological processes. It is helpful to imagine the 'Russian Doll effect': each body maintaining its own space but together creating a whole; each emanating from and attached to a particular chakra which in its turn acts as a porthole. As all the seven subtle bodies enter and leave the body through these chakras or portholes, the smooth flow of energetic information to maintain perfect harmony and balance throughout the whole system is essential.

It is useful to know a little about them in order to understand how the flower essences work their wonders.

Etheric Body or Etheric Lining

Deriving from the base or root chakra, the etheric body is bluish-grey in colour. This is the first subtle body and lies between the physical and other subtle bodies, sustaining the dynamic equilibrium between them. This is one of its key functions.

The etheric body is the exact double, an energetic replica, of the denser visible physical body and contains a blueprint of all the organs. Whether leaving or entering the body, the life force always passes through the etheric body.

The etheric forces are formative and creative, endowing matter with life, form and power. These same cosmic organizing energies are susceptible to control by the mind and will.

The notion that a particular vibration makes a form out of disorganized matter is known as cymatics. Many experiments have shown that certain sounds can create patterns out of a random sprinkling of sand. The classic example is the word 'Om', which forms a kind of mandala. If the etheric body is imbalanced for whatever reason, any problems residing in the subtle anatomy (that is, in the aura and subtle bodies) can filter down and express themselves in the physical body, for the body is the medium through which all electromagnetic radiation and energies play.

The Immunofluidium is an integral part of the etheric body. It is a sort of liquid energy which surrounds and nourishes all the cells in the physical body. It transports energy between the ethereal levels and the physical body, fuelling each cell with life force, or qi. The Immunofluidium flows freely and evenly through the body, maintaining and sustaining good health. When this liquid energy functions properly, genetic disease, viral and bacterial attacks may be kept at bay.

Emotional Body

This band of energy is linked to the solar plexus and heart chakra. In appearance it is brighter than the etheric body, resembling multicoloured clouds in constant motion. It is closely aligned with the etheric body; together they balance the emotions. A strong sense of emotional security and stability at the psychological level is sustained when the emotional body is in balance. Negative emotions dim the emotional body's brilliance, whereas positive feelings of love and enjoyment enhance its colours and sparkle.

Mental Body

This energy band is a vibrant shade of pale yellow, which varies in tone according to mental activity and is like the emotional body but brighter than the etheric. This mental energy enables people to think clearly and rationally. It contains the structure of our thoughts and ideas. Agitation in the mental body blocks the organs of elimination, especially the kidneys. Stress here results in the build-up of toxins in the physical body, which is often linked to allergies. Mental stress and tension also tend to become lodged in the muscular structure – many of us will be familiar with 'the tension headache' or with muscular pain (particularly in the neck and shoulders) when we are stressed.

Astral Body

More intense but softly multicoloured like the emotional body, the astral body is connected to the solar plexus and heart chakras. It encapsulates the entire personality. When the astral body is in balance the individual is more likely to have an intuitive understanding of events and the flow of life. He or she may even glean insight into what lies ahead in the future. The astral body works to collate all past-life experiences, keeping this knowledge and information from spilling into our consciousness in a way that would disrupt our present incarnation. It can be visualized as a transparent shield which sifts and filters out karmic information and disruptive patterns acquired from past lives that reside in our subconscious.

Causal Body

Crystal-clear and intensely blue in appearance, this layer is connected to the throat chakra. The causal body is the seat of our willpower. It facilitates the interaction of the individual with other people and events, allowing us to fulfil our personal destiny. It may be regarded as the gateway to higher consciousness. This body is responsible for organizing past-life information before it is released to the astral body when it is needed or appropriate.

Celestial or Soul Body

Vibrantly luminous and golden, this energy band is connected to the third eye (sixth chakra). It houses our spiritual essence and is, in a sense, the Higher Self which allows the soul to move freely through us. This energy band enters the body through the pineal gland.

Spiritual or Illuminated Body

This energy layer is a shimmering composition of pastel colours which is connected to the heart chakra. It represents a combination and fusion of the whole subtle anatomy with the physical body. Our basic energetic blueprint is housed within this subtle body.

Etheric envelope

This forms a sort of protective outer-coating around the subtle bodies, separating the subtle anatomy from the other energies around us.

Thermal Body

In addition to the ethereal subtle bodies we possess a thermal body which can be likened to a heat source extending beyond the etheric body. The heat is generated by normal cell division and is influenced by our rate of metabolism. It is literally a byproduct of physical activity.

These energy systems are considered separate entities for simplicity's sake, yet they are all interlinked and constantly interact with each other, functioning as an energetic whole. The meridians link up and pass through the organs of the body – it may help to picture the meridians as rivers of energy that are constantly on the move, flowing in and out of one another. There are a further eight energy channels (known as the extraordinary meridians) which hover between the etheric and physical bodies. They act as a sort of energy reservoir, borrowing points from the organ meridians yet forming their own pathways between the nervous and circulatory systems. These meridians relate strongly to our vitality and emotions/states of mind. Their prime function is to feed the main meridians with energy, *qi* or life force. The most important extraordinary meridian travels straight up and down the centre of the body, connecting directly with the major chakras. As we have already seen, these in turn link up with the subtle bodies, and these seven subtle bodies enter and leave the body through the various chakras. The subtle energy system may be visualized as diaphanous layers held in place with thin membranes which separate yet allow them to diffuse into one another.

The aura has its own unique part to play; it is a reflection of the levels of our physical health and vitality. The more balanced and healthy you are, the greater your auric field. This force field can radiate some three to four feet from the body, its energy infusing the whole subtle body systems. In ill health the aura shrinks back close to the body in an attempt to conserve vital energy.

This entire energy system is in a continuous state of motion. You might want to visualize the different energies as swirling mists of colour and light interacting with and receiving information from each other – a multilevelled interfusion; these energies are constantly interchanging, redistributing and rebalancing themselves.

Illuminating the Energies

Scientists have a yet to invent a device that confirms categorically the existence of these subtler energies, although many have turned their minds to it. However, some interesting energetic phenomena have been discovered using special techniques akin to Kirlian photography.

Harry Oldfield has dedicated 15 years of his life to illuminating the subtle energies. While working with Kirlian photography he found that sound and radio frequencies as well as light are emitted from an object. This inspired him to invent the electroscanning method (ESM) – a piece of equipment that surrounds an object or person with an electrical reference field which can be measured three-dimensionally around the body. He feels that fluctuations in this field could reflect what is happening on more subtle levels. For his own private research purposes Harry Oldfield has invented a piece of equipment which seems to make visible some interesting energy effects with light using computer technology. This is known as the PIP technique (Polycontrast Interference Photography).

Oldfield feels that the various swirls of colour he sees in and around the body relate in some way to the subtle energies and possibly the chakras. Over the years he has photographed the energies of literally hundreds of different people and he now feels he can detect the difference between vibrant energy fields belonging to the fit and healthy and the distorted fields which suggest the presence of or potential for illness. Oldfield uses his various detectors widely as a method of diagnosis to investigate the possibility of weakness, stress or disease in the energy field. On numerous occasions these methods have been verified by doctors using orthodox medical procedures such as X-rays and blood tests. Mr Oldfield insists, however, that his work is still in the research stage and has a long way to go before it can be accepted scientifically.

As we shall see in Chapter Four, flowers and their essences seem to interact with and influence the body's energy field in remarkable ways.

CHAPTER THREE

Shock, Stress and Pollution

Each person's whole energy system – aura, subtle bodies, chakras and meridians – forms a sort of personal 'blueprint' or 'body map'. We are all born with this energetic blueprint which, like a thumbprint, is quite unique and different from person to person, however subtly. This energetic pattern holds within it characteristics that endow us with the potential to be as perfect – physically, mentally, emotionally and spiritually – as we can possibly be.

When all the elements of your energy system are in balance you experience a deep sense of contentment and wellbeing. These are the times when life is joyful and everything feels comfortable. Think of those days when you wake up brimming with energy and looking forward to the day ahead. This abundant physical vitality goes hand in hand with a clear, focused mind. You are blessed with a sense of inner calm and cannot be ruffled by other people or the hustle and bustle of life. Deep down you feel safe and secure, as if cocooned from any danger lurking in the outside world, while at the same time totally involved in the here and now. These benefits come from knowing you are following a path or going in a direction that is right for you, one that will bring real purpose and meaning to your life.

For many of us such sensations are usually rare and fleeting. This is because the stresses and strains of living conspire to prevent us from growing to fulfil our potential to be perfect. However, we are all capable of feeling this way most of the time because we are blessed with an intelligence or Higher Self that is aware of this energetic blueprint and knows how to keep the entire energy network in order. In other words, we intuitively or instinctively know what is best for us.

Sadly, we do not always hear or heed the wisdom of this inner voice. In childhood it does not matter too much if our energy systems are thrown off-balance, for there is an abundance of energy or *chi* which can be used to override any disturbance or misalignment. But there comes a point in time when this energy reserve is exhausted and the imbalance begins to become ingrained in the system.

The Higher Self knows when this is happening and sends us warning signals in the form of physical, emotional and psychological symptoms. Typical signs of an energy imbalance are tiredness, feelings of anxiety, irritability and depression, as well as a susceptibility to colds and other infections. If an imbalance is not corrected, it will become firmly entrenched in the energy system and the resulting symptoms will get worse with time. It is my opinion that disease shows itself in the physical body only after disturbances of energy flow have already become crystallized in the subtle structural patterns of the higher-frequency bodies.

I believe that nature holds a cure for every ill, and that the Higher Self will guide us towards certain plants, herbs and flowers that can restore balance in our energetic system. In Chapter Four you will find out how to follow your intuition and choose a combination of flower essences that will displace the disharmony in your energy system.

Before looking more closely at how flower essences work their wonders, let us first look at ways in which our energy systems can be thrown out of kilter.

Shattering the Balance

Shock and stress in their many guises have a devastating effect on the subtle energy system. You can visualize this sudden shock as a pebble being hurled into a tranquil pond, sending ripples or shock waves reverberating through the water or, in this case, the subtle anatomy. This 'pebble', then, can be seen as the root cause of any upset, while the ripples are the physical repercussions of shock. Unlike the pond, however, which becomes still once the pebble has dropped to the bottom, when shock makes an impact on our subtle energy systems the disruptive effects linger unless steps are taken to bring everything back into balance.

As a consequence of shock the subtle bodies are thrown out of alignment and end up becoming either too close or too far apart from one another. When the mental and emotional bodies are not properly aligned to the etheric, for example, we experience feelings of anxiety. When the mental and emotional bodies are too close together we become prone to feelings of frustration and unknown fears, and are unable to make clear-cut decisions. Sometimes the properties of the subtle bodies spill over into each other, this is known as the 'spillage effect'. When the mental body flows into the emotional one, mental lethargy and loss of confidence ensues. Any misalignment in the subtle bodies ultimately filters down to the physical body, where it triggers a range of symptoms depending on which part of the body is affected.

Shock can be divided into two categories: traumatic and long, slow shock.

Traumatic Shock

We live in a world full of horrific events that are often too distressing even to think about. Some of these, such as natural disasters, unpredictable violence and the death of a loved one, are age-old. Others, such as car accidents and bomb blasts which can maim and kill, are relatively recent phenomena. At some time or other we are all likely to experience personally the shock of some traumatic event.

The worst kinds are invariably those that are sudden and unexpected because they take us unawares. As they are not part of our ordinary life, we are totally unprepared for them and they shake us to the very core of our being. The medical profession is only just beginning to appreciate the impact of such shock on our physical and psychological wellbeing. It has come to realize that such trauma gives rise to a range of symptoms resembling those experienced by shell-shocked war veterans. Symptoms can last a lifetime unless steps are taken to redress their far-reaching effects.

The so-called Post Traumatic Stress Disorder (PTSD) is now used to describe the aftermath of shock. The repercussions clearly permeate every level of our being.

Physically, those suffering from traumatic shock feel exhausted and drained of energy. In time the tiredness may lift, but it invariably gives way to all kinds of minor ailments such as stomach upsets, stiff necks and so forth. As such symptoms appear some time after the event has taken place, they often seem to have no apparent cause. Little wonder, then, that those suffering from PTSD are often thought of as hypochondriacs.

Shock has a particularly potent influence on the mind. Concentration becomes difficult, thoughts are blurred and decisions about even everyday issues such as when to do the shopping can pose problems. Emotions are volatile and range from anger and irritability to depression and despair. Sufferers often over-react to events that would not normally upset them, and steer themselves away from any kind of pressure. They may even suffer from panic attacks. Confidence and self-esteem dwindle, making those suffering from shock less inclined to tackle new projects which they would previously have relished as a challenge.

On a spiritual level, many feel compelled to reassess their lives. In the worst cases doubts arise as to whether life is really worth living.

Long, Slow Shock

This is more insidious than traumatic shock, for we are often unaware of its existence and it becomes an integral part of our lives. Long, slow shock can start to take its toll even before we are born. Although safe inside the womb, the developing foetus will detect and react to its mother's stresses. Anxieties about her relationship with her partner and her fears and apprehension about motherhood can all be sensed by her unborn child.

In childhood we may experience stress when deprived of the right kind of love, attention and emotional nourishment. Ironically it can be equally stressful to be swamped by too much love (in the form of overprotectiveness or possessiveness). Parents who threaten to withhold their love unless they are obeyed also create a stressful environment for their offspring. In addition, children whose parents are always quarrelling can suffer the effects of long, slow shock, as will those whose mother or father has a drinking problem or an incapacitating illness. As this kind of stress goes unnoticed and is often present for prolonged periods of time, it becomes so familiar that it appears to be normal. We usually fail even to identify it as shock.

The effects of long, slow shock are cumulative, which means that by the time a person reaches adulthood it has produced the same disruptive effect on the subtle energy system as sudden trauma. Shock and stress set up an abrasive vibration which is at odds with the natural rhythm of the cells and forces them to 'dance to a different tune'. This ultimately affects the smooth and efficient functioning of all the organs and tissues. If left untreated, such distortion in the energy system ultimately manifests itself as a disease of the mind, body and spirit.

The medical profession now agrees that stress can indeed make us more susceptible to illness. This is the reason we often tend to catch cold or fall victim to an infection after a stressful event has taken place, or when we feel overly stressed at home or work. Some forward-thinking physicians believe that negative emotions such as anxiety, fear, anger, frustration and irritability play crucial roles in undermining the body's resistance to disease.

Researchers working in the relatively new field of psychoneuroimmunology (or PNI) are attempting to fathom the link between such negative emotions and various disease states. They suggest that psychological and emotional states undermine our resistance in the way that they interact with our nervous, endocrine and immune systems. Seen from an energetic perspective, shock has the effect of throwing the emotional and mental bodies out of alignment. They leak into each other and, in turn, spill into the etheric body.

As a result of shock or stress the etheric body can no longer hold its boundaries and perform its job of defending the physical body from disturbance in the subtle bodies.

The etheric body is also closely affiliated with the nervous system, which in turn is closely bound to the immune system. This then, is how mental and emotional disturbances act as immunosuppressants, weakening the body's natural defences and resistance to illness.

In cases of severe shock or trauma such as a bereavement or being violently attacked or wounded, the astral and etheric bodies are suddenly and dramatically thrown out of alignment. When this happens the aura breaks and holes appear. These gaps are potentially dangerous as the physical body is no longer fully protected and becomes vulnerable. It is essential to clear the effects of shock out of the system, for if the subtle bodies are misaligned, the *chi* or life force that sustains us cannot filter through and replenish our physical body.

Years ahead of his time, Dr Edward Bach (creator of the Bach Flower Remedies), realized that psychological upsets can be a root cause of disease. Bach was also aware that shock and stress provoke emotional or mental distress by heightening imbalances in the personality. Someone who normally has a tendency towards impatience and who prefers to work at his or her own speed, for instance, will become increasingly irritable, impetuous and prone to outbursts of temper and nervous tension as a result of shock or stress.

Bach described and discovered flower remedies for 38 negative states of mind. These remedies aim to bring you back to a state of emotional equilibrium. In keeping with various ancient philosophies, Bach believed that peace of mind and physical wellbeing go hand in hand.

In his book *Heal Thyself*, Bach wrote:

> We must steadfastly practise peace, imaging our minds as a lake ever to be kept calm, without waves or even ripples, to disturb its tranquillity and gradually develop this state of peace until no event, no circumstance, no other personality is able under any condition to ruffle the surface of that lake or raise within us any feelings of irritability, depression or doubt.

In this book's Encyclopedia of Flower Remedies and Ailment Chart you will find essences helpful for many almost every permutation of shock and stress, including the urban stress that comes of the loneliness, isolation and loss of identity many of us feel as cosy, tight-knit communities disappear and new technology and pollution insidiously change the very nature of our environment. In Chapter Six you will also find excellent first-aid combinations to have to hand in case of sudden shocks and emergencies.

Chemical Pollutants

Clean water, fresh air and natural foods are essential for good health, yet slowly and insidiously they are being polluted by synthetic chemicals.

Car emissions contain a noxious mixture of chemicals which irritate the lungs, trigger asthma attacks, exacerbate chest troubles and increase our vulnerability to respiratory infections. Carbon monoxide competes with oxygen in the blood and can, at high levels, suffocate the tissues. Breathlessness, dizziness, nausea, lethargy and faintness are typical symptoms. The situation is exacerbated during the summer months, for in the presence of strong sunlight the chemicals in exhaust fumes react to form ozone. At ground levels ozone creates smog that can cause eye irritations, headaches and breathing difficulties. It also damages plants.

Even indoors the air may be far from pure. Sealing buildings hermetically in order to conserve energy also encourages a buildup of irritant substances. While cigarette smoke is often the chief offender, chemicals given off by photocopying machines and carpets add to the load. Toxic gases may even evaporate from the adhesives and preservatives used in construction. Polluted air can cause headaches, difficulty concentrating, stinging eyes, sore throats and skin problems as well as lingering coughs and colds, in part because they create a grey etheric mucus-type substance which clogs up our energy system.

Chemicals in our food and water may come from industrial waste flushed into the seas and rivers, whereby they enter the food chain. Some of these synthetic chemicals, such as chlorinated organics, are extremely persistent. After entering the environment they accumulate in the food chain, sometimes building to high concentrations in certain animals. A typical example is PCBs (polychlorinated biphenyls), which are now banned but are still found in many foods, especially fish.

In addition to these long-lived chemicals, a huge number are also in daily use. Most commercially grown fruits, vegetables and cereals are liberally dowsed with at least one, but usually several, different chemicals as they grow and are kept in storage. Some crops may be sprayed with up to six different chemicals before they reach the supermarket shelves.

Particularly worrying is the little-known 'cocktail' effect or combined activity of many different chemicals. Emerging evidence suggests that pesticides and PCBs may act as immunosuppressants, contributing to the incidence of allergies and viral infections.

On an energetic level, chemical pollutants cloud the subtle anatomy, preventing realignment and directly affecting the opening and closing of the chakras. If not cleared from the system they can damage these important energy centres.

Protecting yourself from Chemical Pollutants

- Vitamins A and E help the lungs and air passages to withstand smoke and chemical damage. Together with vitamin C and selenium they work as antioxidants, preventing pollutants from harming the body cells. Vitamin C also helps detoxify pesticide residues, while vitamins A and E protect the liver from chemical abuse and the B-complex vitamins increase efficiency of detoxification systems. The minerals calcium, magnesium and zinc also bolster resistance.
- Ionizers and air purifiers help to remove pollutant particles from the air and plants can help to diffuse office chemicals.
- Buy organically grown foods whenever possible. Alternatively, wash all fruit and vegetables in a mixture of filtered water and 1 tablespoon of cider vinegar.

- Cold-pressed vegetable oils such as sunflower, olive and safflower reduce the absorption of toxins and speed their elimination.
- Select free-range poultry, eggs and game whenever possible.
- Avoid eating organ meats, as chemicals and hormones can concentrate in an animal's liver and kidneys.
- Opt for bottled spring water and invest in a water filter which will extract pesticide residues as well as nitrates and heavy metals from your tap water.
- Flower remedies to combat chemical pollution can be found in the Ailment Chart.
- A specific 'cleansing' recipe can be found in Chapter Seven.

Electromagnetic Pollution

The earth has its own electromagnetic field which pulses, like a heart, at 470 beats per minute or 7.83Hz (beats per second). These pulses are known as the Schumann waves after the German professor who discovered them in 1952.

It is no coincidence that we have in our bodies a pulse that is approximately the same, in the electrical signals – the alpha and beta waves – sent out by our brains. It is thought that this natural electromagnetic pulse may have a role to play in maintaining and sustaining good health. It is well acknowledged that NASA fits its spacecraft with 7.83Hz oscillators to give its astronauts something to make them feel more comfortable – that is, it helps to regulate their sleeping/waking cycles.

Nowadays, however, the earth's natural pulse is being swamped by other forms of electrically and magnetically generated fields. Electromagnetic radiation from overhead power cables and pylons, televisions, computers, VDUs and radio and satellite transmitters is filling the atmosphere with what is commonly known as electronic smog. It may literally blanket the natural signals needed for good health.

Those which are the greatest cause for concern are the so-called ELFs (extremely low frequencies) because they are so similar to those of our own bodies. Particularly strong electromagnetic fields generated by such frequencies may have the power to influence our brainwaves, resulting in various behavioural and physical problems.

Depression, anxiety, irritability, chronic tiredness, headaches, nausea, sweating and indigestion are among the wide range of symptoms that have been attributed to electromagnetic pollution. Offices in particular tend to be filled with a wealth of artificial fields, which may contribute to what is known as Sick Building Syndrome.

Electromagnetic radiation can also occur naturally due to geographic faults (also known as 'geopathic stress') or underground streams and rivers. Ley lines are believed to indicate places where the earth's magnetic field is particularly potent. Such forms of radiation impinge on and affect our own electromagnetic force-field. X-rays, microwaves and even ultraviolet rays from the sun can distort the subtle bodies and, if powerful enough, can also alter the structure of DNA, the genetic material of our cells.

The consequences of continual overexposure to such radiation may not show physically until 20 years after the event.

In his book, *Electromagnetic Fields of Life* the Russian physicist, A S Presman of the Department of Biophysics at Moscow University, explains the detailed experiments he carried out in 1968 which led to his discovery that such radiation was linked to physical problems such as blood disorders, hypertension, heart attacks, sexual dysfunction, lack of energy and nervous exhaustion.

Evidence is emerging that long-term exposure to emissions from VDUs, computers, word processors and television screens can cause chromosomal damage. Studies remain inconclusive and controversial, but some research has linked excessive VDU work with pregnancy problems including miscarriage, stillbirths and birth defects. Embryos are particularly vulnerable to electromagnetic radiation in the first trimester when the cells are rapidly dividing. During this incredible growth spurt, the subtle blueprint has a particularly important role to play in ensuring that everything runs smoothly. It is possible that harmful electromagnetic radiation may damage the blueprint, with far-reaching consequences.

Protecting yourself from Electromagnetic Pollution
- Switch off electrical appliances when not in use.
- Prevent static buildup by filling your home or office with bowls of flowers, sprinkling water on all carpets and wearing natural materials like cotton and silk instead of synthetics.
- Never wear rubber-soled shoes.
- Avoid being in the vicinity of pylons and overhead cables.
- Do not set up home in areas known to be affected by geopathic stress.

Flower remedies to combat electromagnetic pollution can be found in the Ailment Chart. Australian Bush Electro is one suggested combination that works well (*see* study on Electro and radiation in Chapter Eight Proving Essences Work).

Social Poisons

Many of us rely heavily on different kinds of props to boost our energy levels, steady or stupefy our nerves and generally help us to cope with our frantic pace of life. Alcohol, cigarettes and caffeine-laden drinks, however, only provide us with short-lived energy and, once the effects wear off, leave us feeling more depleted than before. These 'social poisons' also have dangerous side-effects.

Alcohol

Alcohol damages cells of the brain and nervous system, giving rise to a wide variety of symptoms ranging from lack of concentration, confusion, memory loss, insomnia or lethargy, to agitation, irritability and exhaustion.

At an energetic level, alcohol loosens and misaligns the subtle anatomy. It has a particularly disruptive influence on the etheric and astral bodies, making them slip out of sympathy with each other, which is why self-control and willpower are weakened. Alcohol also gives rise to a murky, greenish-brown aura congested with a sticky, mucus-like substance.

Cigarettes

Cigarette smoke contains a cocktail of noxious chemical substances, many of which are known to be carcinogenic. The health hazards of smoking are well known, but the harm cigarettes cause the energy system is also significant. Smoke clouds and weakens the subtle anatomy, surrounding it with a fog which dulls and discolours the normally bright, vibrant hues of the aura. It also prevents the aura from cleansing itself. The etheric body is particularly affected by this grey mucus, which undermines the body's first line of defence.

Caffeine

Coffee and caffeine-rich foods and drinks stimulate the adrenal glands into producing adrenaline, a hormone normally secreted in times of stress which gives us a sudden rush of energy and mental focus. The effects do not last long, and when caffeine levels fall we invariably end up feeling as tired as before. Increasing caffeine intake acts as an additional stress, which produces feelings of anxiety, irritability and jumpiness. Excessive caffeine intake has also been linked to breast lumps in women.

From an energetic viewpoint, caffeine disturbs the flow of energy in the meridian system. This affects the etheric body, which in turn causes leakage in the emotional and mental bodies. An imbalance in these energies results in emotional instability and disruption to the nervous system. It also upsets the solar plexus chakra, the seat of emotional balance – and the effects then filter down to the stomach.

Importantly, caffeine actually prevents flower remedies from working by misaligning the subtle bodies.

Certain flower essences help to overcome addiction to these social props, while others counter their negative impact on the subtle energy systems (*see* the Encyclopedia, Ailment Chart and Recipe sections of this book).

Social drugs

The chemical cocktails of recreational drugs, the easy availability of cocaine, marijuana etc. that are now so much part of society is creating havoc with our systems, weakening the immunity and undermining the delicate balance of our physical emotional and psychological health, causing codependence and toxicity in an environment already overloaded with pollution. To survive this toxic climate, we need to keep our bodies as healthy and clear as possible in order to be able to fulfil our potential destiny.

Here a combination of Blue China Orchid (*Aus Liv*) and the No.24 Anti-Addiction remedy (*Him A*) would be helpful.

Illness and Medication

Modern medicines may be essential when it comes to treating physical illness, and they undoubtedly do save lives. On the flip side of the coin, many also have undesirable side effects.

These vary from drug to drug, but they all have a generally disruptive influence on the energy systems. They tend to cloud the subtle anatomy and cause the subtle bodies to separate from one another, at the same time they prevent realignment. They also affect the chakras' function of regulating and dispersing energy – especially the throat chakra, which is particularly susceptible to drugs.

Steroids, for example, create congestion in the solar plexus and heart chakras, preventing the nervous and muscular systems from receiving energy or life force.

Taken in conjunction with orthodox medication, flower essences gently help to buffer these undesirable effects. They can also be taken after a course of medication to realign the subtle bodies and generally rebalance the energy systems.

More importantly, perhaps, flower essences actually allay the need for taking orthodox medication, for if taken soon enough they can help prevent disease from occurring in the first place.

Flower remedies may, for example, negate the need for antibiotics by boosting the body's natural immunity. They help by clearing away physical toxins as well as toxic thoughts, emotions and, last but not least, spiritual toxicity which pollutes the energy system. As a consequence the body's natural defence system is strengthened and becomes better able to repel viral and bacterial invasion.

At present there is increasing concern about the repercussions of using drugs like antibiotics too frequently. It is well recognized that bacteria gradually adapt to any antibiotic, so in using these drugs too much they are made less useful for everyone. Yet in the United States sales of antibiotics have doubled since the mid-1980s, and seven out of ten Americans are prescribed these drugs when they seek treatment for common colds. Is it just coincidence that drug-resistant infections are also soaring?

Resistant germs are hard to treat and can spread through the community. They do not threaten us all equally. A healthy immune system repels most bacterial invaders regardless of their susceptibility to drugs. However, certain people such as the elderly and sick are more vulnerable, and when they contract such bacterial diseases they are harder to treat. While drug companies may see inventing new wonder antibiotics as the ultimate challenge, surely it is better to strengthen our natural immunity and encourage both doctors and patients to stop abusing the weapons we have.

(For a recipe to help boost the immune system, *see* page 335.)

An effective combination is Formula 38 from Him Adit range and Super Immunity from the Pacific Essence Combinations.

Physical Injury

In cases where disease is already manifest and there is a need for surgery, it is good to know that flower essences can help to reduce the effects of such trauma and aid recuperation.

When tissues are cut and injured during an operation or accident, the subtle energy system receives an almighty jolt. Wherever the physical damage occurs it is accompanied by a rupture in the etheric body print. This must be healed along with the tissues to ensure that the damaged area does not remain weak, vulnerable and prone to recurrent problems. For even when the scars have faded, the subtle bodies may still be misaligned.

Before undergoing any operation it is a good idea to take Bach's Rescue Remedy or Five Flower Remedy, or Australian Bush Emergency Essence to ease the shock and trauma. As well as the shock of the operation, anaesthetics themselves also throw you into a state of suspension. This results in feelings of disorientation, unworldliness and dragging tiredness. (*See* page 336 for my recipe for clearing the after-effects of anaesthesia.)

Inheriting Imbalances in the Subtle Energy System

It is important to clear away any imbalance in the subtle anatomy, otherwise it can become etched in the system and passed on to future generations. These inherited flaws in the energetic bodies are referred to as miasms.

The concept of miasms was originally introduced by Dr Samuel Hahnemann, the founder of homeopathy. He was puzzled to find that some patients failed to respond to treatment, while others who improved relapsed after only a short time. He looked at these 'difficult' cases and found a common 'blocking' factor in their personal or family history – such as the presence of certain diseases which have been passed on from one generation to another. He called these blocks 'miasms'.

We might visualize a miasm as a void or lack of life force. They are usually stored in the subtle bodies – especially the etheric, emotional, mental and, to a lesser extent, the astral body. Here miasms may lie dormant for long periods of time, only flaring up occasionally and leading to chronic or acute illnesses, trauma, stress and age-related conditions. A bad fall or emotional shock may easily allow them to filter down from the subtle bodies into the physical anatomy, resulting in the development of various symptoms. As we get older, our natural vitality diminishes, making it easier for miasms to emerge. This could help explain why we tend to become more prone to all kinds of disease as we age.

Miasms

Flower essences help to remove miasms from the system. Once a remedy's life force filters down to the physical level, an immediate rebalancing and readjustment begins to take place. The essences release the miasm from the cells' genetic material and from the subtle bodies, so that it can be discharged from the system.

It may take some time for these shifts to take place, so do not expect miracles to happen overnight.

Dr Hahnemann described three basic types of 'inherited' miasm (psora, syphilitic and sycosis) which he believed to be the underlying causes of chronic disease. Each predisposes a person to a particular range of health problems. Homeopaths have since added many more illness-causing miasms to this list, including tuberculosis, radiation and heavy metals.

Psora

Associated with suppressed skin disease, a psora miasm leads to imbalance in the rhythmic bodily functions and causes general mental and physical irritation. Typical symptoms are tiredness, anxiety, sadness or depression as well as skin disorders, congestion in the tissues and bone structure deformities.

Syphilitic

Associated with suppressed syphilis, this miasm has a destructive effect on all the tissues, especially the bones. Cardiac and neurological symptoms are common. Those carrying this miasm are easily upset, sentimental, irritable and suspicious. This miasm may manifest as meningitis.

Sycosis

Associated with suppressed gonorrhoea, this miasm encourages congestion in the skin, the pelvic region, the joints and the digestive, respiratory and urinary tracts. It may cause fearfulness, nervousness and amorality.

Tuberculosis

This miasm may cause susceptibility to respiratory, circulatory, urinary and digestive problems, resulting, for example, in weight loss and poor circulation.

Those carrying this miasm typically tend to be escapists who feel unable to make decisions or face life's realities. It may also manifest as mental illness and cancer.

Modern Miasms

Most homeopathic research into miasms was conducted in the 1800s and early 1900s, when infectious diseases such as tuberculosis and syphilis were prevalent. Today we are faced with new threats to our health, which derive from modern-day pollutants and are known as 'acquired miasms'.

Petrochemical

Springing from the major increase in petrol and chemical products, the problems this causes are fluid retention, diabetes, infertility, impotence, miscarriage, hair loss/greying hair, muscle degeneration, skin blemishes, or a metabolic imbalance resulting in the storage of fat in tissues. It also blocks assimilation of vitamin K, causing circulatory and endocrine disorders. Those affected find it difficult to resist stress and suffer from various types of psychosis, especially schizophrenia and autism. Leukaemia, skin and lymph cancer can also occur.

Radiation

Associated with the massive increase in background radiation since the Second World War, this miasm primarily affects the skin, connective tissue, circulation and reproductive systems. Symptoms include premature ageing, slower cell division, loss of skin elasticity, rashes, lupus, skin cancer, anaemia, leukaemia, arthritis, allergies, bacterial inflammations (especially in the brain), hair loss, hardening of the arteries, miscarriage, excessive bleeding in women and sterility or a drop in sperm count in men.

Heavy Metals

Resulting from increased levels of toxic metals and chemicals such as lead, mercury, radium, arsenic, aluminium, fluoride and sulphuric acid, the symptoms of this miasm include allergies, fluid retention, an inability to assimilate calcium, viral inflammations and excessive hair loss.

Remedies to combat all these types of miasms can be found in the Ailment Chart. Lotus in particular is excellent as a general aid for miasms.

The following Australian Bush Essences are suggested for the following miasms:

- Tuberculosis: Tall Mulla Mulla;
- Psora: Rough Bluebell;
- Sycosis: Bush Iris;
- Heavy Metal and Petrochemical: Wild Potato Bush;
- Radiation: Mulla Mulla.

CHAPTER FOUR

Essences In Action

Learning to use and prescribe flower remedies

No two people are identical. We may share similar physical characteristics, behavioural tendencies and personality traits but deep down each of us is unique. Our individuality determines the ways in which we cope with and react to any kind of stress in our lives.

Two people may exhibit typical symptoms associated with a frazzled nervous system. Each may be anxious, irritable, on edge and suffering from sleeping problems, indigestion and butterflies in the stomach, but each will be this way for entirely different reasons. One may be going through a marriage break-up while the other may be experiencing a conflict at work. Delve deeper and it will become clear that their problems arise from a certain personality trait or a particular behavioural pattern. For this reason it is essential to treat each person as a unique whole, rather than just addressing his or her symptoms or illness. The beauty of flower essences is that they help us to become aware of elements in our nature which are undermining our sense of wellbeing. They do not work on us, but with us. They bring our attention to any imbalance that exists within, then lend their energetic support so we can release it gently from our lives. In this way we can begin to take responsibility for our own health and happiness.

Know Thyself

As you begin to use flower remedies, you will be embarking on an exciting adventure of self-discovery which will enable you to understand yourself, and why you think and act in certain ways. As the remedies get to work your self-awareness will continue to grow, bringing with it a new freedom to do whatever you wish in life.

In the Encyclopedia section you will see that there are literally hundreds of flower essences from all over the world to choose from. Each is associated with particular qualities or properties. The real art lies in selecting the essences that are best for you. To do this you need to devote some time to thinking about yourself. This may sound narcissistic, but it is an essential part of self-healing.

Reflecting on your own personality is a good starting point. Although this is as individual as your thumbprint, there are certain personality traits or tendencies which prevail in human nature. These characteristics have a strong influence on how you handle and react to stress.

Bach's 12 Personality Types and Remedies

Dr Edward Bach identified 12 key personality traits, and the first flowers he searched for related to these:

> Fear
> Terror
> Mental torture or worry
> Indifference or boredom
> Doubt or discouragement
> Indecision
> Overenthusiasm
> Discouragement
> Weakness
> Self-distrust
> Overconcern
> Pride or aloofness

Take Impatiens, for example. As its name suggests, this flower is for people whose outstanding characteristic is impatience. They tend to rush around and are critical of other people's shortcomings. As a result they are prone to irritability, nervous tension, overexertion and accidents.

In contrast, Clematis relates to quiet, dreamy, absent-minded people who are wrapped up in their own thoughts and fantasies. Their predominant characteristic is indifference. They tend to lack concentration and are susceptible to clumsiness and sleepiness.

Bach often saw human characteristics reflected in the plants themselves. In each flower family you will find remedies describing many permutations of the basic personality traits. Although some may seem very similar, if you read the descriptions carefully you will see there are subtle differences. You should look for flower essences whose qualities reflect the way in which you see yourself. The remedies will help to emphasize your positive characteristics while tempering negative tendencies which can lead you into trouble.

It is important to remember that such tendencies are not fixed. With the help of flower essences we can alter certain aspects of our personality for the better.

A welcome side-effect of cultivating your better qualities and tempering the less attractive ones is that your relationships with others will be easier and more fulfilling. Many people seem to end up in partnerships that begin beautifully but then, when the magic has faded, become unworkable. When you become truer to yourself, you will automatically draw to you the sort of people who possess qualities you genuinely admire and find attractive. All relationships, be they intimate or purely platonic, will be fun and mutually satisfying.

While personality affects the way we handle other people and life in general, our constitution determines how resilient or susceptible we are to becoming ill. Constitution is best defined as temperament and state of health. It is your genetic inheritance which has been modified by experiences in life and the environment. While a strong constitution can withstand considerable pressure without flagging, a weaker one is more susceptible to illness.

If, for example, all your grandparents died of old age and your parents have been healthy all their lives; if your mother was healthy throughout her pregnancy (she didn't smoke, drink, etc.), if your parents' marriage was happy and your birth uneventful, you should be blessed with a strong constitution.

If, on the other hand, your grandparents died at early ages of cancer or heart disease, one of your parents had tuberculosis as a child and the other suffered from asthma and eczema, then your chances of inheriting a weak constitution are far greater.

Take heart, you can still escape the worst of a poor inheritance if your parents were happily married, they took good care of their health and brought you up with plenty of love and a nourishing diet.

Similarly, you may have inherited a potentially strong constitution but if your parents were always arguing and your emotional needs were neglected, your susceptibility to illness will have increased.

In any case, there is no reason to feel lumbered with a flimsy constitution. Flower essences can improve your resilience to every sort of illness in two ways. First, certain essences help to eliminate, at the vibrational level, the inherited genetic weaknesses known as miasms (*see* Chapter Three). Secondly, they can clear away the residual effects of any past traumas as well as the long, slow shock of, for instance, an unhappy childhood, which may have weakened your inherent constitution.

Taking a Case History

Making your own case history is a good way of finding out why you are not feeling as well as you could be. A thorough case history should take into account your personality, constitution, stress – both past and present – to help you to recognize any underlying patterns.

You should list any physical symptoms and psychological problems you would like to treat. These are signs that your mind, body and spirit are out of balance, so it is important to write them all down, no matter how trivial some may seem. They are an expression of need, a call for help from your body.

In addition to noting any symptoms you have at present, it is important to consider your health as a child. Systems that are inherently weak often show up quite early in life. If you frequently caught colds, or suffered from sore throats or ear infections which were treated with antibiotics, your immune system is likely to be a weak area. An allergy to dust mites, pollens or certain foods is another telltale sign. Such immune system weakness does not go away of its own accord although your symptoms may shift to give you that impression.

When a weakness in one system exists, others will compensate for it. Over the years these systems may also begin to exhibit symptoms of upset because they have been overworked or overloaded. Adding stress of any kind may precipitate or exacerbate such symptoms because stress plays on any inherent weakness. If you are not sure what your symptoms are telling you, refer to Chapter Six to discover which systems may not be functioning as well as they should.

YOUR OWN CASE HISTORY

Name   Date
Age   Date of birth
Occupation   Marital status
Children

MEDICAL HISTORY

Health problems of a) mother b) father
Illnesses running in the family
Your health as a child
Your health problems as an adult
Past operations, accidents, injuries
If you are a mother, how did you feel during your pregnancy?
Birth – was it trouble-free or difficult?

PERSONALITY TRAITS

Write down as many different personality traits – good and bad – you can think of that best describe you. For example:
Are you impatient or easy going?
Do you prefer to be alone or crave the company of others?
Be as honest and, if possible, ask someone whom you trust and respect to comment on your character assessment.

LIFESTYLE

Stress levels at home
– low (not noticeable)
– moderate (manageable)
– high (struggling to cope)
– excessive (not coping)
Stress levels at work
– low (not noticeable)
– moderate (manageable)
– high (struggling to cope)
– excessive (not coping)
Shock/trauma/loss
– past
– present
Assess your energy levels
– plentiful
– sufficient
– lacking
– totally drained
Best time of the day
Worst time of the day
Do you smoke?
Do you drink alcohol?
If so how often and how much?
Are you taking or have you recently taken prescribed medication?

Addictions

alcohol	sugar/sweet foods
tobacco	chocolate
coffee	tea
other	

RELATIONSHIPS (describe both good and bad points)

With your mother, father, spouse or partner, children

PRESENT SENSE OF WELLBEING

Physical – do you suffer from recurring health problems?
If so list symptoms, for example: colds and flu (how often, seasonal or consistent throughout the year)
– headaches
– digestive problems
– poor circulation

– poor elimination
– sleeping difficulties
– breathing difficulties
– blood pressure (high or low?)

For women only – describe your menstrual cycle. Are your periods regular, do you experience any pain, premenstrual symptoms, mood swings, any other abnormalities?
Mental – do you have difficulty thinking clearly?
If so, list problems, for example:

poor concentration	weak memory
mental fatigue	absent-mindedness
forgetfulness	learning difficulties
mental chatter	

Emotional – do you feel emotionally calm and content?
If not, list your predominant feelings, for example:

anger	confusion
lack of confidence	depression
irritability	mood swings
tearfulness	night fears

Spiritual – are you happy with and feel in control of your life?
If not, list reasons why, for example:
feeling unfulfilled or empty;
not knowing which path to follow;
confusion about beliefs;
disillusionment with life and others.

WELLBEING QUIZ

Give each subject a score of between 0 and 10
0 = no problem 10 = serious problem

Stress	Trauma
Sleep	Health
Fear	Self-esteem
Thoughts	Emotions
Life changes	State of energy
Outside influences	Childhood
Motivation	Sexuality
Fulfilment	Crisis
Relationships	Other

Choosing Flower Essences

By now you may be wondering how many different flower essences you are going to need to deal with your problems. Go through your personal case history again and underline those symptoms that stand out clearly and strongly. It is best to leave vague and unclear symptoms alone for the moment – you may refer to them later if you cannot make up your mind about which is the most appropriate remedy for you. If you are new to taking flower essences, begin with your psychological and physical symptoms before attempting to deal with any spiritual issues.

Chapter Seven discusses in some detail the different emotional and spiritual symptoms that can indicate the deeper cause of any imbalance or problem you may be experiencing. The Ailment Chart (Chapter Five), too, will show you at a glance which essences are indicated for a whole variety of physical, psychological and spiritual problems.

If, for instance, you are suffering from insomnia you will see ten essences listed in the Ailment Chart. Taking each one in turn, refer to the Encyclopedia section where you will find a fuller description of the essence. You may end up with just one or two that are best suited to your particular type of insomnia.

Using Your Intuition

Read the essence descriptions and determine which ones feel right for you. If you are not entirely sure, follow your intuition. Learn to recognize your instinctive 'yes' to some and 'no' to others. Usually certain essences will tend to catch your eye straight away. They are often flowers you naturally prefer. You may already have chosen them for your garden or they may be the kind you most often buy for your home. These may be the ones you will end up choosing for your combination.

Don't try choosing your essences when you are tired and confused. Come back to it when you are feeling more refreshed and relaxed. Taking a few drops of one of the Emergency or Rescue Remedies beforehand can help you calm down.

By Pendulum

If you feel confident about using a pendulum you can dowse for your essences. Most people find they can become reasonably proficient with a little practice.

A pendulum can be anything from a ring to a quartz crystal on a thin chain or string. Its movements provide answers to the questions you choose to ask. To dowse, hold your pendulum between your thumb and forefinger so that it hangs downwards. Swing it gently back and forth. With practice you will find that when you concentrate or think 'yes' the pendulum will start to move in one direction. When you change this to a 'no' it will start to move in another, probably the opposite, direction. It may swing back and forth or in circles – there are no hard and fast rules.

Once you have your positive and negative responses when you ask your pendulum certain questions (such as 'Is this an appropriate essence for me at this time?') it should give you either a yes or no. If it is indecisive, there may be no clear-cut answer.

Creating Your Personal Prescription

Ideally you should select no more than seven flower essences for your personal prescription. These should be the ones you feel will be most helpful at this particular time.

When purchasing a flower essence from any supplier you will be getting what is known as the Stock Essence. This is a concentrated form which will need to be diluted to the proper dosage level to make your personal prescription. (Full directions for making up your personal prescription are given in Chapter Six.)

The Self-Healing Process

Self-healing is invariably a slow and gradual process, so it is important to be patient.

It may have taken many years for negative behavioural patterns or deeply ingrained emotional states to have become a part of your life, so you cannot expect them to vanish overnight. Similarly, physical problems do not appear without warning. Tiredness and mood changes are early warning signs that our internal balance is disturbed, and other symptoms will follow if we do not take stock of our current situation.

Flower essences are not magic bullets – they are subtle remedies which act as catalysts for change. Don't be concerned if you become more aware of your physical or emotional symptoms when you start the course of treatment. This is natural and shows that the remedies have begun their conversation with the blueprint. My clients often report that a part of them (the Higher Self) is watching the whole process, making them more aware of what their symptoms are telling them.

Often a physical condition or emotional state will clear, only for a deeper emotion to surface. This particular emotion may be associated with an earlier stressful experience or trauma in your life. It is often important to retrace your steps, as if going back in time in order to release that emotion, before you can move forward. This is nothing to be alarmed about. You will not have to relive the emotional intensity or pain of the experience. It is more like being a passive observer who remains detached from what is happening.

Those using the flower essences for physical and psychological problems may find that as time goes on they are drawn to the more spiritually-orientated remedies. It is rather like peeling back the petals of a rosebud until you finally get to the real source of your problems.

Tips on Choosing Remedies for Others

Flower essences are wonderful remedies for babies, young children, animals and even plants because they are so gentle and free from harmful side-effects. They are incredibly effective – and you do not necessarily have to believe in them to reap their benefits!

As babies and animals cannot say how they are feeling, you will have to use your intuition and read the signs to select the most appropriate flower essences. This is not difficult. After all, mothers instinctively know when their children are anxious, irritable, insecure, frustrated or angry.

For babies and young children you will find symptoms such as teething, restlessness, disturbed sleep, night terrors, temper tantrums and colic listed in the Ailment Chart (Chapter Five). Flower essences for these conditions are often best used individually. If you are making a combination, it is best to keep it simple – a mix of two or three flower essences is plenty. It is helpful, too, to have an all-purpose Emergency or *Five Flower Remedy* (*see* pages 145 and 95) on hand for minor accidents or traumas which end in tears, such as falling over or being given routine inoculations.

Pets and other animals can also benefit from being given flower essences, especially those that are deemed to be neurotic or aggressive. (*See* Pets and Animals section in the Encyclopedia.) It is worth bearing in mind that most animals are very sensitive to the emotional states of their owners, so if you are giving remedies to your cat, dog or horse, it may be a good idea to take some yourself as well.

Remedies for shock may be given to plants to aid their growth, reduce infection and minimize the shock of transplanting, pruning or any harm brought on by poor weather or accident.

Combinations

There are now some useful combinations available tailor-made in response to the challenges of today which can help when feeling too stressed to even think of chosing the right essence for yourself

Taking Flower Remedies

It is important to get into the habit of taking a remedy regularly to reap its full benefits. Take two to three drops in the morning (on rising) and in the evening (on retiring). At these times your mind is usually most relaxed and receptive to the essences. It may be a good idea to keep your chosen remedy beside your bed so you remember to take it as you wake up and before you go to sleep. Some people find it helpful to focus on the positive qualities of the essence and visualize their symptoms lifting as they take their remedy.

For severe cases you may need to take the remedy more frequently. In addition to your morning and evening dose, take another one at midday. If the symptoms become more intense or get worse – particularly those of a physical nature such as headaches or skin problems – double the number of drops you would normally take until they clear. Towards the end of the two-month treatment course you may find you need to take the essence less frequently. You may even forget to take it altogether, signifying that you no longer need that particular essence or combination of essences.

Ways to Use the Essences

These flower essences are vibrational remedies, so the best way to experience their effects is to surround yourself with them, both inside and out.

By Mouth

The traditional way of taking flower essences (diluted to the dosage level) is to drop them under the tongue. Placing them under the tongue seems to enhance their absorption. This method also hearkens back to the way ancient healers would sip the dewdrops of flowers to cull their precious benefits. Try to avoid letting the dropper touch your mouth, as this tends to create bacterial growth in the essence.

The drops can also be added to drinks such as herbal teas, spring water and juices, but on no account to coffee or tea.

You may dilute the remedies quite a bit. Rather like homeopathic remedies, flower essences are equally effective, if not more so, when they are very dilute.

On The Skin

Flower essences can also be beneficial when gently rubbed onto the skin. The Petite Fleur therapeutic mists are useful here for spraying on the soft areas of the body. Good places to apply them are your forehead, lips, wrists, soles of the feet and palms of the hands.

This method is useful if someone is unable to take the essences by mouth. He or she may, for instance, be unconscious, in which case it may be helpful to give an emergency, first-aid essence to ease the state of shock (*see* page 76).

Another way to apply the flower essences is to add them, usually at Stock concentration, to compresses, body packs, creams, lotions, ointments and oils.

To enhance the effectiveness of a relaxing massage, add a few drops of one or two of the soothing flower essences to your body oil. Good ones to try are Chamomile, Dandelion, Lavender (FES), or Yellow Ginger (Haii).

Another idea is to add a few drops to your favourite moisturizer or skin cream, one you use every day. Some flower essences are particularly helpful for revitalizing and rejuvenating tired, ageing skin (*see* page 295).

Bath Therapy

You can create a remedy bath by adding a few drops of flower essence to your bath and soaking for up to 30 minutes. In these relaxing conditions the energy of the remedy is readily absorbed into the system. Choose one that is most appropriate to your needs at that particular time. After a fraught day at work you may benefit from an essence to clear your mind and promote relaxation (such as White Chestnut, Chamomile (FES), or Five Flower Rescue (Bach). If in need of a morning pick-me-up, it is best to choose an essence that helps counter lethargy (such as Morning Glory (FES; Haii)). A good way to enhance the benefits of the essences is to add a few handfuls of pure sea salt to the bath as it is running.

For a curative night-time treatment, add five drops of your personal prescription to the bath. Stay in the water for 30 minutes.

Body Splash/Aura Sprays

Splashing or spraying your body with flower essences (diluted with pure spring water) is an effective way of treating sensitive skin conditions such as eczema, cold sores, blisters, blemishes and surface grazes. Add seven drops of essence to a bowl of spring water and, if possible, leave out in the sun for a day. Splash the potentized flower water onto the part of your body needing treatment and allow it to dry naturally. Alternatively you could use an atomizer to spray the diluted essences onto your skin.

For burns, insect stings, animal bites or cuts where there is an element of shock or trauma combine a few drops of an emergency/first-aid combination with an appropriate flower essence (see pages 296 and 301). Spray night and morning, or more frequently for shock.

There are a variety of aura sprays that various essences makers have produced for many eventualities like clearing and protecting yourself from negative and discordant energies (see page 339 to make up your own spray).

Another way to benefit from the essences is to spray your clothes and pillow cases before ironing them. For those who have sleeping problems such as insomnia or nightmares, it may be a good idea to place a few drops of an essence on your pillow before going to bed. This can be particularly helpful for babies and children who have a tendency to wake during the night because of nightmares.

Room Spray

Spraying flower essences into the air is an excellent way to improve the atmosphere of any room. Add 4–5 drops to a 250ml plant spray filled with still spring water and spray the mixture around the room every couple of hours.

Cleansing and protecting essences are beneficial for city environments as well as offices filled with cigarette smoke and chemicals given off by photocopiers and so forth (see page 298 of the Ailment Chart).

This method of using the flower essences is also recommended if you have a cold or influenza, as well as for breathing difficulties brought on by asthma or hay fever. An essence for boosting the immune system can help to protect you from infection if a bacterial or viral epidemic has broken out in your place of work. Some essences are particularly helpful for improving the general atmosphere (*see* pages 383–4).

Storing the Essences

It is important to remember that these remedies are pure energy. They are activated and will start to work on your energy system the moment the combination is made up and the spring water is added.

Being 'vibrationally alive', they are highly susceptible to negative influences in the environment. Always store the essences in tinted glass dropper bottles to protect them from sunlight. Keep them away from any electrical or radiation-emitting appliance such as a television, radio or computer. Don't leave them on your dressing table or in your medicine cabinet next to prescribed medication, essential oils, perfume or herbs. If stored in these conditions the liquid may go cloudy, or a mucus-type substance or tiny specks of impurities may form. If this happens, throw it away.

The best place to keep your personal prescription is beside your bed, provided again it is not sharing a space with a clock-radio or other appliances!

PART TWO

Encyclopedia of Flower Essences

This Encyclopedia section is a compilation of flower essences from all around the world. Each floral family offers a wide variety of different essences, many of which are made from flowers that grow locally or are indigenous to a particular country.

You will notice that the properties of one type of flower, for instance Chamomile, may vary slightly according to the family to which it belongs. Just as wines from different regions have their own distinct characteristics, so have flowers. The same rose growing wild in the hedgerows of Britain may have slightly different qualities to that found several thousand miles away in New Zealand, due to differences in habitat, climate and so forth. The description of each flower essence also depends on the interpretations of the person who discovered and originally prepared it.

The essences listed address a broad spectrum of physical, emotional, mental as well as spiritual issues. You may wonder why it is important to have so many different essences at hand, but once you begin to use the remedies this will become clear. As your awareness expands, there will be times when you find that you need remedies of an increasingly refined or higher vibration.

Flower Essence Families

Africa and the Amazon
Andreas Korte Essences (AKO)

Australia, Japan and Thailand
Bush Flower Essences (Aus B)
Living Essences of Australia (Aus L)
Japanese Essences (Aus LJ)
Flowers of the Orient (FO)

Europe
Bach Flower Remedies (B)
Findhorn Flower Essences of Scotland (F)
Harebell Remedies (Hb)
Light Heart Flower Essences (LH)
Green Man Tree Essences (GM)
Sun Essences (Sun)
Habundia Flower Essences (HUB)
Deva Flower Essences (Dv)
Bloesem Flower Essences of the Netherlands (BL)

India
Himalayan Adita Flower Essences (Him A)
Himalayan Flower Enhancers (Him E)

USA, South America and Canada
Alaskan Flower and Environmental Essences (ASK)
Dancing Light Orchid Essences (DL)
Desert Alchemy Flower Essences (Dal)
Flower Essence Society (FES)
Master's Flower Essences (Ma)
Hawaiian Gaia Flower Essences (Haii)
Pacific Essences of Canada (Pac)
Perelandra Rose and Garden Essences (PVi)
Pegasus Essences (Peg)
Petite Fleur Essences (PF)
Star Peruvian Essences (Peru)

Children
Purely Essences Mother & Baby (PE)
Master Flower Essences for Mother and Child (Ma)

Animals
Master Essences for Pets (Ma)
Sun Essences for Animals (Sun)
Dancing Light Happy Pet (DL)

Sound, Light and Environmental Essences
Sound Wave Essences (SW)
White Light Essences (WL)
Alaskan Environmental Essences (Ask E)

Africa and the Amazon

The Amazon is home to a vast number of different species of flowering plants. In Colombia, for example, over 4,000 species of orchid can be found, many of which live 25–35m (80–115ft) up in the trees. Here, at the top of the tropical rainforests, they obtain sufficient light to support their existence. Their roots have adapted to anchor them to the branches so they have no direct contact with the earth. The continent of Africa has many regions of total wilderness and is also home to many unusual flowering plants, as well as many that have yet to be discovered. It was the promise of such untapped potential that attracted Andreas Korte to these subtropical regions in his quest for new and unique flower essences. The names of some of the flowers from which he prepares his essences are protected because they are so rare – to these he gives only code letters/numbers.

Andreas Korte Essences

Andreas Korte is a researcher and specialist in the field of essences. Brought up in a small village by a forest near Lake Constance in Germany, he has always believed in the flower devas. He regards orchids as queens of the plant kingdom, feeling that they have an exceptionally high vibrational rate and are responsible for creating a link between the cosmos, ourselves and the earth. The orchids often take the form or shape of angels and appear to have human features.

Andreas has invented a gentle, ecological method of preparing essences so that the flowers are not harmed in any way. This involves cleaning and preparing one half of a quartz geode (a naturally occurring stone containing crystals split into two semi-spherical halves) and filling it with natural spring water. He then carefully places the geode into the energetic field of the blossoms and leaves it in the sun for a length of time (which differs from flower to flower). The special crystal formation of the geode acts to focus and capture the energy of the flowers.

Co-author of *Orchids, Gemstones and their Healing Energies*, Andreas is currently involved in research projects in Europe, Africa and South America. With the Delph Essence (*see* pages 65–6) he has conducted research into their effectiveness with water activation, illustrated in his book *Dolphins and Whales* and in the chapter on Proving Essences Work

He has developed a unique method which involves light and multilevelled use of all his essences called Light Treatment, as well as creating combinations which address the mind/body and spirit.

Orchids of the Amazon

Aggression Orchid (*Acinetas superba*) Frees and transforms blockages in lower chakras. Releases basic energy, sexuality, impulsiveness and aggression. This powerful essence should be used sparingly and with conscious positive intent.

Amazon River For loosening energetic blockages, especially in the back. Brings free-flowing energy, understanding and comprehension of the planet. Eliminates most physical blocks.

Angel Orchid (*Epidendron secundum*) For opening up to higher states of consciousness. Brings lightness, stepping up the vibrational rate in order to open us to the higher levels of consciousness in a safe manner and allow communication with our spirit guide (guardian angel).

Angel of Protection Orchid (*Miltonia phalaenopsis*) For fragile, sensitive people who need shelter from hostility and harsh environments. Provides a protective shield for sensibilities and vulnerabilities. Improves communication with our spirit guides.

Channelling Orchid (*Oncidium incurvum*) For increasing direct contact and communication with your spirit guide and universal being and to listen to the 'inner voice'. Allows channelling – the receiving and passing on of messages.

Chocolate Orchid (*Stanhopea wadrii*) For those who need to open themselves to more pleasure and take spirituality too seriously. Freedom from self-imposed limits and structures. Allows you to walk the path of joy.

Colour Orchid (*Oncidium lanceanum*) For those who have a tendency to be sad and think life is grey and hopeless. Helps you to recognize that your thoughts determine perceptions and guide your life experiences. Releases dark thoughts and opens us to life's brightness, love and joy

Co-Ordination Orchid (*Cymbidium lowianum*) Opens us to deep cellular consciousness on the physical level, thereby initiating the self-healing process.

Deva Orchid (*Edidendrum prismato-carpum*) For opening up to communication with devas or the spirits of flowers and trees. Brings integration with the natural environment and an opening up to healing from nature.

Fun Orchid (*Vandas tricolor*) For laughter, harmony and love of life. Increases humour and zest for life. Allows you to see life's problems and idiosyncrasies from a different and wider perspective.

Heart Orchid (*Laeliocattleya hybrid*) Strengthens the heart and solar plexus. For raising self-centredness to the heart level. Harmonizes and balances the emotional body. Transforms ego-centred love to pure spiritual love.

Higher Self Orchid (*Laeliocattleya anceps clara*) For communication and self-knowledge. Connects you to your Higher Self and increases your capacity to act as a messenger. Enhances channelling abilities.

Horn of Plenty Orchid (*Cattleya warscewiczii*) For experiencing infinite, 'universal' love, giving without restriction. Brings the ability to give and receive this love freely. Brings abundance into our lives.

Inspiration Orchid (*Cattleya trianaei*)
For inner inspiration. Helps you get in
touch with higher spiritual levels, bringing
inspiration that can be used creatively.
Helps fulfil our dreams.

Love Orchid (*Oncidium abortivum*) For
opening the heart chakra. Allows energy
and love to flow freely. Opens the heart,
allowing love to be utilized for healing and
compassion. For those pursuing energy or
personal growth therapy.

Past Life Orchid (*Paphiopedilum
harrysianum*) For enhancing self-
knowledge, understanding and inspiration.
Facilitates access to past-life stream of
consciousness – 'the Akashic Records' – to
retrieve lost skills, meanings and stored
knowledge. This essence can help reveal
deep-rooted causes for many emotional
problems.

Psyche or Soul Orchid (*Paphiopedilum
insigne*) For knowledge of life. Allows
access to the subconscious in order to
discover the reason for our existence, our
life's purpose.

Sun Orchid (*Epidendrum chioneum*) For
balance and harmony. Connects us directly
with the energy of the sun by opening and
harmonizing the solar plexus and rebalancing the ego.

Venus Orchid (*Anguloa clowesii*) For
developing the positive qualities of understanding, tenderness, love and listening
skills. Stimulates the female (yin) receptive
energy promoting these qualities.

Victoria Regia Orchid (*Victoria
amazonica*) For explosive energy and transformation. Acting on the first chakra it
brings a powerful release of natural energy,
or kundalini. Liberates from deeply held
fears of life survival. Supports the transformation process of dying and death itself.

Rose Essences

Cinnamon Rose (*Rosa Majalis*) Enables
us not to lose faith when darkness has set
in. Gives us hope when we can see no way
out of present troubles. Opens us to new
possibilities. Helps us heal our emotional
wounds and returns our optimism in the
future to us when all seems dark.

Green Rose (*Rosa Chinesis Viridiflora*)
Alleviates the negative effects of too much
pressure and stress. Restores inner calm
and detachment. Releases tensions and
widens our perspective by renewing the
heart (fourth chakra).

Japanese Rose (*Rosa Roxburgh*) For
those who are too modest and compliant.
Teaches us modesty and humility in love
whilst helping develop our hope for love in
life. Life force energy emerges from hope,
and love is the essence of life, and as we
practice restraint, we learn to use our
thorns only if it is truly necessary.

Provence Rose (*Rosa Centifolia*)
Connects heart and mind, thereby helping
us resolve (apparent) conflicts between our
thoughts and our emotions. Helps those
who only consider love intellectually, who
seek to 'explain' it instead of feeling it. On
the other hand, this rose can also help us
face reality instead of being ruled solely by
our emotions.

Queen of Denmark Rose (*Rosa Alba*)
Relieves emotional distress and tension
when we feel hurt. Helps us to pull the
'thorns' from our heart and alleviates past
wounds.

Sara Von Fleet Rose (*Rosa Rugosa*)
Opens the heart (fourth chakra)
profoundly so we can experience love at its
deepest levels, the kind of love that gives
without expecting anything in return. For a
childlike, cheerful heart.

Souvenir De Philmon Cochet Rose
(*Rosa Rugosa*) Real love requires a unity of
mind, body, and soul. This rose helps
establish that link, connecting the different
energy levels. Heart and mind merge so
that love embraces our entire being. Opens
the door to higher vibrations.

Spring Gold Rose (*Rosa Spinosissima*)
Has an effect on the solar plexus and unites
it to the heart chakra. Allows us to accept

ourselves as we are and to embrace a profound state of love. Restores the energies of the solar plexus (third chakra) and ties them to the heart (fourth chakra), thereby allowing us to accept who we are calmly and dispassionately. Enables us to open our heart without becoming too emotionally involved. It permits us both mental clarity and warm feelings.

Tibetan White Rose (*Rosa Moyusii*) Helps our love for ourselves to grow stronger. Has a grounding effect. Reinforces our self-confidence, inner joy, and zest for life, and allows us to accept ourselves as we are.

Wild Rose (*Rosa* x *Pruhoniciana*) Integrates the energies that flow through us. Opens us to experience a love that embraces all of creation and teaches us to return this love to the earth. In a world full of obstacles, this rose allows us to remain steadfast and true to our own convictions. It helps us to reconnect with Nature and develop a new zest for life. Restores inner stability and power.

Essences of Wild Plants

Almond Tree (*Prunus amygdalus*) Helps us make sense of each stage of life so we can enjoy and develop ourselves more fully. As we recognize that all is relative, we accept the impermanence of material things and lose our fear of the natural ageing process.

Arnica (*Arnica Montana*) A basic essence for any kind of injury, even emotional shock. For re-establishing the connection to the Higher Self, especially after anaesthetics, drug addiction or shock. It smoothes the way so that we can feel whole again.

Basil (*Ocynum basilicum*) Links and harmonizes all the energy centres helping to experience and value each level of being. Strengthens the root chakra.

Bistort (*Polygonum bistorta*) For those whose mind wanders when trying to concentrate. Helps to remain centred and fully present for the task at hand. It promotes mental stability.

Blackberry (*Rubus fruticosus*) For those who have problems initiating projects. Lack of get up and go. Stimulates initiative and strengthens the will. Helps us realize our creative power and to execute projects and follow them through.

Bleeding Heart (*Dicentra spectabilis*) For all affairs of the heart. Offers support to those who have lost someone dear, or when a relationship ends. Allows acceptance of what life brings and consolation when disappointed by creating distance from painful situations.

Borage (*Borago officinalis*) Gives power and courage to confront exhausting emotional situations. Helps us to proceed in life with optimism and rediscover joy in our hearts.

Buttercup (*Ranunculus acris*) Helps us realize our full potential when we lack self-esteem. Reinforces our self-confidence when we encounter high expectations by others, particularly parents or teachers.

Calla Lily (*Zantedeschia aethiopica*) Restores the yin and yang balance in the lower chakras. Helps us to learn to accept and integrate the male and female aspects of ourselves. Enhances self-worth, connection to the earth and creativity.

Chamomile (*Matricaria chamomilla*) For the overstressed, feeling too much is being expected. Especially for those who are easily worked up, have a short temper, and have difficulty calming down again. Reduces tension, relaxes, soothes and calms.

Corn (*Zea Mays*) Ideal for town-dwellers searching for contact with the earth. Brings back life's natural rhythms. Promotes connection with the earth, balances and grounds in order to reclaim our true inner self.

Courgette (*Cucurbita pepo*) Strengthens the second chakra, opening to growth and creativity. For integrating femininity. Brings harmony during pregnancy, enhancing and promoting bonding between mother-to-be and the unborn child.

Daisy (*Bellis perennis*) For integrating many different thoughts, and understanding the whole picture. Ideal for children and adults during the learning process. Helps make it easier to take in and analyse new information.

Dandelion (*Taraxacum officinale*) For reducing stress and tension. Loosens emotional tensions, especially those manifesting in the muscles. Effective addition to massage oils.

Dill (*Anethus graveolens*) Ideal for children of which too much is expected; facing changes, travelling or visiting unfamiliar places. Enables us to digest and process seemingly overwhelming impressions and experiences.

Fireweed (*Epilobium angustifolium*) A pioneer plant that is among the first to grow back after fire or earth clearing has upset the environment. Likewise, this essence restores us at all levels after a trauma such as an accident or a deep emotional shock.

Forget-Me-Not (*Myosotis sylvatica*) Stimulates the subconscious and promotes positive dreaming. Opens up inner communication and creates connections with loved ones. Helps us to integrate memories of those still alive and remember those who are no longer here.

Iris (*Iris germanica*) For accessing and developing creative potential and connection to inner artistic inspiration

Lavender (*Lavandula officinalis*) Calms the mind when agitated or emotionally upset. Its balancing effect restores inner peace and clears and harmonizes our inner thoughts. Helps us reconnect with our spiritual self.

Lotus (*Nelumbo nucifera*) Considered the universal flower which promotes clarity and openness at all levels. Opens and harmonizes all chakras, stimulates the crown chakra gateway to higher energies.

Orange Lily (*Lilium bulbiferum*) For achieving the correct attitude towards sexuality. Brings self-understanding and helps to direct sexual energy towards the heart. Promotes a positive, loving attitude towards intimacy. Activates creative forces, helping overcome considerable obstacles that prevent movement towards goals.

Meadow Garlic (*Allium angulosum*) Calms and soothes all forms of fear. Releases the energies locked up by fear, thereby strengthening our entire system. Also an antidote to psychic attack.

Mistletoe (*Viscum album*) For help with going through a radical process of change. Aids transformation on both the physical and psychological levels.

Morning Glory (*Ipomoea purpurea*) Supports withdrawal and rehabilitation. Helps us become conscious of our bad habits, shortcomings, negative living habits and addictions.

Mullein (*Verbascum thapsus*) Strengthens our connection to our inner guidance, helps us listen to our inner voice and conscience. Aids in the ability to be true to ourselves, gives a healthy sense of perspective, especially in teamwork, allows us to develop ourselves.

Paradise Lily (*Paradisea liliastrum*) Reawakens divine-consciousness and higher realms. Opens the crown (seventh) chakra and fills the body with white light. Aid for meditation and strengthens inner awareness and sense of belonging to 'All That Is'.

Passion Flower (*Passiflora bryonioides*) For raising energy levels so that we can face life's difficult challenges more successfully. Allowing us to step back and see things from a new perspective. Reduces our sense of personal involvement when problems threaten to overwhelm us.

Pink Yarrow (*Achillea millefolium*) For those who are too easily influenced by the emotions of others, it helps protect the heart and emotions.

Red Clover (*Trifolium pratense*) For panic and fear; helps you maintain inner calm and self-control even in emergency situations or in the midst of mass hysteria. You can remain centred and focused whilst others are panicking around you.

Rosemary (*Rosemarinus officinalis*) Strengthens brain function, mental concentration and alertness. For forgetfulness. Helps us to be more aware and conscious of who we are and what is happening in our lives.

Sage (*Salvia officinalis*) 'Purifying'. Cleanses and purifies us at the energetic level. Restores our inner rhythm, especially if suffering from jet lag. Allows us to integrate travel experiences more easily and promotes dawning of consciousness.

St John's Wort (*Hypericum perforatum*) Strengthens the emotional body's defences so that we regain a natural optimism that allows us to think more clearly. Recommended for those suffering from deep-rooted fears and nightmares. Acts like an inner light that illuminates the dark.

Scarlet Pimpernel (*Anagallis arvensis*) Brings spiritual consciousness into everyday life. Through this we experience compassion, self-confidence and are able to integrate into groups.

Self-Heal (*Prunella vulgaris*) Stimulates the body's self-healing powers, especially on the cellular level. Strengthens our will to be healthy. Promotes a sense of well-being and is especially effective when used in a cream.

Sunflower (*Helianthus annuus*) Helps rebuild self-confidence and encourages personal responsibility by harmonizing the energies of the solar plexus. For those in conflict situations with the father figure, both natural and archetypal, or the idea of fatherhood.

Valerian (*Valeriana officinalis*) Calms the body, soul and spirit, allowing sleep and restoration of vital energies when stress or pain has led to insomnia or inadequate rest. Recommended when under major stress and strain.

Violet (*Viola hirta*) For people who feel lonely or isolated in a group. Helps maintain self-identity while increasing openness so you can interact with others better. Develops inner warmth, trust and confidence and helps us remember the past more easily.

White Yarrow (*Achillea millefolium*) For sensitive people exposed to negative environmental influences. It strengthens the light of aura protecting us from negative influences, when disturbed by inner stress or pollution and the presence of strong electromagnetic fields. Increases and strengthens our protective energy shield.

Wild Carrot (*Daucus carota*) Strengthens both inner and outer visual acuity. Good for eye strain. Its calming effect opens us to inner visions so it is an ideal essence for creative visualization or dreams.

Zinnia (*Zinnia elegans*) Helps those who take life too seriously to lighten up. Stimulates childlike humour. Helps us relax and loosen up emotionally, easing any physical tensions and allowing positive forward movement. 'Laughter is the best medicine.'

Wild Plant Extension

Canary Islands Pine (*Pinus canariensis*) Helps free us from deep feelings of shame and guilt. Protects us from the negative thought projections of others and helps us to 'breathe deeply'.

Coltsfoot (*Tussilago farfara*) Enables us to resist harsh physical or emotional environments by strengthening our inner forces. Provides hope and power to endure in the face of obstacles.

Cone Flower (*Echinacea purpurea*) Has a releasing and detoxifying effect on the emotional body, stimulating its defences and dissolving pent-up emotional burdens that have been carried too long. Thus relieved, we get back into life's flow. This essence smoothes the way to restoring emotional health.

Evening Primrose (*Oenothera biennis*)
Shines a light into the darkness of our
deepest fears. Soothes and calms our
emotions so we regain the sense that we are
safe and protected.

Eyebright (*Euphrasia officinalis*)
Sharpens our ability to see clearly, both
physically and inwardly. This essence helps
us act rationally during emotional crises
and also consoles us in times of grief.

Hawthorn (*Crataegus oxyacantha*)
Resolves deep feelings of sorrow or grief,
bringing serenity and permitting our inner
inspiration to flow again. Helps us let go of
the past.

Lemon (*Citrus limon*) Cleanses us at all
levels, bringing new clarity and feelings of
wellbeing. Helps 'restore the soul'.

Maidenhair Tree (*Ginkgo biloba*) Enables
us to resist harsh physical or emotional
environments by strengthening our inner
forces. Provides hope and the power to
endure in the face of obstacles.

Nettle (*Urtica dioica*) Takes the 'sting' out
of conflicts within a group. Helps individuals living or working together to present
different points of view without provoking
hurt feelings.

Paprika Pepper (*Capsicum annuum*)
Sharpens all our senses and sensory
perceptions. This essence strengthens our
energy level.

Pennyroyal (*Mentha pulegium*) Protects
us against external disturbances on the
mental level. Replenishes us with new
energy after a shock so that we can make a
fresh start.

Periwinkle (*Vinca minor*) Has a calming
and balancing effect. It strengthens the
nervous system so that we remain calm
and centred, even in very stressful
situations. Promotes 'nerves of steel'.

Petunia (*Petunia Hybrid*) Helps use
mental energy accurately. Promotes our
ability to focus our thoughts and achieve
both clarity and acuity.

Pot Marigold (*Calendula officinalis*)
Helps us recognize and accept our different
emotional states. This essence enables us to
remain centred and to release energy
blocks caused by shock or trauma.

Primrose (*Primula veris*) Loosens energy
blockages at key points so that our creative
powers begin to flow smoothly again.

Snapdragon (*Antirrhinum majus*)
Promotes our ability to 'strike the right
tone' when expressing our opinion by
harmonizing the fifth (throat or larynx)
chakra so that we express ourselves appropriately and even elegantly.

Sorrel (*Rumex acetosa*) This essence is a
survival artist among plants because it
grows even in extremely polluted environments. Likewise, this essence strengthens
our life force and endurance capabilities.

Turk's Cap Lily (*Lilium martagon*)
Releases emotional blockages that were
formed in childhood when we couldn't
defend ourselves against abuse or bullying.
This essence frees us from uncertainty
about our own abilities and restores our
self-confidence.

Wild Garlic (*Allium angulosum*)
Stimulates our capacity to digest what life
serves up on both physical and emotional
levels. Enables us to release burdens and
emotional blockages so we can enjoy life
again. Helps us remain more consistent
and calm in stressful situations.

Carnivorous Plants

Butterwort (*Alpenfettkraut/Grassette des
Alpes*) Cleanses us at all energy levels,
thereby removing those emotional poisons
that result from negative thought patterns
or excessive criticism and self-doubt. When
burdened by negative thoughts, this
essence helps us extract their harmful
energy from both body and aura.

Sundew (*Rossolis filiforme*) Helps free us
from old negative karmic patterns by
bringing past experiences back into
consciousness so we can release them with

love and understanding. This helps raise our overall energy vibration.

Venus Fly (*Venus Fliegenfalle*) When we feel trapped in a situation and cannot see any way out, this essence helps us develop a broader perspective so that we recognize the relativity of our circumstances. Helps us solve what appear to be insoluble problems.

African and Canary Island Essences

Aloe (*Aloe striata*) Restores life energies in cases of exhaustion. Restores our inner balance and life force when we are spent.

Artemisia (*Artemisia arvensis*) Regenerates our life force energy when it's been depleted after a lengthy illness or a long period of emotional distress. Helps us recover from exhaustion or deep emotional wounds.

Banana (*Musa paradisiaca L*) Strengthens yang energies (masculine, active force). Helps restore male sexual potency. Also helps overachiever personalities express their true feelings openly so they may set more realistic goals in life.

Bird of Paradise (*Strelitzia reginae*) Helps us discover our true 'inner beauty', regardless of outward appearances. Teaches us to accept ourselves as we are and to follow our inner vision unerringly.

Canary Island Bellflower (*Canarina canariensis*) Helps integrate the yin (feminine, receptive) side of one's nature. Provides confidence and security in difficult situations and helps us to develop and admit tender feelings.

Cape Leadwort (*Plumbago auriculata*) Helps set us free from the past, bringing composure when we must address old problems. Its grounding effect allows us to step back and disengage from what's going on around us so we can 'let bygones be bygones'.

Coconut Palm (*Cocos nucifera*) Helps us accept our inner sensitivity while recognizing the need for external protection.

Especially for those who need to develop clear boundaries while maintaining personal harmony and sensitivity.

Blue Gum (*Eucalyptus globules*) Releases and opens us emotionally so that we can accept life for what it is adopting an attitude of 'live and let live'.

Echium (*Echium wildpretii*) Restores our ability to meet life's challenges head-on, freeing us from limiting thoughts and returning us to the road of success. Use it whenever you are tempted to give up on something or someone.

Geranium (*Geranium perforatum*) When everyday life seems dull and grey, this essence restores inner joy and zest for life. Releases negative emotional bonds, adds colour to our life.

Hibiscus (*Hibiscus rosa-sinensis*) Helps us integrate the yin (feminine, receptive) side of ourselves allowing it to vibrate within our being once more. Renews a women's contact with the power and richness of her femininity and sexuality

K9 (the name of this flower is protected) For the immune system. Strengthens and reinforces our 'life force' – the body's natural defence system – on all levels. Antiviral effect. Still being researched.

Milk Thistle (*Sonchus acaulis*) Relaxes and dissolves tensions in stormy times. Helps us gather thoughts calmly so we don't overreact emotionally. Highly effective when combined with massage oils.

Petticoat Daffodil (*Narcissus tazetta*) Allows us to see the 'light at the end of the tunnel' when we feel surrounded by darkness and may have given up hope. Helps us to regain self-confidence and radiate happiness.

Poinsettia (*Euphorbia pulcherrima*) Brings the energies of the heart and throat closer together so that we may express what we truly feel inside. Helps us to talk freely about our feelings to others.

Sensitive Plant (*Mimosa pudica*) Allows us to discover our inner richness and to feel our inner light as we become aware of our personal power. Useful for those who are introverted and who need to open up to the rest of the world.

Swiss Cheese Plant (*Monstera deliciosa*) Strengthens, integrates and balances yang (active) energy and male potency. Helps us accept our yang (masculine) side.

Tree Heather (*Erica arborea*) Reduces emotional dependency on others and helps establish one's own independence and self-acceptance. For those who tend to live life through others.

Vipers Bugloss (*Echium pudica*) Enables us to discover that humour and friendliness take us further than a grim sense of duty or discipline. Develops warm-hearted side and teaches that a smile can often open doors.

Zistrose/Sun Rose (*Cistus albidus*) Strengthens our inner resolve so that we remain centred and able to persuade others in a group to follow us. Assists those who lack assertiveness or 'backbone'.

European Orchids

Cephalanthera (*Cephalanthera rubra*) Helps maintain our focus on the task at hand, if problems develop. It creates a spiritual structure in our mind and strengthens our concentration.

Epipactis (*Epipactis helleborine*) Allows us to dive deep within ourselves in order to bring hidden inner aspects of our personality to the surface, so we can accept them with love. Facilitates access to the subconscious.

Neottia (*Neottia nidus-avis*) Brings suppressed feelings to the surface so they can be transformed in a loving fashion. Removes unjustified emotional fears that we are being wrongly treated or betrayed.

Orchis (*Orchis mascula*) By keeping our feet firmly on the ground, this orchid essence permits us to soar to new spiritual heights in our mind. It assists astral travel while keeping us solidly grounded.

Platanthera (*Platanthera chlorantha*) Helps us see clearly what is spiritually right for us when we must make difficult decisions; a powerful spiritual cleansing agent.

Cacti and Succulent Plants

Cacti are known for their hardiness in extreme climates; their ability to survive with little water and their prickles suggest both their defensive and protective properties. These essences are drawn from plants that are found mainly in South America and Africa

Aura Cleansing Cactus (*Cleistocactus straussii*), South America. For cleansing and regeneration of the aura, especially clears the astral body. Cleanses the astral body of energetic parasites and helps those people whose auric field is too open to cleanse and protect.

Beauty Cactus (*Echinocereus scheeri*), Mexico. Helps us to discover the beauty of our hearts. Nurtures modesty, humility and hope. Develops the natural warmth of the heart, helps us to develop our inner potentials.

Blueberry Cactus (*Myrtillocacyus geometrizans*), USA. Helps us to develop our own potential. On the one hand it aids by helping us to set healthy boundaries and protect the heart chakra, and on the other hand, it encourages us to realize and accept that who we are is good and unlimited in potential.

Earth Star Cactus (*Stapelia desmetiana*) Powerfully cleanses and stimulates the first chakra, connecting it directly with Mother Earth. Clears and releases bottled-up negative emotions, strengthens our sense of self, and grounds.

Formation Cactus (*Mammillaris rubrograndis*), Mexico. Provides protection and stability at all levels, from the cellular to the mental. Stimulates the inner life force and helps to eliminate internal negative energies. Also can be used to cleanse polluted areas around us.

Golden Barrel Cactus (*Echinocactus grusonii*), Mexico. For protection and being centred. When we have been exposed to many different influences, this essence helps us to be centred again. Protects us from environmental influences, and helps one to focus on the essential. Good for those whose work brings them into contact with people.

Grounding Opuntia (*Opuntia dejecta*), Cuba. For a stronger sense of connection to the earth, and for protection. Stimulates the root chakra giving greater stability and assisting us in defending our boundaries.

Here And Now Cactus (*Hylocereus undatus*), Mexico and Central America. Helps us to accept being incarnated; to be here. Stimulates contact with Mother Earth, opens us to an awareness of her love. Brings awareness of her light bodies.

Inside/Outside Cactus (*Pilosocereus pachycladus*), Brazil. Works at the energetic level to protect and regenerate the skin. Expands and opens us up on the surface levels of our consciousness, including the cellular levels of our physical boundaries, i.e. the skin, and makes us aware of the 'inside' and 'outside' of our being.

Inner Cleansing Cactus (*Cleistocactus ritteri*), Bolivia. Stimulates positive inner processes and helps us to digest all the impressions to which we are exposed. It promotes both cleansing and renewal of our innermost processes.

Inspiration Cactus (*Echinopsis oxygona*), South America. Has a deep cleansing effect on our state of mind. It protects us against disturbing thoughts and negative influences, thereby allowing us to develop a clear sense of our own purpose and inner direction.

Joyful Opuntia (*Opuntia cardiosperma*), Paraguay. Brings joy back to our lives, especially at difficult moments when life seems a heavy burden. Restores a sense of optimism and self-confidence when we need to look beyond immediate problems.

Radiation Protection Cactus (*Cereus peruvianus*), Peru. Offers strong protection against all kinds of radiation and negative influences, helps us to develop our full potential, including our intellectual potential.

Release Cactus (*Ceropegia fusca*), Canary Islands. Helps us to recognize and accept our shadow sides. This essence is profound in its effect, reaching the level of cellular consciousness and unconsciousness, dissolving old blockages, which allows the body to realize the trauma of the psyche's old wounds, aiding cellular regeneration.

Life Force Cactus (*Orbea variegata*) Works to protect and regenerate the skin. Helps us to be aware of what is 'inside' and what is 'outside' our being so we can shed old limits and boundaries, thereby allowing us to grow.

Love Cactus (*Seticereus icosagonus*) Has a strong effect on the second chakra (creativity), and helps us become conscious of our creative powers at all levels. It helps us to discover how to achieve a balance between work and play and how to maintain integrity when dealing with others.

Noble Heart Cactus (*Stenocereus marginatus*), Mexico. Promotes better physical posture, reinforcing the spinal column, and also an awareness of our upright nature. Helps us to open and expand the heart chakra, developing sincerity and integrity.

Queen of the Night Cactus (*Selenicereus grandiflorus*) Brings light and hope when we are overly afraid or sorrowful. Helps purify our thoughts and clear our mind as we recognize which parts of our being remain shuttered in darkness. Helps us reconnect with the Light.

Self-Esteem Cactus (*Ferocactus schwarzi*), Mexico. Strengthens our self-confidence and provides energy support for our body's immune system. It promotes positive group energy such as feelings of trust and compassion with those close to us. Confidence in ourselves and others creates a stable basis for co-operation and mutual assistance.

Shadow Cactus (*Caralluma russelliana*), East Africa. Has a releasing effect on the solar plexus, we become conscious of our inner processes and are able to overcome them and move on. We say goodbye to our shadow, learn to accept the death of the past and live in total awareness

Special Essences

Anti-radiation Essence T1 Essence (made at Chernobyl in Russia) The singularity of this essence is that it acts in the opposite way from all other energy essences we have researched. Instead of radiating energy, T1 essence soaks up surplus energy, thereby restoring the organism's energy balance in cases of overexposure or stimulation. Our research has led us to conclude that this essence can be used positively in the following situations: in cases of field lines pollution (high-tension electricity); after X-ray treatments; and in cases of overexposure to electromagnetic nuclear radiation. T1 and Delph (see Dolphin and Whale Essences) together is a powerful combination used to clear radiation in the subtle energy field.

Teide – Volcano Essence This is an environmental essence that was produced on the 'Teide', a 3,716 meter-high volcano on the island of Tenerife. This essence brings our consciousness down to the deepest cellular level. We can then experience our consciousness in the smallest building blocks of matter. It also brings us the experience of both the universal microcosm and macrocosm forces – subject to alterations, i.e., changes.

Essence Skin Creams

Andreas Korte makes a range of Essence Skin Creams which (with the exception of Amazon and RQ7 First Aid Cream) can be personalized by adding a few drops of your own prescription mix (see page 46) or other specially selected flower essences. Each cream uses avocado and wheat-germ oil as part of their base.

Amazon Skin Cream Recommended for massaging into areas of the body when the energy flow is stifled or energetically blocked. For treatment of the back, apply directly on the fossa triangularis of the auricle (the indent at the front and top of the ear).

Delph Skin Cream An energetically strong cream that helps open the heart chakra. It activates and purifies the skin.

Lotus Skin Cream Restores energetic harmony and balance to the skin through its relaxing properties. Based on the Lotus Flower, considered to be the universal flower of peace and harmony.

RQ7 First Aid Cream Contains seven different flower essences. Apply externally in acute emergencies such as shock, and injury to the skin such as cuts and bruising. It also energizes and stimulates and relieves exhaustion or deep fatigue.

Self-heal Skin Cream Stimulates self-healing for irritated or chaffed skin. Ideal for using as an aftershave balm

Venus Orchid Skin Cream Deeply relaxing preparation for the face and body which enhances the gentle side of one's nature and softness of the skin. Recommended for sensitive skin.

The Original Crystal Method of Preparing Essences

This original method dispenses with the need to pick the plants, leaving each and every plant absolutely intact. Through this method the crystal transmits the vibrations of the flowers directly into the water that acts as a liquid medium. Just as in photography a light sensitive film captures a given image, this method allows the subtle energy of the flower to be brought to the crystal, and then the flower vibrations are stocked in the water. The essences prepared this way are of a high vibrational quality.

Korte Energy Balancers

The energy balancers herald a multi-levelled approach to combining essences. Andreas has created a synergistic blend of all the vibrational octaves that his range of essences operate on from mushrooms on the ground level to the higher vibrations of the orchids at the top level.

Forever Young Energy Essence Gives us the feeling of permanent inner youth. Helps us to let go of the fear of aging. Provides an energetic revitalization of our body – reconnecting with the mind and spirit. Lets our inner beauty shine through

Heart/Emotional Energy Balancer Heightens and grows our qualities of the heart. Teaches us to give unconditional love without disempowering ourselves. Supports and nurtures the emotional body. Gives us the wonderful feeling that we are lovable beings.

Jet Lag/Sleep Energy Balancer Balances sleep and rest times. Helps us to regenerate energetically. Supports us during travelling through different time zones

Joyful Sexuality Essence Heightens our emotions and awareness of those beautiful special moments. Helps us to enjoy sensuality with more love and creativity. Connects the experience of body with mind and spirit. Recommended in combination with the Women or Men Energy Balancer Essence.

Men Energy Balancer Strengthens the male energy (yang). Creates balance when men are too achievement-oriented. Helps us to connect with their true inner nature. Aids men to be truly empowered and succeed in manifesting that empowerment in their lives.

Protection Energy Balancer Strengthens our protection shield for the emotional body. Gives us the feeling of distance and protection. Increases our feeling of trust and that we are always protected. Enables our growth into our true power as a unique being

Purification Energy Balancer A deep purifying cleanser, helpful for those times when we feel internally clogged or unclean. Clears energetic blocks and toxins from the subtle body. Gives us the feeling of inner and outer purification and a fresh clear perspective

Regeneration Energy Balancer Revitalizes us when we feel lethargic or weak. Unleashes new energy and power. Gives us the feeling of inner stability and strength. Helps balance our mind, body and spirit in an energetic unity.

Stress Energy Balancer Nurtures us with a sense of calm when we feel we want to explode. Guides us to develop more distance and perspective. Assists in protection of ourselves. Allows us to give more time to ourselves and accept the good things in life.

Women Energy Balancer Increases the female energy (yin). Empowers women to accept their feminine side with joy. Heals emotional pressures; provides emotional stability when we need it. An energetic aid during pregnancy.

Dolphin and Whale Essences

Water Activation with Andreas Korte

A powerful dream called Andreas to make the Delph essence. In it he journeyed to the islands off Brazil where he made the essence, there he experienced the unique communication with the dolphins and tells of their desire to help us. He has been conducting energetic healing of the waterways with Delph and has co-authored a book on dolphins *Dolphins and Whales*.

Delph (*Tursiops truncatus*)

Delph®(Dolphin) is an extraordinary essence that re-energizes and cleanses the whole chakra system and subtle bodies. Produced with the conscious help of free, sea-dwelling dolphins, it has the amazing ability to work on all our chakras at once, stimulating and harmonizing our entire being. The dolphins' message is one of unconditional Love. It is said that dolphins are the guardians of the ancient wisdom and secrets. Like a personal encounter with wild dolphins in the ocean, this essence opens our heart chakra so that we experience Life's unity and the interrelatedness of all living things. Delph has a powerful cleansing effect both on our physical body, which is over 80% water, and spiritually. It is also used for the cleansing and activation of rivers, lakes and seas polluted by industrial or agricultural waste. Recommended for childbirth to ease the trauma of coming into the world. Helps babies to be peaceful and serene.

The Pink Amazonian Dolphin (*Sotalia fluviatilis*) Connects us with the heart of Planet Earth giving us a deep interconnection with our soul which calms and raises the consciousness.

Whale (*Globicephala melas*) This powerful essence should only be used after one has worked with Delph®(Dolphin essence). Please, always test it first! Whales are the keepers of knowledge. They are quite serious but in a loving, fatherly way. Their essence throws our heart chakra wide open so that we can connect deeply with all life forms on earth. This experience, which can be overwhelming for the unprepared, reminds us of our role as caretakers of this planet and our need to live up to our real purpose for being here.

Aura Sprays

Due to the destruction of the ozone layer, we are exposed to radiation that is becoming stronger. We know that this harmful radiation reaches the ethereal body, known as the aura, before it touches our skin. Damage to the physical body only arises after the aura's protective shield has already been considerably weakened. Therefore, PHI has developed an aura spray for strengthening our natural protective shield. It combines gem-energy essences, which absorb harmful radiation and cleanse the aura, with flower- and orchid-energy essences, which deflect radiation away from the body.

RQ 7 (Emergency Spray) PHI has also created a pleasant flower-essence combination emergency remedy for external use, in spray form. When under stress or in situations that cause shock, spray RQ 7 several times around your aura or even directly onto the skin.

Delph-Spray The pleasant and cleansing effect of Delph® is now also available in spray form. It is helpful for cleansing energetically-polluted rooms (offices, treatment rooms, conference rooms, etc.). Delph® creates a better energetic and cleansed atmosphere and promotes the opening of the heart chakra. It is also recommended for use during air travel.

New Developments in Methods of Flower Essence Use

Andreas Korte has a vision for integrating the consciousness of nature into our world and its importance of the infinite balance of nature; how vital it is at this moment on the earth for us to recognize this, and to find a way to become more in harmony with the healing gifts nature has to offer the world. Not only on a personal level, but healing the environment, as well as our social and health structures.

Korte has devised a pyramid of healing, developed from his vibrational range of essences, which include:
- **Crystals** – are in and of the earth, they store vital knowledge and information. Work on our structure and overall energy.
- **Mushroom essences** – grow close to the earth and deal with our negativity. Related to the lower chakras.
- **Flower essences** – Growing from the earth, reaching upwards. Related to the middle chakras.
- **Orchid essences** – Growing 'in the air'. Related to the head/crown and higher chakras.
- **Delph essence** – all-encompassing energy of love and compassion.

A combination these essences, has extraordinary power to cleanse and rebalance the physical being and is part of Korte's light treatment.

Australia, Japan and Thailand

Australia was once part of the southern landmass known as Gondwanaland. The land has a powerful and vibrant energy that has not been weakened by civilization, war or pollution. Native Aborigines have long acknowledged the power of the flower kingdom and have been using flowers to heal emotional imbalance and physical injuries for over 10,000 years.

Bush Flower Essences

Some of the oldest flowering plants in the world can be found growing in the wilderness of the Australian bush. They draw upon and reflect the power, strength and vitality of this extraordinary region. The collection of Australian Bush Flower Essences described below were created by Ian White, a fifth-generation herbalist who spent much of his childhood in the bush learning from his grandmother about the healing properties of Australian plants and flowers. He spent many years travelling and researching the properties of flowers growing in areas as diverse as the Northern Territory wetlands, the Olgas, the Kimberleys, the South Australian deserts, the Victorian heathlands and Sydney's sandstone region before he, together with Kirstin White, developed the Australian Bush Flower Essences in the early 1980s.

The main focus of these remedies is to bring out and cultivate the positive qualities present in everyone. The Waratah flower, chosen to represent this collection of essences, is unique to Australia. It comes from one of the oldest plant groups in the world the origins of which date back 60 million years to Antarctica. Known by its Aboriginal name meaning beautiful, the Waratah has a magnificent red bloom comprising many individual flowers which are tightly packed together.

The Waratah is a survival remedy. It embodies the Australian bush-dweller's qualities of adaptability and the ability to cope with all sorts of emergencies. Ian believes that in the years to come there will be major economic, social, physical and spiritual upheavals which will take us by surprise. The Waratah will help by aiding people to find the courage and strength they need to deal with such change. Ian White has researched and conducted studies into the use of the combinations he has created, especially Electro, which is designed for reduction of radiation (*see* Proving Essences Work page 386); and also studies on a combination for hormonal imbalance in women.

He has further developed a spiritual range White Light Essences inspired by the energy of sacred sites and elemental qualities (*see* section on Sound, Light and Environmental Essences).

Alpine Mint Bush (*Prostanthera cuneata*) For mental and emotional exhaustion, lack of joy, feeling the weight of responsibility. Brings revitalization, joy and renewal.

Angelsword (*Lobelia gibbosa*) For those who are spiritually possessed. Helps in attaining spiritual truth, protection and access to gifts from past lifetimes. Repairs the whole energy field.

Banksia Robur For people who are normally dynamic but are suffering a temporary loss of drive and enthusiasm due to burn-out, frustration or illness. Restores energy and the enjoyment of and interest in life.

Bauhinia (*Lysiphyllum cunninghamii*) For resistance to change and rigidity. Encourages the embracing of new concepts and ideas, bringing acceptance and open-mindedness.

Billy Goat Plum (*Planchonia careya*) For sexual revulsion, physical loathing or self-disgust. Brings sexual pleasure and enjoyment, and acceptance of one's physical body. Good for skin conditions such as eczema, psoriasis, herpes and thrush.

Black-Eyed Susan (*Tetratheca ericifolia*) A remedy for stress. For those always on the go, rushing, constantly striving and impatient. Slows you down, enabling you to turn inward, be still and enjoy inner peace. Balances the adrenal glands.

Bluebell (*Wahlenbergia sp*) For those cut off from their feelings, fearful of emptiness and vulnerable to greed. Opens the heart, encourages sharing and belief in abundance, gives a sense of joy and universal trust.

Boab (*Adansonia gregorii*) For those who adopt family thought-patterns, repeating negative experiences of the past. Releases negative thought-patterns and actions within families. Good for abuse and prejudice.

Boronia (*Boronia ledifolia*) For obsessive thoughts, grieving over recently ended relationships, feeling broken-hearted. Brings mental calmness, serenity, clarity of mind and thought.

Bottlebrush (*Callistemon linearis*) For those going through and overwhelmed by major life changes such as puberty or pregnancy particularly those who are holding on to the past and old habits when approaching the end of a phase in life. Restores the ability to cope with serenity and to be calm by letting go. Good for pregnant women and new mothers who feel inadequate. Assists bonding between mother and child.

Bush Fuchsia (*Epacris longiflora*) For poor ability to learn, dyslexia, stuttering, ignoring 'gut feelings'. Unsurpassed for resolving learning problems, balancing and integrating the left and right hemispheres of the brain. Brings clarity to expression and speech. Develops intuition.

Bush Gardenia (*Gardenia megasperma*) For those caught up in their own world and affairs, taking for granted and being oblivious of those close to them. For stale or failing relationships. Brings passion and renewed interest in a partner; improves communication.

Bush Iris (*Patersonia longifolia*) For fear of death, of materialism, of atheism, addiction to sex and drugs. Brings spiritual awakening and insights, understanding of things beyond the physical. Assists in making transitions in life.

Christmas Bell (*Blandfordia nobilis*) This remedy assists one with mastery of the physical plane and with stewardship of one's possessions. It also helps one to manifest their desired outcomes and is extremely beneficial for anyone experiencing a sense of lack. Promotes openness to new experiences, people and perceptual shifts, and healthy questioning of traditional standards and beliefs. For the heart closed due to expectations or prejudices which have been taught, not personally experienced.

Crowea (*Crowea saligna*) For individuals who continually worry; feeling out of balance. Brings peace, calm, vitality and a sense of being centred and balanced.

Dagger Hakea (*Hakea teretifolia*) For resentment, bitterness towards close family, friends and old lovers. Brings forgiveness and enables feelings to be expressed.

Dog Rose (*Bauera rubioides*) For fearful, shy, insecure people who are apprehensive of others. For niggling fears. Promotes confidence, courage, belief in oneself and a love of life.

Dog Rose of the Wild Forces (*Bauera sessiliflora*) For those who fear losing control, for physical pain with no apparent cause. Brings emotional balance, ability to overcome fear.

Five Corners (*Styphelia laeta*) For low self-esteem and self-dislike. For those who repress or 'hold in' their personality. An important remedy for bringing love, acceptance of oneself and a celebration of one's inherent beauty.

Flannel Flower (*Actinotus helianthi*) For those who dislike being touched, lack of sensitivity, especially in males, an aversion to physical activity and agoraphobia. Encourages emotional trust, sensuality and gentle, sensitive touching. Makes physical activity joyful.

Fresh Water Mangrove (*Barringtonia acutangula*) The healing quality of the essence is to release and heal mental prejudice, allowing the heart to open without prejudgement. As opposed to prejudice caused by personal experience that can be treated with Slender Rice Flower (see below), Fresh Water Mangrove works best for those who mentally reject or have already made up their mind about something without it ever being experienced. This essence has the potential to allow us to fully experience and be open on both a mental and heart level to new perceptual shifts and all the changes occurring at this time.

Fringed Violet (*Thysanotus tuberosus*) For shock and trauma, damage to the aura and lack of psychic protection allowing energy and vitality to be drained by other people and environmental factors like radiation. Poor recuperation. Removes the effects of recent and old trauma, realigns the subtle bodies after shock and gives psychic and energy protection.

Green Spider Orchid (*Caladenia dilatato*) For nightmares and phobias, or those needing acceptance. Brings release from terror and the ability to guard information.

Grey Spider Flower (*Grevillea buxifolia*) For terror, panic, fear of psychic attack and nightmares. Gives faith, calmness and courage.

Gymea Lily (*Doryanthes excelsa*) For proud, dominating and controlling personalities. Brings humility and the ability to let go of control.

Hibbertia (*Hibbertia pedunculata*) For fanaticism, excessive self-discipline, and addiction to acquiring knowledge for self-improvement. Allows you to accept yourself, your own knowledge and experiences. Dispels the desire to be superior to others.

Illawarra Flame Tree (*Brachychiton acerifolium*) For those suffering from a sense of rejection and feeling left out, especially for children undergoing temporary setbacks at school. Fear of responsibility. Brings self-approval and reliance, confidence and inner strength.

Isopogon (*Isopogon anethifolius*) For poor memory, senility, an inability to learn from past experience. For a stubborn, controlling personality. Brings learning from past experiences, retrieval of forgotten skills and memories. Allows you to relate to others without manipulation and control.

Jacaranda (*Mimosifolia*) For those who are changeable, dithering, aimless, scattered, always rushing around and accident prone. Brings decisiveness, quick thinking and a clear mind.

Kangaroo Paw (*Anigozanthos manglesii*) For socially immature, clumsy or gauche individuals who are insensitive to the needs of others. Encourages relaxation, sensitivity, savoir-faire and enjoyment of company.

Kapok Bush (*Cochlospermum fraseri*) For people who are easily discouraged and give up easily, resigned and apathetic. Brings persistence, common sense, practicality and a willingness to apply oneself to any task.

Little Flannel Flower (*Actinotus minor*) For denial of the child within, over-serious adults, precocious children who grow up too quickly. Restores sense of playfulness and joy. For having fun.

Macrocarpa (*Eucalyptus macrocarpa*) For those who are tired, exhausted, burnt out and, as a result, have poor immune resistance. A quick pick-me-up tonic which regenerates the adrenal glands, restoring energy, strength and vitality.

Mint Bush (*Prostanthera striatflora*) For spiritual trial and tribulation, despair, feeling overwhelmed. Brings calmness, the ability to move on, readiness for new beginnings.

Monga Waratah (*Telopea mongaensis*) Promotes strengthening of the will and helps find inner strength, reclaiming of one's spirit, belief that one can break the dependency of any behaviour, substance or person, clears neediness, codependency, inability to do things alone without the support of others, negative conditions of disempowerment, feeling choked or stifled in situations or relationships and feeling not able or strong enough to leave. Addresses the addictive personality, and fosters self-empowerment

Mountain Devil (*Lambertia formosa*) For hatred, anger, jealousy, holding grudges and suspiciousness. Brings unconditional love, forgiveness and happiness.

Mulla Mulla (*Ptilotus atripicifolius*) For trauma associated with fire, heat or even sunburn. Fear of flames, fire and hot objects. Brings a feeling of ease with fire. Releases stored radiation and aids rejuvenation.

Old Man Banksia (*Banksia serrata*) An Aboriginal symbol of female spirituality. For lethargy, low energy levels, sluggish thyroid activity, obesity. Restores energy, enthusiasm, the enjoyment of and interest in life.

Paw Paw (*Carica papaya*) For those overwhelmed and burdened by decision who are unable to resolve problems. Malabsorption of food. For assimilating and integrating new ideas and information. Improves access to the Higher Self for help in problem-solving. Aids the absorption of nutrients.

Peach-flowered Tea-tree (*Leptospermum squarrosum*) For mood swings, lack of commitment to completing projects due to boredom. For hypochondriacs. Brings emotional balance, completion of goals and projects. Encourages trust and taking responsibility for health without becoming preoccupied by it. Balances the pancreas.

Philotheca (*Philotheca salsolifolia*) For an inability to accept acknowledgement, excessive generosity. Brings an ability to accept praise and receive love and acknowledgement.

Pink Flannel Flower (*Actinotus forsythii*) For those who feel life is dull, flat, and lack joy and appreciation for the everyday aspects of life. Aids in feeling gratitude and appreciation, *joie de vivre*, keeping one's heart chakra open.

Pink Mulla Mulla (*Ptilotus exaltus*) For deep hurt, isolation, being guarded and feeling blocked. Helps in overcoming obstacles, opening up and finding forgiveness.

Red Grevillea (*Grevillea speciosa*) For feeling stuck, knowing the goal but not how to attain it. For those who are easily affected by criticism and unpleasantness, too reliant on others. Gives strength to leave unpleasant situations. Encourages boldness.

Red Helmet Orchid (*Corybas dilatatus*) For rebellious, hot-headed, selfish people who resent authority due to a poor relationship with their father. Helps men bond to children; develops sensitivity and respect.

Red Lily (*Nelumbo nucifera*) The sacred lotus embodying Aboriginal spirituality. For daydreamers who are vacant and accident prone. Balances spiritual and earthly aspects, enabling you to be grounded and practical while evolving spiritually. Good for autism and countering the effects of drugs.

Red Suva Frangipani (*Suneiria rubra*) For turmoil, emotional upheaval, sadness. Brings feelings of acceptance, equanimity and nurturing.

Rough Bluebell (*Trichodesma zeylanicum*) For those who lack concern for others' feelings, who are openly malicious. Brings openness, compassion and unconditional love.

She Oak (*Casuarina glauca*) For infertility, especially when there is no physical reason; hormonal imbalance in females, especially PMT. Restores fertility and hormonal balance; aids conception. Helps with fluid retention.

Silver Princess (*Eucalyptus Caesia*) For lack of direction in life, aimlessness and despondency. Gives life, purpose and direction, motivation.

Slender Rice Flower (*Pimelea linifolia*) For racism, narrow-mindedness, and comparing yourself to others. Encourages co-operation, humility, pride, interconnectedness and the ability to see goodness in others.

Southern Cross (*Xanthosia rotundifolia*) For victim mentality; those who think life has been hard on them and feel hard done by; complaining, feeling impoverished. Brings personal power; taking responsibility for situations and being able to effect a positive change.

Spinifex (*Triodia species*) For herpes, chlamydia and surface cuts or grazes. Heals physically by helping you realize the emotional issues involved. Heals skin conditions when applied topically.

Sturt Desert Pea (*Clianthus formosus*) For deep hurt, sadness and emotional pain. A powerful essence that diffuses and allows you to let go of sad memories. Motivates and re-energizes.

Sturt Desert Rose (*Gossypium sturtianum*) This essence is for guilt, including sexual guilt, which can be an emotional trigger for many sexual problems. It is also for having the courage to following your own inner convictions and morality, helping you to follow through with integrity. If we are not true to ourselves, as a consequence we can often feel regret or remorse. It can restore self-esteem that has been damaged by past actions you may have felt guilty about.

Sundew (*Drosera spathulata*) For those under the age of 28 who are vague, indecisive, dissociated, lacking focus and prone to procrastination. Encourages grounding, focus, inspiration, attention to detail, enabling you to live in the present with interest. Speeds recovery from fainting and anaesthetics.

Sunshine Wattle (*Acacia terminalis*) For struggle, feeling trapped in the past and expecting the worst for the future. Brings optimism and an acceptance of the beauty and joy in the present.

Sydney Rose (*Boronia serrulata*) The crowning glory of the Bush Essences, the rare Sydney Rose helps us realize and know, not merely an intellectual level but on a deep heart level, that there is no separation between us, that we are all one. Promotes feeling safe and at peace. Creates heartfelt compassion, tolerance and love for others and the willingness to help and support dissolving feelings of separated, deserted, unloved or morbid creating a sense of unity.

Tall Mulla Mulla (*Ptilotus exaltatus*) For feeling scared and unsafe, lack of integration with others. Brings the ability to interact socially and feel secure with people.

Tall Yellow Top (*Senecio magnificus*) For alienation, loneliness and isolation. Brings a sense of belonging and knowing that you are 'home'.

Turkey Bush (*Calytrix exstipulataI*) For creative block and disbelief in your abilities. Inspires creativity, self-expression and renewed artistic confidence.

Waratah (*Telopea speciosissima*) For black despair, suicidal thoughts, feelings of hopelessness and an inability to respond to crisis. Brings courage, tenacity and adaptability. Strengthens faith and survival skills.

Wedding Bush (*Ricinocarpus pinifolius*) For difficulty in committing to relationships, whether business, social or intimate. Encourages commitment in and to relationships. Restores dedication to life purpose.

Wild Potato Bush (*Solanum quadriloculatum*) For a sense of being physically encumbered and weighed down; for a body that is slow to respond to will. Brings freedom and vitality to move on in life.

Wisteria (*Wisteria sinensis*) Specifically for women who are tense about and unable to enjoy sex for fear of intimacy, frigidity. Also for the macho male. Brings sexual enjoyment and gentleness.

Yellow Cowslip Orchid (*Caladenia flava*) For critical, judgemental, bureaucratic attitudes. Fosters humanitarian concern, impartiality and constructiveness. Enables you to step back from emotions and develop a sense of arbitration. Balances the pituitary gland.

Combination Essences

Abund Essence *Boab, Christmas Bell, Five Corners, Philotheca, Southern Cross, Sunshine Wattle, Bluebell.* Aids in releasing negative beliefs, family patterns, sabotage, and fear of lack, pessimism and poverty consciousness. Clears financial sabotage patterns and in so doing, it allows you to be open to fully receiving great riches on all levels, not just financial. Promotes joyful sharing, belief in abundance and universal trust

Adol Essence *Billy Goat Plum, Boab, Bottlebrush, Dagger Hakea, Five Corners Flannel Flower, Kangaroo Paw, Red Helmet Orchid, Southern Cross Sunshine Wattle, Tall Yellow Top.* This essence addresses the major issues teenagers commonly experience, such as feelings of hopelessness, insensitivity, a sense of not belonging, an 'It's not fair' attitude. Also, rebelliousness and anger; gaucheness, and a sense of alienation and abandonment. For poor relationship with parents/authority figures. Helps with coping with change and enhances acceptance of self, communication, social skills, harmony in relationships, maturity, emotional stability and optimism.

Calm & Clear Essence *Boronia, Bottlebrush, Bush Fuchsia, Crowea, Jacaranda, Little Flannel Flower, Paw Paw, Black-Eyed Susan.* Helps one to find space and have time for oneself, to relax without getting caught up in external pressures and demands, to unwind, contemplation of oneself, enjoy relaxing pursuits and have fun. Encourages clarity, calmness and peace. For those who are always over-committed with no time for themselves, impatient, and irritable. Rushing and worry with mind chatter and insomnia. Fear of making decision and mistakes, stiffness, stomach problems, tension and tiredness, and feeling out of balance.

Cognis Essence *Bush Fuchsia, Isopogon, Jacaranda, Paw Paw, Sundew.* This essence gives clarity and focus when working, speaking, reading or studying. It balances the intuitive and cognitive processes and helps integrate ideas and assimilate information. Clears daydreaming, confusion and being overwhelmed, poor memory, stuttering, ADD & ADHD, imbalances between the right and left hemispheres, procrastination and lack of follow-through in projects.

For enhancement of all learning abilities and skills. Excellent for study or pursuits that require intense focus. It assists problem-solving by improving access to the Higher Self, which stores all past knowledge and experiences.

Confid Essence *Boab, Dog Rose, Five Corners, Southern Cross, Sturt Desert Rose.* This combination brings out the positive qualities of self-esteem and confidence. Clears low self-esteem, guilt and shyness, and also lack of conviction and victim mentality. It allows us to feel comfortable around other people and resolve negative beliefs we may hold about ourselves as well as any guilt harboured from past actions. Helps us to take responsibility for situations and events that occur in our lives, realizing that we have the ability and power not only to change those events, but also to create those we want. Promotes integrity, confidence and personal power; helps one to be true to oneself.

Creative Essence *Bush Fuchsia, Crowea, Five Corners, Flannel Flower, Red Grevillea,*

Tall Mulla Mulla, Turkey Bush. Creative Essence inspires and promotes creative and emotional expression in a gentle and calm way and gives courage and clarity in public speaking and singing. Frees the voice, improving its tone, timbre and melody. Indicated for creative blocks and inhibitions and helps to find creative solutions in all life's pursuits. Helpful for those who have difficulty expressing feelings. For dyslexia, stuttering, TMJ problems, difficulty opening mouth wide, breathing problems.

Dynamis Essence *Banksia Robur, Crowea, Illawarra Flame Tree, Macrocarpa, Old Man Banksia, Yellow Cowslip Orchid.* Renews enthusiasm, passion and joy for life. It is for those who feel 'not quite right', drained, jaded or not fully recovered from setbacks or illness. Lethargy, exhaustion, low energy, sluggish, overweight, weakened immune system. Balances, harmonizes and stimulates the major endocrine glands thereby enhancing one's energy, vitality and wellbeing. Centres and harmonizes one's vital forces. For burnout, temporary loss of drive, enthusiasm and excitement.

Electro Essence *Bush Fuchsia, Crowea, Fringed Violet, Mulla Mulla, Paw Paw, Waratah.* Greatly relieves fear and distress associated with earth, electrical and electromagnetic radiation. Found where ley lines cross or in houses where underground streams run. Feeling drained, flat and sensitive due to electromagnetic overload. Decreases the harmful effects of electrical radiation emitted by meter boxes, overhead power lines, mobile or cellular phones, fluorescent lights and electrical equipment, especially televisions, microwaves and computers. Helps alignment of the body, the broken aura, tiredness, insomnia, and brings one into balance with the natural rhythms of the earth.

Emergency Essence *Crowea, Dog Rose of the Wild Forces, Fringed Violet, Grey Spider Flower, Sundew, Waratah, Angelsword.* Excellent for any emotional or physical upset. It has a calming effect on the mind, body and emotions during a crisis. It quickly eases panic, distress, fear, severe mental or physical stress, nervous tension and pain. Promotes the ability to cope. If a person needs specialized medical help, this essence will provide comfort until treatment is available. Administer this remedy every hour or 10–15 minutes if necessary. For headaches, muscle tension, childbirth, accidents, fear of flying, all injuries and trauma to animals. Also assists with recovery from surgery.

Meditation Essence *Boronia, Bush Fuchsia, Bush Iris, Fringed Violet, Green Spider Orchid, Red Lily, Angelsword.* A wonderful combination to awaken one's spirituality; it allows one to go deeper into any spiritual practice. Enhances access to Higher Self and intuition whilst providing psychic protection and healing of the aura.

For psychic attack, damage to the aura feeling psychically drained. Highly recommended for anyone practising meditation, enhances deeper meditation. Clears spiritual confusion and improves telepathic communication and creative visualizations.

Purifying Essence *Bauhinia, Bush Iris, Bottlebrush, Dagger Hakea, Dog Rose, Wild Potato Bush.* To release and clear emotional waste and residual byproducts, to clear built-up emotional baggage, encourages the mind and body to clear toxic waste. A spring clean for physical toxicity, oedema, feeling weighed down and sluggish, heavy metal toxicity, chemotherapy, imbalance in any organ of elimination – such as constipation. Aids acne, eczema and other skin conditions as well as bad breath and headaches.

Relationship Essence *Bluebell, Boab, Bottlebrush, Bush Gardenia, Dagger Hakea, Flannel Flower, Mint Bush, Red Helmet Orchid, Red Suva Frangipani, Wedding Bush.* Enhances the quality of all relationships, especially intimate ones. It clears and releases resentment, bitterness, blocked or held-in raw emotions, and the confusion, emotional pain, grief and turmoil of a rocky relationship and an inability to relate. When closed and cut off from

feelings, helps one verbalize, express feelings and improve communication. Enhances parental-child bonding and breaks the early negative family conditioning and patterns which effect us in our current adult relationships. For those in intimate relationships a perfect remedy to follow this combination is Sexuality Essence.

Sexuality Essence *Combination of Billy Goat Plum, Bush Gardenia, Flannel Flower, Fringed Violet, Little Flannel Flower, Sturt Desert Rose, Wisteria.* This essence is helpful for releasing shame and the effects of physical or sexual abuse and trauma. It enables the individual to allow one to feel comfortable with, and to fully accept, one's body. For fear of intimacy. Allows one to be open to sensuality and touch and enjoy physical and emotional intimacy. Clears guilt and embarrassment, feelings of revulsion and frigidity, bringing playfulness and fulfilment. Renews passion and interest in stale relationships

Solaris Essence *Combination of She Oak, Spinifex, Mulla Mulla.* An essential first-aid remedy, greatly relieves fear and distress associated with fire, heat and sun – eases the pain from all degree of burns. It also greatly reduces the radiation absorbed from X-rays and the sun. An excellent remedy to have handy during summer and after long exposure to the sun. Applied topically it will help reduce fevers. Reduces the negative effects of fire and heat. For hot flushes, sunburn/ stroke, blisters and burning sensations anywhere on the body.

Transition Essence *Combination of Bauhinia, Bottlebrush, Bush Iris, Lichen, Mint Bush, Red Grevillea, Silver Princess.* This combination helps one to cope and move through any major situational or biological life change, such as moving house or starting a new career, becoming pregnant, or entering menopause. It gives the ability to be open to change and deal with challenges associated with it like fear of the unknown and resistance to change. It brings about an awareness of one's life direction, especially for people who are at a crossroads. Alternatively those who know what they want but do not know how to achieve it will benefit from this combination. It also eases the fear of death as well as helping one come to terms with it. Consequently, this remedy allows one to easily and gently pass over with calmness, dignity, serenity and peace.

Travel Essences *Combination of Banksia Robur, Bottlebrush, Bush Fuchsia, Bush Iris, Crowea, Fringed Violet, Macrocarpa, Mulla Mulla, Paw Paw, Red Lily, She Oak, Silver Princess, Sundew, Tall Mulla Mulla.* Beneficial for distress associated with all forms of travel, particularly addresses the problems encountered with jet travel. It maintains a sense of personal space and enables a person to arrive at their destination feeling refreshed balanced and ready to go. Combats jet lag, motion sickness, fatigue, vertigo, radiation in planes, stiff muscles, weakened endocrine, immune and nervous systems from aircraft engine vibration, physical stress, depleted and drained, static electricity, digestive disorders, dehydration and circulation problems.

Woman Essence *Combination of Bottlebrush, Bush Fuchsia, Crowea, Five Corners, Mulla Mulla, Old Man Banksia, Peach flower.* This essence encourages a woman's own innate strength and beauty through life's physical and emotional cycles and seasons of change, remaining calm and stable, and allowing a woman to discover and feel good about herself, her own body and her beauty. Harmonizes any imbalances during menstruation, pregnancy and menopause. For female hormonal imbalance, infertility, menstrual cramps, PMS, irregular menstruation, candida, hot flushes, weight gain, sluggish, feeling disheartened and weary. Also skin problems, moodswings, hypoglycaemia and for women feeling overwhelmed by pregnancy.

Companion Essences

Autumn Leaves The essence is made only from these leaves. Allows one to hear, see and feel communication from the other side, increases awareness, to be open to the guidance and communication especially of loved ones in the spiritual world. It's important for anyone passing over to be aware that help and guidance are around, especially through the presence of loved ones who have already died; this allows the sense of letting go and moving on in a very profound way. Helps with difficulties in the transition of passing over from the physical plane to the spiritual world. Autumn Leaves is included in the Transition Essence combination.

Green Essence Made from the stems and leaves of traditional fresh green herbs, using the same method as for Flower Essences. Purifying and for emotional distress associated with intestinal and skin disorders, used to harmonize any internal yeast, mould and parasites to the same vibration as one's body. It should be taken orally for a minimum two-week period, five drops three times a day, five minutes before meals. Can also be used topically on the skin. Place seven drops of Green Essence in a dessert bowl of water, splash on the affected area and allow to dry. Do this morning and night for two weeks and refresh every two days. Effective to douche with Green Essence, morning and night for a two week period. It is not recommend that you use Green Essence externally at the same time as internally.

Lichen Essence Helps to be aware of, look for, and go to the Light at the moment of death, rather than being earth-bound in the astral plane. For healing the separation between the physical and etheric body, helps the release of earth-bound energies and encourages transition into the Light.

Australian Bush Creams

These exquisite Australian Bush Flower Essence creams have been blended with a base of pure botanicals, herbal extracts and aromatic oils to provide a deeply nourishing carrier to rehydrate, moisturize and protect even the most delicate skin whilst the gentle yet profound qualities of the flower essences care for your emotions. The deeply penetrating botanicals are rich in antioxidants and can be applied all over your face, hands or body to create, stimulate and encourage the desired healing response.

Calm & Clear Cream *Boronia, Bottlebrush, Bush Fuchsia, Crowea, Jacaranda, Little Flannel Flower, Paw Paw.* Promotes having own time and space, winding down, relaxing and having fun, clarity, calmness and peace for those who are always over-committed, with no time for self. Counteracts impatience, rushing and worry. Helps to find time for oneself, to relax without external pressures and demands, to wind down and enjoy relaxing pursuits

Emergency Cream *Crowea, Dog Rose of the Wild Forces, Fringed Violet, Grey Spider Flower, Sundew, Waratah, Slender Rice Flower and Spinifex have also been added to this cream formulation.* Excellent for any emotional upset. It has a calming effect during a crisis. If a person needs special-ized medical help, this essence will provide comfort until treatment is available. Administer this cream every hour or more frequently if necessary, until the person feels better. For bruises, or other injury to the skin.

Face, Hand & Body Cream *Billy Goat Plum, Five Corners, Flannel Flower, Little Flannel Flower, Mulla Mulla, She Oak, Wisteria.* Encourages love, nurturing, care and touch of your physical body. Helps to deal with any dislike and non-acceptance of one's physical body. Promotes love and nurturing of self, beautiful skin texture and enjoyment of intimate loving touch.

Travel Cream *Bottlebrush, Bush Fuchsia, Bush Iris, Crowea Fringed Violet, Macrocarpa, Mulla Mulla, Paw Paw, Red Lily, She Oak, Silver Princess, Sundew, Tall Mulla Mulla.* This combination particularly addresses the problems encountered with jet travel. Moisturizes and prevents dehydration of the skin. It enables a person to arrive at their destination feeling balanced and ready to go. The use of this essence is beneficial for all forms of travel. Massage on the feet and lower legs during long flights to help prevent DVTS.

Woman Cream *Bottlebrush, Bush Fuchsia, Crowea, Five Corners, Mulla Mulla, Old Man Banksia, Peach-flowered Tea-tree, She Oak.* Harmonizes any imbalances during menstruation and menopause. It allows a woman to feel good about herself, her own body and beauty. Promotes female balance, calmness and stability, and helps with coping with change. Massage on to stomach area during painful menstruation. Combats the dryness of menopause. For moodswings, weariness and physical dislike.

Australian Bush Mists

These Australian Bush Flower Essence mists have been formulated with a base of pure botanicals, herbal extracts and exquisite aromatic oils to create and encourage positive healing environments. The Bush Flower Essences have been blended within a deeply nourishing carrier to rehydrate, moisturize and create protective environ-ments whilst the gentle yet profound qualities of the flower essences care for your emotions. They can be used anytime there is a need to create a safe healing environ-ment, at home, at work, while travelling and with those you love.

Calm & Clear Mist *Black-Eyed Susan, Boronia, Bottlebrush, Bush Fuchsia, Crowea, Jacaranda, Little Flannel Flower, Paw Paw.* Spray this mist to promote calm and help to find time for oneself, to relax without external pressures and demands, to wind down and enjoy relaxing pursuits.

Emergency Mist *Angelsword, Crowea, Dog Rose of the Wild Forces, Fringed Violet, Grey Spider Flower, Sundew, Waratah.* Excellent for any emotional upset. It has a calming effect during a crisis. Spray this frequently if needed, to clear panic, distress and fear.

Sensuality Mist *Bush Gardenia, Flannel Flower, Little Flannel Flower, Macrocarpa, Wisteria.* Encourages the ability to enjoy physical and emotional intimacy, passion and sensual fulfilment.

Space Clearing Mist *Boab, Fringed Violet, Lichen, Red Lily, Angelsword.* Creates sacred, safe space and harmonious environments. Purifies and releases environments with built-up negative, disharmonious or unpleasant emotional, mental and psychic energies. Great for clearing tense situations and environments and restoring balance.

Travel Mist *Bottlebrush, Banksia Robur, Bush Fuchsia, Bush Iris, Crowea, Fringed Violet, Macrocarpa, Mulla Mulla, Paw Paw, Red Lily, She Oak, Silver Princess, Sundew, Tall Mulla Mulla.* This combination partic-ularly addresses the problems encountered with jet travel. It enables a person to arrive at their destination feeling balanced and ready to go. The use of this essence is beneficial for all forms of travel to refresh, sweeten and maintain sense of personal space in closed environments.

Woman Mist *Billy Goat Plum, Bottlebrush, Bush Fuchsia, Crowea, Five Corners, Mulla Mulla, Old Man Banksia, Peach-flowered Tea-tree, She Oak.* Harmonizes any imbalances during menstruation and menopause. It allows a woman to feel good about herself, her own body and beauty. Promotes female balance, calmness and stability, coping with change. Spray mist when experiencing hot flushes. For moodswings, weariness and physical dislike.

Living Essences of Australia and The Life Academy

The Living Essences of Australia are mostly made from flowers that grow in the south-western region of Australia, called the Wildflower State, an area known for its prolific and unique flora. They have been developed by pioneers Vasudeva and Kadambii Barnao who have been conducting far-reaching research into mind-body medicine and the evolution of consciousness for the past 28 years.

The medical results they have been able to achieve through the application of their flower essences have been so successful that their qualifications in holistic counselling and mind-body medicine and flower essence therapy are now recognized by the Australian Government and are equivalent in professional standing to the highest naturopathic and homeopathic qualifications.

Their education programme teaches unique techniques for the application of flower essences along with an in-depth pragmatic understanding of the meta-physical world and the place a human being has within it. With the utilization of this knowledge and the application of these techniques the student is able to go beyond using psychological profiling as the primary tool for the diagnosing and prescribing of flower essences.

By combining the metaphysics of yogic science and traditional Chinese medicine with modern-day science, a deep knowledge of the inner and outer nature of a human being is understood. Upon this foundation, practical, effective diagnostic and treatment techniques are taught that take into account the mind and body of an individual along with their unique evolutionary journey, or to put it another way, their unique life path.

After moving to Australia from New Zealand, Vasudeva began his pioneering research into the native flowers of Australia in 1977. In 1982 Vasudeva and his wife Kadambii started working together, setting up the Australasian Flower Essence Academy and the Living Essences Clinic in Perth, Western Australia. Together they have made and researched over 200 flower essences and developed the Microvita range of creams and lotions for the relief of pain, arthritis, hypertension, stress and lethargy which are now used in hospitals on a professional basis and by orthodox practitioners (*see* page 85). In 1994 this led to the Barnaos being invited to create the first university flower essence course in Perth, WA. Kadambii's work from 1985 with an Aboriginal community brought her into contact with an elder who had been entrusted with the secrets of native folk-healing. He still used the traditional flower sauna, one of the oldest-known forms of flower essence therapy dating back at least 10,000 years. They also initiated research into the benefits of combining flower essences with the ancient Chinese art of acupuncture/acupressure to strengthen the potency of both modes of healing. Their findings led to the creation of some of the world's first Floral Acu-maps, which pinpoint specific flowers for specific acupuncture points. This therapy is proving highly effective in the treatment of pain and stress. In addition, they have pioneered many new flower essence diagnostic techniques such as Baihui diagnosis, Field of Flowers technique and Flower Photography Diagnosis, all of which are taught internationally through their academy's correspondence course and lecture tours.

They researched further and created the Japanese Flower Essences as well as the Combination Living Helpers

The Barnaos feel the future in health is mind-body flower essences. Flower essences work by unlocking the inner wisdom innate within every human being. Faulty attitudes, with the consequent negative reactions to life situations, can cause physical disease, unpleasant mental states and are obstructive in the fulfilment of our desired goals.

Antiseptic Bush (*Calocephalus ass. Multiflorus*) For cleansing oneself from negative influences in the environment which may have built up over some time. Maintains inner sanctity when living among negative or harmful aspects or people.

Balga Blackboy (*Xanthorrea preissi*) For those who are unaware that their personal desires and goals can create emotional or environmental catastrophes. Brings an awareness of the impact your desires may have on others, so that you understand and do not resent any natural obstacles placed in your path. For the maturation of the masculine principle.

Black Kangaroo Paw (*Macropidia fuliginosa*) For those unable to forgive parents for controlling them in the past. Replaces hate and resentment with love and forgiveness.

Blue Leschenaultia (*Leschenaultia biloba*) For those who can be emotional and physical 'Scrooges', self-sufficient, unmoved by the needs of others. Breaks down the walls of selfish isolation, allowing you to see the needs of others and learn to share with them.

Brachycome (*Multifida dilitata*) For lack of empathy, intellectual arrogance, over-criticism and contempt of others. Encourages appreciation of people for who they are, not how intelligent they seem.

Brown Boronia (*Boronia megastigma*) For an overactive mind, working excessively without rest in an attempt to solve pressing problems yet being unable to find adequate solutions. Brings patience and acceptance so you do not worry unnecessarily about things you cannot change, as well as the realization that the journey of life will deliver solutions.

Cape Bluebell (*Wahlenbergia capensis*) For those who have a chip on their shoulder and can be negative, displaying hatred and malice. Confers the ability to let go of the past and be loving and empathetic.

Catspaw (*Anigozanthos humilis*) For depression, sadness and anger caused by the insincerity and selfishness of others. For families and close-knit groups with undefined problems. Helps you to drop expectations of fairness while refusing to let others take advantage, so that they too can learn fairness. Promotes mutual consideration.

Christmas Tree (Kanya) (*Nuytsia floribunda*) For those times when duties and everyday pressures cause you to become distant and avoid your share of the load, causing resentment among others. Helps you to meet your responsibilities and reap the rewards of consistency and shared goals. Brings inner contentment which enhances your enjoyment of your family or group.

Correa (*Correa pulchella*) For those who are too hard on themselves. Teaches acceptance of our limitations and short-comings without regret. Enables us to see how we make mistakes unintentionally, and helps us to do better next time.

Cowkicks (*Stylidium schoenoides*) For the unsuspecting optimist who is devastated by an unexpected crisis and trauma, making him or her the depleted, hopeless victim of circumstance. Helps you to rebuild and pull the pieces back together after a shattering experience to create a wiser perspective.

Dampiera (*Dampiera linearis*) For those who are fearful and unable to relax, blowing all situations out of proportion. Allows you to let go and be open, to let things happen in different ways and allow people their own style.

Fringed Lily Twiner (*Caladenia falcata*) For those who blame others for their misery when thwarted. Also for spoiled children and manipulative parents who can be vengeful and brooding. Allows you to see that selfishness lies at the root of misery. Teaches you to turn your focus away from yourself, and stimulates love.

Fuchsia Grevillea (*Grevillea bipinnatifida*) For those who tend to be two-faced. Brings the realization that hidden negativity is destructive, as well as a release from smugness, anger and a dislike of being exposed.

Fuchsia Gum (*Eucalyptus forrestiana*) For claustrophobia, both physical and emotional. Prevents feelings of panic in confined spaces.

Geraldton Wax (*Chamelaucium uncinatum*) For those who feel trapped and resentful, who feel they are under someone else's thumb (for example a parent who always tries to appease a demanding child). Helps you to become strong enough not to be pressured against your will or influenced by the desires of others.

Goddess Grasstree (*Kingia argenta*) For maturation of the female principle (in both men and women). Brings inner strength, nurturing, sensitivity and loving wisdom that is not emotionally dependent. Releases the female aspect into society.

Golden Waitsia (*Waitsia aurea*) For those who worry about details as well as those needing to accept their present imperfect state of health and wellbeing while convalescing from illness or trauma.

Re-ignites spontaneity and carefree feelings, healing all aspects of the anxiety that is caused by perfectionism.

Green Rose (*Rosa chinensis veridiflora*) For people intolerant of advice when needing to break through a problem, becoming agitated when challenged by new ideas – and stagnating in their isolation. Maintains progressiveness, helping you to embrace new thoughts and ideas, not to stagnate, become negative or blame others for your situation.

Grevillea Golden Glory (*Grevillea tenuiloba*) For those whose trusting, open, relaxed nature has been abused, creating within them an uneasy feeling about the motives of others. Rekindles a sense of trust and confidence to allow other people into your life, and not to expect or worry about being judged.

Happy Wanderer (*Hardenbergia comptoniana*) For those who doubt their abilities and need others for security and support, either emotionally, mentally or physically. Helps you stand on your own feet, knowing you are strong enough to do things by yourself. Clears insecurity.

Hops Bush (*Dodonaea* sp.) For those who cannot sleep or relax due to frenetic energy. Earths excessive, scattered energy, re-establishing a natural and healthy flow which feeds your need for activity without overstimulating you. Brings inner mental and physical peace, restoring your control over life and a balanced states of rest and activity.

Illyarrie (*Eucalyptus erythrocorys*) For those who have been badly hurt and suppress the memory. Allows you to realize that you have the strength to face and deal with any pain, that it is never as bad as you fear and it will not overwhelm you. Useful in past-life therapy to uncover forgotten experiences affecting the present.

Macrozamia (*Macrozamia reidlei*) For balancing basic flows of yin and yang. Balances sexual energy to free blockages brought about by bad experiences such as

rape or incest. Heals and restores all aspects of the male/female – releases blockages, corrects underdevelopment and adjusts hormonal fluctuations.

Many-Headed Dryandra (*Dryandra polycephalus*) For those seen as irresponsible or 'fly-by-night', displaying erratic behaviour and panic. Brings composure and strength. Helps you to confront and deal with life's problems rather than running away from them.

Mauve Melaleuca (*Melaleuca thymifolia*) For the emotional idealist who has been hurt and is sad. Also for the unloved spouse, parent or child. Eases despondence about an uncaring world. Allows you to find fulfilment within and tap into the source of eternal love.

Menzies Banksia (*Banksia menziesii*) For clearing the fear that history will repeat itself, in the form of past experiences of hurt and rejection. Also for psychic paralysis. Allows you to let go of past pain, move on through present pain with courage, and have no fear of new experiences.

One-Sided Bottlebrush (*Calothamnus myrticae*) For those who are over-burdened and depressed, caught up in themselves, complaining about their workload. Brings the realization that others also have burdens to bear and keeps you from getting caught up in the 'poor me' syndrome.

Orange Leschenaultia (*Leschenaultia formosus*) For true survivors, tough-skinned people who have become insensitive and lack compassion. Encourages benevolence and caring and puts you in touch with the softer qualities of life.

Orange Spiked Pea Flower (*Daviesa divaricata*) For those who feel undermined by what others say, feeling angered to the point of violence. Helps you to let words spoken by others pass over you and not destroy your poise. Promotes self-expression.

Pale Sundew (*Drosera pallida*) For unscrupulous people who use people and situations for their own benefit, such as the business shark or ambitious politician. Brings the realization that being manipulative and predatory is senseless and destructive. Increases repulsion to wrongdoing. The essence is conscience.

Parakeelya (*Calandrinia polyandra*) For quiet, passive people who become the unappreciated workhorse in the family, business or community; for deep-seated loneliness and pain that comes of feeling used and uncared for. Helps you to stand up and be respected so you become the inspired worker who can enjoy belonging to the group. For self-esteem and assertiveness.

Pincushion Hakea (*Hakea laurina*) For those who feel their beliefs may be threatened or their logic undermined by new ideas, such as scientists and religious people. Allows you to be open to new ideas, not to fear the views of others, to relax and be more accepting without compromising your own ethics.

Pink Everlasting Straw Flower (*Helipterum roseum*) For those who perceive others' feelings but cannot respond to them emotionally due to feeling 'dry' and depleted. Renews springs of love and joy. Helpful for teachers and caregivers.

Pink Fountain Triggerplant (*Stylidium bulbiferum*) For those losing their inner vital force which keeps us alive, either by a slow draining on the physical level or a rupture in the subtle bodies. Re-ignites the vital flame and restores its dynamism.

Pink Impatiens (*Impatiens* sp.) For the idealist, the moralist who compromises through struggling to maintain his or her standards. Helps you to retain ideals and standards no matter the obstacles, to have determination and creativity to carry on without compromising.

Pink Trumpet Flower (*Gladiolus Caryophyllaceus*) For those who find it difficult to maintain their sense of purpose, who get lost during a thought process or activity. Brings clarity and focus. Harnesses inner strength of purpose and directs it towards important goals. Encourages achievement through new mental directness.

Pixie Mop (*Petrophile linearis*) For sensitive, emotionally needy people who have become hard because they feel let down. Brings the realization that forgiving those who let you down frees your heart, so that you can help others as you would hope to be helped yourself.

Purple Eremophila (*Eremophila scoparia*) Very helpful during relationship upsets. Helps you to gain and maintain serene objectivity amidst very personal issues of the heart, without compromising your richness of feeling and sensitivity towards loved ones.

Purple Flag Flower (*Patersonia occidentalis*) For those who push themselves to their stress threshold, making them feel extremely anxious and unable to relax. Brings healing relaxation of mind and body. Helps you to unwind, releasing built-up pressure and tension.

Purple Nymph Waterlily (*Nymphaea Violeacea*) Helps those wishing to share their treasures with others but finding themselves holding back. Brings selfless service, while making sure you are not caught in emotional traps in your dealings with others.

Purple and Red Kangaroo Paw (*Anigozanthos manglesii*) For clearing negativity and non-constructive criticism, such as blaming others all the time. Encourages you to do something positive and constructive.

Queensland Bottlebrush (*Callistemon polandi*) For clearing a conflict of desires and unsettled behaviour. Allows us the freedom to be ourselves, to know that people and experiences come and go; we do not have to be isolated from them to stay safe.

Red Feather Flower (*Verticordia mitcheliana*) For the laziness and dishonesty that can arise in those who feel life owes them a living. Teaches that it is better to give than to receive; that we should not exploit the goodness of others or feel resentful when they feel they have given enough; to rely on our own energy and resources; to be there for others.

Red and Green Kangaroo Paw (*Anigozanthos manglesii*) For being in touch with the here and now, and realizing that those close to you are a priority. Encourages sensitivity and patience; brings joy.

Red Leschenaultia (*Anigozanthos manglesii*) For those who feel contemptuous of weaker people, are harsh, lacking in sensitivity. Turns harshness and lack of empathy into sensitivity. Helps you to become caring and considerate towards those weaker than yourself.

Ribbon Pea (*Brachysema Aphylla*) For those who feel a sense of nameless dread, but don't understand why. Helps you to rise above the fear and foreboding that prevents you from having a positive attitude and real direction for a fulfilling life. Heals the panicky fear of annihilation.

Rose Cone Flower (*Isopogon formosus*) For those who feel frazzled and touchy, have difficulty coping, are easily disturbed, want to be alone, need space and peace (such as the parents of babies or young children). Helps you to discover peace amidst the storm, releasing tension so you can enjoy being around others.

Silver Princess Gum (*Eucalyptus caesia*) For those who lose interest or give up easily, displaying rebellious and frustrated behaviour. Teaches you to persevere when things are not working out, to keep caring and not rebel – thereby overcoming obstacles and achieving your goals.

Snakebush (*Hemiandra pungens*) For those who give but are motivated by the need to be loved. For people emotionally unsettled and frustrated in love. Helps you to learn to be self-contained and to care for others without seeking anything in return, so easing disillusionment and anxiety.

Snake Vine (*Hibbertia scandens*) For victims of destructive gossip or character assassination. Also helpful during relationship break-ups, when bitter feelings can undermine your self-confidence. Replenishes confidence and appreciation for your own achievements when others are sowing the seeds of negativity and doubt.

Southern Cross (*Xanthosia rotundifolia*) For those with comfortable lifestyles who feel bewildered when life deals them a sudden blow and they have to struggle for survival. Brings a realization of how life is for others and how, one day, it could be for you.

Star of Bethlehem (Australasian) (*Calectasia cyanea*) For resignation, frustration and lack of initiative due to a feeling that there is no hope of improvement. Brings the realization that there is always hope; helping you to see all the solutions life can offer, and to know that you can find happiness by breaking through problems with creativity.

Urchin Dryandra (*Dryandra praemorsa*) For those who feel downtrodden, the underdog in unequal relationships. Encourages you to rise above the feelings of inferiority stemming from ill-treatment by others.

Ursinia (*Ursinia anthemoides*) For idealists who are cynical, critical and frustrated with being part of a group or organization. Allows the bright-eyed enthusiast to see the reality of group dynamics and still retain his or her idealism. Fosters co-operation and productiveness to ensure healthy progress and growth despite problems with selfish members of the group.

Veronica (*Caladenia* sp.) For isolation and alienation stemming from the feeling that you go unnoticed and are misunderstood. Teaches you to relate to others differently, and not to dwell on loneliness and the belief that no one understands you.

Violet Butterfly (*Stylidium maitlandianum*) For those feeling emotionally shattered during and after relationship traumas such as break-ups. Calms flaring sensitivities and emotional pain, speeds emotional recovery, heals the damage and allows you to get on with the rest of your life.

Western Australian Smokebush (*Conospermum stoechadis*) For those feeling pressurized to achieve when they have no desire to, resulting in loss of mental control, nervousness, anxiety, fearfulness and severe stress. In extreme cases, fear of going mad. Promotes mental stability; reconnects mind and body and reintegrates the subtle with the physical aspects. Helpful for concentration, faintness after anaesthesia – promotes quick recovery.

White Eremophila (*Eremophila scoparia*) For developing a broad perspective when messy situations threaten to drag you down. Brings clarity to complexities and difficulties. Helps maintain your equipoise, consistency and direction in life.

White Nymph Waterlily (*Nymphaea Violeacea*) For uncovering your deepest spiritual core. Brings tranquillity for reaching into the soul and using your Higher Self to integrate and respond to life from a universal rather than personal perspective. Helpful for spiritual practices such as meditation.

Wild Violet (*Hybathus calycinus*) For pessimists and worriers who are apprehensive, depressed, complaining and single-minded. Balances caution with the willingness to be carefree and optimistic, to take a chance on happiness.

Woolly Banksia (*Banksia hookeriana*) For those who are losing heart when the struggle seems too much. Rekindles the desire to go ahead with ideals and goals, to face new aspirations without fear of inevitable failure. Helpful during long, tiring, seemingly pointless phases in the journey to reach your higher ambition.

Woolly Smokebush (*Conospermum incur*) Helpful for maintaining forward progress without getting distracted. Offers perspective and humility. Helps you avoid the traps of glamour and self-importance, so that you look at life objectively.

Yellow Boronia (*Megastigma lutea*) For an overactive mind, scattered thinking, those who are easily distracted. Helps you to remain calm and centred so the mind can be focused and follow thoughts through.

Yellow Coneflower (*Megastigma lutea*) For a sense of inferiority and lack of self-esteem. Brings acceptance of inner worth and freedom from the need to seek recognition from others. Prevents situations arising in which you are used.

Yellow Flag Flower (*Patersonia Xanthina*) For those stressed by daily chores, who feel unable to cope with the trying events in life. Brings calmness and brightness during times of stress, to help you to find the fortitude to handle all situations without making life one long, difficult grind.

Yellow and Green Kangaroo Paw (*Anigozanthos manglesii*) For the perfectionist, hard task master, uncompromising parent or boss who is supercritical and intolerant. Teaches tolerance, the value of mistakes and the importance of being nonjudgemental and patient with imperfections.

Yellow Leschenaultia (*Leschenaultia formosus*) For those who always know better – teachers, parents, teenagers who dismiss out of hand the views of others. Helps you to become open to others, to listen, be patient and tolerant.

Australian Orchids

Blue China Orchid (*Caladenia gemmata*) For addictions of one sort or another, the inability to control yourself, feeling overwhelmed or unfulfilled, lack of willpower. Breaks the spell of addiction, strengthens the will, helps you to take back control of yourself. Brings the realization that you no longer need a crutch.

Cowslip Orchid (*Macropidia fuliginosa*) For those with a superiority complex, who crave recognition and overrate their own importance, use arrogant, pompous behaviour and are negative and contemptuous to those who do not acknowledge them. Helps to deflate egos and to reveal the value of interacting with and enjoying people from all walks of life.

Fringed Mantis Orchid (*Caladenia falcata*) For the destructive, psychic predator, or the busybody with an unhealthy curiosity and no conscience. Brings conscience into one's activities; curbs unhealthy curiosity about the affairs of others. Confers the realization that you should only use information for benevolent reasons.

Hybrid Pink Fairy/Cowslip Orchid (*Caladenia* sp.) For those who take others' attitudes too personally, feeling unfairly persecuted or threatened; for oversensitivity, paranoia, tearfulness over small matters. Enables one to get on with life without being concerned with others' reactions. Generates contentment, inner tranquillity and self-contained positivity. Also helpful for PMS and the sensitivity of pregnancy.

Leafless Orchid (*Praecoxanthus aphylla*) For those who feel bogged down – such as the uninspired therapist who is drained, tired and lacking vitality. Promotes attention to central not peripheral needs in yourself and others. Allows you to find the energy deep within to keep positive and active in your work for others without becoming depleted and tired, mentally and physically.

Pink Fairy Orchid (*Caladenia latifolia*) For those who feel panicky due to circumstances, creating mental instability and the feeling of being overwhelmed by the environment. Filters the stress of environmental situations which can cause feelings of panic and being overwhelmed. Calms the inner core and helps to lessen oversensitivity to the environment.

Purple Enamel Orchid (*Elythranthera brunonis*) For those who begin a task feeling unmotivated and useless, then behave like workaholics to prove themselves. Maintains a consistent and healthily balanced energy input – not too much, not too little and not all at once – to gain an equilibrium between rest and work.

Rabbit Orchid (*Leptoceras menziesii*) For those who tend to be superficial and insincere – socialites. Bestows sincerity and straightforwardness, not shallowness and emptiness. Provides the ability to see the rewards of meaningful, honest relationships. Helps you to find your true self.

Red Beak Orchid – Burnout Orchid (*Lypercanthos nigricans*) For the frustrated housewife or husband, lethargic employee, lazy student or truant. Resolves the clash between desire and responsibility that often causes a sense of burden and mental paralysis. Counters lethargy, rebelliousness, boredom and depression.

Shy Blue Orchid (*Cyanicula Amplexans*) For those dedicated to the path of light. Gives a sense of protection and dynamism where powerlessness had prevailed. Focuses spiritual energies that dispel negative forces in the environment.

Wallflower Donkey Orchid (*Diuris magnifica*) For those who feel they are the victim of circumstances, becoming vengeful, cynical, empty and disillusioned. Allows 'letting go' rather than feeling the sickness of revenge. Allows you to take responsibility for making life positive so that you do not live with a chip on your shoulder.

White Spider Orchid (*Caladenia patersonii*) For spiritual, humanitarian people such as volunteer workers with a tendency to introversion, sadness, hypersensitivity, and anguish deep in their souls. Brings love and caring without devastation at the insensitivity and suffering of others. Allows you to empathize while not being brought down by the world.

Russian Essences

With the political and social turmoil in Russia, these remedies reflect the problems that beset the Russian people, and are relevant to all those facing suppression, oppression and the subsequent reactions to these forces.

Made by Vasudeva Barnao, who was invited to the then Soviet Union in 1989 to begin research on essences collected from flowers in the Bush about 125 miles (200km) from Moscow. Their contribution to the essence repertoire is unique and invaluable.

Blue-Topped Cow Weed For the escapist or joker who avoids life's deeper issues – the superficial good-timer who avoids responsibility, lacking empathy, depth of character. Brings a more responsible attitude. Engenders the strength to deal with problems rather than avoid them.

Kolokoltchik For conquering adversity after a long history of struggle when the will to fight has faded. Restores the desire to fight on and not succumb.

Russian Centaurea For brave people who stand up and oppose injustice, regardless of the consequences; for risk-takers who feel opposed or trapped. Teaches that there are times when you cannot act because of negative forces stronger than yourself, when you must keep your flame hidden so as not to attract undue attention from those seeking to destroy you.

Russian Forget-Me-Not For the follower, looking to others for leadership, underestimating his or her own abilities and strengths. Helps you to find hidden strength.

Microvita Creams

The Microvita creams in the Living Essences of Australia range contain specially selected flower essences derived from the flora of the natural pristine landscapes, in combination, cold-pressed and essential oils in an aqueous cream base. These creams and lotions are designed to relieve stressed states of mind associated with physical discomfort, and to bring long-term benefits.

Medical science now recognizes that stress and negative states of mind can alter body chemistry and create physical disease. For instance, recent medical studies prove that depression is a greater cause of heart disease than smoking. Researchers found that in depressed people the blood platelets became more sticky, clogging arteries and veins. Depressed people lose hope, they view life from a negative perspective, lacking optimism and positivity.

Quality of life is dependent on a healthy mind and body

Arthritis Cream Designed to alleviate arthritic pain. Relief should occur within four to eight weeks.

Body Bliss A body lotion that reduces stress and promotes a feeling of well-being and relaxation. Use for conditions where a calming effect would be beneficial, for example, the temporary relief of tension pain and insomnia, and to ease anxiety which causes the tightening of the lungs, apply the lotion to the chest, back and neck.

Body Sports provides an excellent massage medium and has an invigorating effect. A body lotion which is useful for the temporary relief of soft tissue injury and pain. For general muscle pain, energy loss, cramping, sunburn, stiffness, menstrual discomfort, bruising, sports preparation and invigoration.

De-Stress Moisturizer A moisturizing cream with stress-relieving qualities. Using this moisturizer daily can help to ease tension and allow body and mind to relax, as well as improving skin lustre and appearance. For stressed-out adults, fretting babies, over-active children. For anxiety, depression, sleeplessness, devitalized skin.

Pain Cream Concentrate for pain, bruising, cramping. Also used for menstrual or birth cramps. Has invigorating effect. Pain Cream is like a first-aid kit in a bottle for muscular aches and pains and many other conditions where pain and discomfort are a problem. It can be helpful for the temporary relief of the symptoms of pulled muscles, minor sprains and bruising, back and neck pain, headaches, sinus pain, sunburn and insect bites and itches.

Skin Rejuvenation Moisturizer For wrinkled, devitalized skin and stress-related lines. Brings back the vital energy to your face, which is where stress first shows.

Japanese Flower Essences

For the 21st Century

Japan conjures up a vision of wild cherry blossoms displaying drifts of delicate white and pink blossom in the spring, and snow-capped mountain peaks, the most sacred place in the Japanese universe.

The evolution of Japanese flowers takes us back tens of thousands of years to the distribution of the Magnolia and Mahonia, an ancient species of plants older than mankind, the Magnolia especially has been discovered in fossil deposits some five million years old. The study of these plants is a key factor in the hypothesis that North America and eastern Asia were once a continuous landmass.

The Japanese, with their profound affinity with nature and deep love of flowers, have been cultivating the Rose, Magnolia and Chrysanthemum for up to 1,500 years. The Cherry is so much loved and held sacred that in the spring flower festival of Hanami, the Japanese have special celebrations of flower-viewing parties, held under the blossoming trees in the temples' shrines, in honour of the Cherry's vitality. The Japanese marvel at the way the trees burst into bloom, then suddenly, at the height of their magnificence, all the petals fall, which to them is reminiscent of the samurai's graceful and honourable death suggesting qualities of invisibility but also the ephemeral nature of life.

It was when Vasudeva and Kadambii Barnao met with Hidenori Miura, healer, *chi* master and *ikebana* teacher (flower arranging), that inspiration and timing for the birth of Japanese Flowers Essences occurred. Vasudeva feels that every flower in the world has its arena of work, and people's need of certain flowers generally corresponds to the healing properties of the flowers that grow in that area.

There is a distinct speciality to the healing qualities and attributes of the Japanese flowers that the whole of humanity can benefit from; firstly they highlight the strong sense of community responsibility and work collective; secondly they assist in balancing individual expression and personal development of relationships between people.

Fuderindou Flower (*Gentiana zellingeri*) **Manifesting the Goal**. This essence gives the ability to go forward, manifest one's goals or complete plans no matter the fear, disruption or obstacles one encounters. Enhances the positive qualities of courage, manifesting strength and perseverance. Clears procrastination. For those who are despondent, easily discouraged and lack perseverance. It encourages courage and strength to pursue our convictions, being ready to act on our visions and plans for the future and not be waiting eternally for the 'perfect time'. For the person who is more into planning than doing and is discouraged when plans go wrong, feels anxious and helpless and who, as an insurance against failure, is afraid of commitment.

Hitorisizuka Flower (*Chloranthus japonicus*) **To Have Respect**. For respecting the rights of others and the right to enjoy your share of collective resources. It transforms the hearts of tyrants whose desire is to control the hearts, minds and resources of others for their own ends. Encourages integrity, respect for human rights, selflessness dissolving ruthless and controlling behaviour and extreme selfishness. For the insensitive person obsessed with ambition. For selfish 'control freaks'. For those who use people to fulfil their desires and goals. Inspires detachment from desire for fame and power.

Kasumisakura Flower (*Prunus serrulata*) **The Unique Treasure**. For being true to one's individuality amidst community life. It helps one to break free from unhealthy social obligations and stimulates a desire to contribute to the collective welfare using your own unique talents. Encourages social balance, individuality, responsibility. Clears rebellious feelings, and the feeling that your true nature is being compromised due to social pressure and subservience. For the person who is tired and unmotivated because they are always conforming to the social expectations of others, who are rebellious towards collective or social life and feel a sense of frustration and resentment because it is 'not correct' for them to express their individuality within their community. The flower's qualities help the mind to focus on the true welfare of community life, and heals the resentment and rebelliousness created by such pressure.

Kobushi (Magnolia) Flower (*Magnolia kobus*) **The Higher Responsibility** Relieves the burden of feeling overly responsible and frees one from the subconscious fear of things falling apart for oneself and others. It gives strength, calmness and courage amidst chaos. Encourages responsibility in perspective, freedom and calmness.

Chaos and failure are as important to life as order and success and when chaos and failure are accepted as learning opportunities then the birth of new ideas and new understandings manifest. For the person who feels overly responsible for the welfare of others, who feels exhausted and burdened because of the load they carry for others. For the person who feels weighed down because of their own desire for perfection and because they subconsciously fear things going wrong. Frees those with overprotective and overresponsible natures from duties and responsibilities that are not theirs to shoulder. As the healing balance is established, courage, strength and an inner calm and trust in the processes of life is born.

Mitsubatsutsuji Flower (*Rhododendron dilatatum*) **Open to Counsel** Helps to keep an open mind to the advice and ideas of others, and show respect for another's viewpoint, even when possibly faulty. Encourages being open, respectful and tolerant and dissolves obstinate, overly independent, wilful behaviour. For the person who believes that advice from others will be a hindrance rather than a benefit or who is obstinate and self-willed and refuses to listen because they can't trust the advice from others. In bypassing mental blocks due to bad advice in the past, a person is able to view all information on its own merits and can determine its true value.

Mizubasyou Flower (*Lysichiton camtschatcense*) **Wisdom/The Universal Student** This essence is for deepening one's intelligence and expanding one's ability to handle life with spiritual wisdom. Helps parents deal with and understand difficult children so that they may rear them with wisdom and help them so that their deepest goals and wishes are fulfilled. Encourages the positive quality of insightful, wise and inclusive intelligence, and the ability to act inclusively for the benefit of all. Clears problems of lack of true wisdom, exclusive intelligence, and intellectual arrogance. For those whose life is a mess due to intellectual arrogance and who use their intelligence to manipulate in order to satisfy their own ambitions. Gives the realization of the deeper side to intellect, that of true wisdom. This wisdom is all-encompassing and therefore improves the quality of life for all concerned. This understanding of life fills the person with an inner joy.

Murasakikeman Flower (Corydalis incisa) **Love Without End** For letting go of loved ones. Bonds of love are strong, so when separation comes, for example through death, travel or one's child leaving home, a sense of loss, grief and emotional upheaval often ensues. Allows letting go and feelings of inner peace, showing how a beautiful heart does not need to control a person or have them next to them to love them fully. Encourages a selfless love, self-sufficient, inner strength. Aids in recovery from sadness, devastation and loss. For those who feel lost and lonely because of separation from a loved one and who find it hard to re-establish their life after losing that person. Gives an inner peace and a restful heart, helping the person to overcome the trauma of losing a loved one, stimulating the urge to move on with life positively.

Nojisumire Flower (*Viola yedoensis*) **The Gift of Giving** Inspires unconditional benevolence, the desire to be impartial, giving in response to genuine need. This expansion of the consciousness leads to all-round spiritual enhancement. Due to personal desire a person can be partial or selective in their giving, subconsciously giving when there are personal rewards (emotional or physical). If conscious, inevitably giving is used to manipulate a desired response from another. Encourages integrity, unconditional benevolence, compassion. Dissolves manipulative, selfish and insincere behaviour. For those who control personal relationships through their calculated benevolence, for example the parent who gives to their child on the basis of what they achieve or how good they are and not from the understanding of their genuine needs.

Uguisukazura Flower (*Lonicera gracilipes* Miq.) **Self Determination** This essence is for finding the strength to break free from unhealthy relationships. Unhealthy dependency that leads to constant pain is destructive to body, mind and soul. Often one stays in these relationships to try and fix them, or to try to make the other person see their point of view. Encourages self-determination, courage, not blaming, and dissolves trauma, hurt, and dependency. For the person continually hurt or traumatized by their partner, the child continually traumatized by their 'so-called' friends and the person in a destructive codependent relationship who is abused physically or emotionally. This essence evokes courage, independence and forgiveness, freeing the person to go ahead and explore their life.

Wasabi Flower (*Wasabia Japonica*) **The Observant Mind** Gives the ability to perceive the function and purpose of the small parts that make up a bigger whole. Understanding life from this vantage point gives respect and appreciation for all life forms. An inability to do this makes it hard to discover the cause of a problem and take steps to solve it, and is often the cause of learning difficulties. For mental sharpness, comprehension of detail, and problem-solving ability. It stimulates wisdom, providing solutions for the more involved problems. For those who find problem-solving hard, who conceive simplistic solutions to involved problems and become frustrated and confused when tackling problem areas in their own lives. Also for those who understand the problem but are unable to dissect and understand agreements, written or verbal, or find the solution. Inspires you to take one step at a time, allowing the mind to observe the detail of how things work in relation to each other.

Yamabuki Flower (*Kerria japonica*)
Sweetness of Service This essence brings awareness beyond one's self-centred world. It enhances the desire to help, compassion, and service. Clears selfish, uncooperative behaviour and indifference to the hardship of others. For the person who likes to pursue their desires and wishes without interruption
and who refuses or fails to give a helping hand to others in need, yet seeks help from those very people when they experience difficulties in their own life. For those who are totally insensitive to the hardship of others. Inspires heartfelt warmth to stay in touch with the hardship of others, and help out when possible.

Yukiyanagi Flower (*Spiraea thunbergii*)
The Cosmic Student Opens the mind

and frees it from preconceived ideas and opinions. It inspires focus and understanding of how the universe works. Fosters humility, open-mindedness and wisdom. Dissolves arrogant, know-all, attitudes. For the person who feels they have pretty much learned all there is to know on any one subject, the dogmatic opinionated person who sees no point in exploring new sciences or philosophical arenas as they believe their understanding is superior. Gives a true understanding of the limits of the human mind and its ability to understand the universe. This attitude stimulates open-mindedness for all thoughts and opinions, for one understands that no mind has a monopoly on truth or infinitely understands it.

Zazensou Flower (*Symplocarpus foetidus*) **Coming Together** For the carefree joy of sharing oneself with other people. Gives the freedom of uninhibited self-expression while remaining true to yourself, your values and ideals.

Encourages sociability and interest in others. Clears reclusive tendencies, isolation and dislike of people. For reclusive personalities who feel uncomfortable in social situations, and who think human relationships are nothing but trouble. Inspires the joy of sharing and communicating with others. It stimulates social interaction and interest in others.

Flowers of the Orient

'Essences created especially for Women'

The Flowers of the Orient have a special energy appropriate for women. To create the range I journeyed to the Orient, Bali, and in particular Thailand, a country lush with exquisitely perfumed blooms. In its purest unadulterated form, it is a deeply powerful and sensual land that calls to a woman's inner beauty. The essences were made at a sacred site in beautiful gardens with pagodas dedicated to Quan Yin, the Chinese goddess of grace, beauty, love and femininity.

Frangipani (*Plumeria*) Awakens passion and joy. Boosts confidence, inner beauty, and feeling complete as a woman. Works on the sacred fire, awakens a passion for life, the joyousness of being a woman, calling to her inner beauty, bringing confidence in her beauty and feminine self. Feeling complete within herself. Frangipani returns her original state of purity and innocence, which is the true 'spirit of woman'.

Hibiscus (*Hibiscus*) Clears nervous stress, calms, cools and relaxes the nervous system. Invaluable for insomnia. Calms a woman's inner core, works in the sphere of the nervous system. It penetrates through all the subtle anatomy, relaxing, refreshing and chilling out the nerve endings. Supports the *chi* of the nervous system helping to maintain the integrity of the nervous system's network and strengthens the inner matrix that makes up a woman's delicate structure, this being unique to a woman.

Orchid Queen (*Orchidium altissimum*) Helps a woman to have a clear insight into her own unique nature and tap into the wonder of being a woman. The Quan Yin of essences. Helps to tap into free-flowing dancing, magnetic energy of the goddess within. A sacred essence, giving a clear insight into the nature of womaness, and how it is expressed in her own unique way. It heals the female psyche, inspiring the wonder of being a woman, touching the heart and mind with joy and creating a soft strength.

Pink Orchid Strengthens and stabilizes the inner core, expands the aura's magnetism, tingeing it pink, it softens the edges, dissolving overprotectiveness.

allowing positive uplifting energies to infuse the auric field and enhancing attractiveness.

Water Lily (*Nymphaeaceae*) For times of passion, balances sensuality/sexuality and spirituality. Combines night and day, warm balmy nights and hot summer days. For nights of passion. Soft flowing energy gently balances and blends the energy of the chakras especially the heart chakra, allowing a woman to be open to receive, yielding with softness and sensuality. Heightens touching, as well as encouraging the desire to express love through the sensuousness of touching. Guaranteed to send a shiver of delight throughout your partner's entire body right down to his very toes.

Combination Essences

Sensuality Blend *Frangipani*, *Water Lily*, *Orchid Queen*, *Hibiscus* and *Pink Orchid*. A combination of exotic and sensual flowers from Thailand created to bring back the passion into one's life. With its silky smooth energy, it acts as a magnet that sets up a powerful vibration within the body and auric field. A subtle and harmonious blend of spirituality with sensuality. For extra effect use in combination with Spirit Lift Spritz.

Spritzes

Spirit Lift Spritzer A blend of exotic oils of *Tlang Ylang, Jasmine* and *May Chang* combined with essences of *Frangipani, Hibiscus, Orchid Queen* and *Pink Orchid*. Designed to uplift a woman's spirit and enhance her sensuality. Spritz the aura with this evocative and delightful aroma whenever you need to feel sexy and sassy!

Europe

Throughout Europe there exist ancient traditions of healing with plants and flowers. In many countries such as Britain, France and Switzerland, folk remedies handed down from generation to generation are still alive today. Not surprisingly, many of the most renowned herbalists – from Nicholas Culpeper to Paracelsus – came from this part of the world. Dr Edward Bach himself was a native of Britain and prepared many of his remedies from flowers growing in the fields and hedgerows of Oxfordshire. Throughout Europe many others are following in his footsteps.

Bach Flower Remedies

In the 1930s Dr Edward Bach rediscovered the art of healing with flowers and created 38 remedies from flowers growing in the British countryside. After his death his close companion Nora Weeks kept his work alive; she in turn entrusted the Bach Centre to Nickie Murray for many years. Since then it has changed hands again; Judy Howard now runs the Bach Centre and is responsible for preparing the Bach Flower Remedies. To meet increasing demands the company Nelsons, makers of homeopathic preparations, are now involved in their production and Robert Wilson makes the mother tincture.

Julian Barnard and his then wife Martine also prepared a range of remedies according to the dictates of Dr Bach at their home on the edge of the largest area of national park in Britain (Hertfordshire). They were invited to work at the Bach Centre by Nickie Murray in 1984 and were involved in establishing the Bach Educational Programme before setting up their own Healing Herbs company in 1990.

Julian, a medical herbalist, feels it is important to follow Dr Bach's instructions to the word, so he adheres scrupulously to his original methods. He goes to some of the wildest and most inaccessible places to seek flowers, and uses only pure, fresh mountain water to make the essences. His is the only company, as far as is known, who make the remedies with full-strength brandy as did Dr Bach himself. The remedies are strongly endorsed by Nickie Murray.

The remedies have earned a reputation for integrity and quality and Julian now runs a flourishing education programme, and lectures throughout the world.

Agrimony (*Agrimonia*) For those who appear cheerful, jovial and uncomplaining, hiding mental torture and anxieties behind this mask – they may be restless and seek excitement to overcome their worry, or may use alcohol/drugs to dull and forget their pain. Helps us acknowledge and transcend such feelings so real peace and humour can be found.

Aspen (*Populus tremula*) For irrational, vague, inexplicable fears of unknown origin; sudden apprehension, fear of unseen power or force, of sleeping and dreams; headaches, sweating, trembling, sudden faintness, sleep walking/talking, fatigue and anxiety. Brings a sense of security and an ability to trust that we are safe and protected.

Beech (*Fagus Sylvatica*) For those who are critical, dissatisfied, intolerant, unsympathetic, irritable, always finding fault, seeing only the negative side of things; for tension affecting the upper-chest area, jaw and hands. Brings compassion and tolerance, relaxing strict attitudes.

Centaury (*Erythraea Centaurium*) For timid, quiet, kind, gentle, conventional people who are anxious to please. They may have a tendency to lose their identity and direction, be submissive and be exploited. Physical symptoms affect the shoulders and back. Encourages self-determination and an ability to trust and follow our good judgement, to act decisively.

Cerato (*Ceratostigma Willmottiana*) For those who doubt their own abilities, lacking faith in their own intuition and judgement, always asking others' advice, they tend to be mercurial and are easily led astray.

Cherry Plum (*Prunus Cerasifera*) For desperation, fear of being unable to control negative thoughts, feelings and impulses of losing control, suicidal feelings, obsessive fear, delusions, nervous breakdown. Enables us to feel strong and safe enough to deal sanely with issues that scare us.

Chestnut Bud (*Aesculus hippocastanum*) For those who do not learn by experience, repeating the same mistakes over again, always looking ahead and failing to see what is happening. They can be careless, clumsy, slow to learn and inattentive. Enables us to observe, remember and make logical connections which help us make sense of life and formulate wise responses and choices.

Chicory (*Cichorium intybus*) For those feeling empty inside who become manipulative and possessive to get the attention they crave, who dislike being alone, needing their loved ones near to control and direct their activity. For 'the mothering type' as well as children who demand attention. Helps those who are self-pitying, fussy, bossy, critical, smothering, tearful and thwarted. Nourishes by instilling feelings of love and security.

Clematis (*Clematis Vitalba*) For dreamers who are absent-minded, lacking concentration and vitality; for quiet people preferring dreams and fantasy to reality, who are romantic and imaginative but unrealistic, prone to drowsiness, excessive sleep, sensitivity to noise and faintness. Helps transform ideas and visions into actuality, developing talents and creating a life that is interesting and fulfilling.

Crab Apple (*Malus Pumila*) A cleansing remedy for those who feel unclean and polluted, leading to despondency and self-disgust. For those obsessed with and repelled by what is seen as bad in themselves and the environment. Enables us to process impurities and negativity, and create sensible priorities.

Elm (*Ulmus Procera*) For capable people who shoulder responsibility and occasionally take on tasks that are unreasonably demanding, making them feel exhausted, overwhelmed and temporarily inadequate. Enables you to let others handle the excess responsibility, so you are free to enjoy what you are doing.

Gentian (*Gentiana Amarella*) For those easily discouraged by difficulties, who doubt and lack faith in their ability to succeed. For the negativity that breeds feelings of failure, disappointment, scepticism, gloom and sadness. Encourages perseverance and the realization that we cannot fail when our goal is to learn more about ourselves and the nature of life.

Gorse (*Ulex Europaeus*) For times when life seems a misery, bringing hopelessness and despair. For those resigned to feeling nothing can be done to help and that any attempt will be futile. These feelings can result in conditions that apparently cannot be cured, or repeated failure or disappointment. Heals the inner will to see light in the darkness and embrace suffering as a positive aid to self-realization.

Heather (*Calluna Vulgaris*) For whose who feel needy of and greedy for attention of others. They may be obsessed with their own affairs, constantly chattering, unable to bear being alone, seeking sympathy and living off the energy of others. For those who are self-centred, overconcerned with themselves, lacking interest in others, or prone to hypochondria. Enables you to stand alone and find a wider, less self-centred view of life.

Holly (*Ilex Aquifolium*) For when we are enveloped in negative and aggressive emotions such as anger, jealousy, bitterness, envy, rage, suspicion, revenge, hatred, bad temper, contempt, selfishness, frustration. Encourages the ability to show goodwill and love to others, in the awareness that what enhances us enhances all.

Honeysuckle (*Lonicera Caprifolium*) For nostalgia, getting stuck in the grief, regrets and memories of the past, longing for happier days gone by, romanticizing the past. Also for homesickness. Helps us to live in the moment, using past experiences as a guide and solid foundation, rekindling interest in life.

Hornbeam (*Carpinus Betulus*) For temporary feelings of being overwhelmed, mental/physical weariness, lack of energy, boredom, the feeling that everything seems too much, an inability to get up in the

morning and face the day. Also for convalescents. Encourages creation of a balanced lifestyle which is sufficiently stimulating and varied to allow inspiration to flow.

Impatiens (*Impatiens Glandulifera*) For impatient, impulsive people who dislike restraint and are driven by urgency and hastiness, who like working at their own speed, act quickly and are critical of others. For those prone to nervous tension, overexertion and accidents, temper outbursts, irritability, sudden pains and cramps, indigestion. Releases pent-up tension and encourages the patience to enjoy being as well as doing. Brings sensitivity to situations and relationships.

Larch (*Larix Decidua*) For lack of confidence, feeling trapped in self-doubt, inferiority, expecting failure so not bothering to try, hesitating and procrastinating. Also for the despondency and general depression often associated with impotency. Develops our sense of realism about our talents, builds confidence and self-assurance, clears old patterns of limitation.

Mimulus (*Mimulus Guttatus*) For fear of specific or known origin, often undisclosed due to shyness; fear of illness, death, others and being alone. Symptoms may include stuttering, blushing, shallow breathing and oversensitivity to noise, crowds and confrontations. Allows us to value our sensitive disposition and have the strength, courage and safety to enjoy life.

Mustard (*Sinapis Arvensis*) For overwhelming black clouds of depression of unknown origin, causing deep sadness and melancholy that lifts as unexpectedly as it descends. Brings the realization that every day is an opportunity to get more deeply in touch with ourselves, to grieve for what is amiss so healing can occur in preparation for new growth.

Oak (*Quercus Robur*) For strong, reliable, responsible and patient people, who shoulder their burdens without complaining, though have a tendency to take on more than they can manage. Their perseverance can lead to exhaustion, though they find ill health frustrating because it imposes limitations.

Olive (*Olea europaea*) For total mental/physical exhaustion. Useful after prolonged illness or during convalescence, for combating the effects of overwork and overworry, and to help you get through crises such as divorce or conflict.

Pine (*Pinnus Sylvestris*) For those taking the blame for others' mistakes or situations not of their making. For the guilt and self-reproach that has become part of their lives. Also for those who are self-critical, overconscientious and constantly striving, leading to tiredness and depression. Allows forgiveness of shortcomings, releases responsibility, brings true understanding and acceptance of the human condition.

Red Chestnut (*Aesculus carnea*) For those who are fearful and anxious for the welfare of loved ones, anticipating trouble, imagining the worst, being over-concerned about world problems and projecting their anxiety onto others. Develops trust and calm confidence in the ability of others to look after themselves.

Rock Rose (*Helianthenum nummularium*) For fear, panic, feeling paralysed by terror, and the hysteria due to emergencies, sudden illness or accidents. Symptoms include coldness, trembling and loss of control; nightmares. Brings calm so you can respond adequately and appropriately to problems.

Rock Water (*Aqua petra*) For rigidity and self-repression, being ruled by logic and hard on oneself and others. Also for fantasists and idealists prone to obsession, punishing self-discipline and spiritual pride. Facilitates open flexibility and a sense of balance in your approach to life.

Scleranthus (*Scleranthus Annus*) For indecision, moodswings, lack of concentration and balance, restlessness, changeable outlook, problems making oneself understood. Also for those prone to travel sickness. Helps us to discover inner balance so we can become clear and decisive.

Star of Bethlehem (*Ornithogalum unbellatum*) For all forms of shock: sudden and traumatic, long and slow over a period of time, delayed from the past, the shock of birth. Clears shock from the system bringing a sense of being centred, soothed and comforted. Restores the body's self-healing mechanisms.

Sweet Chestnut (*Castanea Sativa*) For anguish and despair, desolation, feeling at the limits of our endurance, that nothing is left but destruction and oblivion – the dark night of the soul. Reveals the light at the end of the tunnel, restoring hope and an awareness that all transforming processes have a purpose. Brings the understanding that we must experience darkness to appreciate the light.

Vervain (*Verbena Officinalis*) For those who are overzealous and forceful in their beliefs, enthusiastically trying to convert others by imposing their own will and ideas. For those who are highly strung, argumentative, strong willed and prone to overexertion, thus setting up a stress pattern for physical tension, muscle strain, headaches, migraines, eyestrain and exhaustion. Releases the stress pattern and built-up tension, enabling us to relax and let others lead their own lives.

Vine (*Vitis Vinifera*) For self-assured, proud, dominating, bossy people who use authority to gain power; leaders who are of great value in emergencies but who can be ruthless in pursuing their goals; tyrants and dictators; those prone to back problems and high blood-pressure. Brings flexibility, allowing us to put our skills and abilities to the general good while letting others develop their potential.

Walnut (*Juglans regia*) For protection from outside influences and from major life changes (puberty, a new career, etc.) which have unsettled our foundations. Helps us to break with the old and those influences that impose on our free will. Enables us to establish new patterns, to break free and be ourselves.

Water Violet (*Hottonia palustris*) For loners who retreat and isolate themselves, appearing aloof and quiet. They are self-reliant and contained, knowing their own minds, seemingly condescending because they believe they are different and special, never interfering with others and intolerant of interference; prone to physical tension, stiffness and rigidity. Brings the ability to ask for help when needed; allows us to appreciate and enjoy others.

White Chestnut (*Aesculus hippocastanum*) For persistent unwanted thoughts, restless mental chatter, congestion, preoccupation, insomnia, confusion, depression, nervous worry and headaches. Quietens and calms mental processes, allowing the mind to function clearly and efficiently.

Wild Oat (*Bromus ramosus*) For feeling uncertain of one's direction in life; dissatisfied, undefined or unfulfilled ambitions; despondency, frustration and boredom. Gives definite knowledge of and clarity to one's purpose in life.

Wild Rose (*Rose canina*) For resignation and apathy; feeling unable to cultivate interest or make an effort; being fatalistic, lacking vitality; prone to dullness and fatigue. Restores motivation, creativity and energy; rekindles enthusiasm.

Willow (*Salix Vitellina*) For resentment and bitterness, blaming others, feeling hard done by, being self-centred and self-pitying, bearing grudges, feeling wronged. Often linked with arthritic problems. Brings the ability to take full responsibility for life in order to make a fresh start. Cultivates optimism and a sunnier disposition.

Special Combinations

Five Flower Remedy (The rescue combination) A blend of *Cherry Plum* for loss of control, *Clematis* for unconsciousness, *Impatiens* for stress, *Rock Rose* for panic/terror, and *Star of Bethlehem* for shock.

Findhorn Flower Essences of Scotland

Scotland conjures up images of mist, and magic, with a wild landscape of rugged mountains and magnificence lochs and a Celtic spirit that like its environment is known for courage, honesty and tenaciousness.

The Findhorn Flower Essences are subtle infusions of Scottish wildflowers which, when used for healing, can enhance spiritual awareness and growth by restoring equilibrium throughout the different levels of being. They are made by Marion Stoker, who first joined the Findhorn Foundation in 1976, then temporarily returned to her native Australia to become a qualified homeopath. Through her study of homeopathy and work with the Australian Bush Flower Essences she came to appreciate the extraordinary healing properties of flower essences. On returning to Findhorn she found the whole region carpeted with gorse in full bloom, and was drawn to preparing an essence from this flower. She decided to use water collected from a local ancient secluded well with known healing properties. The magical energy of the flowers from the Findhorn gardens is well known and the strong connection with the nature spirits has produced some wonderful flower essences.

Marion feels the flowers tend to find her when the time is appropriate. One exception was the rare Scottish Primrose, a plant found only in certain areas on the north coast of Scotland and in Orkney. Marion actively went in search for this flower after receiving a message that its essence had remarkable powers for promoting feelings of inner peace and stillness in times of struggle, strife and conflict.

Apple (*Malus sylvestris*) Keynote: Higher Purpose. Apple helps us to realize our goals and visions positively. In contacting and clarifying our higher purpose and aspirations, and freed from distractions, we focus our willpower and channel our energies into right action.

Balsam (*Impatiens glandulifera*) Keynote: Tenderness. Balsam facilitates love and acceptance of our physical bodies and our sexuality. Illusions of separateness are dissolved when we open to love and nurturing. We experience feelings of warmth, sensitivity and tenderness towards ourselves, and others, and feel safe and present in our world.

Bell Heather (*Erica cinerea*) Keynote: Confidence. Bell Heather helps to access inner strength and resolve to stand one's ground. We become resilient to stress, setback or disappointment when we remain flexible, consolidate our energies and stand firmly grounded and confident in ourselves.

Birch (*Betula pendula*) Keynote: Vision. Birch helps us to broaden our perceptions and transcend limitations of mind. Through expanding our consciousness and seeing the bigger picture we gain understanding and peace of mind. Birch frees our imagination and gives us hope for the future.

Broom (*Cytisus scoparius*) Keynote: Clarity. Broom stimulates mental clarity and concentration. When our thinking is clouded or distracted, we may be hindered in our communication and expression. Broom illuminates the mind and from this brightness frees our thinking and intuition.

Cherry (*Prunus serrulata*) Keynote: Compassion. Cherry helps us to open the heart to love and to transcend limitations of karmic and social heritage, which bind us to past patterns of behaviour. When we let the heart guide us in all our relationships, notions of separativeness dissolve as we identify with the divine essence in everyone and everything. We feel empowered to act with compassion and in the spirit of goodwill.

Daisy (*Bellis perennis*) Keynote: Protection. Daisy helps us to remain calm and centred when we feel overwhelmed by the turbulence of life. With true feelings of trust and of being protected, we are able to maintain our focus with openness and sensitivity and stay on purpose and on course.

Elder (*Sambucus nigra*) Keynote: Beauty. Elder stimulates the body's natural powers of regeneration and renewal. By resonating with the source of our own inner beauty and eternal youthfulness, we connect with true feelings of wellbeing and the circulation of those vital energies that may rejuvenate us.

Globethistle (*Echinops sphaerocephalus*) Keynote: Strength. Globethistle helps us willingly and joyfully make sacrifices that will liberate us on our path. When we reconnect with our inner strength and resilience to do what we must, we can surrender the nonessentials in our lives and discover that letting go and serving the highest good brings us the deepest peace and joy.

Gorse (*Ulex europaeus*) Keynote: Joy. Gorse stimulates vitality, enthusiasm and motivation. When we feel run-down or low, we risk withholding ourselves from fully participating in life by trying to conserve our energies. By reconnecting with the quality of joy and giving ourselves passionately to life, our hearts are uplifted and we are refreshed and renewed.

Grass of Parnassus (*Parnassia palustris*) Keynote: Openness. Grass of Parnassus opens the heart to the healing power of love. Strong emotions, fear or vulnerability may cause us to create protective barriers, which can cut us off from our true feelings. When we allow these powerful emotions to be, and transform them within the heart through love, our soul qualities of peace, joy and serenity can shine through.

Harebell (*Campanula rotundifolia*) Keynote: Alignment. Harebell aligns us to the living of a prosperous life. When we feel lacking, or lose faith in ourselves, or our abilities, we may block the flow of vital energies. We realign our awareness to the spirit of abundance and become open to receiving the limitless energy supply from the Universal Source.

Hazel (*Corylus avellana*) Keynote: Freedom. Hazel can help free us to let go of all limitations which restrict growth, advancement and potential unfolding. Liberated of the need to be in control of the direction and flow of our lives, we find joy and freedom in movement and spontaneity.

Holy Thorn (*Cratageus sp.*) Keynote: Acceptance. Holy Thorn awakens us to the presence of love in our hearts. When we are open and accepting of ourselves, and others, we remove barriers to friendship and love, and free our creative expression.

Iona Pennywort (*Umbilicus rupestris*) Keynote: Transparency. Iona Pennywort brings light into the darkest corners of our souls whereby we can let go of deep fears held in the psyche, which help to create delusions, self-deception and judgement of ourselves, and others. By bringing in the pure light of truth, we can move forward with a new awareness and purity of aspiration.

Lady's Mantle (*Alchemilla vulgaris*) Keynote: Awareness. Lady's Mantle helps us

to access deeper resources of the mind. When we are unable or unwilling to be conscious on all levels, our awareness and understanding become limited. We can call on and bring to light all the power and intelligence which is inherently ours.

Laurel (*Prunus lusitanica*) Keynote: Resourcefulness. Laurel can assist us in manifesting our vision, and in empowering ourselves to find the resources to bring our ideas and ideals into form. When we bring a plan to fruition, we must be able to hold and synthesize many diverse energies. Wise in heart, we trust the spiritual worlds and Universal Source to support all plans which are for the good of all.

Lime (*Tilia platyphyllos*) Keynote: Universality. Lime brings an awareness of our relationship and interdependence with all life on earth. When we open to and anchor universal love in our hearts, feelings of separateness are transformed and we create harmonious relationships in our lives.

Mallow (*Malva sylvestris*) Keynote: Grace. Mallow helps us to 'think in our hearts'. Separation in our thinking and feeling impedes us on all levels. Mallow activates our will to live in right relationship.

Monkeyflower (*Mimulus guttatus*) Keynote: Personal Power. Monkeyflower helps raise our vibrational energy from the lower self, empowering us to celebrate and be who we truly ARE. When we are not fully in our power, we may fear power in others or ourselves. With Monkeyflower we access the source of true power from the Higher Self and find the confidence to act NOW.

Ragged Robin (*Lychnis flos-cuculi*) Keynote: Purification. Ragged Robin aids us in the processes of purification. We allow the free flow of life force and energies on all levels when we remove the obstacles to realizing health and wellbeing.

Rose Alba (*Rosa alba*) Keynote: Power. Rose Alba represents the positive, outgoing, creative Principle. It assists in connecting the mind and the intuition to bring forth deeper insight. When we positively follow our intuitions, right speech and right action follow.

Rose Water Lily (*Nymphaea* sp.) Keynote: Presence. Rose Water Lily helps us to rise above the pressures and demands of daily life which draw us into the depths of the material world. When we lose sight of our spiritual connections, by our aspiration we reconnect with spirit and draw strength from this source from deep within.

Rowan (*Sorbus aucuparia*) Keynote: Reconciliation. Rowan helps us to learn to forgive ourselves, and others and to heal the past. By opening the heart to unconditional healing love we can release our attachments to habitual, inherited or karmically acquired patterns of behaviour and emotions, and live peacefully with ourselves, and others.

Scots Pine (*Pinus sylvestris*) Keynote: Wisdom. Scots Pine helps us to find directions in our search for truth and understanding. When we open ourselves to listening truly, we can access our own inner source of wisdom, and feel guided on our way.

Scottish Primrose (*Primula scotica*) Keynote: Peace. Scottish Primrose brings inner peace and stillness when we are confronted by fear, anxiety, conflict or crisis and helps to restore natural rhythms. When we are at peace in our hearts, unconditional love flows through us, and harmony prevails.

Sea Pink (*Armeria maritima*) Keynote: Harmony. Sea Pink helps to balance the energy centres. When we feel disconnected, or split off from our higher or divine nature, the inflowing life and consciousness energy streams may not be grounded in the material world. Sea Pink assists the flow of conscious vital energies throughout the body.

Sea Rocket (*Cakile maritima*) Keynote: Regeneration. Sea Rocket helps us to open to the experience of abundance in all its forms. When we find our resources drying up, or swinging from 'feast to famine', our insecurities may cause us to accumulate or hoard. We cut ourselves off from the Universal Source. With purity of purpose we can again receive and give freely, trusting all our needs will be perfectly met.

Silverweed (*Potentilla anserina*) Keynote: Simplicity. Silverweed helps us to live lightly in our bodies and on earth, through moderation and self-awareness. When we become caught up in material concerns, we may lose contact with our higher purpose. We can lift our awareness through deep contact with the forces of nature and life to break through into higher levels of self-realization.

Snowdrop (*Galanthus nivalis*) Keynote: Surrender. Snowdrop allows us to access deep inner stillness and to surrender to the processes through which we can release the past. We find hope and, seeing the light at the end of the tunnel, move towards it. Even in our darkest hours we find hope in the revelation of light, the flame of eternal life within.

Spotted Orchid (*Dactylorhiza fuchsii*) Keynote: Creativity. Spotted Orchid helps us rise above our narrow views or insularity to look beyond the imperfections we see. When we are too introspective, we risk becoming pessimistic and our outlook on life reflects these limitations. Spotted Orchid allows us to see freshly to find the beauty and perfection in everything. With a positive attitude, our vision is broadened and we find our own perfect expression.

Stonecrop (*Sedum anglicum*) Keynote: Transition. Stonecrop aids in times of profound personal transformation. We realize change is happening around us and within us at the deepest levels. But this process has its own timing, and we may feel stuck, unable to push through the barriers which hold us back. Stonecrop allows us to release our frustrations and attachments to the past, embrace change and find the point of stillness and peace within.

Sycamore (*Acer pseudoplatanus*) Keynote: Revitalization. Sycamore recharges and uplifts body and soul when we are stressed or worn down. Sycamore helps us to tap into the unlimited energy source of the life force, which radiates, illuminates and energizes our whole being. We can then experience the smooth flow of the energies in ourselves and in our lives.

Thistle (*Cirsium vulgare*) Keynote: Courage. Thistle helps us to find true courage in times of adversity and to respond with positive action. When we encounter fear, our performance can be crippled. Thistle encourages us to access inner strength and to take appropriate action with confidence and certainty.

Valerian (*Valeriana officinalis*) Keynote: Delight. Valerian is uplifting to our mind, body and spirit and helps us to rediscover delight and happiness in living. When we are weighed down in our busy lives by our responsibilities, we may miss the simple joys in life that bring us happiness. Through Valerian we may become more responsive in the moment, lighten up and have fun.

Watercress (*Rorippa nasturtium aquaticum*) Keynote: Wellbeing. Watercress sounds a vibrational note of purification in our bodies. It can act as a powerful cleanser, stimulating our immune systems to clear stagnant energies and overcome disease by refining, transforming and releasing all that is toxic to our health and harmful to our wellbeing.

Wild Pansy (*Viola tricolor*) Keynote: Resonance. Wild Pansy helps clear and illuminate the head and heart channels when the energies they carry have become blocked or diverted. As receptivity, sensitivity and contact are re-established, these connections enable the life energies to flow freely and radiate throughout the whole being.

Willowherb (*Chamaenerion angustifolium*) Keynote: Mastery. Willowherb helps to balance the personality expressing authoritarian or overbearing behaviour by tempering force of personal-ity with true power. Responsible integra-tion of will and power issues is brought forth through love and humility, and the correct use of the will.

Note

As well as the original kit of 38 flower essences listed above, the following seven flower essences were developed and have been well researched over the past few years.

Ancient Yew (*Taxus* sp.) Keynote: Emergence. Ancient Yew helps us to overcome resistances in achieving one's purpose and goals. By breaking unwanted addictive patterns and attachments, we cast off the millstones weighing heavy on the soul. Liberated we emerge with a new attitude, self-reliant and stable, to realize our path and destiny.

Cabbage (*Brassica oleracea*) Keynote: Devotion. Cabbage fosters 'love in action', clarity and accomplishment, bringing complete joy and satisfaction. When lack of motivation and direction causes mental oppression and the dragging of one's feet, Cabbage's dynamism will convert the vision from procrastination to action. Helping us to anchor enthusiasm and perseverance until the job at hand is done.

Elecampane (*Inula helenium*) Keynote: Sensitivity. Elecampane helps us connect with our intuitive power, promoting the divine ability to channel and transmit energies of a higher nature through tranquil, inner development. Enhancing our receptivity to spiritual impression and extrasensory perception, we are able to bring forth and relay love, light and power for the good of all.

Garden Pea (*Pisum sativum*) Keynote: Expression. Garden Pea helps us to benefit from the joy of creativity by aligning our true potential with expression. When self-sabotage, depression or pain associated with stifled creativity is eased and released, the channel is opened for inspiration to flow freely. Spontaneity and beauty arise, tendering gifts of gratitude and expression.

Lichen (*Cladonia coccifera*) Keynote: Liberation. Lichen releases deep-seated patterns and worn-out old issues by transmuting negative karma, which is ripe for resolution. Destructive emotions are then purified, self-punishment, anger and low self-esteem relinquished. An opportunity for appropriate change is available, as we grow towards unity of wholeness in mind, body and soul.

Sea Holly (*Eryngium maritimum*) Keynote: Brilliance. Sea Holly helps us to eradicate self-imposed limitations of shyness and oversensitivity, particularly when it causes us to be fearful, or if our own inner voice is tormenting and critical. Ultimately we restrict our potential to shine. By casting off these boundaries and stepping out we break free, embracing adventure, emerging radiant, enterprising and brilliant.

Wintergreen (*Moneses uniflora*) Keynote: Gladness. Wintergreen initiates the wakening up of consciousness by invoking aid from one's Higher Self. Particularly when we are feeling dispirited and dark, or axed by spiritual loneliness. Reconnecting to our soul ignites optimism and aspiration, whereupon we can maintain a true state of alertness and full consciousness.

Combination Flower Essences

Calm Me Down *Bell Heather, Daisy, Lady's Mantle, Laurel, Monkeyflower, Wild Pansy and Willowherb.* Focus dynamic energy into intelligent creative activity. Foster calmness of mind and body through self-mastery of negative emotions that impede clear thinking, concentration and presence of mind. Integrating mental and emotional bodies aids the ability to pay attention and channel energies into right action.

Clear Light *Birch, Broom, Lady's Mantle, Rose Alba, Scots Pine and Wild Pansy.* For bringing about a peaceful state of mind. By stilling and focusing the mind, Clear Light can assist in attuning to higher wisdom and inspiration, and influence mental clarity and brightness. An excellent aid to meditation and study.

Eros *Balsam, Elder, Gorse, Grass of Parnassus, Holy Thorn, Rose Alba, Sea Pink and Sycamore.* To nurture love, sensitivity and intimacy. Without self-acceptance it is difficult to love and nurture ourselves, or be a loving partner. Relax, enjoy, and be in tune with your body. Also available in Aloe Vera Gel for external application

Femininity *Balsam, Elder, Holy Thorn, Lady's Mantle, Rowan, Scottish Primrose, Sea Rocket and Sycamore.* Providing support for women's issues and cycles. During times of changing rhythms or moodswings, Femininity can help to release tension and restore emotional balance and wellbeing.

First Aid *Bell Heather, Daisy, Scottish Primrose and Thistle.* Calming, soothing relief in any crisis. In times of stress or trauma on any level, First Aid can help to relieve associated fear and anxiety, and ease pain and tension. Also available in Aloe Vera Gel for external application

Healing the Cause *Ancient Yew, Gorse, Lichen, Monkeyflower, Rowan, Snowdrop, Sycamore and Watercress.* Strength and support to get well. Deep seated or longstanding negative emotions hinder the ability to get well. By accepting responsibility for our health, ill fortune can be seen as an agent for beneficial change. Surrender obstacles to wholeness and wellbeing and heal the past and sources of suffering.

Heart Support *Grass of Parnassus, Gorse, Holy Thorn, Rose Water Lily, Rowan, Scottish Primrose, Stonecrop and Wild Pansy.* To heal the heart when affected by trauma or grief. For all issues connected with the heart and love. Feel supported during times of major life changes.

Holy Grail *Balsam, Globethistle, Lady's Mantle and Rose Alba.* To integrate and harmonize the physical, emotional, mental and spiritual bodies. Bring balance and harmony into all aspects of your life through alignment and synthesis of body, mind and soul. Embody and express your full creative potential.

Jetstream *Daisy, Scots Pine, Scottish Primrose, Sea Rocket, Sycamore and Wild Pansy.* To offset the negative effects of travel stress or fatigue. Travel can upset and disturb natural rhythms. Find balance to cope with motion and calm to overcome claustrophobia or fear and arrive feeling 'ready to go'.

Jetstream Spray Mist Alternative to above Jetstream combination essence. To offset the negative effects of travel stress or fatigue. Travel can upset and disturb natural rhythms. Find balance to cope with motion and calm to overcome claustrophobia or fear and arrive feeling 'ready to go'.

Karma Clear *Birch, Holy Thorn, Japanese Cherry, Lichen, Rowan and Snowdrop.* To release the tensions that bring pain, suffering and unhappiness. To heal the past through compassion and forgiveness, and by awareness and understanding of the underlying causes of life's predicaments and ailments.

Life Force *Grass of Parnassus, Gorse, Elder, Sycamore and Valerian.* To overcome tiredness, low energy or burnout. Activating the vital life force and stimulating the body's powers of renewal, Life Force can help to uplift body and soul when fatigued.

Light Being *Gorse, Holy Thorn, Rose Water Lily, Snowdrop, Spotted Orchid, Valerian and Wintergreen.* Be content and enjoy life. Uplifting the spirits when feelings of despair, sadness or hopelessness weigh down on the soul. Identifying with a greater sense of purpose and nurturing an optimistic outlook on life, contentment and happiness can be achieved in the present moment.

Move Freely *Cabbage, Globethistle, Hazel, Holy Thorn, Ragged Robin, Rowan, Stonecrop, Sycamore, Watercress and Willowherb.* Enjoy the freedom of movement. When limitations that restrict ease of movement hold us back, relax, release and go with the flow. Access inner reserves that stimulate resilience, flexibility and graceful, effortless motion

Prosperity *Bell Heather, Cabbage, Elder, Harebell, Laurel, Rose Alba and Sea Rocket.* Manifesting an abundance of wellbeing. Foster a sense of inner security and faith in yourself. Align with the source of universal, limitless supply and manifest your dreams and goals. Recognize your inherent power and follow the keys to success: work with the spiritual laws of money and abundance; affirm creative abundance; experience and feel gratitude for the abundance in your life; magnetize inner resources needed to implement a plan and attract your heart's desire ('hold the vision'); build towards manifesting your ideas and ideals; and follow your inner guidance and intuition.

Psychic Protection *Ancient Yew, Daisy, Iona Pennywort, Rose Alba, Thistle, Watercress and Wintergreen.* For protecting the emotional body against negative forces. To feel centred by creating a safe space in and around yourself. Psychic Protection can help in detaching from negative thought forms or energies when feeling vulnerable, or in overwhelming situations or environments. Also helpful in cutting the ties that bind. Also available as a Spray Mist for external use

Sacred Space *Findhorn Element Essences of Earth, Water, Fire, Air and Ether and pure essential oils of Rose Alba and Frankincense.* Revitalizing and energizing space clearing spray mist, to help clear and transmute negative energies. Use to refresh and energize your personal space, cleanse and purify your aura, promote happiness and harmony around your home, bring forth light, clarity and serenity.

Seasonal Affections *Birch, Elder, Globethistle, Gorse, Ragged Robin, Scots Pine, Snowdrop, Sycamore, and Watercress.* Sunshine in the soul when feeling under the weather. When suffering from intolerances and irritations, release emotional congestion and discomfort. Feel protected and supported, no matter the season or the climate of the times.

Spiritual Marriage *Apple, Elecampane, Holy Thorn, Mallow and Sea Pink.* To integrate and harmonize the masculine and feminine qualities. Balancing the pairs of opposites creates a vital partnership between intuitive/creative self and intelligent/logical self. Dynamic union of our emotions and vision, with reason and action will maximize productivity and happiness.

Sweet Dreams *Birch, Grass of Parnassus, Lady's Mantle, Scottish Primrose and Valerian.* Good night. Sleep well. Relaxing into deep sleep can be difficult when stuck thoughts, emotions, worry, anxiety, or tension agitate or overwhelm us. When we calm our energies, our natural rhythms are restored, and we find balance and peace of mind.

Transformation *Apple, Globethistle, Grass of Parnassus, Iona Pennywort, Sea Pink, Stonecrop and Watercress.* Supporting personal growth and transformation. Choosing transformation means 'shining the light' on what needs to be reformed or changed. We can transform and harmonize seemingly opposing parts of ourselves, cultivate inner strength to persevere and stay on course, and willingly make sacrifices, which will serve our highest good.

Voice Confidence *Elecampane, Garden Pea, Holy Thorn, Lady's Mantle, Rose Alba, Scots Pine, Sea Holly and Thistle.* Express and radiate inner beauty and confidence. Free your expression and let creativity flow by overcoming self-created barriers, inhibitions or fear of failure. With trust, and the motivation to succeed, let the voice be heard loud and clear and performance reflect poise and self-confidence.

Harebell Remedies

The Harebell Remedies are made from the wild flowers from a remote area of southwest Scotland, on the Southern Upland Way. Galloway is a gentle place of rolling hills, quiet lochs and wooded estates, sheltered from the extremes of the Scottish highlands.

It was established by Ellie Web in 1985. A flower essence maker and practitioner for over twenty years, Ellie was inspired to make flower essences after having explored various spiritual and healing paths. When her interest in herbs and natural remedies grew it was natural for Ellie to bringing together nature and healing evolving it into a flower essence therapy for inner wellbeing. Ellie was strongly drawn to making essences from the healing qualities of plants immediately around her. Helped by the strong nature spirit of the place and by her two small daughters, she made Mother essences of many flowers in her large garden and surrounding countryside. The Harebell Remedies are named after one of Scotland's favourite wild flowers, and the essences eventually settled into the set of 64 essences described here. They are made from a mixture of familiar wild flowers and garden favourites. All are made in the purest of habitats far from pollution and wherever possible in places where the flowers are naturally established and abundant. In recent years combination essences, mist sprays and roll-on essences have been added to complete the range.

Alkanet (*Anchusa officinalis*) Inner strength. For the ability to centre and strengthen ourselves in preparation for change. Unifies opposing energies. Helps us move through transformative experiences safely.

Bluebell (*Endymion non scriptum*) Cooling. Deeply cooling, calming and grounding. Works well on a hot temper or in times of over excitement, stress, injury and trauma. A good 'rescue' remedy with a pleasant after-effect.

Borage (*Borago officinalis*) Cheerfulness. Gives emotional strength and courage. A tonic to fortify the heart, renew confidence and promote a cheerful outlook. For the discouraged or downhearted.

Broom (*Cytisis scoparius*) Perseverance. For strength of will and endurance. Supports a calm, mindful response to difficulties. For the ability to start afresh and keep going.

Buttercup (*Ranunculus acris*) Appreciation. Increases capacity for pleasure and fun and helps you to value life in the present moment. Balances negativity, overseriousness, impatience, cynicism and lack.

Chamomile (*Chamaemelum*) Harmony. For emotional stability. Like the herb, the essence calms and soothes, bringing a release of anxiety. Beneficial for deep relaxation and acceptance of a situation.

Comfrey (*Symphytum officinale*) Integration. To make whole. Good for injury, tiredness, memory loss and for balancing natural cycles. Relaxation, repair and renewal. Positive visualization and deep-level healing.

Cornflower (*Centaurea cyanus*) Individuality. Makes us comfortable and happy with our difference. Gives a healthy self-knowledge and worth. Protects sensitivity and special gifts from harmful, ignorant attitudes and institutional conditioning (eg. from schools, hospitals and prisons).

Cymbidium (*Cymbidium*) Self-possession. Gives confidence and strength and allows us to embrace the tiger within. Gives power and potency to the heart. Helps us to overcome fear of disapproval and show our true colour. For a fast and truthful response.

Daffodil (*Narcissus pseudonarcissus*) Uplifting. Lifts us out of a low, inward-looking mental state. Opening up to lighter, brighter energies, and banishing blues, casting out doubts. Depression, tiredness, low self-esteem and S.A.D.

Dandelion (*Teraxacum officinalis*) Relaxing. A deep letting go with profound effect. Release of fear and of being overwhelmed. Gives us a trust in our ability to cope. Turns a 'driven' energy to calm strength and natural vitality.

Elder (*Sambucus nigra*) Assertiveness. Brings self-protection out from a deep place inside. Balances timidity and helplessness. Good for helping us deal with bullies and tyrants. Gives us the strength to say 'no' consistently.

Eyebright (*Euphrasia officinalis*) Perspective. An uplifting essence bringing understanding and gladness. Brings a wider and wiser viewpoint, connecting heart and mind.

Flowering Currant (*Ribes sanguineum*) Flowing. Assists the natural breath. Relaxes tightness and control in the chest and shoulders. Expands and softens the lungs. Warms and opens the heart.

Forget-Me-Not (*Myosotis sylvatica*) Balanced. Emotionally grounded. Helps us remember reality and release fear. Brings us back to earth from flights of fantasy or paranoia. Good for working with dreams.

Forsythia (*Forsythia suspense*) Energy. Brings an awareness of how we gain and lose energy. Helps us to make use of it better. Gives a greater appreciation of life force. Helps us choose energizing activities.

Geranium (*G. Atlanticum*) Manifesting. Makes things manifest and visible. Helps us to bring cherished ideas to reality and see well-grounded plans through to the end. Aids in making us let go of being 'not ready'.

Harebell (*Campanula rotundifolia*) Wildness. Healing separation from nature. Allows us to stay close and connected to the wild spirit within us. Encourages freedom and a gentle strength of character.

Hawthorn (*Crataegus monognya*) Hope. Defends the spirit, bringing hope and deep compassion to sorrow and despair. Protects the heart through grief to recovery.

Heartsease (*Viola tricolour*) Comforting. Helps a closed heart to open or eases an open heart in pain. Comfort for overwhelming emotions. Encourages compassion and self-forgiveness.

Heather (*Calluna vulgaris*) Courage. Helps us facing loneliness and fears in order to grow and find peace. Accepting silences and solitude, feelings of emptiness or lack of certainty.

Honesty (*Lunaria annua*) Openness. Truthfulness and clarity. Can help us to stay present when the truth is complex and emotionally difficult. For confusion, memory blanks or lapses in consciousness.

Hyssop (*Hyssop officinalis*) Anxiety. A tonic to lessen and release the burdens of guilt and blame. Understanding the true reasons behind some of the thoughts and deeds which trouble us.

Iris (*Iris germanica*) Empowering. For coming into one's own personal power. Being our own authority and withdrawing that invested in others. Releasing blocks to creativity and living to our full potential.

Jacob's Ladder (*Polemoneum caeraleum*) Receiving. Learning how to ask for, recognize and receive assistance. Both practical help and spiritual guidance. For when we feel we must resolve all our problems alone.

Jasmine (*Jasminum officinale*) Processing. For absorbing what we need and eliminating what we don't. Stimulates us to be decisive, practical and less confused. For efficiency and self-esteem.

Lady's Mantle (*Alchemilla vulgaris*) Prayer. Awakening or reaffirming a belief and trust in a divine feminine influence. Invoking protection and inspiration. For prayer and meditation.

Lavender (*Lavandula spica*) Serenity. Soothes and cleanses. Brings peace to the mind and balance to the emotions. Can help us to develop a sense of composure, space and healthy detachment.

Lilac (*Syringa vulgaris*) Flexibility. For a relaxed attitude and ease or grace of movement. Opens and aligns our posture. Helps us to surrender; to bend and not break.

Lungwort (*Pulmonaria officinalis***)** Clearing. To create a clean and peaceful space in and around our body (lungs) and mind (psychic space) through meditation and awareness of breathing.

Marjoram (*Origanum vulgare*) Supportive. Enables us to put our trust in creation. Comforts and protects through danger and difficulties. Brings emotional release, especially of fear. Heals lack of security; helps us feel safe.

Marsh Woundwort (*Stachys palustris*) Security. Gaining reassurance and love. For the tendency to worry and fret unnecessarily. For letting go of the distress from unmet needs in the past and being content in the present.

Monkshood (*Aconitum napellus*) Judgement. To help us recognize and banish bad influence from our life. Good judgement in protecting ourselves and our spiritual integrity. To keep us from harm.

Nettle (*Urtica doica*) Connection. Warmth, expression, communication and sharing. For withheld feelings resulting from past hurt, and the cool and distant personality. For easier relationships.

Oriental Poppy (*Papaver orientalis*) Facing. Making the choice to live, to fully be here in the present moment instead of escaping, numbing or pretending. Endurance and joy in being alive.

Pansy (*Viola wittrokiana*) Resistance. Promotes hardy strength and builds up the ability to recover from frequent illness. Use when tired, overwhelmed and vulnerable. Claim the power of the warrior within.

Plantain (*Plantago lanceolata*) Acceptance. For turning resignation or a heavy heart around to grounded strength. For when there is a holding on to negativity preventing good things in the present.

Potato (*Solanum tuberosum*) Calming. For feeling safe, centred and grounded, and calming down from an over-stimulated state. For the feeling of coming home and enjoying the ordinary or commonplace. Use before or after intense experiences.

Primrose (*Primula vulgaris*) Opening. For the release of whatever is held. Lightens and cleanses as though a weight is lifted. For the lifting of any heavy, lethargic or 'poisoned' feeling. Helps with eating imbalances.

Purple Foxglove (*Digitalis pupurea*) Growing. For learning through difficulties and accepting responsibility for life's lessons without becoming bitter. For dealing with wounds and betrayals.

Ragwort (*Senecio jacobaea*) Centring. Surrender to the physical. To build respect for our body's natural wisdom. Calms an emotionally confused and mentally overactive mind. For intuition and trust.

Red Clover (*Trifolium pratense*) Release. Letting go of fear. For shock or fright. Gently calms, soothes and reduces panic or inappropriate reactions. For taking care of our own immediate needs.

Red Rose (*Rosa floribunda*) Passion. For being true to our desires and against shame. For boldness, passion, love and romance. Living with enthusiasm and delight and follow our heart.

Red Rosebud (*Rosa floribunda*) Sensitivity. Openness and tenderness.

Feeling safe to be loved and touched. Good for new relationships and also the passage through puberty. Giving and receiving love and bringing eroticism into whatever we do.

Red Tulip (*Tulipa 'darwinii'*) Outgoing. Being lively without losing one's centre. To overcome shyness or mistrust of the spirited side of our nature. Giving birth to the whole self.

Rhubarb (*Rheum nobile*) Boundaries. Brings awareness of others and their boundaries. Compassion for our insecurities; allowing feelings and silences. Balances uncensored behaviour.

Rosebay Willowherb (*E. angustifolium*) Responsive. Lasting release of old fear and conditioning. Brings awareness of the ways we are numb to others and a willingness to change stubborn and defensive patterns. Sensitivity in relationships.

Rosemary (*R. officinalis*) Remembering. Active remembering means putting back together. To strengthen the power of recall; linking heart and mind. Encourages trust and strengthens bonds.

Rowan (*Sorbus acuparia*) Attachment. For following the path of the heart and deepening attachments to people, places and culture. For positive connection to our ancestors. Drawing on our rich personal heritage.

Sage (*Salvia officinalis*) Enlightenment. For connection with Higher Self. For wisdom and joy. Helps us to find the fool within and not take life too seriously. Practising good judgement whilst retaining a humorous detachment.

Self-Heal (*Prunella vulgaris*) Responsibility. Taking charge of our own wellbeing and nourishment. For inner health, self-love, and acceptance. Trusting the body's self-healing process. Heals self-doubt and confusion.

Snapdragon (*Antirrhinum majus*) Expression. Brings bold expression of emotion. Aids in loosening the facial muscles. Helps us move on from frustration and release anger, fear or sadness held tightly in the face or jaw. For voice work and speech problems.

Snowdrop (*Galanthus nivalis*) Regeneration. Deep cleansing and renewal wherever there is felt to be a loss of innocence. For issues of safety and trust, and healing the child or adolescent inside. For self-forgiveness.

Speedwell (*Veronica officinalis*) Change. To look forward to a new direction so that the trauma, discomfort and disorientation of any kind of travel, big change or crisis are reduced.

St John's Wort (*Hyp. perforatum*) Holding. Calm protection when we are vulnerable. An essence to hold and contains us. The effect is to greatly reduce fear. Promotes trust, healing and sleep.

Thistle (*Cirsium vulgaris*) Integrity. To be steadfast in our own truth. Encourages us to have pride and self-respect which empowers both ourselves and others. Balances a compliant nature.

Tormentil (*Potentilla erecta*) Confidence. To bounce back from small setbacks. Cheerfulness and renewal. For countering negative beliefs and turning the other cheek. Not easily defeated.

Violet (*Viola adorata*) Kindness. Allowing the heart to open and bring love into our lives. Letting go of negative critical thoughts. For practising loving kindness towards others. For letting in the love around us.

White Foxglove (*Digitalis purpurea*) Dreamy. To free the mind of thought, making us less aware of time. Encourages us to be more imaginative, dreamy and wild. Use to deepen meditation, explore an altered state or simply loosen up a little.

White Narcissus (*N. actaea*) Spontaneous. To be guided by the heart and the spontaneous child within. For those who think too much. For being aware of our own and others' feelings.

White Rosebud (*Rosa floribunda*) Blessing. To keep us in a state of grace and growth toward fulfilling our potential. For infants and babies in the womb to rest and keep a sense of heaven on earth. For blessing and thanksgiving.

Wild Thyme (*Thymus polytricus*) Purify. To strengthen one's thoughts and intentions. Helps us to reflect on our appropriate motivations and clear the mind of doubts and fears.

Yarrow (*Achillea millefolium*) Protection. Brightens and strengthens our energy field. To allay fears and protect from outside negative influences in situations where we are vulnerable.

Yarrow in Sea Water (*A. millefolium*) Cleansing. Protective Yarrow made in cleansing sea water. Take during and after exposure to radioactive, electrical or chemical pollution. Helps us to release harm.

Combination Remedies

Acceptance & Peace A well-tried combination useful in many situations as well as promoting general wellbeing. *Heather* gives the courage to face fears or difficulties; *Lungwort* promotes a quiet meditative state; and *White Rosebud* encourages appreciation and thankfulness.

Confidence New but already popular this combines three simple essences: *Borage* for emotional strength, courage and cheerfulness; *Tormentil* for the ability to bounce back from small setbacks and for countering negative beliefs; and *Red Tulip* for overcoming shyness and being bold and outgoing without losing one's centre.

Inspiration A new combination to bring a breath of life into whatever you are doing. Contains *Flowering Currant* which relaxes tightness and encourages going with the flow; *Lady's Mantle* to invoke a little divine influence; and *White Narcissus* for spontaneity and being guided by the heart.

Motivation An aid to 'doing' of any kind. *Broom* gives purpose, perseverance and determination; *Oriental Poppy* helps us keep on making that choice to live and to come out of 'stuck' or negative places; *Wild Thyme* is cleansing and strengthening, focusing the mind on appropriate intention and clearing away any doubts and fears.

Physical Trauma Another well-tried combination. A beneficial aid through rescue and recovery from accident, operation or any harm to the physical body. Useful for all kinds of shock. Use long term as an aid to recovery from serious injury or drug abuse. With cooling *Bluebell*; calming *Chamomile*; healing *Comfrey*; and soothing *Red Clover*.

Purify & Cleanse This is one to turn to when you feel unwell. *Jasmine* to help with processing things wisely on both a physical and emotional level; *Lungwort* for awareness of breathing and clearing the space around you; *Primrose* is for cleansing and the release of toxins; and *Wild Thyme* is for purifying thoughts and clearing the mind.

Relaxed & Grounded A useful mix of some favourite essences. *Dandelion* brings a letting go of tension and renewal of trust; *Forget-Me-Not* is for emotional balance with a firm hold on reality; *Lilac* encourages grace of the body and flexibility of mind; *Potato* keeps us calm and down to earth.

Stress Release One of the first Harebell essence 'combinations', it has stood the test of time. Containing *Chamomile* for emotional stability and release of anxiety; *Lavender* bringing peace to the mind and a sense of composure or healthy detachment; *Red Clover* for the release of fear or panic; *Sage* for connection to the Higher Self who is wise and able to find the humorous side to life; and finally *Self-heal* for staying focused on and taking charge of one's own wellbeing.

Travel 'Travel' has been made for many years and proved useful to promote a calm and positive experience of journeys and life changes of any kind. With *Potato* for calming down from over stimulation; *Speedwell* to encourage looking forward to the new direction so disorientation is reduced; and *Yarrow* to brighten our own energy and protect from any negativity along the way.

Uplift A popular combination as a party essence or general daily tonic. Contains *Bluebell* which is joyful as well as being cooling and grounding; *Daffodil* to lift and open up to lightness and brightness; *Hyssop* helps with releasing any troubled thoughts; *Primrose* lightens, cleanses and dispels lethargy; and *Sage* gives wisdom and humour.

Seasonal Combination Remedies

Twenty-five ml combinations to take over several weeks. Begin when you feel the need, which does not always coincide with 'official' season change.

Autumn Reflection *Heather, Honesty, Hyssop, Rowan and White Foxglove flower essences.* To deepen and enrich, a time of completion, of gathering in, of sifting and sorting. Take stock and prepare for turning inwards. Process and release the past, mourn your losses. Protect and hold the seed of the coming year. Take any time from late August onward.

Spring Renewal *Primrose, Lungwort, Snowdrop and Wild Thyme.* To lighten, cleanse and renew as winter's dark mantle is shed. Clearing and purifying for both body and mind. Promotes release of negativity and a lightening of thoughts. Take as early as January till about May.

Summer Love *Buttercup, Eyebright, Geranium, Sage and White Rosebud.* Time to run with life, let go of negativity, lack, and of being overserious. Appreciate and think of others, create a little happiness. Feel your heart, enjoy your life, watch things happen, and give thanks. Take from May onwards. Take forever.

Winter Strength *Jasmine, Pansy, Selfheal, St John's Wort and Yarrow.* To give strength through the winter months. Take from November through to about February/March. A time to draw on inner resources. The remedy supports positive action to process things wisely, protect ourselves and build up resistance.

Mist Sprays and Roll-on Remedies

Peace & Harmony Rollette *Essences of Chamomile, Forget-me-not, Heartsease, Heather, Lavender, Lungwort, Marjoram and White Rosebud.* With *essential oils of Lavender and Chamomile* for calmness and peace of mind. A soothing topical flower essence which is convenient to carry around and safe for children to use. An all-round beneficial blend for many of life's fearful, anxious moments. Has proved a useful aid for calm travel or peaceful sleep.

Scottish Wildflower Mist *Essences of Broom, Harebell, Rowan, Thistle and Wild Thyme; bringing qualities of strength, integrity and freedom. With the sweet and mysterious essential oil of Bog Myrtle.* A subtle hint of the Scottish countryside to use as roomspray or personal mister.

Space Cleansing Spray *Essences of Jasmine, Lungwort, Primrose and Wild Thyme. With the fresh and uplifting Bergamot essential oil.* A purifying blend which helps to dispel stale air and negativity from rooms. Useful for cleansing the home or workspace. Especially beneficial after the use of electrical equipment – computers and televisions etc.

Light Heart Flower Essences

The Light Heart Flower Essences are created by spiritual healer, flower essence maker and therapist, Rose Titchiner. Rose has been working with flower essences for the last 33 years, in search of answers to the many mental, emotional and spiritual questions of this time. She has created the Light Heart Essences, in partnership with those in spirit who inspire and work with her. These essences are made from flowers, trees and plants grown organically in the 2½ acres surrounding Rose's home in Suffolk, or in nearby wildflower meadows and wildlife habitats. Some essences incorporate gems and crystals, some are environmental essences and some are made solely with light and intention. The Light Heart Essences ask us to look at what governs our choices and our reactions and at whether we allow our choices to be dictated by fear, judgement and conditioning, or whether instead we allow ourselves to experience our peace, our love, our joy, our truth and our innate wholeness and goodness. They encourage us to realize that we are the powerful authors of our experience.

Light Heart Single Essences

At the Heart of Being Heart of Sacred Oak (*Quercus*). Centred stillness and deep connection within to our core timeless self. For knowing that all that we seek lies within us, whether that be wisdom, strength, love, worth, abundance or happiness; experiencing our essential wholeness. For remaining centred and undisturbed by external changes, events, or attack; deep integrity and self-worth.

Beauty in the Eye Orchid (*Phalaenopsis hybrid*) For seeing the true beauty of people and thing with discernment and without prejudice or judgement – particularly if we've held back from embracing someone or something. For discerning the difference between real or illusory dreams when yearning for 'better things'. Knowing what to embrace and what to change or move on from.

Bluebell Grove (*Scilla non-scripta and selenite*) Connection to the healing grove, to nature and stillness; making time and space for deep peace, relaxation and rest, to restore our energy and re-inspire our spirit (particularly when exhausted or stressed). For laying aside cares and responsibilities to settle deeply into the inner sanctuary and peace of our being.

Blue Delphinium (*Delphinium sp.*) Speaking out. For the courage to speak our truth with honesty and integrity; listening for the words to say, for when to speak and when to stay silent; listening to others (both verbally and non-verbally); listening to the voice of our heart; releasing inhibitions around speaking, singing, writing and listening.

Blue Salvia or 'Blue Enigma' (*Salvia guarantica*) Revealing with love the truth behind the mask or smokescreen – our own and other people's; seeing through confusion and mixed messages; clarity of thought and insight; for adults and children who need to trust their clear sight and sensing, even when their vision or understanding is not upheld by others.

Celandine (*Ranunculus ficarius*) Joy, lightness. For joyful appreciation and expression; for seeing beauty and light in the world; restoring trust in goodness; allowing ourselves to be uplifted into joy when gloomy, negative or grumbling; for joyful music, song and speech; awareness of the energy and perceptions we reinforce with our words, tone and pitch.

Cherry Plum Fruit (*Prunus serasifera*) For staying peacefully centred and un-reactive, right in the heart of strong feeling; 'being with' that feeling, and following it with curiosity to uncover the love, under-standing and compassion that lies at the heart of feeling; knowing it is safe to feel, without fear, judgement, suppression, escape or reaction.

Childs Play – Inspirational Light Essence. For laughter, joy, fun and play; learning how to play and to use our imagination to create a world that is wonderful, miraculous, joyful and funny; developing a sense of humour; loosening control; lightening up; trusting that it's safe to be spontaneous; enjoying playing the fool.

Comfrey (*Symphytum aspermum*) Dynamic patience and stillness; recogniz-ing and embracing the opportunity, gifts and learning within our present experience or situation; knowing that everything happens at the right time – and that where we are now, and how we are is precisely where we need to be for our continuing understanding and growth.

Crab Apple Fruit (*Malus pumila*) For allowing our body to return to its innate state of innocent health and vitality, by letting go of the belief that we are guilty of creating disease or damage through some failing on our part; letting go of self-judgement and feelings of failure around our physical condition. For experiencing our essential purity.

Crimean Snowdrop (*Galanthus plicatus*) Healing the memory of trauma and shock held in our being, in an environment or in material objects. For a return to pure essence of being, beyond reaction; healing our perception of traumatic events and experiences; learning to stay deeply in our centre of peace, unshaken by sudden or powerful life experiences.

Cyclamen (*Cyclamen hybrida*) Self-nurture. For making time and space to nourish our body, mind, heart and soul; nurturing our core energy and dreams; making time to centre and connect with how we're feeling; choosing from the heart and nurturing our dreams, abilities and creativity. For not letting our life be governed by external demands.

Dandy Lion Sunshine, Rainbow & Dandelion patch (*Taraxacum officinale*) For finding and shining all the rainbow colours of our authentic being into the world; releasing childhood suppression of self-expression; becoming alive to feeling, expressing our feelings with love and sensitivity for ourselves and for others; integration of our solar and lunar expression; for actors, singers etc. For enjoying public performance.

Disciple of the Heart Osier (*Salix viminalis*) For finding flexible, heart-impelled, real ways to structure our life, our work and our organizations; 'getting our act together'; manifesting and realizing our unfulfilled talents and dreams, by developing unique and loving ways to organize our lives, our work and our time; transforming fear of structure into loving and practical self-organization.

Divine Being Common Yarrow (*Achillea millefolium*) and clear quartz. Confidence in our ability to heal; realizing that our body is not a 'physical' body, but an energy body – that energy follows thought, and that we are miraculous, invulnerable, eternal, light beings; experiencing light and peace in every atom and cell of our being, and in our whole life.

Divine Union Jasmine (*Jasminus officinale*) For embracing and reweaving within us of all the rejected aspects of our masculine and feminine expression; integration and synthesis of polarities; balance and wholeness; embodying within

ourselves those qualities that we've allowed others to express for us, or that we've sought in others; inner marriage; becoming our own inner lover.

Father Sun Field Sowthistle (*Sonchus arvensis*) Confidence in independently managing our affairs, and being out in the world; becoming self-supporting; inner strength and robustness; reconnecting with our strong, supportive, inner, father self, particularly after losing one's father or a male partner; finding ways to warm and strengthen our body and spirit through the winter.

Forget-Me-Not (*Myosotis arvensis*) For remembering who we really are; awakening from the dream into reality; remembering the truth; remembering whatever we need at this time: both short-term memory, as well as aspects of our personal or collective history; trusting we'll remember what we need, when we need it; recalling skills, understanding and knowledge.

Grandmother's Arms (*Crataegus monogyna*) Knowing what heals our body, mind and spirit; living at a sustainable, peaceful pace, at one with the rhythms, cycles and true timing of our heart and soul; balancing the needs of our inner child with those of our busy adult self; balancing multiple needs within a community or family.

Green Alexanders (*Smyrnium olustratum*) Connection to the revitalizing *chi* energy of the natural world and the joy of being physically alive and physically active; feeling uplifted and renewed by being out in the natural world, the elements, and the changing weather and seasons; growing confidence and joy in our physicality and robustness.

Golden Blessings (Golden leaves of *Acer platanoides*) Gratitude. For feeling blessed; appreciating all that we have; creating joy, happiness and golden moments; happy with change and 'imperfection'; not needing things or ourselves to be 'perfect' in order to appreciate and enjoy life; contentment; giving and receiving blessings and gifts; knowing we have all we need, day by day.

Goldenrod (*Solidago virgaurea*) Inner authority, self-respect and quiet inner confidence; individual integrity; setting appropriate boundaries; honouring our own inner knowing and integrity in the face of judgement, bullying or social or peer pressure. For peaceful assertion, self-referral and self-responsibility in place of rebelliousness; becoming our own inner father, particularly when we've lost our father.

Heart Flow African Amaryllis (*Amaryllis belladonna*) For opening our hearts to feeling; allowing our feelings to flow freely, moment by moment, through our undefended hearts; embracing all our feelings with love and compassion; moving beyond a fixed identity or personality, to being the movement of living love – the flow of boundless, fluid being; embracing and letting go.

Heart Mother Cyclamen (*Cyclamen* sp. and clear quartz) Balancing nurturing and giving to others, with our own need for nurture, and for 'having a life' beyond caring for others; cutting the apron strings; empowering others to become increasingly responsible for their own wellbeing and affairs; giving 'enough', but not too much; connection to the earth; environmental awareness.

Honesty (*Lunaria annua*) Knowing the power of honesty and loving vulnerability; showing our true face; happy to show our true feelings with love and understanding; embracing the full depth and range of our feelings; trusting our innate goodness and intention; realizing that the true expression of our humanness is a gift of healing.

Horse Chestnut Leaf Bud (*Aesculus hippocastanum*) Embracing with love, our masculine yang energy and a more proactive, empowered way of being; celebration and enjoyment of male physicality and sexuality; inspires men to enjoy and use their physicality and sexuality, with love and respect for themselves and for others; inspires women's love of male physicality.

Inner Fire Fire agate, fire pit, red sandstone & eagle feather. Courage, strength, clarity, accurate vision, decisive action; empowerment; for strong peaceful assertion; bringing an end to situations that are intolerable; setting boundaries, standing one's ground, saying no; knowing when and how to act in order to be effective; moving beyond being a 'victim'.

In the Arms of Love Mixed freesias (*Freesia*) with pink rhodocrosite & rose quartz. For cracking open our heart's defence against love; embracing ourselves and others with the deepest level of unconditional love and compassion; deep self-worth – feeling worthy, 'worth it'; knowing we are all equal at the level of the heart, regardless of whether we are 'able' or 'disabled', 'successful' or 'unsuccessful' etc.

In the Light of Goodness Gorse (*Ulex europaeus*) Experiencing our ever-present goodness and essential worth; standing in the radiant light of our innate goodness at all times; deep self-worth, self-compassion, self-forgiveness; feeling 'worthy' and 'good enough' to have love, friendship, happiness, abundance, and opportunities in one's life; freeing ourselves from the chains of guilt, self-punishment, judgement and prejudice.

Letting Go 'White Pearl' Hyacinth (*Hyacinthus orientalis*) Letting go of deep fears in the human psyche that arise at times of transformation; joy in letting go into an expanded experience of ourselves, stepping into the light – knowing that we are always supported, safe and held by angels, particularly at the point of dying, and at times of powerful transition.

Light Anchor Inspirational Light Essence. Anchoring the light of divine consciousness to transform and heal our personal and collective awareness; hope, courage and certainty that we will complete our journey of healing and transformation at this time; crystal clearing; clearing the energy of suffering from environments (use clear quartz crystals programmed with Light Anchor).

Light Dancer Great Bindweed (*Calystegia silvatica*), Tibetan bowl & Dancers of the Four Directions. Joy; non-attachment; trust; trusting that we're always held in love; unconditional, unpossessive, true love; leaping into the void; embracing and letting go; releasing ourselves and each other from fear-based ties that suppress our expansion and joyful development; seeing what to let go and what to keep; coming into full expression.

Lilac (*Syringa vulgaris*) Steering an instinctive path through complex situations or information; finding a lateral approach to managing complexity and multilevel, multidimensional information; intuitively establishing order within chaos; finding where to begin when facing complex tasks or situations; establishing accessible sense and order in our lives, in our work or when studying.

Living the Dream Inspirational Light Essence. Moving beyond trust and hope into empowerment, clarity of vision and positive action to manifest our dream for ourselves and for the world; knowing that love does prevail; moving from being the dreamer to living the dream; embracing certainty and empowerment whenever we waver or lose hope in our dreams.

Loving Me, Loving You Bell Heather (*Erica cinerea*) Loving who we are, right now; embracing with love and laughter all our 'imperfections'; celebrating our uniqueness; being happy to be real; accepting and showing our humanness; being warm and loving towards ourselves and others; feeling relaxed, unselfconscious, and 'good enough' as we are, right now; true beauty.

One Being Medicine man quartz. For being still, deeply centred, fully present – at one with oneself, and with the One Being in all; deep peace; deepening meditation and attunement to devas, spirits, people, plants and animals; developing true clairvoyance and clairaudience; feeling connected to the world and to life, even when unable to actively participate.

Orange Wallflower (*Cheiranthus cheirii*) Self-appreciation; becoming our own best friend, enjoying our own company; happy to be alone; feeling happy being ourselves around others and in groups; making friends easily; knowing we are the source of love and abundance – that there's no lack, except in our perception; meeting our own needs; integrity in relationships.

Original Innocence Inspirational Light Essence. Recognizing our ever-present, essential innocence and wholeness; self-forgiveness; self-compassion and understanding; recognizing that only our judgement separates us from knowing the perfection and light of our true being; wiping the slate clean for ourselves; knowing that enlightenment lies in our lovingly embracing all of who we are, right now.

Passionate Life Belladonna Lily (*Amaryllis belladonna*), amethyst & quartz. Energy, enthusiasm, courage, adventurousness, motivation, zest for life and new experiences; being passionately alive; overcoming obstacles and setbacks; rebuilding confidence after illness; developing inner strength, and confidence; trusting ourselves and life; knowing we will be supported if we follow our heart.

Peaceful Detachment Common Yarrow (*Achillea millefolium*) & quartz. Peaceful detachment from the emotional energy or suffering of others; peaceful connection to others at the level of their true self, beyond fear, ego reaction and emotional drama; seeing others as autonomous, invulnerable and divinely creative beings; seeing beyond drama to the true essence and purpose of people and situations.

Phoenix Rebirth Common Gorse (*Ulex europaeus*) Forgiveness; truth and reconciliation; embracing anger and grief with compassion and understanding for oneself and others; empowering ourselves to move out of repeated patterns of playing the role of 'victim'; taking responsibility for our part in the picture; peaceful and powerful assertion of human rights; appropriate setting of boundaries.

Physotegia (*Physostegia virginiana*) Integrity in interaction; peaceful, centred response to situations and to others; centred interaction with others – appropriate response unaffected by strong influences, drama or ego dynamics; remaining unswayed by peer or social pressure; separating out what's 'mine' and 'thine'; pausing to centre and check in before acting or reacting.

Pink Cherry (*Prunus* 'Kanzan') For a deep sense of unconditional, tender, compassionate love; heart softening and opening; nurtures and soothes; for unconditional love; inspires tenderness and sensitivity; compassionate self-understanding; being gentle and caring towards oneself and others; bonding with children and our inner child.

Pure Love Paper-White Narcissus (*Narcissus Tazetta*) Learning to give love, be love and be 'in love' every moment of our day; purifying the intentions of our heart; letting go illusions about 'falling in love' and the desire to have someone mirror our beauty and light back to us; realizing what unconditional, non-dependent, real love is.

Purple Hebe (*Hebe* x *franciscana*) made in the snow. Moving from primeval 'flight and fight', defensive instincts, into responding from a place of stillness within the movement of peace; moving beyond the polarity of 'safe' or 'unsafe', into empowered action and interaction – peacefully co-creating our reality and experience; healing defensive reactions arising from trauma or high-stress environments.

Pussy Willow (*Salix daphnoides*) Flexibility born out of responding to the real flow in life – to what is truly comfortable and appropriate, to our inner rhythms and real sense of timing; knowing that life supports us if we support and honour ourselves on a daily basis; connection to intuition and needs; living, loving ease.

Red Clover (*Trifolium pratense*) Experiencing and radiating peace and safety every moment; transforming feelings of panic or anxiety (our own or others) into an experience of deep peace and safety; settling down into our ever-present peace; knowing we are always safe and supported; letting go of the 'what ifs' and peacefully embracing 'what is'.

Red Deadnettle (*Lamium purpureum*) and clear quartz. Knowing the eternal wellspring of love lies within us – that love can never be denied; recognizing that it's only we who reject ourselves and walk away from our love for ourselves and others; transforming the wounds of past rejection with deep self-love; knowing that we are always held in love.

Red Gladiolus (*Gladiolus* sp.) Integrity in sexuality; clarifying our original choice to enter a sexual relationship, or to make love at any time; healing our sexual experience with love and care for each other's sensitivities and timing; reuniting our spiritual expression of love with our physical and emotional experience; celebration of women's sexuality.

Red Poppy (*Papaver rhoeas*) For a fiery sense of self-worth; for constructive use of anger to bring about positive change; setting boundaries without guilt; peacefully embracing anger with love and understanding; recognizing the fears and unmet needs that underpin our anger; moving from 'hopelessness' and being a 'victim', into empowerment and positive action.

Red Quince (*Chaenomeles speciosa* 'Simonii') Willingness to embrace the truth in what others say, and in our life; undefended, unreactive, objective listening to others and to truth; feeling 'big enough' to embrace the truth about ourselves; healing our fear of judgement, with love, understanding and deep self-worth.

Return of the Sun Kingcups Marsh Marigolds (*Caltha palustris*) Bringing the light of divine understanding to heal the deepest wounds of our personal and shared history; healing the denigration and suppression of sensitivity, spirituality and feminine expression in men and women; healing wounds arising from racial prejudice, ethnic cleansing and witch hunts; empowered uprising of feminine expression and sensitivity.

Reunion Ash (*Fraxinus excelsior*) Integration and synthesis of multi-dimensional awareness, left and right brain, masculine/feminine, linear and lateral, within and without, seen and unseen, spirit and matter – duality and oneness within our being; peacefully embracing and integrating expanded awareness beyond our former comfort zones; reuniting opposites, twins and polarities.

Rosebay Willowherb (*Epilobium angustifolium*) Connecting to the spirit and beauty of nature, the natural world, the animals and the earth; peacefully developing awareness of the multi-dimensional reality of life, through communion with the wonders of the natural world; recognizing heaven on earth; gratitude for earth's gifts.

Serene Being White and Gold Phalaenopsis Orchid (*Phalaenopsis* sp.) Centred, unruffled, self-referring, serene, peaceful, undefended, compassionate, self-supporting; fully present; gently breathing deeply; unhurried; taking time to seek clarity and to respond appropriately; essential self-worth; standing our true height; expanding fully within the light of our being; peaceful decision-making; acting as an equal; honouring our integrity.

Sky Blue Comfrey (*Symphytum aspermum*) Infinite, dynamic peace; timelessness; agelessness, experiencing our timeless being, fully alive, constantly new in each moment, untainted and undamaged by time; knowing that we are infinite and that time and death are an illusion; letting go into the infinity of now.

Speedwell (*Veronica persica*) For taking the time we need; timelessness; deep concentration, attention, stillness, focus; slowing down; being fully present – responding to what's needed in the now;

taking time to meet our own needs as well as others'; connection to intuition, understanding and inspiration; knowing there's always enough time for what's really needed.

Stitchwort (*Stellaria holostea*) Commitment to being fully alive, fully inhabiting our body and life, centred in divine peace; experiencing the divine, embodied in us and in all things; vitality, presence, warmth, invulnerability; divine strength; physical confidence, joy in living, fulfilling our soul choice to realize heaven on earth now, at this time.

Sweet Hunza (*Prunus armeniaca*) For embracing the gift of now; finding and creating profound healing, meaning, realization and sweetness in the midst of hardship or suffering; letting go resistance, embracing the opportunity, gifts and understanding offered by our experience; transformation through embrace; encouragement; uplifting; knowing all is well and all will be well.

Sweet Pea (*Lathyrus odoratus*) Knowing we are never alone; recognizing the divine nature of all being and ourselves; connection and communion with friends in spirit and with angels – our brothers and sisters in light; increasingly realizing and embodying our own divine/angelic nature and light; comforting, uplifting, empowering; connection to divine being.

The Mirror of Creation Honesty (*Lunaria annua*) and clear quartz. Recognizing how powerfully creative we are, and how precisely we create our experience and reality through our combined thoughts, feelings, beliefs, actions and reactions; highlighting the choice between peace or fear, abundance or lack – and how our choices are mirrored back to us by our unfolding reality.

The Rose (*Rosa* 'Mme Isaac Periere') Integrating and unfolding all our understanding, qualities and gifts so that we can fulfil our incarnation purpose at this time; developing our skills and full potential; offering our highest expression to the world; being happy to be different, radical or unique in how we live or express ourselves.

True Power Crocus (*Crocus thomasinianus* 'Royal') For realizing that true power lies within us, in the love and truth of our being – that this is power and stature beyond measure, that can never be diminished or taken by anyone; being completely at peace, at one with who we are, true to ourselves, unthreatened; empowered; equal in worth.

Violet (*Viola odorata*) Encourages us to express truth and maintain integrity, boundaries and privacy when in the public eye; resisting the glamour and pressure of image creation; giving of ourselves only as much as we wish; being real; being true to ourselves; valuing our true worth, beyond outside appreciation or recognition.

Wild Cyclamen (*Cyclamen coum*) Inner resourcefulness; self-sufficiency; becoming self-supporting, self-referring and independent; drawing on our own inner strength and counsel; growing up and managing our worldly affairs confidently; for children and adults learning to cope on their own; standing strongly on one's own two feet; enjoying one's own company and counsel.

With Love (*Rosa* 'Sophie's Perpetual') Doing what we love and loving what we do; being wholehearted in our choices; examining our heart about our life choices; creating a life that is truly loving to ourselves; following our heart's desire; giving as much or little as we wish; imbuing with love whatever we do.

Yellow Hyacinth Hyacinth 'City of Haarlem' (*Hyacinthus orientalis*) Respect for others; self-respect; knowing we're all equal in worth, regardless of our achievements or level of understanding; recognizing and appreciating each others' gifts and qualities; essential respect for others at the level of their true self; recognizing our own 'blind spots'; valuing other people's individual journey and timing.

Light Heart 'Truly Divine' Combinations

At One – Meditation Combination. For deep stillness. Being deeply At One with ourselves and with life. For a timeless sense of 'being' and 'being with' the world. For deepening meditation and heightening our awareness, and connection to our intuition and understanding. Grounding and centring. Used regularly, inspires a way of 'living meditation' throughout each day.

Lighter Space – Space Clearing Combination (mist and drops). A powerful blend of space-clearing essences for clearing, transforming and lightening the energy of a place – creating a light, welcoming atmosphere in the home, workplace, hotel rooms etc. For clearing trauma or accumulated mental, emotional, or electromagnetic energy, also for house/laundry cleaning, clearing crystals and jewellery.

Make Love – Sensual Loving Mist. For passionate, openhearted, tender, loving. Encourages deep enjoyment and appreciation of our individual male and female sexuality and physiques. Inspires us to love ourselves just as we are, and to share the gift of our loving, tenderly and playfully, savouring each moment and each touch as we create a deep and loving connection.

Peace in a Storm – Centring Combination. For staying centred and peaceful in a crisis; for peacefully embracing strong emotions (one's own or other people's); remaining peaceful and unshaken by the drama or trauma of events around us. For settling deeply into peace and equilibrium following shock or anxiety.

Self-Worth Inspires integrity and self-worth, encouraging us to love and value ourselves, honour our own understanding and instincts, be true to ourselves, and have the courage to speak out and stand our ground. Restores compassion, self-worth and confidence. Supports us in honouring ourselves and in resisting outside pressure and influence.

Sleep Well (mist and drops). Reassures and settles a busy, fearful or worried mind, encouraging us to let go of emotional tension and restlessness so that we feel relaxed and secure enough to sleep. For settling into deep, peaceful rest and relaxation. For centring and grounding (both adults and children) whenever we feel overactive or over-excited.

Working Harmony –Workplace, Study and Integrity mist. For centred focus and attention. Finding flexible, creative ways to manage complex information and work situations. For listening attentively, without reaction. Promotes greater harmony, co-operation and centred interaction. Inspires integrity, understanding, and the willing-ness to listen to other people's feelings and points of view. For meetings and conflict resolution.

Light Heart Therapeutic Combinations

Forgiveness Forgiveness and self-forgive-ness; compassion and deep understanding of ourselves and others; understanding how we co-created our experience; letting go of old anger, judgement, self-judgement and guilt; moving out of patterns of powerlessness and playing the role of 'victim'; peaceful empowerment; healing old conflicts which seem impossible to reconcile and forgive.

Healing Grief Embracing the full range of our grief, peacefully, without judgement and with love and understanding; uncovering the healing that lies at the heart of grief; making the time and space to grieve; caring for ourselves; healing the memory of trauma and suffering; forgive-ness, connection to spirit; nurturing new beginnings.

Heart of Peace Peaceful Detachment from the drama and trauma of world events, events around us, or in our own lives: choosing peace in place of fear, to create an experience of peace and safety in our own lives and in the world; embracing life's events with divine awareness, peace, trust and empowerment.

Infinite Abundance Knowing we are infinitely blessed with love and abundance – that everything we need is here, right now – there is no lack, except in our perception; knowing life supports us when we support and honour ourselves; making the most of our resources and gifts; knowing we're 'worth it'.

Life Balance Balancing meeting our own needs with meeting the needs of others; nourishing our body, mind and spirit; living life from the heart; honouring our integrity; responding to our inner rhythms and real timing; making the time and space for peace, relaxation, rest, exercise, inspira-tion, eating well, friendship, creativity and fun.

Light Heart Space Clearing and infusing our personal energy field with light; peaceful detachment from the drama and trauma of others; maintaining appro-priate boundaries and energetic integrity; balancing personal needs with the needs of others; taking time to restore our energy and spirit; clarity of awareness; for healers, sensitives, therapists and therapy rooms.

Passionate Life Energy, enthusiasm, courage, joy, adventurousness, motivation, zest for life and new experiences; being passionately alive; overcoming obstacles and setbacks; rebuilding confidence and resilience after illness or setbacks; developing skills and resourcefulness; empowerment; trusting our abilities; following our own instincts and timing; trusting our inner guide and our invulner-able divine nature.

Self Expression Peacefully and clearly expressing our feelings, understanding and perceptions; relaxed, empowered expression; embodying and expressing who we really are, physically, vocally, creatively and in how we live our lives; letting go our fear of being judged; increasing expressive-ness verbally, and through art, dance, singing, acting, writing etc.

Self Healing Confidence in our ability to heal; experiencing our true light, radiantly embodied by every cell of our being; letting go our fear of illness and feelings of guilt in relation to health; understanding what heals our body, mind and spirit; making healing choices in our lives.

Sexual Healing Healing men's and women's experience of sexuality; celebration and love of both male and female sexuality; expressing unconditional love, integrity and embodiment of spirit through sexuality; healing issues arising from past sexual experiences, sexual trauma or abuse; empowered, sensitive, tender sexuality; honouring one's integrity in sexual relationships.

True Beauty Knowing that true beauty shines from within – from the love that we give to ourselves and others, and from our true spirit; being happy to be real; loving who we are right now; letting go judgement about how we look; enjoying the sensuality and aliveness of our being.

Green Man Tree Essences

Our relationship with trees is as old as time itself. For centuries humans have regarded certain trees as having healing qualities, and have revered and cared for them as sacred or even magical beings. Trees are among the most ancient living organisms on this planet. They are protectors and regulators of their surroundings, offering food and shelter to many other forms of life. We now realize that our existence is totally dependent on the great forests and woods that cover the earth. They not only regulate the atmosphere ensuring a life-sustaining balance of oxygen and carbon dioxide, but also control weather systems and enrich the soil.

Trees flourish and survive by adjusting their form to harmonize with the prevailing conditions, and they succeed in maintaining this balance for hundreds, sometimes thousands of years. This ability to be balanced and flexible, to absorb and let go, is a lesson from which we could all benefit.

Each species of tree shows different characteristics and you can sense their particular energies when walking in ancient woodlands or forests. Integrating this energy into our own system helps us to act more responsibly towards nature. The Green Man Essences were created by Simon Lily and his partner Sue as an aid to meditation and self-healing. In traditional British folklore the Green Man is the perfect blending of human and plant life. He is the spirit of nature, an embodiment of fertility, and is celebrated every May Day.

The Green Man range comprises 74 tree essences. The first essence made was from the flowers of the hazel tree, whose qualities encourage the growth of new skills and information.

Alder (*Alnus glutinosa*) Release. Reduces nervousness and anxiety. Brings clarity of mind and eases stress. Increases *prana/chi*.

Apple (*Malus domestica*) Detoxification. Helps the elimination of toxins on all levels and brings in spiritual energies. Transforms negative emotions.

Ash (*Fraxinus excelsior*) Strength. Harmony with your surroundings. Feeling in tune. Brings flexibility and security.

Aspen (*Populus tremula*) Delight. Intuition and intellect; balances over-analysis; calms fears and gives a broader perspective. Brings amusement and wise laughter.

Atlas Cedar (*Cedrus atlantica*) Resilience. For the removal of out-of-date patterns and achieving a personal path. Gives resilience to cope with change and adversity.

Bay (*Laurus nobilis*) Energy. For deep-rooted vitality. Releases blocked and suppressed emotions. Spiritualizes physicality.

Beech (*Fagus sylvatica*) Easygoing. Brings confidence and hope in oneself and one's life. For relaxation and release of held-in trauma. Confidence in self-expression and speaking out clearly.

Black Poplar (*Populus nigra*) Nurture. Creates a powerful peacefulness; a sense of security and inner clarity. Very comforting. Blends all energies.

Blackthorn (*Prunus spinosa*) Circulation. Helps absorption of energies necessary for life. Stabilizes emotions; brings hope and joy. Stimulating.

Bird Cherry (*Prunus padus*) Sensuality. For unblocking deep emotional wounds. For those who have become over-defensive of emotional attachments. Helpful where there are sexual difficulties, mental rigidity and being overcritical or uncomfortable with physicality

Box (*Buxus sempivirens*) Clarity. Strengthens the mind and will. Clears the head and eases irrationality and confusion. Links you with your Higher Self.

Catalpa (*Catalpa* x *erubescans*) Joy. Stabilization of emotions, helps find peace of mind. Reduces anxiety, increases self-confidence in what one can achieve.

Cedar Of Lebanon (*Cedrus libani*) Turmoil. Physically cleansing, a breath of fresh air. Where there is suffering this essence lessens the resistance to needed change. Brings clearer messages from the deep mind and universe regarding appropriate actions. Increases peaceful flow, reduces turmoil.

Cherry Laurel (*Prunus laurocerasus*) Balance of mind. For all problems with the mind and head. Imagination and inspiration used practically. Helps maintain molecular and genetic integrity of the body. Subtle perceptions accessed. Gives high-level protection and support.

Cherry Plum (*Prunus cerasifera*) Confidence. For wisdom and security of the inner self; helps remove fears. Tension and rigid mental concepts are eased. For opening up on emotional levels. Helps shyness.

Copper Beech (*Fagus sylvatica* var. purpurea) Depression. Brings a deep, enlivening sense of peace and detachment from worries. Energizes emotions in a positive, nonaggressive way.

Crack Willow (*Salix fragilis*) Spiritual sun. For letting go and allowing things to happen. Brings a sense of oneness with the world. Aids communications with the Higher Self, the planet and the energies of the sun.

Douglas Fir (*Pseudotsuga menziesii*) Standing alone. For relatedness and finding one's place. Brings spontaneous energy and freedom to be oneself.

Elder (*Sambucus nigra*) Self-worth. Calms aggression, brings stability, love and forgiveness. Balances self-image. For times of transformation and change. Good for fretful children.

English Elm (*Ulmus procera*)
Enthusiasm. Desire to progress, move on.
Re-energizes the mind when fatigued and
balances the heart when feeling drained or
overemotional. Brings clarity for decision
making and study.

Eucalyptus (Cider Gum) (*Eucalyptus
gunnii*) Sustenance. For opportunity;
restoration of energy; smooth integration of
energy; and correct relationship and flow.

Field Maple (*Acer campestre*) Aching
heart. Brings balance to those hearts
reaching for love. For understanding and
contentment when overwhelmed by a sense
of responsibility or remorse for mistakes,
accidents etc. Aligns heart chakra to higher
love.

Fig Tree (*Ficus carica*) Generator. For
expression of needs; soul food; feelings of
emptiness resolved; letting go; dancing;
and energy to achieve.

Foxglove Tree (*Paulownia tomentosa*)
Harmonious flow. For ending of
turbulence; strengthens aura and life force;
brings happiness, relaxation and smooth
waters.

Gean, Wild Cherry (*Prunus avium*)
Soothing. Focuses energy in the physical
and stimulates self-healing. Calms the
heart and mind. Creates a smooth flow of
energy. Useful where there is emotional
pain.

Giant Redwood (*Sequoiadendron
giganteum*) Weight of responsibility. For
those who are too hard on themselves or
on others. Brings a sense of balanced
responsibility, tolerance and relaxation that
allows wisdom the space to develop.
Releases energy blocked in lower chakras.

Ginkgo (*Ginkgo biloba*) The ancient way.
Brings harmonization with the universe;
invisibility; flowing with the tides. For a
smooth flow of emotions and internal
harmonization.

Glastonbury Thorn (*Crataegus
monogyna biflora*) Out of the woods. Helps
find a clearer direction. What feels right to

do and be emerges from indecision and
chaos. This brings immediate relaxation
and release from tension, increasing subtle
information and intuition.

Gorse (*Ulex europaeus*) Integration. Eases
restlessness, frustration and jealousy.
Brings joy from emotional security and
growth. Helps integrate new forms of
energy or knowledge in a useful, personal
manner.

Great Sallow (*Salix caprea*) Soul. Allows
the mind to expand and link with the soul.
Brings an understanding of life purpose.
Energizing. Links to earth energy.

Hawthorn (*Crataegus monogyna*) Love.
Stimulates the healing power of love. For
trust and forgiveness. Helps to cleanse the
heart of negativity.

Hazel (*Corylus avellana*) Skills. For the
flowering of skills. For the ability to receive
and communicate wisdom. Helps all forms
of study; clears away unwanted debris.
Brings more stability and focus in order to
integrate useful information.

Holly (*Ilex aquifolium*) Power of peace.
Agitated states, balance of mind. For
people with a loss of control, panic, lack of
self-worth, unhappiness, loneliness. Active
expression of love.
Non-aggressive, peace-loving yet assertive.

Holm Oak (*Quercus ilex*) Negative
emotions. Relieves emotions and restlessness related to thwarted expression such as
guilt, jealousy, anger etc. Activates personal
creativity and balances emotional and
mental energy.

Hornbeam (*Carpinus betulus*) Right
action. Deep energizing on many levels
clearing blocked or stagnant energies. For
clarity of purpose. Standing up for
personal experience. Increased security in
working with others.

Horse Chestnut (*Aesculus hippocastanum*) Agitation. Harmonizing flows of
energy to and from the individual, eases
agitation caused by contrast and difference.
Brings clarity of mind and a flow of

intuition. Peace. Ability to ground and dissipate excess energy.

Italian Alder (*Alnus cordata*) Protected peace. Brings peace, love and protection for delicate energies. Helps with shyness or overaggression. Courage for new starts.

Ivy (*Hedera helix*) Fear. Eases hidden fears and anxieties. Helps to release true feelings and identify needs. Balances the heart chakra and its nadis.

Judas Tree (*Cercis siliquastrum*) Channelling. Brings access to completely new thought patterns and ideas. Openness and acceptance of very subtle levels of energy and the ability to communicate it to others. For the ability to discriminate and discern the validity of given information.

Juniper (*Juniperus communis*) Doorway. For renunciation of the past; generosity; relaxation; releases old stresses; ancestral patterns; and brings inner versatility.

Laburnum (*Laburnum* x *watereri* 'Vossi') Detoxification. For a balanced release of stress and tension. Increases detoxification processes and the growth of creative potential, optimism, positivity and expression of personal wisdom.

Larch (*Larix decidua*) Will to express. Helps the communication of personal wisdom from new levels of peace and healing. Brings inspiration and creativity. Enhances physical and sexual energy. Balances heart and mind, will and desire.

Lawson Cypress (*Chamaecyparis lawsoniana*) The path. Helps identify correct action and one's true needs. Initiates change in the right direction. Brings increased communication between mind and body, and discipline to attain one's goals and spiritual direction.

Leyland Cypress (*Cupressocyparis leylandii*) Freedom. Helps ease hidden fears and anxieties, increases positive attitudes and sense of humour allowing a sense of freedom in which to grow and feel comfortable. For those who dislike being by themselves.

Lilac (*Syringa vulgaris*) Spine. Eases all energies of the spinal axis. Activates all chakras. Eases tension. Lilac is closely aligned with many different types of nature spirit.

Lime (*Tilea* x *europaea*) Development. For shifting levels of consciousness without disorientation. Calms anxiety where related to practical use of one's psychic and healing potential. Doubts and fears ease. Past programming is lessened.

Liquidambar (Sweet Gum) (*Liquidambar styraciflua*) Sweet tongue. For self-aware dynamic energy. Brings personal energy integrity; care for self and others; and a calm mind.

Lombardy Poplar (*Populus nigra* 'italica') Aspiration. Discrimination; acts of unique creativity; understanding deep drives; inspiration to aspire.

Lucombe Oak (*Quercus hispanica* 'lucombeana') Creative energy. For life-supporting creativity, inspiration, ideas. Increased mental focus. Commitment to act and bring change. Wisdom and compassion.

Magnolia (*Magnolia* x *soulangeana*) Restlessness. Eases restlessness and lack of clarity. Helps to maintain balance when difficult changes have to be made. Increases sense of freedom and relaxation. Learning from past experiences, brings a clearer idea of one's true identity.

Manna Ash (*Fraxinus ornus*) Happy with oneself. Heals the heart and emotions. Brings honesty with oneself about how one feels. Helps with unresolved emotional issues. Increases understanding and access to creative levels of consciousness.

Medlar (*Mespilus germanicus*) Boundless. Brings energy to core personal patterns; motivation, enthusiasm and drive. Boundless energy to achieve goals. Increase in joy and happiness. Total security. Strength, humour, brightness and creative intelligence.

Midland Hawthorn (*Crataegus laevigata*) Expansion. Energizes aspects of the heart chakra and its relationship with personal growth and spiritual awareness. Enthusiasm to enjoy and explore life.

Mimosa (*Acacia dealbata*) Sensitivity. Brings increased awareness of what is going on inside self. Intuition is better understood. Ability to stand up and express oneself. A sense of peace.

Monkey Puzzle Tree (*Araucaria araucana*) Fierce compassion. Calms aggression but allows creative, forceful action. Strongly energizing, earthing, protecting. Perception of cycles of time and space, expanded awareness of continuity and change on this planet.

Monterey Pine (*Pinus radiata*) Connectedness. Helps remove very deep trauma. Artistic blocks eased. Balances emotions, calms anxieties. Brings a deep peace and connectedness to everything. At ease in one's body, physical well-being. Past-life information.

Mulberry (*Morus nigra*) Wrath. Powerful emotions released constructively. Freedom from remorse and past pain. For those hurt by the world and who react with anger and cynicism.

Norway Maple (*Acer platanoides*) Healing love. Brings love and acceptance; healing and nurturing energy for emotional shock and trauma. Lightness, happiness, relaxation. Taking back control of life and power for oneself.

Norway Spruce (*Picea abies*): Trust. Helps in understanding change. Brings lightness and openness to experience. seeing clearly; axis; beacon.

Oak (*Quercus robur*) Manifestation. For absorption and integration of very deep, hidden energy underlying this reality. The desire for stability whilst experiencing the polarities of existence. Brings the ability to manifest one's goals. Channelling energy.

Olive (*Olea europea*) Valour. Warmth; solar energy; truthfulness motivation; passionate clarity.

Osier (*Salix viminalis*) Spiritual void. To contact Higher Self. Energy to adapt, change and grow. Useful when everything seems empty and useless. Brings energy and understanding.

Pear (*Pyrus communis*) Serenity. Helps you be happy to be who you are. Brings clarity, simplicity, confidence. Reduction of stress in the nervous system. Increased enthusiasm, drive and energy. Deep peace.

Persian Ironwood (*Parrotia persica*) Alienation. Brings energy, emotional strength, drive, enthusiasm. Grounds spiritual energy into the physical body. Activates deep-level healing. Connectedness to the highest level of planetary consciousness. Strong sense of connectedness, belonging and joy. For feelings of alienation and weakness.

Pittospora (*Pittosporum tenuifolium*) In two minds. Helps to clarify how one truly feels. Useful when loyalties are divided. Helps find solutions to mental worries and conflicts. Increases perspective and sense of humour.

Plane Tree (*Platanus* x *acerifolia*) Fine judgement. Brings ability to discriminate subtle levels of the truth. Helps prevent introspection, melancholy and over-analysis. Broadens viewpoints and gives a peaceful space to meditate.

Plum (*Prunus domestica*) Empowerment. Helps the highest spiritual energy enter into the material world. Practical solution to problems. Increased awareness of surroundings and effective use of personal power. Self-worth, self-motivation.

Privet (*Ligustrum vulgare*) Old wounds. Works with subtle bodies to repair physical shock and trauma. Creates harmonious vibration that helps to heal on fine levels. Increases life force to allow letting go of old wounds.

Red Chestnut (*Aesculus* x *carnea*) Fear for others. A feeling of serenity and protection at a deep level of being, both for oneself and others. This reduces fear and anxieties and brings a peace and detachment from the worries of what may, but probably won't, be. Helps create a clear, positive, unselfish link with others. Fears and phobias ease.

Red Oak (*Quercus rubra*) Practical support. Energizes the body's structural systems. Growing conviction of one's place and purpose in the world. Clearing of self-doubt and false views. Very practical searching for the spirit.

Robinia (Black Locust) (*Robinia pseudoacacia*) Awakening. For a calm mind; dissolves 'glamour' and obsession. Brings optimism; clearing emotional and mental clutter.

Rowan (*Sorbus aucuparia*) Nature. Attunement to the energies of nature, particularly wood and earth. Enlarges perspectives to a cosmic level, allowing deep understanding of the universe.

Scots Pine (*Pinus sylvestris*) Insight. Helps activate third eye and development of subtle awareness in a balanced way. Brings penetrating insight and increases tenacity and patience. Broadens one's outlook.

Sea Buckthorn (*Hippophae rhamnoides*) Pioneer. Fresh perspectives; uninvolvement; protection from harmful influences; understanding emotions

Sequoia (*Sequoia sempervirens*) Anchor. Creates space to deal with energy blocks, stabilizing our anchor to the planet and opening to the universe. Eases difficult emotions giving clarity of thought

Silver Birch (*Betula pendula*) Beauty. Ability to experience beauty and calmness. Tolerance of self and others. For those who find it difficult to express themselves.

Silver Fir (*Abies alba*) Enthroned. Empowering; going with the flow; transformation; open crown; brightness; brings a flow of healing and creativity.

Silver Maple (*Acer saccarinum*). Moods. Helps balance the flow of energy through the body and regulates mood swings. Realigns the meridians, so useful for acupuncture.

Spindle (*Euonymus europaeus*) Self-integration. For understanding one's true nature and needs. Brings increased sense of security, reducing the need to compare oneself to others. For feelings of superiority/inferiority. Energizes soul, accesses energies of the shadow-self in an integrated, positive way.

Stags Horn Sumach (*Rhus typhina*) Meditation. Energizes brow chakra. Eases flow of information. Balances energies for meditation. Stills mental and emotional processes while allowing clear intuition and communication at deep levels.

Strawberry Tree (*Arbutus unedo*) Quietude. Quietens and clears the mind of all unnecessary thought. Brings stillness and silence, which allows change to occur on deep levels. Energizes the crown chakra. Good for healers and meditation.

Sweet Chestnut (*Castanea sativa*) The now. For focusing and centring in the present moment. Helps release guilt, particularly alienation with physical world. Creates detachment and understanding to regain wider perspective. Finding ways out of difficult situations.

Sycamore (*Acer pseudoplatanus*) Lightening up. Energy levels increase, so helps with lethargy. Brings awareness of the sweetness of life, harmony and relaxation. Lifts heavy moods.

Tamarisk (*Tamarix gallica*) Fire of transformation. Helps in finding spiritual direction, freeing up energies for personal expansion and growth. Deeply cleansing and uplifting, cleanses age-old dross for the true self to emerge.

Tree Lichen (*Usnea subfloridana*) Wisdom. Accesses past knowledge and ancient wisdom. Brings a sense of independence and detachment without isolation. Letting go of things no longer needed in order to grow.

Tree of Heaven (*Ailanthus altissima*) Heaven on earth. Dynamic, energizing, spiritual energies. Maintains integrity of self whilst removing barriers and allowing growth of new levels of awareness. Brings practical spirituality and practical wisdom.

Tulip Tree (*Liriodendron tulipifera*) Spiritual nourishment. Nourishing on spiritual levels, particularly for those feeling restless and dissatisfied or those with addictive tendencies. Helps in finding positive outlets for energy and expression. Artistic. Brings balance for meditation.

Viburnum (*Viburnum tinus*) Reassurance. Support and reassurance. For those who feel unsettled, vulnerable or unhappy. Helps to establish identity and direction, particularly after life-threatening situations.

Walnut (*Juglans regia*) Liberation. For purification, and cleansing; sturdiness; helps in the removal of all sorts of intrusions and influences; brings personal power and integrity; security

Wayfaring Tree (*Viburnum lantana*) Far memory. Recognition of similarities of circumstance and patterns in the present relating to the past. Re-establishing personal boundaries and independence to create a protective space.

Weeping Willow (*Salix* x *chrysocoma*) Ego. For proper use of personal power and energy. Useful for those who get annoyed by others' views and attitudes. Tolerance of others and acceptance of one's own short-comings. Energizing and motivating in a wise, balanced way.

Western Hemlock (*Tsuga heterophylla*) Open grace. For cleansing, clearing, quietening and focusing. Brings serenity; acceptance. For new beginnings.

Western Red Cedar (*Thuja plicata*) Constancy. Brings underlying peace; play of emotions; and belief in oneself. Helps screen harmful influences. For subtle tides of consciousness; steadiness.

White Poplar (*Populus alba*) Starting again. Increases wisdom, joy and content-ment. Heals mind and emotions. Gives energy and courage to recover from emotional setbacks.

White Willow (*Salix alba*) True self. The perception of the self is put in the context of its universal existence. This clarity brings a truer balance within oneself. Ego is cleansed and filled with a sense of bliss and love welling up. Spiritual cleansing.

Whitebeam (*Sorbus aria*) Otherworld. Stimulates finer levels of perception. Understanding of the animal and plant kingdoms. Opens heart and mind to finer levels of creation.

Wild Service Tree (*Sorbus torminalis*) Unfoldment. Brings expansion of awareness and an understanding of motives. Also for past-life healing; self-definition; hidden currents.

Willow Leaved Pear (*Pyrus salicifolia*) Dance of life. Brings security within the self; dance of joy; healing; personal power and vitality; creative living; enjoyment

Wych Elm (*Ulmus glabra*) Attainment. The mind is brought to clarity. There is a more positive, life-affirming outlook. Brings confidence in personal strengths and abilities and peaceful awareness, no matter what state. Meditation touches many subtle realms.

Yellow Buckeye (*Aesculus flava*) Devas. A way to link to devas, elementals and nature spirits in all environments. Modifies personal energy patterns in order to understand different sorts of communica-tion.

Yew (*Taxus baccata*) Protection. Protects from harm by activating the highest spiritual values of survival and protection. Aids the memory and discrimination, helps the immune system and increases energy.

Sun Essences

Sun Essences have a policy of hand-prepared flower essences where living flowers are held in the bowl, in addition to the picked flowers. As the remedy is potentizing, it remains connected to the ongoing stream of life force, which strengthens the healing potential of these English flower essences.

Sun Essences were created by Vivien Williamson, whose passion for flower essences evolved from a decade-long love affair with the Bach Flower Remedies and the unforgettable experience of making her first flower essence – White Chestnut in 1989. She started her company, Sun Essences, in the early '90s and lives near Cromer, a much loved haunt of Doctor Edward Bach.

Right from the beginning Vivien had an intuitive sense that essence combinations would be a significant part of the future of flower essences and with the help of Jane Stevenson (of Sun Essences for Animals), she began developing ranges of blends for people and animals.

Vivian believes that, as in ancient traditions, the rainbow is a bridge between heaven and earth. It is also thought to be the colours of the human soul. As we strive to build a bridge between the needs of our inner self and the demands of this busy world, a good colour balance can enhance our natural life force. With this in mind, Sun Essences has taken care to blend the colours of the flowers chosen, to create a rainbow in each bottle.

These flower essences support an inner radiance, so the soul colours can shine through and we can function more effectively in our daily lives.

An active member of the flower essence community in the UK, Vivien was Chairman of the British Flower and Vibrational Essence Association (BFVEA), and was editor of its Essence Journal. Her book *Bach Flower Remedies and Other Flower Essences* was published in 2000, and during that year Sun Essences was asked by Bioforce to supply the essences for the Jan De Vries range of flower essences. Living Essences and Be Blends are some of her ranges

The English Collection

Living Flower Essences (All individual essences made by Vivien Williamson and Jane Stevenson.)

Alkanet (*Pentaglottis sempervirens*) Calm in a storm. Alkanet can help you to keep your own inner sacred space centred and contained. It becomes easier to focus and communicate clearly, thus finding a way through challenging situations.

Autumn Leaves (All colours) Transition. Some people today find themselves living many lifetimes within their single lifespan, seemingly dying and being reborn to new circumstances, not unlike the cycles of nature. This can be a very challenging process. This essence eases the way through periods of profound personal change and may clarify anything that might be blocking the way.

Bluebells (Mixed Colours) (*Endymion non-scriptum*) Uplifting stillness. Bluebell is nature's panacea. Use whenever life seems full on and you are feeling overwhelmed, vulnerable and finding it difficult to cope with the pressure. Consider also when there is trauma, anxiety, or grief, or when feeling crowded, isolated and depressed by circumstances. Bluebell brings a balanced connection with the Higher Self, stillness and tranquillity.

Chalice Well Renewal. This essence is made with water from the Chalice Well, a red iron spring in Glastonbury. This ancient and deep source of water helps to dissolve imprints from the past. These old patterns can be quite aggressive, draining energy and taking a real hold. This essence brings renewal, unblocking channels of energy and bringing in new light. It is ideal when there is a need to rejuvenate in a natural way.

Copper Beech (*Fagus sylvatica*) Rooted and present. Copper Beech is indicated when you are feeling disorientated, panicky, scattered and unable to focus. There may also be times when you forget where you are or what you've done. These symptoms can drain confidence, as you feel anxious and out of control of your life. Such withdrawal of consciousness from reality, can be a habitual response to unpleasant life circumstances. Copper Beech helps you feel secure and rooted in yourself so nothing can throw you off centre. You will notice that it's pleasurable to be on life's journey, despite the challenges.

Dark Mullein (*Verbascum nigrum*) Supporting mental clarity. This essence is an ideal choice when a clear mind is desirable and there is taxing mental work to be done. It helps the body stay straighter and feel supported, which enhances consciousness and promotes high energy levels. Prevents heavy energies from the surrounding environment from draining or zapping energy, so an aid to vulnerable and sensitive types who need to keep functioning in intrusive situations i.e. busy offices, trains, planes etc.

Double Daffodil (*Golden Dukat*) Abundance. Double Daffodil can help those who have a rigid and constricted attitude and find it difficult to be expressive. It opens the heart to the rich abundance of life and allows in feelings of joy and happiness.

Elderflower (*Sambucus nigra*) Integration of the shadow side. Elderflower can help us come to terms with the dark side that is within us all. It gives a sense of protection as we face this fearful challenge and promotes a deeper understanding and acceptance of the self.

Eyebright (*Euphrasia nemorosa*) Clear sight. Eyebright is indicated when there is a need to live life through someone else, as it is easy to lose your sense of identity and way in life. This essence can bring a wider viewpoint and helps you to embrace new and independent opportunities in life.

Feverfew (*Tanacetum parthenium*) Flexibility. In quick-moving, challenging situations, this essence can help you to 'think on your feet', encouraging the quality of adaptable and flexible thinking. It's an ideal choice when travelling or moving house as it brings out strength and tenacity.

Jack By The Hedge (Hedge Garlic) (*Allaria petiolata*) Fragility. For sensitive, fragile and delicate individuals, easily run down. This essence is ideal when emotional pain e.g. grief, has weakened the constitution, leaving you feeling low. Jack can strengthen the heart, which can bring valuable support to the system's defences. Partners well with Ramsons.

Lady's Mantle (*Alchemilla vulgaris*) Honours the female side. This essence can help protect your sensitive, female side. Ideal for men struggling to be comfortable with their vulnerabilities and holding back emotions through fear. Whatever your sexuality, Lady's Mantle helps give more understanding and acceptance of the feminine aspect.

Lungwort (*Pulmonaria officinalis*) Energizes auric field. Lungwort opens the breath, and connects you more fully with the universal life force which can mend and revitalize your energetic body. This process is gentle and ideal for those of a delicate constitution who need strengthening.

Meadowsweet (*Filipendula ulmaris*) False persona. Meadowsweet is for those who tend to present a false, superficial front. They are usually popular, but their flattering ways are often a guise for control and an insurance that others will continue to like them. This essence helps them feel safe enough with who they are inside to be more genuine with others.

Mixed Poppy (*Papaver*) (various species) Restriction. This essence is indicated when you are restricted by life. Perhaps you are trapped in your head with many pressured thoughts, or you may be hemmed in by physical circumstances you can't change, e.g. elderly people in a home, so escape is not an option. With Poppy essence, pent-up pressure is dissipated and some sense of inner control within the self is regained, despite the situation. Also suggested for animals in kennels and people immobilized by various domestic or work-related circumstances.

Ramsons (Wild Garlic) (*Allium ursinum*) Cleansing and cooling. Ramsons can invigorate the body with an explosion of cleansing white light. If you feel congested, it can 'burn' off the dross and take strength where it is needed. It is helpful in reducing the effects of heat, as it can balance the four elements thus bringing harmony to the system. Ideal for people who become quickly dehydrated, or easily feel overheated.

Orange Hawkweed (*Pilosella auranti-acum*) Realization and rejuvenation. Orange Hawkweed throws off anything that is not 'of the self'. It stops things settling into the system, so can be used as a protection against psychic pollution, or the effects of trauma. It very effectively clears and recharges the system, so is an ideal choice when you are really 'stuck' with life or feeling very low or run down. It creates more inner space and brings an expansion of consciousness, filling the system with renewed energy and light, so is an aid to meditation. You begin to understand the

true self and get a more objective view on life.

Primrose (*Primula vulgaris*) Lightness to one's inner child. This essence is indicated when there is unexplained melancholy or deep sadness, which is often the sign of a repressed inner child. Primrose can gently nurture this crushed spirit bringing comfort, hope and release. It is as if you can start anew, pure, unblemished and refreshed to life.

Snowdrop (*Galanthus nivalis*) Purity. For frozen, numbed or locked-down emotions, perhaps due to past abuse, sometimes sexual. Snowdrop will help to cleanse and purify emotions and move you to a place where you can start again. It brings new light on situations and initiates forgiveness and trust. You can learn to be more open or creative, and connect to loving situations in a new way.

Trine Tree (*Carpinus betulus quercifolia*) Synthesis. A rare form of Hornbeam bearing 'leaves like the Oak' hence its Latin name. This tree can bring strength and endurance when struggling to harmonize opposing aspects of life. It helps you see how it's possible to give equal importance to the diverging needs of the body, mind and spirit, so is helpful during times of personal growth or crisis.

Viper's Bugloss (*Echium vulgare*) Balances loving forces. Viper's Bugloss helps to realign how love flows in the system. When this is out of balance, people may become the perpetrator or victim of manipulative patterns in an effort to get their needs met. This flower can help dissolve these stubborn and distorted patterns, thus helping the loving forces to flow more freely.

Wild Daffodil (*Narcissus pseudonarcissus*) Appreciation of talents. Wild Daffodil is indicated when your talents seem insignificant or do not appear to fit into society. This essence can help the recognition of their worth. Once they are used with this positive attitude, they can blossom and grow with abundance.

White Violet (*Viola odorata*) Acceptance of the spiritual self. This essence is indicated when there is a strong awareness of the spiritual side of life but through a fear of rejection, you deny this aspect of the self. White Violet brings feelings of self-acceptance, truth and trust, so it becomes safer to be open with others.

Yellow Archangel (*Lamiastrum galeobdolon*) Happy on your path. This essence is for when you lose spiritual direction, maybe through rushing to get somewhere or even arrogance. There can be an urge to keep up with everyone else, so maybe you pretend to be other than who you really are. This essence helps you to learn your lessons, and pay more attention to your Higher Self. You become content to move at your own pace, at peace with the self and happy to be where you are on your life journey.

Be Blends Sun Flower Essence

Hand-prepared, the Be Blends are easy to choose and simple to use and are nature's gentle way of soothing our minds and emotions from the various challenges of everyday living.

Be Balanced For when the system needs some tender loving care. This gentle blend eases anxiety, tension and frustration, thereby restoring balance during the natural cycles of life. Also brings essential vitality during times of change and is therefore an ideal choice for women.

Be Calm – The Crisis Blend. This blend of flowers is designed to bring ease during those times when much is demanded and there is extreme anxiety or pressure e.g. shows, interviews, tests or exams. It helps the mind and body relax, thus enabling the individual to feel focused, productive and in control. Use also for mishaps, unsettling news, the acute stages of bereavement etc. Take seven drops on the tongue or sip in water as often as required, the effect being cumulative.

Be Comforted This blend of flowers is designed specifically to comfort and ease the enduring pain of losing a treasured friend or family member. It gives support when moving through the wide range of emotions that are a natural part of the grieving process, such as anger, guilt, blame, sadness or despair. It enables you to come to terms with the loss in your own way, and in time brings hope of a new beginning.

Be Confident This blend of flowers is for those who lack confidence in their ability to achieve goals or perform as well as others. Also suggested for individuals who may have had disappointments or setbacks in life. This essence brings determination and self-belief while staying focused on the task in hand. If needed for a specific occasion, start at least two weeks prior to the event.

Be Courageous If you suffer from everyday anxieties or apprehensions, this blend of flowers helps reduce them to a manageable level, by enhancing feelings of courage and inner safety. They help you to forget the original cause of the problem, which is what often triggers the attack. For particularly difficult conditions these essences may be used to complement and support other treatments, as they stimulate inner strengths.

Be Decisive Ideal for those who worry about making the wrong choice and need to feel more decisive. This blend offers support during times of personal change, as it facilitates a letting go of the past and provides a stable inner centre from which to choose a way forward. If there are issues present that inhibit this progress e.g. extreme fear, these will come to light and can be dealt with appropriately.

Be Focused Lack concentration? Exams? Computer weary? Then this is the one for you. This blend of flowers helps to clear the head, improve motivation, stimulate creativity, and restore interest in daily tasks. If working under pressure, then this essence may be taken more frequently.

Be Free This blend is ideal for letting go of the things that control your life. Depending how serious these habits are, this blend of flowers may either be used on its own or in conjunction with other modalities. This blend supports a positive self-image and is particularly helpful when there has been a setback. It can also boost motivation and the drive to make progress each day.

Be Loving Ideal for dealing with everyday situations that call for greater love, forgiveness and acceptance i.e. relationships, children, at the work place. Particularly helpful when strong feelings emerge and there is a need to diffuse them and gain greater insight. Its effectiveness can be boosted if taken by partners/family members at the same time.

Be Positive Whatever the reason is for feeling down, hopeless, negative or discouraged, this blend of flowers will help you to lighten up and become more positive. Releases the need to focus on personal problems and helps create a new optimistic frame of mind. Life can become more enjoyable, bright and promising.

Be Relaxed A key blend for hectic modern living, so is ideal for those leading demanding lifestyles or with high-pressure jobs. This blend enables you to relax, unwind and feel more refreshed on all levels. It is then easier to enjoy increased focus and productivity in daily life.

Be Resistant This blend of flowers is designed to support the system at times when you might be feeling at a low ebb. Ideal for when you go down with everything that's around and it's hard to shake things off. Gives you a much needed lift, and if taken regularly, strengthens the system.

Be Restful Being unable to settle at night can be a frustrating downward cycle. This blend of flowers helps to overcome restlessness and supports the return of natural patterns, with improved quality of rest. Ideal for people who cannot switch off, and suggested for children who feel unsettled at night.

Be Vitalized Exhausted, no get up and go? Lack staying power? This blend of flowers is particularly useful when feeling drained after a period of overwork. When taken as part of a positive move towards a more holistic lifestyle, this essence will gradually recharge your batteries.

Habundia Shamanic Flower Essences

Shamans of many different spiritual traditions have been communicating with the spirits of flowers and plants in order to learn and understand their healing qualities for many generations.

Peter Aziz has been involved in shamanism for 37 years. He has trained in Pueblo Indian, Kahuna and Hungarian shamanism, is a trained ayahuascero, and has been in retreats in the jungle in which he learned to communicate with the plant spirits. These retreats usually involve eating only one plant, until the spirit of that plant comes to teach its secrets. He is also a qualified homeopath. He has been preparing flower essences since 1987. His inspiration originally came on one of his wilderness retreats, when the flower spirits told him how they wanted to be prepared. He only uses flowers that ask him to use them. They are taken and prepared in a sacred way, using songs taught by the plant spirits, and are thereby imbued with a great deal of power. Peter works as a healer, and has been teaching these shamanic skills for 18 years.

General Remedies

Alfalfa (*Medicago sativa*) Strengthens the root. Self-worth. For honouring and communicating your needs. Earthing.

Aloe Vera (*A. barbadensis*) Soothes emotional pain, shock and emotional traumas, new or old.

Apple (*Malus sylvestris*) Develops the heart. Giving and receiving. Generosity, trust, magnetism.

Artichoke (*Cynara scolymus*) For feelings of weakness, helplessness, impotence and emotional exhaustion, after devastating experiences or long, drawn-out emotionally painful situations.

Bramble (*Rubus*) Teaches us to approach love with respect.

Butterfly Orchid (*Oncidium papilio*) For speaking one's own truth, rather than impressions picked up from others. Clears the psychic gate. Strengthens the tongue and spine.

Chickweed (*Stellaria media*) Being happy with yourself, so you don't need to seek approval from others, and do not attract 'draining' relationships.

Comfrey (*Symphytum officinale*) For letting go of the past, and flowing with new impulses.

Cowslip (*Primula veris*) Strengthens the solar plexus and comforts and uplifts the emotions. For when you are feeling vulnerable.

Cyclamen (*Cyclamen Persicum*) For healing childhood deprivation.

Dandelion (*Taraxacum officinale*) Centring. Understanding one's emotions and the cause of one's reactions. Helps release hatred and resentment.

Date (*Phoenix dactylifera*) Strength of character and vital energy to complete goals.

Dock (*Arcitum Minus*) Quiets and calms. Lessens the ego and fears around one's vulnerability.

Figwort (*Scrophularia nodosa*) For overcoming judgement towards matter. For those who love material existence and see it as a vehicle for spirit.

Fleabane (*Inula dysenterica*) Provides the quiet vitality that allows one to build health. Gives immunity against parasites on many levels.

Ground Ivy (*Glechoma hederacea*) For rebuilding when you have given out too much.

Harebell (*Campanula rotundifolia*) Faith in oneself and one's own judgement. Guards against giving away power and authority to others.

Hedge Woundwort (*Stachys sylvatica*) For healing deep hurts and tapping a source of inner strength.

Honesty (*Lunaria annua*) Maintains peace and beauty amongst stressful surroundings.

Ivy (*Hedera helix*) Patience, strength, stability, rooting. Links one to the Earth Mother.

Jasmine (*Jasminum*) For finding peace, rest and recharging in the darkness. Overcomes fear of darkness, and judgement towards that which is dark in ourselves.

Lily of the Valley (*Convallaria magalis*) Safety, by enshrouding the negative tendencies of the subconscious mind that could draw in trouble.

Madonna Lily (*Lilium candidum*) Opens one to joy, and releases all shame and judgement towards one's sexuality.

Marigold (*Tagetes*) Vitality. A great catalyst in healing. For any difficult conditions which are taking much energy to heal.

Navelwort (*Umbilicus rupestris*) Security, safety, self-esteem. Heals the shock of the umbilical cord being cut too soon.

Papaya (*Carica papaya*) For those involved in therapy and self-discovery,

Papaya helps assimilate experiences faster, and brings out memories and deep feelings.

Rosemary (*Rosemarinus officinalis*) Brings clarity when there is great emotional stress, loss of trust or confusion.

St John's Wort (*Hyp. Perforatum*) Uplifts the emotional body, eases fears and nervousness, and aids calm, peaceful sleep. Good for nightmares.

Snowdrop (*Galanthus nivalis*) New hope. Helps one deal with rejection by finding nourishment within.

Solomon's Seal (*Polygonatum biflorum*) For disappointment. Restores courage, hope and the will to live.

Stonecrop (*Sedum*) Becoming really still inside, so that you grow more easily.

Sunflower (*Helianthus annuus*) True enthusiasm and balanced masculinity. For those who are disconnected from the feelings, stress and deprivation of others.

Sycamore (*Acer pseudoplatanus*) Increased flow of life force. Fertility on all levels.

Tansy (*Tanacetum vulgare*) Causes you to look at yourself and examine your motives, while providing some protection against outside influences.

Trefoil (*Trefolium*) Gives courage to shy, sensitive and nervous people. Also offers protection on the astral when breaking through into new dimensions.

Wayfaring Tree (*Viburnum lantana*) Cleansing and healing the sexual chakras.

Wild Rose (*Rosa* x *Pruhoniciana*) Bringing out the beauty of your wildness. Overcoming limited conditioning and beliefs. Love and appreciation of all life, including self.

Yarrow (*Achillea millefolium*) Strengthens the aura. Protection. Over-identification with other people's energy.

Yellow Iris (*Iris pseudacorus*) Understanding commitment in its true sense, i.e. keeping one's vision, and working towards it with constancy.

Yellow Poppy (*Eschscholzia californica*) Calms emotions and brings clarity of mind. Helps to memorize, synthesize and adapt.

Spiritual Remedies

Arrowhead (*Sagittaria sagittifolia*) Provides the urge to all spirituality, and realigns our dark urges.

Blackthorn (*Prunus spinosa*) Balancing beauty with power. Gives security in showing your inner beauty.

Bluebell (*Endymion non scriptum*) Trust in the source of all abundance. Joy, spontaneity, connection to Pan.

Cherry (*Prunus serrulata*) Overcomes fear of death. Trust in what is beyond material life.

Daffodil (*Narcissus pseudonarcissus*) Good for meditation. Enlivens the spirit, aids connection to one's Higher Self, and allows faster spiritual growth.

Edelweiss (*Leontopodium alpinum*) Opens the crown chakra and attunes us to the highest vibration we can reach. Brings trust in spirit, and helps us know our destiny and true will.

Elder (*Sambucus nigra*) Wisdom to rise above apparent opposites and encompass dualities. Overcomes judgement. Recognizing the importance of all things, each in its own place.

Laurel (*Prunus lusitanica*) Aspiration. Helps break through into higher dimensions.

Oxtongue (*Helminthia echioides*) Builds power and vitality within, while overcoming the urge to give it out too soon.

Pyramidal Orchid (*Anacamptis pyramidalis*) Develops a warrior spirit and urges us to follow our true will.

Scarlet Pimpernel (*Anagallis avensis*) Strengthens and nourishes the navel chakra and etheric body. Brings out resentments. Replenishes creative and sexual energy.

Spearmint (*Mentha spicata*) Opens one to take joy in receiving.

Spinach (*Spinacia oleracea*) Develops a higher octave of the heart chakra, to universal love. For growing out of repeated patterns.

Stinking Hellebore (*Helleborus foetidus*) For breaking out of conditioning and outer pressures to conform, while maintaining a strong, loving heart. Freedom and individuality.

Stinking Iris (*Iris foetidissima*) Withdrawing for spiritual transformation and vision. Makes you unreachable to those who drain you.

Thistle (*Cirsium vulgare*) Spiritual value. Trust in spirit. For maintaining one's spiritual integrity in spite of undermining company.

Tree Mallow (*Lavatera maritima*) Develops the spiritual heart chakra. Allows rapid growth through adversity.

Water Lily (*Nymphaeaceae***)** Provides a sense of space. For detachment, stability and safety, while providing inner nourishment.

Wild Garlic (*Allium ursinum*) Enhances one's projections of power in such a way that they are able to put a stop to any negative energies in their environment.

Wild Pansy (*Viola tricolor*) Develops a strong, loving warm heart. Heals traumas of love, and overcomes feelings of being undeserving.

Magical Remedies

Black Tulip (*Tulipa niger*) Clears the third eye. Brings clarity, perception, vision, and originality.

Black Hellebore (*Helleborus niger*) Re-establishes the barriers of the mind, and clears out invading energies from the mind.

Cuckoo Pint (*Arum maculatum*) Protects the spirit from invading entities, and quickly rebuilds vital energy when it has been lost. A great ally in soul retrieval.

Deadly Nightshade (*Atropa belladonna*) Powerful third-eye stimulant and psychic purge. Clears one from psychic interference. To be used as a single dose when required.

Dittany of Crete (*Origanum dictamnus*) Attunes one to positive astral forces, and opens one to help from the spirit world.

Early Purple Orchid (*Orchis mascula*) Makes one fully aware of one's desires, and one's ability to manifest those desires. Strengthens desire.

Enchanter's Nightshade (*Circaea lutetiana*) Acts on the unconscious, so that you draw towards yourself that which you need, particularly spiritual needs.

Four-Leafed Clover (*Trifolium*) The essence of magic. Expands awareness into new dimensions. Aids connection to nature spirits.

Five-Leafed Clover (*Trifolium*) The essence of the magical dynamic of fire. Will, direction, inner strength, purification. (Caution: this essence responds to your thoughts. Always take it with a clear intention in mind.)

Foxglove (*Digitalis purpurea*) Helps one let go of the material plane, of anxiety about one's material situation, or what is to come. Aids transition into other planes. Good for trance work, inner journeying, and astral projection.

Henbane (*Hyoscyamus niger*) For understanding death and exploring its realms. Prepares one for death initiations. Connecting with spirits of the dead.

Houndstongue (*Cynoglossum officinale*) Brings out hidden powers from the unconscious, releasing inhibitions and restricting dogma.

Ivy-Leafed Toadflax (*Cymbalaria Muralis*) Breaks down inertia on the astral that builds up through desire for power.

Larkspur (*Delphinium Consolida*) Strengthens and clears the aura, particularly the psychic gate. A good protection remedy, it produces a vibration that casts out psychic parasites and external forces.

Lemon (*Citrus limon*) Cleansing and renewal. Removes old, unwanted energies from the person.

Mandrake (*Atropa mandragora*) Connects one with that which is eternal and indestructible within them, and therefore builds confidence by overcoming the illusion of powerlessness.

Marjoram (*Oreganum marjorana*) Restores power, will, and the knowledge of who you truly are.

Mugwort (*Artemisia vulgaris*) Gives control of the astral plane, and trust in the unseen. Helps creative visualization and the positive use of dreams.

Periwinkle (*Vinca minor*) Prevents energy leakage and re-centres one after astral experiences. Focuses energy and prevents dissipation.

Penny Royal (*Mentha pulegium*) A powerful purifier. Activates the crown chakra, earths spiritual energies and unconditional love, and overcomes judgement.

Thornapple (*Datura stramonium*) A very initiating essence that should be taken with clear motivation. Helps movement between different planes of consciousness. Breaks limitations in the mind. Seeing beyond life and death.

Wolfsbane (*Aconitum napellus*) Control of power, and of one's mind. Strengthens visualization and will. Helps awaken latent psychic powers.

Yellow Archangel (*Lamium galeobdolon*) For understanding and accepting the balance of light and dark. Puts one in touch with hidden realms, and helps accept all that one may find in these planes.

Viper's Bugloss (*Echium vulgare*) Understanding primordial powers, and helping them evolve. Helps with the stresses that are due to the emergence of unconscious forces.

Wild Thyme (*Thymus serpyllum*) The essence of feminine power. Creativity, intuition, clairvoyance, and psychic power.

Deva Flower Elixirs

In France there exists a very strong tradition of healing with flowers and plants. The doctrine of signatures and principles of homeopathy are widely accepted due largely to the influence of healers such as Goethe and Paracelsus.

Deva Flower Elixirs were started by Philippe Deroide and Dominique Guillet after they had discovered the Flower Essence Society Essences (*see* page 197). The Deva Essences are made from the blossoms of flowers growing in the Alps and Mediterranean as well a Devas own biodynamic gardens. Only the healthiest flowering plants growing in unpolluted environments are chosen; the garden essences are prepared in creative gardens tended according to organic principles.

At the Gaia Institute (the Deva laboratories) homeopaths research the ways in which flower essences exert their benefits. Around 1,000 therapists contribute to this work where scientific methodology blends with the intuitive approach to glean information about the healing properties of flower essences.

Almond (*Prunus amygdalus*) For those who fear growing old. Strengthens and regenerates the physical body, joy of living, vitality. Helps us to accept the ageing processes and perceive the beauty beyond superficial physical appearances.

Angelica (*Angelica archangelica*) For emergency situations and each time we feel that our lives are at stake. Offers spiritual protection. Strengthens trust and reinforces resistance in difficult moments. Helps us to face the unknown.

Arnica (*Arnica montana*) To be taken after any physical, mental or emotional trauma. Regenerates and consoles. Repairs damages due to shocks or deep traumas. Re-establishes or maintains our contact with the Higher Self.

Basil (*Ocimum basilicum*) For those who fear and conceal their sexuality – especially when sexuality and spirituality are perceived as opposing forces. Brings sexual integration, helping us to harmonize our emotional and sexual desires with our spiritual worth. Eliminates conflicts of sexual or emotional origins within a relationship by helping us to understand their roots.

Blackberry (*Rubus fructicosus*) For those who cannot materialize their projects, who have difficulties putting their ideas into practice. Also for those hampered by inertia, lethargy and mental confusion. Helps us to overcome confused mental states and develop our hidden talents. Recommended to those who meditate, who practise creative visualization and who work on dreams.

Black-Eyed Susan (*Rudbeckier hirta*) For those who fear looking deeply within themselves and who resist all transformation processes. Aids understanding of hidden emotions and repressed aspects of the self, particularly when the mind censors or disassociates itself from certain aspects of the personality.

Bleeding Heart (*Dicentra spectabilis*) For those who go through a painful experience of separation: loss of a loved one, break-up of a relationship. Fosters the emergence of intense emotions which lie heavy on the heart. Brings harmony and detachment.

Borage (*Borago officinalis*) For depressive temperaments. Fosters courage and self-confidence. Helps us to overcome sorrow, sadness and discouragement when facing trials and danger.

Box (*Buxus sempervirens*) For those who lack will, who are shy, perhaps weak and let themselves become dominated by their nearest and dearest. Helps us develop individuality, detaching ourselves from the domination of others by bringing strength, courage and tenacity.

Buttercup (*Ranunculus acris*) For those who are shy and reserved and have doubts about themselves, who don't know how to appreciate their true worth and underestimate themselves. Brings open-mindedness and trust, and promotes self-esteem.

Calendula (*Calendula officinalis*) For those who listen only superficially and who are often hurtful in what they say. Brings receptivity and understanding beyond words, the real meaning of others' messages. Confers warmth, sensitivity and mellowness in all communications.

California Poppy (*Eschscholzia californica*) Particularly for those who focus on outer means of spiritual development rather than harmonizing with the inner source of spiritual experience. Encourages awakening and recognition of one's qualities and personal abilities. Helps us in our spiritual search by developing attention and inner listening. Safeguards against overfascination with spirituality.

Cayenne (*Capiscum annuum*) A powerful catalyst for overcoming inertia, indecision and immobilization. Develops willpower, brings motivation and enthusiasm. Triggers dynamic transformation when 'stuck' in situations so we can move forward.

Chamomile (*Matricaria recutita*) For nervousness, emotional instability and insomnia. Releases emotional tensions felt mainly in the stomach area. Good for hyperactive children prone to mood changes and to extreme emotional reactions.

Corn (*Zea Mays*) For those who live in an artificial environment and need to re-establish contact with the earth (city dwellers). Also for those who tend to shut themselves away when feeling hostile or alienated. Develops the harmonious and balanced relationship between one's social and natural environment.

Comfrey (*Symphytum officinale*) Strengthens and tones up the nervous system. Releases nervous tensions and improves memory. Develops conscious control of physiological processes and improves reflexes. Good for athletes.

Cosmos (*Cosmos bipinnatus*) Allows shy, introverted or hesitant people to express their ideas more clearly and easily, so they can express themselves with calm and composure when facing the public. Helpful for public speakers, actors and writers.

Daisy (*Bellis perennis*) Helps the mind to synthesize information coming from different sources and integrate them into a global perspective. Useful for those who must plan a project or organize an activity.

Dandelion (*Taraxacum officinales*) For those who do too much and need to learn to release their tensions. Frees muscular, mental and emotional tension. Fosters spiritual openness by relaxing the physical body. Advised for athletes and those doing body work such as masseuses.

Dill (*Anethum graveolens*) For those who feel overwhelmed by the pace of life. Helps us to face up to stress caused by excessive stimulation. Brings liveliness and clear thoughts. Promotes assimilation and understanding of complicated or unusual situations.

Eyebright (*Euphrasia officinale*) Helps healers develop perception of a patient's condition, and increases their sensitivity and intuition.

Fig Tree (*Ficus carica*) For coping with the complexity of modern life in a calm, assured manner. Encourages self-control. Develops mental clarity, confidence and memory. Frees hidden fears and helps in resolving relationship conflicts.

Fireweed (*Epilobium angustifolium*) Liberates tensions and worries caused by traumatizing events. A transformation catalyst which leads one towards a new progressive phase. Promotes regeneration and purification.

Forget-Me-Not (*Myosotis sylvatica*) Releases repressed tensions; stimulates memory, quick wit and insight. Develops our connection with the extrasensory spiritual world. Strengthens the mother-child bond during pregnancy.

Fuchsia (*Fuchsia hybrida*) For freeing deep feelings of anger and sorrow, or feelings linked to sexuality which lead to tension, psychosomatic problems or false emotionalism. An emotional catalyst that encourages the emergence, understanding and elimination of repressed emotions, which often stem from childhood.

Hawthorn May (*Crataegus oxyacantha*) Frees one from outer influences, especially those induced by emotional attachments. Relieves emotional stresses linked to relationship problems. Eases the pain and sorrow of separation. Brings inner freedom.

Hibiscus (*Hibiscus sabdariffa*) For women who have lost all contact with their sexuality. Allows the soul's warmth and feelings to permeate one's sexuality. Frees psychological blocks of sexual origin.

Iris (*Oros germanica*) For eliminating the frustration caused by a lack of inspiration or feelings of imperfection. Brings creative and artistic inspiration.

Lavender (*Lavendula officinalis*) For those whose nervous problems arise from having difficulties integrating spiritual steps to their daily life. A harmonizing essence for those subject to nervous tensions caused by excess stimulation. Brings purification, emotional equilibrium.

Lemon (*Citrus limonum*) Stimulates and lightens the intellect by pushing aside emotional interference and co-ordinating thoughts. Fosters analytical reasoning.

Lilac (*Syringia vulgaris*) For balancing the flow of energy in the back. Good for those who are fed up. Regenerates the spinal column, corrects posture and brings flexibility.

Linden (*Tilia platyphyllos*) Develops receptivity to love and imbues all communication and exchanges with respect and cordiality. Brings out qualities of protection, nourishing warmth, softness and calmness. Strengthens the relationship between mother and child.

Lotus (*Nelumbo nucifera*) A universal essence for all aspects of the human being. For blossoming and spiritual harmony. Dynamizes and amplifies other remedies. Encourages reception and spiritual openness. Harmonizes the soul forces and purifies the emotions.

Mallow (*Malva sylvestris*) For accepting the transformation processes that occur in life. For overcoming insecurity and introvertedness. Good for those who feel ill at ease socially. Eliminates tension and stress that arise from a fear of ageing. Develops trust and heartiness in shy people.

Martagon Lily (*Lilium martagon*) Recommended to women with fears linked to sexuality, as well as warlike, aggressive, dominating and authoritative individuals. Develops co-operation, solidarity and the ability to listen to others. Helps group work and the search for a joint success.

Morning Glory (*Ipomea purpurea*) For liberating oneself from harmful habits such as dependence on alcohol, coffee, tobacco. Balances vital strength and tones the nervous system. Regularizes the rhythms of daily life.

Mullein (*Verbascum thapsus*) For those in doubt about which moral values to follow. Encourages awareness of the 'inner voice'. Facilitates and promotes group work by creating unity and developing harmony.

Nasturtium (*Tropaeolum majus*) To be used during 'funny spells', such as when overloaded by work or in a pre-influenza state. Also for those who tend to over-indulge the intellect to the detriment of their physical wellbeing. Stimulates vitality.

Nettles (*Urtica dioica*) For resolving psychological problems encountered in perturbed homes. Relieves emotional stress and brings calmness and courage after a family split or break-up. Strengthens family unity.

Onion (*Allium cepa*) For women who have suffered domestic violence or sexual abuse. Eases the process of introspection and the emergence of repressed emotions in psychotherapy. For emotional liberation and 'letting go'.

Passion Flower (*Passiflora incarnata*) Frees physical tensions, allowing us to consider life's events calmly and serenely. Brings stability and eliminates emotional confusion. Opens us up to higher levels of consciousness. For spiritual balance.

Pennyroyal (*Mentha pulegium*) For those disturbed by others' negative thoughts. Reduces the mental confusion provoked by the ill will of others. For protection.

Peppermint (*Mentha piperita*) For those who tend to be dull-minded due to excess mental activity. Helps us to overcome mental laziness and psychic lethargy. Develops mental clarity and a quick wit; encourages active and awakened thought processes. Good for students and intellectuals.

Pink Yarrow (*Achillea millefolium*) For those who are too emotional or who identify with the emotions of others. Protects against emotional tension emitted from the surrounding environment. Reinforces the emotional structure of those who are oversensitive and easily influenced.

Pomegranate (*Punica granatum*) For emphasizing all the feminine qualities. Helps women to resolve conflicts whose origin is an imbalance between career and family life. Balances feminine creativity.

Quince (*Cydonia oblonga*) For women confronted with power conflicts who have difficulty integrating their outer ambitions – such as professional ambitions – with maternal love. Balances the feminine aspect of the personality.

Red Clover (*Trifolium pratense*) For keeping one's psychic equilibrium. Recommended in emergency situations such as disasters, conflicts. Allows us to remain calm and centred while facing fear, panic or the collective hysteria generated by certain groups or certain collective states of mind.

Rhododendron (*Rhododendron ferrugineum*) For those inclined to sadness, melancholy and discouragement when confronted with a difficult and harsh environment. Brings warmth, consolation and a sense of joy; encourages emotional liberation in the thoracic area (linked to breathing).

Rosemary (*Rosmarinus officinalis*) For those who are disorientated, prone to forgetfulness and drowsiness, find it difficult to be present in their body. Develops clarity of mind and sensitivity. Helpful for introverted and sullen temperaments. For inner peace.

Sage (*Salvia officinalis*) Promotes reflection on the meaning of life's events. Brings understanding, inner peace and consciousness of our spiritual dimension. Allows us to look more objectively at life's experiences.

Scarlet Monkeyflower (*Mimulus Cardinalis*) For those who repress powerful emotions linked to anger and aggressiveness, fearing a loss of self-control or the disapproval of others. Liberates these emotions, helping to resolve power struggles and angry situations in relationships. Frees the vitality that may be concealed by repressed negativity and resentment.

Scotch Broom (*Cystisis scoparius*) For pessimism, discouragement and despair. Helps us to consider life's hardships as opportunities for growth and evolution.

Brings tenacity and perseverance to those who are continually confronted by obstacles.

Self-Heal (*Prunella vulgaris*) A catalyst for inner healing and transformation, enabling us to develop our inner power of healing. Supports us when we are fasting or convalescing. Helps the body assimilate most nutritional substances. Good for those who try many therapies unsuccessfully.

Snapdragon (*Antirrhinum majus*) For those who find it difficult to express their feelings. Encourages us to give voice to our repressed emotions. Encourages verbal 'letting go' and the expression of truth.

Spruce (*Picea abies*) For those suffering from tenseness, austerity and coldness, who lack flexibility and refuse to make compromises or concessions. Brings grace and harmony.

Sticky Monkeyflower (*Mimulus auriantacus*) For integrating love and sexuality, discovering the sacred meaning of all life's aspects. Frees fears and resolves conflict or confusion linked to sexuality and intimacy. Balances out sexual energies.

St John's Wort (*Hypericum perforatum*) For children prone to restless dreams. Offers freedom from nightmares, nocturnal fears, night terrors, feelings of obscurity and the fear of death. For courage, protection and freedom.

Sunflower (*Helianthus annuus*) For resolving conflicts linked to parents or parental images. Balances the ego when it is excessive (vanity) or lacking (low self-esteem). Develops the harmonious expression of our spiritual nature, helping us to work in a creative manner. Encourages our individuality.

Sweet Corn (*Zea mays*) Balance. Balances out and energizes the individual in his/her relationship with the earth (vertical) and with other human beings (horizontal). Develops harmonious relationships with one's social and natural environment by bringing about love and understanding. This essence is advised for those living in an urban environment, especially those confronted by overpopulated environments. For those who tend to shut themselves up when feeling hostile and alienated. For those who live in an artificial environment and who need to re-establish a contact with the earth.

Valerian (*Valeriana officinalis*) To overcome insomnia, stress and nervous irritation. Brings tranquillity and peace.

Watermelon (*Citrullus vulgaris*) For birth: the development of a harmonious and correct attitude before, during and after conception in couples wishing to have a child. Eliminates emotional stress during pregnancy.

White Yarrow (*Achillea millefolium*) For those who feel too vulnerable and those who, through their professions, are confronted with the problems of others. Reinforces the energy structure of the individual and protects against disturbing environmental influences (radioactivity, electromagnetic and the electronic radiation of computers).

Wild Garlic (*Allium sativum*) For eliminating fear, anxiety, insecurity and nervousness. Releases tension around the solar plexus. Strengthens any part of us that is prone to repeated infections and to general weakness.

Zinnia (*Zinnia elegans*) Cheerfulness and joy. For those who are depressed, restless or hypersensitive and need to laugh. Helps us to accept that laughter is a very effective therapy. Releases tensions. Helps adults who have communication problems with their children to rediscover the child within them.

Zucchini (*Cucurbito pepo*) For a harmonious pregnancy: Helps pregnant women balance out their emotions and eliminate physical tensions. Generally stimulates and increases feminine creativity, especially when it has been smothered and repressed due to difficult social and cultural environments.

24 Complementary Essences

Alpine Lady's Mantle (*Alchemilla alpina*) Unconditional love, confidence, protection. For those suffering from, or who have suffered from, the lack of a bond with the mother, who are incapable of expressing tenderness towards their parents, family and those close to them, and who are in permanent need of love. Favours the letting go of repressed emotions. Helpful in rediscovering the capacity to love.

Amaranthus (*Amaranthus caudatus*) Going beyond one's limits. For situations of deep distress. Permits you to overcome feelings of devastation, hostility, solitude and rejection. Helps in confronting and coping with extreme suffering, the most total sense of desolation, hopeless situations in which there is no way out. Reinforces the organism when feeling under attack, weakened or off balance.

Apricot (*Prunus armeniaca*) Joy, plenitude. For intellectual temperaments, with multiple responsibilities, who are subject to rapid mood swings, who are not at ease in their bodies and who display a tendency to hyperglycemia. Helpful in overcoming mental and emotional tension. Facilitates the resolution of inner conflict.

Birch (*Betulus pendula*) Vitality and regeneration. Greater dynamism, revitalization. For overcoming sclerotic tendencies, related to ageing. Helpful for understanding the meaning of one's existence by going beyond rigid attitudes and behaviour

Bistort (*Polygonum bistorta*) Openness, self-control. For remaining faithful to one's own aspirations while recognizing and respecting those of others. Helps in overcoming feelings of disorientation, dispersion and lack of presence. For returning to one's centre. Strengthens those who do not have, or no longer have, their feet on the ground, particularly in times of great change.

Echinacea (*Echinacea purpurea*) Integrity and wholeness. Recommended when the dignity and moral integrity of the being are shattered by violent acts and situations. Helps in recovering one's profound identity through self-respect and self-esteem.

Elder (*Sambucus nigra*) Regeneration, purification, vitality. Helps in overcoming feelings of shame, of dirtiness or of imperfection. For dull temperaments, the withdrawn, submissive person lacking in vitality. For those who reject their body or hide behind false appearances. Recommended when one feels abandoned or filled with uncertainty. For moments when one feels at a loss, when one lacks self-esteem following a shock or a difficult event in one's life.

Eucalyptus (*Eucalyptus globulus*) Enthusiasm, faith in life. For overcoming melancholy, sadness and chagrin provoked by conflict in relationships or by unresolved emotional traumas that remain blocked in the respiratory sphere. Gives help in getting over past traumas and moving on.

Golden Yarrow (*Achillea filipendulina*) Openness, protection. For hypersensitive and vulnerable temperaments, who have a tendency to cut themselves off from the outside world to protect themselves. Favours the growth and development of the personality within an active social-life setting, while preserving individuality and sensitivity.

Greater Celandine (*Chelidonium majus*) Self-expression, exchange, openness. Facilitates communication, exchange and receptivity. For obtuse, obstinate temperaments that are closed in on themselves and have difficulty in communicating.

Hyssop (*Hyssopus officinalis*) Repentance, pardon. For getting over feelings of guilt when one is convinced of having done wrong. Allows one to understand and to go beyond the attitudes and behaviour patterns that are at the root of this guilt.

Jasmine (*Jasmine officinalis*) Purification, self-acceptance. For those who put themselves down, who have a negative image of themselves or who lack self-esteem. For feeling at ease with oneself and at home in the body. Favours the opening of the heart and the rediscovery of one's true spiritual identity. Eliminates toxins, real or imagined.

Lady's Mantle (*Alchemilla vulgaris*) Maternal consciousness, accomplished femininity. For women who reject their femininity in its maternal and nourishing aspects. Attenuates the effects of any shock concerning the genitals. Helps in overcoming feelings of loss, of need or emptiness associated with troubles in the area of reproduction. On another level, strengthens the connection with nature and the earth.

Lily of the Valley (*Convallaria majalis*) Innocence, spontaneity, freedom of action. For those whose lives are dictated by duties, obligations and social conventions. For those who seek the approval of others and are prisoners of external conditioning. For rebellious temperaments, ever on the defensive, who refuse conformity but find themselves dependent on outside conditions which do not correspond to their true nature. Recommended for adolescents who have left the world of childhood too abruptly and cannot find their place in the adult world.

Maple Tree (*Acer campestre*) Vitality, dynamism, fluidity. Favours the balancing out and circulation of energies. For those who feel immobilized, in periods of stagnation. Tones up and revitalizes the organism when energy is not flowing. Recommended in acupuncture.

Mimosa (*Acacia dealbata*) Openness, empathy. For timid temperaments, introverts, independent people who turn in on themselves and cut themselves off from others. Facilitates opening up to others and the world. A flower essence recommended in periods of discouragement and depression, in moments of solitude, when one feels abandoned.

Orange Tree (*Citrus sinensis*) Emotional release. A powerful catalyst used to favour emotional catharsis. Liberates emotional tensions and helps in coping with conflicts related to them. Apeases frazzled emotions.

Pansy (*Viola tricolor*) Interior strength, resistance. For those who feel vulnerable, who lack strength and are subject to repeated infections. Strengthens and protects the organism.

Peach (*Prunus persica*) Altruism, letting go. A healing catalyst that facilitates the liberation of tensions. For those who are overconcerned with their problems and are unable to open up to others and the world. Recommended for external application.

Pear Tree (*Pyrus communis*) Balance, bodily ease. Helps to recentre after all situations of imbalance. Brings balance to the spinal column and favours the alignment of the body in its vertical axis.

Petunia (*Petunia hybrid*) Mental clarity, enthusiasm. For those who lack enthusiasm or are, on the contrary, too exuberant and dispersed in what they are doing to reach a determined goal. Helps for examining priorities, eliminating the superfluous, looking at the essential and getting straight to the point.

Pimpernel (*Anagallis arvensis*) Self-affirmation. For problems related to authority and the father image. For those who have difficulty in taking part, getting involved in the action, and lack willpower.

Tabacum (*Nicotiana tabacum*) Opening of the heart. For nervous temperaments, dry and tense people who have lost all heart connection with their environment. For loss of sensitivity, emotional coldness. For overcoming the mechanistic tendencies of the modern world.

Tansy (*Tanacetum vulgare*) Decisiveness, action. For undecided, slow and apathetic temperaments, who refuse to take action, refusing to get on with things, always putting things off until later, afraid of constraints, of getting involved, and wanting to be left in peace.

Wild Carrot (*Daucus carota*) Perspicacity, sensitivity. Favours the awakening of clairvoyance and parapsychic qualities. For those who are over-mental or over-emotional and do not allow the other psychic faculties to develop.

Wild Cherry (*Prunus avium*) Gaiety, good humour. For pessimistic and gloomy temperaments who see only the negative side of things. For developing a serene and optimistic view of life.

Wood Betony (*Stachys officinalis*) Harmonious sexuality. Helps to resolve inner conflict related to sexuality. Brings balance to sexual expression when it is perturbed (excessive sexual activity, degrading sexual practices). For overcoming compulsive needs provoked by sexual fantasies and desire.

Wood Violet (*Tanacetum vulgare*) Healthy sensitivity. For timid, vulnerable and self-effacing temperaments who like solitude. Cold and reserved in appearance, they are afraid of being exposed and have difficulty in opening up to others. Helps them to communicate and overcome excess.

Combination Essences

Also available as 10 and 30ml sprays. All combination essence bottles and sprays (except 'Assistance') are only available upon request, please note.

Assistance (also available as a cream) Contains the 5 essences that comprise Bach's 'Rescue Remedy' plus Lotus

Positive outcome: Assistance, balance, stability, regeneration.

Patterns of imbalance: Emergencies, crisis situations, shock. A basic combination for use in all crisis situations, in moments of great tension and for getting over hardships of all sorts. Used for remaining calm and collected and for keeping a cool head when confronted with difficulties, it can also be used in a preventive way when some sort of stressful event is expected, to deal with apprehension, fear of losing control or feeling lost and confused, (exams, unusual situations…) (This combination formula is not intended to be used over a long period.)

Physical Ease

Positive outcome: Vigour, suppleness, litheness and ease, gracefulness, psycho-physical harmony.

Patterns of imbalance: Physical and emotional tension. This combination formula is recommended for sportsmen and people who do strenuous physical activity. Taken before and after physical exertions it keeps the body supple and lithe, and the muscles relaxed. It improves co-ordination between the mind and body helping to prepare for action, and favours recovery after strenuous activity. This formula is also recommended for hyperactive people, who tend to do too much, stretching their physical capacities to the limit.

Protection

Positive outcome: Protection, well-adjusted openness to others and balanced sensitivity.

Patterns of imbalance: Vulnerability, fragility, negative influence. This combination formula is recommended for those who feel vulnerable to others and their surroundings. It provides protection from disturbing influences present in the environment. These can be psychic (negative thoughts and intentions) or physical (radioactivity, electric and electro-magnetic pollution, computers). For sensitive people, the easily influenced, those with emotive temperaments who tend to identify too easily with their surroundings. For the extremely sensitive person who tends to withdraw and turn in on himself, it provides protection from negativity in the environment and assistance in overcoming feelings of insecurity.

Balanced sexuality

Positive outcome: Brings balance to emotional life and the heart, healthy and harmonious sexuality.

Patterns of imbalance: Sexual troubles. Brings the emotional life and sexuality into harmony. Makes it easier to express deep feelings and develop an honest appraisal of one's love life. This formula is recommended when there is difficulty in expressing sexuality in a harmonious way, when it becomes predominant to the detriment of other values or is the cause of conflict in a relationship. Brings about a harmonious blending of loving feelings with physical passion, and gives warmth and vitality to sexual expression.

Self Balance

Positive outcome: Spiritual resource, inner peace, groundedness.

Patterns of imbalance: Overwhelmed, stress of city life, disorientation. This formula is recommended for those who live in a difficult environment and suffer because of it. It is for those who have the feeling of being strangers on this earth, for getting back in touch with one's roots and finding inner stability. By helping the soul to express its spiritual nature it makes us aware we can overcome the limitations of the physical world. Used for the stress of city life (sensorial overload caused by too many stimuli, noises, sights; the impression of being imprisoned in crowded places).

Peaceful Sleep

Positive outcome: Calm, relaxation, restful sleep.

Patterns of imbalance: Insomnia, nervousness, mental agitation. This combination formula is recommended for calming children and adults alike when they are unable to relax, have difficulty in getting to sleep or have restless nights (nightmares, disturbed sleep…). Children who tend to have mood swings and extreme emotional reactions, become peaceful and relaxed with this combination formula. It is also recommended for people with hyperactive temperaments who find it hard to wind down at the end of the day, as well as for those whose minds are full of repetitive thoughts or constant worry.

Studies And Tests

Positive outcome: Attention, concentration, creativity, ability to synthesize

Patterns of imbalance: Difficulties in expression and concentration To optimise the intellectual abilities and facilitate verbal expression. Develop intellectual sharpness and the ability to synthesize by favouring global understanding and avoiding focus on details. Helps overcome mental lethargy and express thoughts clearly and with coherence. To arouse creative potential and integrate the learning processes. For research, studies, exam periods, teaching and writing. Recommended for students, researchers, speakers.

Family Unit

Positive outcome: Listening, understanding, fellowship.

Patterns of imbalance: Rejection, lack of understanding, stress and conflict. Strengthens the family unit. Develops emotional bonds. Favours communication, understanding and the expression of deep feelings within a group or family. Helps overcome emotional disorders related to transgenerational conflicts, as well as the resulting suffering and confusion. Favours the understanding and resolution of negative family conditioning that parasitizes community life. Complex recommended when everyday situations tend to create barriers between family or group members.

Pregnancy

Positive outcome: Emotional balance, confidence, vitality, receptivity.

Patterns of imbalance: Hypersensibility, vulnerability, uneasiness. Helps the pregnant woman both physically and emotionally by balancing the emotions and eliminating physical stress. Reduces nausea and soothes gastric disorders. Helps overcome nervous stress and hypersensitivity. Reinforces the bonds with the baby before its born. Facilitates the arousal of maternal qualities and develops confidence in the ability to be a mother.

Evolution

Positive outcome: Courage, clarity, commitment, determination, letting go.

Patterns of imbalance: Inertia, being prisoner of the past, inability to move forward. A complex for periods of change, transformation and self-questioning, when it is necessary to give up old habits in life and behaviour that is not adapted to the present situation and that does not have any reason to continue. Complex recommended in all phase of minor or major transition: moving, change of social environment, change in career, break-ups. To free oneself from past emotional bonds that prevent moving forward. Help remain centred in periods of major change and look towards the future with courage and confidence. Stirs up the will for change and to not remain bogged down in inertia and inaction. To follow one's road outside of all external influence. Recommended when one wants to become free of a self-image that is false and conveyed by others.

Maturity

Positive outcome: Vitality, joy of living, perspective.

Patterns of imbalance: Fear of ageing, loss of interest, stagnation, lack of satisfaction Helps get some distance from life's experiences and develop new meaning. For those who feel that life is behind them and who are feeling bitter, harsh, weary and discouraged. Revitalizes and helps overcome the sclerotic tendencies of age. To overcome the fear of ageing or seeing oneself age. Helps break habits that prevent evolution. Facilitates the passage of menopause and helps women go through this period like a healthy and positive transition.

Adolescence

Positive outcome: Will, enthusiasm, affirmation and self-acceptance.

Patterns of imbalance: Self-withdrawal, rejection of others, feeling of isolation and lack of understanding, lack of satisfaction, apathy, immaturity. This complex helps overcome adolescent identity crisis. For those who don't feel comfortable with themselves. To harmoniously integrate sexual identity. To positively affirm one's individuality and defend ones ideas when confronted with family, social and cultural pressures. To avoid letting the adolescent withdraw into illusory experiences that weaken the will (drugs, abuse of passive situations). For those who are confused as to their future and who still have not found a direction in their life. Frees the creative potential of the individual.

Early Childhood
Positive outcome: Openness, self-esteem, social enthusiasm, creativity.

Patterns of imbalance: Feeling of abandonment, self withdrawal, lack of self-

confidence, timidity or aggressiveness. A complex to facilitate the learning of social skills and encourage the child to open up to the world. To develop harmonious relations with the environment, whether within or outside the family unit. Balances the mother-child relationship. Stimulates the affective warmth and favours tenderness between the child and those around him/her. Develops the spirit of companionship and helps overcome the fear of others. Favours balanced self-esteem. Preserves and encourages spontaneous artistic creativity in the child, especially when the social or environmental context tends to stifle creativity. Recommended in situations of ill-treatment and abandon.

Bloesem Flower Essences of the Netherlands

Water forms a large part of the Netherlands because much as the land has been reclaimed from the sea, so the landmass is laced with waterways. Apart from the cleansing aspect, water has a profound connection with the emotions. The Bloesem essences are made from wild and organic plants, which address issues that living in this water-based environment creates.

Bram and Miep Zaalbergís founded these remedies in 1986 and now produce some 47 essences, a selection of which are included in the repertoire offering some of the first mushroom essences.

Alternanthera (*Alternanthera dentate*) Centred feelings, without fear of expression. Staying centred, undisturbed by people or their issues. To do the work you believe in and bring your higher truth into reality and expand it. Give full expression to what is. For those times when you feel like you come from another planet. To find your direction and life purpose. Self-confidence.

Angelica (*Angelica archangelica*) Protection and help from the spiritual worlds for development. Gives spiritual protection during pregnancy, birth and dying. Stimulates trust in the Higher Self, and reaching beyond your boundaries.

Borage (*Borago officinalis*) Strengthens the heart in difficult circumstances, bringing gladness and joy. Helps with difficulties or discouragement and when you lose faith, it brings strength to the heart. Helps you with spiritual contact so you can receive support. Helpful when you cannot get pregnant, because you cannot meet the unborn spirit.

Evening Primrose (*Oenothera lamarckiana*) This night-blooming flower strengthens the creative forces of the moon. Helps you to rediscover and connect with the source of your self-confidence, beauty and the inner feminine (in both sexes). Gives insight in the old, unknown areas of darkness, such as incest, abuse and problems with sexuality. Helps to solve these problems and brings them into the open.

Foxglove (*Digitalis purpurea*) Eases the mental processes, helps contact the heart. Releases mental structures and behaviour patterns, especially from past lives. To return to the Higher Self as the centre and source of love in your life. Brings playfulness, joy and pleasure in sexuality. Balances the polarities of the Higher Self and the earth.

Ground Ivy (*Glechoma hederacea*) Clears away old emotions, makes you aware of behaviour patterns. For abundance, strength and expansion and a good connection with the earth. Use for personal development, brings out the finer qualities of your being. Gives self-trust and self-confidence.

Motherwort (*Leonurus cardiaca*) The Motherwort flower essence works on family patterns. Helps those who don't feel at home in their family and on the earth. For lack of warmth and love in the family, resulting in becoming hardened, rigid and feeling like a stranger on the earth. Motherwort essence brings its softness and helps you to stay open to the love and support of family and friends in the here and now.

Mycena (*Mycena polygramma*) A mushroom remedy. For a strong and well-grounded connection with the earth. To go forward despite difficult situations, especially when everything around you seems to be in chaos. Mushrooms are good cleansers and help your body to eliminate forgotten emotions, especially everything that is hard to digest and Pluto-related problems.

Peppermint (*Mentha piperita*) For difficult and challenging times. Helps you to digest the problems in your life, and the deep emotions and problems you see in the world around you. Strengthens you and prepares you for many eventualities and difficulties. Gives insight into behaviour

patterns and structures held since birth. Makes you awake and alert. Particularly helpful for emotions and energies which have been accumulated in the area of the stomach and the digestive system.

Purple Flower (*Centratherum punctatum*) Brings light into the energy around the head, allows the mind to relax. Heightens awareness in healing; gives you trust in your work as a healer and bring this out into the world. Reflects the light of your being into the different kingdoms (animal, mineral, plant and human); opens for the power of nature, and for the insight and awareness of your environment.

Red Helleborine Orchid (*Cephalanthera rubra*) Strength in all circumstances. Helps you to find and follow your own path. Opens you to 'higher' energies and healing, when you are unsure about the path of becoming a healer. Connects healers with their Higher Selves when they feel depleted.

Red Henbit (*Lamium purpureum*) Strong earthly bonds and joy in physical activity. Gives clarity in chaotic activities; stimulates organizing with joy: moving, bookkeeping, studying. When you are stuck in chaos, disease, habits or too much work. Strengthens your energy. Apply topically for blockages in the wrists and joints. Promotes self-expression and activity.

Red Poppy (*Papaver rhoeas*) Strengthens the inner woman and the earth connection. A warming and empowering essence when you feel vulnerable as a woman. Increases the inner quality of warmth and love. Supports disturbances like moving, abuse, calamities, and disaster. Calms extreme sexuality (in men and women). Good results for all female problems (from menarche until menopause), as well as insomnia.

Rue (*Ruta graveolens*) Spiritual protection in the psychic realms. Helpful for psychic attack or energy stealing. Especially helpful when this is being done in the area of the crown chakra and the line of connection with the Higher Self. Brings insight in old, deep-hidden, and unknown fears. Gives more strength to act from your intuition. Cleanses old physical problems stored in the body.

Smooth Hawksbeard (*Crepis capillaries*) Balance between action and rest. Brings new energy and vitality, softens rigid structures. For feeling at ease with others. Clears childhood emotions. Helps recharge energy and store it in the bones.

Sneezewort (*Achillea ptarmica*) Gives protection on the spiritual path. To follow your direction, physical and spiritual with certainty and without the need to ask others. To strive for your own highest standards and values and to express these. For taking your own decisions and still being open for the help and advice of others, without getting distracted.

Snowdrop (*Galanthus nivalis*) Releases deep pain and trauma, especially when it originates from not being true to yourself. Can bring some tears. To renew the beauty and importance of the self. Brings a strong sense of trust, and joyful and refreshing new energy after a long dark (emotional) winter.

Sunflower (*Helianthus tuberosus*) This perennial sunflower works on the father principle, both in men and women. The essence helps you stand up for yourself, restores the connection with the father and helps to release long-standing father problems. Strengthens and empowers the solar plexus renewing the connection with the light or sun as centre of your life. Helps with the manifestation of your dreams. Gives strength, vitality and energy. Allows you to do what you always wanted to do with joy and encourages you to stand up for yourself. Dispels limitations imposed by others.

Tansy (*Tanacetum vulgare*) Use for doubt and the inability to make decisions; brings the insight that indecision will result in stagnation. Tansy brings trust and helps to connect you with your Higher Self. Strengthens the heart and gives insight into the deepest core of doubts on all levels of being.

Yellow Star Tulip (*Calochortus monophyllus*) For sensitive people who are not sure about their feelings. Connects you with the truth of your heart. For starting projects that you have been aware of for some time, but not initiated. Brings insight into your feelings connects you with the inner goddess. Gives trust in all changes and stimulates you to act from your Highest Self.

Special Combinations of Flower Essences

4 Elements *Burdock, Impatiens, Stinging Nettle, and Tansy*. Allows openness and warmth towards others, while still being yourself. The contact with your soul and the purpose of your soul becomes clearer. Releases hindrances to your evolution, and helps you stay in your own power and accept others as they are. Gives a feeling of freedom, joy and openness.

Animal Freedom *Mycena, Red Henbit, Snowdrop, Trumpet Vine, Alternanthera, Rue, Smooth Hawksbeard, Foxglove, Clematis, Sensitive Weed*. Helps to free the soul of animals, releasing problems and sufferings animals have taken over from their owner, as well as suffering that the animal has received from humans, both on a conscious and a subconscious level. Many problems they experience are from absorbing their owner's tension and stress. Gives the animal a sense of freedom, calmness and ease, connects it to its original strength, so that it can live its original purpose. For humans the essence has shown good results in situations of epileptic attack, also restores the disturbances of old (sexual) abuse. Good to use after the death of your pet, helping to keep the connection.

Cell Phone Combination *Mycena, Terra, Impatiens*. To protect against the radiation emitted from cell phones. Hold the essence near the phone when you are using it, also drop the essence on the side of your head in the area you hold the phone. If you already have a pain in your head because of overuse of the phone, put a drop on the painful spot several times a day. Also good for those sensitive to electricity and those who work with computers a lot. One drop of the cell phone combination, on a clear quartz to protect you from disturbing electrical and negative frequencies.

Emergency Combination *Angelica, Clematis, Mycena, Red Helleborine and Yellow Star Tulip.* A first-aid remedy for all complaints. First it clears blockages then helps with recovery. Brings peace and calmness in tense situations. Opens the solar plexus. Gives strength in difficult times. Helps with exams, fears, accidents, shock, trauma, moodswings. Recommended use: 2–5 drops straight from the stock bottle under the tongue and/or hold the bottle during prolonged periods of tension. Can be applied locally on the specific area.

Integration Combination *Combination of two mushrooms: Stropharia and Psathyrella candolleana, Angel's Trumpet, Hollyhocks, Impatiens and Pumpkin.* A remedy for integration, protection and the resolution of old emotions which have not been integrated. It helps you to let go of the old and gives insight into how the problem originated. This can be related to past relationships or past misfortunes and abuse. For all situations in which you have been hurt or offended and have lost control over your life. Re-establishes the link to the Higher Self, integrating the various recovery processes and giving protection and confidence.

Living Star Light The Living Star Light is neither a combination nor a flower essence, but a cosmic essence. This essence connects you to the stars. It is an essence from a five-pointed star, with three points directed horizontally, one point directed

down and one point directed up. The essence gives relaxation and releases everything that is not part of your being. It helps you to find wholeness on earth and then deepens the connection of your being with the earth and with the cosmic energies.

Protection *Sneezewort, Greater Celandine, Rue and Sensitive Weed.* Gives spiritual and emotional protection. Brings calmness to the centre of your being when there is tension, stress and uncertainty. Protects against all attacks on all levels. Surrounds and protects with a mantle of light.

Rainbow *Borage, Impatiens, Money plant, Red Henbit and Poppy.* The bridge between heaven and earth; a combination essence for personal development. Stimulates creativity, development and new activities. To start the new directly and forget the old. Opens and helps to overcome barriers that block your development; brings awareness to the process of growth.

The Spiritual Path *Borage, California Poppy and Trumpet Vine.* Helps to find your spiritual direction, particularly when choices were not made from a spiritual point of view and when the material world and material things have become the most important aspects of your life. This combination starts to change the choices you have made in the past and gives you the insight that there is no material world without a spiritual world.

Terra Extra (Emergency Combination) *Angelica, Clematis, Coprinus auricomus mushroom, Red Helleborine and Yellow Star Tulip.* A combination that deals with severe problems for all situations. For those who cannot release their emotions; for those who worry constantly. For excessive stress, Terra Extra helps you to breathe again and makes it possible to move forward in life.

India

India has a very rich floral heritage. The country boasts wide variations in climate, from the icy north to the tropical south, which support the growth of a great variety of flowering plants. In India, flowers are traditionally associated with various deities and with ceremonies, pujas, prayers and other occasions. There are also mythological stories regarding various flowers, clearly indicating the effect of flowers on day-to-day life. Flowers still have a role to play in Ayurvedic medicine, a tradition of healing the principles of which date back at least 2,000 years. Regarded throughout the world as one of the most spiritual of flowers, the Lotus is India's national flower.

The Himalayan Mountains in particular exhibit a spectacular floral show every year. Here the land is still relatively unpolluted and uncorrupted by human activity. It pulses with a vibrancy and life force that is fast fading elsewhere on this planet. Each year the peaks grow a few centimetres, a tell-tale sign of the tremendous upward thrust generated from deep within the earth. Pilgrims have traditionally journeyed to the Himalayas to meditate and seek enlightenment. Many sages of old lived in the Himalayas, while others (including the famous Chinese philosopher Lao Tzu) travelled there to end their days having reached a higher state of consciousness, knowing that their final impressions or images of earth were these eternally snowy peaks. Reaching through the clouds towards the heavens, the Himalayas symbolize the peak of consciousness and the flowers that grow here reflect the extraordinary energies of this land.

Himalayan Aditi Flower Essences

Aditi is the Sanskrit word for 'Earth'. It is also the spiritual name given to the white Lotus flower, representing divine consciousness. For this reason Drs Atul and Rupa Shah chose Aditi as the name for their collection of flower essences.
This husband and wife team are both allopathic doctors who became increasingly interested in complementary medicine. They researched various different therapies before they came across the Bach Flower Remedies. Impressed by the results they achieved with the Bach Remedies, they were prompted to prepare remedies from flowers growing wild on the slopes of the Himalayas and from

other particularly verdant spots in this colourful country.

The Shahs have invented a method of preparing essences *in situ*, so that they can avoid cutting the flowers' stems. This technique involves placing a glass bulb around a flower and pouring water through it. With the intervention of sunlight they have their 'mother tincture'. They try to determine the most auspicious time to do their work and always pray first for permission to collect the essences. The essences are preserved in Ganges water (from the source) as well as brandy. Aware that some people are unable to tolerate alcohol, they are currently looking into making essences with honey.

At their two health centres, where both orthodox and complementary methods work in synergy, the Shahs carry out in-depth research into the properties of their essences. Medical techniques such as X-rays, cardiograms and blood tests are employed to assess the benefits flower essences are bringing to their patients. The Shahs claim to have had much success in treating a broad spectrum of health problems related to stress and tension including infertility, hypertension, breast cancer and arthritis using their own essences as well as others from around the world.

Ashoka Tree (*Saraca Indica*) For those who have gone through great trauma such as a bereavement, disease or failure and are suffering from deep-seated sorrow, sadness, grief, isolation and disharmony. Brings a profound inner state of joy, harmony and wellbeing. Especially good for elderly people.

Bougainvillea (*Bougainvillea glabra*) For evoking meditation when we need to reaffirm our connection with our higher spiritual destiny when anxiety, fear or mediocrity swamp us. Rekindles enthusiasm, interest and emotional well-being, promoting our sense of the sacred in life.

Butterfly Lily (*Hedychium coronarium*) For those who exercise great power over people in an evil or negative way. For seeing clearly what has been done, wishing to be forgiven and making amends. Brings true remorse for wrong-doing, and inner peace.

Cannonball Tree (*Couroupita guianensis*) For overcoming frigidity in women caused by deep fears in the mind concerning sexual expression. To use in sexual therapy for women when a strong desire to conceive is blocked by inexplicable frigidity.

Christ's Thorn (*Ziziphus spina-christi*) For those in a constant state of internal turmoil for no obvious reasons. Relieves the state of negativity in the psyche and resolves conflicts from the consciousness. A redemptive essence.

Curry Leaf (*Murraya koenigii*) For healing ulcers and hyperacidity caused by mental tension and an imbalanced diet (which may include a lot of meat and alcohol). Produces greater relaxation as well as a balanced awareness and concern about diet and lifestyle.

Day-Blooming Jessamine (*Cestrum diurnum*) For those going through great suffering from painful, debilitating diseases. Brings acceptance and transformation of suffering into positive love, kindness and sensitivity to others. Relieves the burden of fear, nightmares and pain.

Drum Stick (*Moringa Oleifera*) For dispelling bitterness, resentment and other pains by building up positive feelings. Also for reducing the desire to smoke and resolving difficult emotions. Good for bronchitis.

Goldenrod (*Solidago virgaurea*) For those who feel insecure and seek negative attention from others in social situations by being naughty, bad or repulsive. Brings real humility, love and mental realism about others and our relationship with them. Eases internal emotional disharmony.

Gulmohar (*Delonix regia*) Spiritual healing for those who have committed acts of sexually-related violence in past lives. Restores deep peace and harmony, letting the sexual energy flow so lovemaking becomes fulfilling once more.

Indian Coral (*Erythrina Indica*) For bureaucrats and those holding positions of power over society who are self-interested, power-seeking, generally arrogant and insensitive. Brings a transformation of consciousness for those wielding political power and gives them wisdom, enlightenment, understanding and peace. Dissolves the blockages of selfishness and impure intentions.

Indian Mulberry (*Morinda citrifolia*) For groups of people in conflict who are antagonistic and hate one another. Alleviates long-held prejudices, hatred and deep disharmony. Good for dealing with the legacy of negative patriotism and social conflict. Brings reconciliation.

Ixora (*Ixora coccinea*) Relationship enhancer for couples lacking direction or suffering a loss of interest and vitality in their sexual energy. Revitalizes and enhances sexual energy and activity. Enhances and brings responsibility, wisdom, calmness and balance into sexual expression.

Karvi (*Strobilanthes callosus*) For changing distorted attitudes towards sex and the expression of sexuality. For problems of sexual performance, or seeing sex as purely for financial gain. Guides us away from pornography and selfish sexual gratification towards more loving, sensitive and equal sexual relationships and practices. Helps with the problems of frigidity or impotence.

Lotus (*Nelumbo nucifera*) A spiritual elixir and aid to meditation. Calms the mind and improves concentration. Gently releases negative emotions, correcting imbalances. Hastens recovery from illness. Aligns and balances the chakras by releasing, adding and directing energies to them. Clears the entire system of toxins. Balances, cleanses and strengthens the aura. Harmonizes interpersonal relationships. Amplifies the effect of other flower essences when used in combination with them.

Malabar Nut Flower (*Adhatoda vasica*) For those who feel superior to others because of nationality or class. Deals with prejudice, deep-seated pride and snobbery. Enhances love and tolerance and understanding of others.

Meenalih For religious or self-righteous people who repress their sexuality, feeling it is wrong or sinful. For impotence caused by guilt about one's body and the pleasure that sexual urges bring. Transforms old fearful attitudes of guilt. Teaches us that true virtue lies in real love, which embraces everything, and that we have the right to a pleasurable and enjoyable sex life.

Morning Glory (*Ipomoea violacea*) For addiction to opiates and nicotine, benefiting those trying to give up drugs at any stage of treatment. Eases nervous discomfort and physical withdrawal symptoms.

Neem (*Azadirachta indica*) Essence of the heart. For bringing overly cerebral people into their hearts, making them more loving, intuitive, understanding and giving, and less judgemental.

Night Jasmine (Newara) (*Jasmine arborescens*) For those who find it difficult to make love successfully. Can be used to foster long-term synchronization between two people or as an instant tonic prior to lovemaking. A sexual enhancer for attuning and integrating lovers' sexual energies.

Produces the state of real pleasure, fulfilment and ecstasy in lovemaking. Revitalizes sexual relationships when taken by both partners.

Nilgiri Longy/St John's Lily/Cape Lily (*Crinum Latifolium*) Specifically for teachers and professionals who are too strict and rigid with students. Helps teachers to make learning more creative and fun.

Office Flower (*Portulaca grandiflora*) For those who work in modern, high-tech offices sitting in front of video display screens the whole day, resulting in mental and nervous stress, frustration and associated skin problems.

Old Maid (Pink) (*Vinca alba*) For women who are too promiscuous as a result of mistaken attitudes towards sex, seeing men as playthings for their own sexual gratification and ego, neglecting love and responsibility in sex. For women who have become brutal and insensitive towards men after being used or abused. Brings a loving, caring attitude towards sex and lovemaking.

Old Maid (White) (*Vinca alba*) For men who are too promiscuous through mistaken attitudes towards sex. Helps men change egotistical, self-centred, insensitive attitudes which make them emphasize their own pleasure above all else. Promotes love, caring and greater control over sexual urges. Stimulates deep concern about a partner's experience of the quality of the shared relationship.

Pagoda Tree (*Plumeria alba*) For those who treat sexual partners as mere objects to satisfy their desire and fantasies, putting their own power and satisfaction above love. Dissolves illusions about sex, corrects channelling of sexual energy and cultivates a loving, caring attitude in lovemaking.

Parrot (Flame of the Forest) (*Butea monosperma*) For public speakers who wish to improve the timing of their elocution and co-ordination between thought and speech. Synchronizes thought, will and speech to improve pronunciation and enunciation. Helps the mind to gain control over the delivery of speech, so enhancing confidence and vocal expression.

Parval (*Trichosanthes dioica*) For hard-hearted people. Opens up the emotions, harmonizing and rekindling compassion and sensitivity towards others. Makes us more spontaneous and joyful.

Peacock Flower (*Poinciana pulcherrima*) For overcoming the effects of long debilitating illnesses or of physical and mental torture. Valuable for any rehabilitation process, such as overcoming drug addiction. Restores the nervous energy flow.

Pill-Bearing Spurge (*Euphorbia plentissima*) For those who are accident-prone, going through a bad patch or feeling powerless to control their own lives. Alleviates the effects of cyclical misfortune and the consequent bitterness.

Prickly Poppy (*Argemone mexiana*) For men who mistreat women sexually, seeing them merely as objects. Brings a caring responsibility and love back to sex without diminishing physical arousal or pleasure. Steers a man towards seeking a fulfilling and caring relationship by teaching that sex can be more fun when responsibly and lovingly undertaken.

Radish (*Raphanus sativas*) For anyone suffering from bereavement and from a sense of being unable to cope. Specifically strengthens and reorders the mind, affording mental objectivity, well-being and comfort following the death of someone very close. Integrates the mind after shock and trauma or bereavement.

Rangoon Creeper (Madhumalti) (*Quisqualis Indica*) Frees those who are captured in soul and will by very powerful gurus or cult leaders.

Red Hibiscus (*Hibiscus*) For enhancing compatibility between people in one-to-one relationships, thus evoking warmth and responsiveness. Restores mental harmony and emotional wellbeing, and indirectly improves sexual interaction.

Red-Hot Cattail (*Acalypha hispida*) For those who have been abused and wronged in past lives. Opens the heart centre, bringing a warm and loving transformation. Dissolves deep-seated blocks of hardheartedness and unforgivingness in the psyche. Restores faith in a universal spirit.

Red Silk Cotton Tree (*Salmalia malbarica*) For those drawn to spiritual paths. Cleanses and transforms the inner intention of such people. Liberates them from spiritual glamour and power-seeking by bringing a purity of spiritual intention, humility, love and appreciation for all people.

Rippy Hillox For those who are negative and fearful about sex because they have had difficult or traumatic sexual experiences in the past; for victims of rape or sexual perversion who find the thought of sex too painful to bear.

Sithihea For those who are self-centred in business and their dealings with others. For anyone whose vanity and insensitivity creates a mental block in his or her awareness of others. Evokes qualities of patience, reasonableness, compassion and integrity. Enhances, sensitizes and balances external, financial and material relationships.

Slow Match (*Careya arborea*) For those who feel badly treated in one-to-one relationships such as a marriage or parent/child relationship, resulting in bitterness and resentment towards the other person. Brings real love, openness, trust and understanding of the other person and a will to keep the relationship good.

Spotted Gliciridia (Rikry Rorshia Flower) (*Glicirida maculata*) For oppressive political leaders. Reforms those who imprison others for their political beliefs, bringing a change of heart as well as enlightenment and wisdom.

Swallow Wort (*Calotropis gigantica*) For those in a state of torment, disharmony and fear in their subconscious minds giving rise to disturbed sleep, nightmares, panic attacks and general restlessness. Alleviates deep disharmony so that peace, wellbeing and courage return.

Tassel Flower (*Calliandra surinamensis*) For deep emotional wounds and disharmony with members of one's own family, particularly for parent/child but also for distant relationships. Fosters forgiveness and aids the reconciliation process.

Teak Wood Flower (*Tectona grandis*) For vagueness, irrational and confused thinking, mental tiredness. For anyone over 60, especially those with senile dementia. Revitalizes and refreshes the mind, enhancing concentration and keeping the mind alert and interested.

Temple (*Plumeria rubra*) For deepening and strengthening the experience of worship; helpful to anyone who has totally rejected religion. Restores true awareness of the universal spirit.

Torroyia Rorshi Plant For those living in urban and industrial cultures. Encourages environmental sensitivity and awareness.

Tulip (*Spathodea campanulata*) For those who are aloof and disinterested in their day-to-day lives and in those around them. For anyone unable to wake early due to the intensity of his or her dreams. Brings a willingness to work and an ability to open up to and interact with others joyfully. Promotes early rising and applying oneself more completely to work and daily tasks. Reduces dreaming and astral travelling, helping one to be earthed and to accept physical life fully.

Ukshi (*Calicopteris floribunda*) For elderly women who used to be glamorous or beautiful but who feel rejected, depressed and resentful in their old age. Helps dissolve resentment, bitterness and isolation. Rekindles self-esteem and a sense of *joie de vivre*.

Vilayati Amli For mild envy of those close to us, making us unable to open up to or share/communicate with family and friends because they seem better than us or due to our own inferiority complex. Brings real pleasure in others' success, encouraging us to love and help others with warmth and caring. Improves relationships, particularly those within the family or among close friends.

Water Lily (*Nymphea alba*) The Kama Sutra among flower essences. A powerful tonic for those with psychological inhibitions about intimacy and sex. Enhances enjoyment of lovemaking by heightening sensuality.

White Coral Tree (*Erythrina variegatis orientalis*) For narrow-minded religious people who tend to be dogmatic, critical and simplistic in their assessments of others, seeing the world in black and white. Liberates us from a state of ignorance, broadening understanding and making us more flexible, loving and real in our religious faith.

White Hibiscus (*Hibiscus*) For anyone who feels blocked, tense and out of tune with his or her spiritual nature. Increases responsiveness to the spiritual world and our own spirituality. Increases our psychic and sensory ability to respond to the higher planes of being – the first step towards self-discovery.

Yellow Silk Cotton Tree (*Bombax ceiba*) For those who long to be free of a subconscious craving for spiritual power. Brings a pure, clear will to do spiritual work selflessly, humbly and without the desire for spiritual power over others.

Combination Essences

The Shahs have formulated combinations to target specific problems, here is a selection below.

Formula 1 First Aid For moments of intense stress, trauma, or emotional shock, helps one to deal calmly under difficult circumstances without panic.

Formula 2 Stress and tension A soothing remedy that brings relief from stress-related disorders such as tense muscles, headaches and anxiety.

Formula 7 Urban Stress Assists with dealing with urban stress.

Formula 14 Environmental Stress For protection against harmful effects of environmental stress caused by radiation from appliances such as TVs, mobile phones and computers.

Formula 17 Sleep Brings relief to insomniacs and those experiencing disturbed sleep by helping the body to rebuild its natural sleep rhythm.

Formula 18 Travel Aid For those constantly on the move who are exposed to different foods, climates, etc. Boosts personal immunity and keeps good health.

Formula 19 Cleansing Aid A multipurpose combination for multilevelled cleansing.

Formula 20 Acne Effective remedy for treating acne which purifies the system.

Formula 23 Menopause Helps women pass through a turbulent phase of menopause smoothly. Diminishes the physical and emotional discomfort caused by menopause.

Formula 24 Anti-Addiction Aid For those who earnestly wish to give up their addictions. Works on the mind to help to achieve a complete release from destructive habits and patterns.

Formula 38 Immunity Booster Enables one to maintain a good state of health by building the body's immunity against disease.

Formula 43 Sinus/Cold Offers relief from the common cold and sinusitis.

Gels

The Shahs have formulated some successful gels that address arthritic conditions and other painful symptoms.

Arthritis Aloe Vera Gel Fast-acting, cooling gel that uses remedies from Himalayan flowers to ease the swelling and discomfort of painful joints.

Floral Relief Gel This gel is made with Indian flower energy essences. Aloe vera juice is added to a gel base. Use to give relief to bites and itchy eczema as well as minor discomforts such as the following:

Backache Apply over the centre of the spine and on either side of spine. It is desirable to apply over the abdominal muscles.

Burns Relieves mild burns. DO NOT apply to open wounds or exposed burnt skin.

Calf pain Apply over the painful area including back of knee and ankle and also apply to the front of the leg.

Headaches For frontal headaches, apply over forehead and on either side of head. For deeper headaches, apply over painful area through hair, back of neck muscles and in the centre of upper part of abdomen.

Heel Pain Apply over the heel and the back of the ankle and to front of heel under the arch.

Injury On any painful area due to injury or sprain. (Not to be applied to open wounds.)

Knee Pain Apply over the painful area of knee joint in the front and back. Also apply to front and back of thigh completely. This is important as it will help you to recover fast.

Neck Pain Directly apply over the painful area and over the muscles starting from back of neck to the base of neck.

Premenstrual Pain Or Painful Menses Apply over lower abdomen and around the navel.

Shoulder Pain Apply over the painful area and also on the neck muscles.

Sneezing Apply on the nose and cheek and also on the forehead. Avoid putting it in the nose or in the eyes.

Toothache Apply externally over the painful side of cheek. Do not apply in the mouth.

Himalayan Flower Enhancers

These essences are made from flowers that grow 3,000m (10,000ft) above sea level in the Parvati Valley of the Himachal Pradesh region of the Indian Himalayas. Their creator is a man called Tanmaya, a former landscape gardener who left his native Australia to spend the next 20 years as a nomad and spiritual seeker in India.

He has always been passionate about flowers, and discovering these flower essences marked a turning point in his life for they brought him out of his reclusive lifestyle.

Tanmaya calls his essences 'enhancers' because of their ability to empower each of the body's main chakras or energy centres. The enhancers shine their light into these centres, dispelling any blockages or stored negativity. The first enhancer he created was for the crown chakra; he named it 'Flight'. Unlike many other prepared essences, the names of Tanmaya's enhancers derive not from the plants themselves but from their therapeutic qualities, such as 'Let Go' or 'Ecstasy'. He makes his 'enhancers' by placing the blossoms directly into pure, locally-produced alcohol – made from wild white roses, mountain spring water, wheat and sugar. The same white rose is the source of his 'Happiness' essence.

Tanmaya believes we can learn a great deal from the flowers growing in the Himalayas: 'They push up through the earth and rocks with such determination and courage... (they) are a celebration and a gift from the earth which share their beauty, individuality and uniqueness willingly with us.'

A further development to Tanmaya's collection is The Astro Essences range which address the particular vibrational energies of the sun and moon in each of the twelve signs of the zodiac.

Flowers of the World

Endurance Date Palm (*Phoenix dactylifera*), Indian olive (*Olea cuspidata*) (Sinai Desert/Himalayas) Eases inappropriate attitudes and belief systems around ageing. Supports youthful vigour, vitality and endurance.

Goddess Purple Orchid Tree (*Bauhinia purpurea*), *Rosa webbiana*, *Ahbizia saman* (India/China) Enhances the goddess, the wise woman. Provokes beauty, grace, receptivity, feminine strength. Connected to the energy of the moon and Venus.

Gulaga Red Mushroom (Australia) A powerful essence for transformation. Ruthlessly exposing and clearing away all that is no longer appropriate or serving us on our journey. Realigning us with our life's purpose. Made during a solar eclipse from a red mushroom at the sacred ceremonial site on Gulaga Mountain, on the far south coast of Australia's eastern seaboard.

Gulaga Crystal Quartz Crystal (Australia) Aligns the mind, crystallizes intention, grounds new vision, strengthens resolve. Brings lightness, clarity and joy.

Gulaga Crystal King Orchid (*Dendribium speciosum*) (Australia) Opens the heart to forgiveness of self and others.

Isan Neem (*Melia azadirachta*) (India) Made from the flowers of an old Neem tree beside the ancient Tantric temples of Khajuraho. Helps integrate body, mind and spirit, creating wisdom referred to by the Zen Master Isan. Good to take after meditation sessions. Strengthens the ability to live one's truth.

Lotus (*Nymphaeaceae*) (India) The philosopher's stone of flowers, a symbol of enlightenment. General tonic and cleanser for the entire system. Activates the crown chakra and enhances all forms of healing; acts as a booster for other flower enhancers, herbs and gem elixirs. Excellent to use in conjunction with meditation. Made under the Taurus full moon.

Morning Glory (*Ipomoea nil* or *Ipomoea purpurea*) (India) Helps you get up and greet the morning with enthusiasm. Enhances vitality and tones the entire nervous system, thus reducing nervous behaviour. Helps break addictive habits such as smoking. Good for restlessness at night.

Rapa-Nui Mira-Tahiti (Easter Island) Evoking ancient earth energy, healing past-life wounds, merging into the wisdom of Gaia. Made with seawater at the oldest sacred site on Easter Island, under the dark of the moon, with obsidian from the island's largest volcano, and the flower of Mira-Tahiti – the last native shrub remaining on the island.

Renaissance Air Plant (*Tillandsia stricta*) (Brazil) Rebirth. Assists in letting go of all that is not real and dissolving into that which has always been. Helps in letting go of emotional attachment to the past. A support for seekers during difficult times, giving understanding that flowering can happen in any moment regardless of external circumstances and conditions. (This essence was made under a full Pisces moon, with Sandra Epstein, co-creator of the Brazilian Rain Forest Essences.)

Repatterning Fungus (Australia) Opens one to receiving new information and grounding it in the body. Rearranges outmoded existing energy patterns to fit with ones current reality.

Tracking Brings clarity to point of disturbance or imbalance in oneself or client, where it may be appropriate to bring healing awareness.

Veil of Dreams Cactus (*Acanthocereus Horridus*) (India) Enhances ability to dream consciously and step through the veil of dreams so that you can understand the mysteries behind dreams. Excellent to take before going to sleep. Brings awareness of dream patterns in the waking state, allowing them to dissolve into the here and now. Use in conjunction with 'Clarity' and 'Blue Dragon' (*see* below) for psychic work.

Warrior Tamarind (*Tamarindus indica*), Grass Tree or Blackboy (*Xanthorrhoea australis*), Plantain (*Musa paradisiaca*) (Australia/India/China) Enhances masculine strength, grounding, courage, male sexuality, strength of purpose. Best taken in conjunction with the flower enhancer 'Ecstasy' (*see* below). For women it helps re-establish the flowing of energy which is stuck in feelings of intimidation and overcriticism, allowing the energy to move in a more creative way. Connected to the energy of the sun and Mars.

Womb With A View Mushroom (Australia) Helps bring consciousness to and erase energetic patterns and imprints received *in utero* that do not serve one.

The Seven Chakras

There are seven Himalayan Flower Enhancers for the seven major energy centres or chakras of the human body. These chakras each have their own particular quality and resonance, and have a corresponding relationship to one of the various glands in the body's endocrine system. Their exact position varies with the individual.

They can be viewed as booster stations, or transformers, for the journey of the energy from the base of the spine to the top of the head, the crown.

First/Base: Down to Earth Himalayan Honeysuckle (*Leycesteria formosa*), Hardy Calanthe Orchid (*Calanthe tricarinata*) Enhances life force energy, connection with the earth, helps with ungroundedness, sluggishness, anxiety around material existence, subtle or hidden fears, psychological wounds around sexuality, low libido, stress and lack of drive. Enhances sexual energy. Balances hyper-excitement, excess energy in the head, i.e. dizziness, mental fatigue.

Second/Hara: Wellbeing Wallflower (*Erysimum melicentae*) Enhances connection with one's power, centring, stimulating creativity and integrating emotions. This chakra is the storehouse of energy and the centre for transforming base energy. Helps diffuse internalized anger, birth traumas, fear of death, imbalances of emotions.

Third/Solar Plexus: Strength Spearwort(*Ranunculas lingua*), Marsh Marigold (Badmia) (*Caltha palustris var. himalensis*) Enhances one's individuality, personal creativity, honesty and self-worth, self-identity, and the power to manifest in the material world. Helps overcome lack of self-esteem, self-doubt, and inability to express one's innate creativity. Dispels feelings of insecurity, lack of personal power, lack of direction and motivation in life, sense of hopelessness, depression and oppression. Helps release early childhood conditioned patterns.

Fourth/Heart: Ecstasy (*Rosa webbiana*) Enhances love, compassion, sincerity, truthfulness, depth of feeling, empathy with all living things, and transpersonal love. Helps with bitterness, jealousy, feelings of contraction, feeling unloved, undernourished, overcritical of others, disillusioned and lack of truth. Enhances feelings of expansion and universal love.

Fifth/Throat: Authenticity

(*Delphiniium incanum*) Enhances expression, verbal communication, appreciation of beauty, creativity, refined experience, questioning, seeking, singing, sharing ideas, stimulating dreams, imagination, embracing humanity. Enhancing conviction and self-authority. Helps in cases of timidity, shyness, fear of speaking one's truth, difficulty in communicating, stress, tension, apprehension, claustrophobia, lack of conviction, stage fright, unwillingness to change.

Sixth/Third Eye: Clarity Columbine

(*Aquilegia pubiflora*), Blue Oxalis (*Parochetus communis*), Wild Thyme (*Thymus serpyllum*) Enhances clarity, awareness, sharpness of intellect, perception, intuition, sense of spirituality, understanding, ability to see into the heart of things, bliss. Sense of universal self. Meditation, insight, and clairvoyance. Aids poor concentration, unawareness, lack of clarity and direction. Helps with headaches, balances excess sexual energy. Dispels isolation, alienation, and feelings of meaninglessness.

Seventh/Crown: Flight Jasmine

(*Jasminum officiale*) Enhances oneness, meditation, prayer, Higher Self, union of mind, body and spirit, sense of formlessness and the ability to experience nothingness. Helps with feelings of separateness, isolation, lack of meaning, feelings of insignificance. Enhances universal love, brotherhood, universal sharing, wonder, awe. Catalyst for all essences. Helps with egocentric, selfish and judgemental attitudes. Gives receptivity and acceptance of the beauty of oneself and others.

Other Himalayan Flower Enhancers

Astral Orchid (*Dactylorhiza hatagirea*) A higher octave of the third eye. For connection with one's Higher Self and channelling.

Aura Cleaning Himalayan Indigo (*Indigofera heterantha*), Baby's Breath (*Gypsophila cerastioides*) Cleans and refreshes the aura, adding a lightness and sparkle to the energy field. Excellent for use in the bath or spraying over the body or around the house.

Blue Dragon (*Corydalis Cashmeriana*) Gentian (*Gentiana ornate*), Prickly Blue Poppy (*Meconopsis horridula*) Enhances focus, concentration and single-pointedness, Excellent for meditation. Pierces straight to the heart of matter, dissolving the illusion of separation revealing only one sky.

Cedar (*Cedrus deodar*) Gives grounding and courage, stability, strength and vitality. Encourages deep roots in the earth so one's branches can reach to the sky.

Champagne Kashmir False Spirea (*Sorbaria tomentosa*) For celebration – particularly good at night. Take with the floral enhancer 'Ecstasy' for a night of celebration, 'Clarity' for a more mysterious night, or 'Down to Earth' and 'Ecstasy' for a night of passionate lovemaking.

Children's Flower (*Androsace Primuloides*), Primula (*Primula gracilipes*), Strawberry (*Frugaria nubicola*) Protective essence for children. Helps the child to maintain their original connection with the natural world. Invokes delight, playfulness, innocence, resilience, a sense of wonder and awe in the mysteries of life. Connects adults with their inner child.

Chiron (*Thermopsis barbata*) Gives insight into the wound which has disconnected us from our essence; the key points that keep us from living our truth/being our true selves. Opens the senses to refined experiences. For healers evokes shamanistic energies and clarifies the point of disconnection in the client. Good for channelling. Can clarify Chiron transits.

Expansion Common Chicory (*Chicorium Intybus*) Specifically for the chest area, opening and releasing tension – bringing expansiveness to the heart chakra and the experience of letting go. Dissolving the perceived boundaries of the heart and merging into the heart of all things.

Gateway Indian Horsechestnut (*Aesculus indica*) Assists in times of transition, rites of passage, dark night of the soul. Gives strength and resilience in times of inner turmoil. Helps you turn within when times are difficult. Can help to appreciate the process, the bigger picture.

Golden Dawn Impatiens (*Impatiens scabrida*) Particularly good for women. Releases old wounds around sexual, psychic and physical abuse from male domination. Centres one in the place of stillness where no wounds exist, and so allows disidentification and gentle healing to happen by itself. For example, can bring awareness to the internal restrictions women place on their feminine side due to mental conditioning from growing up in male-oriented societies.

Gratefulness Jasmine (*Jasminum officiale*) Enhances universal brotherhood and sharing, wonder, awe. Catalyst for all essences. Helps counter egocentric and selfish attitudes.

Happiness Himalayan Musk Rose (*Rosa brunonii*) Provokes a radiance from within that sends a smile, a soothing glow throughout the whole body, relaxing the mind. Gives a deep sense of joy in life. Very supportive for laughing meditations.

Healing Indian Poke (*Phytolacca acinosa*), Musk Orchid (*Herminium monorchis*), (*Polygonatum cirrhifolium*) For healers. Gives the effect of walking through a pine forest, clearing the channels for the healer, centring and bringing them back to their natural relationship with existence. Helps them to be in touch with the basic life-forces in nature; especially helpful to healers working in cities or heavy urban environments. Encourages an instinctive relationship between healer and client, particularly if taken in conjunction with the Heart Essence and the essence most

suitable to the client. Of great help where the life force is weak. Apply directly onto the hara or wherever there is a marked absence of energy.

Heart of Tantra Impatiens (*Impatiens glandulifera*) Creates a circle of light between the sex chakra and around the heart chakra. For men particularly, this bridges the solar plexus with the heart, thus moving sex from being about power to being about love.

Hidden Splendour (*Iris Kemaonensis*) Brings forth the splendour within. For reclaiming your birthright; your inner glory. Helps combat feelings of worthlessness, constriction, insignificance, smallness.

Let Go (*Hackelia Uncinata*) A Pisces flower – dissolving into the moment, relaxation, surrender, 'throwing away the oars and letting the boat take you where it will'. Letting go of past hurts, fears and attachments – moving into the present with empty hands. Good for hypnosis and guided fantasy work.

Nirjara Drumstick Primula (*Primula denticulata*) A deconditioning essence, excellent for all work of deprogramming. When there is conscious intent to change conditioned attitudes and patterns, this essence help to erase outmoded imprints from the cells. Supports transformation. A powerful healing essence.

Nirjara 2 (*Primula macrophylla*) Aids in peeling back the layers of conditioning around our perception of reality – allowing the true face to reveal itself.

Opium Poppy (*Papaver somniferum*) Helping to break free of addictive emotional patterns and compulsive behaviour that keep us in the past.

Pink Primula (*Primula rosea*) Opening the heart to pure delight and the joy of being alive.

Pluto (*Arisaema propinquum*) Diffuses anger and frustration and old patterns of behaviour whilst helping one to identify with the enormous power of change/evolution, rather than clinging to the old patterns that are being broken away. Brings consciousness to the shadow part of the mind. A powerful essence for embracing the disowned, 'darker' side of one's self. In the act of conscious acceptance, these negative aspects lose their grip on the unconscious, and no longer have power in our life. In some people this essence can be initially cathartic. Brings strength and clarity to the aspect where Pluto is placed in the birthchart. Eases Pluto transits.

Purple Orchid (*Roscocea alpina*) A doorway in. Accessing great depths within. Good for those who find it difficult to turn their focus inward, this essence draws the attention away from external distractions, towards profound inner spaces.

Rock Primula Quiet acceptance or connection with one's inner beauty/peace – regardless of what may be going on around you.

Roots and Wings Cedar (*Cedrus deodar*), White Orchid (*Cephalanthera longifola*) Roots and Wings nurtures and reminds us that we are not separate, but one with existence itself. It gives us the courage to live our lives from this place of knowing and understanding. To tread lightly on the earth and interface with all beings through love.

The White Orchid opens wings in our heart, enabling the feeling and recognition of the vast open sky of love that is our nature. Gives courage to live from this heart-space, and meet the world through the eyes of love and openness, rather than through fear and rigidity. The Cedar anchors us to the earth and so supports us to live our truth, knowing that we are one with our Mother Earth. Our bodies are from the earth we are not separate from the earth. Our spirits are love and we are not separate from love.

Sat-Chit-Ananda A combination of *Nirjara, Nirjara 2, Pink Primula, Rock Primula and White Orchid*. Meditation essence. An exquisite support for melting into the heart of existence.

Sober Up Himalayan Honeysuckle (*Leycesteria formosa*) For grounding, balances excess energy in the head, gives stability, solidity and stamina. Has been reported to help give balance and stability to people with a tendency to drug and alcohol abuse and related problems.

Trust Anemone Clematis (*Clematis montana*) A bridge between the vertical and the horizontal dimensions (*see* the structure of the flower itself); the horizontal being the space/time dimension, the vertical being the transcendental/spiritual. Bringing one to a place of trust in the big picture – that one is exactly where one needs to be in this moment. A state of surrender. Also heals wounds between lovers allowing a higher level of union.

Vital Spark Indian Horsechestnut (*Aesculus indica*), *Hackelia uncinata*, Himalayan Musk Rose (*Rosa brunonii*), Himalayan Indigo (*Indigofea heterantha*) Enhances vitality and life force, especially in situations of shock, fear and extreme emotions. Centring. Helps one calm down, relax, let go and surrender to the moment, thereby providing space for healing to take place. Can be given to distressed animals, plants shocked due to replanting etc.

White Orchid (*Cephalanthera longifolia*) A higher octave of the heart chakra. Accessing the angelic realms of the heart, compassion and bliss.

Himalayan Astro Enhancer Essences

These 24 astro essences offer a doorway into the particular vibrational energies of the sun and moon in each of the 12 signs of the zodiac. Many people may be familiar with their sun sign, most commonly referred to as your zodiac sign, but if you have never had a birth chart done, and do not know your moon sign, you can still use these essences

Take the essence of your own sun and moon sign if you wish to increase your conscious recognition of these energies, and/or to reveal that of which you have previously been unaware. Take your sun sign essence to help clarify your direction and add vitality; take your moon sign essence to help clarify your emotions and revitalize flagging feelings,

It can be beneficial to take essence of other sun and moon signs, if your current situation would benefit from a particular energy, or to reveal the energy of that sign. This revelation may be especially pertinent if you have another planet or point (such as the ascendant) in your birth chart, in that sign. Briefly experiencing the energy of a sun or moon sign that is not your own, may also help your understanding of how these energies are experienced by others.

Taking these essences may increase your awareness of the difficulties for each sign. Although possibly uncomfortable, revealing these difficult energies can add insight and assist healing.

Aries Sun essence Lost contact with your inner warrior? Need courage, enthusiasm, a fighting spirit? Starting a new venture? Start your motor, get moving with this essence.

Aries Moon essence Been feeling blue lately? A little down in the dumps? Need a pick-me-up tonic? This essence may provide the fuel to light your fire.

Taurus Sun essence Haven't seen your earth goddess lately? Need stability, or help to push through? Assistance could be at hand with this essence.

Taurus Moon essence Feeling wobbly and need to feel grounded with indulgence, pampering, sensuality on the menu? The rich pastures you need could be in this essence.

Gemini Sun essence Need to communicate? Feeling mentally off the boil? The running shoes in this essence could get you off to a good start.

Gemini Moon essence Need to adapt to changes and movement on your inner life? Feeling stuck for words? Get the words bubbling with this Gemini fizz.

Cancer Sun essence Need to connect with family, put down roots, make a home? Let the mothering influence in this essence help you.

Cancer Moon essence Aching for Mother to nurture and protect you? Feeling numb, closed off fragile or vulnerable? Pick up the emotional grit in the crab shell of this essence.

Leo Sun essence Is the king in you dead? Stuck with your creative projects, need to be fired up? Get motivated and let this essence put the crown back on your head.

Leo Moon essence Lacking warmth, life feels serious? Take heart, contact your courage and playfulness with this sparkler of an essence.

Virgo Sun essence Can't see the wood for the trees? muddling along in disorder and lacking routine? This essence may be the tool to perfect, tune and polish your life.

Virgo Moon essence Feel like you've lost your grip on things, everything feels chaotic? The servant in this essence may sort it all out for you.

Libra Sun essence Looking for compromise? Co-operation with others and team effort not working? The harmony you seek may be in this essence.

Libra Moon essence Feeling off balance and finding relationships with loved ones difficult? Add a dose of peace and beauty with this essence.

Scorpio Sun essence Need to shed some skin and to clear out some debris? Do a spot of research and get to the bottom of it all with this detective essence.

Scorpio Moon essence Wish to add some extra spice or bite to your feelings and emotions? Having difficulty connecting with your gut instincts? Put your feelings under the microscope with this essence.

Sagittarius Sun essence Run out of goals and need a new direction? Got itchy feet and yearn for adventure? Cut loose and seek new horizons with this essence.

Sagittarius Moon essence Feel like you've reached a dead end? Feeling restless and restricted? Feel your body and mind expand with this essence.

Capricorn Sun essence Lack discipline and needing to assume responsibilities? Nothing to work on and not achieving? This essence may provide the 'rope and tackle' to scale your next mountain.

Capricorn Moon essence Life feels out of control and feel unable to go the distance? Ache for a dose of stability and practicality? This essence may provide the 'mountain climbing boots' to get you back on track.

Aquarius Sun essence Searching for a new way and different methods? Do you have unusual ideas and want to change your world? Start the revolution by plugging in to this essence.

Aquarius Moon essence Feeling bored with the old you and fed up with being one of a crowd? Feel like a party? This essence could be the 'lightning bolt' you need.

Pisces Sun essence Struggling with trust in your life and forgotten your source of spiritual nourishment and 'the dreamer' inside you? Dive into your ocean with this essence.

Pisces Moon essence Need a dose of sensitivity and intuition and a rest from worldly affairs? Need to switch off and recharge your flat battery? Jump aboard this essence and float away.

USA, South America and Canada

For hundreds of years before the arrival of European settlers, the vast and colourful North American continent was inhabited by peoples who knew it as Turtle Island. These Native Americans regarded themselves as caretakers or keepers of the land who were responsible for safeguarding its fertility. They saw themselves as belonging to the natural world and also saw it as their duty not to disturb the balance that exists in nature. The idea of splitting up and owning various bits of land was alien to them. The whole of Turtle Island was their home and they regarded it as sacred. Native North as well as South American legends talk of Gentle Giants who once walked upon the earth in times when all was peace and harmony. These 'Giants' were reputedly a highly spiritual people, such was their awareness of the Great Spirit – Gitchi Manitou – in all living things and their deep connection with nature. They are said to have possessed the gift of talking with the energies of animals, flowers, the wind, water and thunder. They also had the ability to utilize these energies for healing purposes. Native American traditions live on and are an inspiration to many of those who seek to explore the healing powers of nature.

Alaskan Flower and Environmental Essences

The Alaskan Flower Essence Project was founded by Steve Johnson in 1984 to coordinate the collection of new flower essences from the extensive ecological regions of Alaska.

Johnson was born and raised in the mountains of Idaho where he developed a deep connection with the natural environment. He spent his childhood playing in the gardens and orchards, walking in the forests and swimming in the nearby lakes and rivers. After graduating from high school he began his career working as a firefighter. He was stationed near the largest wilderness area in the United States where he learned the names and uses of all the local plants. He then transferred to Alaska, a land of vast, unspoiled forests and tundra regions which are home to many unusual species of plants.

Johnson's interest in flower essences was kindled in 1980 when he was given two Bach Flower Remedies and experienced a notable change in his health and emotional being. As a result of this experience he decided to find out as much as he could about flower essences and their mode of healing. During the next three years he trained in auric energy balancing, polarity, reflexology and massage before specializing in using vibrational energies for emotional, mental and spiritual healing.

He began making Alaskan Flower Essences in the summer of 1983, preparing them from the native plants of Alaska which have adapted and flourished over many aeons in a vibrant ecosystem, an environment of extremes from frigid cold to sweltering heat, from long dark winters to summers of perpetual light. These flowering plants reflect the special strength, power and vitality of this land.

Because they have evolved freely, without human intrusion, this community of plants embodies a unique range of vibrational energies and healing qualities that are especially relevant to the growth and evolution of human consciousness.

While the Alaskan Kits 1 and 2 are composed primarily of the essences of flowering trees and plants, and aim to balance the core or fundamental life-energy patterns, Kit 3 features essences from unique and rare plants which work on the subtle or spiritual levels of our being. The majority of essences in these kits come from wild flowers growing in healthy thriving plant communities at the peak of their blossoming stage, while the garden remedies come from blossoms growing in a co-creative garden (nature and the nature spirits co-creating together).

Encapsulating the special energies of Alaska, these flower essences provide significant levels of support for the process of conscious change and transformation and work on issues related to unfolding one's future, opening to higher levels of perception and understanding, and living life in alignment with divine purpose. They are also unique in their orientation towards healing the heart and therefore healing our relationship with each other and all forms of nature.

Johnson further developed combination essences, and Alaskan Feng Shui Sprays to address the toxic buildup in one's surroundings. The Environmental Essences are an interesting exploration into the concept that we are directly affected and influenced by the forces of nature (*see* chapter on Sound, Light and Environmental Essences).

KIT 1

Alder (*Alnus crispa*) For clarity of perception on all levels, allowing our seeing to become knowing, recognizing truth in personal experience. Empowers us to move beyond limited mental programming and respond to higher learning.

Balsam Poplar (*Populus balsamifera*) Releases the pain and emotional tension associated with sexual issues (which block the circulation of energy in the body); resulting from shock and trauma or a lack of grounding, associated with sexual trauma; synchronizes sexual energy with planetary cycles and rhythms.

Black Spruce (*Populus balsamifera*) Allows integration of the eternal into awareness and experience in the present; opens us up to information contained within the archetypes of nature. Helps us to learn the wisdom of the Ages.

Blue Elf Viola (*Viola* sp.) Helps us to understand the seeds of our anger and frustrations; enables us to express anger in a clear and nonviolent way; releases and dissipates the protective energy surrounding unresolved conflicts, bringing the whole process to completion so they can be expressed in a clear and heart-centred way.

Chiming Bells (*Mertensia paniculata*) Peace through understanding one's true nature; joy in physical existence; awakens a spiritual awareness of nature. Good for feeling depressed; despondent; disheartened; no joy in one's day-to-day existence; feeling a lack of support and stability at a basic level. For regeneration, renewal and stability at the physical level of our beings; opens us to the loving energy of the Divine Mother.

Cotton Grass (*Eriophorum* sp.) For letting go of pain held in the body; shock and trauma resulting from an accident or injury of any kind; fixating on one's discomfort rather than on the healing process; unable to completely heal an old injury because of a lack of awareness of what led to its creation. Helps a person come to an understanding of the core issues that led to an accident or injury so that they can release the physical, emotional, and mental trauma associated with it. Restores equilibrium after injury or trauma; shifts our focus from pain to healing. Can be applied topically.

Dandelion (*Taraxacum officinale*) Brings awareness and release of emotional tension and stress held in muscle tissue; and the deeper mental attitudes that lead to chronic muscular tension; increases one's level of body-mind communication to be better able to identify the underlying issues and attitudes. Difficulty releasing emotional energy stored in the body. For use both internally and externally.

Fireweed (*Epilobium angustifolium*) Helps us ground and cleanse old stagnant energy patterns from the body so that new life may enter; good when feeling burned out or have a weak connection to the earth. Strengthens and restores a nurturing flow of energy after a traumatic or transforming experience. Brings new cycles of renewal and revitalization. Useful in emergency situations especially for releasing physical pain, trauma and shock

Forget-Me-Not (*Myosotis alpestris*) Opens our hearts for the release of pain held deep in the subconscious; facilitates the release of fear, guilt, feeling separate; difficulty connecting to the spiritual dimension; helps us to remember our original innocence. To regain true respect and compassion for ourselves, others and the earth.

Foxglove (*Digitalis purpurea*) Releases fear and emotional tension centred around the heart; fear of the unknown; lack of perspective on how to deal with a challenging situation; allows us to see through perceptual constrictions to the 'heart' of the matter. During conflict or difficulty enables our perceptions to expand to connect with the truth of the situation.

Golden Corydalis (*Corydalis aurea*) Creates the ability to get all of one's talents and skills to work together in a focused way; and make sense of how one's life fits together. For positive growth of the personality. Restores full communication between the soul and the personality; reintegrates our identity according to the needs of the soul after an experience of deep transformation.

Green Bells Of Ireland (*Molucella laevis*) For opening our perceptual awareness to the various levels of energy and intelligence that exist in nature; feeling ungrounded; helps us to reconnect with the energy of the natural world and to feel at home on the earth. Helps the newly born greet the earth; strengthens the energetic connection between the physical body and the earth.

Icelandic Poppy (*Papaver icelandica*) For reflecting one's inner radiance to all aspects of life. When survival, sexual, and spiritual aspects of life are not integrated. Supports the gentle unfolding of spiritual receptivity; strengthens our capacity to integrate and radiate spiritual energy into all aspects of our lives. Opens us up to and helps us maintain a spiritual focus in life.

Jacob's Ladder (*Polemonium pulcherrimum*) Helps to bring awareness of our attempts to control the events of our lives and be open to receiving the creative impulses of the soul; allows mental control to evolve into a disciplined acceptance of spirit. Resolves unclarity about intention or motivation. When lacking trust in the spiritual world and trying to 'figure things out' brings you to a place of opening to receive the wisdom that is available in each moment.

Labrador Tea (*Ledum palustre*) For addictions, and when attempting to balance one extreme with another. For imbalance in any area of life. When you have difficulty coming back to centre after a traumatic or unsettling experience. Centres energy in the body and calms extreme imbalances of physical, emotional and mental energy; relieves the stress associated with extremes and helps continually learn a new perspective of balance. Useful in times of emotional catharsis or after traumatic experiences.

Lady's Slipper (*Cypripedium guttatum*) Helps us to gain awareness of subtler energy flows in and around the body. Alleviates resistance to receiving healing energy from others. Fosters the collection, focus and release of energy for healing and regulates circulation in all of the major energy pathways. Works on the chakras and central nervous system and spine – a gentle catalyst.

Monkshood (*Aconitum delphinifolium*) Gives fearlessness. For those who feel vulnerable through lack of well-defined boundaries and who have difficulty allowing contact with others. A powerful and precise essence which increases our ability to interact with others through a stronger identification with our divine nature; strengthens and defines our energy fields so we can create and maintain our physical, emotional and mental boundaries to help us function in accordance with our higher purpose.

Paper Birch (*Betula papyrifera*) Helps us gain a clear perspective of our true purpose; reveals the underlying true and essential self present within. Confusion or disorientation about the direction life should take; unable to connect with deeper levels of insight regarding life purpose. Useful when facing important life decisions, or when lost or uncertain how to proceed, helps us gain a clearer perspective of our life purpose and how to live it.

Prickly Wild Rose (*Rosa acicularis*) For openness, courage and renewed interest in life in the face of adverse circumstances. For lacking trust and faith; feeling hopeless; apathetic and disinterested in life; unable to keep the heart open when involved in adverse circumstances. Allows the heart to open in response to conflict and struggle. Brings courageous interest in life and our hopes to fruition.

Spiraea (*Spiraea beauverdiana*) To overcome resistance to conscious growth and expansion. For feeling unsupported by life; attachment to the way things are, even if they are not to our liking. Brings unconditional acceptance of support, regardless of the form it comes in. To learn to nurture and be nurtured by living things.

Twinflower (*Linnaea borealis*) For those who are defensive or reactive and have difficulty expressing themselves or listening to/understanding others. Improves communication skills, helping us to listen and speak to others from a place of quiet, inner calm and focused neutrality.

Wild Iris (*Iris setosa*) For lack of belief in one's own capacity to create; blocking and disconnected from creative expression because of an unwillingness to share it with others; brings a focused release of creativity, encouraging sharing one's inner beauty and creative energy freely and enables recognition of the beautiful expression of divine creativity.

Willow (*Salix bebbiana*) Brings mental receptivity, flexibility and resilience. Dissolves resistance to taking responsibility for one's actions or for the life one has created; Brings awareness of how thoughts create reality. Helps us remove our resistance to consciously creating our lives and a positive reality from the quality of one's thoughts.

Yarrow (*Achillea borealis*) For strengthening the overall integrity of the energy field; knowing and being the source of one's own protection. For those oversensitive to the environment when the integrity of the aura has been compromised by injury or trauma in this or another lifetime. Use to seal energy breaks in the aura and strengthen the aura and the overall integrity of the energy field and build a protective shield against environmental hazards, such as electromagnetic radiation from computers and fluorescent lights. Helps us know and be the source of our own protection

KIT 2

Alpine Azalea (*Loiseleuria procumbens*) Releases old patterns of self-doubt. Opens your heart to the spirit of love. For living in total unconditional acceptance of yourself; teaches us compassion through understanding. Clears self-doubt and stops us withholding love from ourselves or being unable to have compassion for ourselves

Bog Blueberry (*Vaccinium uliginosum*) Clears conditional acceptance of abundance; attachment to the form in which anything manifests in one's life. Neutralizes the beliefs that limit the experience of abundance on all levels; encourages us to open to the abundance that is offered with acceptance and gratitude.

Bog Rosemary (*Andromeda polifolia*) Nurtures through the process of trust. For deep cleansing and healing of the experience of life, strengthens trust in divine healing and support. Promotes the release of fear and resistance held deep in the heart; helps one let go of any resistance to being healed. Strengthens one's connection with the infinite life-force.

Bunchberry (*Cornus canadensis*) For focusing and directing the power of the will; for mental steadfastness and emotional clarity in demanding situations, especially when easily distracted by or caught up in the emotional turmoil of others. For when we feel we do not have enough time to complete tasks. Strengthens the boundary between the emotional and mental body and promotes coherent thinking

Cassandra (*Chamaedaphne calyculata*) Quietens and calms the mind; clears anxiousness and increases the depth of perception so that we can sense the currents of life. Acts as a catalyst to improve the quality of our relationship with nature. An aid to relax into deeper levels of meditation in order to receive inner guidance.

Columbine (*Aquilegia formosa*) For self-appreciation, cherishing our unique and distinctive personal beauty regardless of how it differs from others'. For projecting a strong sense of self and the ability to project ourselves out in the world for others to see.

Cow Parsnip (*Heracleum lanatum*) For those who feel powerless to direct their lives. Feeling ungrounded and cut off from one's roots; unsure of one's inner direction; or when having difficulty connecting with or adapting to new surroundings after a move. Promotes inner strength; assists with the process of adapting to a new environment. Helps us to thrive wherever we are. Brings contentment with present circumstances and peace of mind during times of intense transition and change.

Grass of Parnassus (*Parnassia palustris*) Brings a high and pure quality of light into the aura for cleansing, purification and protection; attracts nourishment from nature, re-energizing. Helpful for those who have difficulty maintaining energy levels in toxic environments, or who are living and working in crowded, polluted surroundings. Helps us bring past experiences to completion on all levels.

Grove Sandwort (*Moehringia lateriflora*) For feeling a lack of physical and emotional nurturing; weak bonding connections between mother and child; feeling unsupported by the earth. Strengthens the physical and emotional bonds of communication and comfort between mother and child; opens us up to support a nurturing relationship between earth mother and all living beings, and encourages sharing this support with others.

Horsetail (*Equisetum arvense*) For distorted communication with other levels of one's consciousness; difficulty communicating with the Higher Selves of others, including animals. Helps feeling connected; enhances communication with our different levels of consciousness. Through this we are better able to make true contact with others. Improves inter-species communication.

Lace Flower (*Tiarella trifoliata*) For appreciation of all nature and of ourselves; strengthens self-acceptance and our sense of self-worth; realizing the importance of how a unique contribution enriches the contribution to the whole, however humble. Dissolves lack of awareness, acceptance or appreciation of our own natural beauty and intrinsic value; feeling insignificant; unsure of how our personal or professional contributions fit into the whole.

Mountain Wormwood (*Artemisia tilesii*) For healing old wounds; helps us by releasing unforgiven areas in our relationships with others and with ourselves. Dissolves unresolved anger and resentment; forgiving past actions regardless of the intent behind them. Helps to bring all our relationships into balance.

Opium Poppy (*Papaver sominifera*) For when unable to find balance between activity and rest. For finding a balance between doing and being; helps us integrate previous experiments in order to live fully in the present. Balances extremes of activity and rest, being and doing. Clears deep exhaustion; unawareness of past accomplishments; and difficulties in understanding and integrating lessons and experiences so we may live more fully in the present.

Pineapple Weed (*Matricaria matricariodes*) Encourages freedom from injury and risk through harmony with our physical environment. For those unaware of the support and nurturing that is available from nature and also for weak nurturing bond between mother and child; helps to builds affinity between mothers and children. For active young children, mothers and mothers-to-be. Promotes sense of wellbeing during pregnancy.

River Beauty (*Epilobium latifolium*) An essence of emotional recovery, reorientation and regeneration. To help you start over after a devastating experience overwhelmed by grief, sadness, or a sense of loss; shock and trauma from emotional or sexual abuse and to see adverse circumstances as a potential for cleansing and growth. Helps us start over.

Single Delight (*Moneses uniflora*) For those suffering feelings of isolation and loneliness during a dark or depressing time; cloudy inner vision. Links us energetically with other members of our soul family. Opens the heart and reminds us of the support we have always had.

Sticky Geranium (*Geranium erianthum*) For getting out of a rut, or 'unstuck'; frees the many aspects of our potential; helps us to go beyond previous stages of growth. For feeling unfocused, lethargic, or indecisive; resistance to moving on to the next level or stage of an experience; lacking energy to reach our goals; attached to our current level of consciousness and identity. Encourages us to move from procrastination and lethargy to decisive and focused action.

Sunflower (*Helianthus annuala*) For an unbalanced expression of masculine energy in men or women; weak or dysfunctional relationship to the father, or to one's own identity as a father. Strengthens our radiant expression; harmonizes the active, masculine aspect of energy in both men and women. Promotes a functional relationship and teaches us to accept the authority of the Higher Self, without imposing our will on others.

Sweetgale (*Myrica gale*) For emotional energies blocked in lower chakras. For when emotional communication with others is defensive, lacking clarity, and is characterized by conflict, blame, and the assignment of guilt. Aids deep integration and release of emotional pain and tension that undermines the quality of our communication and interactions with others, especially in male/female relationships. Heals the core of our emotional interactions with others. Aids completion of unfinished emotional experiences, enabling us to respond to the present with strength and clarity.

Tamarack (*Larix laricina*) Builds self-confidence through a deeper understanding of one's unique skills and abilities. For a weak sense of self-identity; or those who lack awareness of what they are capable of. Helps us remain centred in the knowledge and self-confidence that our abilities will carry us through challenging times. Encourages the conscious development of individuality.

Tundra Rose (*Potentilla fruticosa*) For hopelessness; lack of inspiration and motivation. For those overwhelmed by the responsibilities they have taken on. Restores hope, courage, inspiration and a love of life. Allows the power of life to be communicated through our living of it; for combating fears of living and dying. Releases deep resistance that has blocked the dynamic expression of spirit in our lives. Encourages a robust expression of joy and enthusiasm to the fulfilment of one's responsibilities.

White Spruce (*Picea glauca*) Unification. For information overload; feeling disintegrated; unable to apply knowledge to life's challenges; difficulty integrating how one feels with how one thinks. Balances intuition, thought and emotion together and unifies them in the present moment. Native Alaskans considered this to be 'the gentle grandfather healer' – a touchstone to our higher knowledge. Brings us to a place of balance and stability. Grounds spiritual wisdom into the body and opens us up to that internal wisdom that will illuminate our current situation.

White Violet (*Viola renifolia*) For highly sensitive people who find contained environments intolerable. For those uncomfortable in closed spaces and constrained environments and those who are fearful of losing their identity in a group or unable to embody their sensitivity in a comfortable way. Supports creation of new energetic boundaries, allowing trust and relaxation to develop regardless of the dynamics of the environment. Opens our hearts to the essence of purity; connects us with the highest in ourselves and in others

Yellow Dryas (*Dryas drummondii*) Support for those who explore the edge of the unknown; for the expansion and clarification and maintaining awareness of self and family throughout dynamic cycles of growth and change. For feeling estranged from one's soul family; unable to sense the connective thread that links one's experiences into a coherent and understandable whole. For the pioneer in us.

KIT 3

Bladderwort (*Utricularia vulgaris*) Brings awareness of truth and shattering illusion through clear internal knowing so that we see only truth. Promotes discernment when faced with dishonesty in others; strengthens our ability to perceive the truth regardless of the confusion that surrounds it. Enables one to make decisions that support one's highest good. Good for those often deceived or taken advantage of or with a lack of discernment.

Blueberry Pollen (*Vaccinium uliginosum*) For abundance. Releases deep patterns of limitation from the mind so we can attract and be open to receive all we need to live life to the fullest. For those with a lack of belief in the concept of abundance; low prosperity consciousness; difficulty receiving from others and from the earth. Helps us expand on all levels to accommodate abundance; facilitates the release of mental and emotional attachments that limit our ability to manifest higher purpose in physical form.

Cattail Pollen (*Typha latifolia*) For standing tall in one's personal truth; helps you to find the courage and inner strength to act in alignment with this truth even during pain and trauma; to follow your chosen path even when feeling unsupported by others and weakened by connections and involvements which no longer serve one's highest good.

Comandra (*Geocaulon lividum*) For clearing disharmonious energies from the heart that limit one's ability to be open to and aware of subtle energies in nature. For those whose visionary abilities are undeveloped or ungrounded and of no practical use, and whose focus of their perceptions is limited to the material aspects of the physical world. Supports maintaining the necessary vision to move through the current dimensional shift; opens the heart to be a bridge between the third and fourth dimensions; helps us develop our potential to see the physical world from a higher perspective.

Green Bog Orchid (*Platanthera obtusata*) Gently releases blocked pain and fear held deep in the heart due to lack of trust in one's deeper motivations. For difficulty communicating from the heart. For coming into true balance with the natural kingdom so that we can fulfil our divine co-creative potential. Expands our awareness, sensitivity and ability to perceive life from a place of openness and neutrality and encourages the development of a heart connection with others.

Green Fairy Orchid (*Hammarbya paludosa*) For accepting oneness through total internal balance. For when there is a core imbalance between the masculine and feminine aspects of the self resulting in difficulty resolving conflicts within the heart. Creates a level of honesty in the heart where nothing is hidden; expands the heart, balancing the inner male/female at the deepest level of the body and being. Releases duality.

Hairy Butterwort (*Pinguicula villosa*) Ascension. Aids acknowledgment or trust in higher guidance and support, especially when confronted with a challenging situation or life lesson; clears lack of awareness of the core issues that need to be addressed in order to resolve a situation. Helps consciously access the support and guidance needed in order to move through threshold points of conflict and transition with grace, ease and deep understanding without creating crisis or illness.

Harebell (*Campanula lasiocarpa*) Removes self-imposed mental and emotional limitations, when feeling unloved and cut off from the Source; looking for love outside of oneself. Allows you to open up your life to receive universal love and the presence of the Divine and give unconditional love.

Ladies' Tresses (*Spiranthes romanzoffiana*) For lack of awareness of the connection between our life lessons and our life purpose; difficulty reconnecting with the body after a serious injury or traumatic experience. Brings deep internal alignment for releasing deeply-held traumas held at the cellular level, helps us reconnect energetically with parts of the body that have been injured or traumatized. Realigns you with your soul purpose in this lifetime.

Lamb's Quarters (*Chenopodium album*) Heals separation when there is a lack of balance and harmony between the mind and heart, the rational and the intuitive. Helps to assimilate information through the heart before interpreting it through the mind. For those who tend to be highly intellectual. Brings the power of the mind into balance with the joy of the heart.

Moschatel (*Adoxa moschatelina*) For those with an overly intellectual focus on life; believing that everything must come through struggle; creating without joy. Teaches us how to accomplish more by grounding our mental focus into the earth. Opens our intuitive connection with the plant kingdom and helps us learn how to co-create with nature through celebration and play.

Northern Lady's Slipper (*Cypripedium passerinum*) Reconnects body and spirit. For a weak body/soul connection; traumatic birth experience; pain and trauma held very deeply in the body. Allows one's being to be touched and healed by infinite gentleness. A positive nurturing energy and a catalyst for adults who need to heal the core traumas of their inner child and the wounds that are being held very deeply in the body. Good for children and babies with birth traumas.

Northern Twayblade (*Listera borealis*) Clears resistance to opening of the subtle aspects of our own consciousness. For when we are unable to integrate our spiritual wisdom and divine nature with our most basic needs. Helps us ground our sensitivity to the subtle realms more fully into our physical body and life experience; helps us enlighten our most basic needs, instincts, and mundane realities with the finest aspects of our spiritual wisdom.

One-Sided Wintergreen (*Pyrola secunda*) Helps sensitive people become aware of how they impact on and are impacted by others. Teaches us how to work in close proximity with others without losing our centre; helps create functional energy boundaries based on awareness of our own sensitivities. Dissolves dysfunctional energy boundaries when strongly influenced by other people's energy. For creating and maintaining functional boundaries that are in alignment with one's highest truth and life purpose, especially when unaware of how one's energy and actions affect others.

Round-Leaved Sundew (*Drosera rotundifolia*) For merging with the source of life; relinquishing identification with your ego, blending ego and divine will. Letting go of resistance to change and attachment to the known, fear of the unknown; when struggle rather than change is preferred. Overidentification with the ego; lack of communication between the Lower and Higher Self. Brings the ego into alignment with divine will.

Shooting Star (*Dodecatheon frigidum*) For developing our connection to inner spiritual guidance for understanding cosmic origins and earthly purpose. When a sense of not belonging on the earth or homesickness for a place that cannot be identified creates an inability to consciously understand why one is here. Strengthens one's connection to inner spiritual guidance; brings a deeper understanding of cosmic origins and earthly purpose.

Sitka Burnet (*Sanguisorba stipulata*) For healing the past on all levels and feelings of internal discord from unknown origins. When unable to locate the source of our problems in life or having difficulty understanding the lessons contained within our learning experiences. Initiates healing completion on all levels – a facilitation essence which helps you identify issues that are contributing to internal conflict, bringing forth the potential in any healing process.

Sitka Spruce Pollen (*Picea sitchensis*) A 'grandfather' essence which acts as a catalyst by supporting the right action for the present moment, fostering a positive relationship with one's power. Dissolves lack of humility in one's relationship to the earth. Clears and expands our energy channels so that we can accept a strong flow of energy in the body. Connects us with ancient archetypes of mastery, male and female power perfectly joined together, clears imbalance between the masculine and feminine expressions of power within an individual. For reluctance to express or exercise one's power for fear of hurting someone. Balances power and gentleness in men and women supporting the balanced partnership with nature.

Soapberry (*Sheperdia canadensis*) Release of constrictions around the heart associated with a fear of the power of nature, fear of one's own power, or fear of using one's power in irresponsible, inappropriate or unbalanced ways. For understanding and integrating intense experiences in nature and helps us move through fear with an open heart. Supports us in channelling the expression of power through our hearts. Harmonizes both personal and planetary power.

Sphagnum Moss (*Sphagnum* sp.) For those who are overly critical and judgemental of the healing journey and obsessing about the day-to-day details of the healing process. For those who are unable to see the positive side of transformational experiences. Helps us release the need for harsh judgement or criticism of our healing journey; enables us to create a space of unconditional acceptance in the heart so that core issues can be brought there for healing, and helps us learn to see with unconditional love.

Sweetgrass (*Hierochloe odorata*) For the cleansing and rejuvenating of the energy blockages in the etheric and physical body and low energy flow during the day. For difficulties in bringing a healing process to final completion. Good for removing negative energies from the home or work environment. Helps to bring one's lessons and experiences to completion on all levels and removes disharmonious energies from our home or work environment

Tundra Twayblade (*Listera cordata*) Supports the release of deep pain, anguish and past trauma held at the deepest level of one's being. Opens the heart to allow unconditional love complete access to areas of the body that need healing – supports the clearing of trauma held at the cellular level of the body, especially dysfunctional patterns held within the collective consciousness (abuse being the most prevalent form of these patterns today).

White Fireweed (*Epilobium angustifolium*) For deep emotional healing of shock and trauma from profound alienation from the body after an experience of sexual or emotional abuse. Calms the emotional body after shocking experience, releasing the energetic imprint of the past emotionally painful experiences from our cellular memory so rejuvenation can begin.

Wild Rhubarb (*Polygonum alaskanum*) Promotes mental flexibility, clearing blocked or undeveloped mental faculties and expanding the channel of communication between the heart and mind. Brings the mind into alignment with divine will through the heart; encourages a relaxation of inappropriate mental control; balances the rational and the intuitive. As a result, new thoughts, plans for action and solutions to problems come about.

New Essences

Angelica (*Angelica genuflexa*) Promotes effortless acceptance of spiritual support in all situations; letting the light into your life, experiencing the protection that comes from within.

Cloudberry (*Rubus chamaemorus*)
Opening to the true source of your being
and reflecting this outwardly for others to
see; for replacing low self-esteem with an
awareness of inner value; helps you see the
light of purity deep within yourself; recognizing the 'angelic' level of your being.

Comfrey (*Symphytum officinale*) Supports
healing on all levels; heals the etheric body
when there has been an injury in this or
another lifetime; promotes the
embodiment of higher spiritual energies
and the expression of our divine potential.

Dwarf Fireweed (*Epilobium adenocaulon*)
Helps transform unresolved issues that are
held at the core of your being; allows you
to be open to and experience transformation with gentleness, pacing and ease;
releases pain and trauma from the past so
you can reconnect with the original joy of
living, helps to fine-tune how we move
through a healing process so we do not
create more difficulties or pain. Encourages
the feeling of 'I have my whole life to live'.

Lapland Rosebay (*Rhododendron
lapponicum*) Penetrating insight into the
self and all of nature; seeing without
distortion; brings a person back to their
senses when they have been looking
outside of themselves for answers; reminds
you to look within for wisdom, knowledge,
perspective, and direction.

Lilac (*Syringa vulgaris*) Aligns the chakras
so that they can more fully receive and
embody light; helps you gracefully raise the
frequency of your energy fields. For raising
energetic vibration in the body; aligning
the chakras to receive and embody light
energy fully.

Pale Corydalis (*Corydalis sempervirens*)
Balances addictive and conditional patterns
of loving; helps you see relationships as
catalysts for spiritual growth and enlightenment; helps you follow the divine plan in
relationships.

Pink-Purple Poppy (*Papaver
somniferum*) Purity in form; helps you
embody and project universal love through

your heart. Helps you maintain balance
during rapid phases of evolution, when
your entire vibrational makeup is
undergoing transformation; enables you to
experience deep levels of integration and
rest while allowing the transformative
process to continue; helps you open to and
embody new information from the Higher
Self that enhances life in the physical
dimension.

Potato (*Solanum tuberosum*) Physical
release: helps you 'thaw out' incomplete
cycles of experience that are being held in
the body; allowing love to penetrate into
every cell of the body and into all manifestations of your being.

Purple Mountain Saxifrage (*Saxifraga
oppositifolia*) Grounding wisdom from the
Higher Self; helps you tune in to higher
frequencies of information.

Purple Poppy (*Papaver somniferum*)
Balance during rapid phases of evolution,
when our entire vibrational makeup is
undergoing transformation; enables us to
experience deep levels of integration and
rest while allowing the transformative
process to continue; helps us be open to
and embody new information from the
Higher Self that enhances life in the
physical dimension.

Red Elder (*Sambucus racemosa*)
Grandmother wisdom (Native American
for wisdom of the ages) helps one view life
from the centre rather than from the
periphery; and open up to your future
potential. Also helps one contract over-
expanded states, i.e. feeling frazzled and
overwhelmed.

Red-Purple Poppy (*Papaver
somniferum*) For balancing extremes
between physical and etheric levels;
blending the survival and spiritual aspects
of life together in a balanced way, supports
us in making full use of our physical
capacities to embody spirit.

Self-Heal (*Prunela vulgaris*) For raising
self-esteem; self-acceptance, and an
expansion of love and compassion for

yourself. Helps strengthen your belief in the body's ability to heal itself. Relaxing and calming, slows one down in order to gain perspective on priorities, especially under pressure to do and decide.

Valerian (*Valeriana officinalis*) Helps you slow down in order to gain perspective on your priorities, especially when feeling pressured to do or decide; promotes harmony in relationships finding a peaceful common ground.

Wild Sweet Pea (*Hedysarum mackenzii*) Increases your sense of your own inner strength and stability; helps bring these qualities to the surface to be offered in balance to others; promotes confidence and ease in your interactions with others.

Yellow Paintbrush (*Castilleja unalaschensis*) Facilitates the release of emotional frustrations and feelings of self-limitation that block our creative expression; helps you open and cleanse the heart so that it may act as a focal point for the sharing of your creative energies

Combination Essences

Calling All Angels (*Angelica, Chalice Well, Chiming Bells, Kunzite*) Calling All Angels is a combination formula that helps you contact the love, guidance, and protection of the angelic realm. It brings a very soft, loving, and serene energy into your heart, physical body and environment. Use it to:

strengthen the knowledge that you are guided, supported, and protected by the angels;

bring more joy and peace in to your life;

make a stronger connection with the divine feminine;

create a sacred and protected space for sleeping and dreaming, especially for children;

come into a stronger awareness of your own angelic nature;

experience the love of the angelic kingdom in your physical body.

Fireweed Combo (*Fireweed, River Beauty, White Fireweed, Dwarf Fireweed*) Fireweed Combo encourages and supports deep processes of transformation and renewal. Helpful to prepare for a transformational experience, especially useful when in the middle of an intense healing process and need extra support to get through it. Enables you to access the support you need to face fears, let go of resistance, and allow the process to move forward through each stage to its completion.

Helps to strengthen your grounding connection to the earth so your energy system will be more stable and better able to cope with change;

shifts the whole transformative process to a deeper level by releasing layers of deep pain and emotional trauma that are being held at the cellular level of the body;

stays engaged with the transformative process until you have resolved all of the issues that are connected to it;

reconnects with the desired levels of joy and happiness that are your birthright.

Add to a bath whenever you need additional support to make it through a period of intense transformation and change.

Guardian (*Covellite, Devil's Club, Round-Leaf Orchid, Stone Circle, White Violet Yarrow*) Guardian creates a powerful force field of protection in your aura. It invokes positive, harmonious energies that help you claim your energetic space, maintain your grounding and feel the protection of strong, healthy boundaries. Especially effective for those who: are overly reactive to influences in your environment;

are ambivalent about being present in their body and on the earth, because they don't feel safe or protected;

work around computers and other electromagnetic equipment or in a toxic environment;

have a tendency to take on or absorb the thoughts and emotions of others;

are unable to embody their sensitivity in a practical and easy way because of a lack of functional boundaries;

are doing healing work that requires them to be in the working, living, or personal energy space of their clients;

have just moved into a new home or neighbourhood and are having difficulty grounding into their new situation;

feel tired or run-down and need to rest and nurture themselves, but can't seem to create the space to do it.

Lighten Up (*Carnelian, Grass of Parnassus, Orange Calcite, Solstice Sun*) A combination formula that increases your ability to embody light. Its overall effect is to uplift, energize, inspire and nourish. Designed specifically for people who suffer from light deprivation, either due to living in extreme northern or southern latitudes, the limitations of their living environment (in a dark house or apartment), or because of the quality of their energy system (energy pathways blocked or undeveloped). It is also helpful for those who are depressed, caught in negative patterns or situations, or feel cut-off in any way from their inner sources of light.
It works on three main levels:

It opens and cleanses the chakras so you can draw more life force energy through appropriate channels already present in your energy system;

It cleanses and expands the energy pathways in your physical body, and amplifies your ability to assimilate light at the cellular level;

It strengthens your ability to integrate experience, thereby increasing the amount of energy that can flow through your body and life.

Use when you are fatigued or feel a chronic lack of energy on the physical level. When you want to enhance the qualities of light in your living and working environments. For Seasonal Affective Disorder. With animals that must be kept inside for long periods, especially during the winter

months. In the classroom, when you are losing your ability to concentrate. On plants to give them extra light and energy during short winter days

Pregnancy Support (*Balsam Poplar, Bog, Devil's Club, Diopside, Emerald, Grove Sandwort Ladies' Mantle, Northern Lady's Slipper*) This formula was inspired by the work and research of Cynthia Abu-Asseff, a flower essence therapist and mother living in Sao Paulo, Brazil. Cynthia started using the Alaskan essences with mothers and babies at a centre called Projeto Renascer in January of 1999. This centre was started in 1991 by a service-oriented spiritual group led by Cynthia's parents. In the years since its formation, it has helped over 1000 pregnant women.

Pregnancy Support is designed to strengthen, stabilize, and balance a woman and the baby growing within her during the entire pregnancy. Its primary action is to help the mother to meet the physical, emotional, and mental challenges that can arise during this life-changing event.

Use to help a woman create and nurture a sacred space in her life and body to support the growth and development of her baby. To assist both the mother and the indwelling soul in clearing any ambivalence they have about being on the earth. Helps mothers strengthen their connection with the earth so they can provide nurturing energy for themselves and their families. Enables women who themselves suffered from a traumatic birth to heal this trauma so they can offer a stronger body/soul connection to their babies.

Develops and strengthen the energetic triad between the mother, father, and baby

Purification (*Black Tourmaline, Fireweed, Portage Glacier, Sweetgrass*) Purification is designed to cleanse and purify your home and work environments as well as your personal energy field. Used to break up and cleanse stagnant patterns of energy on any level. Use to:

release toxic energy from the mind, emotions, and physical body;

revitalize, balance and stimulate the renewal of energy on all levels of your energy system;

break up unhealthy patterns of energy in an environment where there has been addiction, depression, or abuse;

purify and recharge the environment where there is stagnant energy;

release old ingrained habits that are no longer useful, necessary, or contributing to your wellbeing.

Soul Support (*Cattail Pollen, Chalice Well, Cotton Grass, Fireweed, Labrador Tea Malachite, River Beauty, Ruby, White Fireweed*) Soul Support is our emergency care formula. Provides soul support for the whole family in acute stress, for children, and animals. Maintains strength, balance, and stability during any kind of stressful activity or traumatic situation, including:

accidents involving injury, shock, and/or trauma;

emotional catharsis and violent outbursts;

fear of flying and motion sickness;

before, during and after visits to the dentist;

after a fight, argument, or disagreement;

after receiving bad news;

for post traumatic stress;

before and immediately after surgery and during recovery;

for abrupt and/or major changes in plans;

in an animal shelter and for wild animal rescue and rehabilitation work;

for any transition, challenge, or initiation.

Travel Ease (*White Violet, Yarrow, Covellite, Black Tourmaline, Smoky Quartz*) The Travel Ease combination is specifically designed to ease the negative effects of air travel, including jet lag. For those who are environmentally sensitive and have difficulty being confined in small, constricted spaces for long periods of time, supports the establishment and mainte-

nance of functional energy boundaries, enabling us to feel as though we have all the personal space, even on a crowded flight.

The accumulation of 'airborne' pollutants in the auric field during long flights is one of the main contributors to jet lag. This essence maintains the overall integrity of our energy fields, challenged by electromagnetic radiation generated by the plane's avionics and wiring, and by the noise and vibration generated from the plane. Releases any toxic or unwanted energies absorbed during flight.

Addresses the disorientation when travelling to new places and from moving through multiple time-zones, maintains grounding during flight and keeps our body energies synchronized and aligned by constantly updating our energetic system with the earth's energy as we move from one location to another. So we arrive at the final destination, truly there, energetically as well as physically.

For maximum effectiveness, begin taking the Travel Ease combination several days before your flight, at least three times during the flight, and for a few days after you reach your destination. For extended travel, the formula should be taken every hour you are airborne. It will also be helpful if you drink lots of water during the flight, stretch whenever possible, and get plenty of exercise before and after your trip.

Sacred Space Sprays

The Sacred Space Sprays, co-created by Jane Bell and Steve Johnson, were designed primarily for space clearing, an ancient practice brought to life by Denise Linn in her book *Sacred Space*, that helping people to create healthy living and working environments.

These sprays are further developed from the Alaskan Combination Formulas: Calling All Angels, Guardian, and Purification. Added to these are complementary blends of the highest quality essential oils and absolutes, chosen on the basis of their therapeutic qualities, and their ability to ground and enhance the function of each essence combination.

The Sacred Space Sprays were formulated to address the increasing challenge of maintaining our health in this crowded and fast-paced world. Stagnant and toxic energies accumulate in our living and working environments from computers and other electrical equipment, pollution, emotional upsets, illness, clutter and even from previous occupants. Over time these disharmonious energies can have a detrimental effect on our physical vitality, relationships, productivity, creativity, prosperity and general wellbeing. You can cleanse yourself and your surroundings of these unwanted toxins and bring in the fresh, elementally infused energies of nature by using Sacred Space Sprays along with the simple and straight-forward techniques of space clearing.

These sprays were designed to help evolve from a position of being at the mercy of surroundings to having a positive effect on them. The apartments, flats, houses and buildings in which we live and work can become beacons of light that radiate out and positively transform our neighbourhoods, cities, countries and the world.

Calling All Angels Spray *Angelica, Chalice Well, Chiming Bells, and Kunzite Essences with essential oils of Bulgarian Red Rose Otto, Carnation, Alpine Lavender, and Pink Grapefruit.* This spray helps you to contact the love, guidance, and protection of the angelic realm and bring a soft, loving, serene energy into your heart, physical body, and environment. The joyful and calming oils promote the release of tension, and open our hearts to the love and peace of the angels. This spray came out of Jane's work with children who were having difficulty sleeping, and as a result were keeping their parents up as well. Instead of calling out for Mum or Dad after waking up, they would use this spray, say, 'Calling all angels', and fall back into a peaceful slumber.

Invokes the love, guidance, and protection of the angelic realm into a room after it has been space cleared.

Creates a sacred, protected space for sleeping and dreaming – works for pets too!

Strengthens the awareness that all family members are supported and protected by the angels.

Brings the essence of joy and peace into your life.

Makes a stronger connection to the divine feminine.

Guardian Spray *Covellite, Devil's Club, Round-Leaf Orchid, Stone Circle, White Violet, and Yarrow, also contains the essential oils of Hyacinth, Litsea Cubaba, Tangerine, Lime and Melissa.* Guardian helps you create a powerful force field of protection in your aura and environ-ment, enabling you to claim your energetic space, maintain your grounding, and feel the protection of strong, healthy boundaries. The oils enhance the protective and grounding qualities of the essences and add uplifting notes of joy and playfulness. Especially useful for the highly sensitive – often feeling sensitivity is a curse instead of a blessing because we don't know how to keep the energies in our environment from penetrating and depleting us. Guardian reminds us that we are the source of our own protection. Connects us with our inner light, helps radiate this powerful energy outward into our surroundings. This helps us stay open and sensitive, while feeling sealed and protected. For those people who:

need to strengthen their boundaries before entering into another person's living, working, or personal space;

want to invoke an energy of protection into a room that has just been space cleared;

want to set a more relaxed and grounded energy into the environment;

want to preserve the energy that they have just invoked into a space;

would like to decrease the detrimental effects that computers and other electro-magnetic equipment are having on them or their employees.

Purification Spray *Black Tourmaline, Fireweed, Portage Glacier, and Sweetgrass enhanced by the essential oils of Peppermint, Lavender Mailette, Black Spruce, and Frankincense.* Purification cleanses and purifies your home, work environments and personal energy field. Utilized to break up and clear stagnant patterns of energy on any level and contains the four most powerful cleansing and releasing Alaskan essences. The oils enhance the purifying function and add clarifying, sanctifying and refreshing qualities to the spray. The Purification Spray evokes a feeling of cool winds blowing off glaciers. It carries an invigorating blast of ionic energy that washes away tiredness and brings a sense of vital aliveness. This spray transports the purity of the wilderness into our complex man-made environments, awakening our senses and reminding us of our true natures.

Spray to release any kind of stagnant energy that has collected in a room or building – the first step in the space clearing process.

Breaks up unhealthy patterns of energy in a space where there has been illness, addiction, depression, or abuse;

releases toxic energy from the mind, emotions, and physical body;

purifies the energy in your rental car when you pick it up and in your hotel room when you arrive;

revitalizes, balances, and stimulates the renewal of energy on all levels of your home, office, or aura.

Soul Support Spray *Cattail Pollen, Chalice Well, Cotton Grass, Fireweed, Labrador Tea Malachite, River Beauty, Ruby, White Fireweed and essential oil of*

Lavender. Utilizes the soothing and clarifying properties of an organic Lavender oil from Kashmir. Use it to calm, ground, and centre your environment as well as your energy field. It can be used in all of the situations listed above, especially when oral application is impossible or inconvenient.

Travel Ease Spray *White Violet, Yarrow, Covellite, Black Tourmaline, Smoky Quartz and essential oils of Black Spruce, Lavender, and Pink Grapefruit.* The essential oils in the Travel Ease Spray support the cleansing, grounding, and uplifting qualities of the formula. Using the Travel Ease Spray is a refreshing way to keep your energy field strong, clear, and grounded during long flights, train or bus journeys, and when transiting airports, train and bus stations.

Alaskan Flower Essences: Making the Environmental Essences

Shabd-sangeet Khalsa (SSK) has kindly provided some of the original notes she made when making the Environmental Essences. From these one can gain further fascinating insights into these unique essences and the process of attunement and deep connection producers have with the nature kingdom.

As a child SSK would listen to the sound of silence, lie on the ground next to a waterfall and go into the silence beyond her thoughts, hear the music played by trees, and receive profound wisdom while she was 'just being'. Often she would talk to fairies and fell in love with flowers in the garden; she particularly loved the pansies with their happy little flower faces. Compelled to pick the roses and breathe in their fragrance throughout the day she would often sip raindrops from the flower petals – it rained frequently where she lived. SSK felt the natural world deeply. Her desire to commune with the oneness of nature was an ache deep at the core of her being.

She moved to Alaska in 1976 where she studied botany at the University of Alaska and received an undergraduate grant to conduct a taxonomic survey of the wild plants in the arboretum. She marvelled at the wild green orchids in the bogs, and the carnivorous plants in the mosses, tussocks and ponds. SSK lived and breathed flowers, it was her heaven on earth.

In the 1980s she was drawn to the California Flower Essence Society essences (FES) and was amazed by their subtle magic. She felt compelled to begin making her own.

As she listened to the nature spirits in her garden and in the woods and heard the messages from the flowers on how they wanted to be used for healing, she began to make essences with pansies, Johnny-jump-ups, fuchsias and so on.

In 1983 she was introduced Steve Johnson, and as their friendship grew, they started making the Alaskan Flower Essences together. In 1984, they co-founded the Alaskan Flower Essence Project in order to accurately identify each of the wild flowers that were used as essences, as common names can often apply to multiple species and even different genera.

A further development was initiated when in the Arctic winter SSK made the Northern Lights environmental essence, and in the summer she made the Rainbow Glacier, and Glacier River. Together they made the Solstice Sun Essence on the longest day of the year at about midnight with the sun shining brightly between two mountain peaks. They were standing along the banks of the Koyukuk River just south of the Arctic Circle. This was the start of a new concept in making essences and became the range of Environmental Essences.

According to SSK it is important to keeping information about the essences as pure as possible without filtering it through the mind and ego, which changes the information. When opening herself to receive the essence's message she opens her heart, experiencing the flower's essence,

allowing it be expressed in words to convey her experience. She says it is a challenge to bring words to describe such gossamer journeys, words can only give a sense of the essence. Each person who uses an essence can follow the energy of the essence to experience it themselves. It is a delicate line to walk between bringing the energy and information through so that it is not too etheric, but is understandable, and giving free rein to the mind to manipulate the information to fit a personal agenda.

An essence producer has a major responsibility to be aware of when the mistakes of the mind and ego are made as this creates a product of the ego, which is not what a flower essence is about.

Alder 9-9-87 A Crown of light to dwell within. Open, move beyond your resistance. Let this crown of light work within you.

Blue Elf Viola – my garden 9-7-84 Dissipates anger through its calming vibration, it cools the nervous system.

Blue Elf Viola – my garden 9-6-87 Draw upon this source of calm in the midst of intensity.

Butterwort 6-18-88 (SSK made this near Bettles, just south of the Brooks Range.) This essence brings harmony to the inner, subtle levels of your humanity. It connects all aspects of the human self to the Higher Self, more vibrant levels of light. Imagine this as threads you can follow to adjust your state of mind, emotions or general awareness. It feels like the freshness of rain. It feels like you slept all night in a wonderful cleansing rain and you awoke very clear and refreshed. It functions as a vehicle to take you deep inside yourself to leave past deprivations behind, to ascend within yourself as you dive deep into your own heart and consciousness to the experience of, 'I want to be you, I know I am you when I look into your eyes and feel the openness of my heart. I want to envelop you, to merge with you, to flow as the identical light we become in this recognition.'

Cattail Pollen 8-10-87 Courage during emergence. To come forth in growth to be as you truly are. Stand tall in your courage, sway if you must but do not yield to forces outside of yourself. Let your spirit soar while you keep your feet planted on the earth. Stand solid in your truth. This is the essence of standing tall on your truth.

Chiming Bells 6-15-84 Helps you develop the gift of spiritual song. It helps you to open to more life force energy, puts more life into your eyes, opens the heart to the subtle consciousness of the natural world. It helps to shield you from the effects of loud noises.

Combination Poppy – my garden 7-18-89 Joy, willingness to touch into the deep layers of your being to see and share the inner light. To see yourself as separate, compartmentalized is not true. See what is whole, that you are whole and you are a part of the whole.

Crowberry 5-8-91 Feel your own sense of knowing from within your body, your vehicle with which you experience this life. If you resist living in your body this essence will help you sense how much you are in and how much you are out. This essence is a guide for those who are lingering on the outside of their bodies. The essence will guide you into your body.

Crystal Saxifrage, Rainbow Mt 6-4-88 (SSK gave this common name as it had none.) This essence works indirectly with solar energy by bringing it into an etheric crystalline form within the flower. It can assist you in working inter-dimensionally. The purpose is to expand your awareness and to tap into this tiny source of power which acts as a catalyst for intense creative thought, as a preparation for creative breakthrough this crystalline energy helps you access additional energy, especially when you have reached a point where you need to move through a 'tight squeeze' or meet with inertia.

Focus your thoughts at the heart centre, place the essence on the heart centre and bring the energy to the heart. Let the crystalline energy develop in you; bring your thoughts into the centre of the crystals. Allow for the transformation to take place within you, for the creative flow, the opening, expanding intuitive knowing.

Double Shirley Poppy – my garden Abundance. It begins with where you grow, flourish and blossom. You share your nectar, fruits and seeds. Each stage takes place in its own time. While there is growth there are no fruits or seeds to share, but they are developing out of sight while the plant grows them in fertile ground where the earth shares her abundance through the roots, the sky shares its abundance through the sun and rain. The sharing of abundance requires patience. Some flowers bloom while others have gone to seed. In abundance there is variety. The earth is generous and abundant.

Look within; what variety of abundance do you have within and in what stage of development? What are you able to share abundantly with yourself and with others?

Forget-Me-Not 9-4-84 This essence penetrates to your depths to help you bring forth the golden heart within you so you can share this in your life.

Foxglove 9-4-84 This essence assists you when you must navigate through darkness, through tunnel vision. It will help you to be able to see where you are headed because you will be able to follow your inner guidance, your goal will be very clear and precise. Go beyond the forms of darkness, once beyond it you are infinity, you can create what you wish.

Fuchsia – my garden 6-17-84 Abounding joy in having physical form for expression of life. See your inner light, your glow, the rainbows moving all around you. See your own beauty in this creation, you are but another flower in the garden of life. For clarity of mind, breaks the chains of habitual thinking and emotions

Glacier River 7-18-90 The glacial river embodies the process of release from form. The river carries suspended particles of ground-up mountains. The water in this river comes from melting glaciers and snow. The glaciers glide over the mountains and grind the rocks into tiny particles. The mountains are gradually released from their forms. While the mountains were growing the glaciers were forming. During their creation they were also being destroyed. The mountain pieces are so tiny they remain suspended in the torrential waters flowing rapidly downhill. If you feel rigid, non fluid, resistant to change, clinging to the form you assume is 'real' this essence will help you release.

Nothing is set in stone, even if it looks like it is. The river is always flowing even in the deep of winter when the world feels so cold in the far north. The waters still flow, the glaciers still slide over the rocks and the grinding goes on. Be like the river, always flowing, always releasing form into formlessness and movement. You can embody disembodiment during the times you find it difficult to let go. You will find this essence in some of the wild divine flower essence combinations.

Green Bells of Ireland – my garden

These flowers create illusions to fool the mind to bring you to a place of inner openness. The essence expands a silvery light inside you to create neutral space from which to explore the inner worlds. This essence is a beginning step of travelling into the green light energies of nature, which is the expansive self.

Green Fairy Orchid 7-8-87 (SSK gave it this common name as it has none in the taxonomic key for Alaska.) Accepting oneness. Seeing Helpers. You can look at this orchid and not see it. It is tiny and illusive. Once you feel it with your heart you will see it. The green light beckons you onward past the sight of your eyes. This tiny bog orchid helps you to focus in and inward. It is the tiny things in life that help you to see differently. Through this inner focus you are invited into a realm beyond the ego, into the mystical green energies of nature to find the inner light, to let it be focused to a pin point to go through it into

the heart beyond the mind. This helps to set you free, to experience your boundlessness. This essence helps you to see when it is time to see what you have not yet focused on. See the light you are, it grows, and you cannot be separate from the divine except in your mind.

Grove Sandwort 6-21-84 It can assist with regaining balance when experiencing a whirlwind of emotions. It helps settle the emotions of the unborn child when the mother is disturbed, happiness returns. This essence can facilitate developing the bonds and communication between mother and child. It will help you to strengthen your own tie with Earth Mother and to open to being nurtured by her. As you are nurtured so you can nurture.

Harebell (Rainbow Mt tundra) 8-12-87 Connecting open hearts. Connects the hearts of those who love one another. To connect despite barriers. This essence is like an invisible string that keeps the hearts touching, feeling the connection. The connection can be lost if it cannot be felt even when it exists. The heart feels, the head does not. Heart felt connections need to be felt to be kept alive.

Icelandic Poppy 9-4-84 This bright splash of light in the flower's colours helps to reflect your inner radiance. The flower is a solar collector, it collects light and reflects light. It will help you become bold in your life if that is what you need.

Labrador Tea 6-21-84 Clears shadows away from the mind to help one see what is true and to make new choices.

Lambsquarters 7-17-87 Accessing information through the heart before interpreting it in the mind. Expand into and beyond the vastness of time and space. Be connected, be the flow, let your vision, your wisdom and awareness expand beyond the mind. This essence will help you develop a lighter life. Between the mind and its might follow this green light on the path to the heart.

Lilac – my garden 7-3-90 Garden Lilac calls out, 'Reunite yourself, be one with all things.' (The lilac brings in the purple rays, angels slide to earth from the heavens on these beams.) The lilac ray, the Christ ray of light. Strength and joy. This lilac essence brings in the purple ray energies. Within this ray is a full spectrum of the purple and violet hues. It relates to ascension. Not the ascension of leaving the body as in the example of the Christ, but in aligning the chakras, opening the energy pathways to receive light, to embody light and to share light.

Monkshood 7-11-87 This essence helps you to remove your earthly burden, to help you disrobe from the heaviness you carry in your mind, emotions and body. It can teach you to walk in the nudity of truth so you can be clothed in light. The entire plant is toxic, truth is toxic to the ego. When you resist truth it can make you sick. Monkshood shares the calmness of the sanctuarial confines where the focus is on the divine without distractions. You can be cloaked in this calm vibration with this essence which makes it easier to touch the divine in yourself and therefore in others.

Northern Twayblade, Rainbow Mt 7-6-91 Opening to the infinite. Attuning your perceptions to a very subtle level of manifestation. An energy so soft that you cannot develop any resistance to its healing.

Onesided Wintergreen One side of one thing is the other side of another. There is no separation. This essence is to bring you into the awareness that all that you do is affected by others and all that you do affects others. Will you think and behave differently if you are actually cognisant of this, if you can actually feel your connectedness with all?

Opium Poppy Devic Essence 7-6-91 This preparation embodies not only the floral archetype, but also the living presence of the devic energies, consciousness. This essence becomes a living entity, a living potential as an essence. Archetypes are usually well formed unless there is a need for them to be altered.

Pansy – my garden 9-7-84 These flower vibrations spread cheer. They vibrate fearlessness.

Pink Lady's Slipper 6-22-84 Each flower has the ability to stimulate energy in the body, open meridians for the *chi* to flow powerfully. It helps to give clear vibrations to the voice.

Pink-Purple Opium Poppy – my garden 10-4-90 This essence is to help you drink in the elixir of love. Not the emotions, the Big Love, the essence of creation the purity of form and the love of life, the gift of life, the gift of consciousness. This essence is to help you to drink in the nectar of life, of living freely, not bound by form, but allowing form to become your freedom.

The balance grows finer as you become more developed. The universal love can flow into you, through you. Your heart can keep this pure. This will help you to keep your heart pure so the flow through you will be unimpeded. Let it flow, be the flow and then overflow the elixir of life in your life.

Prickly Wild Rose 6-19-84 Fortitude, expansive clarity of spirit.

Purple Saxifrage, Rainbow Mt 5-29-91 This essence is a beacon of light, a receptor for stellar light channelling it into the planetary grid of light. It pulses blue light upward to bring in the needed frequencies. It will help you to clear your own energies so that you can be aligned with the incoming frequencies to assist you with multidimensional living. Do you want to be a clear receiver? It can help open the crown chakra. It will help you make energetic adjustments so you can more readily receive the celestial songs that mingle with the earth elements. It will help you to shift from living solely in rapport with the limited intellect to living in relationship with your limitless, spirit, open heart and ability to manifest beauty on this earth.

Purple Opium Poppy – my garden 7-9-89 This essence is for when you need a break and there is no break. It is for when you go through very challenging and profound growth that brings you closer to spirit. It is for when your entire vibrational blueprint is being rearranged. When you feel so uncomfortable you don't want to be in your body. This vibration is like a vibrational oasis, rest during evolution. Sometimes the internal changes are almost too intense to bear, that is when this essence is really needed.

Rainbow Glacier 8-11-87 Essence of the elements. Time and space frozen in ice. Then and now moving as one in ancient ice. Power and tranquillity. Elements seemingly in opposition come together as one in glacial ice. Ice as mass of moving, melting, flexing, pushing, grinding frozen water. A river of ice moving, imperceptible. Renewal, cleansing. Earth is scraped bare. This essence of the elements contains the energies that create the beginnings of life.

Grain by grain, mountains are ground into tiny flecks of ground up rocks, glacial silt. This is how you move a mountain. If you find there are seemingly insurmountable obstacles in your life this is the essence to use.

Red-Purple Opium Poppy – my garden 10-4-1990 This essence helps to balance the extremes between earth and ether, physical and spirit. When the earthly focus takes too much attention then the balance is lost. When the physical is ignored the balance is also lost. These are meant to function together. Not one to negate the other or to be held in more favour than the other. They are part of the one and together they create a balance for dwelling with spirit embodied, with body respected. Life is a yoga, the coming together of the perceived opposites to find out how they synergize to expand your awareness and help you to evolve as a whole being.

Rhododendron, Rainbow Mt 6-4-88 Pink crystalline energy envelops these flowers, it is more cloudlike, less formed; or more gaseous, etheric and moving than static or structural. This essence will help to reveal small things in all forms. It will help to intensify your awareness of life at this small scale, shift your perception of smallness to equal vastness and then have nothing to do with size at all. It will play with your mind to help you shift and expand and come to perceive this life with freshness, with the not-knowing wisdom of an unconditioned mind. The soft pink light of these flowers and this essence will be like guides for your eyes, for your inner vision.

Single Delight (Toads' Reading Lamp) (*Moneses uniflora*) This flower channels light along the surface of the earth where it grows. It focuses additional light to the earth's grid, which is a natural aspect of nature. This essence will help you to feel connected to those who also walk upon this earth.

Sitka Burnet, Rainbow Mt Healing the past so the constrictions around the heart do not return. This essence will assist you in dealing with internal strife, the kind that results from inner conflicts, lack of inner congruency or lack of time given to oneself. This essence will help sooth you, like an internal massage or a sense of the smoothing of your feathers.

Snapdragon 9-4-84 Helps with healing jaw injuries. This essence contrasts 'good and bad' side, positive and negative, yin and yang to help you be aware of the direction each polarity will take you.

Spireae 6-17-84 Brings the vibrations of the forest's peace and the sensitivity of the heart. Opens one to the love and beauty of flowers, and deep inner strength.

Sweetgrass, Bettles 6-21-88 This essence will make you feel very clean, like you have showered in the cleanest rain and every single facet of your being is very, very clean.

Tundra Twayblade, Rainbow Mt tundra 7-6-91 (SSK gave this its common name.) Seek the green places in the heart they will lead you inward. Listen inwardly. This essence has green light rays as sharp as points to help sharpen your vision. Follow the green light within to expand your heart light. The journey is inward, follow the light inward. The green points of light become crystalline and can be focused in the body to assist with healing. Life begins in the ethers, with thought and energy, your imagination is your tool, like your hands in the subtle playground of the not yet physical form. This essence is an expression of the divine creation in its delicate beauty, and intricate creation. It will show you the power of your heart because as closely as you look at this flower so must you look at yourself.

Twinflower 6-21-84 Helps magnify sound, will help intensify the spoken quiet voice and shows you the power of small thoughts.

Verbena – from my garden

Celebration of light, colour, raindrops, sunlight, life and scent. Joy embodied in beauty. Fairy trumpets. Dancing fairies. Attune your ears to the joy, let the joyful dance touch you. Lighten yourself in celebration, in cosmic dance. Light becomes the perfume of flowers. Drink in the colours and cosmic laughter.

White Spruce Cosmic antennae. Call on the infinite wisdom through the spruce. Feel the support of creation. Access your wisdom. When you have trouble doing so, the white spruce will assist you again and again.

Wild Iris 6-27-84 Opens you to your inner health, balance and strength after a difficult confrontation. It helps to bring solar energy inward for strength so you have energy to develop to your full capacity in your life.

Wild Rhubarb 8-5-87 Clearing the channel between the mind and the heart. Flexibility of the mind is like flexibility of the spine, it keeps new life coming in. It is necessary to learn how to bend. The green light of the flowers helps to cleanse the mind. The more you allow it in the clearer you can become. The mind can stand in the way of living from the heart. This green energy is the energy of the heart, it helps to soften the grip of the mind. If the mind becomes rigid, it will affect your flexibility. Use this essence to keep or increase your flexibility on all levels.

Willow 9-9-87 For a strong energy field that cannot be broken. This is the power of regeneration in great abundance. Bring this strength into yourself.

Wormwood This essence is an etheric map into the heart to heal the human soul so that the evolution is not hindered, but that you may experience the hidden treasures of nature that are in your own nature; there is no separation. It is a journey into the self through healing, or releasing the constrictions around the heart so that your own light may expand and you know your truth. There is no separation. There is limitlessness. There is ultimately the light and bliss, of which we are all expressions.

Zinnia – my garden 9-7-84 This bright red orange flower vibrates powerfully. It can help you to penetrate dense vibration so that you can move through them as though they were not there.

The Dancing Light Orchid Essences

Inspired by the indefinable spiritual nature of orchids, after her work with the Alaskan Essences SSK went on to develop her delightful range of Dancing Light Orchid Essences.

Orchids have an exceptionally high vibrational quality and are said to be 'the queen of the plant kingdom'. They are honoured by shamans and indigenous peoples for their connection to spirit, and they embody the creative intelligence and intentions from Nature.

These essences intend to work with our own blueprints and act as internal guides bringing us back into alignment so that we are able to fulfil our destinies. The human experience is very demanding and oftentimes damaging to the original blueprints we have designed, there is no oasis to go to for realignment so the over-lighting beings assist with the strong intentions and focus through the Dancing Light Orchid Essences.

Imagine a multidimensional blueprint which over-lights and infuses our circuitry with our original blueprints. It takes the struggle out of transformation so one's own intact blueprints are once again accessible and in fact functioning as overlays. Suddenly we can simply realign instead of struggling for ideals of perfection lost.

Balancing Extremes (*Paphiopedilum lowii*) Express the truth and radiance of yourself in balance. Has your uniqueness felt misplaced? Why did you go so far out of balance? What did you lose sight of? In the ecstasy, your self will remain grounded; in the earth plane, you will remember your bliss.

Centred Love (*Bollea coelestis*) This essence embodies heart-centred love. A good essence to use when you want communication to come from the heart. This essence will facilitate heart shifts, for exploring new relationships and new levels within relationships.

Clearing Blockages (*Phragmipedium caudatum*) This essence brings a fresh example of how energy can move most freely through the body. Overall theme: fluidity and flexibility. An analogy in Chinese medicine would be removing blocks to the flow of *chi*.

Clearing Energy Fields Combination Essence Offers energetic support to look within and release. Clears the energies when one feels ready to release, and transform.

Clearing Inner Pathways (*Aeranthes henrici*) My subtle light penetrates and prepares the internal communication paths to enlightenment. This essence excels in clearing our inner pathways to allow information and light to travel.

Dance of Creation Blue Orchid (*Vanda coerulea*) I am the soothing essence of exquisite awareness. My purpose is to tickle your mind and the pathways into your heart so you will join in the merry dance of creation.

Dancing Light Spirit Calypso Orchid (*Calypso bulbosa var. occidentalis*) Embody fluidity. Dance between form and formlessness. This essence holds the pattern of fluidity for you to be able to open your perceptions to move between the manifest and un-manifest. It can transform you.

Defining Edges (*Brassia arcuigera*) Create your personal boundaries without creating separation from others. Creating boundaries provides an important part of your definition of self, as well as strength, safety, and integrity.

Earth Mother Nurtures Environmental essence Earth Mother is a collective of enlightened beings, with a capacity for compassion that is unfathomable. They merge with the form of earth to nurture all beings who dwell here. They are eager to assist us with our journey towards enlightenment; they know that ultimately we all journey together. This essence is an invitation, a welcoming into the heart of the earth.

Essence of the Edge Environmental Essence The Essence of the Edge is for those doing their work at the cutting edge. It is for comprehending the purpose of the edge in your life at present. It is a safety net if you are pushed to the edge of what you can do, understand, cope with, and manifest.

Expanding Awareness (*Phaleanopsis hybrid*) This essence creates a wiggle where there is a tiny opening; it wiggles and keeps wiggling, creating an expanding gap, a space for your awareness to expand. You may feel a quickening as this process gains momentum.

Gossamer Steel/Enduring Love (*Phalaenopsis Texas Star* x *P. Brother Delight*) This essence opens the heart to higher octaves of love. Touch the fine threads of love, let their music resound within. This essence embodies resilience, the strength to endure. This essence is like gossamer steel, born of desire to create the sustainable fineness of love, and to anchor love's higher manifestations.

Graceful Transformations (*Masdevallia coccinea var. harryana*) A caterpillar makes a cocoon wherein it transforms into a butterfly. This essence

assists you in discarding unused energies, thought forms, and emotional patterns. It helps clothe you with your new forms of manifesting self.

Heart to Heart Combination Essence This essence assists in attuning to your truest source of navigation, your heart. An energy emanates from your heart that another heart recognizes as true. 'Let your heart be your guide', is an expression based on universal truth of experience and being. Get to the heart of the matter. Let this essence assist you in going deeper within, through the gateway of your heart, to the heart of your self.

Heart of Nature/Devic Awareness (*Miltonia Jean Sabourin* 'Vulcain') This essence helps you develop an elemental awareness of the life force all around you. The trees, rocks, flowers and other forms are alive with creative cosmic intelligence. Elemental light. Elemental sound. Elemental motion. Elemental breath. Much of this awareness is purely experiential, far beyond thoughts the mind can capture. Let the experience take you; ultimately there will be a story for your mind to know.

Heart Wings Butterfly Orchid (*Psychopsis papilio*) Let your heart fly with the energies of this essence, let the wings of your heart lift you. Perspectives of spirit are unburdened. Feel free, think free, break free and fly free.

Higher Levels (*Paphiopedilum parishii*) Supports transformative growth by helping you release yourself from the accustomed form and allowing movement toward the next higher level of form.

I am In my Body/Expansive Embodiment (*Masdevallia ignea*) Assists with the process of full incarnation, bright with the light of spirit being…a new way of experiencing your spirit-body relationship. Imagine your body full of tiny spaces so the light within you shines outwardly like the sun's rays shining through clouds. The source is the sublime within.

Idiot Glee (*Vanda roeblingiana*) I am the brash youngster, I am the fits of giggles, I am the aches in the face from smiling, I am the tears of laughter. I bring you the most intense, senseless joy that you shall have the good fortune to endure.

I Like Being Me Combination (*Restrepia guttalata and a piece of a granite mountain*). This essence holds a pattern for self-love and acceptance. 'I look to nothing outside of myself for reference as to my self-worth, acceptability, lovability, inner wealth, and inner health. I like being me. That which I am is my unique expression of all possibilities. There is no other like me.'

Infinite Patience (*Paphiopedilum rothchildianum*) This pattern of conscious-ness directly accesses the gaps between your thoughts; drawing on limitless creative intelligence which embodies a deeper level of patience than is generally experienced in life. This is patience to carry one through great and lasting challenges. This is deeper than the patience of the mind; this is like breathing in the infinite.

Light Hearted/Heart Light (*Miltonia hybrid*) This essence supports your emotional body during difficult times so you can avoid falling into the depths of pain and despair, and face your experiences with hope and inner strength.

Lotus Petals of the Heart (*Paphiopedilum hybrid*) This essence helps you open to live life from your heart so you can feel your life more fully; know bound-less joy and possibilities that are not limited by the constraints of mind-centred being.

Lucid Dreaming (*Angraecum eburneum var. typicum*) Take this essence to release yourself from emotional terror. It will also assist you with developing lucidity on all levels. A companion for exploring the vast unknown, which is larger than you can ever know, and yet you may go exploring there.

Manifesting Thought Forms (*Paphiopedilum leeanum superbum*) This essence embodies the immanent patterns of the creative process. Intentions manifest gradually at first as they move through the ethers to where you can notice their shadow and then their form. At some point, one's intention is crystallized into physicality. Enhances the creative process.

Meditative Mind (*Phragmipedium xerophyticum*) How do I learn how to meditate? A quiet mind is like an unusual day of calm flat on the ocean, no waves, just glassy smooth water. A quiet mind is a gateway to pass through. This essence assists you in diving into the deeper levels of the mind to explore self in deeper meditative states, where the true treasures of life reside.

My Heart Knows (*Paphiopedilum tonsum*) Grace is the quality of fitting actions to the circumstances of the moment: knowing in your heart what to do, and when.

My Own Pure Light (*Paphiopedilum Eagle Peak* x *Paphiopedilum niveum*) 'The struggle is gone and I am light.'

My Song Calls Me Home (*Phragmipedium amazonica* syn. richteri) This vibration reunites you with lost or disconnected pieces of your self; from reclaiming bits of your playful inner child to soul retrieval.

New Perceptions Leopard Orchid (*Ansellia gigantean*) Keen focus takes place with this essence. It is about shifting paradigms with effortless ease. See, feel, sense, find and utilize abundance and unexpected opportunity.

Purpose Flows Slipper Orchid (*Phragmipedium ecuadorense*) In the heart one finds the wellspring of life's purpose: upwelling, bubbling, spilling over and trickling with the fluidity of water. Let your purpose well up within, let it be your sustaining pool. This essence helps to manifest the unaltered blueprint of purpose flowing freely.

Radiant Strength Slipper Orchid (*Phragmipedium besseae*) This essence supplies the blueprint for increasing radiance. For those who have lived a lifetime afraid of being seen as the radiant, unique and powerful beings they truly are. The stronger your glow the safer you are as you strengthen your energy field by the radiance of your boundless self.

Reading Energy Fields Star of Bethlehem Orchid (*Angraecum sesquipedale*) When auras blend, information is exchanged. You can use this essence to read your own energy field, and the energy fields of others. Whatever others have been holding onto, you will pick up.

Reveals Mystery Within (*Aeranthes grandiflora*) This essence is an invitation to explore the inner mysteries of the self.

Sacred Sphere (*Phragmipedium Scorcer's Apprentice*) This essence creates a subtle energetic sphere that one can 'be' within, while you engage in your daily activities. It helps you maintain your personal clarity.

Softening the Edges (*Platanthera obtusata*) (a wild Alaskan orchid) For those who handle delicate situations, precious young creatures and objects to help you have the gentlest of touches. Use this essence if you notice the edges of your personality have become sharp or hardened in reaction to disappointing or painful life experiences. It can help you to release and discard any harsh behaviours that cause yourself and others pain.

Unveiling Self (*Oeonia volucris*) Escape your ego's illusions of self – that is little ego. Recognize that True Self dwells in your human form, yet is much greater. Ego is not left behind, it is brought along on the journey of the soul.

Walking Out of Patterns (*Rhyncholaelia digbyana*) This essence is for walking out of the rhythms of old emotional patterning. Feel with your heart, and come into alignment with the purpose of your soul.

Wise Action Blue Sky Orchid (*Cattleya loddigessi var. coerulea*) Use this essence when you want your actions to come from wisdom. It allows you to let the spark of inspiration distil within, so your actions are congruent with your intelligence.

Wondrous Heart (*Vanda javierii*) Have you come to a place in your life where you've lost touch with the sense of wonder you had as a child. This essence will bring you back to that place. 'If you can feel the wonder, you can proceed.'

Combination Essences

Acceptance Essence Accept what is. If you are not accepting 'what is' in the present moment, you are resisting. Resistance does not change the present or past, but instead blocks the flow of your life. The gentle vibration of flowers can help you 'just be'. Allowing 'what is' creates acceptance. To create change, accept things for what they are as a first step: then you will know what is real, avoiding illusion and delusion. From there you can make choices and take action according to what is. Acceptance requires pause in action. The essence holds the energy to pause. In the pause, see 'what is'. In the pause accept 'what is'. You will find yourself in a pool of awareness and of acceptance. Pause in this.

Internal Marriage Combination Essence This essence is like taking a walk hand in hand with someone: yourself. It is about integrating dualities, complementary opposites, female and male energies within; internal marriage. It is not effort, but creativity.

Letting Go *Wild Alaskan River, Unveiling Self, Walking Out of Patterns, I Am In My Body* You will come to the time and space repeatedly in life where letting go of past experiences and emotions is required in order for you to move forward in life with clarity, with an open, light, compassionate heart. This essence will help you release your weighty emotions and thoughts renewing your ability to carry on with a lightened load. Just as solid mountains are eroded away one particle at a time by the elements so too can the embedded charges of body and mental memories be released.

Allow yourself to flow into the new days ahead with renewed fluidity and freedom. As mountains are eroded they become lighter, they rise higher.

Stepping Ahead Now Combination Essence You've done the work; now go forth into that which you have prepared. The elements are in place, the atoms and molecules are arranged correctly, in alignment with your intentions. The canvas is ready to receive your brush strokes. Step ahead now. This essence encourages you to do just that.

Wild Divine Mists

Wild Divine combination essences are effective for shock and trauma for you and your pets (our version of rescue remedy) (*see also* Pets and Animal section) they can help to connect you with your smiles, playfulness, inner peace, and peace of mind. Wild Divine essences can also help you to unfurl your wings, help you to release stressful energies, and are useful for clearing unwanted energies from your spaces.

These combination essences are filled with Alaska's wildness, nature's inspiration, the divine feminine, bits of magic, and senseless glee; plus Alaskan flower, tree, rock, elemental, environmental, wild and garden essences; the Dancing Light Orchid and the 7 Sister Moon Flower Essences, all to help you create movement in your life, to help you heal, grow and meet life's challenges. They'll help you by uplifting, expanding, and nurturing you, and by supporting your inner being and healing. Use them with your pets, plants, kids, friends, and especially for yourself in celebration of your life, health and wellbeing.

Alaska is a treasure of purity and wilderness, a vast unbroken web of forests, mountains, glaciers, and tundra with moose, bear, caribou, sheep, eagles and, of course, the elements. We can't make essences without including the elements of these very powerful environments. Alaska affects us in powerful ways. Alaska's essence is the life force of the land and it is these powerful energies we are sharing.

Angels' Wings Mist *Filled with the laughter and blessings of angels, fairies and flowers, plus Alaska's Elements, Dancing Light Orchids held in the gleeful scents of Geranium, Orange and Ylang-Ylang.* Helps clear away burdensome thoughts, feeling scared or blue and simply need some cheering up, lifts your spirits to a higher perspective. Nurtures your inspiration and wonder.

Mist your feet when your hopes and spirits are low so weighty thoughts won't drag you down. Mist over your head and shoulders to loosen and stretch your wings in preparation to take flight!

Mother's Arms Combination Mist *Contains Alaska Elemental Energies Essence and 8 very feminine essences for nurturing yourself and those around you. plus Lavender and Blue Camomile essential oils.* Formulated to draw in healing nurturing vibrations of the feminine nature, along with the energetic support to deal with urgent situations. Effective for emergencies, shock and trauma; it also evokes the sense of safety, nurturing and healing. Relax into the cosy embrace of these gentle vibrations, that hold you lovingly as if in your mother's arms, which allows a letting go of the of trauma in order to settle into being supported by either friends, the capable hands of health care providers or the sense of safety and healing you feel within.

For fearfulness, panic or terror, stress, or overwhelming feelings; before and after medical procedures to help relieve stress after experiencing fear, pain, due to invasive procedures. Or for children who don't feel safe, are hard to comfort or have trouble with sleep, helps clear your own or your children's emotional energy after frantic escapades. Mist around to allow the flower essences to be evaporated into the aura. Hospitals do not generally allow patients to take any type of remedy by mouth which they do not supply. But often have no objection to a pleasant misting of flower essences.

Protective Shield Mist *Combined from Alaska's Elements, Dancing Light Orchids with Cinnamon, Lemon, and Cedar oils.* Helps to provide relief from stressful energies; it envelopes you in a protective sphere. Protective Shield is particularly helpful to sensitive people for increasing their radiant strength while helping to clear and define their personal space in positive ways. It can help them feel comfortable so they don't feel the need to withdraw from people and stressful environments and situations. It is especially helpful for pregnant women whose sensitivity increases as gestation progresses – important for newborn babies and their mother when they re-enter the world together.

For highly sensitive children and adults, and those who are empathic or unable to distance other's emotions from their own. For easing their subtle distress in crowds because they feel the energies of other people's words, thoughts and emotions remaining in their aura.

Sacred Space Mist *This potion is infused with thundering waters, the clearing wind and other forces of nature from Alaska's clean, remote wilderness as well as Dancing Light Orchids blended with purifying Cedar, Sage, and Lavender oils.* Designed for cleansing and clearing unwanted energies from around yourself and your immediate environment to help you expand your space, and clear the air around you. Mist when your personal or mental space feels like it is shrinking, to help you hold your ground, expand and define your boundaries and re-establish harmonious flow. Draws in the power of nature to help unblock and reorder the flow of *chi* while avoiding chaos during the process. Also useful to release disincarnate beings from very old buildings and landscapes.

Still Mind Mist *Combination of Alaska's Elements, and Dancing Light Orchid Essences; with Marjoram and Tangerine oils.* Invaluable when troubled by thoughts going around in your head, keeping you awake at night. Enables you to be a human being rather than a human doing, allows you to live each day opening to fully experience each moment.

Gently touches your body and mind with the stillness found on the high peaks and glaciers in Alaska's wilderness, where the quiet is so profound that the vibrations of tundra flowers seem like noisy chatter. This combination contains the secret wisdom and vibrations from nature to move you into the higher levels of your mind. Here you can live with a sense of inner quiet and emptiness, enabling you to perceive and receive from the sensory to the cosmic.

Young Heart Mist *Contains Alaska's Elements, Dancing Light Orchids and Rose Geranium oil.* Young Heart contains the magic you knew when you were small, it holds vibrational patterns to nurture or rekindle a healthy sense of wonder, angel dust to give lift to the wings of your heart, inspirational seeds for your lofty ideas, and the silent chiming music made by joyful fairies dancing on Scottish Bluebells.

Use to rejuvenate your inner fountain of youth. Take it to your work or play place to lift your spirits when things get too serious, too competitive; when you or others around you start to feel and act old at heart For when you feel weak and tired, disheartened, disappointed, fed up, angry or generally unhappy, been sick for a short or a long time. Healing occurs more readily and deeply when the joy and magic of your heart is nurtured.

Desert Alchemy Flower Essences

The desert is an environment of extremes, with an abundance of heat from the sun and little water. Throughout history people wishing to strengthen their sense of spirituality have spent time in the desert. Key words to describe the energy of the desert are adaptability, individuality, expansion and inner security.

The plants inhabiting this place have evolved amazing strategies for adapting to the formidable climate in order to survive. Some only bloom at night, while others can produce leaves within six hours of a rainfall although they can continue to photosynthesize without foliage at all if necessary.

Desert Alchemy was founded in 1983 by Cynthia Athina Kemp Scherer with a view to researching and making essences from desert flowers. The inspiration for making a flower essence from desert plants came to Cynthia while driving through the Arizona desert one day. She found herself in the midst of a whole forest of Saguaro cacti, some standing 15m (50ft) tall with great arms that seemed to reach towards the heavens. She felt as if the Saguaro cacti were communicating with her and giving her a message to make flower essences, though at the time she did not even know what flower essences were.

Out of this experience grew the Desert Alchemy Essences, created from 119 individual flowers, which capture the extraordinary qualities of the plants growing wild in this harsh environment. With an emphasis on survival, these essences are perfect for crisis situations, helping us to adapt and cope in extremely demanding situations. They encourage shifts in our perspective which enable us to deal with and embrace any emergency as an opportunity for change and growth.

Agave (*Century Plant*) The 'late bloomer' essence, Agave helps us own our level of mastery and manifest our inner beauty and strength into daily life.

Aloe (*Aloe*) Cultivates patience and surrender to our healing process. It is excellent if we feel resistance to allowing things to surface, helping us feel supported from within.

Arizona Sycamore (*Platanus wrightii*) For those who experience life or relationships as confining or entrapping, Arizona Sycamore helps us to find inner freedom. It is excellent for those who feel confined or limited by their bodies.

Arizona White Oak (*Quercus Arizonica*) Arizona White Oak helps us if we believe that in order to grow we must struggle. It fosters strength through stability and continuity and helps us to feel deeply rested through surrender.

Arroyo Willow (*Salix lasiolepis*) Restoring a consciousness of personal will, Arroyo Willow helps us responsibly create our life experiences while remaining flexibly true to ourselves.

Bear Grass (*Xerophyllum tenax*) Fosters our knowing that no outside influence can overpower our deeply held intentions. It keeps us steadily centred in our hearts.

Big Root Jatropha Excellent for 'growth spurts'. Big Root Jatropha encourages a feeling of security as great inner expansion takes place. It helps us to feel safe enough to allow change to happen without the need to control everything.

Bisbee Beehive Cactus (*Coryphantha vivipara var. Bisbeeana*) Bisbee Beehive helps take us to the core of an issue and feel grace and healing energy at a cellular level. It is very often indicated for recovery of sexual or physical abuse.

Black Locust (*Robinia pseudoacacia*) Those who disregard others around them and insist upon their own way can find a softening effect from this flower essence. It helps balance masculine assertiveness with feminine yielding and nurturing.

Bloodroot (*Sanguinaria canadensis*) Bloodroot is for those who exclude themselves, or feel ostracized, from a group or community, usually because of deep feelings of unworthiness. It helps heal the wounds of rejection and free us from the bonds of unworthiness.

Bougainvillea Bougainvillea relaxes the body and deepens our breathing, encouraging feelings of peace and ease. By provoking self-reflection and inner listening, crisis is met with stillness and nonreactivity.

Bouvardia (*Bouvardia ternifolia*) Bouvardia fortifies our will to confront life directly and consciously, changing emotional reactivity and avoidance patterns into positive response and action. An excellent essence for denial.

Bright Star (*Echinacea purpurea* 'Leuchtstern') Bright Star is indicated when we are unable to say 'No' to an entangling situation or person. It helps us have healthy boundaries by trusting that we deserve what we want.

Buffalo Gourd (*Cucurbita foetidissima*) Buffalo Gourd helps us maintain a deep inner place of healing and calm while participating in external activity. The keyword here is balance, knowing that 'I Am the centre.'

Camphorweed (*Heterotheca subaxillaris*) While gently diffusing old patterns, Camphorweed brings a sense of purpose and appropriateness, helping us to stay on track, feel grounded and bring things into

manifestation. It is excellent for when we find ourselves caught up in adrenaline-producing situations.

Candy Barrel Cactus (*Ferocactus*) Fostering mental and emotional calmness, Candy Barrel helps us recognize our inner wisdom and uncover long-stored abilities.

Cane Cholla Cactus (*Opuntia imbricata*) Cane Cholla Cactus helps us leap to a new perspective when we struggle with an issue and insist upon defining it in such a way as to block its resolution.

Canyon Grapevine For issues of autonomy, Canyon Grapevine brings appreciation of others as interdependent rather than competing. This essence helps us find a balance between dominance and dependency and encourages us to see obstacles as opportunities.

Cardinal Flower This flower essence helps us to redirect sexual energy into other usable forms of energy. It is excellent during menopause, or for those who allow the five senses to dictate their responses rather than mastering their bodies and senses.

Cardon Cactus (*Pachycereus pringlei*) Powerful energy is released as repressed feelings of inadequacy and inferiority are unlocked. Helps us accept our shadow side so that it becomes a source of strength and confidence.

Claret Cup Hedgehog Cactus (*Echinocereus triglochidiatus var. melanacanthus*) Clarity and focus are the key words for this hedgehog cactus. This is an excellent essence for manifestation, meditation or any situation requiring mental steadiness and acuity.

Cliffrose (*Purshia mexicana*) Cliffrose helps us unite our will, our intention and the power to act. It is for those of us who are always meaning to manifest an altruistic goal but never quite manage to do so.

Compass Barrel Cactus (*Ferocactus cylindraceus*) Compass Barrel Cactus helps us move through an emotional state by lightening up and letting go, trusting our inner wisdom to point the way.

Coral Bean (*Erythrina* herbacea) Coral Bean helps overcome a drug-like dulling of the survival instinct. It stimulates focus and will in facing or recovering from dangerous situations.

Cow Parsnip (*Heracleum maximum*) This essence is for transforming insecurity into a deep sense of self and surrender to divine will. It is for an underlying sense of inability to direct our lives.

Creosote Bush (*Larrea tridentata*) Supports us in releasing what is unexpressed or held in which is usually at the root of self-imposed separation from others. It brings us a sense of being freed. Often used for resolving the feeling that something is missing in life.

Crown of Thorns For those who believe that they must pay a price for love, or that everything worthwhile is difficult to obtain, this essence helps us to know that abundance is our birthright. It is also excellent for those who are invested in the perspective of good and bad, or positive and negative.

Crownbeard (*Verbesina encelioides*) For those with a defeatist attitude, or those who experience the world as unsupportive or hostile, Crownbeard helps us to keep faith and optimism. It helps us to transmute fears of hostility and find purposeful expression.

Damiana (*Turnera aphrodisiaca*) When we feel inadequate, weak, emotionally needy or detached from the flow of vital life force, Damiana relaxes and restores our radiant fullness of energy and sensuality.

Desert Broom (*Baccharis sarothroides*) When we want to accomplish something but all parts of our being are not in alignment with our desire, Desert Broom helps us to find resolution and readiness to take the next step. Resolution is the key word for this essence, especially when we want to go deeply into a matter but

something holds us back.

Desert Christmas Cholla Cactus (*Opuntia leptocaulis*) This cholla cactus helps us communicate our limits with humour and ease, especially if we get caught up in other people's needs or expectations. It is wonderful support when we have too many demands upon us and feel overextended.

Desert Holly (*Acourtia wrightii*) Desert Holly helps us live in a heart-centred state, opening easily to love rather than working at it. It is excellent for those who feel stifled by smothering love or for those who live from their heads rather than from their hearts.

Desert Jointfir (*Ephedra californica*) Activates our will and our innate healing resources, bringing directedness, vision and determination. Through confidence in our self-healing abilities, we learn to escape potentially damaging situations.

Desert Marigold (*Baileya multiradiata*) When we think that someone else has power over us, Desert Marigold helps us recognize how we actually give the power to them. For taking responsibility and transforming victim consciousness.

Desert Sumac (*Rhus kearneyi subsp. kearneyi*) Desert Sumac helps us transform the pain of loneliness and separation by seeing beyond the superficial differences in people. It is for those who feel they are on the outside looking in in social relationships.

Desert Willow (*Chilopsis linearis*) With Desert Willow, we are supported in feeling respite and in having a perspective of abundance. It is helpful for perfectionism and inflexibility, fostering a perspective of comfort and ease.

Devil's Claw (*Harpagophytum procumbens*) Devil's Claw activates our natural sense of morality. This essence supports us in taking responsibility for owning and expressing who we really are, separate from the projections of others. It is useful if we find ourselves using attractiveness or personal magnetism to manipulate others, or if we try to become who we think others want us to be.

Dogbane (*Apocynum*) Dogbane helps us to access the courage to follow our rebellious instincts, which is an important part of growth and change. For the fear that our rebellion will hurt or damage others, and the fear that we cannot take care of ourselves if we leave home. This is the essence to support self-confidence.

Dyssodia (*Dyssodia pentachaeta*) This yellow flower helps us to assimilate and clarify information, knowledge or wisdom. It helps us to bring things through into consciousness that are felt or sensed but not yet known.

Evening Star (*Mentzelia decapetala*) Evening Star is wonderful for problems of intimacy in relationships due to doubt about our emerging identity. It encourages us in shifting from outer dependence to self-reliance with confidence and quiet surety.

Fairy Duster (*Calliandra eriophylla*) Fairy Duster balances the tendency to swing between high and low energy states. We can use this essence when we have inflated expectations or build castles in the air. It is excellent for nervous excitability and overreactivity to stimuli.

Fire Prickly Pear Cactus (*Opuntia spp.*) This prickly pear cactus helps us redistribute energy (or focus) if we are concentrating too much attention on one part of our lives (or bodies) to the detriment of the whole.

Fishhook Cactus (*Mammillaria microcarpa*) Fishhook Cactus is for those who hide behind noncommunication. It is especially indicated for the fear of risking in communication. It supports us with confidence in public speaking, intimate relationships or for speaking foreign languages.

Foothills Paloverde (*Cercidium microphyllum*) An essence of choice for those of us who are judgemental of ourselves or others, Foothills Paloverde supports us in quieting our minds and finding perfection within ourselves, just as we are. It is also helpful if we feel at the mercy of our emotions.

Hackberry (*Celtis pallida*) Hackberry helps us if we have resistance to feeling grief. Sometimes we have an idea of how long it is appropriate to grieve, but our feelings don't match.

Hairy Larkspur (*Delphinium parryi*) For those with a compulsion or addiction for sweet things, this essence helps us untangle our association of sweet things with a sense of reward. It is excellent for helping us to clarify the difference between desire and self-nurturance.

Hedgehog Cactus (*Echinocereus engelmannii*) Hedgehog Cactus helps us sort out the difference between self-nurturance and overindulgence. It intensifies empathetic perceptions, bringing us closer to nature.

Hoptree (*Ptelea trifoliata*)For those of us who become too easily distracted by the needs of others, Hoptree supports us in staying in alignment with our purpose and remaining focused on what is essential to us. It is excellent for anxiety about boundary making.

Indian Root (*Aralia racemosa*)Do you find yourself trying too hard and making things complex? Indian Root helps us value simplicity. It releases deep seated fears that block our free-flowing creative expression.

Indian Tobacco (*Nicotiana trigonophylla*) This peace fostering essence supports us when we view growth processes as hindrances rather than opportunities. It brings a heightened perception of depth and meaning, assisting us to see below the surface of things.

Indigo Bush (*Psorothamnus fremontii*) Indigo Bush helps anchor our spiritually achieved ideas into daily life. It warms the heart and brings the light of clear seeing or inner sight to an area that needs it.

Inmortal (*Asclepias asperula*) Inmortal goes to the core of shame and self-esteem issues. It is excellent for resolving feelings of despair, feeling that problems are insoluble, and feeling inadequate. It helps us know the magnificence that we really are.

Jojoba (*Simmodsia chinensis*) For the overly sensitive individual who finds it hard to cope with the mundane, Jojoba brings a sense of ease and security. This grounding essence helps us to participate in daily life and relationships.

Jumping Cholla Cactus (*Opuntia fulgida*) Fostering inner balance, Jumping Cholla Cactus is an antidote for frenzied rushing around. It helps us respond rather than react to life.

Klein's Pencil Cholla Cactus (*Cylindropuntia kleinae*) This cactus essence encourages our creativity and growth in dealing with a relationship that feels stuck. It is excellent for when we stay in a relationship that is not supporting our growth in some way.

Lavender Wand Penstemon For those who have an inability to deal with emotionally charged issues, this flower essence helps enhance our ability to move into and through difficult issues. It helps bring emotional objectivity and transforms attitudes of struggle and difficulty into ones of confident ease and steadiness of intention.

Lilac (*Syringa*) For those who nostalgically cling to the past or to old ways of being, Lilac helps us to let go. It is a cleansing essence that helps us realize that we are complete or finished with something.

Mala Mujer (*Cnidoscolos angustidens*) Mala Mujer helps the positive expression of feminine qualities, releasing emotional tensions and bringing a lighter, more honest quality to our overall self-expression. It is for when we are bitchy, venomous, shrewish, or grouchy. (Guys! This means you too!)

Mariola (*Parthenium incanum*) If we have a false persona, Mariola restores the congruence of our inner experience and outer expression, provoking our essential honesty and enthusiasm.

Mariposa Lily (*Calochortus eurycarpus*) Self-mothering brings joy and freedom, healing separation and alienation. We become receptive to human love.

Melon Loco (*Apodanthera undulata*) Melon Loco helps step down the intensity of our emotions in order to bring us back into our bodies. It helps us have emotional sensibility, responsibility and balance.

Mesquite (*Prosopis spp.*) Opening ourselves to abundance and pleasure, Mesquite amplifies compassion and warmth. This is a great essence for loners and for those who feel an inner barrenness.

Mexican Shell Flower (*Tigridia*) This essence supports our willingness to confront life and its possibilities. It is excellent for 'coming out of your shell'.

Mexican Star (*Milla biflora*) Mexican Star helps us embody strong, self-contained individuality. By knowing that our inner strength is our foundation for survival, we enjoy our uniqueness rather than feeling isolated by it.

Milky Nipple Cactus (*Mammillaria heyderi*) The Milky Nipple Cactus person demands constant attention from others. This 'weaning' essence calms, gives a sense of belonging to the earth and transforms dependence into self-nurturing autonomy.

Morning Glory Tree (*Ipomoea carnea*) This essence is excellent for becoming conscious of issues of ancestral addictions. It facilitates a conscious chance to change patterns that may be latent or active from our families of origin.

Mountain Mahogany (*Cercocarpus*) Mountain Mahogany provides a gentle but firm push toward our next stage of development. Helpful when we become complacent.

Mullein (*Verbascum thapsus*) Mullein is for when we need to recognize and accept our dark side without feeling overwhelmed by it. We become emotionally self-nurturing, especially when external support isn't available. It brings a sense of security, purpose, protection.

Ocotillo (*Fouqueiria splendens*) If we have subconscious or unexpressed feelings that erupt in uncontrolled ways, Ocotillo gives insight into and acceptance of our emotions without feeling victimized by them.

Oregon Grape (*Berberis aquifolium*) When we are never quite satisfied by our performance, the Oregon Grape helps us develop trust for ourselves and others. An important essence for helping to restore hormonal balance, it supports us in overcoming fear of emotional hostility.

Organ Pipe Cactus (*Stenocereus thurberi*) This cactus helps us survive the dark night of the soul wherein we question our foundations for being. It supports in dealing with mundane aspects of our lives while we allow deep transformation to take place.

Palmer Amaranth (*Amaranthus palmeri*) For those who focus on inessential things rather than getting to the root of the matter, Palmer Amaranth enhances insights as we awaken to a deeper perception of our being. This essence helps us to nourish our roots so we can flower and fruit.

Pencil Cholla Cactus (*Cylindropuntia ramosissima*) For confusion, feeling lost or overwhelmed by details. It helps us focus continually in a specific direction and find steadiness with our intention. It brings clarity and surrender into and through obstacles.

Periwinkle (*Vinca minor*) Periwinkle helps us to integrate and contemplate where we have come from in order to provide wisdom and understanding for the next phase of life. It is excellent when we attempt to forge on ahead into a new project or aspect of our lives without learning from where we have been.

Pink Pond Lily (*Nopalxochia phyllan-thoides*) This is an essence to use for self-deception or when we cling to old ways of perceiving ourselves or others. It is excellent for those who have a deep feeling of being unsafe as it fosters total knowing that there is only trust, perfection and safety in being.

Pomegranate (*Punica granatum*) Pomegranate embodies the primal urge to produce, create, procreate and care for. It is excellent for difficulty in giving or receiving maternal support due to a lack of childhood nurturance. It helps when we try hard but get nowhere because our commitment isn't total or right.

Prickle Poppy (*Argemone pleicantha*) This flower essence helps us to be in touch with our natural rhythms and cycles, both physically and emotionally. It is for those who have a taskmaster attitude towards themselves that creates blockages to the natural flow of life energy, and may manifest in joint tension or rigidity. It is excellent for those who are overly controlled.

Prickly Pear Cactus (*Opuntia*) The key word is adaptability. Its qualities help us surrender to the flow of life's events. It is excellent for culture shock.

Purple Aster (*Symphyotrichum patens*) For those whose hard-working efforts create the feeling that they are isolated and that progress is small and difficult, this flower essence changes the feeling of pursuing a goal to feeling as if you are drawn to it. This is the essence of choice for performance anxieties.

Purple Mat (*Nama demissum*) Purple Mat helps us take risks so we can stay true to ourselves and others. For when we secretly harbour our feelings or needs for fear of being rejected or ridiculed if they were openly exposed.

Queen of the Night Cactus (*Epiphyllum oxypetalum*) The Queen of the Night can help us sink deeply into the intuitive root of our being to ground our subtle sensitivities. It helps us open to the qualities of the moon in our daily life, experiencing the blissful perspective of deeper understanding, feeling and sensuality.

Rainbow Cactus (*Echinocereus pectinatus*) Rainbow Cactus is a searchlight to illumine something dark or held in. Releasing petrified emotion without becoming entangled in it, we emerge bright, free and whole. It is excellent for meditation or regression work as it facilitates easy movement from one state of consciousness to another.

Ratany (*Krameria parvifolia*) If we are pulled between two choices, Ratany enables us to recognize, follow and communicate the truth in our hearts.

Red Root (*Ceanothus azurea*) For those of us who feel guilty because others suffer and we do not, Red Root helps us release enmeshment. It is also for situations in which we are motivated by superstitions or other unconscious forces.

Red-Orange Epiphyllum (*Orchid Cactus*) This essence facilitates grounding of goddess energy into worldly existence. An excellent essence for manifestation.

Sacred Datura (*Datura metaloides*) Sacred Datura facilitates seeing beyond our present view of reality to a more comprehensive, visionary state. When appropriate, it supports us in letting go of a known or familiar reality, such as a relationship or job, without feeling threatened.

Saguaro Cactus (*Carnegiea gigantea*) Saguaro helps us know and trust our inner wisdom and authority. It restores the will to live, to heal and to be the best that we are. It assists us in accessing the perfect inner father who encourages us on in life.

Salsify (*Tragopogon porrifolius*) If we have difficulty in bringing a project or some aspect of ourselves to fruition or completion, Salsify supports us in the maturation process. It is excellent for finding all the vital elements for growth and the expression of our full potential.

Sangre de Drago (*Croton lechleri*) This flower essence helps us to create good

psychic boundaries based upon appropriate discrimination and natural morality. It is excellent for those who are afraid of their psychic nature as it fosters the acceptance of sensitive abilities with grounded practicality.

Scarlet Morning Glory (*Ipomoea hederifolia*) Some of us think about what we will do in the future but never begin to make it reality. For those who have difficulty giving form to their creative impulses, this flower essence stimulates us to get going, making future potential into present reality. It also helps keep us focused if we become caught up in excitement that pulls our focus in other directions.

Scorpion Weed (*Phacelia tanacetifolia*) The strength of innocence and direct confrontation overcomes fear and paralysis. Scorpion Weed helps us with many types of fears: of the consequences of our actions; of our past mistakes; of not being forgiven. It is especially useful when we externalize our fears or when we create monsters out of them.

Senita Cactus (*Cereus schottii*) The grandparent's perspective opens the flow of emotion without pain, without bitterness from the past or expectations for the future. Senita helps us access from within us a soft, sweet support for letting go of old perspectives that keep us locked into unsettled emotions.

Silverleaf Nightshade (*Solanum elaeagnifolium*) Silverleaf Nightshade helps us in recognizing that we have the power to hurt as well as heal. It is used for fear and paralysis created by our minds that keeps us from owning our own power.

Smartweed (*Polygonum hydropiper*) Smartweed is for those who believe that since they were hurt before they will be hurt again. These people hide away and withdraw from perceived dangers of being with others. It encourages openness and willingness to receive love and encouragement from others.

Soaptree Yucca (*Yucca elata*) Soaptree Yucca activates our assertiveness in the expression of our own will or intention, especially if we tend to allow the will of another to dominate us. It helps us to keep sight of our long-term goals with faith, perseverance and endurance.

Sow-Thistle (*Sonchus asper*) Sow-Thistle helps us deal appropriately with obnoxious behaviour, whether our own or that of others. It helps us deal with feeling intimidated by dominating personalities. It is also excellent if we find ourselves wanting a relationship so badly that we don't give the other person the space they need.

Spanish Bayonet Yucca (*Yucca aloifolia*) An excellent essence to help us when we experience indecisiveness, hesitation or fear in facing challenges. It provokes a unification of our will with our intention.

Spineless Prickly Pear Cactus (*Opuntia tuna*) With Spineless Prickly Pear, we discover that all we need for survival is contained within us and that we don't need anything outside of us to 'Be'. We find strength in vulnerability.

Staghorn Cholla Cactus (*Opuntia versicolor*) This cholla cactus activates our innate capacity for self-ordering and reconstruction after a time of transformation and change. It helps us see that change occurs in harmony with our own unique soul plan.

Star Leaf Star Leaf helps us be simply and purely ourselves, without the need for external approval. It frees up self expression for those who do not recognize or accept their unique contribution to life.

Star Primrose An excellent essence for those of us with a poor self image, Star Primrose is helpful if we blame our negative feelings on an outside source while simultaneously denying such feelings exist. It is also an essence of choice for those of us who are confused about sexuality and spirituality, or who repress sensuality and put energy into occult, mystical or mental pursuits.

Strawberry Cactus (*Echinocereus stramineus*) For those of us who are expecting things to go wrong or be difficult, Strawberry Cactus encourages us to let go and allow our hearts to transmute difficult emotions. We know that there is perfection in each moment and each situation, and we begin to live in joy.

Syrian Rue (*Peganum harmala*) An energetic 'truth serum', Syrian Rue is for all issues of lying, being lied to, betrayal, telling the truth, and trustworthiness. It helps us know and trust in our own truth, regardless of external pressures.

Tarbush (*Flourensia cernua*) Tarbush strengthens inspiration and motivation to change something that has been accepted as a limitation or condition of life. It helps us to identify and release deeply imprinted assumptions or beliefs that work subconsciously.

Teddy Bear Cholla Cactus (*Opuntia bigelovii*) A cuddly looking cactus, Teddy Bear Cholla helps with deep fears of intimacy and allowing others close enough to see our perfection. It is also for when we feel impatient with our perceived level of growth or development.

Theresa Cactus For those who hide behind serving others, this cactus fosters a deep sense of self-care. It helps us change conditional giving into unconditional service.

Thistle (*Cirsium occidentale*) For those who experience a lack of trust or faith in their spiritual connection, Thistle helps us let down our defensiveness and recognize grace in our lives.

Thurber's Gilia (*Ipomopsis thurberi*) For all types of fears that paralyze us, this is the essence of choice. Also for resolving the frustration of our limitations and the paradoxical fear of living without our limitations.

Violet Curls Violet Curls helps us release, one by one, congested emotions. It supports us in expressing our emotions as they arise so as not to create a backlog of them. We lighten up and are able to have a calm detachment.

Violet Soldier For those who feel defeated and unable to survive a transformational experience, Violet Soldier helps us find a will to live, to heal, and to overcome all obstacles. Victory is the key word, victory of the spirit over all possible conditions of external existence.

White Desert Primrose (*Oenothera delatoides*) White Desert Primrose is for those who are overly influenced by what others think is right for them. It helps us see through others' projected images and ideals to realize forms of self-expression that are in harmony with our essential nature. It enhances belief in ourselves and discernment of our own unique soul pattern.

White Desert Zinnia (*Zinnia acerosa*) Those who have a discouraged attitude towards life and who believe that they can never quite get ahead can use this flower essence. It helps bring the ability to laugh at ourselves or a situation and open ourselves to lightness, merriment and renewal.

White Evening Primrose (*Oenothera pallida*) This flower essence has a grounding effect for those who feel disconnected from their sense of spirituality. It helps us to be spiritually receptive by being more present in our bodies and in touch with our childlike sense of innocence.

Whitethorn Whitethorn helps us be more gentle with ourselves. It brings a sense of optimistic freshness and helps our thinking to move in new, innovative directions. It helps release us from succumbing to old

patterns and habits, especially if we have continued to act them out after initially recognizing them. It is useful for calming adrenaline excess.

Wild Buckwheat (*Polygonum convolvulus*) This is the essence to use when you compare yourself to others and set yourself apart from them. When we focus on the differences between us in relationships we isolate ourselves. Wild Buckwheat helps us to find and focus on what we have in common, and helps us to blend and harmonize with others.

Windflower (*Anemone pulsatilla*) When we feel highly energized at one moment and then depleted in the next, Windflower facilitates a more balanced distribution of energy.

Wolfberry (*Lycium pallidum*) Releasing deep sadness from the past, helps us to allow grief to take us to a transpersonal experience. When we experience that something is shifting around inside ourselves but we don't know what it is, Wolfberry helps us to be at peace and allow the process without insisting upon defining it.

Woven Spine Pineapple Cactus (*Neolloydia intertexta*) This cactus loosens old emotional tensions in the body when we are overburdened by the 'shoulds' of life, helping us become our own best friend. For regeneration of energy after exhaustion, burn-out, travel, or illness.

Zephyr Lily (*Zephyranthes*) This is the essence of choice to use for present or past traumas, whether physical, emotional or mental. It allows deep peace and calm as we heal from shock or trauma.

Flower Essence Society

The Flower Essence Society has been in existence longer than almost any other flower remedy organization (the exception being the Bach Flower Centre). It was established in 1979 by Richard Katz with a view to gathering together information and research regarding newer flower essences and educating the public through classes and publications. In 1980 he formed a professional partnership with his wife, Patricia Kaminski, and together they not only administer the Flower Essence Society but through their company Flower Essence Services, prepare an extensive range of high quality North American flower essences known as the 'FES Quintessentials.' They are made from flowers wildcrafted from pristine natural habitats in California and other parts of North America, and from organic gardens and wild areas on their 17-acre centre, Terra Flora, located near Nevada City in the foothills of California's Sierra Nevada mountains, a place of granite peaks studded with golden quartz and sparkling rivers.

Katz and Kaminski have devoted particular attention to researching their essences thoroughly, using extensive case studies and clinical reports by practitioners, and by studies of the essence plants, including morphological and botanical characteristics. They also conduct seminars and practitioner training and certification programmes, write and publish newsletters and books, including their comprehensive Flower Essence Repertory. Flower Essence Society membership provides a communication network for those teaching, researching and practising in this field.

The FES essences are currently being used by thousands of practitioners and lay people in more than 50 countries around the world. As Katz and Kaminski have said, flower essences are not panaceas, but catalysts which stimulate and energize the inner transformative process, while leaving us free to develop our own innate capacities. Just as food nourishes the body, so can flower essences nourish and heal the soul. They are a harbinger of a new alchemy of the soul, one which incorporates ancient wisdom with a modern awareness of the human psyche and of nature.

Professional Kit

Aloe Vera (*Aloe vera*) For people who have an abundance of fiery energy but tend to overuse it and literally burn out – workaholics who neglect their emotional and physical needs. Brings a sense of renewal and rejuvenation, restores nourishment. Balances creative activity and centres vital life energy.

Alpine Lily (*Lilium parvum*) For women who have difficulty accepting their femininity, lack of connection, awareness or rejection of female body, who may be susceptible to reproductive and sexual problems. Encourages a radiant and self-assured feminine identity, physical presence grounded in the female body

Angel's Trumpet (*Brugmansia candida*) For those who fear death, who resist letting go of physical life, and crossing the spiritual threshold. Brings spiritual surrender at death and times of deep transformation or transition, opening the soul to the spiritual world.

Angelica (*Angelica archangelica*) For those who feel cut off, bereft of spiritual guidance and protection feeling like a spiritual orphan. Encourages feelings of being protected, guided and cared for, especially in times of crisis. Good for birthing, dying, festive celebrations and other major life passages.

Arnica (*Arnica mollis*) For deep-seated shock or trauma which may become locked into the body and prevent full healing recovery. For accidents and violent experiences where the soul or Higher Self dissociates from the physical body. Brings conscious embodiment, especially during shock or trauma, and aids recovery. Helpful for treatment of psychosomatic illnesses which do not respond to other treatments, and for dysfunction or latent illness deriving from past trauma or stress. Aids recovery from deep-seated strain, post-trauma, or scarring.

Baby Blue Eyes (*Nemophila menziesii*) For those who are unsure of themselves and unable to trust in the goodness of others and the world – defensive, insecure, with a cynical mistrust of the world. Estrangement from higher spiritual authority and lack of support from the father or other masculine influences in childhood. Restores innocence and childlike trust, feeling supported and loved, especially by male figures; and a recognition of goodness in others, the world, and faith in the providence of spiritual beings.

Basil (*Ocimum basilicum*) For those who have a tendency to separate the experience of spirituality from that of sexuality. They may be secretive about sex, regarding it as sinful while finding illicit sexual practices attractive and compelling, typically leading to clandestine behaviour, bifurcated relationships or sexual addiction. Integrates sexuality and spirituality into a sacred wholeness.

Blackberry (*Rubus ursinus*) For those who have lofty visions and desires but are unable to put them into action, concrete or viable activities; often lacking the ability to organize their intentions into specific goals and priorities creating procrastination. Also for poor circulation and sluggish metabolism. Aids competent manifestation in the world, and directs willpower and enables one to take decisive action.

Black-Eyed Susan (*Rudbeckia hirta*) For those who avoid or repress parts of their personality or traumatic episodes from the past, for instance rape or incest, often experiencing emotional amnesia and paralysis, addictive or hypnotic behaviour due to loss of consciousness. Awake consciousness, enables you to acknowledge all aspects of the self and to achieve penetrating insight.

Black Cohosh (*Cimicifuga racemosa*) For those caught in relationships and lifestyles that are abusive, addictive or violent with dark brooding emotions, congested or toxic psychic forces. Gives us the courage to confront rather than shrink from abusive or threatening situations, transforming the negativity, gaining power and balance in destructive circumstances fostering clear and contained psychic forces.

Bleeding Heart (*Dicentra formosa*) For a tendency to form relationships based on fear or possessiveness; for emotional dependence which leads to a lack of freedom in the relationship, neediness; emotional codependence. Sufferers may feel tremendous pain and brokenheartedness by loving someone who is emotionally distanced or no longer present. Brings the openhearted ability to love others unconditionally, and emotional freedom.

Borage (*Borago officinalis*) For heavyheartedness, depressive behaviour, or lack of confidence in the face of difficult circumstances. For those who feel discouraged or disheartened in times of grief, sadness or other adversity. Uplifts the heart, gives buoyant courage, rekindles a sense of optimism and enthusiasm.

Buttercup (*Ranunculus occidentalis*) For those who feel humbled and lack self-worth, or are self-deprecating and unable to acknowledge or experience their uniqueness and inner light. Brings recognition of the inner light which is a source of healing and peace. Relieves you from the need to judge yourself by conventional standards of achievement and success. Helpful for children who may be physically handicapped or impaired.

Calendula (*Calendula officinalis*) For those prone to being argumentative, who have a tendency to use cutting or sharp words and lack receptivity when communicating with others, verbal abuse. Gives warmth and benign compassion; encourages receptivity in conversations.

California Pitcher Plant (*Darlingtonia californica*) For those who fear their instinctive desires; they may lack strength and physical vigour, be listless, anaemic, with poor digestion or unable to assimilate nutrients properly. Restores earthly vitality, balancing instinctual desire so these energies can strengthen physical vitality.

California Poppy (*Eschscholzia californica*) For those seeking false forms of light, who become attached to illusion or grandeur, or higher consciousness, 'spiritual glamour' or psychic experiences. Balances the forces of light and love, encouraging more self-responsibility and quiet inner development. Encourages a radiant heart-centred spirituality; strong interior alignment for values and choices.

California Wild Rose (*Rosa californica*) For apathy or resignation, passivity; not wanting to take full responsibility or to experience the pain or challenge of life. For those who recoil from relationships which may involve taking emotional risks or who feel socially alienated. Brings the ability to care for and give oneself to life and to others. Kindles enthusiasm for doing and serving.

Calla Lily (*Zantedeschia aethiopica*) For confusion or ambivalence about sexual identity or gender. Brings acceptance and clarity of sexuality and sexual identity and individualized integration of masculine and feminine qualities. Heals wounding due to cultural gender bias.

Canyon Dudleya (*Dudleya cymosa*) For those who exaggerate the relevance of psychic experiences; attracted to mediumism, channelling and experiences which spark off psychic fantasies; prone to neglecting daily activities. Encourages inner contentment which dispels the necessity for psychic excitement and addiction to trauma drama lifestyle. Balances psychic and physical energies; grounded presence in everyday life; positive charisma.

Cayenne (*Capsicum annuum*) Fiery and energetic, inwardly mobile. For those prone to stagnation, complacency, feeling stuck or immobilized, unable to make any progress or change, caught in a pattern of procrastination and resistance. Ignites and sparks the soul, encouraging our capacity to initiate and sustain spiritual and emotional development and capable of change and transformation.

Chamomile (*Matricaria recutita*) For those easily upset, moody, irritable and unable to release emotional tension, often leading to insomnia and tension that leads to stress in the stomach or solar plexus. Releases tension, encouraging serenity, emotional balance and a sunny disposition. Also good for children's stomach complaints, which are often emotionally based.

Chaparral (also known as Creosote Bush) (*Larrea tridentata*) For disturbed dreams or psychic toxicity when overexposed to violent or chaotic images. Important remedy for modern civilization. Clears post-traumatic stress and physical toxicity due to drugs. Important psychic cleanser which works especially through the dream life to cleanse the psyche. Balanced psychic awareness, deep penetration and understanding of the transpersonal aspects of oneself.

Chrysanthemum (*Chrysanthemum morifolium*) For fear of ageing and mortality, overidentification with youthfulness or attachment to fame and fortune, the material world. For midlife crisis. Brings a shift towards identifying with what is truly eternal, a higher spiritual identity and a transcendent soul.

Corn (*Zea mays*) For disorientation and stress, particularly in urban environments; helpful for those who feel uncomfortable living in congested, chaotic environments, preferring rural or uncrowded areas. Helps you stay centred and in alignment with the earth, with your feet firmly on the ground.

Cosmos (*Cosmos bipinnatus*) For those who find it difficult to organize their thoughts into words. Unfocused, disorganized, overwhelmed by too many ideas, their speech is rapid and inarticulate. Brings integration of ideas, harmonizes thinking and speaking patterns to bring more coherency.

Dandelion (*Taraxacum officinale*) For those who have a natural intensity and love for life but who tend to overstretch themselves, overstriving and hard-driving, making themselves overly tense, rigid or stiff, especially in the muscles. Encourages listening to bodily messages. Allows release of tensions from the body and emotions, bringing dynamic, effortless physical energy.

Deer Brush (*Ceanothus integerrimus*) For mixed or conflicting motives, deceiving ourselves by lack of honesty or polite responses not based upon genuine feelings in our relationships with others and in the affairs of daily life. Brings gentle purity, clarity of purpose and sincerity of motive, with actions that are allied with one's true feelings. Helps the soul attain purity so that it radiates truth and harmony.

Dill (*Anethum graveolens*) For when the senses are overwhelmed and over-stimulated; for hypersensitivity to the environment, sensory congestion. Enables us to absorb and experience the fullness of life, especially sensory impressions, heightened awareness of taste, touch, hearing, sight, smell, etc.

Dogwood (*Cornus nuttallii*) For emotional trauma stored deep within the body – often springing from physical or sexual abuse or harsh physical living circumstances – which can cause the body to feel awkward and ungainly. Also for those with self-destructive, accident-prone tendencies. Evokes a sense of gentleness, graceful movement, physical and etheric harmony in the body and inner sanctity.

Easter Lily (*Lilium longiflorum*) For those in conflict about their sexual identity leading to an imbalance towards either prudishness or promiscuity, virgin/whore split in psyche. Cleanses the conflict, conferring the ability to integrate sexuality and spirituality; enhancing the inner purity of the soul.

Echinacea (*Echinacea purpurea*) For feeling shattered by severe trauma or abuse, loss of dignity, profound alienation. Poor immune function. Restores a sense of true identity and dignity. Maintains self-integrity and immunity, maintaining a strong sense of self, especially when challenged by stress or disease.

Evening Primrose (*Oenothera hookeri*) For feeling rejected and unwanted due to past abuse or childhood neglect; avoiding commitment in relationships; fear of parenthood; sexual and emotional coldness and repression. Brings awareness and healing of painful early emotions absorbed from parents; ability to be open, express emotional warmth and presence, and be able to form deep, committed relationships.

Fairy Lantern (*Calochortus albus*) For immaturity, helplessness, dependency – the eternal child, delicate and needy, lacking inner strength to face the world or shoulder responsibility. Brings about a positive integration of child identity and a mature, independent adult. Use during childhood and adolescence for retarded phases of physical or emotional development.

Fawn Lily (*Erythronium purpurascens*) For withdrawal, isolation, self-protection;

those who are highly developed spiritually who find it difficult to cope with the stress and strain of modern society and lacking the inner strength to participate in community and family. Encourages acceptance and involvement in the world, and the ability to share spiritual, healing gifts with others.

Filaree (*Erodium cicutarium*) For disproportionate worry and those who become too enmeshed in or overly concerned with the mundane affairs of daily life, wasting energy on small problems. Unable to gain a wider perspective in daily life; hyperfocus on small details. Helps give a cosmic overview and puts life into perspective, unleashing inner strength and reserve.

Forget-Me-Not (*Myosotis sylvatica*) For feelings of isolation, lack of awareness of spiritual and karmic connections with others. Loneliness and isolation due to death of a loved one; soul myopia. Encourages awareness of our relationship and responsibility to everyone. Good for maintaining a conscious link with lost loved ones.

Fuchsia (*Fuchsia magellanica*) For hyperemotionality and those who mask their true feelings (such as pain and deep-seated trauma) with false emotions and misdirected psychosomatic symptoms and responses to pain and stress. Brings genuine emotional vitality. Allows expression of deep and intense feelings and enables emotions such as grief, deep-seated anger or rejection to be encountered and transformed.

Garlic (*Allium sativum*) For those who are fearful, weak, due to parasitic influence, or easily influenced, prone to low vitality and tend to be mediumistic by nature. Brings a sense of wholeness which imparts strength and active resistance to adverse influences and a resilient and vital response to life. Good for poor immune response and vulnerability to infection.

Golden Ear Drops (*Dicentra chrysantha*) For those who suppress painful and toxic memories and trauma from the past

(especially childhood) which affect present emotional life and identity. Encourages being in touch with one's inner child as a source of spirituality. Stimulates remembrance and ability to understand core experiences that define emotional history; releasing these traumatic memories so the past can become a source of strength and nourishment, wisdom and insight.

Golden Yarrow (*Achillea filipendulina*) For those with a tendency to withdraw from society or artistic involvement due to profound oversensitivity, avoiding the limelight or performance, becoming hardened to cope with vulnerability. Dependence on drugs for protection or social masking. Shields and protects, allowing you to stay open, whilst staying self-contained and balanced without compromising your integrity and health.

Goldenrod (*Solidago californica*) For those easily influenced by family or others, subject to peer pressure or susceptible to social expectations, unable to be true to themselves or to establish their own values and beliefs. Conforming to social norms to win approval and acceptance, such people may one day resort to antisocial or obnoxious behaviour as in adolescence. Encourages a strong, well-developed, secure sense of individuality, greater strength and inner conviction.

Hibiscus (*Hibiscus rosa-sinensis*) For when sexual expression becomes cold and unresponsive – often due to prior sexual exploitation or abuse. Inability to enjoy sexual experience. Particularly for women profoundly affected and offended by stereotyped images of female sexuality. Kindles sexual warmth, vitality and responsiveness, the integration of the soul's warmth and the body's passion.

Hound's Tongue (*Cynoglossum grande*) For those who tend to see the world in materialistic terms, becoming weighed down or dulled by an overly analytical worldly view with the accompanying heaviness or torpor in the physical body. Promotes holistic, balanced thinking;

encouraging lively thoughts, integration of imagination and intellect. Restores a sense of wonder and reverence for life. Stimulates the ability to perceive the physical world with spiritual clarity.

Indian Paintbrush (*Castilleja miniata*) For creative people who suffer from low vitality, exhaustion and other forms of physical illness during their work because they are unable to stay grounded and energized, unable to bring creative forces into physical expression. Helps the physical body to be lively, energetic, exuberant and healthy while using creative potential.

Indian Pink (*Silene californica*) For those who take on too many activities at once, becoming tense, emotionally volatile, depleted and unable to see the self as a centre of activity. Whose psychic forces, which are easily fragmented by too much movement, are frayed and overwhelmed during multilevelled activity. Assists in becoming centred and focused even under stress, or high levels of activity; so as to manage and co-ordinate diverse activities.

Iris (*Iris douglasiana*) For those feeling dull, unable to feel inspiration, lacking creativity and feeling weighed down by the ordinariness of the world. Encourages perception of beauty, making everything seem alive and vibrant, and a deep soulfulness and inspired creativity which is in touch with the higher realms. Brings radiant, iridescent vision in all aspects of life.

Lady's Slipper (Yellow) (*Cypripedium parviflorum*) For those estranged from their inner authority, unable to integrate and align their higher spiritual purpose and direction with real life and work, leading to nervous exhaustion and sexual depletion. Calms and restabilizes the nervous system, helping to regain inner composure and spiritual strength, integrating spiritual purpose with daily work, integration of spiritual vision with vital forces in the root and creative chakras bringing spiritual power into the body.

Larkspur (*Delphinium variegatum*) For those in positions of leadership who are distorted by self-aggrandizement and who feel over-burdened by duty or inflated with self-importance, unable to motivate or inspire others. Encourages charismatic leadership qualities, contagious enthusiasm and joy in serving others.

Lavender (*Lavandula officinalis*) For nervousness and overstimulation of mental or spiritual forces which deplete the physical body; for those who are highly strung and wound up, typically suffering from headaches, vision problems, neck and shoulder tension and insomnia. Soothes and teaches moderation. Brings spiritual sensitivity, encouraging a highly refined awareness intact with stable bodily health.

Lotus (*Nelumbo nucifera*) For spiritual pride – those who regard themselves as spiritually correct and who are out of touch with ordinary personality and humble tasks. An all-purpose remedy for enhancing and harmonizing the higher consciousness. Enables an expansive and inclusive spirituality, with the ability to synthesize diverse life experience in service to the spiritual world.

Love-Lies-Bleeding (*Amaranthus caudatus*) For intensification of pain and suffering due to isolation; profound melancholia due to the overpersonalization of one's pain. Brings transcendent consciousness, the ability to move beyond personal pain, suffering or mental anguish by finding larger, transpersonal meaning in such suffering; compassionate awareness and vision of and attention to the meaning of pain or suffering. Helps develop compassionate acceptance of life karma.

Madia (*Madia elegans*) For those who are easily distracted, unable to concentrate, and having trouble living in the present, splintering activity so that it is unproductive. Also for seasonal distress, when hot weather can make you feel listless and distracted. Brings precision thinking, disciplined focus and concentration.

Mallow (*Sidalcea glauscens*) For insecurity in relationships, an inability to trust and paralysis in reaching out to others or radiating warmth, resulting in social barriers. Removes barriers and helps us trust our inner feelings. Encourages warm openhearted sharing and friendliness.

Manzanita (*Arctostaphylos viscida*) For those who have an aversion to their body and feel estranged from the physical world. Often drawn to punishing dietary regimes, such people often feel ill even if they are following perfect health programmes, and have eating and sleeping disorders. Softens attitude to physical matter, encourages a spiritual identity that is fully integrated with the physical body and a positive involvement in the world.

Mariposa Lily (*Calochortus leichtlinii*) For those alienated from their mother or the mothering instinct due to abandonment, abuse or trauma in childhood. Heals the trauma and encourages our ability to nurture and show caring attention to others. Strengthens maternal instincts, warm and positive mother-child bond. Restores the inner child.

Milkweed (*Asclepias cordifolia*) Neediness and emotional regression, dulling the consciousness due to extreme dependency on drugs, alcohol, food as a means of escaping from self-awareness, also creating dependency or sickness to receive attention. Brings independence, strength, self-reliance and a healthy ego; nourishes at the deepest level.

Morning Glory (*Ipomoea purpurea*) For 'night owls' with erratic eating and sleeping rhythms who have difficulty getting up in the morning with the inability to fully enter the body. Feeling hungover, dull and toxic perhaps making them susceptible to nervous depletion and poor immunity. Also for addictive habits. Encourages attunement with rhythms to restore natural energy and sparkling life-force, so that we are refreshed and in touch with life.

Mountain Pennyroyal (*Monardella odoratissima*) For difficulty thinking clearly and making rational decisions because of unconscious absorption on the negative

thoughts of others – negative programming, psychic contamination or possession. Cleanses the mind to promote clear, positive thinking and mental integrity.

Mountain Pride (*Penstemon newberry*) For fear and withdrawal when faced with challenges, vacillation and lack of assertiveness making us unable to take a stand for what we believe in. Cultivates a courageous warrior-like spirituality and attitude which confronts, takes positive action and transforms.

Mugwort (*Artemisia douglasiana*) For those prone to fantasy or projection, who display irrational, hysterical, over-emotional behaviour, who are out of touch with reality. For those who have an overactive psychic life and are unable to distinguish or integrate transphysical experiences. Integrates psychic dreams and balances experiences so we can glean greater insight into the affairs of daily life. Encourages warm and expansive soul qualities

Mullein (*Verbascum thapsus*) For those feeling weak and confused, unable to tune in to or hear their inner voice and lacking in decisiveness, confused, prone to lying or deceiving themselves and others. Develops a strong sense of inner conscience, truthfulness and moral fortitude.

Nasturtium (*Tropaeolum majus*) For intellectuals who think too much and deplete their life force and emotional verve from too much study. Restores warmth, vitality and radiant energy.

Nicotiana (Flowering Tobacco) (*Nicotiana alata*) For numbing of the emotions accompanied by mechanization or hardening of the body; inability to cope with deep feelings and finer sensibilities. Blunted feelings, shallow breathing. Brings inner peace which is deeply centred in the heart; deep breathing, integration of physical and emotional wellbeing through harmonious connection with the earth.

Oregon Grape (*Berberis aquifolium*) For paranoid, fearful people who see others and the outside world as hostile and unfair, and have defensive behaviour and antagonistic projection. Helps cultivate trust and positive expectation in the goodness of others. Good for tension and ill will that predominates in many urban environments.

Penstemon (*Penstemon davidsonii*) For those who feel persecuted or victimized, or who pity themselves for having been dealt an unfair hand in life and are unable to bear life's difficult circumstances – they may be disabled or may have lost a loved one, their home or possessions. Develops inner strength, courage, and resilience in the face of hardships. Fosters an enduring and persevering attitude.

Peppermint (*Mentha piperita*) For mental dullness and lethargy, craving stimulation or food only to feel sluggish afterwards – unbalanced and under-active metabolism depletes mental forces. Imparts mental clarity and vibrancy and a warm metabolism balanced with cool head forces.

Pink Monkeyflower (*Mimulus lewisii*) For shame, guilt, unworthiness, fear of exposure and rejection, masking feelings and hiding your real self from others. For fear of anyone seeing your pain, possibly due to childhood trauma or abuse. Brings self-acceptance and forgiveness, the ability to let go of the past as well as emotional openness to experience and risk the love and affection of others.

Pink Yarrow (*Achillea millefolium var. rubra*) For those who are overly sympathetic towards others and excessively vulnerable to their emotional influence, with an overly absorbent auric field, dysfunctional merging with others, giving rise to emotional confusion. Imparts appropriate emotional boundaries and greater objectivity and containment, teaching how we can radiate love.

Poison Oak (*Toxicodendron diversiloba*) For fear of intimate contact, being violated.

For those who put up a hostile front, protective of personal boundaries; reactive or rejecting in relationships so driving away intimacy. Brings emotional openness and vulnerability so others can make close contact possibly through touch. Especially for men who fear being too open.

Pomegranate (*Punica granatum*) For women torn between career and home life, feeling confused and compromised, especially between values of career and home. Such psychological tension can affect sexual organs. Enables women to see their destiny and choices more clearly, encouraging joyful expression of feminine creativity, active productivity and nurturing.

Pretty Face (*Triteleia ixioides*) For those feeling ugly and rejected because of their physical appearance, such as those born with deformities or whose features are ungainly. Allows inner beauty to radiate within; brings acceptance of our own appearance despite handicaps or blemishes.

Purple Monkeyflower (*Mimulus kelloggii*) For fear of the occult, or of any spiritual experience; fear of retribution or censure if one departs from religious conventions of family or community, apprehension or avoidance of threshold experiences due to fear-based beliefs or ritual abuse. Brings inner calm and clarity when experiencing any spiritual or psychic phenomenon; the courage to trust in one's own spiritual experience or guidance; love-based rather than fear-based spirituality.

Quaking Grass (*Briza maxima*) For those who have difficulty finding their place in the work or family setting. Inability to compromise, over-attachment to personal will and desire in social situations. Helps individuals maintain their identity without being subservient or overexerting their ego. Harmonious community consciousness, flexible and receptive in group work.

Queen Anne's Lace (*Daucus carota*) For those who close their eyes to what is really happening, denying the subtler levels of

The process of making Flower Essences

Right: Roses – mother essences in the process of creation by my flower essence diploma students.

Below: Mother essences in the process of creation in the Himalayas

Above: Process of connection with the aura of the flower in Thailand

Above right: Himalayan mother tincture in the process of being enhanced by the light of the Himalayan moon

Left: Camomile

Below: Water crystals of camomile essence

Above: Water crystal of people consciousness when expressi love and appreciation

Left: Water crystals of the love expressed between husband and wife *bove:* Angel Orchid   *Below:* Inspiration Orchid

Above: Waratah

Left: Sturt Desert Pea   *Below:* Boab

Above: Fringed Violet   *Below:* Billy Goat Plum

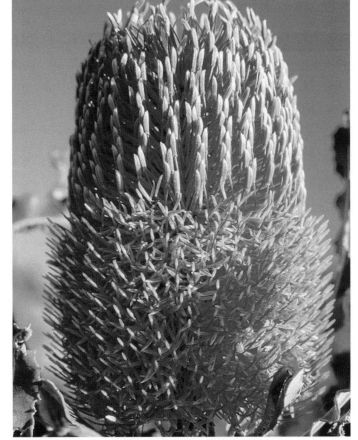

Above: Gymea Lily
Left: Paw paw
Right: Menzies Banksia

Above: Pincushion Hakea

Below: Star Of Bethlehem

Above: Silver Princess

Below: Illyarie

Rabbit Orchid

Start's Spider Orchid

Pink Fairy Orchid

Donkey Orchid

Geraldton Wax

Orange Spiked Pea

Wild Violet

Orange Leschenaultia

Northern Twayblade

Wild Iris

Northern Lights

Right: Lotus

My Song Calls Me Home

Graceful Transformation

Heart Light/ Light Hearted   Hearts Wings

Orchid Queen

Hibiscus

rab Apple Blossom

ed Chestnut

Cerato

Above left: Apple Blossom
A*bove:* Quince Blossoms
Left: Harebell Flower
Below left: Wild Garlic
Below: Bleeding Heart

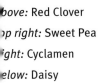
above: Red Clover
top right: Sweet Pea
right: Cyclamen
below: Daisy

bove: Lily of the Valley
bove right: Nootka Rose
ght: Purple Magnolia
ft: Poppy

Star Tulip

Shooting Star

Echinacea
Left: California Poppy

Tiger Lily

23

Above: Claret Cup Hedgehog Cactus   *Below:* Rainbow Cactus

Golden Gulaga

Ecstasy

Above: Strength

Right: Pluto

Above: Faith and Courage

Above: Nature Communication

Left: Ancient Wisdom

Above: Rose Madame Louis Levique

Right: Inoncencia
Coca

Kirlian Photography

Photographs showing the energetic effects of Cherry Plum essences dropped onto a crystal, starting with a control without any essence, progressing to a few minutes later when the drops have been administered to the crystal.

Above left: Control   *Above:* Immediate

Left: after 2mins   *Below:* after 4 mins

Effect of essences on the subtle anatomy

My aura and subtle bodies after a long day at a trade show in Switzerland; the grey and dull areas indicated exhaustion due to contact with so many people; the pink around the eye and nose indicates an open and activated third eye.

The effect after taking vibrational essences (Star Traveller from Soundwave Essences) the whole aura and subtle bodies are brighter, clearer and refreshed. The column of bright yellow light is the effect just after taking the essences when spiritual energy was drawn down into the crown and third eye chakra.

Harry Oldfield's electro-scanning machine 'photographs' the aura and imbalances in the body's energy field. The red/pink areas in the neck and right shoulder regions, indicate congestion in the throat chakra and a buildup of muscular tension. Clare had a slight sore throat and a long motorway journey. The turquoise with yellow indicate a person who heals through changing consciousness.

This shows the colour change in the energy field when Clare held pansy flower essence – an antiviral remedy. The red/pink areas are lessening, clearing the throat and discharging negative energy out through the right side. This also shows pansy's ability to bring violet-coloured energy into the auric field from above, to heal imbalances.

EEG of the effect of dolphin essences

31

A representation of the process of connecting with the energy of essences

Photo 1: SSK before taking Acceptance – drops placed on the crown, tongue and heart

Photo 2: Subtle bodies of the orchids appeared at the 13th chakra as an entry point into the aura.
Two orchids were present in combination to make the essence blend into one unified subtle body.

Photo 3: The orchid essence Acceptance was released through the 13th chakra by the orchid essence subtle body as light which softly flowed down through the chakras into the heart chakra.

Photo 4: At the heart chakra the essence of Acceptance pooled, and then moved outward as ripples on a pool of water. Sit in this softly reverberating pool of watery light allowing yourself to be infused with perceptions of Acceptance wisdom.

reality. Projection or lack of objectivity in psychic awareness; distortion of psychic perception or physical eyesight due to sexual or emotional imbalances. Helps clear the vision, bringing spiritual insight while keeping both feet on the earth, integrates psychic faculties with sexual and emotional aspects of self.

Quince (*Chaenomeles speciosa*) Loving strength and firm loving; integration of masculine initiating power and feminine nurturing qualities. Inability to catalyse or reconcile strength and power with affection and tenderness; dysfunctional or inconsistent parenting or leadership behaviour. For difficulty in combining nurturing and gentle qualities with discipline and objectivity. Helps us to use our loving nature in a way that does not compromise our essential dignity and strength.

Rabbitbrush (*Chrysothamnus nauseosus*) For those easily overwhelmed by details; unable to cope with simultaneous events, fuzzy consciousness that is unable to register details. For combining focus and attention to detail with wide-ranging perspective stimulating a lively and alert mental field. Encourages our capacity to integrate details while simultaneously being aware of the total situation.

Red Clover (*Trifolium pratense*) For those whose individuality is challenged by mass consciousness, feeling swept away on a tide of mass hysteria and anxiety, easily influenced by panic around them or other forms of group thought. Encourages awareness of our behaviour, helping us to maintain calm and steadiness, especially in emergencies.

Rosemary (*Rosmarinus officinalis*) For those who tend to be forgetful and absent-minded with poor learning ability because their spirit feels insecure about being here, loosely incarnated in body, lacking physical/etheric warmth, with their feet and hands often being cold and devitalized. For traumatic out-of-body spiritual experiences. Brings the ability to feel warm and secure. For feeling vibrant with a healthy embodiment.

Sage (*Salvia officinalis*) For a tendency to see life as ill-fated or undeserved, unable to perceive the higher purpose and meaning in life events. Enables you to learn and reflect about life experience which brings insight, wisdom and inner peace. Helpful during transitions and phases in life when you need to step back and consider the events that are unfolding. Gives wisdom derived from life experience and the ability to assess and understand life process from a higher perspective.

Sagebrush (*Artemisia tridentata*) For those who cling to proof of their existence by overidentifying with illusory parts of the self, needing to purify and cleanse the self and release dysfunctional aspects of the self and surroundings. Encourages us to become more aware of our essential identity, to be true to ourselves – thus capable of transformation and change.

Saguaro (*Carnegiea giganteus*) For rebellious tendencies – conflict with authority – sense of separateness or alienation from the past and reacting against your past. Brings awareness of what is ancient and sacred and an ability to learn from elders and an understanding of your culture, lineage or tradition, in order to embrace and understand the past.

Scarlet Monkeyflower (*Mimulus cardinalis*) Patterns of imbalance: fear or repression of intense feelings; inability to act upon issues of anger and powerlessness for fear of intense feelings/ repression of powerful emotions /inability to resolve issues of power or anger/fear of exploding in a blind rage. Needing to be seen as nice rather than real. Gives courage to acknowledge and confront such feelings. Imparts emotional depth and honesty, direct and clear communication of feelings especially anger or disappointment – integration of our emotional 'shadow'.

Scotch Broom (*Cytisus scoparius*) For those disheartened, anxious and depressed by uncertainty and upheaval in the world/pessimistic and despairing of your role in larger events. Gives tenacity and strength, cultivating hope, a positive view and optimistic feelings of the world's future.

Self-Heal (*Prunella vulgaris*) For those unable to take responsibility for their own healing and wellbeing, lacking in spiritual motivation for wellness and good health, overly dependent on external help. Encourages belief in your own capacity for recovery and an awareness and ability to tap into your own healing potential: a vital and healthy sense of self.

Shasta Daisy (*Chrysanthemum maximum*) For overanalytical people who have a tendency to see information as separate pieces rather than parts of a whole, artificial or mechanized intelligence. Gives insight into the larger patterns of mental and emotional experience and helps us to synthesize these patterns into a living wholeness, a holistic consciousness. Helpful for those involved in writing, teaching, research and other intellectual professions.

Shooting Star (*Dodecatheon hendersonii*) For feeling profoundly alienated, not at home on earth nor a part of the human family; disturbed birth trauma. Obsessed with extra-terrestrial existence. Brings the ability to find the right earthly connection and to be warmed with caring for all that is human and earthly. Humanized spirituality, cosmic consciousness.

Snapdragon (*Antirrhinum majus*) For energetic people with powerful wills and libidos who tend to repress these tendencies – prone to verbal aggression and hostility; sarcasm, lashing criticism, tension around the jaws (teeth-grinding). Misplaced snapping, biting or eating behaviours. Encourages a lively, dynamic, healthy libido and communication which is emotionally balanced.

Star Thistle (*Centaurea solstitialis*) For socially reclusive, lonely people who find it difficult to trust and be generous; those who tend to hoard or guard their material possessions due to a fear of lack, feeling malnourished at a deeper level. For an inability to give freely and spontaneously, miserly or hoarding tendencies. Brings feelings of security and a sense of abundance. Encourages the ability to give and share.

Star Tulip (*Calochortus tolmiei*) For men who deny their softer, receptive side, or women who have built a shell of protection around themselves. For the inability to cultivate quiet inner presence, lack of attunement or soul insight, unable to meditate or pray. Increases sensitivity and receptivity. Encourages quiet inner listening, serene soul disposition, ability to listen to higher worlds, especially in dreams and meditation.

Sticky Monkeyflower (*Mimulus aurantiacus*) For fear and repression of sexual intimacy and contact, often compensated for by seeking superficial sexual encounters. Balanced integration of human warmth, encourages ability to express deep feelings of love in sexual relationships.

St John's Wort (*Hypericum perforatum*) For those sensitive to light/fair-skinned/easily burned/adversely affected by heat and light/prone to environmental stress including allergies/vulnerable to psychic attack at night leading to bed-wetting and night sweats. For psychic and physical vulnerability, deep fears and disturbed dreams. For depression due to lack of contact with spiritual world. Gives protection and strength, illuminated consciousness, light-filled awareness and strength.

Sunflower (*Helianthus annuus*) For inflated ego, arrogance and vanity or low self-esteem and self-effacement resulting from a distorted sense of oneself. Poor relations to father or solar aspects of self. Encourages sense of unique individuality, balancing receptivity and nurturing self-expression, spiritualizing the ego and infusing a sun-radiant personality with outgoing qualities.

Sweet Pea (*Lathyrus latifolius*) For wanderers who have difficulty with caring, committed relationships. For an inability to form bonds with social community. Also for a sense of homelessness which may stem from moving around frequently as a child as well as from living in urban and suburban environments, disconnected from the natural world. Kindles feelings of being at home. Encourages commitment and forming connections with others and the earth.

Tansy (*Tanacetum vulgare*) For sluggish, lethargic people who are indecisive, prone to procrastination, appearing lazy, indifferent and nonchalant with habits which undermine or subvert real abilities and talents. They may often be exposed to much chaos, confusion, emotional instability and even violence in childhood and respond by withdrawing and restricting their energy. Encourages straightforward responses to others and life. For being purposeful, decisive and goal-oriented.

Tiger Lily (*Lilium humboldtii*) For over-aggressive yang forces, hostile, competitive people who strive against others rather than working for the common good. A feminine flower which makes inner peace and harmony the basis for relationships with others, encouraging co-operation and positive social interaction.

Trillium (*Trillium chloropetalum*) For excessive ambition, greed and lust for possessions, power and material wealth. Poverty consciousness that leads to overly-materialistic focus. Cultivates altruism, balances energy and brings inner purity. Secure sense of personal welfare and financial wellbeing; brings the ability to serve and give to others.

Trumpet Vine (*Campsis tagliabuana*) For lack of vitality, an inability to be assertive or speak clearly due to feeling intimidated and shy. Also for speech impediments. Encourages articulate, lively, colourful free-flowing speech, an ability to express feelings verbally, dynamism in social situations.

Violet (*Viola odorata*) For those who are profoundly shy, reserved, aloof and lonely. They may long to share themselves with others but hold back for fear of being overwhelmed. They are delicate, have highly perceptive sensitivity, elevated spiritual perspective; socially responsive but self-contained. Allows interaction with others while protecting individuality.

Yarrow (*Achillea millefolium*) For extreme vulnerability to thoughts or the negative intentions of others, overly absorbent of negative influences, psychic toxicity, easily affected by surroundings and depleted and prone to environmental illness or allergies. Protects with a shield of light. Rebuilds vitality and solidity by repairing the aura. Creates a luminous and strong auric field, compassionate and inclusive sensitivity, refined and flexible psychic forces.

Yellow Star Tulip (*Calochortus monophyllus*) For insensitivity to the feelings and the sufferings of others, and lack of awareness of the consequences of your actions. Brings compassion and caring. Encourages empathy with and sensitivity to the suffering of others.

Yerba Santa (*Eriodictyon californicum*) For internalized grief and melancholy, deeply repressed emotions, feelings constricted in the chest, particularly in the heart and lungs. They may appear to be wasting away and are susceptible to chest congestion, pneumonia, tuberculosis, addiction to tobacco. Lightens the heart. Allows the emotions to flow freely, with the ability to harmonize breathing with feeling. Brings the capacity to express a full range of human emotions, especially pain and sadness; positive melancholy and soul depth.

Zinnia (*Zinnia elegans*) For those who are over-serious and sombre, too earnest, lacking humour and spontaneity. Workaholic tendencies. Encourages childlike qualities of playfulness, laughter and humour.

Combinations

Yarrow Environmental Solution

Flower essences of Yarrow, Pink Yarrow, Golden Yarrow, Arnica and Echinacea, with Yarrow and Echinacea tinctures, in a sea salt water base. For exposure to nuclear radiation and other forms of noxious environmental or geopathic stress including radiation from VDUs, X-rays, radiation therapy and other invasive electromagnetic fields. Originally developed in response to requests after the Chernobyl nuclear plant disaster in 1986. Directly counters the destructive effects of radiation on the human energy field by acting as a shield, so imparting powerful vitalizing and restorative properties. Counteracts pollution, or other geopathic stress; residual effects of past exposure; dysfunctional immune response; allergic hypersensitivity. Enhances our physical and etheric vitality, and brings self-regulating and adaptive immune response to environmental stresses.

Self Heal Cream

This world-renowned skin cream awakens the inner vital forces necessary for healing on all levels: physical, emotional and spiritual. Contains Self-Heal flower essence which is especially indicated for those who have lost belief in their own capacity to be well and is beneficial for those who face great healing challenges, whether physical, mental or spiritual. Self-Heal is an excellent remedy to enhance other flower essences and therapeutic programmes and the inner commitment to be well; it acts as a catalyst in the journey to mind-body health. It affirms the self and draws from the deep wellspring of life, to aid true recovery and restoration. Use alone or add your own essences of choice to personalize your cream. Used for its therapeutic and regenerative qualities, it has an anti-inflammatory property and can soothe the irritation caused by eczema and oversensitive skin.

© Flower Essence Society, used with permission.

For more detailed flower essence profiles please refer to the Flower Essence Repertory, available in print. An online Repertory with database cross-referencing and plant photographs is available to members of the Flower Essence Society at www.flowersociety.org.

Master's Flower Essences

Remedies for Inner Wellbeing

These essences are made exclusively from the blossoms of flowering fruit trees from local orchards and blossoming plants from vegetable gardens. The ancient yoga teachings explained that the food we eat affects our state of consciousness. Heavy, processed food brings the energy down and creates toxins, which in turn causes fatigue and eventually contributes to bodily distress and illness. Pure, fresh food, such as fruits and vegetables, uplift the consciousness and provide energy.

This is also the philosophy of the world-renowned metaphysician Paramhansa Yogananda (1893–1952, author of *Autobiography of a Yogi*), who came to the United States in 1920 to teach practical, scientific techniques for self-improvement. He taught that food fortifies us on spiritual and psycho-emotional levels and also supplies nutritional benefits. Cherries, he explained, possess a vibration of cheerfulness and raspberries contain kindness.

If food has such power, how much more so do the blossoms, containing 90 per cent of the life force of the plant. Commissioned by J Donald Walters, a direct disciple of Yogananda, Lila Devi Stone developed Master's Flower Essences in the foothills of the Sierra Nevada Mountains just outside Nevada City, California in 1977, making them the oldest essence line outside the UK. (The tropical essences – Pineapple, Coconut, and Banana – are prepared on the Hawaiian Islands, and Date is made in the desert of Southern California.) Three decades of research, analysis, case studies and direct testimonials, from health care professionals to lay people, confirm the potency of these 20 essences.

Lila says,

> 'When we feel distressed by attitudes that block our highest
> potential, it is natural to want to rid ourselves of them. Even more
> so do we want to live in those states that are our true nature. Flower
> essences work by stimulating and encourage us to manifest those
> positive qualities which we already possess in our own delightfully
> unique way. This process is accomplished through the supportive
> interaction of the essence with our own readiness and willingness
> to make needed changes in our lives and attitudes.
>
> That is their great strength and immense beauty.'

She proposes that the essences help people to become 'masters of their own lives'. Master's Essences are an excellent first line to work with, because of their simplicity and straightforwardness. A branch of this essence line, Yogananda's Spirit-in-Nature Essences – http://www.Spirit-in-Nature.com – is becoming nationally known in India. Particularly recommended for children, these essences enhance their clarity of energy and bring forth their unique talents. The Master's line is especially supportive of the dynamic between mother and child (*see* page 271). Animals also respond positively to essences (*see* special section for Pets and Animals page 278).

Almond (*Prunus amygdalus*) Self-control, moral vigour. For the power to rebound vigorously from every setback in life. For calming the mind and nerves. Use when you need to be more inward, less affected by environment and circumstances. Good in times of activity and high demands on your energy reserves. Promotes synchronicity of body/mind/spirit, and restores a sense of balance and moderation.

Apple (*Malus domestica*) Healthfulness. For more inner peace amid life's swirl of activity. To be always 'calmly active and actively calm'. For clarity, receptivity and healthy attitudes. For inharmonious states of mind, including hypochondria, worry and doubt, and recurring negative emotions such as anger and fear. Helps bring clarity, receptivity and joy. Restores a sense of wellbeing to one's thoughts and outlook on life. Unlocks the spring of true health and vitality, providing the motivation to take better care of oneself.

Avocado (*Persea Americana*) Good memory. For a retentive mind, important for every kind of success. For the ability to develop mental skilfulness and concentrate wholly on anything you do. Brings focus and recollection of details; inspiration for new projects and challenges for the mind (such as exams) as well as a greater awareness of life's purpose. An attitude of 'Now I get it!' Also for learning from one's mistakes and delighting in the learning process.

Banana (*Musa* x *paridasiaca*) Humility rooted in calmness. For self-honesty and self-forgetfulness. For projecting your energy outward, away from yourself. For a calm, nonreactive attitude, for perspective and not getting overly involved, especially where emotions are concerned. For objectivity and a having a healthy distance from people and circumstances. To be able to let others have the last word and be able to 'agree to disagree'. Excellent for promoting harmony in close relationships.

Blackberry (*Rubus fruticosus*) Purity of thought. To free yourself from every thought that is foreign to your higher nature. Brings kindliness, mental clarity, optimism, and the ability to see the good within oneself and others. Helps us to be inspirational, incisive and direct yet gentle, and supportive of our environment and of all living things. Encourages true friendships and harmony in life.

Cherry (*Prunus avium*) Cheerfulness. For a more light-hearted, less heavy attitude toward life. For being more solution-oriented. A life-brightener! Encourages seeing the good in every situation, being hopeful, inspiring to others, optimistic, positive, light-hearted, even-minded. Helps whenever there is a lack of energy, enthusiasm, and interest in life.

Coconut (*Cocos nucifera*) Greater spiritual awareness. For a clearer, more spiritual focus in life. For the energy to endure, or to rise above, every test. For completing tasks, living up to one's highest potential. Helps us to see solutions, and to welcome and offer support for meeting any kind of challenge. Often called the 'walking tall' essence, which means to become aware that you are bigger than any of your tests.

Corn (*Zea mays*) Mental vitality. For being always awake and prepared. Brings initiative to projects, rekindling enthusiasm and, through awakening the will, and provides unlimited energy to accomplish anything you desire. For living in the moment, and especially for 'new beginnings' of any kind: a new job, a new home, a new relationship, or starting a new year at school.

Date (*Phoenix dactylifera*) Sweetness and tenderness. To view all living things as our own, including strangers. For overcoming judgmental, negative attitudes or thoughts of separateness from others. Encourages discrimination, receptivity, open-mindedness, and sensitivity to others' feelings, allows us to be easy to talk to, welcoming, magnetic, and warm-hearted. Good for people who work with the public. Also for self-nurturing when life seems harsh.

Fig (*Ficus carica*) Flexibility and self-acceptance. For the ability to relax, no matter how heavy your responsibilities. To soften too strict a sense of discipline, toward oneself and others. For those too hard on themselves, with unrealistic expectations and difficulty with change. Brings a sense of humour, fluidity, self-liberation, and the ability to go with the flow and be at ease with people.

Grape (*Vitis* sp.) Love and devotion. To awaken the feelings of the heart and to love others spontaneously, whether that love is returned or not. For developing selfless love and all true and noble qualities. Many people, especially in crowded cities, feeling disconnected, alienated and vulnerable, experience the need for this essence through loneliness, isolation, or unfulfilling relationships. For weathering the death of a loved one, divorce, separation, neglect, and abandonment issues. Brings a realization of the source of love within, loving without condition, demand or expectation, patience with others' shortcomings.

Lettuce (*Lactuca sativa*) Calmness. To have greater calmness and inner strength when confronting the difficulties in your life. Also for clear communication skills and promoting creativity, self-expression, and expansiveness. For an inner sense of restfulness and dynamic, energized stillness. For restlessness, inability to concentrate, excitability, repressed and troubled emotions, Dispelling emotional turmoil, replacing it with even-mindedness. Confers the ability to speak one's truth, restores clear communication skills, and creates a productive, clear-thinking environment for highly creative people. Freedom to experience the more subtle states of relaxation.

Orange (*Citrus sinensis*) Enthusiasm, Hope and joy. Excellent for blasting through obstacles. For 'seeing the light at the end of the tunnel'. For deeply ingrained present and past abuse issues, physical, sexual or emotional, either past or present. Gives a sense of restored energy, resilience, lightness, banishing mild to severe depression and melancholy, and for culti-vating an inner smile.

Peach (*Prunus persica*) Unselfishness. For the ability to extend your generosity toward others and include them in your own happiness. Brings concern for the welfare of others, maturity, nurturance, consideration, deep compassion, sensitivity and empathy.

Pear (*Pyrus communis*) Emergency use, creates peacefulness. A 'must' for emergency situations, accidents, trauma, physical and/or emotional shock, or crisis, surgery, childbirth complications, extreme grief and any situation which throws us off balance; uncontrollable thoughts and nonproductive habit patterns. Also for balance and harmony throughout the day. For minor to monumental auric distur-bances. Restores peace of mind and a sense of rhythm, proportion and balance. For living fully in the present moment; gives an

ability to handle crises and awakens our ability to handle life's upsets.

Pineapple (*Ananas comosus*) Self-assurance, for building self-esteem. For those who feel undermined by the criticism of others. Helpful for people in the work world where their identity is reflected back to them by money and job issues. Fosters confidence, prosperity and abundance. For a strong, healthy sense of self that is neither a superiority nor an inferiority complex.

Raspberry (*Rubus idaeus*) Kind-hearted-ness and compassion. Raspberry teaches us that kind-heartedness opens the heart and allows us to forgive our own failings. For those feeling easily hurt, touchy, overreac-tive, insensitive – who lash out, lack understanding and judgement, are clouded by emotions, blame others and feel resentful and bitter. Fosters taking respon-sibility for our words and actions; for sympathy, benevolence, generosity, and the desire to help others heal their hurts; for releasing old wounds.

Spinach (*Spinacia oleracea*) Simplicity. For stress, feeling burdened or overwhelmed, and for trust, to replace suspicion. For a sense of wonder, a free spirit, a playful nature, and a love of adventure. Helpful for people who are stressed, overworked, or have endured an unhappy or dysfunctional childhood. Allows us to be straightforward, easily understood, and uncomplicated, even with numerous responsibilities.

Strawberry (*Fragaria*) Dignity. For centring and grounding and the ability to draw respect from others. For a sense of poise and inner beauty. For those who are guilt-ridden, regretful, self-blaming, undeserving, or unsure of themselves. They may have a history of emotionally abusive parents, Also for psychic over-sensitivity and for healers who tend to absorb the problems of their clients. Brings strength, stateliness, and self-worth. Allows us to leave a dysfunctional childhood in the past.

Tomato (*Solanum lycopersicum*) Strength and endurance. To support you in standing up for your beliefs. Tomato is for fear of any nature, severity and duration, nightmares, and also for working on addictions. Allows us to know there is no failure, only another chance to succeed. Encourages belief in oneself, invincibility, psychic protection, and immunity from the effects of large cities, crowds, and negative environments.

The Essential Flower Essence Handbook (also in Italian, Spanish, and Japanese, as well as in English in India) is also the text for her widely acclaimed home study tri-level comprehensive course.

Hawaiian Gaia Flower Essences

Hawaii is renowned for its wonderfully exotic subtropical species of flowers, many of which were reputedly introduced by the migrating Polynesians when they discovered the islands and settled there some 1,600 years ago. Inspired by the beauty of these islands, some suggest they may be the remainder of ancient Lemuria/Oceania, a mythical land that is said to have existed some 50,000 years ago. They speculate that some of the endemic Hawaiian Flower Essences such as Koa and Hawaiian Sandalwood have properties which help to enhance spiritual awareness, and these species could date back to these times.

The Hawaiian people traditionally turned to herbs for healing wounds and easing digestive problems. Internal illness was believed to be induced by evil spirits which weakened the *mana* or spiritual life-force in a person. Their medicine men or *Kahunas* treated illnesses by holding a ceremony called a *ho'oponono* in which they used herbal potions with rituals to clear psychological disharmony within the family and so appease the spirits. The Hawaiians as a race of people recognized and were respectful of the spirit of life present in the plants, trees and rocks, referred to in the Western world as fairies or devas.

Natural medicine came into Cathie Welchman's life in the early 1990s when she was cured of a chronic allergy to wheat. Becoming interested in complementary medicine, she trained in crystal therapy, reflexology, aromatherapy and hypnotherapy. She became intrigued by gem and English flower essence making, which she still does. However there is a certain something about the inspiring and magical atmosphere that draws Cathie back to Hawaii repeatedly.

The plants on Hawaii grow super-abundantly, due to the subtropical climate, the rich volcanic soil and the magnetic power rising from the still active volcanoes. These 62 essences have been gathered from amongst over 50,000 tropical plants on the main Hawaiian islands of Oahu, Maui, Big Island and Kauai. Many of the flowers used for the essences, such as Noni, Sandalwood, Ti and Koa, come from plants that were traditionally used by the native medicine men (*Kahunas*) for healing disease, wounds and mental afflictions. The essences have absorbed and now embody the islands' magnetic healing qualities. The original mother essences were made with Hawaiian mineral water, drawn from deep artesian wells sunk beside the highest volcano, Mauna Loa, on Big Island.

The Hawaiian essences come from the lava desert, high altitude grasslands, tropical jungles, tree parks, the beachside and water sites. Cathie found the essences both potent and reflective of the primal forces of nature or *mana* which have been absorbed and reflected by plants. They offer a simple, safe way of returning us to health and happiness, resolving stress, despair and confusion, communication, vulnerability and relationship issues.

Aloe (Panini-awa 'awa) (*Aloe*) Aura repair. This essence protects one from lower astral interference, and helps to close holes in the etheric body caused by the effects of psychotropic drugs.

Angel's Trumpet (Nana-honua') (*Brugmansia candida*) Calling spirit. Stimulates reintegration on all levels of the personality. For those people who have lost touch with their intuitive side and focus only on the physical side of existence, and have a great fear of death, or anything otherworldly.

Banana Poka (Passion flower) (*Passiflora bryonioides*) Lack of control. Stimulates co-operation and brings a sense of calm to those exhibiting wild, hyperactive or out-of-order behaviour, such as toddlers or teenagers. Dietary advice should also be sought.

Blue Ginger (*Dichorisandra thyrsiflora*) Fear of known things. Stimulates courage and strength in nervous people to be able to face their everyday fears. These include fear of the dark, spiders, needles, animals, heights, strangers etc.

Bougainvillea (*Nyctaginaceae bougainvillea*) Enthusiasm. Encourages inspiration, purposefulness and enthusiasm. Discourages feelings of anxiety, fear or guilt.

Chenille (*Acalypha hispida*) Severing emotional ties. Cuts emotional ties formed through duty, base desires, programming or emotional blackmail, that bind one to an unhealthy, negative or harmful relationship.

Chinese Violet (*Asystasia gangetica*) Keeping it all together. Gives those who habitually overstretch their energies the wisdom of knowing when to say no, and to act on the need for rest, pleasure and holidays, despite the pressures of work and others' demands and neediness.

Cotton (Ma'o) (*Gossypium tomentosum*) Fearing the worst. Stimulates the ability to anticipate the future in a positive manner, and meet future challenges with courage and optimism. Lessens negative expectations, fear and apprehension of what might happen.

Crepe Myrtle (*Lagerstroemia indica*) Speak out without fear. Essence encourages those who are shy or nervous to state their needs, and speak up for themselves without fear or embarrassment.

Crown Flower (*Calotropis gigantea*) Independence. Instils courage and inner strength in those who are afraid of being on their own. This essence helps people to overcome the need to use emotional blackmail and states of ill health to maintain their overdependence on others.

Cup of Gold (*Solandra maxima*) Fear of the unknown. Opens the heart to bring deep inner calm and security in the face of constantly perceived danger. Decreases fear of fear.

Hau (*Hibiscus tiliaceus*) Calming extreme nervous stress. A calming, soothing and balancing essence for those overcome by extreme negative emotions.

Heliconia (*Heliconia caribaea*) Attention-seeking issues. Encourages acceptance of others' needs and talents, without feeling jealous, inferior or of lesser value.

Hibiscus (*Hibiscus*) Releasing memory of abuse. Realigns and restores emotional balance in those who are frigid or unresponsive in intimate relationships, due to past trauma from sexual abuse or exploitation. Heals soul loss and spiritual shocks.

Hina Hina Ku-Kahakai (*Heliotropium anomalum*) Empowered lady. Restores self-esteem, self-worth and the ability to make choices for one's own needs. Especially helpful for those women who have given up their lives and wishes completely to follow the desires of their spouse or children.

Ili'ahi (*Santalum*) Releasing stuck energy. Stimulates mental and emotional flexibility. It also amplifies the effect of other essences. For those with rigid, inflexible ways, that lead to escalating levels of stress, and difficulty in being able to unwind at the end of the day.

Ilima (*Sida fallax*) Dispelling illusions. Releases narrow-minded tendencies and hostility towards the spiritual views of others, due to cultural programming or religious dogma.

Impatiens (*Impatiens wallerana*) Calming anger. Encourages patience and tolerance in those who get easily annoyed and aggressive with others and the little problems of everyday life.

Ixora (*Ixora* sp.) Accepting change. Encourages interest and enthusiasm in present circumstances. Helpful for those who find it difficult to adjust to changing circumstances because they want to keep living in the past.

Jacaranda (*Jacaranda mimosaefolia*) Focus. A magically calming essence that stimulates decisiveness, clear-headedness and the ability to focus. Good for ditherers and those who constantly change their mind.

Jatropha (*Jatropha integerrima*) Spirit of fairness. Restores self-esteem and an ability to assert one's individual rights. Helpful for those whose kind and gentle natures have led to them being bullied, abused, unappreciated and used as scapegoats.

Kamani (*Calophyllum inophyllum*) Cleansing negative energies. Strongly positive essence for protecting a person or sacred place from profanity, or ignorant, negative or insensitive people. Neutralizes negative energies.

Koa (*Acacia koa*) Feeling fulfilled. An inspirational essence that promotes optimism and contentment at the deepest level of being. It eases the state of inner emptiness and deep pain and depression that people suffering from a lack of childhood nurturing or soul loss can't help returning to whenever life becomes temporarily more difficult.

Kukui (*Aleurites moluccana*) Emotional support. Promotes calmness and understanding. It dissipates emotionally- charged situations, agitation and deep-seated, subconscious fears. It is particularly helpful for toddlers, children and teenagers going through stubborn phases, or experiencing 'growing-up' difficulties or hormonal changes.

Kou (*Cordia subcordata*) Maintaining personal boundaries. Stimulates strong personal subtle boundaries around those who are easily affected by the negative energies of others, especially when in crowds or bars.

Lani Ali'i (*Allamanda cathartica*) Making the right decision. Instils inspiration, willpower and wisdom for making important decisions. Helpful for those in authority who are unnerved by their responsibilities.

Mai'a (Banana) (*Musa paradisiacal*) Balancing male sexual energies. Encourages balance in male libido. Also helps to overcome tendencies towards sexual obsession or perversion.

Mango (*Mangifera* spp.) Lightness of spirit. Increases one's ability to utilize cosmic rays for energy needs, and lessens the desire for dense foods such as meat.

Milo (*Thespesia populnea*) Self-esteem. An essence to restore self-worth to those who have been held in a restrictive environment for some time, such as a mental institution or prison. Essence increases the ability to be able to act in an independent, positive and decisive manner within the human community.

Morning Glory (*Ipomoea tunoides*) Revitalize. Rebalances the natural pattern of sleep and daytime alertness. Essence breaks the vicious circle of repeatedly stimulating more instant energy with addictive substances such as coffee, coca cola, or sugar, which then leads to a feeling of tiredness and irritability upon awakening.

Mountain Apple (Ohi-a-'ai) (*Myrtaceae*) Vulnerability. Stimulates the ability to overcome a weakened immune system through increasing the strength and determination of the mind's powers.

Naio (*Myoporum sandwicense*) Balancing appetite. Guides the soul to satisfy true inner needs instead of mollifying the outer symptoms of an emotional problem. Increases willpower to break addiction to comfort food.

Naupaka-Kahakai (*Scaevola taccada*) Moving on. Helps one to seek inspiration in the present and future, whilst gently encouraging release of the past. For those who want to move forward, but haven't been able to achieve closure or peace of mind due to personal injustices, bereavement problems or unfinished relationship issues.

Noho Malie (*Thevetia peruviana*) Calming agitated minds. Instils peace and calm in those who quickly become fearful and agitated for the smallest of reasons.

Noni (*Morinda citrifolia*) Faith in yourself. Stimulates invincible self-confidence and faith in yourself, particularly when you are being undermined by people who are gossiping behind your back. The essence prevents easily overwhelmed people from being pressured into acting against their will.

Nui (*Nucifera*) (Coconut) Perseverance. Helps sensitive people to develop a protective outer shell, so that they can reach their greatest potential. For those who lack endurance, find it hard to meet challenges, or to make tough decisions.

Ohai-Ali'i (*Poinciana*) Empathy. Encourages a greater awareness and understanding of the feelings of others. Helpful for people who are so self-involved that they don't listen to anyone, and are out of touch with those around them.

Ohia Lehua (*Metrosideros macropus*) Facing challenges. Helps one to master new skills and face challenges. Brings resilience, determination and an increased resolve to those who give up too easily. Helps to overcome addictions.

Orchid Tree (*Bauhinia*) Change. Stimulates the impetus to make necessary changes. Assists those who do not know how to change, even though they want to, and know they should.

Papaya (Paw paw) (*Carica papaya*) Clear head. Helps in the assimilation of information, even where there is prior fatigue present. Stimulates the clarity of mind needed for taking exams or making big decisions.

Pa-Nini-O-Ka (Night-blooming cereus) (*Hylocereus un-datas*) Light in the night essence helps to balance night and daytime energies. Alleviates fear of the dark or the sunlight.

Pink Ginger (*Alpinia purpurata*) Hugs. A wonderful essence to revive warm interactions with others. Especially helpful for those who never share their feelings with others. Also for those who have become emotionally cold and insensitive, due to past trauma.

Pink Waterlily (Day blooming) (*Nymphaea Odorata*) Feeling safe. Reinstigates trust in oneself, and releases apprehension in intimate relationships. Releases old patterns of feeling inherently unsafe that have been instigated by past experiences.

Plumbago (*Plumbagor auriculata*) Family issues. Restores love, empathy and respect to family relationships. Reduces animosity or lack of caring between family members.

Pohuehue (*Ipomoea pes-caprae*) Mother issues. Puts those who have been hurt by their mother's behaviour in touch with their own deep inner self, where love always resides.

Protea (*Protea* sp.) Openness. Encourages openness of emotions and expression, especially in those who are unable to fully express their feelings, even with those closest to them.

Pua-Kenikeni (*Fagraea berteriana*) Overcoming hedonism. Releases psychological cravings for sensual overindulgence or dips into directionless apathy, restoring a balance and purpose to life.

Pua Male (*Stephanotis*) Marital harmony. Enhances co-operation, communication and compromise in close relationships. Instils respect for each other's differences.

Pua Melia (Frangipani/*Plumeria*) T.L.C. Empowers, motivates and strengthens resolve to look after your own health and personal needs. For those who put everyone else's needs and demands before their own, eventually resulting in a breakdown of their own health and wellbeing.

Pukiawe (*Styphelia tameiameiae*) Zest for life. A revitalizing essence that decreases apathy, and encourages the desire to improve your quality of life.

Red Ginger (*Alpinea purpurata*) – Increasing sexuality. Enhances a healthy interest in sensual pleasures. Increases libido in both sexes by opening the base chakra and deepening a sensitivity in bodily desires.

Rose Apple (Ohi'a loke) (*Syzygium jambos*) Inner compromise. Instils an inner acceptance to be content with what one has. Helps those who think true happiness can only be found through money, partners, homes, career or other external things.

She Oak (Ironwood) (*Allocasuarina* sp.) Mother instinct. Promotes an emotional balance needed for optimum fertility in both sexes. Clears any feelings of inadequacy, lack of confidence or other subconscious emotional blocks. Promotes the need for adequate hydration. Take two or three drops of essence in a glass of water twice daily for at least three months.

Spider Lily (*Crinum asiaticum*) Childhood issues. Works on the inner child to help release damaging emotional programming learnt during childhood. Especially helpful for children or adults with painful memories instigated by parents or those in authority.

Spider Orchid (*Brassia*) Emotional blackmail issues. Stimulates respect and understanding of others' needs and kindness. Increases give and take, and lessens the need to bully, threaten or use emotional blackmail tactics.

Star Jasmine (*Jasminum multiflorum*) Overperfectionism. Essence encourages an inner acceptance and contentment with what talents and abilities you have. Helpful for those who make themselves unhappy by being overcompetitive, too perfectionist and highly critical of themselves and others.

Stick Rorrish (*Stenogyne caliminthoides*) Confusion. Restores communication between the mind, body and subtle bodies. Use for personality integration and soul loss problems.

Strelitzia (Bird of paradise) In crisis. Offers support and inner strength on a day-to-day basis to those who are exhausted, traumatized and at the end of their tether.

Ti (*Cordyline fruticosa*) Banishing negativity. A powerful essence to remove negative energies or neutralize curses. Also for overstimulation of the mind by circumstances or external environment.

'Uala (*Ipomoea batatas*) Releasing trauma. An essence to restore communication in a child or adult who has suffered a trauma, and is unable to express their feelings of shock, grief, frustration or helplessness.

Yellow Ginger (Awapuhi-melemele)
(*Hedychium flavescens*) Releasing the past.
A magical essence for gently releasing
knots of disharmony in the subtle bodies
or subconscious mind, that have become
stuck there due to repressed or unhealed
present and past life traumas. Essence also
links with liver issues. Helps to restore the
sensitivity to the senses.

Wiliwili (*Erythrina sandwicensis*)
Lessening autocracy. Brings in wisdom,
altruism and understanding. Dissolves
selfish motives. Helps to release a superiority complex. Helps those who have a
tendency to be arrogant, bossy and insensitive.

Pacific Essences of Canada

These are the first Canadian essences and are made by Sabina Pettitt from the
plants and marine life of the Pacific Northwest.

On moving to Vancouver Island, in the Canadian province of British
Columbia, Sabina was excited to discover new kinds of plants, and began making
some of them into vibrational medicines. The Arbutus trees of the west coast of
Canada were among the first to catch her attention. The Arbutus essence acts as a
spiritual tonic; one of the qualities it promotes is wisdom.

Sabina is a Doctor of Traditional Chinese Medicine and for nearly 25 years
has been researching the essences in the context of their specific resonance with
the meridian pathways with which each essence interfaces. Because each of the
meridians has specific physical, mental, emotional and spiritual correspondences
(or signs and symptoms of imbalance) using essences in conjunction with this
ancient knowledge impacts on the whole person and produces remarkable
healing effects.

In 1983 Sabina formed Pacific Essences and proceeded to research the plant
energies that attracted her. By 1985 she had researched 24 Wildflower remedies
and 13 Spring Flowers and to date has developed 48 flower essences in her range.

One day when walking along a sandy beach Sabina came across a Sand Dollar
(a type of sea urchin). She knew instinctively that this Sand Dollar had to be
made into a remedy to treat a friend with a rare form of skin cancer. To capture its
essence she placed the Sand Dollar in a glass of seawater and left it under a
pyramid in the sun. This incident marked the beginning of her work with
essences from the ocean, from which a whole new realm of energetic medicine
began to unfold.

With her husband and life partner, Michael, Sabina is credited with making
the first sea essences on the planet and introducing this whole new range of
healing frequencies to the vibrational medicine pharmacopoeia and there are now
24 sea essences in the Pacific Essences Repertory.

They are about transformations in consciousness and are indicated for major
breakthroughs, for they help us to contact the basic rhythms of the universe when

we are going through change. Sabina's sea essences differ from her flower remedies in that they come from salt water, which is very similar in composition to our own blood plasma and seems to have a special affinity for the body. In Chinese medicine the water element is related to reproduction, growth and maturation. At the level of the spirit it is linked to *chi* or psychic strength, which leads us through obstacles to growth. It is also the symbol for the unconscious.

Sabina proposes that, by their very nature, sea essences reveal the unconscious and strengthen consciousness in order to move forward towards a unique unfolding. Each essence is very precise and powerful. Being quick-acting, they usually have quite noticeable results.

In conjunction with her husband, Michael, a gifted energy healer, she has also researched the essences in relation to their impact on the chakras. These are the *prana* vortices of energy at specific locations on the physical body which literally act to download the life force into the physical. Each of her essences (Wildflower, Spring Flower or Sea Essence) is also linked to particular chakras and meridians.

In developing the understanding of energy as both preceding and affecting matter, a clear sense of how essences can impact on physical conditions became apparent for her. Like Dr Edward Bach she sees that it is fundamental that we treat the patient and not the disease. She trains her students to really listen to the patient and to be open to what their body/mind wants rather than having preconceived notions of which essence should work based solely on symptoms. Involving the patient in the cure is fundamental to work with essences. We cannot practice Energy Medicine® in the same way as chemistry based medicine.

Native Wildflowers – Kit 1

Bluebell (*Endymion non scriptus*) For giving up constraints, releasing old programmes, opening the channels of communication, engaging in what is fulfilling. Helpful for emotionally-caused speech disorders, autism. Combats shyness. Boosts low energy, combats fatigue, alleviates fear, strengthens the will and ability to breathe during panic or anxiety attacks. Chakra: throat. Meridians: lung and kidney.

Blue Camas (*Camassia quamash*) For acceptance and objectivity. Balances the intuitive and rational, unifies and balances the left and right brain. For the creative person who is impractical, and the down-to-earth person unable to access his or her intuition. Also for dyslexia, learning disabilities, inability to learn from experience. Releases stored memory from past lives. Chakras: solar plexus and throat. Meridians: kidney and bladder.

Blue Lupin (*Lupinus rivularis*) For clear and precise thinking. Links the pineal gland (organ of spiritual perception) with the pituitary gland (organ of metabolic control and balance). Also for toxin-related headaches and digestive disorders. Eliminates confusion about who we are. Alleviates depression, frustration and despair. Focuses attention and simplifies issues. Chakra: base/root. Meridian: liver.

Easter Lily (*Erythronium oreganum*) Truth, purity, integrity. Helps to integrate different aspects of our personalities, allowing open and honest self-expression. Eliminates social masks. For bypassing acquired personas of illusion, duplicity and dishonesty. Also effective for premenstrual syndrome and gynaecological imbalances. Chakras: heart, third eye and crown. Meridians: kidney and bladder.

Fireweed (*Epilobium angustifolium*) For realizing the abundance of love, both within and without. For emotional experiences recorded in the heart. Eases a broken heart, clears emotional wounds, coldness and the inability to feel. For embracing new relationships without residue from past ones. Loving, surrender. Improves circulation, softens muscle fascia in chest and upper back. Chakra: heart. Meridian: heart.

Goatsbeard (*Aruncus Sylvester*) For meditation, creative visualization, and the power to visualize oneself in a deep state of relaxation, being calm and relaxed in stressful situations. Resolving tension by creating inner alignment before action. Activates thymus to deal with stress. Strengthens immune system, white blood cell production. Helps to rejuvenate our body's chemistry. Chakra: third eye. Meridians: small intestine and spleen.

Harvest Lily (*Broadiaea coronaries*) Community, relationships, social interaction. Encourages expansion and awakening. Supports group energy and the ability to see another's point of view. For problems linked to reproduction, elimination, digestion, absorption, respiration and heart. Chakras: solar plexus and crown. Meridians: triple warmer and heart protector.

Hooker's Onion (*Allium cernuum*) For freedom, inspiration, spontaneity. Replaces blocked energy and heavy feelings with being refreshed and light-hearted. Nurtures creativity. Remedy for the spirit. Potential for releasing birth traumas and resolving the emotional attachment between mother and child. Chakras: all. Meridians: all twelve.

Orange Honeysuckle (*Lonicera ciliosa*) Inner direction, expression and identity. For crisis of personal identity and related physical tension. Releases creative blocks, diffuses anger and frustration. Evokes peaceful creativity. Useful for the turmoil of the teenage years. Also a powerful tonic for digestive disorders. Chakras: hara or sacral and solar plexus. Meridian: triple warmer.

Plantain (*Plantago major*) For releasing mental blocks and drawing off negativity. Purifies and cleanses the effects of poisonous thoughts, attitudes and resentment. Also for blood and liver disorders; any physical toxicity resulting from emotional or mental poisons, such as migraines and indigestion. Chakras: hara or sacral and crown. Meridians: liver and gallbladder.

Salal (*Gaultheria shallon*) For holding grudges or resentment. Releases power to forgive yourself and others; to let go. Clears stress and allows you the freedom and joy to experience the embodiment of the spirit in mysterious ways. Chakra: heart. Meridians: heart and small intestine.

Snowberry (*Symphoricarpus albus*) For accepting life as it is at the moment, dissolving resistance to what is – even when it is painful. Being here now. Also helpful for chronic fatigue and seasonal affective disorder. Chakras: crown and heart. Meridians: kidney and bladder.

Native Wildflowers – Kit 2

Arbutus (*Arbutus mensiesii*) Spiritual tonic – enhances qualities of depth and integrity. For homesickness or abandonment. For hanging on tightly while letting go lightly. Also benefits the lungs when their energy is depleted by sadness. Chakra: crown. Meridians: lung and liver.

Candystick (*Allotropa virgata*) Physical tonic – releases pelvic tension and promotes pelvic alignment. Releases blocked energy surrounding the experiences of abortion, miscarriage, birth, sexuality. Transforms self-anger and frustration to honour of self despite trauma. Survival and free will. Also for injuries to the sacrum and pelvic girdle, any insult to the reproductive system.

Chakras: hara or sacral and throat. Meridians: kidney and bladder.

Chickweed (*Stellaria media*) 'For clear and precise thinking' and acknowledging and experiencing timelessness, being fully present and able to respond. Allows free and easy expression. Works on gallbladder channel to release tension and give up resentment and control. Useful for losing excess weight that is caused in part by old emotional baggage. Good for health practitioners. Chakras: throat and base or root. Meridian: gallbladder.

Death Camus (*Zygadenus venenosus*) Spiritual rebirth: Awareness of spiritual connection with all life, for new beginnings, transformation and change. Alleviates stress and worry in times of transition. Helpful for new jobs, relationships, adventure. Assists self-cleaning efforts such as fasting, examining beliefs. Chakras: hara or sacral and heart. Meridians: lung and kidney.

Grass Widow (*Olsynium douglasii*) Releases old beliefs and limited patterns, and the fear of being judged by others. Challenges mental structures and beliefs (linked to family, work, religion) that are not working for us. For fear of letting go. Also helpful for digestive problems and food intolerance. Chakra: heart. Meridians: stomach and large intestine.

Nootka Rose (*Rosa nutkana*) For expressing love, laughter and joy. Kindles enthusiasm. Reminds us that the life of the soul does not begin with birth or end with death. Excellent for spiritual crisis, abuse, abandonment, psychic, emotional or physical assault. Reintegrates the psyche after assault, heals fragmentation after years of self-abuse – such as with drugs, alcohol. Chakras: all. Meridians: all twelve.

Ox-Eye Daisy (*Chrysanthemum leucanthemum*) For vision and the visionary. 'Total perspective; for being centred.' Brings a greater perspective when we cannot see the woods for the trees. Dissolves the blockage of fear which prevents clear sight. Develops better vision.

Benefits the eyes and ears. Chakra: third eye. Meridians: heart protector and kidney.

Pipsissewa (*Chimaphila umbellate*) For making decisions. Clears ambivalence and indecisiveness. Releases worry and confusion around choices in life. Benefits the area of the brain involved in choice. Chakras: solar plexus and throat. Meridians: spleen, liver and kidney.

Poison Hemlock (*Conium maculatum*) For letting go, moving through transition periods without getting stuck and holding on to old structures and beliefs. Dissolves emotional, mental, physical paralysis arising from periods of major change. Releases rigid feelings, ingrained thought patterns, no longer relevant unconscious thoughts. Also beneficial for constipation, fluid retention, weight problems, paralysis of the physical structure or nervous system, stalled labour during the birthing process. Chakra: crown. Meridian: gallbladder.

Salmonberry (*Rubus spectabilis*) A physical tonic – for spinal alignment and structural balancing. Works on bone, muscles and fascia. Helps chronic misalignments of physical structure due to injury. Chakra: third eye. Meridian: bladder.

Twin Flower (*Linnaea borealis*) Acceptance and compassion. Clears judgement and a critical attitude towards everything. Teaches discernment to make choices without criticizing others. Fosters optimism, humility, and peace of mind and heart. Chakras: base and heart. Meridians: liver and gallbladder.

Vanilla Leaf (*Achlys triphylla*) For affirmation and acceptance of oneself. Replaces self-loathing with self-esteem. A grounding remedy of exuberance, joy, acceptance. For skin disorders and any problem rooted in self-denigration and lack of self-love. Chakras: third eye and crown. Meridians: lung and large intestine.

Spring Flowers – Kit 3

Camellia (*Camellia sasanqua*) A catalyst for opening up to new attitudes which reflect one's true inner nature. Replaces guilt and shame with openness and flexibility. Stimulates expansion and vision beyond self-inflicted limitations, and expression of our uniqueness and inner power. Releases cell memory of earlier experiences in this life. Accesses self-trust and creates shifts in attitude. Chakra: solar plexus. Meridian: large intestine.

Forsythia (*Forsythia suspense*) Catalyst for change. Provides motivation for transforming old useless thought and behaviour patterns which may be self-destructive (such as addictive and self-destructive habits: mental, emotional and physical addiction, especially to alcohol, drugs and tobacco). Liberates dysfunctional relationships. Detoxifies the liver. Chakra: crown. Meridian: gallbladder.

Grape Hyacinth (*Muscari racemosum*) For times of external shock, despair and stress. Allows one to step back from the situation while harnessing inner resources to meet the challenge. Replaces shock and trauma with balance. Dissolves hopelessness, despair and depression. Eases stress felt in the stomach and aids breathing in times of stress. Also for bumps, bruises, accident shocks and all forms of trauma. Chakra: third eye. Meridians: stomach and lung.

Lily of the Valley (*Convallaria majalis*) For freedom of choice by discovering the simplest form of behaviour. Replaces sophistication and overcontrol with innocence. An emotional tonic that helps us to see with simplicity through the eyes of a child. Used in Europe as a cardiac tonic. Brings inner radiance and vitality. Chakra: throat. Meridian: heart.

Narcissus (*Narcissus pseudo-narcissus*) For identifying and resolving conflicts by going to the centre of the problem or fear. Slays internal dragons, calms butterflies in the stomach, and alleviates worry. Clears obsessive thinking, connects us to the impulse for survival, assists in feeling grounded. Also promotes digestion and eases digestive disorders (such as excess stomach acid, ulcers, gas). Chakras: base/root and hara/sacral. Meridian: stomach.

Periwinkle (*Vinca major*) Helps us to be responsible for our own depression and thereby dispel it. Lifts the dark cloud of depression, moves us to a place of inner knowing. Calms the mind and clears confusion and the memory. Also for hypertension, haemorrhaging, nervous disorders especially anxiety and seasonal affective disorders. Chakras: hara/sacral and crown. Meridian: heart.

Polyanthus (*Primula* x *polyantha*) Dissolves blocks to abundance and transforms attitudes of inadequacy into those of worthiness and willingness to receive. Increases sense of self-worth, abundance and gratitude. Also benefits the respiratory and elimination systems. Chakra: base. Meridians: large intestine and lung.

Purple Crocus (*Corcus tomasinianus*) Enhances ability to tune in to all aspects of pain, grief or loss in order to release and resolve the tension and restriction associated with these feelings. For embracing issues; beneficial for those who turn their blocked energy against themselves after grief, or heartache causing life-threatening disease. Helps tension in the upper back and shoulders, releases the heaviness related to loss and grief. Also assists the lungs. Chakra: throat. Meridian: lung.

Purple Magnolia (*Magnolia soulangeana*) Promotes intimacy and non-separateness, enhances all the senses. Replaces withdrawal, coldness and frigidity with open intimacy. Elevates sexuality to its fullest potential for intimacy and nonseparateness. Benefits the senses of smell, touch and feeling. Also a remedy for the spirit. Chakras: solar plexus and crown. Meridian: heart protector (circulation/sex).

Snowdrop (*Galanthus nivalis*) For letting go, having fun and lightening up.

Combines enthusiasm and joyful exploration of life. Embodies qualities of personal power and leadership. Dissolves energy blocks and personal holding patterns that prevent the free flow of energy or *qi*. Strengthens the will to dissolve paralyzing fear, attracts hope and release. Physically good for paralysis problems – arthritis, multiple sclerosis, poliomyelitis, cerebral palsy. Chakras: base, solar plexus and crown. Meridians: kidney and bladder.

Viburnum (*Viburnum carlesii*) Strengthens our connection with the subconscious and our psychic abilities. Excellent aid to channelling, meditating or centring. To hear and trust the intuitive voice within. Clears self-doubt and insecurity. Fosters clarity of sight. Affects the ears and ability to listen. Helps relax the nervous system. Chakra: third eye. Meridians: spleen and triple warmer.

Windflower (*Anemone pulsatilla*) A spiritual tonic providing grounding and inner security. Provides the security necessary to express our spiritual being, allowing the soul to dance. Balances scattered and spaced-out feelings. Also for stomach disorders, both physical and emotional – for nourishment on all levels. Chakras: throat and heart. Meridian: stomach.

New Flowers – Kit 6

Alum Root (*Heuchera micrantha*) The power of the small; manifestation of 'godness'; ability to move in a pattern without having to do it 'your way'; willingness to choose 'to be'. Clears conflict and power struggles in relationships, moves a judgemental attitude to easygoing acceptance, creating trust, grace and beauty. Chakras: heart. Meridians: heart protector.

Douglas Aster (*Aster subspicatus*) 'Endless expansion while maintaining our centre; savouring life experience, living fully and consciously connected to our source, promotes courage and adaptability.' Releases attachment to the ego, attracting expansion, generosity and radiance. Helps with staying centred, whatever turbulence is encountered, and in the face of many demands. Chakras: heart. Meridians: kidney, governing vessel.

Fairy Bell (*Disporum smithii*) Light-hearted release from murky thoughts; expands willingness to follow one's guidance; eases depression. Helps through the pain of a healing crisis emotionally and physically, sometimes has a mild sedative effect. Thaws frozen feelings and frozen body patterns. Physically frees the lungs and eases breathing. Can be used to assist the newborn to take its first breath, and help others breathe through the feelings of despair. Dissolves ambiguity and resistance bringing a lightness of being. Chakras: third eye. Meridians: lung.

Fuchsia (*Fuchsia*) For recreation, letting go of dysfunctional patterns; being the change we wish to see in the world. Helps the slow phlegmatic types to 'lighten up' and move, and the fast, busy, overdoing types to slow down, 'chill out' and relax. A remedy of balance which peels the layers of programming of acceptable behaviour patterns and attunes to our own inner rhythms. Behavioural shifts occur as a level of self-actualization is experienced. A constitutional remedy for the water element, tonifies and nourishes the kidney and bladder channels. Chakras: sacral. Meridians: kidney, bladder.

Indian Pipe (*Monotropa uniflora*) Reconciliation with others and making peace with oneself with reverence for all of life. Allows standing alone in closeness, to be able to be fully in a relationship whist maintaining and expressing our own unique qualities of being. Fosters self-respect, banishes negative self talk, feelings of worthlessness, so that we can find and live our life purpose. A constitutional remedy for the metal element, aiding self-expressing in the world, and gives the ability to recognize and claim what is valuable. Chakras: root. Meridians: lung, conception vessel.

Pearly Everlasting (*Anaphalis margaritacea*) Commitment and lasting devotion; opening to the mysteries of life; transformation through service. Deepens connections with another, reminding us that when connected on the soul level it's easy to remain beautiful in the eyes of the beloved. Shifts and transforms anger and brings the earthy 'stuff' into perspective. Encourages us not to throw the baby out with the bathwater in relationships. Helpful for those unwilling or unable to make deep and lasting commitments. Chakras: third eye, navel. Meridians: liver, gallbladder.

Poplar (*Populus tremuloides*) For contacting spirit; for the ability to transmit healing energies; to improve choice-making; attunes to the gentleness of nature. Connects with the triple warmer channel, harmonizes the energy flow spiralling upwards from hara through the heart to the crown and tunes the physical body to a higher frequency. Chakras: throat, back neck. Meridians: triple warmer.

Red Huckleberry (*Vaccinium parvifolium*) To experience the power of introspection, to be able to withdraw from the madding crowd, the rush and business of daily life, allowing ourselves to go within with ease, reminding us of the power of nourishment when taking time to digest, and the wisdom of regeneration contained in hibernation. For being not doing, attuning to the cycles of nature on the planet and in our body. Helpful for preventing SAD, by resting in the winter months. Chakras: solar plexus. Meridians: gallbladder, stomach.

Silver Birch (*Betula pendula*) Enhances the ability to receive and to conceive; softens the need to control; dispels suffering and develops humility. A catalyst for balancing the female energy, strength in yielding. Physically for healing the reproductive organs. Emotionally and spiritually helps with conception when there are mental and emotional blocks that stand in the way. Also can be used to eliminate power struggles in relationships, especially when one person needs to be in control, and trying to play many roles simultaneously, clears self-sabotaging behaviour, making it easer to create agreement and harmony. Chakras: heart. Meridians: spleen.

Wallflower (*Cheiranthus*) For hopelessness, endurance, preparedness; attuning to our own inner rhythms. Dispels the sense of hopelessness when feeling misunderstood and can help us find the right means to make ourselves understood. Helps us to honour and delight in the many manifestations of divinity in form. The medicine of saints and mystics, it fosters an appreciation of the individual who can step to the beat of a different drum. Wallflower essence enters into the solar plexus chakra, it cleanses the imprint of old emotional pain resulting from feeling like 'the ugly duckling'. For Sensory deficits and autism. Chakras: solar plexus. Meridians: stomach, spleen.

Weigela (*Weigela florida*) For integrating experiences on the physical and emotional planes. For realizing that others are both our teachers and mirrors who reflect our own negative and positive energy patterns. Clears disassociation, fosters trust and integration. Also for accidents and unexpected physical/emotional traumas. Chakras: throat and third eye. Meridians: liver and gallbladder.

Yellow Pond Lily (*Nuphar polysepalum*) Allows us to float free of emotions and attachments; fostering a secure sense of self, feeling strong and secure in one's path; blesses relationships. Through the bladder channel grants the ability to see things anew, to release emotional patterns so we are able to move forward fearlessly without being at the mercy of our feelings. Connects the throat chakra and allows us to express ourselves purely and without artifice, helps us to centre and perceive differently and act on our new information. Chakras: throat. Meridians: bladder

Sea Essences – Kit 4

Anemone (*Anthopleura elegantissima*) For acceptance of ourselves and others by helping us to take responsibility for our own reality, allowing us to be organized by the universe. Aligns the mental body with higher soul purpose. Empowerment versus victim mentality. Releases karmic blockage in the solar plexus. Also for physical pain, allowing movement through pain rather than resistance to it. Helps eye problems. Also for overcontrolling both emotionally and mentally; for those prone to tension, muscle spasms and injuries. Chakra: solar plexus. Meridian: liver.

Barnacle (*Balanus glandula*) For attuning with the feminine aspect of the self in order to develop complete trust. Embodies wisdom, nurturing, fertility and abundance. Also for the female reproductive system, especially cysts and fibroids. Regulates hormone production and release. A powerful birthing remedy. Chakra: heart. Meridian: small intestine.

Brown Kelp (*Nereocystis luetkeana*) For shifts in perception leading to clarity. For those who get in their own way because of fear and confusion. Balances energy between the base/root and crown chakra. Also dissolves back tension, helps bladder infections and ear problems – especially fluid imbalance of the middle, inner ear. Chakras: base/root and crown. Meridian: bladder.

Jellyfish (*Aurelia aurita*) A birthing and rebirthing essence. Dissolves resistance that causes pain, helping us to be fluid and flexible and let go into the experience rather than be rigid and stuck. Spiritually connects us to the rhythms of our own being. Helps self-expression and depression. Also works against arterial plaque and hardening of arteries. Dissolves bitterness and hardness on the mental and emotional level before physical manifestation of disease occurs. Chakra: throat. Meridians: heart and heart protector.

Moon Snail (*Polinices lewisii*) Cleanses the mind and lets in light. Eliminates physical toxins which cloud the mind. Helps cultivate innocent wonderment instead of rigid thought structures. A helpful tool for meditation, illumination and inner journeys. For mapping unconscious territory in order to harness and explore creative expression. Chakra: hara/sacral. Meridian: triple warmer.

Mussel (*Mytilus edulis*) For releasing the burden of anger, enabling one to stand up straight. Transforming anger, it allows creativity and inner radiance to shine through. Excellent for a 'victim consciousness' that prevents our alignment with inner power and strength. Resolves irritability, frustration and anger. Also relaxes neck and shoulder tension and eases headaches and dizziness. Helpful for whiplash; promotes the flow of bile and aids digestion. Chakra: hara/sacral. Meridian: gallbladder.

Pink Seaweed (*Coranilla vancouveriensis*) A grounding remedy for the patience needed before new beginnings, to harmonize thought before action. Helps us to move out of our 'comfort zone' into the new and challenging. Softens and allows change to occur with grace. Helpful when beginning new jobs, schools, relationships and experiences. Physically strengthens the bones and teeth; aids constipation. Chakras: hara and solar plexus. Meridian: heart protector.

Sand Dollar (*Dendraster excentricus*) For 'coming to your senses', awakening to reality versus illusion. For positive thinking that helps us to overcome the underlying cause of disease in the physical body. Effective for bronchitis, asthma, throat problems and self-expression. Chakra: throat. Meridian: lung.

Sea Palm (*Postelsia palmaeformis*) For breakthroughs in consciousness. For those who hurry for no reason, who are busy, preoccupied and controlling but not really allowing themselves just to be. For activity, being busy, and preoccupied which is a hindrance to success and meaningful relationships. For those who crave nurturing and emotional/ physical nourishment. Also helps digestive problems and eating disorders. Chakra: heart. Meridians: stomach.

Starfish (*Pisaster ochraceus*) A grief remedy. For willingly giving up the old and allowing the experience of being empty and releasing attachment. For appreciating our own unique soul path. Helps us to remember that 'to everything there is a season and a time for every purpose under heaven'. Stimulates a deep spiritual connection with those we love. Chakra: crown. Meridian: large intestine.

Surfgrass (*Phyllospadix scouleri*) For courage, strength and power rooted in stability and flexibility. Encourages integration of opposites by embracing paradox. Brings us the courage to be. For achieving goals that reflect our life's purpose, not our ego's desires. Alleviates fear and integrates courage. Strengthens will and gives a second wind. Also benefits kidney disease, infections, calcifications, inflammations. Balances the adrenal glands, enabling adrenaline to be used in a life-supporting way: stress without distress. Chakra: heart. Meridian: kidney.

Urchin (*Strongylocentrotus purpuratus*) For safety and psychic protection. For charting unknown territory, such as past-life regressions. A spiritual essence that expands the mind to access stored memories from early childhood or a previous life. Also for the effects of childhood abuse which have created self-abuse patterns (e.g. alcoholism, eating disorders, suicidal tendencies). Helps to dispel panic attacks, and respiratory problems that arise from feeling unsafe. Chakras: crown and solar plexus. Meridian: spleen.

Sea Essences – Kit 5

Chiton (*Mopalia muscosa*) For gentleness which serves to break up and to dissolve blockages and tension. Rigidity, promotes gentleness and flexibility. Primarily a physical remedy, helps us to live softly in our bodies instead of tightening up under stress. Remedy for whiplash or other neck injuries, also for dysfunction of the thyroid gland causing holding patterns in the body e.g. excess weight. Helps us to be more flexible within our body/mind structure. Useful before going into a situation where emotional distress exists. Helps move beyond limitations of cultural conditioning and rigid beliefs, encouraging the full creative expression of the liver channel. Allows you to receive new information, perceiving something in a new way and change course acting on this insight. Chakras: throat. Meridians: liver.

Coral (*Pocillopora meandrina*) For living in community; respect for self and others. Allows us to retrieve ancient memories, lost connections with the earth and how to be human. Helps us to remember we are not enemies only those who have agreed to play roles in our own script of learning and evolution. Cleanses old 'stuff' held in the solar plexus so we are not held back by emotionally-charged memory patterns. Connects with the kidney channel and is potent for the brain and the central nervous system, the kidneys are where the inherited *qi* resides. It affects physical growth and mental potential and is appropriate for CNS disease such as post-polio syndrome, Parkinson's, MS etc. Also encourages cell adaptability, so with those who have lost part of their brain function, the viable cells will be able to take over the function of the missing cells. Chakras: solar plexus, throat. Meridian: kidney.

Diatoms (*Amphipleura pellucida*) Repatterning cellular memory; letting in the light. To be used when the purpose of a cell has been forgotten, as in cases of cancer and degenerative disease, helps to enlighten the cells and assist with its return to normal if that is the soul's intent. Chakras: heart. Meridians: heart.

Dolphin (*Stenella longirostris*) Appreciation for all that is, brings a playful, light-hearted, dancing energy. Dolphins are considered water creatures' manifestation of angels. For those who feel profound alienation and loneliness with a sense of deep loss and abandonment. A remedy of the heart and mind, expansion and transformation and connects with the limbic system where we experience pleasure and joy. Opens the heart, moving energy through the crown to the higher dimensions in order to expand consciousness. Chakras: sacral, solar plexus, heart, throat, third eye, crown. Meridians: spleen, heart.

Hermit Crab (*Pagurus granosimanus*) The ability to enjoy 'aloneness'; contentment and sensitivity. For help through the dark night of the soul when our aloneness feels overwhelming. Aids understanding and reconnection with our soul whose journey is always alone, individual and unique, which brings freedom and easy self-integration physically, emotionally and mentally in all situations. Diminishes fear, and those so insecure that they are unable to enter or maintain authentic relationships. Quiets the mind, and helps feeling comfortable with the self wherever we are. Chakras: throat. Meridians: stomach.

Rainbow Kelp (*Iridaea cordata*) Alignment of front and back brain i.e. reactivity and sensibility; alchemical transformation. A remedy for depression, mental confusion, helps to release, relax and attune to a higher perspective and connect to our light source. Connects with the third eye chakra and hara, the adrenal glands, 'the fight or flight response' and fear states. With its affinity with triple warmer channels it balances all the other meridians and regulates the body temperature. Harmonizes the extrovert and introvert and therefore has an impact on social relationships. Chakras: navel, third eye. Meridians: triple warmer

Sea Horse (*Hippocampus*) Energizing the spine and central nervous system; accessing the 'wild one' within. No matter what physical form we have chosen this remedy allows us to express unique talents and abilities and let go of notions of how men and women 'ought' to be. Physically for disease or dysfunction of the CNS, communication between the brain and motor or sensory function. Benefits the lungs, assisting utilizing of *prana* or *qi* whilst breathing. Good for athletic and physical endurance. Resolves stiffness of the spine through the effect on the governing vessel which also allows dispersion to all other meridians as needed. Chakras: root, sacral. Meridians: lung, governing vessel.

Sea Lettuce (*Ulva lactuca*) Embracing and healing the shadow; for dispersal and elimination of toxins. Affords the ability to recognize, heal, and transform those faults, flaws of the ego that we hide even from ourselves. Known to Native Americans as the 'eater of filth' sea lettuce detoxifies, purifies and releases, acting as a blanket which soothes and heals the lower abdomen as well as being useful for the reproductive organs or bowels. Resonance: Purification. Chakras: solar plexus. Meridians: small intestine, stomach.

Sea Turtle (*Chelonia mydas*) For persistence, grace, commitment. Benefits the spleen and assists in its functions of transformation and absorption of nutritive *qi*. It helps those who tend to be 'spaced out' and underground to reconnect with solid earth energy, to get out of their heads and into being in their bodies and living on the earth. At the spirit level helps find the 'spark of divinity' in our souls and connection to the Source. Chakras: heart. Meridians: spleen, heart protector.

Sponge (*Myxilla incrustans*) Everything is unfolding in perfection; nothing happens to me without my consent. Filters impurities from the mind and spirit so freedom can be experienced. Helps us to let go and embrace life fully and gives the ability to dance between the two polarities of attachment and detachment. For those who tend to absorb the energies of others and have no way of transmuting them. Connects with the stomach channel, assists with digestion and absorption of emotions and ideas. Connects with the bladder channel by maintaining energy reserves and fluid balance and by maintaining the position of active participation and passive observation. Chakras: crown. Meridians: stomach, bladder.

'Staghorn' Algae (*Lessoniopsis littoralis*) Holding ground (sense of self) amidst turbulence and confusion; accessing higher consciousness. An aid to reconnecting with our own divinity when feeling lost or alone. For attunement and perception and is beneficial for the eyes. Awakens spiritual clarity, promoting steadfastness and gentleness. Works on the gallbladder channel and physically on tight and painful shoulders. Improves co-ordination, mentally aids clear thinking, decision-making when making life-supporting choices which benefits physical and emotional health. Chakras: root. Meridians: gallbladder.

Whale (*Globicephala macrocephalus*) Enhances ability to communicate through vibration and sound; expansion of human consciousness; ability to contact the record keepers. A remedy for healers, an aid to expanding, enhancing and transmitting the healing ability as well as receiving and interpreting subtleties of nature revealing knowledge of our roots, path in life and future possibilities. Physically a general tonic, that tonifies the circuit of *qi* in the governing and conception channels which directly influences all the other meridians as well as the mind/body connection. Chakras: third eye, crown. Meridians: conception vessel, governing vessel.

Abundance, Balancer and Heart Spirit Combinations

While doing the early research on individual essences three combination formulas emerged – Abundance, Balancer, and Heart Spirit balancer. These combinations address moving through stress, acting from grace and ease, and attracting prosperity.

Sabina created the Abundance Program, a 22-day journey of using the essence with specific intention. Heart Spirit gifted us with healing for the heart at all levels. The ancient Egyptians had an image of a person's heart being weighed against a feather on a set of scales at the door to the next life. Only if your heart is lighter than the feather can you proceed into the next world. This is the gift of Heart Spirit.

These combinations have been one of the most exciting additions to Pacific Essences repertory.

Their gift is that they work at so many levels. When a number of essences are combined in a formula the whole becomes greater than the sum of the parts and the impact is far bigger than when they are used individually.

Abundance Discover your inner connection with the source of all that is and manifest your heart's desire in any area of your life. Abundance essence connects us to the source of all manifestation, allowing use of the principle of creation in our daily life so that we are 100 per cent responsible and accountable for the reality that we experience. Helps to tap into the potential that 'I create my own reality' and reinforces the understanding that we are each the author of our lives instead of the audience in our lives. Aligns body, mind, emotions, and spirit to act in a unified manner to achieve individual goals while forging a connection with the larger flow of all of life. It is an essence of transformation of consciousness.

The 22-day Abundance program consists of an essence, oil, and a spray. The abundance program is a commitment to yourself. Its purpose is to create a new framework for manifesting abundance at any and all levels of your life. Choose your focus, whether it's money, relationships, work, family, health, or any area where you are experiencing lack or scarcity.

Each exercise is designed to release 'stuff' which no longer serves you, or to assist you in creating a particular experience of abundance in your life. Essentially the program, coupled with that of the Abundance essence and oil, will repattern cellular memory so that you can experience your own inner power to manifest exactly what you want.

Heart Spirit Embrace life wholeheartedly – with joy, compassion and generosity. Dissolves old heart pain, encourages us to truly embrace the 'spirit of the heart'. The 'spirit of the heart' is love, light, laughter, and joy. It is peace, allowing, embracing, acceptance, comfort and enthusiasm. The primary effect is to raise the vibrational frequency of the heart centre to its highest level, promoting self-worth and lending new meaning to the dignity of being human, allowing us to interact with each other with grace. It is much needed at this time. Heart Spirit is an essence, oil and spray.

Balancer Maintains centre in stressful situations. Restores balance and harmony. The Balancer essence harmonizes the body/mind in any situation of psychic, emotional, or physical overload. It allows us to shift our attention, regaining perspective and balance. It resets homeostatic mechanisms in the physical body, calms the mind, and dissolves turbulent emotions. It feels like immersing yourself in a cooling, soothing waterfall and emerging rejuvenated and refreshed. A powerful adjunct to a first-aid kit, Balancer offers immediate, safe, and effective results. It balances excess or deficiency in any of the channels or chakras. Balancer is an essence, oil and spray.

Nine Synergistic Formulas

As a result of the phenomenal success of these first three combinations, Sabina introduced nine new synergistic formulas in 2003. These combinations are designed to be 'user friendly' for people who know little or nothing about essences. Already they are proving to meet a growing need on the planet for gentle medicine.

Being True Worth Recognizing who we are with the freedom to express who we are in our daily lives and relationships. Transcending cultural programming/ brainwashing. Physically nourishes lung and large intestine, and enables the receiving of new vibrant energy and the release of old toxic energy. Emotionally welcomes new feelings, releasing old emotional patterns that don't serve. Mentally embraces new thoughts and attitudes, dissolving crystallized thought forms, and spiritually brings grace.

Cellular Memory Supports and enhances the innate intelligence of each cell, coaxes each atom to perform impeccably to maintain balance and harmony to survive, and to contribute to the survival of the whole. Reminds each cell of its *dharma* (purpose) and unique contribution to the whole being. Physically restores memory of cellular purpose, activates and enlivens our own unique DNA blueprint. Emotionally dispels discouragement. Mentally brings inner peace and knowing that it is all unfolding perfectly. And spiritually it embraces the divine

Fearlessness Ability to move into love and the heart centre, what is not love is fear. Encourages the ability to stop time, shape shift, broadcast energy from the heart instead of adrenaline and fear vibes. Physically nourishes adrenals, supports kidneys. Emotionally promotes nonattachment. Mentally creates clarity, and spiritually awakens consciousness.

Forgiving Gives the freedom to disconnect from any and all 'old and painful' stuff by letting go of any blame or shame that we might attribute to ourselves or others. Forgiving is the ultimate gift to ourselves and restores our own sense of self-empowerment and self-direction. For 'control freaks', it is the ultimate and optimally healthy form of control. Physically cleanses every cell memory of any perceived harm from others. Emotionally dissolves bitterness, resentment, fear, and hostility. Mentally erases resentment, and spiritually frees our soul to dance the dance we came here to perform.

Kids' Stuff For all the fears (imagined and real) and dramas and traumas of childhood when we can't get into bed at night until we are sure there is nothing or no one hiding under the bed or in the closet. For when we think the 'sky is falling in' or 'it is all our fault' when parents are fighting or when one of them gets sick, when 'bad stuff' happens. Restores innocence and harmony and 'acceptance of what is' with calm detachment and light-heartedness. Physically tickles the heart with a feather. Emotionally restores innocence, brings joy and delight. Mentally dispels seriousness, promotes spontaneity. Spiritually helps us to know the spirit within, nourishes inner security and self-referral

Optimal Immunity Strength and protection for body/mind/spirit: physical, emotional, mental, and spiritual safety. Physically strengthens spleen, increases white blood cells. Emotionally protects against psychic and/or emotional attack. Mentally prevents toxic thought patterns and eliminates old ones. Spiritually fosters safety and protection at all levels of being and a warrior spirit.

Optimal Learning Helps to access and decode information with ease and promotes the ability of the brain to function holistically and to access more of its potential. Practically assists with learning disabilities like dyslexia and Attention Deficit Disorder (ADD) and in the bigger picture it can help those of us who repeat the same mistakes over and over and over again. Physically promotes wholeness and integration in the brain. Emotionally destroys fear and restores self-esteem. Mentally promotes mental acuity and perception, and spiritually is a reminder that the incarnated soul is here to learn

Radiant Beauty Switches on the light of our inner beauty and illuminates the body and mind so that through whatever the shape, size and physical features of the 'vehicle' we are driving in this lifetime, we appear beautiful to all who perceive us and perhaps mostly 'we accept and appreciate who we really are'. Physically enlivens the *Shen*, and nourishes spirit. Emotionally dissolves and erases 'ugly' emotions. Mentally catalyses 'beautiful' thoughts. Spiritually balances among the five spirits – *Shen, I, Po, Chi*, and *Hun* allowing us to connect with the divine; accepting, expressing and allowing others to see who we really are.

Super Vitality For rejuvenation and revitalization of body/mind/spirit. Enhances stamina and promotes peak performance. Useful for athletes to encourage peak physical performance or for anyone whose natural vitality of the sex chakra is diminishing, and for anyone who is feeling the effects of aging. Physically it's revitalizing. Emotionally it is harmonizing. Mentally it restores optimism and optimal neurological function. And spiritually it is renewing.

Perelandra Rose and Garden Essences

Back in 1976 Machaelle Small Wright established the Perelandra Garden, a nature research centre, with a view to researching and discovering the principles and dynamics of co-creation between man and nature. Tucked away in 22 acres of woodland at the foothills of the Blue Ridge Mountains of Virginia, she has succeeded in creating a garden environment which is integrally balanced with nature in such a way that every living thing enhances the life and health of everything else. Plants growing here flourish without the use of organic or inorganic pesticides, nor does Machaelle remove insects by hand. The state of balance provides a niche for the insects who, given their proper place, do not act in a destructive manner. The garden has now reached a level where all its inhabitants do truly enhance the life and health of one another.

Like many Machaelle feels there is an intelligence in nature which serves to keep everything in balance. She communicates directly with the nature spirits, devas and the nature intelligences (the intelligent levels of consciousness within nature) in order to obtain specific information on how to create a balanced environment. It is said that the deva of each plant type holds the architectural blueprints of that plant.

The Perelandra Rose and Garden essences grew from this co-creative relationship and are one result of the work being done in this research centre. The essences benefit additionally by being made from the flowers of vegetables, herbs and other plants growing in this unique garden.

The first eight Rose Essences (Set 1) were developed in 1984. Made from the roses in the Perelandra garden, these essences function with one another to support and balance an individual's physical body and soul as he proceeds in day-to-day evolutionary process. As we move forward in daily process, there are mechanisms within us which are set in motion to facilitate our periods of growth. The Perelandra Rose Essences help stabilize and balance us and our process mechanisms.

The next set of 18 Garden Essences is made from flower petals of vegetables, herbs and flowers grown in the Perelandra garden. Their balancing and restorative patterns address physical, emotional, mental and spiritual issues that we face in today's world.

The Perelandra Rose Essences (Set 2) were developed in 1992. The eight essences are made from roses growing in the Perelandra garden and address the specific functions within the body that are activated and/or impacted during a deep expansion experience. Here, one is not simply processing ordinary, everyday occurrences, rather one is faced with an experience that is new and challenging to the present balance and functioning of the body. When faced with this kind of expansion, the body is required to function in ways that are new, and with patterns and rhythms yet to be experienced. The Rose Essences II address this expansion phenomenon by fine-tuning, balancing and stabilizing the specific steps of the process one must go through to expand.

The Perelandra Essences are one meaningful way the extraordinary benefits derived from this special balanced, natural environment can be shared with mankind.

Garden Essences

Broccoli (*Brassica oleracea italica*) For the power balance which must be maintained when one perceives oneself to be under siege from outside. Stabilizes the body/soul unit so the person won't close down, detach and scatter.

Cauliflower (*Brassica oleracea Botrytis*) Stabilizes and balances the child during the birth process. Stabilizes the body/soul balance in the adult.

Celery (*Apium graveolens dulce*) Restores balance in the immune system when it is being overworked or stressed and during long-term viral or bacterial infections.

Chives (*Allium schoenoprasum*) Re-establishes the power one has when the internal male/female dynamics are balanced and the person is functioning in a state of awareness within this balance.

Comfrey (*Symphytum officinale*) Repairs higher vibrational soul damage that occurred in the present or a past lifetime.

Corn (*Zea mays*) Stabilization during universal spiritual expansion. Assists transition of experience into useful, pertinent understanding and action.

Cucumber (*Cucumis sativus*) Rebalancing during depression. Vital reattachment to life.

Dill (*Anethum graveolens*) Assists the individual in reclaiming power balance one has released to others. Releases victimization.

Nasturtium (*Tropaeolum majus*) Restores vital physical life energy during times of intense mental-level focus.

Okra (*Abelmoschus esculentus*) Returns ability to see the positive in one's life and environment.

Salvia (*Salvia divinorum*) Restores emotional stability during times of extreme stress.

Snap Pea (*Pisum sativum*) Rebalances child or adult after a nightmare. Assists in ability to translate daily experience into a positive, understandable process.

Summer Squash (*Cucurbita* sp.) Restores courage to the person who experiences fear and resistance when faced with daily routine. Releases shyness and phobia issues.

Sweet Bell Pepper (*Capiscum annuum*) Restores inner peace, clarity and calm when faced with stressful times. Stabilizes body/soul balance during times of stress.

Tomato (*Solanum lycopersicum*) Cleansing. Assists the body in shattering and throwing off that which is causing infection or disease.

Yellow Yarrow (*Achillea*) Supplies emotional protection during vulnerable times. Its support softens resistance and assists the integration process.

Zinnia (*Zinnia*) Reconnects one to the child within. Restores playfulness, laughter, joy and a sense of healthy priorities.

Zucchini (*Cucurbita pepo*) Helps restore physical strength during convalescence.

The Rose Essences

Ambassador Pattern. Aids the individual in seeing the relationship of the part to the whole, in perceiving his pattern and purpose.

Betty Prior Stabilizes and balances the delicate rhythm of expansion and contraction of the cranial bones during the expansion.

Blaze Improved Climbing Rose
Softens and relaxes first the central nervous system, then the body as a whole, thus allowing the input from an expansion experience to be appropriately sorted, shifted and integrated within the body.

Chicago Peace Stabilizes movement of and interaction among the cranial bones, cerebrospinal fluid and sacrum during an expansion experience.

Eclipse Acceptance and insight. Enhances the individual's appreciation of his own inner knowing. Supports the mechanism which allows the body to receive the soul's input and insight.

Gruss an Aachen Stability. Balances and stabilizes the body/soul unit on all physical/emotional/mental/spiritual (p.e.m.s.) levels as it moves forward in its evolutionary process.

Nymphenburg Strength. Supports and holds the strength created by the balance of the body/soul fusion, and facilitates the individual's ability to regain that balance.

Orange Ruffles Receptivity. Stabilizes the individual during the expansion of his sensory system.

Peace Courage. Opens the individual to the inner dynamic of courage, which is aligned to universal courage.

Royal Highness Final stabilization. The 'mop-up' essence which helps to insulate, protect and stabilize the individual and to stabilize the shift during its final stages, while vulnerable.

White Lightnin' Synchronized movement. Stabilizes the inner timing of all p.e.m.s. levels moving in concert and enhances body/soul fusion.

The Rose Essences II

Maybelle Stearns Stabilizes and supports the sacrum during an expansion experience.

Mr Lincoln Balances and stabilizes the cerebrospinal fluid pulse while it alters its rhythm and patterning to accommodate the expansion.

Oregold Stabilizes and balances the cranials, central nervous system, cerebrospinal fluid and sacrum after an expansion process is complete.

Sonia Stabilizes and supports the cerebrospinal fluid pulse after it has completed its shift to accommodate the expansion.

Tiffany Stabilizes the cranials as they shift their alignment appropriately to accommodate the input and impulses of expansion.

This material is reproduced by kind permission of Machaelle Small Wright, Perelandra Guide to Rose and Garden Essences, © 1992, and Perelandra 1995–6 catalogue, © 1995, Perelandra Ltd.

Pegasus Essences

Fred Rubenfeld, the owner of Pegasus products, was introduced to the world of vibrational healing when he went to work in the diamond industry in New York. While surrounded by gemstones and crystals he began to learn about and experience the healing effects of the stones he worked with. In 1983 he was among the first to open a mineral and crystal store, selling gem elixirs in New York. He then expanded into the world of flower essences when he took over the Pegasus company. Fred has now created a phenomenal 'remedy bank' which offers a vast range of over 500 flower essences and more than 300 gem elixirs, as well as star light elixirs from the stars and planets.

The Pegasus range is made up of contributions from all over the world: Lily from Africa; Holy Thorn from Glastonbury; Creeping Thistle from Scotland; and many flowers from Tahiti etc. The company is based in the Rocky Mountains in a town called Love Land, near Boulder, Colorado, a sparsely populated area with an abundance of wildlife and rich gold and quartz deposits. Geographically it is the centre of North America. People living here seem to derive a great deal of energy from the land, which is conducive to good health.

Fred believes the secret of making good essences and elixirs is to welcome participation from all kingdoms – floral, mineral, elemental, planetary, and extra-terrestrial – while detaching ourselves mentally and emotionally from the process of making essences.

To make his flower essences he uses a special quartz crystal bowl and sunlight that is filtered through xenon gas before hitting the water. The gas acts as a filter, reputedly eliminating any harmful effects of the sun's rays.

The essences are potentized by a geometric shape called a metaform, an aquarian pyramid filled with crushed quartz. This process is carried out after the essence is made, again after it is bottled and once again prior to shipping, to clear any negativity and ensure a safe journey and long shelf life.

At this particular time these essences aim to deal with and provide the energy needed to cope with issues, destruction, change and disaster. Flowers and crystals in particular, Fred Rubenfeld maintains, can assist with these issues. He feels there is something quite unique about the urban flowers that push themselves up through the sidewalks of New York. They show a determination to move through obstructions, a strength of spirit that is appropriate for dealing with the issues of today, and indicative of the tenacity needed to work through the kinds of obstacles we face daily.

He also feels that at this time there is greater awareness of the higher realms, as there was in biblical times and even earlier. At a time when so much life on earth is in jeopardy, flowers and gems are providing some possible solutions. For example, elephants are now being saved thanks to the discovery of a new substance that comes from a bean plant and can be worked to look like ivory. Its qualities are captured for the first time in Fred Rubenfeld's Tagua Essence. Here are some of his vast range of flower essences as well as his roses collection.

Agave Yaquiana (*Maguey Lechugilla*)
Affects the unconscious decisions people make based upon deep-seated beliefs about separation, loneliness, aloneness, etc. that are often the legacy of past-life information and experiences. When taken repeatedly it helps loosen the hold of these hidden or unconscious belief-patterns.

Aloe Eru (*Aloe campem*) Helpful in closing holes in the etheric body due to other entities and, to a lesser extent, due to an individual's own experiences. Soothes after severing an association with a negative entity.

Alyogyne Huegelli (Blue Hibiscus)
Increases the capacity of the crown chakra to assimilate and work with information. For accessing the 'cosmic computer'. Can increase understanding of the nature of kundalini energy as it moves through the spine.

Bird of Paradise (*Strelitzia*) For under-standing flight, movement. Brings a realization of the interconnectedness among people and communities. Useful in people-management and for the appropri-ate use of new technology and its impact on freedom – for humour created around relationships and freedom.

Blazing Star (*Liatris* sp.) Can awaken expressive energies felt as a buildup of energy in the heart which then pours through the hands and fingertips, especially the middle finger. Useful in utilizing the energy of love for healing.

Blue Witch (*Solanum umbelliferum*) Has the ability to create energy shifts in chakras 4–9 (the 8th and 9th chakras reside in the subtle bodies), beginning at the heart and extending upwards before returning. May provide a deeper understanding of the higher dimensions.

Butterfly Lily (*Hedychium thyrsiforme*) For attuning to the process of transformation as symbolized by the butterfly; increasing awareness of this transformation for the human race. For those involved in group work when they are faced with insurmountable obstacles. Brings encouragement, strength of purpose and the ability to let go of stress.

California Baylaurel (*Lauris nobilis californica*) Opens the mind and gives a feeling of flexibility to the mind and nervous system. Helps overcome rigid mindsets, ideas and body armour, bringing wisdom. Soothes and relieves.

California Buckeye (*Aesculus californica*) Strengthens one's ability to understand and work with vision. May provide attunement to one's purpose as well as to ecosystems, agriculture and nature spirits. Increases third-eye abilities.

Calypso Orchid (*Calypso bulbosa*) Helps one climb through several spiritual levels simultaneously. Enhances the ability to communicate with the Higher Self or one's guides; encourages teachers to be drawn to you. Cleanses and opens the crown chakra.

Cape Honeysuckle (*Tecomaria capensis*) Can bring co-ordination between the physical body and chakras 4–8. May intensify psychic abilities and a shift in the emotional body. Balances the energies of grief, loneliness and other difficult emotions.

Caterpillar Plant (*Phacella Mutabilis*) Brings encouragement to access and receive spiritual gifts of which one is not aware. Makes it easier to assimilate and integrate psychic abilities when they start to appear.

Choke Cherry (*Prunus virginiana*) Brings illumination to a lack of clarity in ourselves and our relationships. Sheds light when we need to see the problem, chasing away the darkness, ending confusion and clarifying motivations.

Clarkia (*C. purpurea*) Brings some affiliation with the energies of forgiveness, especially in relation to physical aspects and the influence of our genetic structures. Brings greater awareness of genetic structures and our ability to work with them.

Coralroot (Spotted) (*Corallorhiza maculata*) Brings greater awareness of the role of disease in our lives, the need to recognize and understand the lesson of disease on subtler levels so that the disease no longer needs to manifest physically. It may reduce the influence of antibiotics which can last for a long time after taking them.

Creeping Thistle (*Onopordum Acanthium*) Produces tendrils of light and energy from the seventh chakra, causing a temporary blending or bringing of new energies in many different forms and directions. Can make a bridge from the seventh to the heart to the base chakra. Brings clear internal healing energy to the physical body and steps up vibrational transference from other subtler levels to the physical, which can be a joyful experience.

Curry Leaf Tree (*Murraya Koenigii*) A catalyst for things already happening in one's life. Spiritual practices become clearer. Encourages synergy in relationships, especially within the family. Brings playfulness and a sense of relaxed purpose.

Dayflower (*Commelina*) Allows access to greater light, which is especially helpful for the physical body and those using light therapy, and for a greater awareness of the connection between the sun and the earth. Benefits those seeking to reduce their food intake and increase their attunement to light.

Desert Barrel Cactus (*Ferocactus alamosanus var. pottsii*) Assists those seeking to understand boundaries, where they begin and end, where their relationship to someone begins and ends, where and how they relate to the whole of humanity. Helps us to confront the sadness and separation sometimes felt during our spiritual journey between ourselves and our soul family.

Dragon Flower Cactus (*Huernia macrocarpo*) Assists the capacity to apply spiritual principles to the physical realm. For balancing the physical aspects of the body properly. Especially helpful in movement and exercise.

Dutchman's Breeches (*Dicentra Cucullaria*) Enhances the release of emotional residues into the aura which can then be cleansed easily by movement, water or air. Can also clear away residues from negative environments.

Easter Lily Cactus (*Echinopsis multiplex*) For deeper attunement to chaos and the balance of perfect symmetry. Improves communication through gesture and movement.

Elephant's Head (*Pedicularis groenlandica*) Creates a vibrational link to the energies of the angelic kingdom and those associated with humanity's own development. Strengthens the ability to perceive and work with earth energy. For deeper attunement and awareness of angelic or spirit guides; for wisdom.

Everlasting (*Antennaria rosea*) Helps to moderate a shift in consciousness which contains repressed memories from childhood or past lives. Increases self-esteem and self-recognition of spiritual progress. Encourages positive energy.

Gardenia (*G. jasminoides*) For emotional shifts from accepting one's consciousness

in a new way; greater attunement to knowledge received in the recent past. Excellent for student/teacher relationships. Creates a sense of peace, caring and compassion.

Gentian (*Gentiana simplex*) Improves the ability to communicate on many levels. Improves speaking abilities for deeper insights and connection with others. For future expression.

Gilia-Scarlet (*Ipomopis aggregata*) Gives deep strength to those seeking an understanding about how they populate the earth and share it with others. Enhances the possibilities of the spiritual aspects of sexuality. May assist in treating mysterious skin complaints. Enhances empathy with the plant and animal kingdoms. Encourages harmony.

Green Gentian (*Frasera Soecuisa*) Awakens psychic gifts of an expressive nature. Working with the sixth chakra, these gifts can project mind-energy. The accelerated and enhanced ability to project energies of love from a group to many beings will assist the earth at this time.

Green Rein Orchid (*Habinaria sparsifolora*) For seeing the continuity of patterns of emotions – a common thread running through lifetimes – particularly for understanding one's parents and early upbringing. Benefits both therapist and patient when used for depressive states or co-addictive energies.

Heliconia (*H. Flava*) Creates energy spirals which can influence the left and right balance of the subtle bodies. The brain and spine are positively affected. Helps to gain ideas and put them into form, accepting the results and making the necessary internal changes. Strengthens the 7th–10th chakras.

Holy Thorn (*Euphorbia milii*) Opens the crown chakra, bringing a greater willingness to work with a universal energy connection. Allows a deeper attunement to any particular spiritual avenue. It is best to have a specific being or ideal in mind when taking this essence. Forms a bond with the essential energy behind the spiritual idea or ideal. Best used by itself.

Hooded Ladies' Tresses (*Spiranthes romanzoffiana*) Maintains higher states after peak experiences, catalytic change or catharsis so they continue in a constant but less intense fashion. Brings a slight strengthening of psychic gifts.

Hydrangea (Green) (*Hydrangea macrophylla*) Works in many ways to combine energies of the chakras, balancing them and allowing them to intermingle and transmute energies in useful ways. For visualizing and awakening the different chakras.

Indian Pipe (*Montropa uniflora*) Balances the flow of energy between chakras, so enhancing movement. For establishing a clear contact with higher vibrations in channelling. Releases stress/ strain in the back.

Kinnick-Kinnick (*Arctostaphylos uvaursi*) Allows one to connect consciously more easily to others and to break any unnecessary connections. Assists one to move with ease and more freedom and to alleviate unwanted past-life connections.

Lemmon's Paintbrush (*Castilleja lemmonil*) May bring a deeper level of connection to our higher energies. Especially useful in creating a deeper understanding of our interaction with society or communities. For social interaction.

Leopard Lily (*Lilium parvum*) Strengthens our ability to improve self-image. For expressing ourselves clearly and allowing our inner nature to shine through. Especially helpful for public speakers and writers who have an alternative viewpoint.

Lobivia Cactus (*L. aracnacanthus*) For attuning the heart to an awareness of the Christ principles manifest in your relationship to the earth. May bring a feeling of deeper groundedness and awareness of another, enhancing the interchange of energies between you both.

Milkmaids (*Dentaria californica*) Dissolves critical attitudes towards oneself and others. Brings sweetness, love, acceptance and self-esteem. Helps the heart understand and appreciate goodness and positive qualities so one can let go of judgements and move back to spiritual love.

Mock Orange (*Philadelphus lewisii*) Increases the ability to coordinate in deep states of relaxation and meditation. Useful in forming new ideas. Reduces stress.

Monkeyflower (*Mimulus aurantlacus*) Helps emotional clearing, especially with issues of denial and addictive states. Enhances ability to absorb light directly, providing deep nurturing for the 2nd and 3rd chakras.

Monvellea Cactus (*M. Spegazzini*) For attuning to and understanding the symbolism of the breast and genitals. Brings attunement to moonlight and the unconscious.

Mountain Misery (Kitkitisi) (*Chamaebatia foliolosa*) Increases the ability to stick with a task. To modify old ways so new energies can be brought in. Assists in discovering additional inspiration and deeper understanding of a project.

Mountain Pride (*Penstemon newberryi*) Brings awareness of base chakra energy and understanding of the emotional connection with spirituality. May bring greater acceptance of sexuality and sexual feelings. Restores a clearer sense of one's connection to the earth energy.

Myrtlewood Tree (*Umbellularia californica*) For projecting healing capacities across long distances. Useful in transferring information about healing work.

Neoporteria Cactus (*N. paucicostata*) Strengthens your higher potential by assisting a deeper contact of the soul with incoming energy. Clarifies and focuses the soul's energy for understanding how to put this into action. For overcoming procrastination and getting going when you see where you wish to go. May create a deeper and stronger connection to and awareness of your soul group. Enhances motivation.

Noble Star Flower Cactus (*Stapelia nobilis*) For blending of love energies and an awareness of the consequences of eating meat. Assists in giving up meat and adopting a lighter, vegetarian diet out of love and willingness to assist all animals. Brings a sense of love and compassion for the animals that are consumed for food.

Old Maid (Pink/White) (*Catharanthus roseus*) Brings greater understanding of and clarity about what is truly important in life. For working with the inner child. Brings acceptance and forgiveness of parents and of older plaguing patterns. Increases our connection with all things.

Orange Flame Flower Cactus (*Norocactus horstii*) Assists in understanding and releasing anger, to enable us to see how it can improve relationships by creating greater enthusiasm. For understanding our deliberate attempt to be alone and separate in ways that are self-forgiving. Aids an understanding of the differences among people and brings a willingness to release negative attitudes.

Owl's Clover (*Orthocarpus purpurascens*) Brings out joy and an appreciation of artistic expression and talent. Endeavours to develop self-expression, especially those of the dream state. Brings optimism to those out of touch with, depressed about or lacking confidence in their artistic expression.

Pegasus Orchid Cactus (*Epiphyllum*) For evolving a new creation of destiny and purpose which affects this life and future lifetimes. May bring a shift in the way we create new kinds of relationships, which allows the chance for a deeper connection and intimacy between both partners. For future relationships.

Pine Drops (*Pterospora andromedea*) For a clearer perspective on the entire nature of difficult relationships. To realize the higher aspects within any relationship. For

increased understanding of the genetic structure and code for individuals. Combines well with alternatives to antibiotics.

Plumeria (*P. obtusa*) Brings a deep awareness of one's roots, connection to the human family and attunement to one's ancestors. Useful in group meditation, especially across great distances, in world peace meditation and harmonic convergence.

Prickly Poppy (*Aregemone polyanthemos*) Increases the ability to love in the face of various obstacles, creating a love bond that transcends time and space. Enhances past-life recall in those consciously seeking it. Can increase forgiveness of our own past-life actions and those of others. Assists absolution of those creating war, famine and disease.

Protea (Pink Mink) (*P. neriifolia*) Helps to focus energy in one particular direction. Aids in receiving information from past lives, especially concepts and ideas, integrating them into current ways of thinking. Increases telepathy.

Purple Nightshade (*Atropa purpurata*) Calms and relieves irritation, especially that brought on by trying too hard. Soothes jangled, burned-out nervous states and relieves the emotional disturbance brought on by coffee and other stimulants.

Rattail Cactus (*Aprocactus flagelliformis*) Enhances the capacity to reach into multi-dimensions, across time and space to extract information including a new knowledge relating to one's cultural heritage. Assists in transcending time and creating a deeper connection to time-flow in the future.

Rattlesnake Plantain Orchid (*Goodyera oblongifolia*) For issues relating to aggressive or male-orientated tendencies. Helps men deal with anger and aggression. Helps women seeking a greater male/female balance in their manner of speech, approach to men, how they are seen and the way they see themselves.

Red Ginger (*Alpinia purpurata*) Brings the ability to spiritualize many physical characteristics. Opens the base chakra to spiritual energy. Deepens understanding and acceptance of the male/female balance within. Useful for martial arts and dance. Enhances sexuality, Tantra and Taoist, the union of male/female with the earth.

Red Mountain Heather (*Phyllodoce breweri*) For improving the ability to perceive and work with different forms of sound such as music. Brings greater attunement to the inner voice and vibration of all kinds. Enhances our capacity to love and recognize ourselves in all things. Brings a deeper attachment to all forms of vibration.

Shasta Lily (*Lilium washingtonianum*) Speeds up the etheric bodies. Promotes greater awareness of one's role in serving to heal the earth. Helps in understanding and utilizing the energies available in different power spots, like the site of the Joshua Tree and Sedona, which have in the past been a source of revelation to many.

Sierra Rein Orchid (*Habenaria dilatata*) Has an excellent capacity to transmute emotion, so that deeply buried or denied feelings can surface. Especially effective for depression or sadness.

Snowplant (*Sarcodes sangunea*) Creates a deeper understanding of incoming light and energy, especially for hands-on healers. Strengthens the aura and subtle bodies; supports changes in one's life: new job, new home, new relationships.

Spider Lily (Red) (*Lycoris radiata*) Increases ability of the nadis to reach other dimensional areas. Helps the nadis in the base of the spine to transform and transfer energy from the interdimensional regions, especially the etheric body. Improves the ability to open and close the chakras at will, for taking in what is useful and rejecting that which is not beneficial. Benefits those seeking to strengthen the digestive organs, the sexual reproductive organs, the kidneys and skin.

Starflower (*Trientalis latifolla*) Assists those working with others to understand the truth better, even when it is blocked in their consciousness. Stimulates the 2nd chakra.

Star Thistle (*Centaurea solstitialis*) Helpful for radiating energy. Useful for therapists working with patients, encouraging a higher spiritual awakening in both. Activates the 9th and 10th chakras.

Sulcorebutia Cactus (*S. aremacea*) Creates a vortex of energy within an individual to increase one's focus and alignment with one's own capacities – those associated with the soul, centre of the universe and universal purpose or earthly manifestation. Helps remove obstacles from one's path and may be useful to those who respond poorly to certain holistic treatments.

Swamp Onion (*Allium validum*) Brings a powerful cleansing, usually beginning at the top and working down through the body, from head to toe. Creates an awareness of higher energies associated with such cleansing – a powerful universal energy pouring lovingly through you. Especially useful for cleansing the subtle bodies of things like psychic debris which stand in the way of greater evolution.

Sycamore (*Ficus sycamorus*) Eases stress and overcomes problems of too much or too little discipline. Gives us a handle on life, so we know when to let go.

Tagua (*Phytelephas macrocarpa*) Encompasses the beautiful aspects of elephant ivory in plant form. Brings a sense of great power, longevity, increased memory, strength of purpose, kindness and a deep awareness. Allows direct connection to higher realms. For being aware of how we can release old ways and come to new ones.

Tree Opuntia (*O. consolea falcata*) Assists in maintaining a willingness to change, even when we are comfortable at certain levels of existence. Reminds us to shift and offers us the physical energy for the rapid change necessary at this present time.

Trillium Red (*Trillium rubrum*) Assists in amplifying and grounding our natural healing abilities. Enhances our ability to understand another's life lesson, to recognize what may be beneficial to his or her change and how it may be our own learning experience. Assists those who are bored in their jobs, bringing new ideas into form.

Waikiki Rainbow Cactus (*Epiphyllum*) For seeing our own self-expression act as a deeper connection to others. Enhances self-worth.

Washington Lily (*Lilium washingtonianum*) Increases our innate ability to love unconsciously and universally. Creates a deeper understanding and acceptance of spirituality in its different forms in those approaching difficult spiritual change in life. Strengthens the etheric and astral bodies. Brings spiritual perseverance.

Woolly Sunflower (*Eriophyllum lanatum*) Benefits those working with the sun's energy. Represents the gentler, subtle, female-related aspects of the solar principle. Strengthens the 3rd chakra.

Roses

Fred has further developed a range of roses and feels that of all of the plants that contribute to humanity on earth, the rose family is at the apex of the potential healing available for most people. They sit at the top of the flower essence world much in the same way that diamonds offer the greatest healing in the mineral kingdom.

Long ago, in Lemuria times it is said that the rose family was being worked with by many guides and helpers to ensure their healing attributes were available to humanity in the future. Legend has it that a primary light being, *Cha-a-ra* was instrumental in this group work. In acknowledgment of this, greater healing energy has been brought through the rose family.

Angel Face Rose (rosy purple) Appreciation. This rose is utilized to deepen appreciation of beauty, the opportunity to awaken higher chakras, and infuse positive helpful energies into people. It acts as a conduit, in appreciating the beauty of this rose, higher vibrational qualities will be enhanced for most people, awakening those spiritual principles in their lives and putting them into action. A natural contact with guides and helpers occurs

Beauty Secret Urban Stress. This rose essence helps to ease stress and stimulates balance in city environments.

Bella Portugaise Rose (light salmon, pink, peachy and creamy shades) Grace and Beauty. Confers aspects of grace, inner confidence, and kindness to those who do not necessarily work with such energies normally. It was especially developed for men to ward off or shift energies that would eventually give rise to the utilization of powerful harmful technologies for war on the planet. Helps to find inner courage and strength, to bring ideas to create a more peaceful society, a way of coexisting and learning from each other. When people are trapped in busy schedules, too much to do, drawn in different directions, it helps to find an inner sense of calm in the busy schedule.

Buff Beauty Urban Stress. This rose essence stimulates the intellect to better deal with city pressures. It will open the heart, allowing people to adjust to urban living at the heart chakra level.

Cabbage Rose (*Rosa Centifolia*, medium pink) Intimate Relationships. Helps change in attitudes towards sexuality, aids understanding the intimate relationship between love and sex. Encourages a new deeper appreciation of the physical bodies, enhancing sexual performance, whilst releasing unconscious shame, guilt, and various energies associated with negative sexual patterns from the past. When planning to marry, it helps to dispel previously held belief patterns and f ind new ways of loving and accepting each other.

Charles de Mills (rose/purple flowers) Humility. This rose induces courage within people to reveal their true nature. An obvious application is in the acting profession, particularly with method acting, where one utilizes past-life experiences, early childhood experiences, to help shape character. As one's true nature is revealed, it's possible to step back and look at oneself in a new light. Reminds people of their own inherent beauty, allows them to forgive and love others. The result is the emergence of a true humility, and to understand one's place in the universe and receive the highest wisdom from the true source.

Green Rose (*Rosa chinensis viridiflora*) Psychic Balance/Channelling. Enhances all psychic abilities. Develops spiritual healing. One can become a conscious or trance channel. Improves emotional stability, especially for psychics.

Koenign Van Daenmark (*Rosa Alba*) Left/Right Brain. The etheric, mental, and spiritual bodies are aligned, making it easier to make decisions and recognize destructive elements within the physical body. The left brain is stimulated so that mathematical, computer, and language skills are activated. Excellent for use with colour therapy.

Old Blush China Rose (blush pink) Wisdom and Mercy. This rose derives from many naturally occurring blends, and has it roots in ancient Chinese history. In recent times, its focus has been to gain greater wisdom and awareness on how to direct and utilize love for the highest good in society. In Confucian times, wisdom was tempered with mercy and deeper levels of understanding. It helps to recognize past lives lived in ancient China, connect and draw on the wisdom from these lives, making this available at a positive and helpful level for those individuals now alive in China. Tuning into past lives associated with China, with awareness of balance and beauty, helps to see how this energy might be appropriately utilized to assist others, in a caring way.

Reine des Violettes Rose (cerise then violet) Loving Will. A fascinating plant providing interesting and stimulating qualities to connect to higher levels of consciousness and develop a deep understanding of God, directly from one's heart. Assists in creating a powerful loving presence and helps to connect to others, plants and animals. It allows a sense of forgiveness to manifest in the heart. Powerfully energizes and strengthens many characteristics in the physical body. Clears issues based on scarcity, struggle, or various habit patterns from humanity. Enable one to switch it off and receive energy from a spiritual force, a guiding light or a true path of awareness and awakening.

Rosa Alba (Maiden's Blush, blush pink) Releasing Shame. Helps develop a deep sense of self, and ability to allow the higher energies to make their way into the human consciousness. This rose strongly stimulates the astral body; past-life connections and blocks may come up, relating to shame and aspects that have prevented a deeper awareness of subtler energies being available. With repeated use this confers a deep sense of lovability, and acceptance of love within. It is extremely helpful to take this flower essence just before going to sleep, and invite a dream in which you might feel and sense God's true nature in relation to you

Rosa Alba Semiplena (white) Deep Forgiveness. Creates a deeper sense of compassion and the ability to forgive and to have a deep sense of caring. When releasing sadness in deep emotional cleansing, tears may result. These tears can carry away toxicity, and deeply buried energies, such as pesticide, metals, various hormonal imbalances. To cry cleansing tears can be a very powerful healing experience.

Rosa Arkansana (bright red)
Acceptance. Provides a newfound ability to love where love previously was denied due to a past life experience. Allows an individual to accept that love is present deep within, and that it has always been there to draw on. An obvious application is inner city, places where there is little exposure to nature. Inspires bringing nature into the city or urban environments, and find ways in which this most naturally and easily can be introduced. In addition, as one begins to open a more conscious love, the deep levels of sadness can be healed. Helps one understand the entire process of accepting deeper love.

Rosa Banksia Lutescens (yellow)
Divine Intellect. Opens the intellect to the divine. Activates the solar plexus chakra and enhances mental faculties.

Rosa Beggeriana (white, N. Persia)
Increased Intuition. Stimulates intuition and psychic sight. Increased insight into personal issues.

Rosa Brunoni (Himalayan Musk Rose, white) Higher Purpose. Brings the capacity to enhance spiritual wisdom in humans. This encourages a conscious awareness of the need for deeper spiritual connection and contemplation of the important attributes within spiritual teaching or spiritual wisdom. Brings dogged persistence and a willingness to address issues. As shifts occur awareness of higher purpose on earth comes through; simultaneously a wonderful positive joyful feeling occurs. As the individual surrenders to divine purpose, it fosters awareness of one's place in the universe and the sheer joy of being.

Rosa Californica (pink, California)
Outgoing and Friendly. This elixir can be very useful for introverted personalities, helping to overcome problems and phobias around small, enclosed places.

Rosa Canina (Dog Rose) Enthusiasm. For those who need a change and more interest in life. And those who have lost the spark, and have become resigned to their lot. Helps positive change.

Rosa Carolina (Pasture Rose, rosy pink)
Family Forgiveness. For self-forgiveness, where it relates to family matters. Relieve the need for revenge or retribution, so deeper acceptance of the soul family can result. Families tend to travel across the karmic landscape in groups, frequently reincarnating to work on issues, to heal them and change them. Many issues will be brought into greater clarity and it will be easier to have the patience to allow these issues to naturally unfold. Brings a sense of forgiveness for all of the buried aspects in one's family, so one that memories of earlier childhood incidents are cleared.

Rosa Centifolia Cristata (pink)
Enhanced Love. Combines emotion and the understanding of universal love. For the increase of consciousness so deeper states of meditation can result, in the better understanding of religious concepts. Emotional difficulties and blocked feelings dissipate. This is likely to give individuals far greater ability to love. One may experience a natural release of emotional blockages, and a tendency to open the astral body. This opens, when it is fully cleansed, so understanding of the future, not always conscious, but as a gut feeling, can occur

Rosa Chinensis Mutabilis (flowers opening yellow inside, orange outside, becoming coppery-salmon on the second day, then crimson as they age) Higher Creative Force. Integration of higher subtle bodies; the mental into the astral, to some extent into the emotional. However, there is a higher component, sometimes found in the astral body and the mental body, strengthened by the mental functioning. Producing a sense of deep relaxation felt in the neck and shoulders, eases tensions, and positively affects the gallbladder and bladder meridians

Rosa Centifolia Parvifolia (pink, violet, Europe) Divine Purpose. Helps to open the crown chakra to assist in understanding one's divine purpose. Positively stimulates the dream state.

Rosa Chinensis Minima (Fairy Rose, rosy pink) Devic Perception. Associated with the devic orders, the fairy kingdom, and the devas working with small plants, and fungi. It allows individuals a deeper sense of the joy in connecting with this realm. When welcoming and attuning to this energy it enables engaging with the childlike self and to be able to see with the eyes of the child, and recognize energy in a more fluid, open way.

Rosa Chinensis Serratipetala (red, pink in cooler climates) Universal Love. Creates a deep sense of fearless love, when entering into dangerous situations; finding love in ways that they would not normally be available. Where society has taught to hate, dislike, shun, or judge. When releasing prejudice, it shows the interconnectivity amongst all; as one recognizes how much alike we are. Then we are able to love, honour, appreciate other cultures, particularly helpful when travelling. Awakens the root chakra, fourth or heart chakra, and the ninth chakra.

Rosa Cinnamomea (pink, purple, Eurasia) Mental Insight. Balances philosophical issues. The intellect is stimulated to transcend the mundane, e.g., if someone felt that the philosophies of the East and West were incompatible, this essence would generate the intuitive insight to show the compatibility of these teachings.

Rosa Complicata (brilliant pink with a white centre) Easing Fear. Unconsciously eases fears, helping you to acknowledge them. In relation to self-image, to demonstrate how ideas about oneself can leaves one vulnerable to fears of others when fears are transferred. This often takes place unconsciously in childhood, it's natural that children will tend to absorb the fears of their parents. Valuable for becoming more aware of your own fears or habit patterns, and how they may be unconsciously transferred to your children.

Rosa Coriifolia Froebelii (white) Higher Manifestation. Stimulates and opens the crown chakra allowing stored childhood energies into our consciousness, draws in higher energies to be received at the appropriate chakra level, relieving stress that develops as a result of the sense of this communication not made clear enough.

Rosa Corymbifera (white/pink, Asia) Calm/Peace. Releases stress stored in head, neck, or shoulders. Better understanding of spiritual, religious, or philosophical ideals occurs.

Rosa Damascena Bifera (pink, Europe) Addictive Personality. For the addictive personality and for overcoming addictions. Opens the third chakra.

Rosa Damascena Versicolor (white/pink, Europe) Thought Addiction. Enhances telepathy, and other intuitive processes are better understood and utilized. It can lessen overreliance on thought, logic, and reason in one's life.

Rosa Ecae (yellow, Asia Minor, Turkestan) Astral Balancer. This flower helps to overcome philosophical prejudices or preconceptions which naturally increases intuition and insight. It can be a strong balancer for the astral body.

Rosa Eglanteria (bright pink) Opens Heart. Awakens the heart energy connecting it to higher spiritual wisdom. Some people may be pushed to states of despair as they feel a powerful love inside. Helps us recognize that as love increases, wells up, or strengthens it creates focus, and the need for the person to be useful or valuable. Springing from a deep awe of many aspects of life, it focuses in the heart to awaken deeper levels of acceptance of God's energy in all things. Forgiveness for mistakes made in life occurs, breaking habit patterns, and finding new ways to struggle less with habits. At the higher vibrational level, it provides a sense in individuals of deep appreciation of many aspects of the world, a sense of sweetness or benefit to life.

Rosa Farrerii Persetosa (pink, China) Artistic Ability. This elixir opens the heart and the crown chakras, stimulating artistic ability.

Rosa Fendleri Woodsii (pink, white, US) Overcomes Shyness. Helps overcome acute introversion and fear of meeting people. It will also improve one's insight, and enhance one's negotiating skills.

Rosa Foetida Bicolor (yellow/orange) New Aesthetic Sensibilities. Encourages a sense of beauty in art, shifts consciousness because of seeing with new eyes, and seeing in ways not previously seen before, making new associations. When overstimulated it is helpful for brain fatigue and difficulty with assimilation of new knowledge. Applicable when seeking to develop a new aesthetic sense, deepen understanding, shift judgement. Brings the ability to re-evaluate, re-prioritize and let go of judgements. Aids perceiving beauty, art or magnificence of life, musical and dance forms, and graphic arts. Helps to transform landscape, urban or rural, change various living conditions by working with feng shui and a sense of balance.

Rosa Forrestiana (pink) Creative Imagination. Engages imagination, perceiving and exploring new areas. Imagination without constraint. Encourages an abundant source of inspiration and creativity. The uplifting energies of creativity are valuable and useful to help people to feel excited about life, and feel a sense of accomplishment leading to new ideas, new ways of relating to others. A light-hearted playful essence.

Rosa Gallica Officinalis (red, France) Spiritual Rejuvenation. Promotes mental and emotional balance. Powerful opening of the heart chakra. Stimulates joy and spiritual rejuvenation.

Rosa Gymnocarpa (Little Woods Rose, pink) Psychic Function. Helps blend different parts of the personality, accepting them in a loving way, and allowing psychic abilities, and paranormal abilities to naturally blossom and strengthen. Especially for those with a clairsentience ability or those who work with psychome-

try, or kinesthetic abilities. Develops acceptance of the buried hidden abilities, the shadow self, and the willingness to blend these aspects with other parts of one's life. Encourages self-acceptance as well as the loving self, the judgemental self, integrating these aspects that have previously created disharmony or stress.

Rosa Hardii (yellow, Europe) Inner Joy. Can attune individuals to their own inner awareness, light, and energy. Brings a greater connectedness to life, the sun, and the fairy kingdom. Also brings a greater understanding of the need for joy, and an awareness of the light and joy around and within.

Rosa Horrida (white, Europe) Universal Love. Cleansing of spiritual sadness. Brings an awareness of humanity's struggles and helps show how they can be overcome. Helps achieve forgiveness for the human condition

Rosa x Harrisonni (Harrison's Yellow Rose, Yellow Rose of Texas) – Honest Communication. Pioneering, finding freedom, accepting personal responsibility, and a willingness to share this with others. In the revelation of truth, finding ways to be more honest with oneself, and share this with others, even if this causes some temporary disharmony. Encourages clarity within finding areas of denial so that a way of deeper honesty can be revealed. Confers a level of warmth, as the devas associated with this rose share loving energy, encouraging people to find a way of being clear in their communications with each other.

Rosa Helenae (white) Higher Truth. Devas associated with this plant are very adaptable; and are programmed with information from the Lemurian times, helps to adapt to many different energies. At the subtle level, it is important for humanity to draw in new concepts to work with as needed, and having gained sufficient knowledge, find the next level of awareness. Aids the understanding of different absolute truths and relative truths. Helps to ascertain the specific aspects of truth in your life, and is helpful for understanding and growth, and let go of past-held belief patterns.

Rosa Hemispherica (yellow, Sulfur Rose) Energy Generation. Aids blending of different energies within, at the physical and etheric level. The blending together of the male and female aspects of the self results in many different approaches in life, and different ways of being. This enables flexibility. It is valuable for self-healing, to integrate and work with energies of all different types, and bring a sense of self-love and the capacity to assist our own healing throughout life.

Rosa Hugonis (yellow, China) Visions. This elixir helps to stimulate visions as well as literary and linguistic skills.

Rosa Kamchatka (red, Siberia) Perseverance. It activates the ability to focus and persevere and strengthens the will.

Rosa Laevegata (Cherokee Rose, white) Enhanced Healing Ability. Encourages and strengthens the sixth chakra, opening the third eye, bringing a deeper sense of clarity, and at the same time, an awareness of an inner silence, and the capacity to receive energy from many levels. Hands-on healing or energy work will be accelerated and assisted. With repeated use, a deeper sense of connectedness and understanding of humanity and its role on earth develops. As adaptability increases, the capacity to fit into other societies, learn other languages, and adapt to their customs develops which can assist multicultural bridging or capacity to expand horizons.

Rosa Longicuspis (white, Himalayas) Creativity. This essence will open the brow and crown chakras and the kundalini. It activates creative and artistic sensitivities.

Rosa Macrantha (light pink, Europe) Energy Blocks. Use it to release blockages in the meridians and nadis.

Rosa Macrophylla (red, Himalayas) Greater Love. This is the most powerful rose essence on the planet. Opens the heart chakra. Native to the Himalayas.

Rosa Maximowicziana (white) Shifting Boundaries. Using this rose can assist individuals in understanding themselves better, where they have walled off or allowed various aspects of their own personality, consciousness, or things that they are interested in to become segmented, to become in some sense denied or unavailable. To make such an energy more available in a loving, welcoming, accepting fashion is likely to be enhanced for nearly everyone using this flower essence.

Rosa Moschata (Musk Rose, white) Improving Relationships. Awareness of compassion, caring, and the love felt in the Higher Self. Clears self-blame, in which an individual is unaware of how they are creating a deeper separation by holding judgemental beliefs. The heart begins to open in new ways, in order to incorporate love from one's Higher Self.

Rosa Moyesii Life Purpose. This flower can energize the evolutionary process, either of reincarnation, or the process of successive levels of self-awakening that a soul goes through. Gives one the concentration to overcome many earthly distractions in the accomplishment of one's life purpose. Reawakens a sense of joy in being on the earth, having the capacity to do good in the world.

Rosa Multibractea (light pink) Life Purpose. Enhances the ability to have a sense of one's own sacred work, and appreciate what we are here for and how work can be of maximum utility and value to others. Typical flashes and awareness of this higher purpose will tend to occur early in life, perhaps at age three or so; then as a more defined purpose, focalizing around age 28. A deep sense of forgiveness and love must be felt and at the same time a deeper sense joy

Rosa Multiflora (white) Earth Sensitivity. Creates a powerful connection to Mother Earth, and the ability to assist our life path through a deep self-love. As the heart is opened when working with these energies, a deep sense of peace or calm develops, a sense of timelessness and patience develops when waiting to see how things will unfold. Enhances psychic awareness of earth changes, the properties of plants and animals. Brings attunement to the weather, and encourages the ability to perceive the weather before it manifests. Produces a healing effect that can be transmitted to others, stimulating the healing abilities through the use of sound or working with sound from the human voice.

Rosa Multiflora Carnea (pale pink variety) Unconditional Love. The Lemurians developed and worked with this flower. It holds the energy unconditional love that is an aspect or manifestation principle of the earth's energy. If we resonate with this sense of earth's unconditional love, it awakens unconditional love within.

Rosa Nutkana (pink, U.S.) Self-Denial. Useful in bringing forth denied emotions. Aids in creating more loving relationships. Promotes greater inter-generational understanding and bonding.

Rosa Odorata (white, pink, or yellow) Integration. Awakens the root chakra with energy that bubbles up through the rest of the body. Shows how integration can occur, brings energies from many different sources, learned from past lives, this life, integrating and utilizing it for the problem at hand, giving rise to new possibilities, and new applications. Helpful in group activity, corporations, or wishing to change what is established, especially when struggling with bureaucracies, and seeking to understand systems as they are. It's helpful in order to be patient and to see things from other people's point of view, then find the right steps to take in order to deal with the situations. Also brings joy and strength to gardeners, to those who wish to work with roses, through attunement.

Rosa Paulii (white, clove scented) Shifting Ego. Allows a deeper sense of love and humility. For those who wish to help others, but don't want to be in a position of obligation or constant interaction. Releases the desire or need for appreciation. Encourages a deep understanding or appreciation of God's energy, not asking anything in return, allowing opportunities on many levels which can lead to all kinds of pleasurable and wonderful aspects in life.

Rosa Pendulina (*Rosa Alpina*) (pink to purple) Risk Taking. Allows people the opportunity to take risks more easily, share energies with each other in ways they have not previously. Opens us to new ways of loving, feeling and working, with love as a result. Risk taking can be pathological in some individuals, with the addiction to dangerous sports or activities that risk life and limb. Helps to modify these practices, see them in a different perspective and find ways of achieving the same sense of thrill or life-awakening, without bodily danger.

Rosa Primula (pale yellow) Spiritual Healing. Accelerates the development of spiritual wisdom when applied to healing, and counselling that comes from the heart, where a deeper loving energy is established. This can shift consciousness to awaken the Christ-like principles. Discovering an inner Christ-knowledge depends on people's own particular perception. It awakens the crown chakra; connecting through the body into the heart, allows a deeper fuelling of heart energy from incoming energy through the crown chakra. But this energy must have some point of focus or some particular quality of assistance, either to assist or help someone.

Rosa Pterogonis Group Healing. Develops a deeper sense of group identity and a sense of that group being loving and helpful to others. Useful to teams who seek healing or give assistance to others, in esoteric or practical healing: a hospital staff or a group of hands-on healers. Those who are studying and working with healing energy of any kind may find a level of unconscious competition between the members. Helps to relieve this, bringing people to a state of harmony as they work together. At the gross physical level provides rapid healing from surgery, other forms of interventions in the body, and ways in which the healing would be speeded up.

Rosa Roxburghii (pink, Japan, China) Meditation Enhanced. This is to be used for enhancing meditation and all right-brain type activities.

Rosa Rubrifolia Interpersonal Relationships. Imparts greater conscious will in one's ability to manifest love in the world. Stimulates the heart on the etheric level.

Rosa Rugosa Alba (white, China) Isolation. This is to be used for getting through periods of isolation, such as when in retreat with fasting or meditation.

Rosa Sericea (white, Himalayas) Spiritualizes Intellect. This elixir will open up the kundalini, the crown, heart, and base chakras. It also clears blockages from the meridians. The intellect is spiritualized, and there is more communication with one's Higher Self and guides.

Rosa Sericea Pteracantha (white, Wingthorn Rose) Higher Purpose. Gives a deep understanding of the principle of tough love. This can be the capacity to love in a way that can produce dramatic change, like installing new habit patterns, modes of thinking and feeling. Some individuals who go through a shift around the age of 28 experience deep levels of sadness and lost opportunity. This essence gives an innate sense of joy, strength, and awareness of greater possibilities. Develops an intuitive sense of what is appropriate in our life, what we are here to learn and do, and who we are here to meet, but have for some reason denied of unconsciously avoided. Simply becoming aware of that pattern can be of tremendous value to individuals and save them a great deal of time and effort.

Rosa Sinowilsonii (white, China) Clairaudience. Activates psychic hearing (clairaudience).

Rosa Spinossima Altaica (white) Interconnection. Utilized in assisting individuals with deep transformation and their ability to connect to other people, to feel a sense of commonality or bridging at a heart level. For people who find themselves isolated, separate, alone, perhaps in a place of darkness and struggle, it encourages understanding and receiving of the energy from this flower. As a flower essence it encourages a sense of camaraderie, shared oneness, loving energy between people. Works with the issue of loneliness, to help the individual to understand that they are inherently connected, that they are not alone.

Rosa Stellata (mauve) Vibrational Reception. Encourages communication with guides and helpers, to allow new sources of coherent, well-integrated information to be better transmitted, as if one's antennae are strengthened. Creates the release of inherent belief patterns blocking these energies. Fears will be eased, and better understood. For fear of intimacy. Enables speaking personal truths regardless of the consequences; and results in enhanced telepathy, and contact with other beings, guides and helpers. Allows vision from a higher perceptive; has a profound effect in helping an individual to see issues which they had previously held back.

Rosa Sweginzowii (bright pink) Higher Group Interaction. Shifts the nature of love people experience, making it more physical. Helpful in relationships of all types – business, personal, or family. Creates clarity in one to one and group interaction.

Rosa Villosa (pink/red, Eurasia) Creative Visualization. This can stimulate dreams, astral projection, and creative visualization.

Rosa Virginia (pink, U.S.) Inner Calm. Assists individuals in projecting an inner sense of stillness and calm into their words as they speak them. Charisma will be encouraged and amplified.

Rosa Webbiana (pink, Himalayas) Earth/Angelic Attunement. Use this major essence to attune to the earth's crown chakra. Stimulates the super-conscious and rapport with angelic realms. Opens the heart chakra and psychic abilities, especially channelling faculties.

Rosa Woodsii (Mountain Rose, pink) Energetic Connection. Enables better personal contact, communication, and awareness. For most individuals, this energy extends from the navel area, integrating energies of the second and third chakras. Relates to emotional connection, specifically in relationship to business or pleasure, and the ability to see yourself in someone else. At a higher vibrational level, one can perceive the good nature in another, and see it as intrinsically lovable. This helps with negotiation, to see somebody else's point of view, understand their consciousness, desires, needs; and then be able to meet them halfway. Perceiving this deeper level sometimes involves letting go of aspects of yourself in order to truly see the other person as deeply lovable, as well as yourself.

Rosa Xanthina (golden yellow, N. China) Creative Visualization. For creative visualization, meditation, and hypnosis practices. It will help healers remove negativity, and it also opens the heart.

Seven Sisters Rose (*Rosa multiflora platyphylla*) Youthfulness. There is a natural affiliation between this rose and the star system of the Pleiades. As people work with these energies, they discover all kinds of shifts, sometimes a reminder of an ancient lifetime associated with the Pleiades. Shifts at a physical level will reduce the ageing effect, resulting in greater youthfulness, inherent strength, and other energies of a positive helpful nature will result.

Sterling Silver Rose (silvery lavender) Law of Reflection. Helps with working out issues in relationships, especially understanding more deeply and consciously the law of reflection. Allows seeing things from different points of view, and perspectives, helps in holding a dualistic vision. Awakens higher consciousness, and the awareness that love can bridge apparent opposites. Encourages a deeper acceptance of oneself.

White Bath Rose (*Rosa Centifolia Mucosa Alba*, White Moss Rose) God Awareness. Develops a deeper understanding and awareness of past lives, and the last intermissive period. Promotes connection to God and awareness of God's love. This energy connects with the heart and higher spiritual reality. Above all else it is a direct awareness of God's love.

Petite Fleur Essences

The Petite Fleur essences are created by Judy Griffin, a fourth-generation flower essences maker on her Italian mother's side; she is a master herbalist and professional gardener who has already written five books on these subjects.

She is a scientist with a PhD in nutrition from the University of Alabama who has also spent time studying various disciplines with Chinese, Indian, Native American and Mediterranean peoples.

These essences were developed in response to Judy's recognition that 80 per cent of disease prevalent in Western society is related to stress. This brought her to the realization that any treatment which focuses on just one aspect of illness will always be incomplete. A more holistic approach is needed which addresses mind, body and spirit.

The Petite Fleur Essences are used internationally by progressive medical and chiropractic physicians as well as health care practitioners. The original 60 wildflower essences affect the attitudes connected to our emotions and fears and their related endocrine responses. The Native Texans strengthen the essential character – a form of fine-tuning – and clear inappropriate models and, together with wildflower essences, focus on enhancing the immune system by correcting unstable emotional signals which trigger the 'fight or flight' stress response. Essences in the Antique Rose collection enhance the nervous system, while the Master Essences awaken consciousness by aiding personality transitions and helping us to focus on the here and now so we can fulfil our destiny. They also work to harmonize all chakras. These can be used as enhancers in association with the Native Texans and Antique Roses.

In the words of Judy Griffin,

> 'Mother nature awaits with open arms to transcend physical, emotional and mental limitations as we expand our conscious awareness and oneness with the Eternal Life Force.'

Judy has continued to develop the range and brought out the New Native Texans which address immune system issues and the New Antique Roses which expand their work with the nervous system.

In her work with hospitals and hospices she has shown how supportive the Petites can be with cancer (*see* page 389). She has also created special blend combinations appropriate for common-day problems.

Judy has also designed Feng Shui Spays, especially to cleanse, harmonize, balance and enhance life and the environment as well as attracting positive and abundant energy.

African Violet (*Saintpaulia* sp.) Promotes nurturing, love from within and the release of endorphins which bring feelings of elation and ease pain. Helps heal wounds.

Amaryllis (*Hippeastrum L.*) For anxiety about the future. Brings clarity about the future, helps overcome fears of what may lie in store and enhances intuitive abilities. Also treats parasites.

Anemone (*Coronaria coccinea*) For when life is hard, a struggle and you cannot experience pleasure. Also helps regenerate tissue damaged by scarring or burning.

Azalea (*Rhododendron oblongifolium*) For those who are left-brain dominated and wish to be more creative. Enhances creativity and visualization, bringing forth latent talents.

Babies' Breath (*Gypsophila paniculata L.*) For those who reject new ideas by thinking 'it won't work'. Encourages childlike faith and innocence. Eases congestion in the lungs; benefits asthma and emphysema.

Bachelor's Button (*Centaurea cyanus*) For those who keep looking back and are afraid to release the past. Brings beginner's luck and an ability to complete projects.

Helps release suppressed tears and eases oedema.

Bamboo (*Chamacdorea erumpens*) For those who are not sure what to do next. Helps in planning career, setting goals, learning to have fun. Eases intestinal upsets, lack of colonic acidity.

Basil (*Ocimum basilicum*) For critical people, high achievers who feel they are not good enough. Encourages self-nurturing habits. Helps purify the blood.

Begonia (*Begonia Ceae odorata.*) For having a belief in limitations. Encourages letting go and the realization that even global problems can be solved. Acts as a diuretic for the kidneys. Helps the sensory nerves.

Bouquet of Harmony (blend) For uncontrolled thoughts and emotions when the imagination runs riot. Helps discipline the mind, focusing attention and bringing a sense of direction.

Bougainvillea (*Nyctaginaceae glabra*) For guilt, fear of reprisal. Helps others enjoy life and fulfil their desires. Eases local aches and pains.

Chamomile (*Anthemis nobilis*) For those who swallow their hurt, feeling misunderstood. Brings counsel. Good for indigestion and a sluggish gallbladder.

Crepe Myrtle (*Lagerstroemia indica*) For those who are afraid to speak their mind or of seeming foolish by expressing themselves incorrectly. Brings the realization that rage often underlies such fears. Fosters the ability to release this anger in a creative way and to speak only words of kindness.

Crossandra (*Influndibuoiformis*) For people who are insecure and fearful of new ideas or any major changes in life, not wanting to rock the boat. This personality is prone to gastrointestinal stagnation and toxicity, and also to catarrh. Helpful in any new situations over which we have no control – such as having a baby, moving to a new job or environment. Encourages you to 'go for it'.

Daffodil (*Narcissus nuegelia*) For quiet, timid, shy people who try to please everyone, placing themselves under constant tension and anxiety which causes symptoms like heart palpitations. Their aversion to anger and angry scenes may stem from being intimidated by explosive or violent parents. Helps you to feel more at ease with yourself and others, not needing to appease others all the time.

Dianthus (*Caryophyllaceae chinesis*) For apathetic people who claim they 'don't care', feeling uncared for and separate from humanity, disinterested in life and having nothing to look forward to. They are withdrawn and often anaemic. Helps us to view life in a brighter way, rekindling enthusiasm and self-nurturing.

Garden Mum (*Chrysanthemum morifolium*) For critical, bitter thoughts which often affect the liver and gallbladder. Aids the flow of bile. For those secretly wishing the worst for everyone else and always looking for a scapegoat. Enhances love for mankind, and acceptance of people as they are. Brings compassion.

Iris (*Pallida*) For mental strain that stems from being overanalytical and logical, left-brain dominated, having an explanation for everything, prone to violent behaviour. Releases latent creative abilities, allowing us to feel carefree and humorous. Encourages carefree feelings, promotes a sense of humour. Helps regulate bloodpressure, temperature and breathing.

Japanese Magnolia (*Magnolia verbanica*) For women who are unhappy, feeling dependent on men, vulnerable and used. Also for sufferers of premenstrual syndrome, headaches, fluid retention. Brings a sense of independence, equality and security. Eases physical problems.

Jasmine (*Jasminum nudiflorum*) For loners, those who rebel against authority and find it difficult to get on well with others. They may be prone to accidents such as bone fractures due to a weakness in skeletal structure. Eases bursitis and cartilage/bone/tendon disease. Replaces feelings of alienation with diplomacy. Helps you to find peace in your environment.

Lantana (*Camana*) For those who are quiet, artistic, oversensitive, easily hurt and shy. They may be sensitive to allergens – hay fever sufferers. Helps us to become more independent and assertive, feeling less threatened. For commanding respect.

Lemon Grass (*Cymbopogan citratus*) For those who need nurturing, often rejected by parents, feeling that love hurts and being drawn to painful relationships. Eases pain and promotes self-nurturing, learning to trust and reach out to love. Enhances the absorption of vitamin A.

Ligustrum (*Oleacea privit lucidum*) For an inability to be assertive or express anger, leading to apathy or haughtiness, fatigue and lack of spontaneity. Also for energy leaks from the aura, internal bleeding, liver toxicity, weak eyes, immune deficiency, hypothyroidism. Releases repressive feelings, rekindles optimism and encourages self-expression. Eases physical symptoms.

Lilac (*Syringa vulgaris*) For those with a tendency to hold grudges. Also for tumours, growths and cancers. Helps forgiveness of self and others, releases the past.

Lily (*Lilacea longiflorum*) For those who are anxious about the outcome of everyday affairs and the future, fearful of not being in control of their destiny. Typically such people bite their fingernails or demonstrate other compulsive behaviour. Also for colds, flu, autotoxicity, skin diseases and allergies. Releases anxiety and fear. Helps to boost the immune system.

Magnolia (*Magnolia grandiflora*) For those lacking self-appreciation or belief in themselves, feeling undeserving. For problems with the assimilation of nutrients and protein. Increases self-confidence and boosts self-image, so you can prosper and grow.

Marigold (*Tagetes patula*) For guilt about sexual permissiveness, sexual guilt, confusion about sexual role or identity. For

impotence, hormone imbalance, prostate problems, sterility and frigidity. Balances male and female aspects of the self so we can accept both sides of ourselves without feeling threatened.

Morning Glory (*Convolvulacea*) For those deluding themselves with the idea of a golden past, romanticizing better times and making the present seem unpleasant. Also for uric acid accumulation and bowel problems. Helps us to find faith in ourselves and in the future. Aids circulation and eliminatory systems.

Moss Rose (*Portulaccea floreplens*) For those feeling they need more of anything – money, possessions – giving rise to anxiety and the feeling that they lack something. They may also be prone to weight problems. Also helps problems of pancreatic function, irregular glucose absorption, poor digestion of starches and fats, and proteolytic enzyme production. Enables a change of outlook, seeing yourself as sufficiently providing for your needs.

Mushroom (*Shitake*) For feeling insecure about changes in life, leading to procrastination and resistance. Also for discomfort in the feet, ankles, calves, spine and neck. Helps you to become more independent and adaptable.

Narcissus (*Cyclamineus*) For those who are withdrawn and introverted, living in their own world and reluctant to share themselves with others. Prone to migraine, tension and neuralgia. Enhances feelings of pleasure and security, promoting warmth and affection.

Onion (*Allium cepa*) For those who are narrow-minded, holding one-sided opinions and becoming critical of others' views and habits. Cultivates tolerance, compassion and the ability to listen. Also helps treat viral infections and fevers.

Orchid (*Orchidium sphacelatum*) For those (often high achievers) who silently punish themselves for past failures. May suffer from numbness and nerve degeneration. Helps us to become less workaholic and more interested in loved ones and the community.

Pansy (*Viola tricolor*) For those experiencing a deep-seated sense of grief over the loss of a loved one. Affects adrenal and kidney function. Brings transcendence over grief, pointing the way to new outlets for our loving nature and generosity. Helps in the elimination of toxins.

Penta (*Pentas lanceolata*) For selfish, self-reliant people who are inconsiderate of others, withholding love and thinking that love hurts. They often suffer from low blood-pressure. Also for vertigo, lack of oxygenation. Eases pain and promotes feelings of wellbeing and self-love, making for a more delightful partner or spouse.

Peppermint (*Mentha* x *piperita*) For those who live in fear of losing loved ones, possessions, health, security, of having little control over their emotions. May suffer inner conflict related to an incomplete relationship with their mother. Builds confidence and a sense of control; fosters the ability to visualize a future in which their desires are fulfilled, making life feel safer. Also aids protein digestion and treats gastric ulcers.

Periwinkle (*Vinca rosea*) For clearing past experiences. Clarifies goals, affords a greater overview of life and boosts energy levels. Heals and regenerates.

Pine (*Pinus sylvestis*) For those who only remember mistakes of the past, experiencing guilt, punishment and pain. For fatigue brought on by poor absorption of nutrients; for aches and mood swings. Cultivates inner strength and perseverance, so we can learn positive lessons from past misfortunes.

Pink Geranium (*Pelargonium* x *hortorum*) For those who appear tense, suppressing their anger and intense emotions. Linked to spastic colon, liver/gallbladder trouble, and muscular spasticity. Eases emotional pain, bringing laughter and enjoyment of life.

Pink Rose (*Rosa chinesis*) For those with a 'fat' complex, always trying the latest diet, rejecting themselves. Also for those who are genuinely overweight or plagued by cellulite. Promotes a better self-image and a perspective that acknowledges and focuses on what can be changed.

Poppy (*Hunnemannia*) For demanding, selfish people who can be jealous and covet others' belongings. Also for mucoid colitis, constipation and tuberculosis. Cultivates generosity and service to others.

Primrose (*Primula vulgaris*) For those rejecting love as not being good enough, having a romantic and idealistic view of what 'love' should be. Physically manifests as diabetes, hypoglycaemia. Cultivates an appreciation of relationships and an acceptance of love.

Ranunculus (*Asiaticel*) For mental instability, imbalance in the brain expressed as schizophrenia, violence, rage, psychosis. Sufferers may have been abused in childhood and/or deprived of tender loving care by their mother. Also for premature birth, epilepsy, poor muscle tone and immature nervous system. Restores a balance of energy to the pleasure centres of the brain.

Red Carnation (*Caryophyllacea rosa*) For those with an inferiority complex, feeling unworthy and lonely, unable to accept success. Prone to lymphatic congestion, swollen glands, skin afflictions, hair loss and baldness. Enhances self-image and feelings of worthiness.

Red Rose (*Rosa chinesis*) For gloominess and occasional depression. Replaces negative thoughts with enthusiasm and joy.

Rose of Sharon (*Althea officinalis*) For those who are idealistic, straightforward, honest, highly creative and successful but sometimes feel burdened by responsibilities and want to escape from reality. Indicated for heart action – angina pectoris. Attracts just rewards for creativity.

Salvia (*Salvia coccinea*) For self-dislike and feeling ugly. Brings constructive changes to one's self image. Improves acne, warts, moles, birthmarks and other blemishes, and skin diseases.

Shrimp (*Beloperone guttata*) For those who are dissatisfied with themselves, disliking and feeling lumbered with their lifestyle, keenly aware of others' achievements and assets. This attitude upsets the immune system's ability to handle everyday stress. Also for combating the ageing process. Speeds the process of change and allows creative ideas to flow.

Stock (*Matthiola incana*) For tense, nervous, hyperactive types – dependent on nicotine and other chemicals – susceptible to physical exhaustion and mood swings because they are unable to pace themselves. Slows down and balances out energy, enabling completion of projects.

Sunflower (*Helianthus annus*) For those feeling separated from the universal spirit, rejected and left to fend for themselves – persecuted, fearing death, feeling suicidal. Brings a sense of responsibility for actions. Integrates the personality and soul/spirit.

Tiger's Jaw Cactus (*Faucaria tuberculosa*) For those who like sitting and watching others do the work. Essentially immobilized by fear of failure to the point of apathy and laziness. May be spoiled and inconsiderate or a 'nonparticipant' (out of hypochondria). Brings the motivation to be confident and productive.

Vanilla (*Vanilla planifolia*) For those overwhelmed by negative energy from others and themselves, feeling tired, depressed and irritated for no apparent reason, needing to withdraw from a situation or individual. Also for neurological overload or psychic attack. Offers protection against such influences, helping you stay clear and in control of your individual environment without unnecessary interference.

Verbena (*Verbenaceae*) For inner turmoil, frustration, impulsive action. Induces a meditative feeling of inner peace. Allows mind and body to relax and regenerate.

Wandering Jew (*Setcreasea purpurea*) For those who are easily discouraged, lacking discipline, giving up easily. Prone to inflammation or neuritis /shingles. Helps us to achieve greater confidence and self-discipline so projects can be completed; to learning patience and tolerance.

White Carnation (*Caryophyllaceae*) For those who are stubborn and headstrong, resulting in constant anxiety, tension and mood swings. Adrenal hormone upsets (the fight-or-flight syndrome). Eases fear of failure, balances desire and releases anxiety. Brings contentment.

White Hyacinth (*Hyacinthus*) For shock and trauma, especially that of birth which is linked with feelings of uncertainty and insecurity. Nervous exhaustion. Releases the shock of emotional and physical trauma (e.g. accidents, operations and violence). Enhances sense of self-reliance.

White Petunia (*Solanaceae*) For those who have difficulty making decisions and acting on them, unable to synchronize thoughts, concentration and body movements. For dyslexia, stuttering – and also past negative programming. Aids coordination and the synergy of right and left brain function.

White Rose (*Rosa alba noisette*) For those attracting negativity from others, feeling undefined fears. For 'psychic attack', and also loss of memory. Offers protection from negative thought-forms; cultivates self-confidence and ability to feel comfortable with anyone.

Wisteria (*Wisterea macrostachya*) For those who are unaware of loving feelings, not feeling love at all. Opens us up to receive and give unconditional love. A heart tonic for enjoying everyone.

Zinnia (*Zinnea elegans*) For those feeling unloved, hurt and angry, critical of themselves and others, bitter at being deprived of nurturing attention. Often affected by arthritic or rheumatic pain. Heavy metal toxicity. Encourages self-nurturing, releases bitterness and cultivates generosity.

Native Texans

Aster (*Callestyshus*) Promotes strength within and gentleness without. Increases powers of concentration and encouragement to promote loyalty and honesty in others. Stimulates the immune system to cleanse the internal environment of toxins in cases of disease.

Carrot (*Daucus carota*) Enhances initiative for developing healthy disciplines and organizing priorities so that ambitions are realized through natural rhythm and cycles. Improves the properties of mucus in respiration and reproductivity, enhancing fertility.

Christmas Cactus (*Schlumbergera*) Lends psychological support to help us focus on what is right for ourselves and others. Reinforces strengths and helps healing of others from the heart. Supports genetic strengths and natural talents to enhance wellbeing. Compensates for inherent character weaknesses.

Columbine (*Aquilegia skinneri*) Enhances ability to think and act independently, dropping role models imposed by others. Helps an infant to become independent of its mother's immune system, increasing antibody efficiency and destruction of bacteria.

Dill (*Anethum graveolens*) Releases fear of abandonment and death. Clears self-alienation and denial of feelings. Allows effective thinking and channelling of our 'self'.

Echinacea (*Echinacea pupura*) Purifies thoughts, clarifies visions, refines judgement and understanding. Enhances resistance to viral toxicity.

Gaillardia (*Pulchela*) Enhances determination to succeed by overcoming obstacles. Lightens the personality through the joy of overcoming. Boosts immune system, enhancing resistance to viruses and toxicity.

India Hawthorn (*Rhaphiolepis indica*) Works with group karma, dispels confusion, accents impersonal love by expressing this through deed and example. Loving all as one.

Knotted Marjoram (*Marjorana hortensis*) Enhances clarity of thought to work out details when change is needed. For avoiding premature action, aiding a calculated transformation. Enhances immune system's defence mechanisms.

Kalanchoe (*Blossfeldiana*) Helps correct ingrained illusion of opposites, such as good and bad consciousness, creating dualism, polarity in personality and separation. Mends this fragmentation so we can see our blind spots.

Meadow Sage (*Salvia clevelandi*) Aids expression of strong emotions such as anger without transgressing or being vindictive. Allows us to express emotions and feelings without being controlled by them.

Mexican Oregano (*Poliomentha longiflora*) Enhances ability to understand quickly and respond to new situations correctly, teaching by example and drawing to one experiences that develop character. Helps lubricate and cleanse the skin.

Rose Campion (*Verbascum chapsus*) Strengthens the body's natural defences when there is a congenital weakness which is karmic. Develops character by uprooting old, ingrained patterns that prevent movement forward. Creates liberation in the subconscious.

Silver Lace (*Polygonum auberti*) Aids contemplation and learning from setbacks, seeing them as a potential for growth rather than failures. Helps us to ride the waves and know when to advance or to retreat. Aids synthesis of interferon, the body's antiviral agent.

Snapdragon (*Antirrhinum majus*) Increases perception and discernment. Helps us to recognize what brings us into alignment with others and define guidelines so that we can clarify and refine plans with reasonable expectations. Enhances internal and external judgement, raising consciousness of the immune system.

Antique Rose Collection

Alfredo de Demas Assists command over body and mind to affect constructive habits. Tunes the mind with the environment. Affords clarity of perception and grounding for those who are 'air-headed'.

Fortuniana Aids realization and penetration of universal truths. Leadership qualities emerge, inspiring co-operation in others by integrating the universal soul's desires with personal desires. Enhances intuition or sixth sense.

Lady Eubanksia Expands inner awareness. Brings integration of mind, body and spirit – the expression of all talents in a new and unique way. A previous reclusive person will realize goals through others, emerging as a teacher of wisdom and understanding.

Old Blush Enhances stamina, catalysing inner strength and the ability to keep going. Allows creativity to be expressed and adapted to every aspect of life and health, so that we accomplish more in life than seemed possible. Strengthens willpower to integrate motor pathways and neural systems to initiate muscular contraction.

Viridiflora Helps those who are extra-sensitive to their environment by maintaining alignment of their personal power centres. Enhances grounding and personal power, feeling centred and integrated by clarity of purpose.

Master Remedies

Bluebonnet (*Lupinus texensis*) For those awakened by the call of their own destiny, the quest for one's true identity revealing great powers within. Increased inner awareness creates important changes (eg career, relationships and health) that foster our service to humanity.

Gardenia (*Rubiaceae uasminicdes veichii*) Integration of personal life with future goals. Encourages long-range planning; awakens teaching, writing and speaking talents so concepts can be translated into reality. Dreams come true. Nourishes creativity, inspiration and achievement, encompassing home and family as well as the environment and career.

Indian Paintbrush (*Castilleja*) Brings the source of spirit and light into daily life, so that every challenge is met with a consciousness of success. Confers wisdom and a positive attitude, transforming and illuminating health, career and relationships. Makes every day a miracle.

Yellow Rose (*Rosa c.* x floribundas) For the reformer who has chosen the life of service, who desires to serve society unselfishly. Helps us to be attuned to the times and environment, so that our good works benefit and improve the established order and are an inspiration to others. 'Love isn't love until you give it away.'

New Native Texans Essences

The Native Texans are varieties of flowers from around the world that have naturalized in the extremes of the Texas climates. They are of benefit in the communication of the immune system.

Anise Hyssop (*Hysopus anisum*) Enhances public speaking and teaching abilities, alleviating 'butterflies' in the stomach before a performance. Indicated for those who have chronic headaches, dizzy spells or stomach aches with stabbing or fluttering pain. For overcoming a speech impediment, combines well with Daffodil and Silver Moon.

Borage (*Borago officinalis*) Aids those who feel they must be self-sufficient and stand alone in their career or personal life. Indicated for those with structural difficulties with feet, ankles and hips. Combines well with Viridiflora and Mushroom to enhance balance and agility.

Catnip (*Nepita cataria*) Brings people closer together enhancing friendships and common bonds. Indicated for those who feel socially inhibited or in unfamiliar social situations. It softens perceived boundaries, eliminating apprehension, promoting contentment.

Cinnamon Basil (*Ocimum basilicum*) Fortifies those who buckle under adversity, or feel they can't go on under present circumstances. Indicated for those who suffer from weak knees and lower back pain. To enhance new potentials and personal growth, combine it with Gaillardia and Madame Louis Levique.

Curry (*Helichrysum italicum*) Aids those who have to think on their feet. Enhances new potential by freeing the mind of linear thought patterns. For those who want to figure their life out in advance or lack spontaneity. Combines well with Christmas Cactus and Mexican Oregano. It's indicated for migraine headaches resulting from tension and decreased circulation.

Daylily (*Hemerocallis auranthiaca*) Helps planning major changes in personal life or career. Indicated when one's job affects the future of others. Can help the process of brainstorming to overcome social, economic and political problems. It is beneficial for sufferers of chemical sensitivities and environmental pollution.

Delphinium (*Delphinium cultivars*) Aids focus or completion projects. It helps those who suffer from low blood sugar affecting attention span and memory. Eradicates the effects of parasitic infection when combined with Amaryllis. Also combined with Alfredo de Damas for hand to eye coordination problems.

Bronze Fennel (*Foeniculum vulgare*) Helps overcome limitation affecting the imagination and planning centres. Aids those who want to create; enhances visualization. Bronze Fennel strengthens mental and psychic abilities, enhancing clarity and direction. Combines well with Azalea, Autumn Damask and Echinacea to enhance creative pleasures.

Foxglove (*Digitalis purpurea*) Attracts fulfilling personal relationships, enhancing compassion and sensitivity for others. Indicated when the heart beats out of control or poor circulation is indicated. For cardiovascular congestion or irregularity. Combines with India Hawthorn and Wisteria to attract good working relationships.

French Lavender (*Lavendula reverchon*) Helps us appreciate and focus on the blessings in our lives. It also releases the need for more or bigger and better. Combine French Lavender with Christmas Cactus, apply to temples for headaches or the outside of the ears to decrease congestion.

Iberis Candytuft (*Iberis sempervirens*) Encourages regeneration and self-healing by activating the light inherent in each cell. It enhances a balanced mineral pattern within the cell, allowing the tissues to be bathed with nutrients. Works wells with Crossandra to facilitate transition and lifestyle changes.

Lobelia (*Lobelia inflata*) Teaches us to create boundaries with others. It's for those who have difficulty saying no. Combine with Snapdragon for discernment and with Country Marilou to reduce the need to please others or be liked by peers.

Mexican Brush Sage (*Salvia Leukantha*) Enhances our ability to be unique. Indicated for those adversely affected by peer pressure. Gives us permission to be who we really are, combining well with Aquilegia Columbine to help drop the roles others give to us. It is indicated for red itchy skin, combine with Salvia.

Mexican Hat (*Ratibida columnaris*) Brings prosperity, combining well with Indian Paintbrush for a success consciousness. Fimbriata and Fairy Rose will help fulfil our needs.

Purple Garden Sage (*Salvis officinalis purpurea*) Helps focus on what is valuable and true in love and relationships. It is indicated when relationships are tested by external conditions. Helpful when sinusitis, viruses and profound sweating or heat flashes occur. Combine with onion and thyme to counteract viral complaints.

Rain Lily (*Cooperia penduneulata*) Reconciles lovers and rifts in relationships. It's indicated when one feels slightly left out in relationships. Combine with Marquis bocella to encourage long-term relationships.

Red Malva (*Malva slyvestris manritanica* x *hibiscus rosa sinensis China*) An essences that helps us to stay centred and in tune to receive guidance and channelling. This guidance will be focused on spiritual development. Combine with Dill and Verbena to calm the desire to withdraw from others or isolate.

Rosemary (*Rosmarinus officinalis*) Encourages an endorphin release associated with pleasant memories and releases past painful memories when combined with Bachelor's Button and Morning Glory. When others misunderstand us, Rosemary will bring out the best in us.

Salad Burnet (*Poterium sanguisorba*) Overcomes depression from unfulfilled desires in relationships. When the romance fades, it's time to surrender to the nurturing this essence provides. As melancholy lifts, nutrient uptake and dispersion increases, enhancing blood volume and neuromuscular response. Combines with Fortune's Double Yellow, Daffodil and Chamomile as an anti-inflammatory heart tonic.

Soapwort (*Saponaria officinalis*) This essence opens the channels for inner hearing to increase the inner wisdom of the 'still small voice' within. It detoxifies fatty deposits, affecting cardiovascular health and lymphatic drainage. Combines with Pink Rose to reduce cellulite or feelings of heaviness.

Spike Lavender (*Lavandula latifolia*) Aids those who need to practise the art of co-operation instead of domination. It helps to reduce lung congestion and bronchial spasms and is indicated for frequent sighing and a heaviness in the chest.

Sweet Annie (*Artemisia annua*) Benefits those who wish to enhance their public image. Indicated to draw out the best in personal appearances especially when unexpectedly in the public eye when it's not natural to be in the limelight. This essences also aids ageing gracefully.

Tansy (*Tanacetum vulgare*) Tansy protects the aura of the spiritual warrior. Indicated for those affected by environmental chemicals and pollution. This may include emphysema, pleurisy and bronchitis. Combined with Old Blush and Verbena it enhances energy and muscle tone.

Texas Dandelion (*Taraxacum officinalis*) Frees the psyche from fretful dreams and those who wake up with a feeling of falling into their body. It enables one to receive answers in dreams and to remember dreams.

Thyme (*Thymus vulgaris*) Draws all those that inspire, aid, and encourage our greatest achievements. This essence attracts unseen beneficial elementals such as griffins, devas, nymphs and fairies. Combines with Onion and Sage essence to guard the immune system against viral invasion.

Wild Wood Violets (*Viola odorata*) This essence helps the personality choose endeavours that benefit society. The path of modesty and non-interference allows the mind to enter the wholeness of the universe and predict the evolution of events to follow.

Wild Oats (*Avena fatua*) Enhances and develops a sense of humour. We can let go and laugh our way past inhibitions holding back our natural growth. Also indicated for the 'blues' and for children who are sad. Combined with Dianthus, Red Rose and Fimbriata to let the good times roll.

Yarrow (*Achillea millefolium*) Used to potentize the Petites. Add 2 or more drops to an essences combination to receive the benefits of the 10,000 lotus petal flowers within. It reduces auto-immune reactions and inflammatory responses adversely affecting the immune system and central nervous system.

New Antique Rose Essences

Archduke Charles Enhances intimacy, allowing us to feel safe when touched. May help those who withdraw or push people away who get too close. For those who avoid total commitments, always finding a reason to move on. Touches the heart where true intimacy grows unhindered by intellect and desire. In the body, it encourages the structural stability of the skin, arterial and stomach lining.

Autumn Damask Helps develop constancy in faith. For those who have experienced many disappointments in past relationships, now hesitant to become involved again. This essence helps with learning from past disappointments and in becoming more discerning in relationships. This will attract fulfilling relationships, as well enhance nutrient uptake in the body cells.

Cecil Brunner Encourages those who withdraw or hold back from entering new relationships. It helps overcome fear arising from new challenges. Beneficial for those who are easily persuaded to define boundaries creating realistic goals in relationships. Creates security in reaching out and connecting with others. When ability to love is unhindered, it attracts those who will assist with achieving the highest goals.

Champney's Pink Cluster The rose of integrity, teaches us to love through respect rather than passion alone. We connect with others by recognizing and honouring the love that created each person. Seeing through the eyes of love allows us to accept ourselves as we are as well as others. Through acceptance we are transformed. Forgetting about changing others we share love in the best way possible. Enhances the resting potential of the nerve calls, encouraging muscles to relax and regenerate.

Cherokee Rose This essences opens the crown chakra to stimulate creative ideas. It enhances the endocrine balance of the pituitary, pineal and hypothalamus to regulate menstrual cycles and reduces fluid retention and female complaints. For men it enhances protein metabolism and muscle strength as a new vision of oneself is created.

Country Marilou This rose unlocks inner joy to promote vitality and regeneration, releasing inner strength and security which is ageless. Helps to release uncomfortable feelings and perceptions from the body. Beneficial for those who form nodes of neuronal tissue and neuritis affecting healthy neuronal tissue.

Fairy Rose Promotes passionate connection with every life form, links the first and seventh chakras. A transpersonal experience witnessed in a dreamlike state. Nature spirits may be seen enabling the experience of learning to think, feel and seeing life as nature does. Bloom with the roses or fly like an angel, but your life will never feel ordinary again. Indicated for those who tap Mother Nature's power to heal others.

Fimbriata Encourages a passion for life. Indicated when the need is to release non-productive relationships. It opens the mind and heart to new possibilities activating the law of attraction. Even in friendships it enhances contagious enthusiasm, forming new alliances with those of like mind. May also encourage pathways enhancing the synergistic harmony affecting organ function.

Fortune's Double Yellow This essence calms excessive desires and attracts our greatest good, gently reminding us we always have what we need. It discourages envy and feelings of lack. Aids a tendency for hypertension and tension headaches, nurtures those separated from loved ones by distance. Soothes an aching heart with a feeling that time is on our side.

Gruss an Aachen Encourages us to withdraw from partnerships and relationships that require us to settle for less than the best. Quality, not quantity, will open the heart to fulfilment. During transition time, frequent awaking at night or food craving may be experienced. It encourages us to walk with a good heart and run with success.

Louis Philippe Offers hope to those who feel love has passed them by. Overcoming hopelessness by surrendering to the love within. Affirm truth and call on the heart to receive its greatest good. Encourages growth of receptor sites activating cardiovascular flow, enhancing the feeling of love. This warmth not only provides new life for the blood, but also new love to bless your life.

Madame Alfred Carriere Encourages prophetic dreams, for seeking answers in dream time. Enhances parasympathetic responses to stimulate the body to heal itself, transcending time and difficulty. Since dream time dispels opposites, the subtle body is able to function without inner conflict. The spirit seeks freedom like a bird seeks flight, and this rose invites you to allow your intellect to rest and seek answers from the depths of your subconscious.

Madame Louis Levique This essence increases the desire for service and devotion, surrendering the need to be in control. Helps to neutralize toxins blocking the free flow of *chi*. By letting go, we also let go of insecurities behind control issues. As we learn to be part of nature we will better serve it. Surrender to the present moment of grace.

Maggie Maggie helps to see the truth in situations before it becomes apparent. Hidden aspects can only been seen and felt from the heart. Your heart will guide you as it has the capacity to 'see' and feel what is best for you. The seat of the soul is in a peaceful heart, content with all things, lacking none. Maggie calls on our greatest capacity to see through the masque of the personality to the soul level.

Marie Pavie Encourages following the heart's desire in love for when thoughts deny what the heart knows is right. It can ignite the flame in burnt-out relationships. Also for recovering from deep disappointments in family relationships causing a feeling of loss and grief. Encourages recovery from post-viral syndromes and symptoms of aching and malaise.

Marquis Boccela The constant bloom of perpetual love encourages long-term relationships building intimacy through trust. For when one is searching but not attracting kindred spirits to share joy with. In the body, this essence affects the subtle energy inherent in the nervous system. The energy communicates sensory messages to the subtle body and impacts the sensory organs. Especially useful for those stressed by a busy schedule, replenishing vitality and increasing acuity.

Silver Moon Subdues a restless mind, obsessive thoughts, fearful dreams, and constant mind chattering. From a quiet mind pure awareness emerges. Restless energy often affects the heart chakra causing stuttering and an increased need for personal attention and admiration. An imbalanced fire element can exaggerate the sense of importance and the need to be 'different'.

Rose Oil Petite Fleur Essence Combinations and Sprays

The Petites provide a combination of aromatherapy and their special qualities and properties to encourage healing, releasing underlying sources of stress. They gently encourage us to let go of past and present pain, while gaining wisdom from each experience. Petites open the heart by reconnecting the inner joy and harmony within the body. They encourage self-esteem and release energy by reducing emotions created under stress and expectations. Specific blends have been created to address particular general day-to-day challenges.

The Rose Oil Combinations have been designed over the past 26 years for hospitals, pain and therapeutic clinics in the US, Europe, and Canada. The blends (described in *Country Living* magazine, June 2000) are made from organically grown aromatic herbs and roses, distilled on site, and hand separated without chemicals to produce the purest products.

The blends have been used at Baylor Hospital's Healing Environment Program in Dallas, Texas since 1999; the Bone and Joint Hospital in New York City and many hospitals and clinics in the US and UK, and now are available in sprays for topical use.

Abate Anger (*Orchidium sphacelatum*) Reduces pent-up anger, road rage, disappointment, outbursts, and tantrums. Beneficial for stress induced hypertension, headaches, and tense shoulders.

Allergy (Echinacea – *Echinacea purpurea*) Reduces sensitivity to allergic reactions. Use daily for seasonal allergens, asthma and environmental reactions. Reduces symptoms of sneezing, wheezing, runny nose, itchy eyes, and sinus drainage.

Cold Flu (Periwinkle – *Vinca rosea*) Antiviral, antibacterial essences and essential oils prevent and reduce symptoms of viral cold and flu.

Cravings (Gaillardia – *Pulchela*) Reduces obsessive compulsive habits and addictive behaviour. Apply 2 times every day or as often as needed. Add Harmony blend 2 times daily; add Self Image to increase self-worth 2 times daily.

Deep Sleep (Madame Alfred Carriere – *Rosa chinensis*) Promotes better sleep patterns, reduces fretful dreams and insomnia. Apply at bedtime and rub 2 drops on each earlobe to increase REM time and wake up refreshed. Repeat as needed if awakened during the night.

Energy (Old Blush Rose – *R. chinensis*) Increases mental and physical stamina and alertness during long workdays and workouts. Feel the power. Enhances stamina,

Fatigue (Geranium – *Pelargonium* x *hortorum*) Reduces mental stress and chronic fatigue, fibromyalgia and mild depression, achiness, and jet lag.

Female Balance (Japanese Magnolia – *Magnolia* x *soulangeana*) Reduces menopausal and PMS symptoms, dark moods and crankiness.

Harmony Blend (Antique Roses) Reduces anxiety, nausea, physical and emotional trauma, and welcomes peace of mind. Used by cancer patients before and during treatment of chemotherapy, bone marrow, and stem cell transplants, and anxiety disorders.

Inner Strength (Red Malva – *Malva slyvestris manritanica* x *hibiscus rosa sinensis China*) Develops strength during challenging and adverse times. Enhances personality development and maturity, increasing motivation and self actualization. Used in clinics and hospitals to increase flexibility and mobility for bones, spine and joints, bone density, and structural correction.

Learning Skills (Delphinium – *Delphinium cultivars*) Increases alertness, focus, and concentration for adults and children. Apply before school and study .

Male Power Increases self-worth, enhancing the determination to put ideas into action. Creativity and vitality increases as the soul's purpose is expressed through the personality.

Manage Pain (Country Marilou – *Rosa 'ausmary'*) Reduces symptoms of chronic and acute pain, neuralgia, and inflammation. Used in pain clinics and hospitals for neuropathy, sickle cell anaemia symptoms, joint pain, rheumatoid arthritis, shingles, and auto-immune symptoms.

Maternity (White Jasmine – *Jasminum nudiflorum*) Enjoy the thrill of a child of your heart growing within you. Adjust to the many physical and emotional changes during pregnancy. Prepare for a joyous birth. Used for gestational diabetes and difficult pregnancies.

Passion (Morning Glory – *Convolvulacea*) Enhances productivity; increases attraction for passionate and like-minded relationships. Used in clinics to reduce depressed low energy and apathetic symptoms.

Recall Memory (Texas Bluebonnet – *Lupinus texensis*) Enhances cognitive functions, study habits, and sensory perception.

Recovery (Sunflower – *Helianthus spp.*) Enhances the body's wisdom to catalyse innate healing after acute or prolonged illness. Emphasizes strengths rather than character weaknesses. Used for chemically dependent support after treatment; after chemotherapy, radiation, antibiotic and antiviral drug therapy.

Reduce Stress (Verbena – *Verbenaceae hortensis*) Reduces physical, emotional, environmental, and mental triggers of stress. Used in clinics to reduce herpes virus symptoms.

Regenerate (Tiger's Jaw – *Saucaria tigrina*) Reduces tendency to scar, regenerating cell growth in tissue.

Self Esteem (Magnolia) Enhances self-appreciation and success consciousness: self-esteem, self-worth and self-satisfaction.

Stop Smoking (Stock – *Matthiola incana rosa*) Reduces compulsive urges, breaking habits and addictive patterns, benefits hyperactivity and ADD.

Weight (Vanilla orchid – *Vanilla planifolia*) Reduces compulsive behaviour and the need for 'comfort food'. Beneficial for those who perceive themselves heavy.

Fung Shui Sprays

Petite Fleur Fung Shui Sprays are a combination of flower essences made by a steam-distilled and hand process method with purely organically grown flowers and herbs specially formulated to catalyse potentials and enrich the mind, body, and soul. The flower essences are mixed with essential oils to produce sprays for specific conditions designed to promote balance in your environment and enhance peace of mind.

Attraction Spray Encourages opportunities to enhance and nourish career, family and love relationships. Spray on clothes, in family and meeting rooms.

Clearing Spray Dissolves negativity, upsets, disappointments, procrastination and electromagnetic build-up. Spray rooms, work areas and yourself.

Enhancement Spray Increases prosperity, knowledge, health and career recognition. Spray study areas, doorways and corners of rooms.

Harmonize and Balance Spray Reduces stress and anxiety. Harnesses beneficial energy to recharge stagnant areas. Spray inside car and elsewhere to encourage peace and quiet.

Star Peruvian Essences

Andean Orchids of Machu Picchu

In the Vilcabamba Sacred Mountains in and around Machu Picchu, Peru, grow many species of orchids that have within their matrix the ability to affect global consciousness. They resonate to a frequency which can be directly translated by the vibrational bodies of all who encounter them.

Traditionally orchids are considered the most evolved species of the plant world carrying in their DNA the information of all the other plants. One of the main purposes of the Andean orchid flower essences is to assist us in balancing our energies as we go through shifts into expanded consciousness.

Growing wild and free in nature's laboratory, at an altitude of 10,000ft, the Andean orchids are well adapted and very happy in their environment. They are growing on energetic ley lines, at the sacred centre of Machu Picchu and they have a strong energetic field.

Created by Star Riparetti and Roger Valencia in 1994 the Andean orchid flower essences open and expand our hearts. Love is a magnet which draws all things to it. Star's passion is vibrational medicine, she was chief technician and director of the school of Nuclear Medicine at the cancer foundation of Santa Barbara before working with essences. Roger is an avid botanist who was born in Cuzco, in Peru, and with his passion for wild orchids, along with the fact that he is fluent in Quechua, the language of the indigenous population of Peru, he was instrumental in the creation of the Andean Orchids Project with Star.

Ancient Wisdom (*Lycaste longepetalia*) Discover Soul Purpose. Enhances awareness and openness to the wisdom of the ancients that is returning now to earth. This is an important dream essence. Apply to the back of the neck as it aids in opening the chakras so that we can remember ancient truths and also remember who we are. It assists in discovering soul purpose, and awakens us to our divine potential.

Anchoring Light (*Sobralia dichotoma*) Grounding Planetary Light Work. Useful when we are consciously serving as a divine instrument for anchoring light, connecting ley lines and healing the planetary grids. This essence lubricates the pathways so that energy can flow, enabling us to be more effective conductors of the new frequencies entering the planet. Good to use when feeling overenergized, as it brings grounding energy. Apply on head to bring energy in, or on feet to ground and anchor energy.

Balance and Stability (*Habenaria*) Emergency Remedy. Harmony. A broad spectrum essence. It helps us to feel balanced in our environment. For any kind of stress or emergency situation and when feeling out-of-balance. Brings stability throughout. Assists in adapting to the new high planetary frequencies. For working with planetary healing and disharmonic energy patterns.

Divine Child (*Ponthieva Montana*) For Sensitive Children and Adults. This essence is especially effective for the very sensitive beings that are being born now. Also, for reconnecting with gifts that were suppressed in the past. It is now safe to be sensitive and to stay in the realm of delight and express our divine brilliance. Good before and during pregnancy, to connect with the soul of the new child. It is especially good for the newborn. Put a drop on pulse points and the third eye.

Divine Goddess (*Masdevallia veitchianna*) Intuition and Deep Issues. Aids in birthing, attuning to the divine goddess energies, acknowledging the feminine as the source of creativity. Helps in developing intuition and building self-esteem. An extremely powerful essence for deep issues. On a physical level, this essence is useful for shifting PMS and hot flushes; while the heat may still be there, what shifts is your attitude to it.

Eternal Youth (*Epidendrum ibaguense*) Rejuvenation and Regenesis. This is called the Wiñay Wayna orchid, which means forever young in Quechua. Promotes rejuvenation, by retaining our cells to remember the optimum frequency of life, and by raising our resistance beyond disease and aging into super-health and youthfulness. This essence can be put on the skin and can help with the effects of premature aging of the skin. Use every day and add to all your creams, lotions and potions.

Faith and Courage (*Odontoglossum*) Protection. This essence creates a protective frequency around us, rather like having a powerful, yet gentle watchdog at the edge of our energy field. It helps us to wake up to our inner courage. Take it when you feel vulnerable, in order to build up a field of protection, or when you need more faith and courage. Excellent for use in hospitals. It also helps to protect from all the X-ray and negative electromagnetic frequencies.

Freedom/Libertad (*Xylobium* with 24 carat gold) Manifestation. For freedom on all levels, especially to express ourselves, and freedom to manifest our truth. It assists in realigning us to our original divine blueprint. The frequency of gold added to the Xylobium works synergistically and assists in opening dimensional doorways. Regardless of what other essences we are taking, Freedom/Libertad is

here to assist us as we cross the threshold and take the first steps of ascension.

High Frequency (*Peurothallis*) Meditation. Heart and Lungs. A high-frequency essence. Aids in opening channels to the highest dimensions. For meditation, flower essences facilitate your highest conscious and unconscious desires. This essence is also useful for issues around heart, and lungs and it can lift us out of grief and sadness.

Nature Communion (*Trichoceros parviflorum*) Connection to Nature. Enhances your level of consciousness and your connection to the nature kingdom and your connection to your physical body. It is also good for fertility. Use when working in the garden or walking, as it assists us in communing with nature. It synergistically enhances herbal preparations. It is also useful when you have been inside too long or in front of the computer.

One Heart (*Epidendrum cuscoense*) Acceptance, Love and Unity. This essence is about oneness, unity, unconditional love. Connects us to the heart frequency for unification and acceptance. One Heart is great for balancing male/female energies within oneself, for increasing telepathy and nonverbal communication. This is an excellent essence to share with groups.

Red Union (*Maxillaria*) Oneness. Addresses integrated, sacred sexuality. A catalyst to move us to a new level of union, with ourselves, or with a partner. Rejoice in fulfilment conjoined to make one soul. This love in itself is an instrument for peace in the world. Use alone for tantra. It is for taking sexuality to a higher level.

The Higher Chakra Trilogy

This trilogy of essences, Gold+Silver/White, Zeal Point, and Awakened Thymus, is useful in preparing for the activation of the higher chakras. These essences can be used on their own or in any combination. Using all three of them, and doing numeric harmonic sequencing, can be very powerful.

Magenta Zeal Point Chakra
(*Epidendrum Federicci Guillemi*)
Expression Through the Voice. Assists in
opening, balancing and releasing the
Magenta Zeal Point chakra, which is
located at the base of the skull. It balances
the body, mind and emotions and assists in
moving kundalini energy through the
body. It opens us to the next level of
initiation. Zeal Point Chakra helps us to
speak our truth. The colour magenta
indicates it is an entry point into a new
evolution.

Gold+Silver/White Chakra (*Sobralia
Setigera*) Balanced Light Body. Peace,
Serenity Harmony. This orchid essence
encompasses two chakras. The gold chakra
is like a halo above the head. The wisdom
of the gold chakra is love and acceptance.
This chakra cascades out to the silver/white
chakra encompassing the luminescent light
body. This Gold+Silver/White chakra
essence contains the new energies for us to
access the space where truth and peace
flow out of our hearts. Assists our subtle
bodies in sustaining balance, tranquillity,
peacefulness, divine contentment.

Awakened Thymus (*Erythrodes Simplex*)
High Heart, graciousness. This essence is
useful for telepathy, and connecting the
third and sixth chakras. The thymus,
empowers loving communication and is
also called the high heart. Useful when
healing with voice and sound. The thymus
receives spiritual life force energies and
transforms them for use in the etheric,
subtle body and physical vehicle. The
essence will strengthen and nourish it.

Peruvian Flowers

About Face (Dandelion – *Taraxicum
officinale*) Facing Issues. Helps us face
issues we have been avoiding, keeps us on
track and it alleviates procrastination.
Addresses actual physical problems like
acne on the face. Add Eternal Youth and
About Face to a cream or oil. It is also good
for liver balance and de-tox, especially if
alcohol has been used to numb feelings.

Allows us to face ourselves as we are and
continue to grow.

Bushilla Good for female issues, especially
reproduction at any stage. This essence is
made together with Arbildo Murayari
Mozombite, a shaman from the Pulcalpa
Jungle, a vegitalista, curandero and
perfumero, who has said it is also an
important and valuable essence for men.

I Am Generosity (Chijchipa – *Tagetes
multiflora*) Grand Fortune. This essence is
a treasure. It is about prosperity consciousness and manifestation, affluence and
abundance. We are also reminded to give
generously.

I Am Gratitude (Yuyu/Mustard –
Brassica) Holy Grace. This essence reminds
us of the rich rewards, and of our holy.
This essence magnifies the higher octave
love energy and we are filled with gratitude
The essence was made in Peru (Chaska
Land).

Inocencia Coca (Coca – *E. Coca*)
Shifting Patterns. Stamina. The Coca leaves
are used extensively for ceremony and
healing in Peru and is multifaceted. It is
invigorating and used to increase stamina.
It balances appetite and metabolism, in
addition to shifting addictive patterns. Use
for dieting, rejuvenating and raising the
metabolism. Coca helps strengthen the will
and intent. It aligns us with our source of
joy, passion and effectiveness, and our true
service. Aids psychic ability. It is also very
good for altitude sickness.

Integration (Mutuy – *Cassia hookeriana*)
Open and Clear Mind. Balances the mental
and emotional bodies, works with the
pancreas. Sweetness, self-esteem. Useful for
integrating shifts, during chaotic times.
According to Maximo, the 87-year-old
medicine man who helped make the
essence, it helps soothe your head when
you are scared.

Mango Paradise (Mango – *mangifera*)
Celebration of Life in the Physical Form.
This essence is about robust sexuality,
sensuality. It is about jubilance and

enthusiasm. It is also primal, uncompli-cated and earthy, free of belief systems. This essence is a gift and a celebration of life in the physical form.

Master Teacher (Chiri Sanango) Expansion. Considered a Master Teacher plant in the jungle. It can connect us with the deva of healing. For expansion, and about temperature regulation. People have reported that hot flushes have disappeared after using this essence. Cold extremities warm up as it regulates temperature, and supports the blood and bones.

Purification (*Muòa* – High Andean Mint) Sanctify. Cleanse. Assists connection with our guides, and in passing through the veils of the other dimensions. Use it for balance, especially during purification. Good for cleansing and clearing. Use this essence to sanctify and purify in a multitude of ways. Also good for altitude sickness.

Strength and Chi (Fava – *Vicia fabia*) Wellbeing and vitality. The essence facili-tates all functions of brain activity, including memory, energy and sense of wellbeing. It is useful for balancing hormones. Strength, energy and radiant vitality come from being in balance. Good for menopause, supports a parasite cleanse. Creates and sustains balance in your subtle bodies.

Sublime Chocolate (Cacao – *Theobroma cacao*) Balance Metabolism. This essence balances metabolism. Excellent to use when you crave chocolate. Good for women during their menstruation. Helpful for remembering dreams and stimulates psychic abilities. Provides energy after meals. Etheric endorphins. Assists in clearing ancient DNA. Assists connection to Mayan and Incan cultures, awakening, and getting in touch with the ancestors. Chocolate correlates with pleasure, enjoying a rich history.

Wild Feminine (Wild Potato – *Solanum diploide*) Uninhibited. Spontaneous. Nourishing. The Wild Feminine brings all of our aspects together whether our gender is male or female expressing our unique diversity as we choose. It also has a nurturing feminine quality to it. It helps to anchor important feminine aspects of us in a new way.

13th GATE (Cantu Flower – *Cantua buxifolia*. Open Portals. The 13th Peruvian essence. This essence carries hummingbird medicine and has been found to be a very pleasant and peaceful essence, smoothing edges during these interesting accelerated times. Helps with changing frequencies. Made at the sacred Lake Titicaca, from the Cantu flower, which is the national flower of Peru. It helps us navigate through the portals, octaves and gates that we are moving through.

Santa Barbara Flowers

Be Nurtured (White Ceanothus – *Ceanothus leucodermis*) Soothes the soul. Called Mother's Milk, as it is filled with the divine mother's energy. Feel safe and nurtured. The essence is especially good for children and babies. We are surrounded with an abundance of love from a higher realm, feel nurtured by nature.

Creation/Focus (Jacaranda – *Jacaranda mimosaefolia*) Creative Vision. Assists our ability to hold the energy to dream the new dream. Supports creative vision and staying focused. Stimulates new ideas. Great when working on computers. Helpful for studying. Creation/Focus was made as the comets were entering Jupiter – in a super force-field of meditation. It was a second bloom in one season for this tree – the Jacaranda very strongly offered itself during this time for this important essence.

Dance (*Bougainvillea*) Grace, beauty and brilliance. Gives assistance for flowing through life gracefully. It gets us moving. Good for all forms of sacred movement, especially dancing. Take it for dancing through life gracefully. Also, use it in relationships, which are dances of harmony and perfect rhythm. Dance the journey into the self, and then to this is the cosmic dance. Try dancing at dawn with your eyes looking east. Activate your imagination and awaken. Experience spontaneity, and naturalness. Feel good for no particular reason – or any reason!

Deep Breath (Eucalyptus – *Eucalyptus niphophila*) Divine Inspiration. This essence is about breathing. It opens and expands the chest and the lungs, and makes sure you remember to breathe. Breathing connects all systems in our bodies. Inspires us to breathe air/life into the soul. The best way to get more air is to exercise outside. Do complete inhalations and exhalations to eliminate the carbon dioxide. Mastery of breath is mastery of health. This essence will assist in the journey.

Early Bloomer (Oxalis – *Oxalis stricta*) Family Harmony. Trust. This essence assists in adapting to accelerated, early growth and maturity. Use our advancement to awaken to our divine potential and become a positive instrument. Great for children and teenagers who are advancing at an accelerated rate.

Emancipation (Tobacco Flower – *Nicotiniana*) Physical and Emotional Wellbeing. Freedom from anything that has power over us. Liberation. Release cravings gracefully (especially nicotine and marijuana). Tobacco is grounding and good for travelling between worlds. The tobacco flower essence cleans the meridians. If you are choosing to quit smoking, this essence assists with grace and ease.

For Giving (Acacia) For Giving and Receiving and Worthiness. For giving and receiving gracefully. This essence reminds us to give and receive from the heart to assist in moving into the frequency of forgivingness and for forgiving ourselves. Know that you are perfect. Also useful when working with allergies. For release. Give, and you receive. It is time to transcend the need to forgive anyone for anything.

Full Moonlight (Lavender – *Lavendula*) Full Moon Energy. Excellent for addressing full moon sleeplessness or feeling out of sorts. This essence helps to balance full moon energy so it can be harnessed and used beneficially, creatively and peacefully.

God/Goddess Unity (Banana Flower – *Musa* x *paridasiaca*) Masculine Balance. For merging of the male/female and bringing unified oneness in our sexuality. This essence assists gender healing at very deep levels, and balances the first chakra. Banana flower essence is useful for dealing with sexual issues in relationships, enabling us to view them from a higher frequency.

Graceful Shift (Fennel – *Foeniculum vulgare*) Change with Ease. An excellent essence when you are going through great changes. Useful for balancing physical energy when going through dimensional shifts. Should an influx of light cause discomfort, this essence will address it. Excellent for grounding. Fennel addresses nausea, and butterflies in the tummy.

Initiation of the Heartlight (Pink Lotus – *Nelumbo*) Openheartedness. Reach a new level of openheartedness. This essence will help us to recognize any judgement we may still have. Sometimes you will feel warmth in your heart after taking the essence. In ancient Egypt, the Lotus is associated with resurrection, rejuvenation, and eternal life. It is said to have mind-altering capabilities. The Pink Lotus is also associated with Lakshmi, the Hindu goddess of spiritual wealth, spiritual abundance, and spiritual evolution.

Inner Guru (Purple Sage – *Salvia leucophylla*) Inner Guidance; Higher Self; Individuality. The Purple Sage essence helps access that part of us that knows the answers; the sage within. Be your own guru. Knowingness. Omniscience.

I Remember (Rosemary – *Rosemarinus officinalis*) Remembering; Clarity. This essence deals with remembering on all levels. 'I remember who I am, I remember my gifts, I remember what I came here to do, I remember how to manifest.' (I even remember where my keys are.) Excellent for clarity in all realms. Certainty of self. Creativity, inner peace that creates prosperity, to heal oneself, and to be one with spirit. It also strengthens the immune system. Awakens the full memory of our own potential. When we remember what we are really supposed to do in life, it can restore our health. When we remember what all of humanity is supposed to do, we can heal the world.

Let Go and Trust (Oregano – *Oreganum vulgare*) Release. Helps us let go of attachments. Release with ease the things that no longer serve us. It is good for use during a cleanse. It is excellent for birthing. It is also like an etheric colonic; it gets rid of gunk in our auras. Space is created for something new.

Light Navigator (California Pepper Tree – *Schinus molle*) Interdimensional Journeys. The Molle tree is a Peruvian native plant. This essence can take us to places where we are connected on the inner planes. It helps us to know our direction. It lights the path, and is good for meditation. Take it alone, or in combination with other essences. There is a very strong grandmother connection with this essence. Inner vision lights the path to know our direction. It is a direct portal to Peru. It assists in time, and interdimensional travel.

Magic Healer (Plantain – *Plantago lanceolata*) Accelerated Healing. Is a catalyst for healing the body, especially the skin. It aligns body, mind, and spirit. Use alone or to boost other healing modalities. It works like magic to accelerate healing. Use on plants to balance insect population.

Male Strength (Agave – *Agave americana*) Power; Virility; Enhances Masculine Aspects. This essence speaks for itself. There are positive reports about this essence's effectiveness. It is also useful for women who wish to be more in touch with their masculine aspects. Addresses issues of power and virility.

My Passion (Passion Flower – *Passiflora bryonioides*) In the Moment; Compassion. Teaches us to be in the moment and love that moment, then it becomes our passion (eg. studying, lovemaking, artistic endeavours) and brings out its highest aspects. Expands awareness and ability to recognize magic. Receives, circulates and broadcasts energy.

Open Mind/Future Vision (Mugwort – *Artemisia vulgaris*) Dreams; Visionary. This essence has many qualities. For clairvoyant dreams and divinatory acuity; it increases our visionary capabilities and insights. Heightens openness and spiritual perceptions. Mugwort is a good on pressure points and meridians. Stimulates and expands our sensibilities.

Pure Joy (Orange Blossom – *Citrus sinensis*) I am SO Joyous!; Renewed Enthusiasm. This essence takes us an octave higher. Brings excitement and enthusiasm. Gives us a boosts in conjunction with other essences.

Solar Power (Sunflower – *Helianthus annuala*) Heart Opening; Personal Power; Sovereignty. The flower of the Incas. It brings forth our personal power at its highest level and brings strength through an open heart. Reminds us to stand up straight. Assists with father and fathering issues. It reflects the solar energy.

Soul Family (Blue Ceanothus – *Ceanothus thyrsiflorus*) Precious Connection; Births and Deaths. This essence helps to unify soul groups, or tribes. It is especially good for hospice work and for individuals during the death process, and those assisting them. It will guide the dying person out of the crown chakra when they are ready to leave their body. So they may go directly into their soul group at the moment of transition.

Sweet New Beginnings (Pink Jasmine – *Jasminum polyanthum*) Clarity and Ease with New Things. Useful for remaining balanced during these new, ever-changing times and energies. Take it each time you feel a shift to another octave. Helps us remain connected to the Divine as we expand. With this essence, we can go through change from a clear vantage point, because it provides clarity.

Zania (Zinnia – *Zinnia elegans*) Fun; Playful; Lighten Up; Be Zany. This essence helps us relax and open up and be less serious. We can see things in a brighter, more colourful light. It encourages relaxation and fun.

Combinations

Attention Formula Focused and Peaceful. This essence is said to be of great value to children and adults with ADD & ADHD. It assists in staying attentive, focused, relaxed and peaceful. Helps concentration. Some children have been able to stop prescribed medication completely.

Brilliant Student Studying. We have taken our broad spectrum anti-stress, stabilizing essence, Balance & Stability, and added Faith & Courage and Clear Quartz to amplify the effects with universal love. Works like magic. The rescue remedy for the new millennium. Use whenever you are off-balance. Good for everyone, kids, pets, plants, adults and teenagers. If you can't decide what essence to take, then take this one. Put 7 drops in a glass of water and sip it during acute situations. If you only have one essence, keep this one with you.

Radiant Sensuality Love. A magical Star Flower & Gemstone Essence blend that encourages a loving atmosphere. Take this ecstatic, synergistic combination to enhance your romantic mood. It covers a beautiful range of sexual vitality and sensuality. Marvellous for drawing your beloved to you. Put four droppers full in your bath. Immerse yourself in the essence. Cherish yourself, and each other.

Shield of Light Safe and Protected. Creates a protective vibrational frequency around you. Valuable for healers. Use when working with computers. Useful for travelling in cities, and around high tension wires and airports. It is especially valuable to use (for patient and visitor) in hospitals. Also on the perimeters of the house, yard, office, etc. (inside and out) to build a shield of light.

Soul Purpose Dreams. Take when you have questions regarding direction, and divine will. Your dreams will help determine your direction and choice. Discover what contributions you have for the world and by listening for the answers, find your purpose. Have clarity, and make clear choices. Physical healing often comes about when you discover your soul path. This essence helps you direct and remember your dreams.

Super Immune Wellness and Purification. A combination of flower and gemstone essences and the powerful rose-coloured salt from the Sacred Valley of the Incas. Good for any physical healing and for strengthening the immune system via the electrical system, allowing the body to concentrate full time on the physical – thus speeding up recovery time. Take when the first symptom appears. It is useful for radiation exposure and protection on any level: diagnostic, therapeutic, accidental or employment-related. It will enhance and accelerate any healing modality.

Travel Solution Airplanes and Altitude. Helps adaptation to the changes that take place while travelling. This super balancing essence helps with altitude and jet lag, and assists with flying trepidation. It protects from electromagnetic radiation and strengthens coping abilities. Helpful to start taking a day or two before you leave, and continue during your journey as necessary.

Sprays

Angel Rejuvenation Spray Facial Spray, Aura Cleanser, Room Clearing.
Ingredients: Eternal Youth and Essential Oils of Frankincense, Lavender and Geranium
Angel Spray lifts the spirit to a higher vibration, brings immediate clarity and

positivity. It feels really good, use it often for rejuvenation.

Cool Flash Spray Make Menopause Merry. Spray your face and body.
Ingredients: Balance and Stability, Divine Goddess, Freedom/Liberation, Graceful Shift, Master Teacher, Strength and Chi, Sublime Chocolate, Wild Feminine, Moonstone and Pink Tourmaline. Essential Oils: Clarysage, Lemon and Geranium.
This spray can facilitate a light, gentle, easy, graceful and empowering menopause. The essences and oils in it have been known to balance metabolism and temperature. Considered to be beauty oils, bacteria, hormone regulators and morale boosters. Excellent for the skin and keeping wrinkles at bay. They can improve sleep and dream recall in this deeply profound, powerful time of life.

Crystal Clear Spray Spray your Hands and Face and your Space.
Ingredients: Rose-coloured salt from Maras, Peru. Essential Oils of Lavender, Frankincense and Mint. Flower Essences include: Balance and Stability, Faith and Courage, Purification, Freedom/Libertad and Be Nurtured.
Crystal Clear Spray is great for clearing crystals. Deeply cleanses our aura leaving it radiating and pure and is excellent for clearing energy in a room. Brings one in touch with their light body and the anchoring of the Higher Self into the physical body. Spray your hands after doing healing to clear the energy.

FAB Spray Focused. Awake. Brilliant.
Ingredients: Ancient Wisdom, Creation/Focus, Faith and Courage, I Remember, Inner Guru, Inocencia Coca, My Passion, Kyanite and Purple Tourmaline. Essential Oils: Lemongrass, Peppermint and Rosemary.
Use this Spray while you are studying or need to focus. Use it to help clear your head. Promotes alertness when driving and begin to feel foggy. This combination is effective in many dimensions.

Happy Pet Spray
Ingredients: Balance and Stability, Be Nurtured, Faith and Courage, Nature Communion, Clear Quartz and Kyanite. Lavender Essential Oil.
Animals (wild and domestic) respond well to vibrational essences. This combination is effective for all kinds of pet upsets including moving, any accidents and travel. Use to speed the recovery process. Spray their bed or their space. Spray your hands and pet them. Add the drops to their water or put it on their paws. Put it directly in their mouths or on their fur.

Super Immune Spray Purify and Protect
Ingredients: Balance and Stability, Faith and Courage, Freedom/Libertad, Magic Healer, Master Teacher, Purification, Strength and Chi, Emerald, Pink Coral, Red Coral, White Coral, Dark Green Aventurine, Yellow Agate and the powerful high-vibration Rose-Coloured Salt from Maras, Peru. Plus Essential Oils of Eucalyptus and Oregano.
Super Immune Spray is good to have when an immune boost is needed. It is especially good when those around you have colds or flu. Take it and spray it around if you are in the hospital, whether you are staying or visiting.

Flower Essences for Babies and Children

Many of us remember a childhood that was simpler than today, when we were satisfied with inventing our own games, creating something out of nothing, and what was expected of us was clearer and more defined. The major change has been in the speed of communication, the exchange of information that has dramatically accelerated, resulting in us all having to step up a gear in order assimilate, and process this more rapidly in order to cope.

Although children become familiar with this faster pace of life, the extra stresses and strains of contemporary life demand new ways of handling the problems with which parents as well as children are increasingly confronted. Here its makes sense to use the flower essences for both the parent and child with emphasis on mother, baby and child, as the first few years are when the patterns of response to the world become set.

Purely Essences have created remedies for mother and newborn baby and Lila Devi, producer of the Master Flower Essences, has also addressed this special relationship between mother and children.

Most mothers know that the more stressed she is, the more the child reacts and the less likely she is to be able to handle situations calmly. What creates more tension is the knowledge she not doing it right, giving her the feeling of not being 'a good mother'. This is where flower remedies tailor made for such moments are invaluable.

As parents, we realize the more we are able to interact with our child in an understanding and intelligent way, the better equipped they are, by example, to grow into emotionally balanced, assured adults.

Purely Essences Mother & Baby

This range has been created to support the journey from pre-conception through pregnancy, birth and into new life together as a family.

A special and delightful range of essences designed for perhaps the most important and delicate stages of our lives; which are how we arrive on this planet and what set of circumstances and parents we have chosen for this particular incarnation. Our birth, determines our future. If that event was positive and supportive and our arrival welcomed and handled with sensitivity then it's more likely that our adult life will follow suit.

Debbie Sellwood and Shelley Sishton, having worked with essences for many years, were drawn together to create Purely Essences after meeting on Clare Harvey's inspirational training course, at the International Federation for Vibrational Medicine.

Following their deepest intuitive guidance they were led to bring Mother & Baby essences into being, in partnership with Mother Nature as the director of proceedings.

Connecting mother and father to their innate sense of parenting, their eternal wisdom and source of unconditional love, these essences invite all the family to honour their part in welcoming a new soul to Mother Earth as well as honouring themselves.

As the evolution of consciousness continues on earth, so the vibration of incoming soul energy is changing to speed up the reawakening of ancient wisdom within those already incarnated. Assisting not only those who raise and nurture these children, Mother & Baby essences help these higher vibrational souls to incarnate into a clearer energetic space, stepping between the dimensions with greater ease and peace, to live their truth and their destiny.

Created with pure intention, light and love, around a magnificent natural pond filled with water lilies in full bloom, these essences have a strong connection with the element of water. As the moment drew near for the essences to be born, the pond was blessed and ceremoniously decorated with a medicine wheel under the guidance of resident nature spirits.

Also in preparation for the new essences, orchids, crystals, sacred stones from Sedona in the USA and the Nullabor Plain in Australia, were intuitively laid out. During meditations, while each essence was then being imprinted, Debbie and Shelley were shown unique combinations of the energies of these and other flowers, plants, trees, crystals, animals, and spiritual beings including devas and angels, linking together in love for each other.

Conception and Prenatal

Pregnancy Partner Clears cluttered emotional energies from the womb to create a joyful and sacred space for conception within which the baby can grow. Uniting mum and baby in pure love, this essence prepares both for birth and beyond.

Childbirth

Birthing Companion Offering the mother an invitation to relax into the innate wisdom of her body during labour, Birthing Buddy supports mum through what can be an intense physical and emotional experience. Rather than mum trying to control the process, this essence encourages mum – and baby – to ease into the journey.

Postnatal
Nursing Mother Assisting all mothers, not just those who wish to breastfeed, this essence enhances the nurturing and bonding instinct with baby. It instils a relaxed yet confident approach to feeding and handling, whether this is naturally or by bottle.

Soothe Baby Blues The period following birth can be a vulnerable time. This essence restores emotional balance, encouraging self-nurturing qualities. Enables mum or dad to then manage the daily demands and family life without feeling overwhelmed.

Parenting
Hello Dad Helps make the transition to fatherhood (from pre-conception through pregnancy onwards) and to embrace the role in new ways leaving preconditioned expectations behind to approach being a dad with an open heart and mind.

Mum's Everywhere To help mum – at any time of life – to honour herself and to balance her own time and space with the needs of her family. It helps her maintain a healthy balance of giving and receiving, bringing new perspectives on old ways, of responding to life situations.

Baby and children
Welcome Baby Spritz Embracing a light and playful link between heaven and earth, this spritz offers a sense of peace and reassurance, inviting baby to feel welcome and much loved here on earth.

Sibling Support Helps siblings feel safe and still loved with the arrival of a new baby. Encourages them to feel comfortable, balanced and reassured within the new family set-up. To accompany all stages of conception, pregnancy, birth and beyond

Safe Place Spritz Offers a grounding, soothing, peaceful energy to keep mum, developing baby and the family free of emotional and environmental energetic clutter. Creating a sense of calm and security, it can be used in the home, the car, and in the birthing room/hospital. Encourages more peaceful sleep, for mum and all the family.

Master Flower Essences for Mother and Child

by Lila Devi-Stone

Most mothers know the more stressed they are, the more the child reacts and the less likely she is to be able to handle situations calmly. What creates more tension is the knowledge that she is not doing it right, giving her the feeling of not being 'a good mother', so flower remedies tailor-made for such moments are invaluable.

As parents we realize the more we are able to interact with our child in an understanding and intelligent way, the better equipped they are, by example, to grow into emotionally balanced, assured adults. This is where the Master Flower Essences come into their own.

A beautiful range of essences from the blossoms of flowers, fruits and vegetables based on the principle of the metaphysician Yogananda that 'You are what you eat'.

Created in 1977 by Lila Devi-Stone to enable becoming 'masters of our own lives' by manifesting those qualities that we already possess in our own unique way, these essences are recommended for families and are exceptionally supportive of the unique dynamic between mother and child. It is this important interrelationship that has led Lila to research for solutions within the Masters essence range.

As these essences lend themselves to this special interaction, it is beneficial for both to take essences simultaneously as it not only clears any difficulties the child is experiencing with coping with life but helps the mother understand more fully how to help so that she is part of the solution and not part of the problem.

Almond Essence (*Prunus amygdalus*)
Mother: In control, balance and moderation. For being spread too thin, overindulgence in food, substances, activities etc. Helps to find the middle way, calms mind and nerves, syncs the mind/body/spirit.
    Child: Out of balance. For excess, feelings of being out of control. Balances emotional extremes, helps find inner balance, the middle way. Beneficial for pre-teens.

Apple Essence (*Malus domestica*)
Mother: Healthy mindset. Clears worry, doubt, toxic emotions such as anger, jealousy or fear, cultivates a positive outlook, a nourishing and abundant attitude.
    Child: Healthy and happy. Good during illness or when the thought of illness is present, especially when emotional upset creates physical symptoms. For periods of discouragement. Helps to maintain wellness when overwhelmed by emotional issues.

Avocado Essence (*Persea Americana*)
Mother: Clarity, absent-mindedness, forgetful and feeling dull and flat, without direction, brings clarity and focus, sense of purpose, learning from past mistakes. Feeling alert and alive.
    Child: Learning, focus and concentration. For the child who forgets his chores, manners etc. Helps with school work, homework, exams, sharpens concentration, fosters a love for learning, enthusiasm about homework and aids creativity and the development of musical or artistic endeavours.

Banana Essence (*Musa paradisiacal*)
Mother: Oversensitivity, stepping back, observing, a nonreactive attitude. Clears anxiety, being overwhelmed, loss of perspective, not seeing the wood for the trees, or being caught up in others' negativity.
    Child: Going bananas, calm and thoughtful, gaining perspective and for the child who needs to centre less on him/herself and be more caring, relating better with family, siblings and friends.

Blackberry Essence (*Rubus fruticosus*)
Mother: Positive thoughts. Clears negative thinking, unkind thoughts, fault finding, bluntness or pessimism. Brings purity of thought, optimism and compassion, seeing the good in oneself and others.
    Child: For worry and negative thoughts and behaviour. For the child stressed by exposure to negative influences often through the media such as disturbing movies or TV programmes or people, nightmares, thoughts of uncleanness. Good for the 'terrible twos'.

Cherry Essence (*Prunus serrulata*)
Mother: Cheerful, optimistic, positive, and lighthearted, clears moodiness, feeling contrary, somewhat out of control emotionally. Brings inspiration and seeing the good in life.
    Child: Happiness, brings a happy mood, for the child who is prone to periods of withdrawal and sadness. For disappointment. Helps to heal the trauma of divorce

or separation, imminent or past. Aid for bedwetting.

Coconut Essence (*Cocos nucifera*)
Mother: Uplifted and determined, clears lack of endurance, escapism, giving up, making excuses, avoidance, helps completion of tasks, living up to highest potential, determination, ready to take the next step.

Child: Being positive, helps deal with sibling rivalry, challenge or struggle in school or peer dynamics. Develops maturity, and ability to make healthy choices in difficult situation and in life.

Corn Essence (*Zea mays*)
Mother: Energy and vitality. Clears blocked energy, sluggishness, resistance, procrastination and lethargy. Aids enthusiasm, joy, living in the present, initiating projects, saying yes to life's challenges and new beginnings.

Child: New start. Alertness, helpful for new beginnings, new school year, new friends, moving house and home, gives encouragement for periods of procrastination and bursts of energy for 'study blues'. Aid for car sickness.

Date Essence (*Phoenix dactylifera*)
Mother: Tolerance and receptivity. Open-minded, easy to talk to, self-nurturing, clears intolerance, irritation and the tendency to be critical. Develops a warm, welcoming nature.

Child: Sweet nature and tenderness. For the child that can be overcritical and judgemental of other children or siblings. Fault finding, whining and sometimes clinging. Brings sweetness and ease. Encourages self-nurturing when life seems harsh. Date brings out the tender side in children who tend to be whiney or clingy.

Fig Essence (*Ficus carica*)
Mother: Self-nurture and flexibility. Helps with going with the flow, being at ease with self and others. For those who are too hard on themselves, prone to self-judgement, unrealistic expectations, trying too hard, and who are tense and overextended and finding it difficult to change. Encourages

relaxed healthy self-nurturing, boundaries and energy to move forward.

Child: Its OK! for the child who is too hard on him/herself or tries too hard, unsatisfied with accomplishments even when noteworthy. Good for nail-biting and thumb-sucking, helps children develop a positive overview about themselves.

Grape Essence (*Vitis* sp.)
Mother: Love and compassion. Patience with other's shortcomings. Clears strong negative emotions, jealousy, resentment, feelings of abandonment, grief and vulnerability due to separation, divorce or death. Helps to find forgiveness and that inner source of love.

Child: A Loving nature. Great for tantrums and any attitude that is not loving. Clears stubborn, self-willed moods and any bullying tendencies or attitudes. For the child who keeps saying NO!

Lettuce Essence (*Lactuca sativa*)
Mother: Calm and clear. Inner quiet and ability to speak one's truth. Clears restlessness, nervousness, excitability and agitation, crowded thinking, lack of concentration and indecision. Unblocks creativity, self-expression, success in undertakings. Aids sleep.

Child: Settled and chilled. For children who are too wound up, running on nervous energy, prone to restlessness, agitation and sleeplessness. Helps them to play or study constructively, good for exam nerves to calm and steady the mind. Dislike of salad.

Orange Essence (*Citrus sinensis*)
Mother: Joy. Banishes depression, hopelessness, and despair, any past or present emotional/physical abuse trauma, headaches. Renews hope, helps to resolve conflicts and endure difficulties. Cultivates an inner smile.

Child: Smile. For the child that can be sad and moody, dispels discontentment and periods of depression, helpful during teething. Good for emotional issues resulting from accidents to the head and for conflict resolution between family and peers, for restoring a sense of excitement.

Peach Essence (*Prunus persica*)
Mother: The mothering essence. Concern for others, empathy, nurturing from wholeness rather than from neediness. Clears overinvolvement and tendency to smother. Balances mothering, equilibrium of response.

Child: Sharing and co-operation. Promotes the sense of sharing and co-operation with other children, i.e. with favourite toys and prized possessions. Excellent for helping the weaning process be a positive experience for infants.

Pear Essence (*Pyrus communis*)
Mother: Emergency rescue remedy, for any kind of crisis, physical or emotional. Being thrown off balance during traumatic events, accidents, illness, childbirth and postnatal depression. Clears shock, and fear, giving peace of mind, and stability during major changes.

Child: Shock remedy. Rescue for accidents, sudden illness and crisis situations. Helps with toilet training, learning of new positive habits. For the fidgety and restless child who has a hard time listening in school or at home.

Pineapple Essence (*Ananas comosus*)
Mother: Brings self-esteem and assurance, and feelings of confidence and empowerment. Clears dissatisfaction. If you are unhappy with your job it helps you to match your career with your talents. For strong identity, clarity with money issues, and the ability to attract abundance.

Child: Shyness and confidence, helps the child to 'untie the apron strings'. For being singled out by peers for being different in some way. For the painfully shy child, gives self-esteem.

Raspberry Essence (*Rubus idaeus*)
Mother: Brings kindness, generosity, forgiving, and willingness to turn the other cheek. For the easily hurt and touchy who take things too personally, and tend to overreact. Releases old emotional wounds. Promotes understanding and generosity of spirit.

Child: Easily hurt, oversensitive and reactive. For the child who is easily hurt especially for youngsters who in reaction can hurt others. Nurtures a kind and giving nature.

Spinach Essence (*Spinacia oleracea*)
Mother: Simplicity and trust. For mothers who are stressed out, overwhelmed, worried and distrustful. Brings a childlike sense of joy, clearing dysfunctional childhood patterns. Bringing a carefree spirit and *joie de vivre*.

Child: Stressed out. For the child who is too grown up, overly serious. For times of stress, exhaustion, feeling over-responsible, distraught and overwhelmed. Restores innocence and a sense of fun.

Strawberry Essence (*Fragaria*)
Mother: For dignity and a grounded, quiet strength and sense of self. Dissolves guilt, feeling unworthy and undeserving. Clears history of emotionally abusive, dysfunctional childhood. For those who are psychically oversensitive. Brings poise, grace, and feeling comfortable with one's body.

Child: Good self-image. For children who have trouble letting go of being a baby. Nurtures a deep sense of self-worth, and brings clarity of a positive self-image. For the child dealing with divorced parents.

Tomato Essences (*Solanum lycopersicum*)
Mother: Makes you into Superwoman, knowing no failure and seeing all challenges as only another chance to succeed. Self-belief, invincibility, courage. Clears fears, nightmares, defensiveness, addictions, defeatist attitude, other's negative energy, and the stress of city life and travelling.

Child: Brings an 'I can do anything' attitude, mental strength, courage, helps to dissolve fears, nightmares. Encourages a child to move forward in their life when anxious, nervous, hesitant or unwilling.

The Teenage Years

I've found that in my practice The Australian Bush Remedies are most acceptable to this age group as mostly anything with an Aboriginal connection is considered cool! Australian Bush combination Adol is especially designed for those donkey years when teenagers really don't know how to handle themselves or really what's happening, the boys especially can become day-dreamy, procrastinate, sleep till lunch time, or aggressive or rude with communication going out the window.

For girls when reaching puberty and developing their curves, Woman Essences taken with Adol works wonders for this delicate stage.

For the pressure of exams a combination that's stood the test of time with all exams, is Cognis, which has helped them sail through, with great results. It clears learning problems, helps with assimilation, integration and focused thinking, especially when distracted, scattered and feeling overwhelmed. Also invaluable for accident-prone teenagers, at the clumsy stage when hormones are playing havoc with their emotions.

Environmental and Electromagnetic pollution

This is a more recent phenomena; in our age of rapid technological advances and wizardry childhood has radically changed, most children, especially teenagers, are totally computer literate, mobiles double up as cameras, virtual reality and cyber space are part of their everyday existence. The health implications of this increasing exposure to radiation and electromagnetic energy on developing brains is just beginning to register, as our children spend more and more time in front of the TV, or playing with their Play Stations, surfing the net, researching school projects, emailing, or just chatting or texting with their friends on their mobile phones. More evidence of the possible link to cancer with the use of mobile phones is coming to light. So it seems important to protect the health of our children.

Ian White, creator of The Australian Bush Essences, and a father himself, was concerned about this growing problem and developed the **Electro Combination** to protect against and clear the side effects of electromagnetic pollution.

A Return to Nature and Childlike Innocence by Peter Tadd

The most significant change in the flower essence world in the last decade is the growing appreciation that using essences as remedies for specific ills is also an entry into deepening our relationship with nature. This is the very reason that environmental essences are finding their way into the sets of a growing number of essence makers. These essences put us in touch with the 'spirit of the place'. I focus on nature because in this context we are speaking not of natural beauty alone but Invisible Intelligences. As adults becoming more aware and more capable of sensing these subtleties, we are in fact returning to a state of childlike innocence.

Being in a state of awareness, being present, calm and in harmony with our environment is a most worthy goal. Yet in this same time period, life has become more stressful because we are surrounded by greater numbers of disharmonious forces, environmental hazards, and unnatural electromagnetic and microwave forces which invade our auras. We are looking at visuals made up of square fragments, which no longer offer the etheric light bridge to our eyes, but digitalized pictures that interrupt this subtle life-giving flow. Therefore, essences are more than ever important for us. But what about our children?

One recent and exciting development in the essence world has been the recognition that today's children are in need of help, perhaps more than ever before. They are more vulnerable than adults to the stress factors mentioned above. Indeed, many children are suffering from greater and greater academic demands that challenge their right to be children, open and curious. This pressure is magnified for very creative and gifted children. Some essence makers, such as Rose Titchener, Ian White, and Sabina Petitte, are now including essences in their lines which meet the specific requirements of children. Rose's Light Heart Essences include 'Child's Play', while Ian's Australian Bush Essences include the Adol Essence, and Sabina's 'Pacific Essences', 'Kids Stuff'.

Lila Devi Stone's Master's range has designed essences for the special dynamic between mother and child and Purely Essences are for mothers and their babies. One other maker, Ann Callaghan, has also devoted her essences entirely to children: Indigo Essences.

Why should we consider essences for children and how do they operate differently than for adults? Children are very open to the subtle energies of etheric forces found in homeopathic remedies and in flower essences. Their etheric bodies are not so dominated by rigid mental states, nor weighed down by years of emotional scarring. Thus the results of homeopathic and flower/mineral/animal essence treatments are more easily or dramatically seen in children. This is to say that the auras of children are more easily imprinted – in the same way that some children remain open to 'invisible friends' and some see fairies.

Let us take a moment to look at the aura of a child. A young child's aura is undeveloped. The chakras are not fully opened in the lower three centres. Children are their surroundings, and up until the age of seven they have not yet constructed a mental optic by which to observe life.

Thus certain aspects of a very young child's aura are very open to spiritual dimensions. In an infant the crown chakra is aligned to the Divine, as it is unfettered by self-denial or authoritarian belief systems. If a child can remain open to the Light through to the age of nine the likelihood for continued access to spiritual realms is very strong. This is to say that the child knows that she or he is a 'being' or a soul. The material world is the stage or playground but they retain this essential identity of self.

This is in part due to interplay of the chakras in these developing years. There exists in the area of the hip sockets two very important minor chakras. These are the eyes of the child. They combine with the solar plexus and the third eye chakras and provide the integration of hormonal and ego development, socialization skills and visual and psychological perspectives. As the child grows, this integration can continue with unbroken direct contact with the kingdoms in nature and of the heavens. This is rare but in the cases when children have access to nature and are allowed to wander outside and to wander inside – daydream that is – they retain this ability to be at one with the all that is natural. It is actually this fluidity of movement that most resembles the spiralling patterns found in nature, its whirlpools in streams, cloud patterns, rock flows that form the very basis for the now acclaimed modern chaos theory. This freedom of nature in the child aligns them to the intelligence in nature and to their own creativity. Where this is not the case then an intervention is needed and that can direct us to including the root chakra in our treatment protocol.

Ann Callaghan's Indigo Essences (*see* resource listing) are one of the few lines, as well as Lila Devi's Master's Mother and Child and Purely Essence's Mother & Baby range, to have appeared on the horizon specifically designed for children. They are as effective for adults working with the inner child. For example, Light Hearts Original Innocence Combination. There are many to choose from in the global flower essence world which help us to re-connect with our inner self as well as that innate state of childlike wonder.

What I like about the Indigos is that they have a unique effect on the root chakra because they are not plant derived. The root chakra has two placements, and one is in the perineum aligned with the mineral element. This point is vital to our sense of 'grounding' or for the child incarnating. The fact that this essence line is created from stones and crystals uniquely can help some children feel 'ok in their bodies' and, more than that, these essences strengthen the white light or vital sheath of the etheric body. Moreover, this can mean many things but it gives the child a sense of solidity and clarity.

To sum up, technology is pushing our families and us in one direction. The benefits of the IT world are obvious; the negatives are not always so evident. Essences can be of the greatest value to us, as a way back home, as a means to bring our children back to their birthright as sensitive creative beings. Nature awaits and is never far away.

PETER TADD is known for his clairvoyant skills, analysing essences for makers and developers worldwide and his role for many years as the quality control person and lecturer for I.F.E.R. (My original flower essences company). His present work is a further study and teaching of how essences enhance the aura and chakras, including and especially the transcendental chakras.

Flower Essences for Pets and Animals

An important area in many of our lives is the relationship with our pets and how bonded and fond of them we can become. They provide companionship and can be a positive source of unconditional love. Many of us have an intuitive communication with our cats, dogs or horses, for example in the way they seem to know how we feel and the exact time that we will be arriving at home. We feel drawn to keep them healthy and happy, especially as they can often take on our negative emotions and need to be cleared and protected from this in order to maintain their balance. My Turkish Van cat, Picchu, often alerts me to the fact that my aura needs cleaning by intensely looking around my aura and whilst vocalizing her observations, flicking her legs in sequence to suggest shaking off the negative energy. She is only satisfied when we have both been spritzed. This is where flower essences come very much into their own.

Master Essences for Pets

Master Essences are also invaluable for treating pets and animals. Likewise, pets and animals who are free from the mental interferences that often plague the human mind, also respond quickly and dramatically when given flower essences. Case after case shows that animals, possessing a rich instinctive nature and a wide range of emotions, are able to adapt more easily to a life of domestication with the assistance of these essences.

Lila Deva Stone's book *Flower Essences for Animals* elucidates her essence line and provides the text for her widely acclaimed bi-level pets and animals course.

Almond (*Prunus amygdalus*) For pets who are confined, who pace, or display repetitive behaviours.

Apple (*Malus domestica*) For pets who were the runt of the litter or who tend to pick up worrisome attitudes from their owners.

Avocado (*Persea Americana*) Helps pets with alertness, training and responding to commands.

Banana (*Musa* x *paridasiaca*) Good for pets who are easily agitated or who tend to bully other pets in the home. Also to reinforce the positive behaviour of an already calm animal.

Blackberry (*Rubus fruticosus*) For pets who are ill or older and can no longer care for themselves. It is good to spray this essence in the litterbox area for cleanliness.

Cherry (*Prunus avium*) For pets when they get grumpy, or act listless and disinterested in their surroundings (be sure to rule out medical causes).

Coconut (*Cocos nucifera*) For aging pets who are adapting to limited movement or range of physical abilities and for overcoming any difficulties in adjusting to domesticated life.

Corn (*Zea mays*) For older pets, Corn helps them to act younger again and supports recovery from illness and surgery.

Date (*Phoenix dactylifera*) Helps pets express their natural sense of friendliness and, for those who are domineering, to be more accepting of other household pets.

Fig (*Ficus carica*) This essence aids pets in training and also helps them overcome bad habits. Good for pets who have had multiple homes or been confused by inconsistent training.

Grape (*Vitis* sp.) For pets who have been abandoned, or who feel threatened by other animals in the household; for strays and feral animals. To ease territorial disputes, dominance issues, and helping animals who are jealous or possessive.

Lettuce (*Lactuca sativa*) Good for pets, especially younger animals who are easily riled or who bounce off the walls, especially with strangers or guests.

Orange (*Citrus sinensis*) For pets who have lost an animal or human companion, are nearing their own time of passing, or are dealing with ongoing physical pain. Orange is imperative for grieving animals who have been unnaturally altered, such as declawed or debarked (not including spaying or neutering).

Peach (*Prunus persica*) Good for pets who are demanding or unusually needy, and for animals who were weaned too early and tend to chew or suckle on clothing.

Pear (*Pyrus communis*) Good for pets any time their regular routine is disturbed, including vet visits, car travel, or nearing their time of passing (especially good for their owners at this time as well). This is a good essence to keep on hand at all times.

Pineapple (*Ananas comosus*) For pets, especially show animals, to take pride in their accomplishments, and for multi-pet households, as well as for the runt of the litter.

Raspberry (*Rubus idaeus*) For pets who are extremely sensitive and seem to be good listeners. Also for pets who tend to feel slighted. This remedy is especially helpful for inappropriate urination (as opposed to spraying) and soiling problems.

Spinach (*Spinacia oleracea*) To restore a pet's youthfulness, good for post-surgical procedures and for any kind of stress in the household.

Strawberry (*Fragaria*) To support pets in their growing expressions of likes and dislikes, the flourishing of their personalities, and their innate charm. Helps with the imminence of their passing.

Tomato (*Solanum lycopersicum*) For pets who cower or retreat, especially from any loud noises. Also for animals who have been previously mistreated, including those with an unknown history.

Sun Essences for Animals

Sun Essences for Animals is based in Cromer, Norfolk, close to where Dr Bach lived and worked. Since the 1980s, Jane Stevenson, an experienced flower essence practitioner, has provided individual consultations for people with emotional problems, and discovered this pure and natural remedial method to be extremely effective and rewarding. Jane also found that she was increasingly treating animals with flower essences. Her love of flowers and affinity with animals culminated in the development of a unique collection of flower essence blends, designed to alleviate the key emotional and behavioural problems experienced by animals.

As a co-founder of 'Sun Essences' making a range of flower remedies, (*see* page 124) with her passion for helping animals it was Jane's wish that they all also have the opportunity to benefit from flower essence therapy. A natural result was the creation of 'Sun Essences for Animals' and Jane feels privileged to continue this important work so close to the original roots of Dr Bach, who felt that every household would benefit from his Bach Flower Remedies.

Jane is currently dedicated to helping animals and works closely with vets, trainers, animal sanctuaries and the RSPCA (Royal Society for the Prevention of Cruelty to Animals).

The Natural Way To Happy, Healthy Pets

Anyone who has a pet or works with animals knows that animals can suffer with emotional as well as behavioural problems. They can experience the same range of emotions as us: fear, rage, sadness, anxiety, jealousy etc. The flower essence blends can help by promoting calm, balanced and well-adjusted behaviour.

Flower essences are frequently used to help alleviate emotional problems because they can gently soothe an animal, without masking their true nature. Veterinary clinics, training clubs and rescue homes use flower essences as an effective way of helping animals with emotional and behavioural problems. It suggests that these natural products can be used alongside other treatments and have no known side effects. Natural, simple and safe to use – just add to food and water.

Apathy Natural help for animals who are lethargic, miserable or weary. Useful for when an animal's disposition seems low, down in spirits, miserable or apathetic. Also consider during times when the animal may be overtaxed and an extra tonic is required e.g. pregnancy, lactation, old age, during convalescence etc.

Distress Natural help for animals who are: frightened, anxious or alarmed. Use for alarming or distressing events, as it can initiate a calming process. Can also be used to relax an animal prior to, or during, particularly upsetting situations e.g. accidents, emergencies, travelling, thunderstorms, fireworks, 'show' nerves, visits to the vets or farriers etc.

Dominant Natural help for animals who are impulsive, stroppy, stubborn. This blend has been developed especially to help balance the nature of headstrong, stubborn or bossy animals. Also suggested for jealous, impulsive, unmanageable and possessive behaviour.

Highly Strung Natural help for animals who are boisterous, frisky or scatty. Blended specifically for overactive, scatty, frisky, boisterous and excitable animals. Other indications may be restlessness and attention-seeking behaviour. This blend can also be helpful for training animals who display erratic behaviour.

Pining Natural help for animals who are relocating, alone or bereaved. For pining and lonely pets who are left 'home alone' (e.g. while the owner is at work) or for unhappy or bereaved pets who may have lost an owner or animal companion. Also use for 'relocation', i.e. adjusting to a new home, kennel accommodation, 'separation anxiety' etc.

Timid Natural help for animals who are submissive, ring-shy, nervous. Helpful for animals who may be generally fearful, sensitive, frightened, spooked or insecure. Also indicated for low confidence, nervousness or withdrawn and submissive behaviour.

Dosage instructions for Timid; Dominant; Highly Strung; Pining; Apathy;

Large Animals (Horses, Goats, etc)
12 drops 3 times daily

Medium Animals (Dogs, Cats, etc)
7 drops 3 times daily

Small Animals (Rabbits, Guinea Pigs, Birds, etc)
3 drops 3 times daily

Dosage instructions for Distress Blend

Large Animals (Horses, Goats, etc)
12 drops every 10–30 minutes until calm, then 3 times daily if required

Medium Animals (Dogs, Cats, etc)
7 drops every 10–30 minutes until calm, then 3 times daily if required

Small Animals (Rabbits, Guinea Pigs, Birds, etc)
3 drops every 10–30 minutes until calm, then 3 times daily if required

Instructions for use and administration

The essences should be added to food, treats or water. They can also be rubbed onto gums or the drops can be shaken onto fur to be licked off. For birds (particularly), the essences can be put into a spray mist bottle and sprayed onto the feathers.

Only use one blend at a time, except in certain 'emergency' situations for example, if the animal is frightened during the firework season/thunder storms/a sudden traumatic experience/show nerves etc. In this instance the Distress Blend can be used alongside one of the other blends – use every 10 minutes, if required.

If the animal isn't already taking a blend during the firework season it is advisable to give them the Distress Blend 3 times daily for up to 2 weeks before November the 5th or New Years Eve, and for a few days after, until the fireworks season is over.

N.B. Flower essences are not a substitute for correct veterinary care.

Dancing Light Happy Pet

Happy Pet is a blend of Alaska's Elements, and Dancing Light Orchid Essences

Gentle first-aid support for animals large or small, to assist with emergencies, shock, trauma, fear, injuries, trips to the vet, pregnancy and birth, sickness, death, sadness, recovery from abuse, wild animal rescue and rehabilitation, and other transitions. Keep several bottles on hand as the unexpected is bound to take place. Using Happy Pet yourself when you give it to your pet may help you both feel more relaxed, trusting, bonded and a bit cosier together. When helping a new pet to adjust to new people and surroundings mist the areas where your pet will sleep and play.

Alaskan Animal Care Combination

Alpine Azalea, Black Tourmaline, Chiming Bells, Cotton Grass Horsetail, Jadeite Jade, Lady's Slipper. Animal Care is intended for use in animal rescue work, although it can be given to any animal in need. It is most valuable when it is integrated into the initial care provided to any animal that arrives at an animal shelter, treatment centre, veterinarian clinic, or sanctuary. This formula is also a must when adopting a 'rescue' animal.

Use Animal Care for domestic animals who:

live in large cities, are restricted from normal contact with nature, and are alone for much of the day;

have been voluntarily given up to an animal care shelter because their owners can no longer care for them;

have been abandoned and then rescued off the street after a prolonged struggle for survival;

have lived in conditions where the care given them was inadequate, the living environment toxic, and the relationship with their humans abusive;

are exhibiting self-aggressive behaviour.

Use Animal Care for wild animals who:

are brought to a clinic because they have been injured or their habitats have been damaged or destroyed;

are agitated, irritated, and exhibiting aggressive behaviour, which may be endangering themselves, other animals, or humans;

have lived for some time in pet shops, and subsequently in the homes of people, in isolation from other members of their own species;

must be kept in captivity in a shelter, sanctuary, or zoo, because their injuries cannot be fully healed, and need to be handled in order to receive treatment

are suffering from 'toxic' interference from their contact with the public and need to release this energy so they can be released back into the wild.

Animal Care Spray

Animal Care Spray contains small amounts of organic Lemon Grass and Roman Chamomile essential oils. These enhance the calming effects of the formula and add their refreshing qualities to the spray, which can be misted around the animal, on its bedding, and in its immediate environment. This spray is particularly useful when working with injured animals or those behaving aggressively

Sound, Light and Environmental Essences

Sound Wave Essences

The Original Source of Sound

Sound, particularly harmonious sound, is essential to our nature and has a profound healing effect on our wellbeing. Even in nature birdsong stimulates seedlings to open their pores in order to encourage absorbing of nutrients and therefore profuse growth.

Each person vibrates at their own unique frequency and it was understood by the ancient peoples, especially the aboriginals, that every person had their own note or individual song and that the point when we felt most out of tune was when we had forgotten how to sing our song. Sound Wave essences help to restore the spin and vibration of the chakras so that they can shine with their pure colours again.

Sound Wave Essences are created in Star House, a building built on the principals of sacred geometry, designed by Keith Critchlow, with the ancient sound of 'OM' built into its very structure. Using crystal bowls tuned to each chakra these essences are made during significant phases of the moon and on the solstice. Thus essences are available processed either by using SUN (active principle) or MOON (receptive principle) energies.

The Sound Essences, created in 1997, were the inspiration of myself and Colette Prideaux-Brune, therapist and gifted intuitive healer of 20 years; both of us have trained extensively with shamanistic medicine men and women of Central and South American Traditions.

The concept of creating sound essences sprang from my connection with Beautiful Painted Arrow in 1993, and his work with original sacred sound, whilst simultaneously, during her dream time, Colette was listening and absorbing the original teachings of sound. But it was not until 1996, after I was inspired to make a sacred site essence on Machu Picchu, and Colette made an essence at the sacred site of Palenque in Mexico that the Sound Wave Essences were born. The essences were created with both the light of the sun and energy of the moon and relate to the seven major chakras of the body plus an eighth chakra above the head.

The sun by its nature is naturally expansive and the moon by its nature is naturally reflective giving the essences these inherent qualities. Everyday living causes the colours of the chakras to become dull, and stress, shock or trauma can leave toxic residues behind. These dense energies clog the chakras and stop them vibrating in their pure frequencies causing more rapid aging. The Sound Wave Essences help to restore the spin and vibration of the chakras so that they can shine their pure colours again. These special sets of eight essences that vibrate with the chakras are made by a process of sympathetic resonance by encapsulating sound waves from quartz crystal bowls and colour in water, remembering that water has the ability to hold a memory, and are in fact literally liquid sound!

Sun essences help on the conscious level with:
Processing the changes in patterns held within the mental and emotional levels.
Accessing information held within the body at a cellular level, repatterning cells and shifting consciousness.
Intensifying creativity, imagination and intelligence.
Stimulating and waking up the chakras into action and reaction.
Helping to access silent knowledge within so we remember who we truly are.

Moon essences help the subconscious level with:
Lighting up awareness of our dreamtime.
Reflecting back our original blueprint.
Switching on cellular intelligence.
Activating the inner ear so that our soul's message is audible.
Heightening all of the senses.

The Liquid Sound Essences

Heart of the Earth – Base Chakra. This gateway connects us directly to the heart of Mother Earth, the feminine principle. Roots of energy travel down the legs into the ground, creating stability and security. This forms a solid foundation for the luminous energy and chakra system to anchor itself into the body. The doorway to the heart of the earth simultaneously grounds and protects us whilst enabling us to deal with the unique relationship to our tribal roots.

Sacred Void – Sacral Chakra. The void is not empty but contains both elements of the sacred fire and water. Alchemically blended, these two vital forces create a state of dynamic balance that provides the fuel to empower our dreams, reconnecting to the waters of life, it renews, refreshes and deals with issues around our own birth, returning us to that sacred place of innocence.

Warriors' Path – Solar Plexus Chakra. Strengthens the inner core, the column of light that embodies the principles of solar light. Connects us to the universal warriors energy, the vehicle for both the solar and lunar qualities inherent in the male and female form. When in balance it allows access to the courage that abounds in the universe, and reflects back our unique interaction with all life, enabling us to move forward with empowerment along our true path.

Listening Heart – Heart Chakra. To walk the path of the heart is to walk the path of the soul, hearing the inner whispering of our soul's voice. Circulating its wishes through the compassionate spirit of the heart, the soul reveals the nature of its true self. This is the key to opening the doorway to the heart of the universe, whilst simultaneously hearing the imperceptible teachings of the cosmos.

Divine Purpose – Throat Chakra. The instrument of speaking one's truth and trusting in the clear expression of our soul's journey. Enables us to call back the threads of our timelessness and reconnects us with our lives on the planet. Opens the doorway to the divine purpose of the universe.

Perceiving Spirit – Third Eye Chakra. To perceive the web of life as an indivisible matrix that holds the blueprint of all time. The awareness of spirit behind all things cuts through illusion and opens perception to the space between the worlds.

Universal Present – Crown Chakra. Eminessence, essence of spiritual consciousness, in the present, is the moment that holds all time. The portal to the heavens, illuminating and guiding our passage towards who we are becoming. Aiding the mastery and transcendence of time.

Star Traveller – Eighth Chakra. The golden orb of spinning light held in the luminous energy field above the head contains the imprint of our next incarnation waiting to be born. To become a star traveller through time and space, journeying to the union with our original source.

Ways the Essences Can Be Used

Place on the chakras. Put the bottle onto or close to the relevant chakra.

On the skin. The energy of the remedies can be absorbed through the skin and can be applied to anywhere you feel you need it e.g. on a chakra, lips, forehead, wrist, soles of the feet or palms of the hands.

By mouth. Dilute 10 drops to 2 tablespoons of pure spring water or take 7–10 drops under the tongue. You can also take them in herb tea or fruit juice.

In the bath. A couple of drops will be enough when the bath has finished running.

On your altar: Place the bottles on your altar to effect a certain aspect of your spiritual practise.

Combinations

Eclipse Spritz A unique blend of frequency essences, essential oils of Jasmine and Ylang Ylang with May Chang oil from China and sacred site energy essences from Machu Picchu, Palenque and the Pyramids of Guimar have been included in this special spritz. The spritz clears discordant and electromagnetic energy and has a cleansing, uplifting and refreshing effect on the aura and subtle bodies. By clearing the subtle bodies' electromagnetic field it enables one to move through energy smoothly and cleanly without picking up the residue and negativity that usually clings to the subtle anatomy through the daily interaction with discordant energies. One then feels clean, centred, protected and in control of one's personal space, facilitating clarity of thought and emotional calm. It aids by shifting the vibrational patterns of the body, fine-tuning its frequency and generally raising its overall vibration as well as the subtle anatomy. Aids meditation and attunement to one's Higher Self.

Integrate Combination and Spritz

This combination essence is a blend of the Sun and Moon essences especially designed in a sequence that encourages balance and integrates the male and female polarities.

For the alchemical balance within the cellular structure. As the ancient male and female archetype guidelines are dissolving there is a need for a new perspective and envisioning on how these energies are intermingled and then ultimately expressed. It is important in this time of transition that this delicate alchemic balance is achieved without getting caught by the limitations of the previous traditional concepts. It is vital that this happens with mutual respect and honour whilst maintaining the integrity of both polarities. The Integrate essence and spritz maintains you in a state of dynamic balance while completing the transformation process and helps you to discover the purpose of your soul.

Sun and Moon Rebalancers

(Male/Female) The rebalancers are a combination of all eight remedies specially formulated to harmonize the energy of the chakras, assisting with their stability and realignment. The Sun Rebalancer particularly re-strengthens and nourishes while activating what we are aware of in the present, at a conscious level.

Whilst the Moon Rebalancer reflects what is going on at the subconscious level. By using both combinations the two aspects of inner and outer (Male and Female) are brought together in an alchemical dance of light. Any disruption in the coordination of this alchemical dance creates an instability that contains within it the seeds of disease. These sound rebalancers activate the cell's innate ability to re-coordinate itself, readjusting and holding the correct dynamic pattern, as we move through the discord of daily life.

Transmute Combination This combination represents the interwoven energy of the male and female fully harmonized and integrated with the finer vibrations of the higher chakras.

For the transmutation of the cellular structure into the matrix of the subtle levels. Now equal in balance and strength a sacred marriage can occur between the male and female energy. This fusion ignites the spark of the soul and creates momentum to move the soul forward. The Integrate and Transmute essences can be used separately or together. The Rebalancers create a solid foundation to anchor the male and female energy, Integrate weaves them together in an alchemic dance and Transmute creates a dynamic fusion which results in the sacred marriage within the soul.

Combination Treatment Kit

Many of us are experiencing difficulty in regaining our balance as a direct result of the earth wobbling on its axis. As our usual point of reference has shifted it is important to reset our vibrational patterning to the new matrix. With this in mind the Integrate and Transmute Kit has been developed with a treatment pattern included.

White Light Essences (Australian Bush)

The White Light Essences have been brought through by spirit to help us invoke and access the realm of nature and spirit within ourselves so as to more fully explore and understand our spirituality and fulfil our highest potential.

This project has taken Ian White over four years to complete and has led him on a journey to some of the most remote and sacred locations around the world. During the past 20 years he has researched and developed the Australian Bush Flower Essences and they have been a stepping stone to bring him to the point in his growth and spirituality where he has been able to make the White Light Essences. They were made with the utmost integrity, humility and love.

Air Essence Air Essence helps one to maintain a balance between an intellectual arc and an emotional approach, whilst also aiding discrimination and discernment. Whenever you are needing to make a decision within an emotionally-charged situation, the Air Essence will enable you to feel stable, more in control and empowered. Consequently it is an excellent remedy for people going through emotional stress and trauma. The Air Essence has the potential to bring out a person's spirituality to the highest degree with integrity and passion, while at the same time allowing one to bend and alter his or her reality in a very profound way. The remedy enables people to understand that they are indeed a miracle and all their actions are miraculous. Yet it hinders one from becoming conceited from this knowledge, rather allowing them to remain humble and lighthearted. The Air Essence honours, acknowledges and reflects our uniqueness, holiness, sacredness, and perfection.

Angelic Essence This essence enables us to be more open to receiving the angelic tones of inspiration, love, awareness, communication, guidance and instruction. The angels help us in all our activities, especially in work and service. This essence enables one to aspire beyond the physical and realize that the spiritual exists in everything and to transcend the deceptive illusion of the physical, while also keeping us connected to the mundane. This essence allows closer contact with the angelic realm. Taking this essence invokes protection of an angelic kind, and of any specific angel.

Angelic Essence helps to connect to and access all of the earth's ley lines and energy points. It provides a key to ancient knowledge but future wisdom. This remedy removes the emotional blockages in people with selective hearing, where there are things they don't particularly want to hear – or see! resulting in them having to 'see and hear' everything, whether they like it or not! Produces a sense of empowerment in relationships and stressful situations by creating mental clarity, alleviates and clears our past patterns and blockages, allowing us to respond appropriately rather than reacting.

Devic Essence The Devic Essence assists with spiritual self-nurturing bringing devotional caring quality within us for others and nature. Fosters a sense responsibility and protection in our life. The Devic Essence releases a purplish pink and orange band of colour within one's auric field that has an uplifting effect on our psyche. Enables contact and communication with nature, and ability to listen to any message from the plant kingdom and attunes you with qualities such as healing, from the devic kingdom. Helps to earth the ungrounded person who feels out of control connecting them back to nature. Soothes and calms those stressed out, wound up, stuck for time or feeling disconnected. Recommended for people who are obsessive or insecure in relationships who carry too many expectations. It will help them to feel safe and secure.

The Devic Essence can also be considered for people close to passing over, helping them to attain acceptance and to be clear in the understanding that there is much more beyond our limited reality.

Earth Essence The Earth Essence fosters a strong connection, respect and reverence to nature, the Ancients, the nature spirits, the earth, the life force, life and the origins of life. This essence also helps to heal internal structure and order in life and is an important grounding remedy, especially for those involved in spiritual work. This essence centres, grounds and helps us to find our direction and proceed forward with clarity and focus. It creates a sense of deep restfulness especially in the heart and base chakras. Emotionally it helps to bring stability to relationships and those having problems committing to one.

Earth Essence establishes a connection with the Manu (overlighting energy) of a country. By helping you to energetically access that country, the Earth Essence allows you to be more effective in your work and helps open the doorway to wherever you want to direct your spiritual work on the planet – with or without a visa!

Fire Essence The Fire Essence has a strong connection with a primordial time at the very beginning of intelligence on earth and can open people to their most ancient source; back to the moment when the soul originally chose the life purpose for its earthly incarnations. Unlocks the most sacred part of an individual, revealing one of the last bastions of inner secrets and ancient knowledge that a person possesses – their original and ongoing life paths. When this is revealed an individual will be left with a 'fiery' sense of purpose and direction and be inspired and motivated to follow their life path and fulfil their highest destiny. There is no middle ground with this essence, nowhere to go except forward.

Before working with this essence it's important to be clear that you want irreversible change, and from deep in the heart or soul be prepared to move forward no matter what the consequences. It is only then that this essence will work. The Fire Essence reveals the big picture

For the full potency it should be taken only after working with the Water Essence. The Water Essence will pave the way and allow an individual to experience the deepest action of the Fire Essence. Secondly, it is important to find the right sound vibration to work with it.

Higher Self Essence The Higher Self Essence funnels and channels energy of the highest order into one's very core, where it will radiate out and expand dramatically. Those balanced in their spirituality will have the possibility to be totally expanded. This essence helps us to be aware of what is beyond the physical experience and tap into sources of ancient wisdom and knowledge.

Our Higher Self is comprised of every lifetime we have ever had and this essence offers the opportunity to help a person connect with these earlier incarnations. When taking this essence, the most likely time you will tap into these past lives will be in the dream state, in meditation, or daydreaming. Then you will be able to beam back the energy of whatever it is that you need from that past time. It's advisable to take this remedy when feeling very grounded and balanced. If not, you may have trouble being anchored in the present, as you may be shifting between the past and present extremely quickly. Higher Self Essence can also open dimensional doorways and allow one to enter/access alternate realities. Thus further highlighting the powerful potential of this essence.

Water Essence This remedy integrates the element of water within you, attuning to its vibration and to the nature spirit of water – the undine. It allows intense experience of your own emotional disharmony so that it may be purified and released. An appropriate essence for those not choosing, or unable, to let go of aspects from the past. It releases the past and helps those who are emotionally closed off after a negative or traumatic experience. A day or two of strong emotional release is most likely in the form of tears. This release is nothing to be afraid of. This remedy, together with the element of water, is very nurturing and cleansing, and encourages us all to be more open to receiving. Water Essence illuminates the conscious mind to reveal and initiate the release of our deepest, most ancient, negative karmic patterns and it can dissolve the boundaries of a person's perceptions and realities.

Environmental Essences

There is a growing awareness that taking responsibility for our environment is very much part of our stewardship as cohabiters on this planet. Essences created from the energy of the environment, the elements and sacred places are a new departure in the development of essences. I first became fully aware of the powerful energy held within a sacred place when in 1996 I spent a full moon night in the sacred mountain city of Machu Picchu, in Peru.

In preparation the whole day was spent in ceremony with the guardian and shaman of the sacred city and that night, whilst making an essence on the ancient temple altar, I was left in no doubt about the existence of the mountain *Apu* (spirit) who made its presence very clear to me. There was no way that the essences would have been made had I not approached with respect and asked permission and co-operation. This essence is included in the Eclipse Spritz from the Soundwave Essence range.

Alaskan Environmental Essences

The creation of these essences begins with the identification of specific elemental qualities in the environment with which we wish to enter into a co-creative healing agreement. An attunement from our hearts communicating love and blessings to the devic and elemental beings that represent these qualities is the start of the process. When requested, the energies are transferred into the bowl of prepared water, the environment responds resulting in a totally unique essence, where the vibrational qualities it contains can never be duplicated in exactly the same way.

How the Alaskan Environmental Essences Work

When taken internally, these essences stimulate and support change and trans-formation at the most basic level of the energy system. They are very catalytic in their actions and are often indicated when a strong, cleansing energy is needed to awaken or bring vitality to someone who is not responding to other therapies or modalities. They also provide a strong base of support for our healing work with flower essences, lending energy and vitality to the healing processes catalysed by the flowers.

The Alaskan Environmental Essences are very effective tools for space clearing. This process involves cleansing and releasing old energies from our living and working environments and then recharging and revitalizing these spaces with fresh, clean energy from nature. Space clearing with Environmental Essences is an especially useful process for those living in crowded and polluted urban areas where the natural elemental forces have been weakened or dissipated all together.

Environmental Essences can also be used to provide balance and stability for those involved in emergency situations such as natural disasters where the environment itself is in transition.

Chalice Well Made in the Chalice Well Gardens of Glastonbury, England, with water from the Chalice Well, this essence connects us to the profoundly personal and eternal support that is constantly available from the angelic, elemental, plant and mineral kingdoms. It reminds us that we are not alone – we are a part of the entire web of life and All That Is, and we can draw upon this matrix of support whenever we are struggling and need help to take the next step on our life path.

Full Moon Reflection This essence was made on a cold, clear, full moon night, in a canyon overlooking Kachemak Bay. An essence of reflected light – the sun's light reflected by the full moon off the water of Kachemak Bay and into the snow-filled canyon. This essence penetrates deep into the subconscious to bring forth that which lies unresolved beneath the surface. It offers us an opportunity to let our shadow-self be illuminated by the light of our conscious awareness.

Glacier River An essence of solarized water prepared below the terminus of the Gulkana glacier in the central Alaskan range. This water emerges from the base of the glacier carrying suspended particles of ground-up rock from mountains eroded by the constant pressure and movement of glacial ice. This essence embodies the process of perpetual release from form. It helps us release patterns of feeling,

thinking and doing that have become rigid and unyielding.

Greenland Icecap An essence of solarized glacier water prepared on the Greenland ice sheet over an area where two of the earth's continental plates come together. The Greenland Icecap essence contains the intense energy of convergence, the energy of the natural movement of the earth's crust translated upwards through thousands of feet of ice. This essence helps us remain flexible and feel supported as we move through deep inner change.

Liard Hot Springs This essence was prepared from mineral hot springs water on a clear –35°F day at Liard Springs in northern B.C., Canada. An essence of cleansing, recreation and renewal, that brings us back in touch with the innocent truth of who we really are – spiritual beings who have come to this earth to learn.

Northern Lights This essence was made on a windy subzero arctic night under a swirling green display of Northern Lights. An essence of reaching beyond ourselves into the fundamental creation forces of the universe. For cleansing and repatterning our energies, at a very deep level. Helps us release energies from the heart which have been allowed to obscure our original life patterns.

Polar Ice This essence was prepared on the Arctic Ocean ice pack near the North Pole. An essence of transition and the completion of cycles; for achieving a more patient understanding of the subtleties of time; helps us stay present in a place of pure waiting, with no anticipation of what is to come.

Portage Glacier This essence was prepared on the banks of Portage Lake near the terminus of Portage Glacier in south-central Alaska. A powerful and catalytic energy that helps us release what is unnecessary and inappropriate in our lives from the mental, emotional, etheric, and physical bodies. Use it to revitalize and balance the entire energy system.

Rock Spring Prepared from a spring high in the Talkeetna Mountains of south-central Alaska, the water from this spring emerges from the centre of a sheer rock face and cascades down to a pool at its base. Rock Spring is an essence of hope and miracles! It embodies the constant proof that everything is possible. It is an essence that can help us find our way through seemingly insurmountable obstacles with infinite patience and neverending trust.

Solstice Sun This essence was prepared on the 'night' of June 21/22, as the midnight sun danced along the peaks of the Brooks Range in the northern interior of Alaska. Solstice Sun catalyses our ability to access and circulate a stronger current of light energy throughout the physical body. It opens the heart and the energy pathways of the body in preparation for a 'peak' experience, and helps a person integrate such an experience after it has taken place.

Stone Circle Prepared within a naturally occurring circle of stones located high in the Talkeetna Mountains of Alaska. The formation of energy created by this circle of stones has immense healing power. Stone Circle introduces a highly balanced and protective energy into the aura that invites us to relax, rest, and replenish our vital forces. This essence is especially helpful for those doing energy balancing work with people and spaces, as it will enable them to maintain their openness and sensitivity without absorbing or 'taking on' any of the energies they are being asked to clear.

Tidal Forces This essence was prepared with creek and seawater on Kachemak Bay during a full 24-hour, 22-foot tidal cycle. An essence of rhythm and balance, of loss and gain, of adapting ourselves to the swiftly changing currents of life. Helps us release the old and receive the new with constant and unyielding fluidity. Soothes and balances overly emotional, fiery states of being; washes away mental resistance to change; helps us accept what is in the present moment.

PART THREE

CHAPTER FIVE

Ailment Chart

Essence Key

Africa and the Amazon
Andreas Korte Essences (AK)

Australia
Australian Bush Essences (Aus B)
Living Essences of Australia (Aus L)

Europe
Britain
Bach Flower/Healing Herbs (B)
Findhorn Essences (F)
Green Man Essences (GM)
Habundia Shamanic Essences (HUB)
Harebell (Hb)
Light Heart Essences (LH)
Sun Essences (Sun)

France
Deva Essences (Dv)

Netherlands
Bloesem Flower Essences (BL)

Japan
Japanese Essences (Australian Living
Essences, Japan) (Aus LJ)

India
Himalayan Aum Essences (Him A)
Himalayan Enhancers (Him E)

Thailand
Flowers of the Orient (FO)

USA
Alaskan
Alaskan Essences (Ask)
Alaskan Environmental Essences (Ask E)
Dancing Light Orchid Essences (DL)
Wild Divine (WD)

Arizona
Desert Alchemy Flower Essences (DAl)

California
Flower Essence Society (FES)
Master Flower Essences (Ma)

Colorado
Pegasus Flower and Rose Essences (Peg)

Hawaiian
Hawaiian Gaia Flower Essences (Haii)

Texas
Petite Fleur Essences (PF)

Virginia
Perelandra Rose and Garden Essences
(PVi)

Canada
Pacific Flower and Sea Essences (Pac)

South America
Star Peruvian Essences (Peru)

Sound and Light Essences
Sound Wave Essences (SW)
White Light Essence (Australian Bush)
(WL)

Babies and Children Essences
Masters Mother and Child Essence (*Please
refer to section in Encyclopedia*)
Mother & Baby Essences
Purely Essences (PE)

Animal Essences (*Please refer to section in
Encyclopedia*)
Alaskan Animal Essences
Sun Animal Essences

Physical

Abuse: Emergency Essence (Aus B); Cotton Grass, Tundra Twayblade (Ask); Letting Go, I Like Being Me, Unveiling self (DL); Mother's Arms, Protective Shield, Young Heart, Wise Woman (WD).

Accidents: Rose Bay Willow Herb (Ask); Emergency Essence, Fringed Violet, Mountain Devil (Aus B); Rock Rose, Star of Bethlehem (B); Arnica (Dv); Dogwood, Love Lies Bleeding (FES); 'Uala (Haii); Pear (Ma); Grape Hyacinth, Weigela (Pac); Magic Healer (Peru); Acceptance, Earth Mother Nurtures, Mother's Arms, On Angels' Wings, Birch Forest (WD).

Aches: Bluebell, Crowea, Five Corners, Tall Yellow Top (Aus B); Earth Mother Nurtures, My own Pure Light (DL); Dandelion (FES); Mussel (Pac); Solar Power (Peru); Birch Forest, On Angels' Wings, (WD).

Acidity (Excessive) *See also* **Digestive problems**: Crowea (Aus B); Chamomile (FES); Curry Leaf (Him A); Narcissus (Pac).

Acne *See also* **Skin problems**: Billy Goat Plum, Five Corners, Spinifex, Sundew (Aus B); Dandelion, Self-Heal Cream (FES); Formula 20 Acne (Him A); Mussel (Pac) Salvia (PF).

Addictions (Symptoms): Bush Iris, Monga Waratah, (Aus B); Hedgehog Cactus (DAl); Morning Glory (FES, Him A, Him E); Fairy Lantern, Five Flower Formula, Mallow, Nicotiana (FES); Pua Kenikeni (Haii); Forsythia, Nootka Rose, Urchin (Pac); Craving Combo & Spray, Stop Smoking Combo & Spray (PF); Emancipation, Inocencia Coca (Peru).

Addictions (Withdrawal) *See also* **Caffeine problems**: Boab, Boronia, Bottlebrush, Dog Rose of the Wild Forces, Monga Waratah, Sundew, Waratah, Wedding Bush (Aus B); Morning Glory (AK); Harmonizing Addictive Patterning (DAl); Angelica, Nicotiana (FES); Pua-kenikeni (Haii); Anti-Addiction Remedy (Him A); Forsythia (Pac); Purple

Nightshade (Peg) Craving Combo & Spray (PF) Sober Up (Him E) Master Teacher (Peru).

Adrenals: Black-Eyed Susan, Macrocarpa (Aus B); Chamomile (FES); Rainbow Kelp (Pac); Shrimp Flower, White Carnation (PF); Still Mind (WD); Strength and Chi (Peru).

Ageing: Bottlebrush, Five Corners, Mulla Mulla, She Oak, (Aus B); Almond Tree (AK); Almond (Dv); Mallow (Dv, Hb); California Wild Rose, Hibiscus, St Johns Wort, Star Tulip (FES); Country Marilou (PF).

Allergies: Bush Iris, Dagger Hakea, Fringed Violet, Tall Mulla Mulla (Aus B); Sneezease (Aus L); Yarrow Environmental Solution (FES); Manifesting Thought Forms (DL); Grass Widow (Pac); Balance and Stability (Peru); Allergy Combo & Spray, Lantana (PF).

Altitude Sickness: Inocencia Coca, Purification (Peru).

Anaemia: Bluebell, Five Corners, Kapok Bush, Red Grevillea, Waratah (Aus B); I Like Being Me, Gossamer Steel (DL); Dianthus, Sunflower (PF).

Anorexia Nervosa: Boab, Dagger Hakea, Five Corners, Paw Paw, Waratah (Aus B); Black-Eyed Susan, Fairy Lantern, Manzanita, Pretty Face (FES); Sea Palm, Sea Urchin (Pac).

Appetite Disorders: Peach-flowered Tea-tree (Aus B); Urchin (Pac); Craving Combo, Mist (PF); Inocencia Coco (Peru).

Arthritis: Purifying Essence, Mountain Devil (Aus B); Azurite, Ohai-ali'i (Haii); Snowdrop (Pac); Managed Pain Combo & Spray, Zinnia (PF).

Assimilation (of Nutrients): Dog Rose, Paw Paw, Peach-flowered Tea-tree (Aus B); Centred Love, Earth Mother Nurtures (DL); Self-Heal (Dv, Hb); Blackthorn (GM); Star Jasmine (Hb); Sublime Chocolate (Peru); Magnolia, Autumn Damask (PF).

Asthma: Bluebell, Bush Iris, Dagger Hakea, Fringed Violet, Sturt Desert Pea, Tall Mulla Mulla (Aus B); Eucalyptus (FES); Light-Hearted (DL); Sand Dollar (Pac); Babies' Breath Allergy Combo & Spray (PF).

Bacterial and Viral Infections: Black-Eyed Susan, Dagger Hakea, Illawarra Flame Tree, Mountain Devil, Spinifex, Sturt Desert Pea (Aus B); Manifesting Thought Forms (DL); Wild Garlic (Dv); Brown Kelp (Pac); Colds & Flu Combo & Spray, Thyme, Onion (PF).

Back Problems: Amazon River, Noble Heart Cactus (AK); Menzies Banksia (Aus L); Centaury, Vine (B); Lilac (GM), Red Oak (GM); Brown Kelp (Pac); Indian Pipe (Peg); Cinnamon Basil (PF) Deep Breath (Peru); Chicago Peace, Maybelle Stearns (PVi).

Blood Disorders: Bluebell, Bottlebrush, Dog Rose, Little Flannel Flower, Pink Mulla Mulla (Aus B); Blackthorn (GM); Awapuhi-melemele/Yellow Ginger (Haii); Periwinkle, Plantain (Pac); Basil, Salad Burnet; Louis Philippe (PF).

Blood Pressure – High: Bluebell, Crowea, Five Corners, Hibbertia, Little Flannel Flower, Mountain Devil, Mulla Mulla (Aus B); Vine (B); Periwinkle (Pac); Rain Lily (PF).

Blood Pressure – Low: Five Corners, Kapok Bush, Southern Cross, Tall Mulla Mulla (Aus B).

Blood Sugar (Balance): Peach-flowered Tea-tree (Aus B); Iris (FES); Delphinium, Primrose, Weight Combo & Spray (PF).

Boils/Abscesses: Billy Goat Plum, Dagger Hakea, Mountain Devil, Sturt Desert Pea (Aus B).

Bones (Healing): Gymea Lily and Sturt Desert Rose (Aus B); Pink Seaweed, Salmonberry (Pac); Jasmine, Inner Strength Combo & Spray (PF).

Breathing Troubles: Sneezease (Aus L); Five Corners, Sundew, Sunshine Wattle, Tall Mulla Mulla, Tall Yellow Top (Aus B); Eucalyptus, Rhododendron (Dv); Yerba Santa (FES); Fairy Bell, Polyanthus, Sand Dollar (Pac); Allergy Combo & Mist (PF).

Bronchial Conditions: Dagger Hakea, Red Suva Frangipani, Spinifex, Sturt Desert Pea (Aus B); California Pitcher Plant (FES); Drum Stick (Him A); Deep Breath (Peru); Polyanthus, Sand Dollar (Pac); Allergy Combo & Spray, Babies' Breath, Spike Lavender (PF); Smiles and Giggles, Young Heart (WD).

Bulimia: Billy Goat Plum, Crowea, Five Corners, Grey Spider Flower, Paw Paw, Sturt Desert Rose (Aus B); Black-Eyed Susan, Manzanita (FES); Sea Palm, Urchin (Pac).

Burns: Mulla Mulla (Aus B); Aloe Vera (FES); Flora P Gel (Him A); Anemone, Regenerate Combo & Spray (PF).

Caffeine Problems (*See* **Addictions**): Coffee (Haii); Morning Glory (Him A, AK); Purple Nightshade (Peg); Sublime Chocolate (Peru); Cravings Combo & Spray (PF).

Cancer: Purifying Essence before and after chemotherapy, Emergency, Electro before and after radiation therapy (Aus B); My Song Calls Me Home (DL); Lilac, Harmony Blend Combo & Spray, Periwinkle, Recovery Combo & Spray (PF) (*see* section on proving essences work with reference to Petite Fleur); Diatoms (Pac); Super Immune (Peru).

Catarrh: Bush Iris, Dagger Hakea, Fringed Violet (Aus B); Yerba Santa (FES); Polyanthus (Pac); Eucalyptus, Jasmine (PF).

Cellulite: Billy Goat Plum, Bottlebrush, Bush Iris, Dagger Hakea, Purifying, Tall Mulla Mulla (Aus B); Pink Rose Soapwort (PF).

Chemical Sensitivities: Allergy Combo & Spray, Daylily, (PF).

Childbirth: Balsam Poplar, Green Bells of Ireland, Grove Sandwort, Hairy Butterworth, Shooting Star, Sticky Geranium (Ask); Billy Goat Plum,

Bottlebrush, Dog Rose, Crowea, Emergency Essence, Kapok Bush, Macrocarpa, Wild Potato Bush (Aus B); Star of Bethlehem (B); Angelica (BL); Pomegranate (FES); Pear (Ma); Barnacle, Candystick, Hookers Onion, Jelly Fish (Pac); Birthing Buddy (PE); Divine Goddess, Sweet New Beginnings (Peru); Maternity Combo & Spray (PF); Cauliflower (PVi); Sacred Void (SW); Wise Woman (WD).

Childbirth – Premature: Emergency Essence, Fringed Violet, Sturt Desert Rose, Sunshine Wattle, Waratah (Aus B); Poison Hemlock (Pac); Ranunculus (PF); Sacred Space (WD).

Chron's Disease: Crowea, Paw paw (Aus B); Snapdragon, Yarrow (PF).

Circulation Problems: Tall Mulla Mulla (Aus B); Queen Anne's Lace (FES); Blackthorn (GM); Awapuhi-melemele/Yellow Ginger (Haii); Fireweed (Pac); Morning Glory, Soapwort, Louis Philippe (PF); Stepping Ahead Now, Unveiling Self (DL).

Cleansing: Butterwort, Inside/Outside Cactus, Sage (AK); Green Essence, Purifying Essence (Aus B); Expansive Embodiment, Graceful Transformations, Letting Go (DL); Ragged Robin (F); Lungwort, Primrose, Yarrow in Seawater (Hb); Formula 19 Cleansing Aid (Him A); Apple, Blackberry (Ma); Moonsnail (Pac); Dutchman's Breeches, Sourgrass, Swamp Onion (Peg); Wise Woman (WD);

Colic: Black-Eyed Susan, Crowea, Paw Paw (Aus B); Chamomile (FES); Sage (PF).

Colon Spasm: Bottlebrush, Crowea, Grey Spider Flower (Aus B); Barnacle (Pac); Bamboo (PF).

Common Cold: Black-Eyed Susan, Bush Iris, Illawarra Flame Tree (Aus B); Yerba Santa (FES); Radiant Strength (DL); Formula 43 Sinus/Cold (Him A); Colds and Flu Combo & Spray (PF).

Constipation: Bottlebrush (Aus B); Letting Go, (DL); Barnacle, Pink Seaweed, Poison Hemlock (Pac); Poppy (PF).

Convalescence/Recuperation: Dynamis Essence (Aus B); Golden Waitsia (Aus L); Hornbeam (B); Radiant Strength (DL); Elder (F); Self-Heal (FES); Lotus, Peacock Flower (Him A); Magic Healer, Integration (Peru); Recovery Combo & Spray (PF); Happy Pet (WD).

Cramps (Muscle): Black-Eyed Susan, Bottlebrush, Crowea, Grey Spider Flower, Tall Mulla Mulla (Aus B); Impatiens (B); Anemone (Pac).

Cystitis: Bottlebrush, Dagger Hakea, Dog Rose, Mountain Devil, Mulla Mulla (Aus B); Surfgrass (Pac).

Cysts (on Ovaries)/Fibroids: Bush Iris, Mountain Devil, She Oak (Ovarian), Slender Rice Flower, Sturt Desert Rose (Aus B); Pomegranate (FES); Barnacle (Pac).

Detoxification: Arnica, Inner Cleansing Cactus; Inside/Outside Cactus (AK); Purification (Ask, Peru); Purifying Essence (Aus B); Clearing Energy Fields, Letting Go (DL); Apple, Laburnum (GM); Awapuhi-melemele/Yellow Ginger (Haii); Primrose (Hb); Morning Glory (Him A); Apple, Blackberry (Ma); Blue Lupin, Moonsnail, Sea Lettuce (Pac); Coralroot (spotted), Pine Drops, Sourgrass (Peg); Daylily, Soapwort, Clearing Mist (PF); Ramson's Wild Garlic (Sun).

Diarrhoea: Black-Eyed Susan, Bottlebrush, Kapok Bush, Paw Paw (Aus B); Acceptance, Heart of Nature (DL); Barnacle (Pac).

Digestive Problems: Crowea, Dog Rose, Peach-flowered Tea-tree (Aus B); Peppermint (BL); Chamomile, Sage (FES, AK); California Pitcher Plant (FES); Mango, Naio (Haii); Orange Honeysuckle (Pac); Red Spider Lily (Peg); Moss Rose (PF).

Dizziness/Faintness: Bush Fuchsia, Crowea (Aus B); Aspen, Clematis (B); Expansive Embodiment, Radiant Strength (DL); Sober Up (Him E); Mussel (Pac).

Drug Toxins (Discharging): Purifying Essence (Aus B); Arnica (AK); Morning Glory (FES); Apple (GM); Inocencia Coca (Peru).

Dyslexia: Bush Fuchsia (Aus B); Young Heart (DL); Blue Camas (Pac); White Petunia, Enhance Learning Combo & Spray (PF); Attention Formula (Peru).

Ear Problems: Bush Fuchsia, Bush Iris, Spinifex, (Aus B); Star Tulip (FES); Brown Kelp, Ox-eye Daisy, Viburnum (Pac); French Lavender (PF).

Eczema: Billy Goat Plum, Green Essence, Spinifex, (Aus B); Vanilla Leaf (Pac); Salvia (PF).

Elimination (*See also* **Digestive Problems**): Purifying Essence (Aus B); Star Jasmine (Hb); Narcissus, Polyanthus (Pac).

Endocrine System: Dynamis Essence (Aus B)
   Adrenals: Macrocarpa (Aus B)
   Hypothalamus: Bush Fuchsia (Aus B)
   Ovaries: She Oak (Aus B)
   Pancreas: Peach-flowered Tea-tree (Aus B)
   Pineal: Bush Iris (Aus B)
   Pituitary: Yellow Cowslip Orchid (Aus B)
   Thymus: Illawarra Flame Tree (Aus B)
   Thyroid: Old Man Banksia (Aus B)
   Testes: Flannel Flower (Aus B); Lotus (AK, FES), Cherokee Rose (PF)

Energy: Life Force Cactus (AK); Dynamis Essence, Macrocarpa, Old Man Banksia (Aus B); Essences of Energy, Leafless Orchid, (Aus L); Gossamer Steel, Manifesting Thought Forms, Lotus Petals of the Heart (DL); Life Force (F); California Pitcher Plant (FES); Bay (GM); Flowering Currant, Nasturtium (Hb); Longevity, Vital Spark (Him E); Cherry, Corn (Ma); Bluebell, Goatsbeard (Pac); Cape Honeysuckle (Peg); Tonic – Nasturtium (PVi); Energy Combo & Spray (PF).

Environmental Cleansing: Aura Cleansing Cactus, Delph, Formation Cactus, Life Force Cactus, Ti (AK); Grass of Parnassus, Sweetgrass, Yarrow (Ask); Space Clearing Mist (Aus B); Reading Energy Fields, Clearing Energy Fields (DL); Ti, Kamani, (Haii); Madame Louise Levique (PF), Sacred Space, Protective Shield, On Angels' Wings (WD)

Epstein Barr Virus (ME): K9 (AK); Banksia Robur, Macrocarpa, Peach-flowered Tea-tree, Sturt Desert Pea (Aus B); Diatoms, Snowberry (Pac); Fatigue Combo & Spray, Marie Pavie (PF).

Exhaustion: K9, Aloe Vera (AK); Macrocarpa (Aus B); Elm, Vervain (B); Staghorn Cholla Cactus, Whitehorn, Woven Spine Pineapple (DAD); Radiant Strength, Reading Energy Fields, (DL); Sterlitzia/Bird of Paradise (Haii); Artichoke, Ground Ivy (HUB); Corn (Ma); Fatigue (PF).

Eye Problems *See also* **Sight (Enhancing)**: Alder (Ask); Bush Fuchsia, Red Suva Frangipani, Sunshine Wattle, Waratah (Aus B); Queen Anne's Lace, Star Tulip (FES); Cotton (Haii); Nasturtium, Speedwell (Hb); Anemone, Ox-eye Daisy (Pac).

Fatigue: Dynamis Essence (Aus B); Radiant Strength, Reading Energy Fields, (DL); Life Force (F); California Wild Rose, Indian Paintbrush, Lavender, Yerba Santa (FES); Corn (Ma); Diatoms, Snowberry, Bluebell (Pac); Fatigue Combo & Spray (PF)

Fertility (Problems): She Oak, Woman (Aus B); Pomegranate (FES); She Oak/ Ironwood (Haii); Blackberry, Lady's/ Mantle, Rose-red (Hb); Barnacle (Pac) Borage (BL).

Fevers *See also* **Common Cold**: Mulla Mulla (Aus B); Onion (PF)

Fibromyalgia: Pink, Self Image Combo & Spray, (PF)

Fluid Retention: Bottlebrush, Bush Iris, Dog Rose, She Oak (Aus B); California

Pitcher Plant (FES); Poison Hemlock (Pac); Bachelor's Button, Japanese Magnolia, Yarrow (PF); Wild Feminine (Peru).

Frigidity: Canary Island Bellflower, Courgette (AK); Sexuality Essence, Wisteria (Aus B); Lehur (Haii); Cannon Ball Tree, Ixora (Him A), Barnacle (Pac); Marigold (PF).

Gall Stones: Dagger Hakea, Mountain Devil (Aus B); Mussel (Pac); Garden Mum (PF).

Glandular Fever *See also* **Epstein-Barr Virus**: K9 (AK); Formula 38 (Him A).

Hair Loss/Baldness Red Carnation (PF).

Hay Fever: K9 (AK); Black-Eyed Susan, Bush Iris, Dagger Hakea, Fringed Violet, Hibbertia (Aus B); Sneezease (Aus L); Allergy Combo & Spray (PF).

Headaches: Black-Eyed Susan, Emergency Essence (Aus B); Aspen, Vervain, White Chestnut (B); My Own Pure Light (DL); Awapuhi-melemele/ Yellow Ginger (Haii); Meadowsweet (Hb); Clarity (Him E); Orange (Ma); Blue Lupin, Mussel, Plantain (Pac); Abate Anger Combo & Spray, Anise Hyssop, Curry, Fortune's Double Yellow, Japanese Magnolia (PF).

Healing (Self): Coordination Orchid, Wise Woman (AK); Self-Heal (AK, Dv, FES, Hb); Bog Rosemary (Ask); Spinifex (Aus B); Star of Bethlehem (B); Aloe (DAI); Manifesting Thought Forms, New Perceptions (DL); Star Tulip (FES); Gean/Wild Cherry, Norway Maple (GM); Healing (Him E); Self Healing (LH); Cellular Memory, Fairy Bell (Pac); Creeping Thistle, Milkmaid (Peg); Master Teacher, Magic Healer (Peru); African Violet, Bouquet of Harmony Combo & Spray, Madame Alfred Carriere, Recovery Combo & Spray (PF); Birch Forest, On Angels' Wings (WD).

Heart Irregularity: Emergencies (Aus B); Foxglove (PF).

Heart Problems: Foxglove (Ask, Hb); Bluebell, Flannel Flower, Waratah (Aus B); Borage, Rosemary (Hb); Jelly Fish (Pac); Radiant Strength (DL); Rose of Sharon (PF) Young Heart (WD).

Herpes: Spinifex (Aus B); Marigold, Reduce Stress Combo & Spray (PF).

Hormone Imbalance – Female: She Oak, Woman (Aus B); Evening Primrose, Mala Mujer (DAl); Pomegranate (FES); Female Balance (LH); Barnacle (Pac); Cherokee Rose, Female Balance Combo & Spray, Marigold (PF); Strength & Chi (Peru).

Hormone Imbalance – Male: Flannel Flower (Aus B); Marigold (PF).

Hyperactivity: Cognis Essence (Aus B); Chamomile (Dv); Nasturtium (FES); Hibiscus (FO); Banana Poka (Passion flower) (Haii); Lettuce (Ma); Stock (PF).

Hypertension (Stress related): Periwinkle, Surfgrass (Pac); Abate Anger Combo & Spray, Fortune's Double Yellow (PF).

Immune System (Boosting): K9 (AK); Wild Garlic (AK, Dv); Illawarra Flame Tree, Macrocarpa (Aus B); My Own Pure Light (DL); Gorse, Watercress (F); Echinacea, Garlic, Lavender, Love Lies Bleeding, Morning Glory (FES); Ivy, Yew (GM); Mountain Apple/Ohi a-ai (Haii); Hawthorn, Pansy (Hb); Formula 38 Immunity Booster (Him A); Fleabane: (HUB); Optimal Immunity (Pac); Super Immune Combo & Spray (Peru); Gaillardia, Echinacea, Rose Campion, Silverlace, Snapdragon (PF); Celery (PVi); Be Resistant (Sun); Smiles and Giggles (WD).

Impotence: Banana, Swiss Cheese Plant (AK); Boronia, Crowea, Five Corners, Flannel Flower (Aus B); Earth Mother Nurtures (DL); Larch (B); Queen of the Night (DAl); Ixora (Him A,); Grape (Ma); Marigold (PF).

Incontinence: Bottlebrush, Crowea, Dog Rose, Dog Rose of the Wild Forces (Aus B); Manifesting Light Forms (DL); St John's

Wort (FES); Surfgrass (Pac); Tiger's Jaw Cactus (PF).

Indigestion (Dyspepsia): Sage (Ak); Crowea, Dog Rose, Paw Paw, Peach-flowered Tea-tree (Aus B); Chamomile (FES, PF Ak); Sea Palm (Pac); Ligustrum (PF).

Inflammations: Surfgrass (Pac); Manage Pain Combo & Spray, Red Carnation, Yarrow (PF).

Influenza: Bush Iris, Flannel Flower, Illawarra Flame Tree, Jacaranda, Paw Paw (Aus B); Super Immunity (Pac); Colds and Flu Combo & Spray, Lily (PF).

Injuries: Cotton Grass (Ask); Emergency Essence (Aus B); Crisis Relief Essences (Aus L); Love Lies Bleeding (FES); Earth Mother Nurtures (DL); Pear (Ma).

Insomnia: Valerian (AK, Dv,); Boronia, Calm and Clear Essence (Aus B); Hops Bush (Aus L); White Chestnut (B); Heart of Nature, Meditative Mind (DL); Chamomile (Dv, FES); Sweet Dreams (F); Black-Eyed Susan, Dill, Lavender, Mugwort, St John's Wort (FES); Awapuhi-melemele/Yellow Ginger (Haii); Formula 17 Sleep (Him A); Sleep Well (LH); Lettuce (Ma); Full Moonlight (Peru); Deep Sleep Combo & Spray (PF); Alaska Birch Forest, Still Mind (WD).

Itching: Black-Eyed Susan, Bluebell, Dagger Hakea, Fringed Violet, Red Grevillea, Rough Bluebell (Aus B); Floral Pain Gel (Him A); Vanilla Leaf (Pac).

Jet Lag: Travel Essence (Aus B); Jetstream (F); Travel (Hb); Travel Solution (Peru); Fatigue Combo & Spray (PF); Sacred Space (WD).

Kidney Problems: Dog Rose, Grey Spider Flower (Aus B); My Heart Knows, Higher Levels (DL); Surfgrass, Coral, Fuchsia (Pac); Red Spider Lily (Peg); Begonia, Pansy (PF).

Laryngitis: Bush Fuchsia, Flannel Flower, Mountain Devil, Red Helmet Orchid (Aus B); Purpose Flows (DL); Snapdragon (Hb); Sand Dollar (Pac).

Liver Disorders: Dagger Hakea, Mountain Devil, Slender Rice Flower, Sunshine Wattle (Aus B); Awapuhi-melemele/Yellow Ginger (Haii); Speedwell (Hb); Forsythia, Plantain (Pac); Ligustrum (PF).

Long-Term Illness: Bottlebrush, Kapok Bush, Spinifex, Waratah, Wild Potato Bush (Aus B); Acceptance, Clearing Blockages, Higher Levels, Manifesting Thought Forms, Stepping Ahead Now (DL); Peacock Flower (Him A); Coralroot (spotted) (Peg); Alaskan Birch Forest, Mother's Arms, On Angels' Wings, Smiles and Giggles, Wise Woman, Young Heart (WD).

Lung Imbalance: Red Suva Frangipani, Sturt Desert Pea, Sundew, Tall Mulla Mulla, (Aus B); Eucalyptus, Yerba Santa (FES); Flowering Currant (Hb); Arbutus, Fairy Bell, (Pac) Spike Lavender (PF).

Menopause: She Oak. Woman Essence (Aus B); Heart Wings (DL); Alpine Lily, Borage, Easter Lily, Fuchsia, Hibiscus, Mariposa Lily, Pomegranate, Rosemary, Tiger Lily (FES); Women's Balance (LH); Orange Honeysuckle (Pac); Female Balance Combo & Spray (PF) Smooth Hawksbeard (BL) Divine Goddess, Strength & Chi (Peru) Formula 23 Menopause (Him A) Cardinal Flower (DAI).

Menstruation – Absence of: She Oak, Woman Essence (Aus B); Evening Primrose, Fairy Lantern, Mugwort, Pomegranate (FES); Female Balance Combo & Spray (PF).

Menstruation – Irregular: Woman Essence (Aus B); Evening Primrose, Fairy Lantern, Mugwort, Pomegranate (FES); Female Balance Combo & Spray (PF); Wise Woman (WD).

Menstruation – Pains: She Oak, Woman Essence (Aus B); Black Cohosh, Love Lies Bleeding, Pomegranate (FES); Sublime Chocolate (Peru); Manage Pain Combo & Spray (PF).

Meridian Balance: Northern Lady's Slipper (Ask); Crowea (Aus B); Clearing Blockages (DL); Silver Maple (GM).

Metabolism (Rebalancing): Black-Eyed Susan, Crowea, Mulla Mulla, Old Man Banksia (Aus B); Nasturtium, Peppermint, Rosemary, Snapdragon (FES); Sublime Chocolate (Peru); Cherokee Rose (PF).

Miasms: Boab (Aus B); Lotus Essence (AK, Dv, FES, Him A); Clearing Energy Fields (DL).

Heavy Metals: Purification (Ask); Purifying, Wild Potato Bush (Aus B); Letting Go (DL); Awapuhi-melemele/ Yellow Ginger (Haii); Bloodroot, Daffodil (Peg); Daylily (PF).

Lymphatic System: Bush Iris, Purifying Essences (Aus B); Clearing Energy Fields (DL); Awapuhi-melemele/ Yellow Ginger (Haii); Red Carnation (PF).

Petrochemical: Purifying Essence (Aus B); Garlic (FES); Almond (Peg); Daylily (PF).

Psora: Bluebell, Dagger Hakea, Green Essence, Mountain Devil, Rough Bluebell, Spinifex (Aus B); Eucalyptus, Garlic (FES); Camphor (Peg).

Radiation & Electromagnetic: Electro Essence (Aus B); Radiant Strength, Reading Energy Fields, Clearing Energy Fields (DL); Garlic (FES); Bloodroot (Peg); Faith & Courage (Peru); Recovery Combo & Spray (PF); Protective Shield, Sacred Space (WD).

Syphilitic: Boab, She Oak, Sturt Desert Rose (Aus B); California Poppy, Chaparral, Iris-Blue Flag (FES); Bells of Ireland, Celandine, Four-leaf Clover (Peg).

Syscosis: Black-Eyed Susan, Dagger Hakea, Illawarra Flame Tree, Mountain Devil, Spinifex, Sturt Desert Pea (Aus B); Dandelion, Lilac (FES).

Thyroid: Old Man Banksia (Aus B); Chiton (Pac).

Tuberculosis: Sturt Desert Pea, Sunshine Wattle, Waratah (Aus B); Blackberry, Eucalyptus (FES); Cotton, Hops, Live Forever, Red Clover (Peg).

Migraine: Emergency (Aus B); Awapuhi-melemele/ Yellow Ginger (Haii); Orange (Ma); Plantain (Pac); Narcissus, Curry (PF).

Miscarriage/Termination: Candystick, Sea Lettuce (Pac).

Morning Lethargy: Banksia Robur, Dynamis Essence (Aus B); Hornbeam (B); Centred Love, Walking Out of Patterns, Manifesting Thought Forms, Meditative Mind (DL); Morning Glory (FES, Him E); Rosemary, Tansy (FES); Energy Combo & Spray (PF); Young Heart, Smiles and Giggles (WD).

Mosquito Bites: Green Essence, Mountain Devil, Mulla Mulla, Paw Paw, Spinifex (Aus B); Garlic (FES).

Mucous Colitis: Bottlebrush, Kapok Bush, Peach-flowered Tea-tree, Spinifex (Aus B); I Like Being Me (DL) Snapdragon (FES).

Multiple Sclerosis: Bluebell, Gymea Lily, Hibbertia, Isopogon, Rough Bluebell, Southern Cross, Spinifex (Aus B); Dandelion; Snowdrop (Pac).

Muscular Disorders: Crowea (Aus B); Dandelion (AK, Ask, Dv, FES, Hb); Vervain (B); Anemone, Salmonberry (Pac); Champney's Pink Cluster, Manage Pain Combo & Spray, Pink Geranium (PF).

Nasal Congestion: Bush Iris, Dagger Hakea, Fringed Violet, Tall Mulla Mulla (Aus B) California Pitcher Plant, Eucalyptus, Jasmine, Yerba Santa (FES); Colds & Flu Combo & Spray, Purple Garden Sage (PF).

Nausea: Crowea, Dagger Hakea, Dog Rose, Paw Paw (Aus B); Chamomile (FES); Corn (Ma); Harmony Blend Combo & Spray (PF); Windflower (Pac).

Neck and Back Stiffness/Whip Lash: Noble Heart Cactus (AK); Bauhinia, Black-Eyed Susan, Bluebell, Gymea Lily, Southern Cross, Sunshine Wattle, Tall Yellow Top (Aus B); Dandelion (Dv, FES); Iris (FES); Pau Pilo (Haii); Meadowsweet (Hb); Chiton, Mussel (Pac); Manage Pain Combo & Spray (PF).

Nervous Exhaustion: Angelsword, Black-Eyed Susan, Dog Rose of the Wild Forces, Fringed Violet, Jacaranda, Old Man Banksia, Paw Paw (Aus B); Buffalo Gourd, Fairy Duster (DAl); New Perceptions, Clearing Energy Fields (DL); Lady's Slipper (FES); Alder (GM); Artichoke (HUB); Fatigue Combo & Spray (PF).

Nervousness: Hibiscus (FO); Black-Eyed Susan, Dog Rose, Jacaranda (Aus B); Aspen (B); Whitehorn (DAl); Idiot Glee (DL); Chamomile (Dv, FES); Wild Garlic (Dv); Comfrey (FES; Hau (Haii); Almond, Banana, Lettuce, Pear (Ma); Alaskan Birch Forest, Still Mind, Mother's Arms, On Angels' Wings, (WD).

Nervous System (Tonic): Bush Fuchsia, Crowea (Aus B); Fairy Duster (DAl); Angelica Comfrey (Dv, FES); Morning Glory (Dv, FES, Him E); Arnica (FES); Hibiscus (FO); Pear (GM); Hau (Haii); Viburnum (Pac); Madame Alfred Carriere (PF); Blaze Improve, Oregold (PVi).

Neuritis: Country Marilou (PF).

Obesity: Bluebell, Bush Iris, Crowea, Dog Rose, Five Corners, Fringed Violet, Old Man Banksia, Wild Potato Bush (Aus B); I Like Being Me, Letting Go (DL); Evening Primrose, Golden Rod, Hound's Tongue, Nicotiana, Pink Monkeyflower, Tansy (FES); Poison Hemlock (Pac); Craving Combo & Spray, Pink Rose, Gruss an Aachen, Weight Combo & Spray (PF); Wise Woman, Still Mind, Sacred Space, Protective Shield (WD).

Pain (Relief): Cotton Grass (Ask); Bottlebrush + Emergency Essence, Dog Rose of the Wild Forces (Aus B); Illyarrie, Menzies Banksia (Aus L); Heart of Nature, Clearing Energy Fields (DL); Love Lies Bleeding (FES); Gean/Wild Cherry (GM); Foxglove (Hb); Floral P Gel, Day-blooming Jessamine (Him A); First Aid + Gel (F); Pear (Ma); Anemone (Pac); Bougainvillea, Manage Pain (PF); Happy Pet, Still Mind, Mother's Arms (WD).

Paralysis: Bush Fuchsia, Crowea, Grey Spider Flower, Wild Potato Bush (Aus B); Radiant Strength, Earth Mother Nurtures (DL); Scottish Primrose (F); Poison Hemlock, Snowdrop (Pac).

Parasites: Life Force Cactus (AK); Green Essence, Purifying Essence (Aus B); Garlic (FES); Fleabane (HUB); Amaryllis (PF).

Pelvic Inflammatory Disease (PID): Billy Goat Plum, Fringed Violet, Spinifex, Wisteria (Aus B); Pomegranate (FES); Snowdrop (Hb).

Physical Strength/Growth: Dynamis Essence (Aus B); Milky Nipple Cactus (DAl; Higher Levels, My Own Pure Light, Unveiling Self (DL) Tomato (Ma); Inner Strength Combo & Spray (PF) Zucchini (PVi); Smiles and Giggles, Wise Woman, Young Heart, (WD).

Postnatal: Woman (Aus B); Nursing Mother, Sooth Baby Blues (PE).

Pregnancy & Problems (eg Morning Sickness): Courgette (AK); Pregnancy Support (Ask); Bottlebrush, Dagger Hakea, Dog Rose, She Oak (Aus B); Earth Mother Nurtures, Heart of Nature (DL); Watermelon (Dv, FES); Forget-me-not, Zucchini (Dv); Chamomile, California Wild Rose, Calla Lily, Evening Primrose, Mugwort, Pomegranate (FES); Rosebud-white (Hb); Corn, Pear (Ma); Pregnancy Partner (Peg); Maternity Combo & Spray (PF); Divine Child (Peru).

Premenstrual Syndrome: Woman Essence (Aus B); Immortal, Mala Mujer, Tar Bush (DAl); Pomegranate (FES); Pear, Grape (Ma); Easter Lily (Pac); Female Balance Combo & Spray (PF); Wise Woman (WD).

Protection From – Pollution: Guardian (Ask); Angelsword, Fringed Violet, Space

Clearing (Aus B); Sneezease (Aus L); Radiant Strength, Earth Mother Nurtures, Letting Go (DL); White Yarrow (Dv); Clearing Spray, Reduce Stress Combo & Spray, Tansy (PF); Alaskan Birch Forest, Protective Shield, Sacred Space (WD).

Protection From – Radiation: White Yarrow (AK, Dv); T1 (AK); Guardian (Ask); Electro Essence (Aus B); Radiant Strength, Earth Mother Nurtures, Letting Go (DL); Environmental Solution (FES); Yarrow in seawater (Hb); Regenerate Combo & Spray (PF); Alaskan Birch Forest, Protective Shield, Sacred Space (WD).

Psoriasis: Aloe Vera (AK, FES); Billy Goat Plum, Green Essence, Spinifex, (Aus B); Vanilla Leaf (Pac); Savia (PF).

Psychosomatic Illness: Peach-flowered Tea-tree (Aus B); Strawberry Cactus (DAl); Reading Energy Fields, Walking Out of Patterns, Earth Mother Nurtures, Manifesting Thought Forms (DL); Canyon Dudleya, Fuchsia, Purple Monkeyflower, Yerba Santa (FES); Apple(MA); Still Mind (WD).

Puberty: Adol Essence, Bottlebrush (Aus B); Walnut (B); Fairy Lantern, Sagebrush, Saguaro, Sticky Monkeyflower (FES); Mallow, Rosebud-red (Hb); Almond (Ma); Orange Honeysuckle (Pac).

Radiation Problems and the Effects of Cancer Treatments: Radiation Cactus, T1 (AK); Electro Essence, Mulla Mulla (Aus B); Yarrow Special Formulae (FES); Recovery Combo & Spray (PF).

Regeneration: Champney's Pink Cluster, Country Marilou, Regeneration Combo & Spray, (PF).

Reproductive Problems – Female: She Oak, Woman Essence (Aus B); Alpine Lily, Pomegranate (FES); Candysticks, Silver Birch (Pac); Red Spider Lily (Peg); Female Balance Combo (PF); Wise Woman (WD).

Reproductive Problems – Male: Flannel Flower (Aus B); Pomegranate (FES); Red Spider Lily (Peg).

Respiratory System: Five Corners, Sundew, Sunshine Wattle, Tall Mulla Mulla, Tall Yellow Top (Aus B); Acceptance, Lotus Petals of the Heart (DL); Eucalyptus (FES); Grape Hyacinth (Pac); Babies' Breath (PF).

S.A.D (Seasonal Affective Disorder): Lighten up (Ask); Seasonal Affections (F); Diatoms, Grape Hyacinth, Periwinkle, Red Huckleberry, Snowberry (Pac).

Scar Tissue: Little Flannel Flower (Aus B); Aloe Vera (FES); Anemone, Regenerate Combo & Spray (PF).

Sexual Diseases (Chlamydia, Herpes): K9 (AK); Billy Goat Plum, Spinifex (Aus B); Pomegranate (FES).

Shingles: Manage Pain Combo & Spray (PF).

Shock: Arnica (AK, FES); Cotton Grass, Fireweed, Soul Support (Ask); Emergency Essence, Fringed Violet (Aus B); Rescue Remedy (B); Gossamer Steel, My Song Calls Me Home (DL); First Aid (F); Self-Heal (FES); Privet (GM); 'Ulua (Haii); First Aid Remedy (Him A); Grape Hyacinth (Pac); White Hyacinth (PF); Mother's Arms (WD).

Sight (Enhancing): Eyebright (AK); Red Suva Frangipani, Waratah, Sunshine Wattle (Aus B); Dancing Light Spirit (DL); Queen Anne's Lace (FES); Cotton (Haii); Anemone, Ox-eye Daisy (Pac).

Sinusitis: Bush Iris, Dagger Hakea, Fringed Violet (Aus B); Sneezease (Aus L); Eucalyptus (FES); Formula 43 Sinus/Cold (Him A); Allergy Combo & Spray (PF).

Skin Lesions: Mulla Mulla, Spinifex (Aus B); Defining Edges (DL); Anemone, Regenerate Combo & Spray (PF); Protective Shield (WD).

Skin Problems: Inside/Outside Cactus (AK); Billy Goat Plum, Spinifex (Aus B); Office Flower (Him A); Gilia Scarlet, Red Spider Lily (Peg); Archduke Charles, Lily, Salvia, (PF).

Smoking (Effects of): Morning Glory (AK, FES, Him E); Purifying Essence (Aus B); Nicotiana (FES); Drum Stick (Him A); Stop Smoking Combo & Spray (PF).

Speech Problems: Bush Fuchsia, Flannel Flower, Red Grevillea (Aus B); Mimulus (B); I Like Being Me (DL); Petunia, Snapdragon (Hb); Parrot Tree (Him A); Anise Hyssop, White Petunia (PF).

Spleen: Boronia, Dog Rose, Pink Mulla Mulla (Aus B); Goatsbeard (Pac).

Spinal & Structural Problems: Noble Heart Cactus, Valerian (AK); Black-Eyed Susan, Gymea Lily, Tall Yellow Top (Aus B); Lilac (Dv); Corn (FES); Laburnum (GM); Ma'o, Ohai-ali'i (Haii); Sunflower (Hb); Indian Pipe, Salmonberry (Peg); Borage, Cinnamon Basil, Inner Strength Combo & Spray, Mushroom, Orchid (PF).

Sunburn: Solaris Combo, Mulla Mulla, (Aus B).

Swelling: Bush Iris, Dog Rose, Old Man Banksia, She Oak (Aus B); Bachelor's Button, Red Carnation (PF).

Teeth-Grinding: Black-Eyed Susan, Dagger Hakea, Red Grevillea (Aus B); Morning Glory (FES); Hibiscus (FO).

Teething (Babies): Emergency Essence (Aus B); Pink Seaweed (Pac).

Tension: Dandelion (AK, Dv, FES, Hb); Emergency Essence (Aus B); Purple Flag Flower, Rose Cone Flower (Aus L); Impatiens, Vervain, Water Violet (B); Cherry Plum (B, GM); Comfrey, Forget-Me-Not, Spruce (Dv); First Aid (F); Chamomile (FES, Hb); Lavender (FES); Fig, Pear (Ma); Abate Anger Combo & Spray (PF); Alaskan Birch Forest, Smiles and Giggles (WD).

Throat (Sore): Bush Fuchsia, Bush Iris, Flannel Flower, Hakea, Illawarra Flame Tree, Mountain Devil, Old Man Banksia, Spinifex, Sturt Desert Pea (Aus B); Blue Camas, Sand Dollar (Pac); Colds & Flu Combo & Spray (PF).

Tiredness: Dynamis Essence (Aus B); Leafless Orchid (Aus L); Aspen, Hornbeam, Pine (B); Tansy (FES); Almond, Corn (Ma); Fatigue Combo (PF).

Travel Sickness: Travel Ease (Ask); Travel Essence (Aus B); Travelease (Aus L); Jetstream (F); Travel (Hb); Formula 14 Travel Aid (Him A); Corn (Ma).

Tonsillitis: Bush Fuchsia, Bush Iris, Flannel Flower (Aus B); Sand Dollar (Pac).

Toxicity/Toxaemia: Purification (Ask); Bottlebrush, Purifying Essence (Aus B); Reading Energy Fields (DL); Ragged Robin (F); Chaparral (FES); Coffee (Haii); Apple, Blackberry (Ma); Blue Lupin (Pac); Coralroot (Spotted) (Peg); Crossandra, Pansy, Daylily (PF); Alaskan Birch Forest (WD).

Ulcers Peppermint (Pac).

Vitality/Revitalization: Alpine Mint Bush, Crowea, Dynamis Essence, Macrocarpa, Wild Bush Potato (Aus B); Essences of Energy, Leafless Orchid, Pink Fountain Triggerplant (Aus L); Smooth Hawksbeard (BL); Dancing Light Spirit (DL); Almond, Morning Glory (Dv); Nasturtium (Dv, Hb, FES); Gorse, Sycamore (F); Tansy (FES); Blackberry (Hb); Endurance (Him A); Apple (Ma); Super Vitality (Pac); Energy Combo & Spray (PF); Orange Hawkweed (Sun); Young Heart, Happy Pet (WD).

Viral Infections: K9 (AK); Black-Eyed Susan (Aus B); Wild Garlic (Dv, FES); Pansy (Hb); Colds & Flu Combo & Spray, Echinacea, Purple Garden Sage, Onion, Thyme (PF).

Warts: Billy Goat Plum, Five Corners, Green Essence (Aus B); Salvia, Wild Wood Violets (PF).

Weight Control: Boronia, Bottlebrush, Dog Rose, Monga Waratah, Peach-flowered Tea-tree, Purifying Combo (Aus B); Expansive Embodiment, Manifesting Thought Forms (DL); Hound's Tongue, Yerba Santa (FES); Mango, Naio, (Haii); Tomato (Ma); Chickweed, Chiton,

Poison Hemlock, Urchin (Pac); Dayflower (Peg); Inocencia Coca, Sublime Chocolate (Peru); Craving Combo & Spray, Gruss an Aachen, Weight Combo & Spray (PF).

Psychological

Abandonment: Yellow Top, Illawarra Flame Tree (Aus B); Mesquite, Milky Nipple Cactus (DAl); Acceptance, Gossamer Steel, Heart to Heart (DL); Tall Grape, Strawberry (Ma); Arbutus, Nootka Rose, Sea Palm (Pac); Mother's Arms, On Angels' Wings, Smiles and Giggles (WD).

Abundance: Abund (Aus B); Ground Ivy (BL); Prosperity, Sea Rocket (F); At the Heart of Being, Infinite Abundance (LH); Double Daffodil (Sun).

Abuse (Emotional): White Fireweed (Ask); Confid Essence, Emergency Essence, (Aus B); Mountain Mahogany (DAl); Earth Mother Nurtures (DL); Martagon Lily, Scarlet Monkeyflower (Dv); Black Cohosh, Black-Eyed Susan, Bleeding Heart, Echinacea, Morning Glory, Oregon Grape, Purple Monkeyflower, Snapdragon, Tiger Lily (FES); Elder, Italian Alder (GM); Elder (Hb); Orange, Strawberry (Ma); Urchin (Pac); Happy Pet, Mother's Arms, Sacred Space, On Angels' Wings, Protective Shield (WD).

Abuse (Self): Billy Goat Plum, Five Corners (Aus B); Bisbee Beehive Cactus, Kleins Pencil Cholla Cacuts (DAl); Clearing Energy Fields, I Like Being Me, Lotus Petals of the Heart, Stepping Ahead Now (DL); Dogwood (FES); Fig (Ma); Forsythia, Nootka Rose (Pac).

Accident, Prone to: Jacaranda, Kangaroo Paw, Red Lily (Aus B); Impatiens (B); Ulua (Haii); Pill Bearing Spurge (Him A,) Avocado (Ma); Still Mind (WD).

Adaptability: Angel of Protection Orchid (AK); Bauhinia, Freshwater Mangrove, Slender Rice Flower, Waratah (Aus B); Prickly Pear Cactus (DAl); Clearing Energy Fields, Graceful Transformations, Higher Levels, Reading Energy Fields, Manifesting

Thought Forms (DL); Aloe Vera, Golden Yarrow (FES); Healer (Him E); Fig (Ma); Douglas Aster, Coral, Diatom (Pac).

ADD/ADHD: Cognis (Aus B); Blue Camus (Pac); Attention Formula (Peru).

Addiction Withdrawal Symptoms: Morning Glory (AK); Boab, Boronia, Bottlebrush, Dog Rose of the Wild Forces, Monga Waratah, Sundew, Waratah, Wedding Bush (Aus B); Letting Go (DL); Angelica, Sagebrush (FES); Nirjara (Him E); Tomato (Ma); Nootka Rose, Urchin (Pac); Purple Nightshade, Rosa Damascena Bifera (Peg).

Addictive Behaviour: Boab, Boronia, Bottlebrush, Monga Waratah, Dog Rose of the Wild Forces, Sundew, Waratah, Wedding Bush (Aus B); Blue China Orchid (Aus L); Rose Damacea, Hedgehog Cactus, Tarbrush (DAl); Gossamer Steel, Unveiling Self, (DL); Morning Glory (Dv, FES); Nicotiana, Scarlet Monkeyflower (FES); Tulip Tree (GM); Morning Glory, Pua kenikeni (Haii); Drum Stick, Opium Poppy (Him A); Almond, Tomato (Ma); Forsythia, Urchin (Pac); Monkeyflower Bush, Rosa Damascena Bifera (Peg); Emancipation (Peru); Craving Combo & Spray, Stop Smoking Combo & Spray (PF); Still Mind, Wise Woman (WD).

Adolescence: Adol (Aus B); Banana Poka/Passion Flower, Kukui (Haii).

Aggression: Aggression Orchid (AK); Mountain Devil, Rough Bluebell (Aus B); Buffalo Gourd,(DAl); Centred Love, Higher Levels (DL); Grape (Ma).

Alcoholism: Morning Glory (AK); Boab, Boronia, Bottlebrush, Dog Rose of the Wild Forces, Monga Waratah, Sundew, Waratah, Wedding Bush (Aus B); Clearing Energy Fields, Radiant Strength (DL); Chrysanthemum, Mountain Pennyroyal (FES); Kou (Haii); Sober Up (Him E); Nootka Rose, Urchin (Pac); Craving Combo & Spray (PF).

Anger: Blue Elf Viola (Ask); Mountain Devil (Aus B); Fuchsia Grevillea, Orange Spiked Peaflower (Aus L); Holly (B);

Compass Barrel Cactus, Foothills Paloverde, Star Primrose (DAl); Gossamer Steel (DL); Fuchsia, Scarlet Monkeyflower (Dv, FES); Willowherb (F); Snapdragon (FES); Kukui, Impatiens (Haii); Nettle (Hb); Wellbeing (Him E); Almond, Apple, Lettuce (Ma); Mussel (Pac); Orange Flame Flower Cactus (Peg); Abate Anger Combo & Spray (PF); Smiles and Giggles (WD).

Anorexia Nervosa: Boab, Five Corners, Monga Waratah, Peach-flowered Tea-tree, Dagger Hakea, Waratah (Aus B); Manifesting Thought Forms, Radiant Strength (DL); Black-Eyed Susan, Manzanita (FES).

Anxiety : Emergency Essence, Calm & Clear Combo (Aus B); Purple Flag Flower, Woolly Smoke-Bush (Aus L); Red Chestnut (B); Hoptree, Strawberry Cactus (DAl); Clearing Energy Fields (DL); Wild Garlic (Dv); Scottish Primrose (F); Filagree (FES); Alder (GM); Kukui, Plemomele Fragrans (Haii); Chamomile (Hb); Banana, Tomato (Ma); Periwinkle (Pac); Mother's Arms, On Angels' Wings, Smiles and Giggles, Still Mind, (WD).

Apathy: Dynamis Essence, Kapok Bush, (Aus B); My Own Pure Light, (DL); Gorse (F); Blackberry, California Wild Rose, Tansy (FES); Tulip (Him A); Orange (Ma).

Apprehension: Water Violet (Aus L); Crowea, Dog Rose, Tall Mulla Mulla (Aus B); Aspen (B); Cotton/Ma'o (Haii); Tomato (Ma); Mother's Arms, Wise Woman (WD).

Argumentativeness: Bush Gardenia, Dagger Hakea, Isopogon, Rough Bluebell (Aus B); Expansive Embodiment, Acceptance (DL); Banana (Ma); Still Mind,(WD).

Arrogance: Gymea Lily, Rough Bluebell, Slender Rice Flower (Aus B); Larkspur (FES).

Attachment: Cotton Grass, River Beauty, Sweetgale (Ask); Bottlebrush, Monga Waratah (Aus B); Letting Go (DL); Banana (Ma); Douglas Aster, Yellow Pond Lily (Pac).

Attention Seeking: Helicona (Haii).

Autism: Bluebell, Boronia, Flannel Flower, Red Lily Sundew (Aus B); Expanding Awareness, I Like Being Me (DL); Bluebell, Blue Lupin, Wallflower (Pac).

Balance (Emotional): Labrador Tree (Ask); Crowea, Dog of the Wild Forces (Aus B); Hops Bush (Aus L) Scleranthus (B); Smooth Hawksbeard (BL); Buffalo Gourd, Fairy Duster, Fire Prickly Pear Cactus (DAl); Balancing Extremes (DL); Chamomile (FES); Forget-Me-Not, Red Tulip (Hb); Almond, Apple, Pear, (Ma); Fuchsia, Balancer (Pac); Balanced (Sun).

Bereavement: Emergency Essence + Red Suva Frangipani (later Sturt Desert Rose) (Aus B); Acceptance, Earth Mother Nurtures, Graceful Transformations, Infinite Patience, Lotus Petals of the Heart, Stepping Ahead Now (DL); Forget-Me-Not (FES); Radish (Him A); Healing Grief (LH); Grape (Ma); Purple Crocus, Starfish (Pac); Be Comforted (Sun).

Bitterness: Dagger Hakea, Pink Mulla Mulla, Southern Cross (Aus B); Holly (B); Willow (B, FES); Clearing Blockages, My Heart Knows, Unveiling Self (DL); Mugwort (Hb); Bearing Spurge, Drum Stick, Slow Match, Ukshi (Him A); Raspberry (Ma); Jelly Fish (Pac).

Blame: Dagger Hakea, Mountain Devil, Southern Cross (Aus B); Green Rose (Aus L); Star Primrose, Rue (DAl); Infinite Patience, Softening the Edges (DL); Grape, Raspberry (Ma).

Bonding (Developing): Soul Support (Ask); Bottlebrush, Red Helmet Orchid, Woman (Aus B); Radiant Strength + Centred Love, Lotus Petals of the Heart (DL); Linden (Dv); Mariposa Lily (FES); Plumeria (Peg).

Brain (Left and Right Imbalance): Bush Fuchsia (Aus B); Balancing Extremes, Expanding Awareness (DL); Rainbow Kelp (Pac); Koenign Van Daenmark (Peg).

Breaking Bad Habits/Addictions: Bottlebrush, Boronia, Monga Waratah

(Aus B); Hairy Larkspur (DAl); Cravings Combo & Spray (PF).

Broken Hearted: Bleeding Heart (AK, FES); Boronia, Waratah (Aus B); Acceptance, Clearing Inner Pathways, Gossamer Steel, Heart Wings, Higher Levels, Light Hearted, My Heart Knows, Stepping Ahead Now, (DL); Heart Support (F); Love Lies Bleeding (FES); Field Maple (GM); Heartsease (Hb); Autumn Damask (PF).

Burn-Out: Dynamis Essences, Macrocarpa (Aus B); Earth Mother Nurtures, Meditative Mind (DL); Fairy Duster, Whitehorn, Woven Spine Pineapple Cactus (DAl); Gorse, Life Force (F); Aloe Vera, Lavender (FES); Hibiscus (FO); Take Time (LH); Purple Nightshade (Peg); Mother's Arms, Protective Shield (WD).

Calming – Emotions: Lavender, Red Clover, Valerian, Wild Garlic (AK); Dog Rose of the Wild Forces, Mint Bush (Aus B); Many-Headed Dryandra, Yellow Flag Flower (Aus L); Fairy Duster, Indian Tobacco (DAl); Nettles (Dv); Chamomile (Dv, FES, Hb); Lettuce (Dv, Ma); Daisy (F); Indian Pink (FES); Gean/Wild Cherry (GM); Bluebell, Lavender, Marjoram, Red Clover (Hb); Lotus (Him A); Yellow Poppy (HUB); Purple Nightshade (Peg).

Calming – The Mind: Lavender (AK); Calm and Clear (Aus B); White Chestnut (B); Candy Barrel Cactus (DAl); Meditative Mind (DL); Ragwort (Hb); Yellow Poppy (HUB) Take Time (LH); Almond, Banana, Lettuce (Ma).

Caring: Bush Gardenia, Flannel Flower (Aus B); Immortal, Mesquite (DAl); Centred Love, Earth Mother Nurtures, Lotus Petals of the Heart, (DL); Poison Oak, Sunflower (FES); Lucombe Oak (GM); Peach (Ma); Mother's Arms, Wise Woman (WD).

Childbirth (Attitude Towards) *See also* **Pregnancy**: Delph (AK); Grove Sandwort (Ask); Bottlebrush, Dog Rose, She Oak, Sunshine Wattle (Aus B); Earth Mother Nurtures, Radiant Strength +

Centred Love (DL); Evening Primrose (FES); Noni (Haii); Birthing Buddy, Pregnancy Partner (Peg); Maternity Combo & Spray (PF).

City Stress: Corn (AK); Calm and Clear (Aus B); Antiseptic Bush, Pink Fairy Orchid (Aus L); Radiant Strength, Sacred Sphere (DL); Pink Yarrow, Sweet Corn (Dv); Environmental Solution Special Formula, Indian Pink, Nicotiana, Sweet Pea, Yarrow (FES); Office Flower, Torroyia Rorshi Plant, Urban Stress Remedy (Him A); Beauty Secret, Buff Beauty (Peg); Reduce Stress Combo & Spray (PF); Sacred Space, Protective Shield (WD).

Clarity (Of Mind): Eyebright (AK, Sun); Bladderwort, Bunch-berry Twinflower (Ask); Alder (Ask, GM); Boronia, Bush Fuchsia, Isopogon (Aus B); Essences of Clarity, Pink Trumpet Flower, White Eremophila (Aus L); White Chestnut (B); Red Henbit (BL); Candy Barrel Cactus, Star Primrose (DAl) Dill, Fig Tree, Peppermint (Dv); Expansive Awareness, Meditative Mind, New Perceptions (DL); Daisy (Dv, Hb); Deerbrush, Madia, Mountain Pennyroyal (FES); Box, Pittespora (GM); Kou, Nana-honua (Haii); Apple, Avocado, Banana, Blackberry, Lettuce, Pineapple (Ma); Brown Kelp, Blue Lupin (Pac); Learning Skills Combo & Spray (PF); Still Mind (WD).

Claustrophobia: Grey Spider Flower (Aus B); Fuchsia Gum, W. A. Christmas Tree (Aus L); Balancing Extremes, Clearing Energy Fields, Expanding Awareness, Expansive Embodiment (DL); Glastonbury Thorn (GM); Authenticity (Him E); Apple (Ma).

Commitment: Relationship Essence, Wedding Bush (Aus B); Compass Barrel Cactus, Prickly Pear Cactus (DAl); Basil, Evening Primrose (FES); Acceptance, Centred Love, Heart to Heart, Purpose Flows, Internal Marriage, My Heart Knows (DL); Pearly Everlasting (Pac).

Communication: Bush Fuchsia, Flannel Flower (Aus B); Fishhook Cactus (DAl); Centred Love, Heart to Heart, (DL);

Cosmos, Linden, Zinnia (Dv); Calendula (Dv, FES); Broom (F); Scarlet Monkeyflower (FES); Jade Vine, 'Ulua (Haii); Authenticity (Him E); Lettuce (Ma); Gentian (Peg).

Complaining: Dagger Hakea, Mountain Devil, Paw Paw, Southern Cross (Aus B); One-Sided Bottlebrush, Wild Violet (Aus L); Higher Levels, Infinite Patience, Wise Action (DL).

Compulsiveness: Boronia (Aus B); Filagree (FES); Clearing Energy Fields, Light Hearted, Stepping Ahead Now (DL).

Concentration: Rosemary (AK); Cognis, Jacaranda, Sundew (Aus B); Essences of Clarity (Aus L); Scleranthus (B); New Perceptions (DL); Broom (F); Madia, Peppermint (FES); Teak Wood Flower (Him A); Avocado, Lettuce (Ma); Learning Skills Combo & Spray (PF); Still Mind (WD).

Confidence (Increasing): Buttercup, Self-Esteem Cactus, Sunflower (AK); Confid Combo, Dog Rose, Five Corners, Illawarra Flame Tree (Aus B); Snake Vine (Aus L); Larch (B); Cerato (B, FES); Buffalo Gourd, Cardon, Ephedra, Hedgehog Cactus (DAl); My Heart Knows, My Own Pure Light, Radiant Strength, Wise Action (DL); Borage (Dv, Hb); Bell Heather, Voice Confidence (F); Mullein, Trumpet Vine (FES); Catalpa, Cherry Plum (GM); Cymbidium (Hb); Pineapple (Ma); Be Confident (Sun).

Confusion: Cognis (Aus B); White Chestnut (B); Blackberry (Dv); Broom, Daisy (F); Dill (FES); Higher Levels, My Heart Knows, New Perceptions, Unveiling Self, (DL); Box (GM); Stick Rorrish (Haii); Teak Wood Flower (Him A); Avocado, Corn (Ma); Still Mind, On Angels' Wings (WD).

Contempt: Mountain Devil, Rough Bluebell; Slender Rice Flower (Aus B); Cowslip Orchid (Aus L); Holly (B); Softening the Edges (DL).

Contentment: Pink Flannel Flower, Sydney Rose (Aus B); Christmas Tree (Aus L); Bluebell, Rose – wild (Hb); Acceptance, Reveals Mystery Within, Purpose Flows (DL); Chickweed (HUB).

Control (Loss of): Red Clover (AK); Southern Cross (Aus B); Cherry Plum, Rock Rose (B); Desert Marigold, Hop Tree, Sacred Datura, Star Primrose, Strawberry Cactus (DAl); Balancing Extremes, Wise Action, (DL); Daisy (F); Chinese Violet (Haii); Self-Heal (Hb); Almond, Fig (Ma); Sea Palm (Pac).

Coping (With Problems/Challenges): Bauhinia, Paw Paw, Waratah (Aus B); Rose Cone Flower, Yellow Flag Flower (Aus L); Peppermint (BL); Cow Parsnip, Immortal, Jojoba, Spineless Prickly Pear (DAl); Defining Edges, Expanding Awareness, Infinite Patience, New Perceptions, Meditative Mind, (DL); Fig Tree (Dv); Milkweed (FES); White Poplar (GM); Dandelion (Hb); Chinese Violet, Ohai Lehua (Haii); Radish (Him A); About Space (Peru).

Courage: Borage (AK, Dv, Hb); Monkshood, Prickly Wild Rose (Ask); Dog Rose, Green Spider Orchid, Grey Spider Flower, Waratah (Aus B); Menzies Banksia (Aus L); Mimulus (B); Sacred Datura, Saguaro (DAl); My Heart Knows, Purpose Flows (DL); Thistle (F); Black Cohosh, Mountain Pride, Penstemon (FES); Italian Alder, White Poplar (GM); Wiliwili (Haii); Swallow Wort (Him A); Tomato (Ma); Surfgrass (Pac); Summer Squash (PVi); Be Courageous (Sun).

Cravings: Craving Combo & Spray (PF).

Creativity: Iris (AK, Dv, FES); Inspiration Cactus, Inspiration Orchid (AK); Golden Corydalis, Sticky Geranium, Wild Iris (Ask); Creative Essence, Turkey Bush (Aus B); Essences of Creativity, Pink Impatiens (Aus L); Rainbow (BL); Indian Root (DAl); Dance of Creation, Expansive Embodiment, New Perceptions (DL); Broom, Garden Pea, Holy Thorn (F); Indian Paintbrush (FES); Holm Oak, Lucombe Oak (GM); Creative/ Focus (Peru).

Crisis: Emergency Essence, Waratah (Aus B); Cowkicks, Crisis Relief (Aus L); Aloe, Ephedra (DAl); Lucid Dreaming, (DL); Angelica (Dv); First Aid (F); Speedwell (Hb); Pear (Ma); Be Calm (Sun); Mother's Arms, Protective Shield (WD).

Criticism: Sphagnum Moss (Ask); Purple and Red Kangaroo Paw, Yellow Cowslip Orchid (Aus B); Brachycome, Yellow and Green Kangaroo Paw (Aus L); Beech, Chicory, Impatiens (B); Aloe, Foothills Paloverde, Mala Mujer (DAl); I Like Being Me, Meditative Mind, Sacred Sphere (DL); Calendula, Snapdragon (FES); Ulua (Haii); White Coral Tree (Him A); Date, Figs, Grape (Ma); Garden Mum (PF)

Cynicism: Sunshine Wattle (Aus B); Ursinia, Wallflower Donkey Orchid (Aus L); Wondrous Heart (DL); Spotted Orchid (F); Baby Blue Eyes (FES); Blackberry (Ma); Jelly Fish (Pac); Young Heart (WD).

Daydreaming: Red Lily, Sundew (Aus B); Clematis (B, FES); Sacred Datura (DAl); Lucid Dreaming (DL); Rosemary (Dv); St John's Wort (FES); Avocado (Ma); Still Mind (WD).

Death: Transition Essence (Aus B); Cardon, Klein's Cholla Cactus (DAl); Henbane (HUB); Sierra Rein Orchid (Peg); Dill, Transitions Combo & Spray (PF); Soul Family (Peru); Devic Essence (WL).

Delinquency: Adol, Red Helmet (Aus B); Unveiling Self (DL); Saguaro (FES); Macadamia, Stick Rorrish (Haii).

Denial: Bluebell, Sturt Desert Rose (Aus B) Cardon, Klein's Cholla Cactus (DAl); Clearing Inner Pathways, New Perceptions, Reveals Mystery Within (DL); Sierra Rein Orchid (Peg); Dill (PF).

Dependency: Dog Rose, Monga Waratah, Red Grevillea, Southern Cross (Aus B); Canyon Grape Vine (DAD); Expansive Embodiment, Letting Go, My Heart Knows, Stepping Ahead Now (DL); Black Cohosh, Bleeding Heart, Fairy Lantern, Milkweed (FES); Chenille (Haii); Orange (Ma).

Depression: St John's Wort (AK), Borage (AK, Dv); Dynamis, Waratah (Aus B); Essences of Positivity, Red Beak Orchid (Aus L); Mustard (B, FES); Larch, Pine (B); Bisbee Beehive Cactus, Immortal, Rainbow Cactus (DAl); Higher Levels, Idiot Glee, Light Hearted, Manifesting Thought Forms, (DL); Zinnia (Dv); Black Cohosh, Olive, Scotch Broom, Yerba Santa (FES); Copper Beech, Sycamore (GM); Blackberry, Daffodil, Primrose (Hb); Orange, Peach (Ma); Grape Hyacinth, Periwinkle, Rainbow Kelp (Pac); Red Rose (PF); Cucumber (PVi); Smiles and Giggles (WD).

Deprogramming Dysfunctional Patterns: Northern Lights (Ask); Nijara (Him E); Fuchsia, Weigela (Pac).

Despair: Mint Bush, Waratah (Aus B); Cherry Plum, Gorse, Sweet Chestnut (B); Pine (B, FES); Indian Tobacco (DAl); Heart to Heart, Heart Wings, My Heart Knows, Wondrous Heart (DL); Scotch Broom (Dv); Elm (FES); Broom (Hb); Mother's Arms, Smiles and Giggles (WD).

Doubt/Despondency: Kapok Bush, Silver Princess (Aus B); Mauve Melaleuca (Aus L); Larch (B); Hornbeam (B, FES); Tansy (BL); White Desert Zinnia (DAl); Scotch Broom (FES); Cherry (Ma); Mother's Arms (WD).

Determination (Lack of): Inspiration Cactus (AK); Kapok Bush, Peach-flowered Tea-tree (Aus B); Pink Impatiens (Aus L); Uguisukazura – Flower (Aus LJ); Cardon, Ephedra (DAl); Purpose Flows, Stepping Ahead Now (DL); Penstemon (FES); Ohia Lehua (Haii) Coconut (Ma).

Dishonesty: Flannel Flower, Sturt Desert Rose (Aus B); Fuchsia Grevillea, Red Feather Flower (Aus L); Devil's Claw, Syrian Rue (DAl); Higher Levels, Unveiling Self (DL); Basil, Deerbrush (FES); Manna Ash (GM); Wiliwili (Haii); Honesty (Hb); Autumn Damask (PF).

Disillusionment/Disappointments: Southern Cross, Sunshine Wattle (Aus B); Snake Bush, Wallflower Donkey Orchid

(Aus L); Sacred Datura (DAl); Centered Love, Expanding Awareness, Light Hearted, Lotus Petals of the Heart, Wondrous Heart (DL); Gentian, Star Tulip (FES); Pink Pond Lily (PF).

Disorientation: River Beauty (Ask); Bush Fuchsia (Aus B); Pencil Cholla Cactus, Queen of the Night, Staghorn Cholla Cactus (DAl); Heart Wings, Expanding Awareness (DL); Corn, Indian Pink, Madia (FES); Stick Rorrish (Haii); Avocado (Ma).

Divorce: Bleeding Heart (AK); Emergency Essence, Relationship Essence (Aus B); Pear (Ma).

Dogmatic: Hibbertia (Aus B); Vine (B); White Coral Tree (Him A); Soaptree Yucca (DAl); Heart of Nature, Lotus Petals of the Heart (DL); Willowherb (F); Tiger Lily (FES); Hinahina-ku-kahakai (Haii); Houndstongue(HUB); Anemone, Sea Palm (Pac).

Dominating/Dominated: Gymea Lily (Aus B); Vine (B); Soaptree Yucca (DAl); Heart to Heart (DL); Willowherb (F); Tiger Lily (FES); Hinahina-ku-kahakai, Jacaranda (Haii); Grape, Peach (Ma); Anemone, Sea Palm (Pac).

Dreams – Disturbed: Forget-Me-Not (AK); Grey Spider Flower (Aus B); Lucid Dreaming, Meditative Mind (DL); Sweet Dreams (F); Black-Eyed Susan, Chaparral (FES); Pa-nini-o-ka (Haii); Texas Dandelion (PF); Still Mind (WD).

Ego (Balance): Sun Orchid (AK); Isopogon, Rough Bluebell (Aus B); Lace Flower, Round-Leaved Sundew, Sitka Spruce Pollen (Ask); Foothills Paloverde, Mountain Mahogany (DAl); Balancing Extremes, Higher Levels (DL). Sunflower (Dv); Chrysanthemum, Larkspur, Sunflower (FES); Weeping Willow, White Willow (GM); Thanksgiving Cactus, Water Poppy (Haii); White Narcissus (Hb); Flight (Him E); Dock (HUB); Douglas Aster (Pac); Charles de Mills (Peg); Still Mind, Wise Woman (WD).

Emergencies: Arnica (AK); Soul Support, Fireweed, Labrador Tree, River

Beauty, White Fireweed (Ask); Emergency Essence (Aus B); Crisis Relief (Aus L); Rock Rose (B); Red Clover (Dv); Heart of Peace, Peace in a Storm (LH); Pear (Ma); Mother's Arms (WD).

Emotional Blockages: Shadow Cactus, Earth Star Cactus (AK); Bluebell, Pink Mulla Mulla (Aus B); Compass Barrel Cactus (DAl); Clearing Blockages, Clearing Energy Fields (DL); Baby Blue Eyes, Dandelion, Golden Ear Drops (FES); Bay (GM); Amazon Swordplant (Haii); Apple, Grape, Lettuce, Orange (Ma); Water Essence (WL).

Emotional Cleansing/Release: Borage, Inner Cleansing Cactus, Neottia, Release Cactus, Tree Heather (AK); Fireweed (Ask); Purifying Essence (Aus B); Emotions in Balance (Aus L); Mycena (BL); Clearing Inner Pathways(DL); Lavender, Onion (Dv); Chapparal, Deer Bush, Evening Primrose, Golden Ear Drops, Self-Heal, Yerba Santa (FES); Apple (GM); Chenille (Haii); Marjoram (Hb); Moonsnail (Pac); Monkeyflower Bush, Swamp Onion (Peg); Water Essence (WL).

Emotional Detachment: Pink Yarrow (AK); Sweetgale (Ask); Tall Yellow Top (Aus B); Emotions in Balance (Aus L); Mesquite (DAl); Heart Wings, Radiant Strength + Centred Love, (DL); Bleeding Heart, Love Lies Bleeding, Tansy (FES); Sweet Chestnut (GM); Cup of Gold, Kukui (Haii); Green Rein Orchid (Peg).

Endurance: Banksia Robur, Macrocarpa (Aus B); Willow (Ask); Cardon, Soaptree Yucca (DAl); Radiant Strength, Expansive Embodiment, (DL); Penstemon (FES); White Poplar (GM); Endurance (Him E); Coconut, Corn, Orange (Ma).

Energy Boost : Amazon River, Victoria Regina Orchid (AK); Lady's Slipper, Lighten Up (Ask); Banksia Robur, Dynamis, Old Man Banksia (Aus B); Fire Prickly Pear Cactus (DAl); Earth Mother Nurtures, Radiant Strength (DL); Arnica, California Wild Rose, Cayenne (FES); Bay, Buffalo Cactus, Hornbeam (GM); Pukiawe (Haii); Healing (Him E); Red Spider Lily

(Peg); Young Heart (WD). Energy Combo & Spray (PF) English Elm, Medlar (GM); Cherry, Corn (Ma).

Enthusiasm: Joyful Opuntia (AK); Old Man Banksia (Aus B); Wondrous Heart, I Like Being Me, My Own Pure Light, (DL); Gorse (F); Bougainvillea (Haii); Passionate Life (LH); Cherry, Corn, Orange, Spinach (Ma).

Escapism: Bunchberry (Ask); Red Lily, Sundew (Aus B); Blue-Topped Cow Weed (Aus L); Essence of the Edge, Lucid Dreaming (DL); Basil, Blackberry, California Poppy, Canyon Dudleya, Milkweed (FES); Oriental Poppy (Hb); Coconut (Ma).

Expressing – Feelings: Poinsettia (AK); Dagger Hakea, Flannel Flower (Aus B); Fishhook Cactus, Ocotillo, Rainbow Cactus (DAl); Reading Energy Fields, Heart to Heart (DL); Fuchsia, Onion, Scarlet Monkeyflower (Dv); Snapdragon (Dv, Hb); Golden Ear Drops, Indian Paintbrush, Pink Monkeyflower, Trumpet Vine (FES); Birch, Holm Oak, Ivy, Larch, Mimosa (GM); Crepe Myrtle (Haii); Bluebell, Weigela (Pac); Blazing Star, Owl's Clover (Peg); Marie Pavie (PF).

Expressing – Ideas: Bush Fuchsia, Turkey Bush (Aus B); Defining Edges, Reveals Mystery Within (DL); Cosmos (FES); Parrot (Him A); Owl's Clover, Trillium Red (Peg); Crepe Myrtle (Haii).

Extroversion *See* **Introversion**.

Family Pressures/Stress: Boab, Dagger Hakea, Relationship Essence (Aus B); Cat's Paw (Aus L); Canyon Grapevine, Mesquite, Organ Pipe Cactus (DAl); Expanding Awareness, Infinite Patience, My Heart Knows, Softening the Edges (DL); Nettles (Dv); Fairy Lantern, Red Clover, Sweet Pea, Tansy, Walnut (FES); Chenille, Chinese Violet, Plumbago (Haii); Safe Space (PE); Plumeria (Peg).

Fathering: Sunflower (AK); Flannel Flower, Red Helmet Orchid (Aus B); Mountain Mahogany (DAl); Baby Blue Eyes, Quince, Sage, Saguaro (FES) Hello

Dad (PE); Solar Power (Peru).

Fear – General: Queen of the Night Cactus (AK); Dog Rose, Dog Rose of the Wild Forces, Mulla Mulla (Aus B); Dampiera (Aus L); Cherry Plum, Red Chestnut, Rock Rose (B); Scorpion Weed (DAl); Clearing Blockages (DL); Scottish Primrose, Thistle (F); Blue Ginger, Cup of Gold (Haii); Chamomile, Sweet Pea (Hb); Day-blooming Jessamine (Him A); Apple, Spinach, Tomato (Ma); Fearlessness (Pac); Rosa Complicata (Peg); Mother's Arms, On Angels' Wings, Protective Shield (WD).

Fear – Specific: Bog Rosemary, Tundra Rose (Ask); Dog Rose, Green Spider Orchid, Mulla Mulla (Aus B); Menzies Banksia (Aus L); Mimulus (B); Indian Root, Thurber's Gilia DAl); St John's Wort (Dv); Black-Eyed Susan, California Pitcher Plant, Fawn Lily, Pink Monkeyflower (FES); Red Chestnut (GM); Avocado, Bougainvillea, Cotton, Ma'o (Haii); Cymbidium, Heather (Hb); Protective Shield, Still Mind (WD).

Flexibility: Lamb's Quarters, Wild Rhubarb, Willow (Ask); Glacier River, Greenland Icecap (Ask E); Bauhinia, Isopogon (Aus B); Rock Water, Vine (B); Desert Willow, Foothills Paloverde (DAl); Dance of Creation, Graceful Transformations, Reading Energy Fields, Softening the Edges (DL); Quaking Grass, Rabbit Bush (FES); Ash (GM); Ili'ahi (Haii); White Coral Tree (Him A) Fig (Ma); Feverfew (Sun).

Focus (Mental): Bunchberry, Golden Corydalis (Ask); Sundew (Aus B, Aus L); Essences of Clarity, Hops Bush, Pink Trumpet Flower, Yellow Boronia (Aus L); Fire Prickly Pear Cactus, Hedgehog Cactus (DAl); New Perceptions (DL), Madia, Peppermint, Shasta Daisy (FES); Hazel (GM); Avocado, Blackberry (Ma); Learning Skills Combo & Spray (PF); Be Focused (Sun); Still Mind (WD).

Forgiveness: Blue Elf Viola, Mountain Wormwood (Ask); Dagger Hakea, Mountain Devil, Slender Rice Flower (Aus B); Correa, Pixie Mope (Aus L); Pine (B);

Immortal (DAl); Letting Go, Lotus Petals of the Heart, Softening the Edges (DL); Rowan (F); Elder, Hawthorn (GM); Hyssop (Hb); Raspberry (Ma); Salal (Pac); Clarkia, Prickly Poppy (Peg); Lilac (PF); Forgiveness (F) For Giving (Peru).

Freedom: Mountain Wormwood (Ask); Bottlebrush, Wild Potato Bush (Aus B); Rainbow Cactus, Tarbrush (DAl); Hearts' Wings, Unveiling Self, Wondrous Heart, (DL); Sea Holly (F); Leyland Cypress (GM); Spinach (Ma); Be Free (Sun); Freedom (Peru).

Frustration: Blue Elf Viola (Ask); Banksia Robur, Wild Potato Bush (Aus B); Silver Princess Gum, Snake Bush, Ursinia (Aus L); Holly (B); Acceptance (DL); Blackberry, Indian Paintbrush, Iris, Wild Oat (FES); Gorse (GM); Ulua (Haii); Cymbidium (Hb); Almond, Blackberry (Ma); Mussel (Pac); Verbena (PF).

Greed: Bluebell, Bush Iris (Aus B); Lotus Petals of the Heart (DL); Goldenrod, Star Thistle, Trillium (FES); Grape, Peach (Ma).

Grief: Red Suva Frangipani, Sturt Desert Pea (Aus B); Honeysuckle, Star of Bethlehem (B); Hackberry (DAl); Bleeding Heart (Dv, FES); Borage, Golden Ear Drops (FES); Hawthorn (Hb); Ashoka Tree, Radish (Him A); Healing Grief (LH); Grape, Orange, Pear (Ma); Starfish (Pac); Be Comforted (Sun); On Angels' Wings (WD).

Group Dynamics: Scarlet Pimpernel, Violet (AK); Slender Rice Flower (Aus B); Martagon Lily, Mullein (Dv).

Guilt: Sturt Desert Rose (Aus B); Pine (B); Jumping Cholla Cactus (DAl); Golden Ear Drops, Mullein, Pink Monkeyflower (FES); Sweet Chestnut (GM); Bougainvillea (Haii); Hyssop (Hb); Meenalih (Him A); Peach, Strawberry (Ma); Rosa Alba (Peg).

Happiness: Joyful Opuntia (AK); Mountain Devil, Sunshine Wattle (Aus B); Cherry, Apple Star of Bethlehem (Aus L); Heart Wings, Idiot Glee, I Like Being Me (DL); Valerian (F); Manna Ash, Norway Maple (GM); Happiness (Him E); Peach (Ma).

Hate Mountain Devil (Aus B); Black Kangaroo Paw, Cape Bluebell (Aus L); Holly (B); Black Cohosh, Oregon Grape, Snapdragon (FES); Indian Mulberry (Him A); Grape (Ma).

Healthy Mindset: Boronia, Crowea (Aus B); Apple (Ma).

Honesty *See* **Dishonesty**: My Heart Knows, Reveals Mystery Within, Wise Action (DL); Pineapple, Spinach (Ma).

Hope: Cinnamon Rose, Japanese Rose (AK); Sunshine Wattle, Waratah (Aus B); Star of Bethlehem (Aus L); Gorse, Sweet Chestnut (B); New Perceptions, Wondrous Heart (DL); Snowdrop (F) Cherry, Orange, Tomato, (Ma); Beech Young Heart, On Angels' Wings (WD).

Humour (Lack of): Zinnia (AK FES); Little Flannel Flower (Aus B); Compass Barrel Cactus (DAl); Idiot Glee, Wondrous Heart (DL); Valerian (F); Leyland Cypress, Pittospora (GM); Blackberry, Fig, Spinach (Ma); Zania (Peru); Smiles and Giggles (WD).

Hurt/Pain: Cotton Grass, Ladies' Tresses, River Beauty, White Fireweed (Ask); Sturt Desert Pea (Aus B); Illyarrie, Mauve Melaleuca, Menzies Banksia, Violet Butterfly (Aus L); Aloe (DAl); Hawthorn May (Dv); Heart Support (F); California Wild Rose, Chamomile, Golden Ear Drops, Pink Monkeyflower, Yerba Santa (FES); Beech, Field Maple, Mulberry (GM); Comfrey, Heartsease, Nettle (Hb); Tassel Flower (Him A); Raspberry (Ma); Weigela (Pac); Mother's Arms, On Angels' Wings (WD).

Hyperactivity: Black-Eyed Susan, Jacaranda (Aus B); Dance of Creation, Infinite Patience (DL); Morning Glory (FES); Hibiscus (FO).

Hypochondria: Peach-flowered Tea-tree (Aus B); Heather (B); Earth Mother Nurtures, My Own Pure Light (DL); Fuchsia, Purple Monkeyflower (FES); Apple, Fig (Ma); Tiger's Jaw Cactus (PF) Mother's Arms (WD).

Identity Crisis: Violet (AK); Columbine, Monkshood, Tamarack, Yellow Dryas (Ask); Five Corners, Philotheca (Aus B); Kasumisakura Flower (Aus LJ); My Heart Knows, My Own Pure Light, Unveiling Self + Gossamer Steel (DL); Milkweed, Quaking Grass (FES); Magnolia (GM); Strength (Him E).

Immaturity: Dog Rose, Kangaroo Paw (Aus B); Unveiling Self (DL); Fairy Lantern (FES); Young Heart (WD).

Impatience: Aggression Orchid (AK); Black-Eyed Susan (Aus B); Impatiens (B, Haii); Aloe (DAl); Infinite Patience, Meditative Mind (DL) Calendula, Poison Oak (FES); Lettuce (Ma).

Impetuousness: Kangaroo Paw (Aus B); Impatiens (B, FES); Wise Action, Infinite Patience (DL); Verbena (PF).

Inadequacy: Confid Essence (Aus B); Evening Star, Hackberry, Immortal, Queen of the Night (DAl); Acceptance, I Like Being Me, Internal Marriage, Unveiling Self + Gossamer Steel (DL); Buttercup, Evening Primrose, Goldenrod, Star Thistle (FES); Peach, Strawberry (Ma).

Incest (Effects of): Bottlebrush, Dagger Hakea, Flannel Flower, Red Helmet Orchid, Wisteria (Aus B); Macrozamia (Aus L); Balancing Extremes, Clearing Blockages, Clearing Energy Fields, I Like Being Me, Letting Go, Reading Energy Fields (DL); Black Cohosh (FES); Mother's Arms, Protective Shield, Sacred Space (WD).

Indecision: Jacaranda, Paw Paw, Sundew (Aus B); Centaury, Scleranthus (B); Ratany, Soaptree Yucca (DAl); My Heart Knows, New Perceptions, Purpose Flows, Reading Energy Fields. (DL); Cayenne (Dv); Cayenne, Mullein, Tansy (FES); English Elm, Glastonbury Thorn, Pittospora (GM); Coffee, Papaya (Haii); Apple, Lettuce, Strawberry (Ma); Pipsissewa (Pac); White Petunia (PF); Still Mind (WD).

Independence: Angelsword, Southern Cross (Aus B); Kasumisakura Flower (Aus LJ); Defining Edges, Essence of the Edge, Expansive Embodiment, Walking Out of Patterns (DL); Box (Dv); Bleeding Heart, Fairy Lantern, Milkweed (FES); Crown Flower (Haii).

Inferiority: Buttercup (AK, FES); Dog Rose, Five Corners, Hibbertia (Aus B); Urchin Dryandra, Yellow Cone Flower (Aus L); Cardon (DAl); Defining Edges, I Like Being Me, Unveiling Self (DL); Spindle (GM); Vilayati Amli (Him A); Pineapple (Ma).

Infertility Distress: She Oak, Woman Essence (Aus B); She Oak/Ironwood (Haii); Woman's Balance (LH).

Inherited Behaviour Patterns: Fireweed (Ask); Boab (Aus B) Boab (Aus B); Larch (B); Tarbrush (DAI); Black Cohosh (FES); Macadamia, Ohai-ali (Haii); Nirjara (Him E); Agave Yaquinana (Peg) Reveals Mystery Within + Walking Out of Patterns,(DL) Release Cactus (AK) Inocenicia Coco (Peru).

Inner Child Spider Lily (Haii); Cyclamen:(HUB); Kids stuff (Pac); Primrose (Sun); Sacred Void (SW).

Inner Strength: Monga Waratah, Southern Cross, Waratah (Aus B); Essence of Inner Strength (Aus L); Pink Orchid (FO) Inner Strength Combo & Spray (PF).

Insecurity: Dog Rose, Tall Mulla Mulla (Aus B); Happy Wanderer (Aus L); Bouvardia, Cow Parsnip, Mala Mujer (DAl); Wild Garlic (Dv); Mallow (Dv, FES); Rosemary, Star Thistle (FES); Goldenrod (Him A); Strength (Him E); Strawberry(Ma); Viburnum (Pac).

Insensitivity: Flannel Flower, Kangaroo Paw, Red Helmet (Aus B); Orange Leschenaultia, Red and Green Kangaroo Paw, Red Leschenaultia (Aus L); Heart to Heart, Reading Energy Fields, Softening the Edges (DL) Calendula (Dv); Yellow Star Tulip (FES); Awapuhi Melemele, Kamani (Haii); Lady's Smock (Hb); Indian Coral, Sithihea (Him A); Peach, Raspberry (Ma).

Inspiration: Iris, Inspiration Cactus (AK); Boronia, Turkey Bush (Aus B); Parakeelya (Aus L); Dance of Creation, Dancing Light

Spirit Wondrous Heart (DL); Iris (Dv, FES); Revelation (F); Rose White (Hb); Blackberry, Cherry, Grape (Ma); Choke Cherry (Peg).

Integrity: Sturt Desert Rose (Aus B); Liquidambar (GM).

Intellect (IQ Booster): Cognis Combo, Isopogon (Aus B); Purpose Flows + New Perceptions (DL); Lemon (Dv); Cosmos, Nasturtium, Peppermint (FES); Avocado (Ma).

Intimacy: Orange Lily (AK); Flannel Flower, Wisteria (Aus B); Fishhook Cactus, Klein's Pencil Cholla Cactus, Teddy Bear Cholla Cactus (DAl); Gossamer Steel, Radiant Strength + Centred Love (DL); Sticky Monkeyflower (Dv, FES); Eros, Holy Thorn (F); Hibiscus, Pink Monkeyflower (FES); Sensuality Blend, Spirit Lift Spritz, Waterlily (FO) Pink Ginger, Pink Waterlily (Day Blooming) (Haii); Grape (Ma); Cabbage Rose (Peg) Archduke Charles, Passion, Passion Combo & Spray (PF).

Intolerance: Bauhinia, Slender Rice Flower (Aus B); Green Rose, Yellow and Green Kangaroo Paw, Yellow Leschenaultia (Aus L); Beech (B); Impatiens (B, Haii); New Perceptions, Expanding Awareness, Infinite Patience (DL); Yellow Star Tulip (FES); Date (Ma).

Introversion: Five Corners, Gymea Lily, Tall Mulla Mulla (Aus B); White Spider Orchid (Aus L); Expansive Embodiment, My Own Pure Light, Unveiling Self (DL); Mallow, Rosemary (Dv); Fawn Lily (FES); Plane Tree (GM); Rhubarb (Hb).

Intuition: White Spruce (Ask); Bush Fuchsia, Bush Iris (Aus B); Queen of the Night (DAl); Lotus Petals of the Heart, My Heart Knows (DL); Mimosa, Stags Horn Sumach (GM); Fig (Ma); Viburnum (Pac).

Irrational Behaviour: Shadow Cactus (AK); Aspen (B); Scarlet Monkeyflower (FES); Box (GM); Stick Rorrish (Haii).

Irresponsible Behaviour *See* **Responsibility**: Wise Action (DL).

Irritability: Black-Eyed Susan (Aus B); Leafless Orchid (Aus L); Beech, Impatiens (B); Light Hearted (DL); Poison Oak, Snapdragon (FES); Mussel (Pac); Vanilla (PF); Date (Ma); Smiles and Giggles (WD).

Isolation: Single Delight (Ask); Illawarra Flame Tree, Pink Mulla Mulla, Tall Mulla Mulla, Tall Yellow Top (Aus B); Green Rose, Veronica (Aus L); Water Violet (B); Creosote Bush, Mariposa Lily (DAl); Stonecrop (F); Love Lies Bleeding, Sweet Pea (FES); Persian Iron Wood (GM); Flight (Him E); Hermit Crab (Pac); Cape Honeysuckle (Peg).

Jealousy: Mountain Devil (Aus B); Red Feather Flower (Aus L); Holly (B, FES); Desert Holly (DAl); Centred Love, I Like Being Me, Walking Out of Patterns (DL); Pretty Face, Trillium (FES); Holm Oak (GM); Apple, Grape (Ma); Fortunes Double Yellow (PF); Still Mind (WD).

Joy: Borage, Chocolate Orchid, Joyful Opuntia (AK); Churning Bell, Tundra Rose (Ask); Apple Mint Bush, Little Flannel Flower, Sunshine Wattle (Aus B); Essences of Positivity, Pink Everlasting Straw Flower, Red and Green Kangaroo Paw (Aus L); Aloe, Strawberry Cactus (DAl); Idiot Glee, Dance of Creation, Lotus Petals of the Heart (DL); Rhododendron (Dv); Gorse (F); Angel Trumpet, California Wild Rose (FES); Catalpa, Gorse (GM); Ashoka Tree, Parval (Him A); Happiness (Him E); Apple, Orange, Spinach Ma); Vanilla Leaf (Pac); Rosa Hardii (Peg); Pure Joy (Peru); Young Heart, Smiles and Giggles (WD).

Lack of Commitment: Inspiration cactus (AK); Kapok Bush, Peach-flowered Tea-tree, Wedding Bush (Aus B).

Lack of Direction: Inspiration Cactus (AK); Silver Princess (Aus B); Wild Oat (B).

Laughter (Tonic): Fun Orchid (AK); Little Flannel Flower (Aus B); Zinnia (AK, Dv, FES, PVi); Strawberry Cactus (DAl); Idiot Glee (DL); Spirit lift Spritz (FO); Cherry (Ma); Smiles and Giggles (WD).

Laziness: Kapok Bush (Aus B); Red

Feather Flower (Aus L); Purpose Flows (DL); Peppermint (Dv); Corn (Ma); Sycamore (Peg); Tiger's Jaw Cactus (PF).

Learning Ability: Daisy (AK); Bush Fuchsia, Cognis, Isopogon (Aus B); Chestnut Bud (B); New Perceptions (DL); California Wild Rose, Cosmos, Madia, Peppermint, Rabbit Bush (FES); Hazel, Judas Tree (GM); Blue Camas, Optimal Learning (Pac); Silver Lace, Learning Skill Combo & Spray (PF).

Lethargy (Mental): Banksia Robur, Macrocarpa, Old Man Banksia (Aus B) Corn (Ma) Red Beak Orchid (Aus L); Blackberry (Dv); Peppermint (Dv, FES); Broom (F); Cosmos, Tansy (FES); Sycamore (GM); Pua-kenikeni,(Haii); Tiger's Jaw Cactus (PF).

Listening: Alpine Mint Bush, Bush Gardenia (Aus B); Listening Heart (SW).

Loneliness: Violet (AK); Illawarra Flame Tree, Tall Yellow Top (Aus B); Parakeelya, Veronica (Aus L); Chaparral, Mesquite (DAl); My Song Calls Me Home (DL); Bleeding Heart, California Wild Rose, Nicotiana (FES); Heartsease (Hb); Grape, Date, Peach (Ma); Alaskan Birch Forest, Mother's Arms (WD).

Love (Ability to): Heart Orchid, Love Cactus, Love Orchid (AK); Tundra Rose (Ask); Bluebell, Mountain Devil, Rough Bluebell (Aus B); Black Kangaroo Paw, Mauve Melaleuca, Pink Everlasting Straw Flower (Aus L); Organ Pipe Cactus, Teddy Bear Cholla Cactus (DAl); Centred Love (DL); Field Maple, Hawthorn (GM); Daffodil, Rosebud-red, Self-Heal (Hb); Malabar Nut Flower, Neem (Him A); Grape, Peach, Pear, Raspberry (Ma); Reine de Violettes Rose (Peg); Cecil Brunner, Champny's Pink Cluster (PF); Mother's Arms (WD).

Male/Female Balance *See also* **Sexuality** Calla Lily (AK); Green Fairy Orchid, Sitka Spruce Pollen (Ask); Internal Marriage (DL); Niu (Haii); Rattlesnake Plantain Orchid, Red Ginger (Peg);

Spiritual Marriage (F); God/Goddess Unity (Peru).

Manic Depression: Black-Eyed Susan, Dog Rose of the Wild Forces, Peach-flowered Tea-tree, Emergency Essence (Aus B);); Balancing Extremes (DL); Chamomile, Mustard (FES); Copper Beech (GM); Stick Rorrish (Haii); Orange (Ma); Periwinkle (Pac).

Manipulative Behaviour: Isopogon (Aus B); Fringed Lily Twiner, Pale Sundew (Aus L); Chicory (B, FES); Devil's Claw, Klein's Pencil Cholla Cactus (DAl); Wise Woman (DL); Chenille, Crown Flower (Haii); Grape (Ma); Viper's Bugloss (Sun).

Marital Harmony: Wedding Bush (Aus B); Internal Marriage (DL); Pua Male (Haii); Indian Pipe (Pac).

Maternal Instincts, Lack of: Bottlebrush (Aus B); Quince (Dv); Mariposa Lily (FES).

Maternal Instincts, Unfulfilled *See also* **Mothering**: Evening Primrose (FES); Earth Mother Nurtures (DL); She Oak/Ironwood (Haii).

Memory (Improving): Rosemary (AK); Rosemary (AK, FES); Isopogon (Aus B); Comfrey, Fig Tree, Forget-Me-Not (Dv); Broom (F); Rabbit Bush (FES); Yew (GM); Comfrey, Eyebright (Hb); Ulei (Haii); Teakwood Flower (Him A); Avocado (Ma); Periwinkle (Pac); Still Mind (WD).

Male: Inner Strength: Banana (Haii); Male Strength (Peru); Male Power Combo & Spray (PF).

Men – Relating to Women: Relationship Essence (Aus B); Milky Nipple Cactus (DAl); Heart to Heart, Softening the Edges (DL); Mai'a/ Banana, Spider Lily (Haii); Rattlesnake Plantain Orchid (Peg).

Mental Chatter: Knotgrass, Wild Carrot (AK); Boronia (Aus B); White Chestnut (B, FES); Star Primrose (DAl); Meditative Mind (DL); Cosmos (FES); Papaya (Haii); Lettuce (Ma).

Mental Harmony: Jacob's Ladder, Willow (Ask); Boronia, Crowea, Jacaranda (Aus B); Alaskan Birch Forest, Still Mind (DL); Nasturtium (FES); Cherry Laurel (GM); Spider Lily (Haii); Curry Leaf, Red Hibiscus (Him A); Iris (PF); Pear (Ma); Dark Mullein (Sun).

Mental Illness: Emergency Essence (Aus B); W.A. Smoke Bush (Aus L); Indian Root, Sacred Datura (DAl); Yerba Santa (FES); Stick Rorrish (Haii).

Mood Swings: Crowea, Peach-flowered Tea-tree (Aus B); Scleranthus (B); Cherry (Ma); Buffalo Gourd (DAl); Balancing Extremes (DL); Chamomile (Dv); Bell Heather, Femininity (F); Mustard (FES); Silver Maple (GM); Cherry (Ma); Stock (PF).

Mothering: Nursing Courgette, Pumpkin (AK); Grove Sandwort, Northern Lady's Slipper, Spiraea (Ask); Bottlebrush (Aus B); Goddess Grasstree (Aus L); Desert Holly, Mala Mujer, Milky Nipple Cactus (DAl); Mariposa Lily (DAl, FES); Earth Mother Nurtures (DL); Linden (Dv); Iris, Milkweed, Pomegranate (FES); Niu, Noni, Pohuehue (Haii); Peach (Ma); Barnacle (Pac); Mother, Soothe Baby Blues, Mum's Everywhere (PE); Mother's Arms, Wise Woman (WD).

Motivation: Inspiration Cactus (AK); Silver Princess (Aus B); Mountain Mahogany, Tarbrush (DAl); Purpose Flows (DL); Neoporteria Cactus (Peg).

Negativity (Clearing): Inner Cleansing Cactus, Inspirational Cactus, Life Force Cactus, Release Cactus (AK); Space Clearing Mist (Aus B); Antiseptic Bush, Essences of Positivity, Purple and Red Kangaroo Paw (Aus L); Crab Apple (B); Crown of Thorns, Ephedra (DAl); Clearing Blockages, Clearing Energy Fields, Clearing Inner Pathways, Letting Go (DL); Black Cohosh, Mountain Pennyroyal, Pink Yarrow, Yarrow (FES); Holm Oak (GM); Kamani, Spider Lily (Haii); Forget-Me-Not, Lungwort, Snapdragon (Hb); Christ's Thorn (Him A); Blackberry, Banana, Cherry, Orange (Ma); Sand Dollar (Pac);

Okra (PVi); Sacred Space, Protective Shield (WD).

Nervous Breakdown: Emergency Essence, Waratah (Aus B); Cherry Plum (B); Fairy Duster (DAl); Hau (Haii); Orange (Ma); Periwinkle (Pac).

Nervousness: Dog Rose, Emergency Essence, Waratah (Aus B); Fairy Duster (DAl); Chamomile, Dill, Garlic, Lady's Slipper, Lavender, Nicotiana (FES); Hibiscus (FO); Horse Chestnut, Pear (GM); Hau (Haii); Almond, Banana, Lettuce, Pear (Ma); Purple Nightshade (Peg) Still Mind (WD).

Newborn Babies: Navelwort (HUB); Welcome Baby, Sibling Support (PE).

Night Fears: Emergency Essence (Aus B); St John's Wort (Dv, Hb); On Angels' Wings (WD).

Nightmares: St John's Wort (AK Dv, FES); Green Spider Orchid, Grey Spider Flower (Aus B); Rock Rose (B); Crab Apple (B, FES); Jumping Cholla Cactus, Whitehorn (DAl); Lucid Dreaming (DL); Pa-nini-o-ka, Passion Flower (Haii); Swallow Wort (Him A); Tomato (Ma); Barnacle, Urchin (Pac); Rose of Sharon (PF).

Obsession: Boronia (Aus B); Rock Water (B).

Oppression: Boab, Southern Cross (Aus B); Clearing Energy Fields, Expanding Awareness, New Perceptions, Walking Out of Patterns (DL); Tormentil (Hb).

Optimism: Inspiration Cactus, Joyful Opuntia Cactus (Ak); Sunshine Wattle (Aus B); Wild Violet (Aus L); Gorse (B, FES); Strawberry Cactus (DAl); Heart Wings, Wondrous Heart, Young Heart (DL); Scotch Broom (Dv); Spotted Orchid (F); Gentian, Penstemon (FES); Blackberry, Cherry (Ma).

Overexcitement: Calm and Clear (Aus B); Meditative Mind, Dancing Light Spirit (DL); Lavender (Dv); Canyon Dudleya (FES); Potato (Hb); Lettuce (Ma).

Over-Intellectual Behaviour: Crown of Thorns, Desert Holly (DAl); Nasturtium (FES); Spinach (Ma); Rosa Damascena Versicolor (Peg).

Overreacting: Crowea (Aus B); Emotions in Balance (Aus L); Vervain (B); Jumping Cholla Cactus, Ocotillo, Saguaro Cactus (DAl); Balancing Extremes, Essence of the Edge, Wise Action (DL); Love Lies Bleeding (FES); Raspberry (Ma).

Oversensitivity: Aura Cleansing Cactus, Inner Cleansing Cactus, Blueberry Cactus (AK); Angelsword, Fringed Violet, Pink Mulla Mulla (Aus B); Common White Spider, Hybrid Pink Fairy (Cowslip) Orchid, Pixie Mope (Aus L); Mimulus (B); Balancing Extremes, Defining Edges, Radiant Strength, Sacred Sphere (DL); Pink Yarrow, Zinnia (Dv); Daisy (F); Lady's Smock (Hb); Strawberry (Ma); Protective Mind, Sacred Space, (WD).

Overwhelmed (Feeling): Dill (AK, Dv, FES, Hb); Dog Rose of the Wild Forces, Mint Bush, Paw Paw (Aus B); Essence of Relaxation, One-Sided Bottlebrush, Pink Fairy Orchid (Aus L); Elm, Hornbeam (B); Buffalo Gourd, Jumping Cholla Cactus, Immortal, Pineapple Cactus, Woven Spine (DAl); Clearing Energy Fields, Radiant Strength, Reading Energy Fields (DL); Daisy (F); Cosmos, Hornbeam, Larkspur, Red Clover, Scotch Broom (FES); Chinese Violet, Nani-ahiahi (Haii); Almond, Spinach (Ma); Protective Shield, Sacred Space (WD).

Nurturing *See* **Mothering**: Earth Mother Nurtures (DL); Mother's Arms, Self Nurture (WD).

Panic: Red Clover (AK, FES); Calm & Clear, Dog Rose of the Wild Forces, Emergency Essence (Aus B); Pink Fairy Orchid, Yellow Leschenaultia (Aus L); Pencil Cholla Cactus (DAl); Buttercup (Hb); Sithihea (Him A); Vital Spark (Him E); Pear (Ma); Bluebell, Urchin (Pac).

Paranoia: Red Clover (AK); Angelsword, Dog Rose, Mountain Devil (Aus B); Hybrid Pink Fairy (Cowslip) Orchid (Aus L);

Oregon Grape, Purple Monkeyflower (FES); Cup of Gold (Haii); St John's Wort (Hb); Spinach (Ma).

Patience: Rock Spring (Ask); Black-Eyed Susan (Aus B); Brown Boronia, Yellow Leschenaultia (Aus L); Impatiens (B); Indian Tobacco (DAl); Infinite Patience (DL); Pine (GM); Buttercup (Hb); Ivy (HUB); Sithihea (Him A); Pink Seaweed (Pac); Coconut, Grape, Lettuce (Ma).

Perfectionism: Boronia, Hibbertia, Yellow Cowslip Orchid, (Aus B); Golden Waitsia, Yellow and Green Kangaroo Paw (Aus L); Acceptance, (DL); Star Jasmine (Haii); Fuchsia (Hb); Fig (Ma).

Perseverance: Kapok Bush (Aus B); Woolly Banksia (Aus L); Kolokoltchik (Aus L); Gentian (B, FES); Soaptree Yucca (DAl); Purpose Flows (DL); Scotch Broom (Dv, FES); Mountain Pride, Penstemon (FES); Nui/Coconut (Haii); Broom (Hb); Orange (Ma); Washington Lily (Peg).

Pessimism *See* **Optimism**: Sunshine Wattle (Aus B); Water Violet (B, FES); Heart Wings, Wondrous Heart (DL); Indian Mulberry, Malabar Nut Flower (Him A).

Poor Mother/Father Image: Sunflower (AK, FES, Dv); Grove Sandwort (Ask); Bottlebrush, Red Helmet Orchid (Aus B); Milky Nipple Cactus, Mountain Mahogany (DAl); Mariposa Lily (DAl, FES); Baby Blue Eyes, Quince, Saguaro, Scarlet Monkeyflower (FES); Strawberry (Ma); Barnacle (Pac); Old Maid Pink/White (Peg).

Positivity: Essences of Positivity (Aus L); Cotton/Ma'o, Bougainvillea (Haii); Be Positivity (Sun).

Possessiveness: Bluebell (Aus B); Chicory (B); Harebell (F); Bleeding Heart, Trillium (FES); Grape (Ma).

Pre-Cancerous Emotional State: Release Cactus (AK); Dagger Hakea, Southern Cross, Sturt Desert Rose (Aus B); Clearing Blockages, Clearing Energy Fields, Clearing Inner Pathways, Manifesting

Thought Forms, Shadow Cactus (DL); Nani-ahiahi (Haii); Purple Crocus (Pac).

Prejudice: Bauhinia, Boab, Freshwater Mangrove, Slender Rice Flower (Aus B); Acceptance, New Perceptions (DL).

Pride: Five Corners, Gymea Lily, Slender Rice Flower (Aus B); Vine (B); Poppy (Hb); Malabar Nut Flower (Him A); Banana, Pineapple (Ma).

Procrastination: Jacaranda, Paw Paw, Red Grevillea, Sundew (Aus B); Fuderindou Flower (Aus LJ); Larch (B); Pencil Cholla Cactus (DAl); Purpose Flows, Stepping Ahead Now (DL); Cabbage (F); Cayenne, Tansy (FES); Blackberry (FES, Ma); Coconut, Corn (Ma).

Protection From Negative Emotions/Thoughts: Aura Cactus, Earth Star Cactus, Golden Barrel Cactus, Life Force Cactus (AK); Angelsword, Fringed Violet (Aus B); Walnut (B); Sacred Sphere (DL); Pennyroyal, White Yarrow (Dv); Pink Yarrow (Dv, FES); Psychic Protection (F); Mountain Pennyroyal, Oregon Grape (FES); Yarrow (FES, Hb); Kamani (Haii); Light Heart Space (LH); White Rose (PF), Protective Shield, Sacred Space (WD).

Protection From Others' Negativity: Aura Cleansing Cactus, Inspiration Cactus, Life Force Cactus (AK); Angel of Protection Orchid (AK); Angelsword, Fringed Violet, Space Clearing (Aus B); Shy Blue Orchid (Aus L); Walnut (B); Sacred Sphere (DL); Psychic Protection (F); Fawn Lily (FES); Kamani (Haii); Tomato (Ma); Protective Shield, Sacred Space (WD).

Protection From Stress: Angel of Protection (AK); Yarrow (Ask); Black-Eyed Susan, Calm and Clear (Aus B); Earth Mother Nurtures, Essence the Edge, Meditative Mind (DL); Pink Yarrow (Dv); Corn, Fawn Lily, Sweet Pea (FES); Kamani, Ti (Haii); Urban Stress Remedy (Him A).

Puberty: Adol Essence (Aus B); Expansive Embodiment, Graceful Transformations, Unveiling Self (DL); Alpine Lily, Angelica, Calla Lily, Fairy Lantern, Morning Glory,

Pretty Face (FES); Almond (Ma).

Purification: Aura Cleansing Cactus, Inner Cleansing Cactus, Formation Cactus, Inside Outside Cactus (AK); Purification (Ask); Purifying Essence, Space Clearing (Aus B); Purifying (Peru).

Radiation Problems: Radiation Protection Cactus, T1 (AK); Electro Essence (Aus B).

Rape (Effects of): Billy Goat Plum, Emergency Essence (Aus B); Macrozamia (Aus L); Clearing Energy Fields, Defining Edges, Letting Go, Radiant Strength (DL); Rippy Hillox (Him A); Pear (Ma); Mussel (Pac); Wise Woman (WD).

Rebelliousness: Red Helmet Orchid (Aus B); Red Beak Orchid, Silver Princess Gum (Aus L); Dogbane (DAl); Balancing Extremes, Wise Action (DL); Saguaro (FES); Almond (Ma); Young Heart (WD).

Rejection: Illawarra Flame Tree (Aus B); I Like Being Me, My Own Purple Light (DL); Black Cohosh, Bleeding Heart, Evening Primrose, Holly, Oregon Grape, Pink Monkeyflower (FES); Ukshi (Him A); Raspberry (Ma); Lemon Grass (PF); On Angels' Wings, (WD).

Relationship to Oneself: Beauty Cactus, Bird of Paradise, Love Cactus (AK); Relationship Essence (Aus B); White Desert Primrose (DAl); I Like Being Me, Internal Marriage, Unveiling Self (DL).

Relationship Problems: Mountain Wormwood, Sweetgale (Ask); Bush Gardenia, Relationship Essence, Wedding Bush (Aus B); Emotions in Balance; Purple Eremophila, Rabbit Orchid (Aus L); Gossamer Steel, Heart to Heart, Internal Marriage (DL); Hawthorn May (Dv); Scottish Primrose (F); Bleeding Hearts (FES); Day-Blooming Water Lily, Jade Vine, Kukui, Night-Blooming Water Lily (Haii); Sweet Pea (Hb); Slow Match, Vilayati Amli (Him A); Almond, Grape, Lettuce, Pear, Strawberry (Ma); Alum Root (Pac); Sterling Silver Rose (Peg); Mari Pavie (PF).

Relationships – Breakups: Bleeding Heart (AK); Twinflower (Ask); Emergency Essence, Relationship Essence (Aus B); Snake Vine, Violet Butterfly (Aus L); Heart Klein's Pencil Cholla Cactus (DAl); Acceptance, Letting Go, Light Hearted (DL); Bleeding Heart, Hawthorn May, Nettles (Dv); Support (F); Amazon Sword Plant (Haii); Raspberry, Strawberry (Ma).

Relaxation: Zinnia (AK); Calm and Clear (Aus B); Essences of Relaxation, Dampiera, Hop's Bush, Purple Flag Flower (Aus L); Vervain (B); Indian Root, Indian Tobacco (DAl); Dancing Light Spirit (DL); Dandelion (Dv, FES); Dill, Lavender (FES); Buttercup, Meadowsweet, Sage (Hb); Curry Leaf (Him A); Lettuce, Fig (Ma); Mussel (Pac); Zania (Peru); Relaxation Combo & Spray (PF); Be Relaxed (Sun); Alaskan Birch Forest, Mother's Arms (WD).

Repressed Emotions: Bluebell (Aus B); Rainbow Cactus (DAl); Chaparral (DAl, FES); Balancing Extremes, Clearing Blockages, Unveiling Self, Walking Out of Patterns (DL); Black-Eyed Susan, Fuchsia, Golden Ear Drops (FES); Awapuhi Melemele, Nani-ahiahi (Haii); Red Hibiscus (Him A); Self Expression (LH); Snowdrop (Sun).

Resentment: Mountain Wormwood (Ask); Dagger Hakea (Aus B); Black Kangaroo Paw, Geraldton Wax (Aus L); Compass Barrel Cactus (DAl); Gossamer Steel, Letting Go (DL); Oregon Grape, Scarlet Monkeyflower (FES); Drum Stick, Slow Match, Ukshi (Him A); Raspberry (Ma).

Resignation: Kapok Bush (Aus B); Star of Bethlehem (Aus L); Gorse (B); Tarbrush (DAl); Heart Wings, Perceptions, Wondrous Heart (DL); Wild Rose (FES); Plantain (Hb).

Resolution: Desert Broom (DAl).

Respect: Hitorisizuka Flower (Aus LJ); Bramble (HUB).

Responsibility: Colour Orchid, Golden Barrel Cactus (AK); Many-headed Dryandra, Southern Cross, Yellow Cowslip Orchid (Aus B); Blue-Topped Cow Weed, Red Feather Flower, Wallflower Donkey Orchid (Aus L); Kobushi (Magnolia) Flower (Aus LJ); Scleranthus (B); Ocotillo (DAl); Giant Redwood (GM); Strawberry (Ma).

Restlessness: Black-Eyed Susan, Red Grevillea, Wild Potato Bush (Aus B); Christmas Tree, Red Beak Orchid (Aus L); Agrimony, Scleranthus (B); Meditative Mind (DL); Zinnia (Dv); California Poppy, Morning Glory (FES); Hibiscus (FO); Magnolia (GM); Swallow Wort (Him A); Be Restful (Sun).

Rigidity: Bog Blueberry (Ask); Bauhinia, Hibbertia, Isopogon (Aus B); Beech, Rock Water, Water Violet (B); Prickly Pear Cactus (DAl); Expansive Embodiment, Letting Go (DL); Spruce (Dv); Cherry Plum (GM); Ohai-ali'i (Haii); Nilgiri Longy/St John's Lily/Cape Lily (Him A); Fig (Ma); Mussel, Twinflower (Pac).

Sadness: Colour Orchid, Geranium, Queen of the Night Cactus (AK); Sturt Desert Pea (Aus B); Cat's Paw, Mauve Melaleuca (Aus L); Gentian, Mustard (B); Rhododendron (Dv); Idiot Glee (DL); Borage (Dv); Wolfberry (DAl); Blackberry, Cherry (Ma); Smiles and Giggles (WD).

Sarcasm: Snapdragon (FES); Blackberry (Ma).

Scattered Thinking *See* **Focus (Mental)**: Golden Barrel Cactus (AK); New Perceptions (DL); Peppermint (Sun); Still Mind (WD).

Self-Critical Behaviour: Bird of Paradise (AK); Alpine Azalea, Columbine, Lace Flower (Ask); Billy Goat Plum, Confid (Aus B); Pine (B); Foothills Paloverde, Indian Tobacco (DAl); I Like Being Me (DL); Buttercup (FES); Giant Redwood (GM); Star Jasmine (Haii); Forgiveness (LH); Pineapple (Ma); Twinflower (Pac); Milkmaids (Peg).

Self-Discipline: Hibbertia, Wedding Bush (Aus B); Blue China Orchid (Aus L); Rock Water (B); New Perceptions, Purpose Flows (DL); Lawson Cypress (GM);

Almond, Fig (Ma); Surfgrass (Pac); Sycamore (Peg).

Self-Esteem: Beauty Cactus, Self-Esteem Cactus (AK); Buttercup (AK, FES, Sun); Columbine, Tamarack (Ask); Confid, Five Corners, Sturt Desert Rose (Aus B); Yellow Cone Flower (Aus L); Evening Star, Immortal (DAl); My Heart Knows, Unveiling Self (DL); Echinacea, Sagebrush, Sunflower (FES); Red Oak (GM); Milo (Haii); Daffodil, Star Jasmine, Thistle (Hb); Ukshi (Him A); Hidden Splendour, Strength (Him E); Self Esteem, Self Worth (LH); Sea Palm, Vanilla Leaf (Pac); Milkmaids (Peg); Self Image Combo & Spray (PF).

Selfishness: Bluebell, Rough Bluebell (Aus B); Blue Leschenaultia, Fringed Lily Twiner (Aus L); Yamabuki Flower (Aus LJ); Heather (B); Mala Mujer (DAl); Silverweed (F); Fawn Lily, Trillium (FES); Peach (Ma).

Self-Pity: Southern Cross (Aus B); One-Sided Bottlebrush (Aus L); Chicory (B).

Self Shame/Disgust: Billy Goat Plum (Aus B); Sexual Healing (LH).

Sensitivity to Emotionalism: Angel of Protection Orchid (AK); Pink Yarrow (AK, FES); Angelsword + Fringed Violet (Aus B); Reading Energy Fields (DL); Golden Yarrow (FES); Nui/Coconut (Haii); Protective Shield (WD).

Sensitivity to the Environment: Aura-Cleansing Cactus, Formation Cactus, Radiation Cactus (AK); Electro Essence, Radiation Essence (Aus B); Pink Fairy Orchid (Aus L); Sacred Sphere (DL); Yarrow Special Formula (FES); Nui/Coconut (Haii); Environmental Stress Remedy (Him A); Tomato (Ma); Protective Shield, Sacred Space (WD).

Sensitivity To Negative Thought Forms: Angel of Protection Orchid, Aura-Cleansing Cactus, Inspiration Cactus, Pennyroyal, (AK); Red Grevillea, Space Clearing Mist (Aus B); Clearing Energy Fields (DL); Chaparral, Golden Yarrow, Mountain Pennyroyal, Oregon Grape (FES); Sacred Space, Protective Shield (WD).

Separation/Loss: Murasakikeman Flower (Aus LJ).

Sexual Abuse: Balsam Poplar (Ask); Emergency Essence, Flannel Flower, Sexuality Essence (Aus B); Macrozamia (Aus L); Bisbee Beehive Cactus (DAl); Clearing Energy Fields, Graceful Transformations, I Like Being Me, Letting Go, Radiant Strength (DL); Onion (Dv); Dogwood, Evening Primrose, Mariposa Lily, Pink Monkeyflower, Purple Monkeyflower (FES); Hibiscus, Mai'a/Banana (Haii); Prickly Poppy, Rippy Hillox (Him A); Orange, Strawberry (Ma); Nootka Rose (Pac); Snowdrop (Sun); Mother's Arms, Protective Shield (WD).

Sexual Hang-Ups: Sexuality Essence, Wisteria (Aus B); Clearing Inner Pathways (DL); Basil, California Pitcher Plant, Evening Primrose (FES); Day-Blooming Water Lily, Mai'a/ Banana (Haii); Water Lily (Him A); Down to Earth (Him E); Sexual Healing (LH); Grape (Ma); Mussel (Pac); Marigold (PF).

Sexual Insecurity/Inhibitions: Aggression Orchid, Basil, Fire Lily (AK); Balsam Poplar (Ask); Sensuality Mist, Sexuality Essence (Aus B); Expansive Embodiment, New Perceptions (DL); Hibiscus, Martagon Lily, Sticky Monkeyflower (Dv); Calla Lily, Easter Lily, Rosemary, Sticky Monkeyflower (FES); Bird Cherry (GM); Day-Blooming Water Lily, Pua Kenikeni (Haii); Karvi, Meenalih, Old Maid – white and pink (Him A); Madonna Lily (HUB); Sexual Healing (LH); Purple Magnolia (Pac).

Sexuality, Acceptance of: Arum Lily, Banana, Calla Lily, Red Hibiscus (AK); Billy Goat Plum, Sexuality Essence (Aus B); Acceptance, I Like Being Me (DL); Basil, Pomegranate (Dv); Eros (F); Alpine Lily, Manzanita (FES); Bird Cherry (GM); Niu, Lehur (Haii); Courgette, Rose – red (Hb); Madonna Lily (HUB); Candystick (Pac); Lobivia Cactus, Mountain Pride (Peg).

Sexual/Sensuality Revitalization: Canary Island Bellflower (AK); Sensuality Mist (Aus B); Queen of the Night (DAl);

Dance of Creation (DL); Hibiscus, Lady's Slipper (FES); Sensuality Combo, Spirit Lift, Water Lily (FO); Red Ginger, Night-Blooming Water Lily (Haii); Ixora, Night Jasmine, Water Lily (Him A); Red Ginger, Shasta Lily (Peg); Passion Combo & Spray (PF); Mango Paradise, Red Union (Peru).

Sharing: Bluebell (Aus B); Purple Nymph Water Lily, Christmas Tree (Aus L); Zazensou Flower (Aus LJ); Jojoba, Star Primrose (DAl); Earth Mother Nurtures, Heart to Heart (DL).

Shattered Feelings: Emergency Essence, Sturt Desert Pea, Waratah (Aus B); Cowkicks, Violet Butterfly (Aus L); Lotus Petals of the Heart (DL); Echinacea, Sagebrush (FES); Strength, Vital Spark (Him E); Purple Crocus (Pac); Mother's Arms, On Angels' Wings (WD).

Shock: River Beauty, White Fireweed (Ask); Emergency Essence (Aus B); Crisis Relief (Aus L); Five Flower Remedy, Star of Bethlehem (B); Sacred Sphere (DL); Arnica (Dv, FES); Ulua (Haii); Red Clover (Hb); First Aid Remedy, Radish (Him A); Vital Spark (Him E); Heart of Peace (LH); Pear (Ma); Mother's Arms, On Angels' Wings (WD).

Shyness: Confid Essence, Dog Rose (Aus B); Mimulus (B); My Own Pure Light, Unveiling Self, (DL); Box, Buttercup (Dv); Sea Holly (F); Mallow, Violet (FES); Cherry Plum (GM); Red Tulip (Hb); Pineapple, Strawberry, Tomato (Ma).

Sleep (Disturbed): Boronia, Calm and Clear, (Aus B); Lucid Dreaming (DL); Sweet Dreams (F); Chamomile (FES); Awapuhi-melemele/Yellow Ginger (Haii); Formula 17 Sleep (Him A); Lettuce (Ma); Deep Sleep Combo & Spray (PF).

Spaced-Out (Feeling): Sundew (Aus B); Clematis (B, FES); Pink Fairy Duster (DAl); Rosemary (FES); Avocado (Ma); Sea Turtle (Pac); Copper Beech (Sun); Alaskan Birch Forest, Still Mind (WD).

Stability/Strength: Noble Heart Cactus, Grounding Pountia (AK); Emergency Essence (Aus B); Essences of Inner Strength, W. A. Smoke Bush (Aus L); Red Henbit (BL); Radiant Strength (DL); Black Poplar, Horse Chestnut (GM); Coffee (Haii); Cedar (Him E); Cherry, Pear, Tomato (Ma); Narcissus, Pink Seaweed, Surfgrass (Pac); Inner Strength Combo & Spray (PF); Salvia (PVi).

Strength: Red Grevillea, Waratah (Aus B); Goddess Grass Tree, Happy Wanderer, Russian Forget-Me-Not (Aus L); Mimulus (B); Organ Pipe Cactus, Spineless Prickly Pear (DAl); Radiant Strength (DL); Box (Dv); Cymbidium, Elder, Red Tulip (Hb); Apple, Banana, Coconut, Date, Tomato (Ma); Inner Strength Combo & Spray (PF).

Stress: Dandelion (AK); Labrador Tea (Ask); Crowea, Emergency Essence (Aus B); Purple Flag Flower, Yellow Flag Flower (Aus L); Staghorn Cholla Cactus (DAl); Dill, Nettles, Valerian (Dv); Stress Release (F); Aloe Vera, Corn, Nicotiana, Self-Heal, Sweet Pea (FES); Alder (GM); Cotton, Hau (Haii); Dandelion (Hb); Almond, Spinach, Tomato (Ma); Goatsbeard, Surfgrass (Pac); Mock Orange, Sycamore (Peg); Harmony & Balance Spray, Reduce Stress Combo & Spray (PF); Sweet Bell Pepper (PVi).

Stuttering: Cognis (Aus B); Silver Moon (PF).

Subconscious (Clearing): Queen of the Night Cactus, Epipactis, Sage (AK); Horsetail (Ask); Forget-Me-Not (AK, Ask); Boab (Aus B); Tarbrush (DAl); Clearing Blockages, Clearing Energy Fields, Clearing Inner Pathways, Reveals Mystery Within + Walking Out of Patterns (DL); Chaparral, Mugwort (FES); Awapuhi-melemele/Yellow Ginger (Haii); Swallow Wort (Him A); Lily of the Valley (HUB); Blackberry (Ma); Moonsnail, Poison Hemlock (Pac); Agave, Yaquinana (Peg).

Suicidal Thoughts: Waratah (Aus B); Cherry Plum (B); Higher Levels, Lotus Petals of the Heart (DL); Orange (Ma); Urchin (Pac); Sunflower (PF); On Angels' Wings (WD).

Superiority: Hibbertia, Yellow Cowslip Orchid (Aus B); Mitsubatsutsuji Flower

(Aus LJ); Heart Wings (DL); Malabar Nut Flower (Him A); Banana, Pineapple (Ma).

Tantrums: Dog Rose of the Wild Forces, Kangaroo Paw, Mountain Devil, Rough Bluebell (Aus B); Smiles and Giggles,(DL) Grape (Ma) Scarlet Monkeyflower (FES)

Tenderness: Venus Orchid (AK); Bluebell, Flannel Flower (Aus B); Softening the Edges (DL); Noni (Haii); Date (Ma).

Tension: Dandelion (AK); Emergency Essence (Aus B).

Terror: Emergency Essence, Green Spider Orchid, Grey Spider Flower (Aus B); Rock Rose (B); Rainbow Cactus, Teddy Bear Cholla Cactus (DAl); Tomato (Ma).

Tolerance *See* **Intolerance**: Black-Eyed Susan (Aus B); Acceptance, Infinite Patience, (DL) Mitsubatsutsuji Flower (Aus LJ).

Trapped (Feeling): Venus Fly Trap (AK); Red Grevillea, Sunshine Wattle (Aus B); Geraldton Wax, Russian Centaurea (Aus L); Honeysuckle, Larch (B); Arizona Sycamore (DAl); Expansive Embodiment, Hearts Wings, Higher Levels (DL); Cayenne (Dv); Stonecrop (F); Corn (Ma).

Trauma: Northern Lady's Slipper, River Beauty, Soul Support (Ask); Emergency Essence, Fringed Violet (Aus B); Star of Bethlehem (B); Snowdrop (BL); Zephyr Lily (DAl); Fireweed (Dv); Arnica (Dv, FES, AK); Dogwood, Echinacea, Golden Ear Drops (FES); Beech, Larch, Monterey Pine (GM); Awapuhi Melemele, Kamani, Ulua (Haii); Ashoka Tree, Radish (Him A); Pear (Ma); Hyacinth (Pac); White Hyacinth (PF); Mother's Arms, On Angels' Wings (WD).

Travel: Travel Ease (Ask); Travel Essence (Aus B); Travelease (Aus L); Jetstream (F); Fatigue Combo & Spray (PF).

Trust, Lack of: Flannel Flower, Southern Cross (Aus B); Bog Rosemary, Prickly Wild Rose, White Violet (Ask); Flannel Flower (Aus B); Golden Glory Grevillea (Aus L); Centaury, Red Chestnut (B); Ephedra, Saguaro Cactus, Syrian Rose (DAl);

Reading Energy Fields, My Heart Knows (DL); Angelica, Buttercup, Mallow (Dv); Baby Blue Eyes, Oregon Grape (FES); Hawthorn, Norway Spruce (GM); Bamboo Orchid (Haii); Marjoram, Ragwort, Rosemary, Snowdrop, White Narcissus (Hb); Slow Match (Him A); Lettuce, Spinach (Ma); Camellia (Pac); Let Go & Trust (Peru).

Turmoil: Crowea, Emergency Essence, Red Suva Frangipani (Aus B); Ephedra (DAl); Higher Levels, Graceful Transformations, Meditative Mind (DL); Red Clover (FES); Tormentil (Hb); Christ's Thorn (Him A).

Understanding Problems: Shadow Cactus (AK); One-Sided Wintergreen (Ask); Bush Iris, Pink Flannel Flower (Aus B); Pine (B); Bisbee Beehive Cactus (DAl); New Perceptions, Reading Energy Fields (DL); Love Lies Bleeding (FES); Indian Coral, Malabar Nut Flower, Neem, White Coral Tree (Him A); Raspberry (Ma); Milkmaids, Pine Drops (Peg); Still Mind (WD).

Unloved (Feeling): Sydney Rose (Aus B); Mauve Melaleuca (Aus L); Holly (B, FES); Crown of Thorns, Mariposa Lily, Mesquite (DAl); My Own Pure Light, My Song Calls Me Home (DL); Grape (Ma); Sea Palm (Pac) Mother's Arms, On Angel's Wings (WD).

Victim Mentality: Southern Cross (Aus B); Charlock, Urchin Dryandra (Aus L); Centuary (B); Coral Bean, Immortal, Ocotillo, Star Primrose, Woven Spine Pineapple Cactus (DAl); New Perceptions, Radiant Strength (DL); Canyon Dudleya, Larkspur, Love Lies Bleeding (FES); Strawberry (Ma); Mussel (Pac); Dill (PVi); Viper's Bugloss (Sun).

Violence: Soul Support (Ask); Emergency Essence, Mountain Devil, Rough Bluebell (Aus B); Orange Spiked Pea Flower (Aus L); Black Cohosh, Dogwood, Scarlet Monkeyflower (FES); Stick Rorrish (Haii); Mussel (Pac).

Vitality/Uplifting: Life force Cactus (AK); Lighten Up (Ask); Dynamis Essence

(Aus B); Essences of Energy (Aus L); Life Force (F); Spirit Lift Spritz (FO); Puklawe (Haii); Energy Combo & Spray (PF); Be Vitalized (Sun).

Vulnerability: Angel of Protection Orchid (AK); Emergency Essence (Aus B); Buffalo Gourd, Pencil Cholla Cactus, Spineless Prickly Pear (DAl); White Yarrow (Dv); Grass of Parnassus (F); Golden Yarrow, Pink Monkeyflower, Sticky Monkeyflower (FES); Viburnum (GM); Mountain Apple/Ohi-a-'ai (Haii); Pansy, (Hb); Cowslip (HUB); Apple, Grape (Ma); Yellow Yarrow (PVi); Lady's Mantle (Sun); Mother's Arms, On Angels' Wings; Protective Shield (WD).

Willpower: Blackberry (AK); Bunchberry (Ask); Boronia, Bottlebrush, Monga Waratah, Southern Cross (Aus B); Blue China Orchid (Aus L); Mitsubatsutsuji Flower (Aus LJ); Aloe, Coral Bean, Desert Marigold, Pencil Cholla Cactus (DAl); Manifesting Thought Forms (DL); Box (Dv, GM); Cayenne (Dv, FES); Blackberry, Mountain Pride, Tansy (FES); Willowherb (F); Hinahina-ku-kahakai (Haii); Broom, Pansy, Sunflower (Hb); Solomon's Seal (HUB); Corn, Tomato (Ma); Snowdrop, Surfgrass (Pac); Ettringite (Peg).

Women – Accepting Femininity: Beauty Cactus (AK); Woman Essence (Aus B); Acceptance, Dance of Creation, I Like Being Me (DL); Quince (Dv); Femininity (F); Pomegranate (FES); Frangipani, Orchid Queen, Sensuality Blend, Spirit lift Spritz (FO); Hinahina-ku-kahakai, La'au'-aila, Lehua (Haii); Woman's Balance, True Beauty (LH); Rattlesnake Plantain Orchid (Peg); Wild Feminine (Peru); Sacred Void (SW); Wise Woman (WD).

Women – Relating To Men: Relationship Essence (Aus B); Internal Marriage, Gossamer Steel (DL); Baby Blue Eyes (FES); Water Lily, Sensuality Blend, Spirit lift Spritz (FO); Hinahina-ku-kahakai (Haii); Rattlesnake Plantain Orchid (Peg).

Women – Strengthening Femininity: Bellflower, Canary Island Pumpkin, Venus Orchid (AK); Woman Essence (Aus B); Queen of the Night, Star Primrose (DAl); I Like Being Me, Radiant Strength (DL); Zucchini (Dv); Femininity (F); Alpine Lily, Mariposa Lily, Pomegranate (FES); Frangipani, Orchid Queen, Sensuality Blend, Spirit Lift Spritz (FO); La'au'-aila, Lehua (Haii); Lady's Mantle (Hb); Woman's Balance (LH); Wise Woman (WD).

Worry: Crowea, Emergency Essence (Aus B); Brown Boronia, Golden Waitsia (Aus L); Agrimony, White Chestnut (B); Jumping Cholla Cactus, Melon Loco (DAl); Filaree, Garlic (FES); St John's Wort (Hb); Apple, Spinach (Ma); Narcissus, Pipsissewa, Urchin (Pac).

Working Harmony: Calm and Clear Mist, Space Clearing Mist (Aus B); Lighter Space Mist, Working Harmony Mist (LH); Clearing Mist, Harmonize and Balance Mist (PF).

Spiritual

Abandoned (Feeling): Chalice Well (Ask E); Illawarra Flame Tree, Tall Yellow Top (Aus B); Mesquite, Queen of the Night, Saguaro Cactus (DAl); Earth Mother Nurtures (DL); Angelica (FES); Persian Ironwood (GM); Grape, Strawberry (Ma); Mother's Arms, On Angels' Wings (WD).

Abundance; Abund Combo (Aus B); Bluebell (HUB); Abundance Program (Pac); Enhancement Fung Shui Spray (PF); I Am Generous (Peru).

Acceptance: Tidal Forces (Ask E); Bauhinia, Bottlebrush (Aus B); Eucalyptus (AK); Green Fairy Orchid, Icelandic Poppy (Ask); Five Corners, Red Suva Frangipani (Aus B); Pin Cushion Hakea (Aus L); Acceptance, Dancing Light Spirit, My Heart Knows (DL); Mallow (Dv); Shooting Star (FES); Norway Maple (GM); Rose Apple/ Ohi'a loke (Haii); Chamomile (Hb); Day-Blooming Jasmine (Him A); Apple, Date, (Ma); Anemone, Snowberry, Windflower (Pac); Eclipse (PVi); Sterling Silver Rose (Peg) White Violet (Sun).

Alignment: Chiming Bells, Paper Birch (Ask); Angelsword, Bush Iris, Crowea (Aus B); Internal Marriage (DL); Lotus (Dv, FES); Apple, Harebell, Sea Pink (F); Pine (GM); Hawaiian Tree, Passion Flower (Haii); Gulaga (Him E); Almond, Strawberry (Ma); Viridiflora (PF); Still Mind (WD).

Astral Travel: Orchis (AK); Meditation Essence, Red Lily (Aus B); Lucid Dreaming (DL); Wayfaring Tree (GM); Kou (Haii); Mouse Ear Chickweed (Hb); Foxglove, Mugwort, Periwinkle (HUB); Strawberry (Ma); Rosa Ecae (Peg).

Attunement (Higher Realms): Angel Orchid, Angel of Protection Orchid, Channelling Orchid, Deva Orchid (AK); Meditation Essence (Aus B); Arnica (Dv); Clear Light (F); Angelica, Forget-Me-Not (FES); Judas Tree (GM); Nana-honua, Nani-ahiahi, Pa'u-o-hi-iaka (Haii); Dittany of Crete (HUB); Staghorn Algae, Poplar (Pac); Angel Face Rose, Holy Thorn, Indian Pipe, Rosa Chinensis Minima, Spider Lily, Tagua (Peg); High Frequency, Purification (Peru); Heart of Nature, Meditative Mind (WD); Angelic Essence (WL).

Aura: Aura-Cleansing Cactus, White Yarrow (AK); Aloe Vera, Pennyroyal (AK, FES) Guardian (Ask); Angelsword, Crowea, Fringed Violet, Grey Spider Flower (Aus B); Clearing Energy Fields, Radiant Strength, Reading Energy Fields, Sacred Sphere (DL); Arnica, Yarrow Special Formula (FES); Pink Orchid (FO); Panini-awa'awa (Haii); St John's Wort, Yarrow (Hb); Aura Balancing and Strengthening Formula (Him A); Aura Cleansing (Him E); Pear (Ma); Aloe Eru, Dutchman's Breeches, Okenite, Snowdrop (Peg); Angel Rejuvenation Spray, Crystal Clear Spray (Peru); Ligustrum, Vanilla (PF); Protective Shield (WD).

Awareness: Rosemary (AK); Full Moon Reflection (Ask E); Meditation Essence (Aus B); Expanding Awareness, Higher Levels, New Perceptions (DL); Forget-Me-Not, Mullein (Dv); Wild Service Tree, Wych Elm (GM); Anemone, Viburnum (Pac).

Balance – Male/Female: Calla Lily (AK); Green Fairy Orchid, Sitka Spruce Pollen (Ask); Bush Fuchsia, Crowea (Aus B); Centred Love, Gossamer Steel, Internal Marriage, (DL); Niu (Haii); Almond (Ma); Red Ginger (Peg).

Balance – Sexuality/Spirituality: Bush Iris, Flannel Flower, Red Lily, Wisteria, (Aus B); Star Primrose (DAl); Internal Marriage (DL); Water Lily (FO); Red Ginger (Peg).

Being Here – Resistance to: Here and Now Cactus (AK); Sundew, Tall Yellow Top (Aus B); I Like Being Me, My Song Calls Me Home (DL); Fawn Lily, Manzanita, Milkweed, Shooting Star (FES); Awapuhi-melemele/Yellow Ginger (Haii); Oriental Poppy (Hb).

Belonging: Chalice Well (Ask E); Tall Yellow Top (Aus B); Cow Parsnip (Ask); Jojoba, Milky Nipple Cactus, Star Primrose (DAl); Earth Mother Nurtures, My Heart Knows (DL); Baby Blue Eyes, Sweet Pea (FES); Monterey Pine (GM); Maize (Hb); Arbutus (Pac); Chin Cactus (Peg); Alaskan Birch Forest (WD).

Blocked Spirituality: Meditation Essence (Aus B); Indian Root (DAl); Clearing Blockages, Heart Wings, Lotus Petals of the Heart (DL); Cayenne, Lotus, Star Tulip (FES); White Hibiscus (Him A).

Body/Soul Balance: Apple Rose Hybrid (AK); Pineapple Weed (Ask); Billy Goat Plum, Bush Iris (Aus B); Expansive Embodiment (DL); Great Sallow (GM); Red Hibiscus (Him A); Gruss an Aachen (PVi).

Boundaries: Blueberry Cactus, Inside/Outside Cactus (AK); Guardian (Ask); Angelsword, Boab, Flannel Flower, Fringed Violet (Aus B); Defining Edges (DL); Corn (FES, PVi); Kou (Haii); Rhubarb (Hb); Isan (Him E); Strawberry (Ma); Nymphenburg (PVi).

Catalyst: Dynamis Essence (Aus B); Stepping Ahead Now (DL); Cayenne, Tansy (FES); Gratefulness (Him E); Camellia

(Pac); Curry Leaf Tree, Hooded Ladies' Tresses (Peg).

Centring: Red Clover (AK); Crowea (Aus B); Alternanthera (BL); Buffalo Gourd, Candy Barrel Cactus, Whitehorn (DAl); Centered Love, Balancing Extremes (DL); Daisy (F); Indian Pink, Lotus, Yerba Santa (FES); Sweet Chestnut (GM); Alkanet, Gypsy Rose, Potato (Hb); Vital Spark, Well-Being (Him E); At the Heart of Being (LH); Pear, Tomato (Ma); Douglas Aster, Ox-Eye Daisy, Viburnum (Pac).

Death and Dying: Victoria Regina Orchid (AK); Forget-Me-Not (AK, FES); Bottlebrush, Bush Iris, Red Suva Frangipani, Transition Essence (Aus B); Hackberry, Sacred Datura (DAl); Graceful Transformation, Letting Go (DL); Snowdrop (F); Angels' Trumpet, Chrysanthemum (FES); Blackberry (Hb); Soul Family (Peru).

Chakra Balance: Delph (AK); Crowea (Aus B); Lady's Slipper, Lotus (FES); Lilac (GM); Lilac, Rhubarb (Hb); Chakra Tonic Formula (Him A); Balancer (Pac); Blue Witch, Hydrangea, Indian Pipe, Red Spider Lily (Peg); Higher Chakra Trilogy (Peru); All Sound Wave Essences.

Channelling: Channelling Orchid (AK); Judas Tree (GM); Astral Orchid (Him E).

Change (Major): Mistletoe (AK); Bauhinia, Bottlebrush (Aus B); Buffalo Gourd, Tarbrush (DAl); Acceptance, Higher Levels, Transformations (DL); Graceful Heart Support (F); Elder, Lawson Cypress (GM); Wiliwili (Haii); Ixora (orange, white, pink) (Him A); Corn, Tomato (Ma); Brown Kelp, Poison Hemlock (Pac); Tree Opuntia, Washington Lily (Peg); Graceful Shifts, Sweet New Beginnings (Peru).

Cleansing: Delph, Inner Cleansing Cactus, Inside/Outside Cactus (AK); Fireweed, Laird Hot Springs, Portage Glacier (Ask); Purifying Essence, Space Clearing Mist (Aus B); Clearing Blockages, Clearing Energy Fields, Clearing Inner Pathways (DL); White Willow (GM); Lotus (Haii); Apple, Blackberry (Ma).

Commitment: Here and Now Cactus (AK); Wedding Bush (Aus B); Prickly Pear Cactus, Teddy Bear Cholla Cactus (DAl); Peach (Ma).

Compassion: Love Orchid (AK); Bluebell, Rough Bluebell (Aus B); Beech (B); Immortal, Mesquite (DAl); Lotus Petals of the Heart (DL); Cherry (F); Poison Oak, Sunflower, Yellow Star Tulip (FES); Lucombe Oak, Monkey Puzzle Tree (GM); Ohai-ali'i/Empathy (Haii); Parval (Him A); Peach, Date, Raspberry (Ma).

Confidence: Paper Birch (Ask); Confid Essence (Aus B); My Heart Knows, Purpose Flows (DL); Red Oak, Spindle (GM); At the Heart of Being (LH); Pineapple (Ma).

Courage: Cattail Pollen, Yellow Dryas (Ask); Black-Eyed Susan, Borage (FES); White Poplar (GM); Wiliwili (Haii); Tomato (Ma); Peace, Summer Squash (PVi); Warriors Path (SW).

Denial: Bluebell, Bush Fuchsia, Pink Mulla Mulla, Red Lily (Aus B); Wolfberry (DAl); Unveiling Self (DL); Deerbrush, Nicotiana (FES); Blackberry (Ma); Sierra Rein Orchid (Peg); Dill (PVi).

Destiny: Inspiration Cactus (AK); Pink Mulla Mulla, Silver Princess (Aus B); Lady's Slipper, Shooting Star (FES).

Dignity: Confid Essence (Aus B); My Own Pure Light, Radiant Strength (DL); Lady's Slipper, Shooting Star (FES); Banana, Strawberry (Ma); Wise Woman (WD).

Direction: Silver Princess (Aus B); Orchid (BL); Pencil Cholla Cactus, Spanish Bayonet Yucca, White Desert Primrose (DAl); Purpose Flows, Stepping Ahead Now (DL); California Wild Rose, Chrysanthemum (FES); Glastonbury Thorn, Lawson Cypress, Tamarisk (GM); Bamboo Orchid (Haii); Gypsy Rose, Speedwell (Hb); Avocado (Ma); Surfgrass (Pac); Ambassador (PVi); Yellow Archangel (Sun); Warriors Path (SW).

Dream Time: Lucid Dreaming (DL); Madame Alfred Carriere (PF).

Empathy: Common White Spider Orchid (Aus L); Heart to Heart, Reading Energy Fields (DL); Raspberry (Ma).

Empowerment – General: Beauty Cactus (AK); Sitka Spruce Pollen (Ask); Confid Essence (Aus B); Desert Marigold, Klein's Pencil Cholla Cactus, Silverleaf Nightshade, Saguaro Cactus, Thurber's Gilia (DAl); My Own Pure Light (DL); Laurel, Monkey Flower, Thistle (F); Norway Maple, Plum (GM); Pua Melia/Frangipani (Haii); Mandrake, Marjoram (HUB); Tomato (Ma); Solar Power (Peru); Warriors' Path (SW); Fire Essence (WL).

Empowerment – As a Woman (Femininity): Confid Essence Southern Cross (Aus B); Mala Mujer, Melon Loco, Queen of the Night (DAl); Pomegranate (Dv); Calla Lily, Mountain Pride, Pomegranate (FES); Frangipani, Orchid Queen (FO); Hinahina-ku-kahakai (Haii); Goddess (Him E); Wise Woman (WD).

Empowerment – As A Man (Masculinity): Confid Essence, Southern Cross (Aus B); Mountain Mahogany (DAl); Agrimony, Calla Lilly, Larkspur, Mountain Pride, Nicotiana, Sunflower (FES); Solar Power (Peru) Male Power Combo & Spray (PF).

Emptiness: Sunflower (AK, Sun) Abund Essence (Aus B); Mauve Melaleuca, Wallflower Donkey Orchid (Aus L); Spineless Prickly Pear (DAl); Meditative Mind (DL); Sagebush (FES); Osier (GM); Grape (Ma); Alaskan Birch Forest, Still Mind (WD).

Enlightenment: Bush Iris, Pink Flannel Flower, Sydney Rose (Aus B); Lotus Petals of the Heart, Meditative Mind (DL); 'Ili'ahi, Lotus (Haii); Indian Paintbrush (PF) Alaskan Birch Forest, Still Mind (WD).

Etheric Body: Red-Purple Poppy, Sweetgrass (Ask); Banksia Robur, Fringed Violet (Aus B); Expansive Embodiment, Sacred Sphere (DL); Panini-O-ka (Haii); Shasta Lily, Sourgrass (Peg); Protective Shield, Sacred Space (WD).

Faith: Waratah (Aus B); Higher Levels (DL); Harebell (F); Angelica, Baby Blue Eyes, Borage, Gorse (FES); Bamboo Orchid (Haii); Broom (Hb); Red-hot Cattail (Him A); Spinach (Ma).

Freedom: Stinking Hellebore (HUB).

Focus Cephalanthera (AK); Cognis (Aus B); Ixora (Haii); Avocado (Ma).

Getting Out Of Your Own Way: Shadow cactus (AK); Black-Eyed Susan (Aus B); Stepping Ahead Now (DL); Canyon Dudleya, Fawn Lily, Sagebrush (FES); Hoptree, Teddy Bear Cholla Cactus (DAl); Revelation (F); Tree of Heaven (GM); Banana (Ma); Brown Kelp (Pac); Eclipse (PVi).

Grounded (Feeling): Earth Star Cactus, Grounding Opuntia, Here and Now Cactus, Orchis (AK); Northern Twayblade (Ask); Red Lily, Sundew (Aus B); Melon Loco, Milky Nipple Cactus (DAl); Bell Heather (F); Corn, Fawn Lily, Rosemary, Shooting Star, St John's Wort, Sweet Pea (FES); Black Poplar, Persian Iron Wood (GM); Buttercup, Maize, Plantain (Hb); Strawberry (Ma); Anchoring Light, Balance & Stability (Peru); Narcissus, Pink Seaweed, Windflower (Pac); Heart Of The Earth (SW); Alaskan Birch Forest (WD); Earth Essence (WL).

Growth: Inside/Outside Cactus, Mullein (AK); Golden Corydalis, Fireweed Combo, Spiraea (Ask); Bush Iris, Mint Bush, Yellow Cowslip Orchid (Aus B); Arizona White Oak, Indian Tobacco, Teddy Bear Cholla Cactus (DAl); Graceful Transformations, New Perceptions, Stepping Ahead Now (DL); Scotch Broom (FES); Gorse (GM); Mango (Haii); Bindweed (Hb); Tree Mallow (HUB).

Guidance: Rose of Sharon (AK); Mullein (AK, FES); Meditation Essence (Aus B); Calling All Angels, Hairy Butterworth, Monkshood, Shooting Star (Ask); Angelica, (FES); My Heart Knows, My Own Pure Light (DL); Coconut, Spinach (Ma); Inner Guru (Peru); Still Mind, Wise Woman (WD).

Humanitarian Feelings: Amazon River (AK); Sydney Rose, Yellow Cowslip Orchid (Aus B); Common White Spider Orchid (Aus L); Ocotillo (DAl); Expanding Awareness (DL); Naupaka-kahakai (Haii); Parval (Him A); Yellow Silk Cotton Tree (Him E); Yellow Rose (PF).

Humility: Japanese Rose (AK); Gymea Lily (Aus B); Woolly Smokebush (Aus L); Wondrous Heart (DL); Golden Rod, Yellow Silk Cotton Tree (Him A); Banana (Ma).

Incarnation: Here and Now Cactus, Psyche Orchid (AK); Iceland Poppy (Ask); Flannel Flower, Bush Iris, She Oak (Aus B); Defining Edges, Expansive Embodiment, I Like Being Me (DL); Lotus, Shooting Star (FES); Mamane (Haii).

Independence: Confid Essence (Aus B); Uguisukazura Flower (Aus LJ); Evening Star (DAl); Tree Lichen (GM).

Inner Conflict: Blue Elf Viola (Ask); Ratany (DAl); Internal Marriage (DL); Fawn Lily (FES); Pear (GM); Noho Malie (Haii); Gateway (Him E); Blackberry (Ma).

Inner Beauty: Bird of Paradise (AK); Paw Paw, Wild Potato Bush (Aus B); Frangipani, Orchid Queen (FO); Rock Primula (Him E); Radiant Strength (Pac); Beauty Cactus, Bella Portugaise Rose (Peg).

Inner Harmony: Aloe Vera, Sun Orchid Love Cactus, Lavender (AK); Lotus (AK, FES); Shooting Star, Twinflower (Ask); Black-Eyed Susan (Aus B); Immortal (DAl); Lotus Petals of the Heart (DL); Sea Pink (F); California Poppy, Star Tulip (FES); Ash, Foxglove Tree (GM); Pear (Ma).

Inner Strength: Golden Barrel Cactus (AK); Wild Sweet Pea (Ask); Confid Essence, Emergency Essence (Aus B); Agave, Arizona White Oak (DAl); Radiant Strength (DL); Globe Thistle (F); Penstemon (FES); Pink Orchid (FO); Ash (GM); Hidden Splendour, Well-Being (Him E); At the Heart of Being (LH); Inner Strength Combo & Spray, Christmas Cactus (PF); Nymphenburg (PVi); Tomato (Ma).

Innocence: Forget-Me-Not (Ask); Little Flannel Flower (Aus B); Devil's Claw (DAl); Wondrous Heart (DL); Deer Bush (FES); Blackberry, Spinach (Ma); Lily of the Valley, Moonsnail (Pac); Young Heart (WD).

Insight/Clairvoyance: Hoop Petticoat Daffodil, Platanthera (AK); Meditation Essence (Aus B); Hearts Wings, Meditative Mind, New Perceptions, Reading Energy Fields (DL); Pine (GM); Black Tulip, Wild Thyme (HUB); Blackberry (Ma); Chiton, Virburnum (Pac); Madame Alfred Carriere (PF); Eclipse (PVi).

Integration: Passion Flower, Sage, Tibetan White Rose, Wild Rose Hybrid (AK); Golden Corydalis, Opium Poppy, Sweetgale, Solstice Sun, White Spruce (Ask); Crowea, Slender Rice Flower (Aus B); Queen of the Night (DAl); Graceful Transformations (DL); Holy Grail (F); Basil, Lotus, Lady's Slipper, Shasta Daisy (FES); Gorse, Spindle (GM); Angel's Trumpet (Haii); Isan (Him E); Apple, Orange (Ma); Integration (Peru); Lady Eubanksia (PF); Blaze Improved Climbing Rose, White Lightnin' (PVi); Integration Combination, Integrate Spritz (SW).

Integrity: Love Cactus, Noble Heart Cactus (AK); Sturt Desert Rose (Aus B); Deer Bush, Echinacea (FES); Tree of Heaven (GM); Sithihea (Him A); Thistle (HUB); Strawberry (Ma).

Intuition: Lamb's Quarters, White Spruce (Ask); Bush Fuchsia, Bush Iris (Aus B); Queen of the Night (DAl); Expanding Awareness, Meditative Mind, New Perceptions, Reading Energy Fields (DL); Eyebright (Dv); Elecampane(F); Forget-Me-Not (FES); Horse Chestnut, Mimosa, Stags Horn Sumach (GM); Sunflower (Hb); Neem (Him A); Fig (Ma); Poplar, Viburnum (Pac); Inner Guru (Peru).

Journey (Spiritual): Lotus (AK, FES) Chocolate Orchid (AK); Mint Bush (Aus B); Teddy Bear Cholla Cactus (DAl); Lawson Cypress (GM); Cup of Gold, Lotus (Haii); Calypso Orchid, Star Thistle (Peg) Divine Purpose (SW); Air Essence (WL).

Karmic Problems: Sundew (AK); Boab (karma between individual people), Bluebell, Red Lily, Waratah (karma generally) (Aus B); Lucid Dreaming (DL); Karma Clear (F); Forget-Me-Not (FES); Awapuhi-melemele/Yellow Ginger (Haii); Rose Campion (PF); Higher Self Essence (WL).

Learning Life's Lessons: Isopogon (Aus B); Sage (FES); Magnolia (GM); Coral Root (Spotted) (Peg).

Letting Go Bottlebrush (Aus B); Dampiera, Wallflower Donkey Orchid (Aus L); Agave, Indian Root, Lilac, Rainbow Cactus, Strawberry Cactus, (DAl); Expanding Awareness, Letting Go (DL); Bleeding Heart, Sage Brush (FES); Crack Willow, Privet, Tree Lichen (GM); Marsh Woundwort, Ragwort (Hb); Let Go (Him E); Fig, Raspberry (Ma); Salal, Sea Palm (Pac); Sycamore (Peg); Madame Louise Levique (PF).

Listening (Inner Voice): Higher Self Orchid, Mullein (AK); Twinflower (Ask); Bush Fuchsia (Aus B); Candy Barrel Cactus (DAl); Heart of Nature, My Heart Knows (DL); Calendula, Star Tulip (FES); Banana, Date, Peach (Ma); Orange Ruffles (PVi); Listening Heart (SW); Fire Essence (WL).

Manifestation: Early Purple Orchid, Enchanter's Nightshade (HUB); Rosa Coriifolia Froebelii (Peg).

Materialism: Bluebell, Bush Iris (Aus B); Hedgehog Cactus (DAl); Rose Water Lily, Silverweed (F); Chrysanthemum, Hound's Tongue, Trillium (FES); Foxglove (HUB).

Meditation (Aid): Horsetail, Paper Birch (Ask); Meditation Essence, Angelsword (Aus B); White Nymph Waterlily (Aus L); Meditative Mind (DL); Blackberry (Dv); Clear Light (F); Angel's Trumpet, Fawn Lily, Star Tulip (FES); Lotus (FES, Him A); Stag's Horn Sumach, Tulip Tree (GM); 'Ili'ahi, Koa (Haii); Bougainvillea (Haii, Him A); Chamomile, Lavender, Nasturtium, Salpglossis, Scarlet Pimpernel (Hb); Blue Dragon, Isan, Lotus, Sat-Chit-Ananda (Him E); At One (LH); Banana, Grape, Lettuce (Ma); Deer's Tongue (Peg); Higher Frequency, Light Navigator (Peru); Still Mind (WD).

Meridian Balance: Northern Lady's Slipper (Ask); Crowea, Slender Rice Flower (Aus B); Silver Maple (GM).

Motivation: Opium Poppy, Tundra Rose (Ask); Silver Princess (Aus B); Mountain Mahogany (DAl); Purpose Flows (DL); California Wild Rose, Tansy (FES); Thornapple (HUB).

Nature Awareness/Attunement: Alpine Azalea, Chiming Bells, Cassandra, Green Bells of Ireland, Green Bog Orchid, Moschatel, Northern Twayblade, Spiraea (Ask); Bush Fuchsia (Aus B); Deer Bush (B); Heart of Nature (DL); Sweet Corn (Dv); Poison Oak, Yellow Star Tulip (FES); Ash, Lilac, Rowan, Whitebeam, Yellow Buckeye (GM); Harebell (Hb); Four-Leafed Clover (HUB); Spinach (Ma); Poplar (Pac); Gilia Scarlet (Peg); Nature Communication (Peru); Alaskan Birch Forest (WD); Devic Essence (WL).

Nurturing: Grass of Parnassus, Lighten Up, Spiraea (Ask); Bluebell (Aus B); Hedgehog Cactus, Mariposa Lily (DAl, FES); Earth Mother Nurtures (DL); Quince (FES); Tulip Tree (GM); Water Lily (HUB); Grape (Ma); Be Nurtured (Peru); Mother's Arms, On Angel's Wings (WD); Angelic Essence (WL).

Oneness (Universal): Green Fairy Orchid (Ask); Sydney Rose (Aus B) Organ Pipe Cactus, Queen of the Night (DAl); Expanding Awareness, Lotus Petals of the Heart (DL); Crack Willow (GM).

Opening Up: French Lavender, Passion Flower (AK); Icelandic Poppy (Ask); Pink Mulla Mulla (Aus B); Dampiera (Aus L); Unveiling Self (DL); Dandelion Lotus, Passion Flower (Dv); Lime, Scots Pine (F); Mugwort (FES); Ilima (Haii); Jacob's Ladder (Hb); Wild Pansy (HUB); Avocado, Tomato (Ma); Poplar (Pac).

Passion: Pink Orchid (FO); Passionate Life (LH); Fairy Rose, Passion Combo & Spray, (PF).

Past (Letting Go): Release Cactus, Shadow Cactus (AK); Bottlebrush (Aus B); Cape Bluebell (Aus L); Honeysuckle (B, FES); Indian Tobacco, Wolfberry (DAl); Letting Go, Reveals Mystery Within, Walking Out of Patterns (DL); Rowan (F); Chrysanthemum, Forget-Me-Not (FES); Juniper, Mulberry (GM); Ixora (Haii); Marsh Woundwort, Mugwort, Rosebay Willowherb (Hb); Prickly Poppy (Peg).

Past Life (Overspill): Dog Rose of the Wild Forces, Green Spider Orchid (Aus B); Clearing Energy Fields, Reading Energy Fields (DL); Kukui, Noho Malie (Haii); Agave Yaquinana, Caterpillar Plant (Peg); Higher Self Essence (WL).

Past Life Problems: Past Life Orchid (AK); Black and White Spruce (Ask); Pink Mulla Mulla (Aus B); Clearing Energy Fields, Lucid Dreaming (DL); Evening Primrose (FES); Monterey Pine (GM); Naupaka-kahakai, (Haii); Gul Mohar, Red-hot Cattail (Him A); Cuckoo Pint (HUB); Agave Yaquiana, Everlasting, Prickly Poppy (Peg); Higher-Self Essence (WL).

Peace (Inner): Chiming Bells, Cow Parsnip (Ask); Black-Eyed Susan, Crowea (Aus B); White Nymph Waterlily (Aus L); Agrimony (B); I Like Being Me, Lotus Petals of the Heart (DL); Scottish Primrose (F); Sage (FES); Black Poplar, Holly, Italian Alder (GM); Naupaka-kahakai (Haii); Lavender (Hb); Butterfly Lily, Gulmohar, Indian Coral (Him A); Heart of Peace (LH); Pear (Ma); Sweet Bell Pepper (PVi); On Angels' Wings (WD).

Perception: Bush Iris, Freshwater Mangrove (Aus B); Cane Cholla Cactus, Indian Root Sacred Datura (DAl); Expanding Awareness, New Perceptions (DL); Sagebush, Shasta Daisy (FES); Lani ali'i/Alamanda (Haii); Brown Kelp (Pac); Choke Cherry (Peg); Maggie (PF).

Perseverance: Kapok Bush, Wedding Bush (Aus B); Teddy Bear Cholla Cactus (DAl); Wondrous Heart (DL); Mountain Pride (FES); Coconut, Orange (Ma); Washington Lily (Peg).

Perspective: Valerian (Ask); Bauhinia, Freshwater Mangrove, Paw Paw (Aus B); Cane Cholla Cactus (DAl); New Perceptions (DL); Rabbitbrush (FES); Jacaranda (Haii); Sea Buckthorn (GM); Banana (Ma); Death Camas, Twin Flower, Pearly Everlasting (Pac); Green Rein Orchid (Peg); Perceiving Spirit (Peru).

Power: Sitka Spruce Pollen, Soapberry (Ask); Southern Cross, Waratah (Aus B); Desert Marigold, Spineless Prickly Pear (DAl); Radiant Strength (DL); Rose Alba (F); Mountain Pride, Quince, Trillium (FES); Plum (GM); Ivy-Leafed Toadflax (HUB); Tomato (Ma) Chives, Dill (PVi).

Preparation: Mint Bush, Sundew, Yellow Cowslip Orchid (Aus B); Wise Action (DL); Marsh Woundwort (Hb).

Pretending: Boronia, Little Flannel Flower (Aus B); Cane Cholla Cactus (DAl); Canyon Dudleya (FES).

Protection – General: Angel of Protection Orchid, White Yarrow (AK); White Violet (Ask); Angelsword, Fringed Violet (Aus B); Sacred Sphere, (DL); Angelica (Dv); Psychic Protection (F); Mountain Pennyroyal (FES); Yarrow (FES, Hb); Italian Alder (GM); Kamani (Haii); Monkshood, St John's Wort (Hb); Lemon (HUB); Tomato (Ma); Urchin (Pac); Protective Shield, Sacred Space (WD).

Protection – From Psychic Attack: Aura-Cleansing Cactus (AK); Yarrow (Ask); Angelsword, Boab, Fringed Violet, Grey Spider Flower, Lichen (Aus B); Radiant Strength, Reading Energy, Sacred Sphere (DL); Red Clover (Dv); Psychic Protection (F); Garlic, Pennyroyal, Purple Monkeyflower, St John's Wort (FES); Yew (GM); Pa'u-o-hi-iaka, Ti (Haii); Elder (Hb); Deadly Nightshade, Larkspur (HUB); Tomato (Ma); Urchin (Pac); Rosa Sericea Pteracantha (Peg); Vanilla (PF); Protective Shield, Sacred Space (WD).

Psycho-Spiritual Balance: Victoria Regina Orchid, Paradise Lily (AK); Angelsword, Bush Fuchsia, Crowea

(Aus B); Balancing Extremes (DL); Creeping Thistle, Green Rose (Peg).

Purification: Five-Leafed Clover (HUB).

Purpose: Inspirational Cactus (AK); Ladies' Tresses, Paper Birch, Shooting Star (Ask); Silver Princess (Aus B); Orchid (BL); Hoptree, Soapberry Yucca, Spineless Prickly Pear (DAl); Purpose Flows (DL); Ancient Yew, Apple, Bell Heather (F); Buttercup (FES); Great Sallow (GM); Bougainvillea, Plumeria (Haii); Geranium, Monkshood (Hb); Avocado (Ma); Cellular Memory (Pac); California Buckeye, Pegasus Orchid Cactus, Sulcorebutia Cactus (Peg); Ancient Wisdom (Peru); Viridiflora (PF); Ambassador (PVi); Divine Purpose (SW); Fire Essence (WL).

Quest: Silver Princess (Aus B); Wild Oat (B); Red Oak (GM).

Quietness: Twinflower (Ask); Black-Eyed Susan, Dog Rose of the Wild Forces (Aus B); Meditative Mind, Sacred Sphere (DL); Strawberry Tree (GM); Almond, Banana, Lettuce, Strawberry (Ma).

Reality: Willow (Ask); Red Lily, Sundew (Aus B); Angelica (FES); Oak (GM); Nijara 2 (Him E).

Rebuilding/Repatterning Life: Prickly Wild Rose (Ask); Bottlebrush, Sunshine Wattle (Aus B); Cowkicks (Aus L); Echinacea (FES); Repatterning (Him E).

Relationships: Heart Orchid (AK); Relationship Essence (Aus B); Gossamer Steel, Heart to Heart, Unveiling Self (DL); Plumbago, Red Ginger (Haii); Almond, Grape, Lettuce, Pear, Strawberry (Ma); Pegasus Orchid Cactus (Peg); Red Union (Peru); Angelic Essence (WL).

Releasing Old Patterns: Inner Cleansing Cactus, Inspirational Cactus, Releasing Cactus (AK); Blueberry Pollen (Ask); Boronia, Bottlebrush (Aus B); Foothills Paloverde, Immortal, Tar Bush, Whitehorn (DAl); Walking Out of Patterns (DL); Ancient Yew, Lichen (F); Fairy Lantern (FES); Lime (GM); Rosebay Willowherb (Hb); Nijara 2 (Him E);

Raspberry (Ma); Fuchsia (Pac).

Self-Acceptance: Here and Now Cactus, Self-Esteem Cactus, Spring Gold, Sun Orchid (AK); Tamarack (Ask); Five Corners, Philotheca (Aus B); Aloe, Hedgehog Cactus, Ocotillo, Teddy Bear Cholla Cactus (DAl); Acceptance, I Like Being Me (DL); Black-Eyed Susan (Dv); Holy Thorn (F); Baby Blue Eyes, Buttercup, Purple Monkeyflower (FES); Gean Wood Cherry, Norway Maple, White Willow (GM); Cornflower, Heather (Hb); Fig (Ma); Indian Pipe, Windflower (Pac); Creeping Thistle, Milkmaids (Peg).

Self-Doubt: Alpine Azalea (Ask); Confid Essence (Aus B); Happy Wanderer, Snake Vine (Aus L); Evening Star (DAl); My Heart Knows (DL); Buttercup, Mullein (Dv); Bell Heather (F); Elder (GM); At the Heart of Being (LH); Pineapple (Ma).

Self-Forgiveness: Sturt Desert Rose (Aus B); Foothills Paloverde (DAl); Acceptance, I Like Being Me (DL); Birch (GM); Raspberry (Ma); Prickly Poppy (Peg).

Self-Healing: Co-ordination Orchid (AK); Self-Heal (AK, FES); Bog Rosemary, Soul Support (Ask); Five Corners (Aus B); Manifesting Thought Forms (DL); Tracking (Him E); Self Healing (LH); Fairy Bell, Rosa Hemispherica (Pac); Rosa Laevegata (Peg); Master Teacher, Strength & Chi (Peru).

Shadow (Dark Side): Cinnamon Rose, Shadow Cactus (AK); Bush Iris (Aus B); Sweet Chestnut (B, FES); Cardon, Crown of Thorns, Mesquite (DAl); My Own Pure Light, Unveiling Self (DL); Black Cohosh, Scarlet Monkeyflower (FES); Ohelo (Haii); Heather (Hb).

Soul – Awakening: Psyche Orchid (AK); Bush Iris (Aus B); Expanding Awareness, Unveiling Self (DL); Black-Eyed Susan, Cayenne (Dv); Wintergreen (F); Great Sallow (GM); Avocado, Coconut (Ma); Listening Heart (SW).

Soul – Damage Soul Support (Ask); Sacred Sphere (DL); Ancient Yew, Iona

Pennywort (F); Hibiscus, Stick Rorrish (Haii); Comfrey (PVi); On Angels' Wings (WD).

Soul – Listening to: Jacob's Ladder (Ask); Angelsword (Aus B); Mesquite, White Desert Primrose (DAl); Lotus Petals of the Heart (DL); California Poppy (Dv); Wintergreen (F); Mullein, Yellow Star Tulip (FES); Great Sallow (GM); Nana-honua (Haii); Still Mind (WD).

Spiritual Balance/Cleansing: Piatanthera (AK); Lotus (AK, FES); Chiming Bell (Ask); Angelsword, Crowea (Aus B); Expansive Embodiment, Lotus Petals of the Heart (DL); Pine, Tulip Tree (GM); Rosa Gallica Officinalis (Peg).

Spiritual Glamour: Bush Iris (Aus B); Radiant Strength (DL); California Poppy, Canyon Dudleya (FES); Robinia (GM); Ragoon Creeper, Red Silk Cotton Tree (Him A).

Stability: Formation Cactus, Grounding Opuntia (AK); Crowea, Sundew (Aus B); Ash (GM); At the Heart of Being (LH); Cherry, Pear, Tomato (Ma); Balance & Stability (Peru); Gruss an Aachen, Royal Highness (PVi).

Subconscious/Superconscious: Full Moon Reflection (Ask E); Angelsword, Paw Paw (Aus B); Rainbow Cactus (DAl); Lime (GM).

Subtle Body Balance: Delph (AK); Grass of Parnassus, Lady's Slipper, Sweetgrass (Ask); Angelsword, Crowea (Aus B); Expansive Embodiment, Sacred Sphere (DL); Holy Grail, Sea Pink (F); Lotus (FES); Privet (GM); Marquise boccela, Wisteria (PF); Protective Shield (WD).

Surrender: Kapok Bush (Aus B); Arizona White Oak, Hoptree, Prickly Pear Cactus (DAl); Acceptance, Letting Go (DL); Snowdrop (F); Angel's Trumpet, Love Lies Bleeding (FES); Naupaka Kahakai (Haii); Grape, Banana (Ma); Madame Louis Levique (PF).

Therapist's Balance: Lady's Slipper, Northern Lady's Slipper (Ask); Leafless Orchid, Snake Bush (Aus L); Purple Flower (BL); Cardon, Crown of Thorns, Desert Holly (DAl); Balancing Extremes, Sacred Sphere (DL); Eyebright (Dv); Calendula, Mallow (FES); Strawberry Tree (GM); Frangipani/Plumeria, Pua Melia (Haii); Bougainvillea (Him A); Healing, Tracking (Him E); Grape (Ma); Leopard Lily, Washington Lily (Peg); India Hawthorn, The Fairy Rose (PF); Alaskan Birch Forest, Sacred Space (WD).

Transcendence: Meditation Essence (Aus B); Immortal, Rainbow Cactus, Wolfberry (DAl); Graceful Transformations, Higher Levels, Stepping Ahead Now (DL); Birch, Revelation, Stonecrop (F); Love Lies Bleeding (FES); Lotus (Him A); Grape (Ma); Star Traveller (SW).

Transformation: Mistletoe (AK); Fireweed Combo (Ask); Bottlebrush, Transition Essence (Aus B); Chiming Bells, Fireweed, River Beauty (Ask); Bisbee Beehive Cactus, Sacred Datura (DAl); Graceful Transformations, Manifesting Thought Forms, Unveiling Self (DL); Black-Eyed Susan, Cayenne, Fireweed, Mallow (Dv); Transformation (F); Love Lies Bleeding (FES); Elder, Tamarisk (GM); Koa (Haii); Day-Blooming Jessamine (Him A); Stinking Iris (HUB); Pearly Everlasting (Pac); Butterfly Lily, Sulcorebutia Cactus, Tree Opuntia (Peg); Graceful Shifts (Peru); Transmute Combination (SW).

Transition: Cow Parsnip, Purple Poppy (Ask); Fireweed Combo, Polar Ice, Soul Support (Ask E); Bauhinia, Bottlebrush, Transition Essence (Aus B); Rainbow Cactus, Ratany (DAl); Graceful Transformations (DL); Stonecrop (F); Angel's Trumpet, Filaree, Mugwort, Star Tulip (FES); Gateway (Him E); Corn (Ma); Poison Hemlock (Pac); Gruss an Aachen (PVi); Autumn Leaves (Sun).

Transparent Shield: Coconut Palm, White Yarrow (AK); Green Spider Orchid (Aus B); Sacred Sphere, Radiant Strength

(DL); Pink Orchid (FO); Protective Shield (WD).

Truth: Bladderwort, Cattail Pollen (Ask); Angelsword, Sturt Desert Rose (Aus B); Ratany, Syrian Rue (DAl); My Heart Knows, My Own Pure Light (DL); Plane Tree (GM); Ilima (Haii); Butterfly Orchid (HUB); Blackberry (Ma); Maggie (PF).

Unconditional Love: Delph, Horn of Plenty Orchid, Sarah van Fleet, Love Cactus, Love Orchid (AK); Alpine Azalea, Harebell, Sphagnum Moss (Ask); Bluebell, Dagger Hakea, Mountain Devil, Rough Bluebell (Aus B); Uguisukazura Flower (Aus LJ); Heart to Heart (DL); Rose Chinensis Serratipetala (Peg); One Heart (Peru); On Angels' Wings (WD).

Understanding Why: Psyche/Soul Orchid (AK); Spinifex (Aus B); Sweet Chestnut (B); Expanding Awareness, Lucid Dreaming, My Heart Knows (DL); Sage (Dv); Birch (F); Rowan (GM); Coconut (Ma); Coral Root (Spotted) (Peg); Madam Alfred Carriere (PF); Perceiving Spirit (SW); Wise Woman (WD); Fire Essence (WL).

Universal Being (Connection): Channelling Orchid (AK); Bog Rosemary (Ask); Angelsword, Green Spider Orchid, Paw Paw, Sydney Rose (Aus B); Meditative Mind (DL); Star Tulip (FES); Ginkgo (GM); Nana-honua/Angel's Trumpet (Haii); Calypso Orchid, Christ Thorn (Peg); Alaskan Birch Forest, Still Mind (WD).

Universal Timing: Pink Flannel Flower (Aus B); Mountain Mahogany (DAl); Infinite Patience (DL); Star Traveller (SW).

Universal Will: Bluebell (Aus B); Hoptree (DAl); Heart of Nature, My Own Pure Light (DL).

Uplifting: Lighten Up (Ask); Air Essence (WL).

Vision: Boronia, Turkey Bush (Aus B); Dance of Creation (DL); Birch (F); Queen Anne's Lace (FES); Hawks Weed, Nasturtium (Hb); Gulaga Crystal (Him E); Ox-Eye Daisy (Pac); Rosa Hugonis (Peg); Creation/Focus, Open-minded/Future Vision (Peru).

Visualization: Boronia, Meditation Essence (Aus B); Blackberry (Dv); Lotus (FES); Wolfsbane (HUB); Goatsbeard (Pac); Hydrangea (Green) (Peg); Creation/Focus (Peru).

Wisdom: Lotus (AK, FES, Haii); Black Spruce, Purple Mountain Saxifrange, Red Elder, Sitka Spruce Pollen, White Spruce, (Ask); Angelsword, Bush Fuchsia, Paw Paw (Aus B); My Heart Knows, Wise Action (DL); Clear Light, Scots Pine (F); California Poppy, Sage, Saguaro (FES); Hazel, Tree of Heaven, Tree Lichen (GM); Sage (Hb); Indian Coral, Spotted Gliciridia (Him A); At the Heart of Being (LH); Date, Pineapple, Raspberry (Ma); California Baylaurel, Elephant's Head, Old Blush China Rose (Peg); Ancient Wisdom (Peru); Sage (Sun); Wise Woman (WD); Angelic Essence, Fire Essence (WL).

Worthlessness: Beauty Cactus, Sensitive Plant, Self-Esteem Cactus (AK); Five Corners, Philotheca, Sturt Desert Rose (Aus B); Candy Barrel Cactus, Hedgehog Cactus, Immortal, White Desert Primrose (DAl); I Like Being Me, My Own Pure Light, Unveiling Self (DL); Elder (GM); Daffodil (Hb); Alfalfa (HUB); Pineapple, Strawberry (Ma); Being True Worth, Indian Pipe (Pac).

Warrior Spirit: Pyramidal Orchid (HUB); Warriors Path (SW).

CHAPTER SIX

Specific Recipes For Your Own Use

If you do not feel sufficiently confident about choosing flower essences to make your own personal prescription, here are some recipes to help with common ailments for you to try.

Note: All the recipes in this book are for your personal use. They are simplified versions of my professional recipes, which are also available directly from me (*see* Useful Addresses). Many flower essence producers have created some very successful combinations that are well worth taking.

Making Up A Remedy

To make up your own remedies you will need several standard 20ml dropper bottles (*see* Useful Addresses for suppliers), some spring water, a little brandy and some adhesive labels. It is a good idea to label each bottle with details like your name, the date you made the combination, a brief description of what this particular mix is for and the flower essences it contains.
  • Rinse through a 20m1 stopper bottle with spring water.
  • For each recipe, put 2 drops of each of the essences listed into the bottle.
  • Add 1 tablespoon of brandy to the mix. This is used purely as a preservative.
    If you have a sensitivity to alcohol you may wish to use apple cider vinegar,
    vegetable glycerine or clear honey as a substitute for the brandy.
  • Fill to the brim with spring water.

This is your course of treatment for the next two months. Two bottles of this mix will last about two months. After a month it may be a good idea to stop taking the essence and review your condition. The emotional state, physical discomfort or other issue you were working on may have eased or even disappeared. If not, continue taking the combination until the course is completed. It is worth remembering that even when you have finished taking the remedy it will still be acting in your system for some time.

On regaining your balance there may be no need for further remedies for the time being. Alternatively you may become aware of another issue that is troubling you. In this case you will need to select appropriate remedies for your next prescription.

Fighting Off Disease and Stress

Stress Buster

An excellent de-stressor for when you are feeling overstimulated and over-whelmed – in short, burnt out – by stressful situations and environments. Brings calmness, filtering out the stress from all situations. Restores balance and resilience. You can add 2 drops of Office Flower (Him A) to combat stressful office environments.

Black-Eyed Susan (Aus B)
Pink Fairy Orchid (Aus L)
Macrocarpa (Aus B)
Fairy Duster (DAl)
White Carnation (PF)

Energy Booster

A re-energizer and revitalizer for when you feel drained, tired or fatigued. Restores deep-seated vitality and helps you to learn to work with consistency to avoid becoming depleted either physically, emotionally or mentally. You can add 2 drops each of Bay (GM) and Vital Spark (Him E) for extra potency.

Banksia Robur (Aus B)
Leafless Orchid (Aus L)
Cherry (M)
Forsythia (Hb)
Vanilla (PF)
Macrocarpa (Aus B)

Environmental Protector

For those feeling overwhelmed and sensitive to a city environment, whose nerves are frazzled by the fast and frantic pace of life. For those living and working in crowded and polluted surroundings. Vulnerability to electromagnetic radiation from computers, fluorescent lights, pollution and other noxious substances often manifests as allergic reactions.

This combination boosts and protects the energetic system against all kinds of environmental hazards. Eases stress and allows you to remain calm, centred and grounded. Add 2 drops of Pink Fairy Orchid (Aus L) for extra potency.

Grass of Parnassus (Ask)
Yarrow (Ask, FES)

Dill (FES)
Indian Pink (FES)
Viridiflora (PF)
Radiation Cactus (AK)
Ti (AK)
Mulla Mulla (Aus B)

Protection From Chemical Pollutants

This combination cleanses and detoxifies the system of environmental pollutants such as chemical residues and heavy metals, clearing vibrational debris and impurities from the body, mind and emotions. It also offers protection from pollution, rebuilds a suppressed immune system to alleviate allergic problems and guards against bacterial infections. Add 2 drops each of Star Tulip (FES) and Lily (PF) for extra potency.

Portage Glacier Environmental Essence is available from Alaskan Flower Essences.

Portage Glacier (Ask)
Sweet Grass (Ask)
Fringed Violet (Aus B)
Wild Potato Bush (Aus B)
Lotus (FES)
Crossandra (PF)
Daylily (PF)

Immune Boost

Boosts immune resistance to all kinds of infections and speeds recovery. Restores balance to the immune system when it is overstressed or overworked; gives you greater mental control over your immune system. Builds resistance to auto-toxicity, enhances the body's natural defence network and invigorates the production of white blood cells and interferon to fight viral or bacterial attack and infection which has over-powered the system. Add 2 drops each of Knotted Marjoram and Snapdragon (PF) for extra potency.

K9 (AK)
Macrocarpa (Aus B)
Silverlace (PF)
Gaillardia (PF)
Echinacea (Haii)
Celery (PVi)

Infection Fighter

For helping to shake off viral infections such as colds and flu. Eases the chills and aching associated with the pre-influenza state. Helps fight off infection by clearing viruses out of the system. Especially beneficial for respiratory and throat infections as well as fevers. Add 2 drops each of Thyme (PF) and Tomato (PVi) for extra potency.

Spinifex (Aus B)
Thyme (PF)
Babies' Breath (PF)
Nasturtium (Dv)
Drum Stick (Him A)
Echinacea (PF)
Onion (PF)

Anaesthetic Clearing Mix

Clears the effect of anaesthetic from the system. Acts as a tonic for a stressed nervous system and stimulates the cleansing of impurities and toxicity from the blood and lymphatic system. Releases the subtle anatomy from the shock and trauma of going through an operation. Enhances resistance to infection from bacteria and viruses, as immunity is weakened by an operation of any kind. Add 2 drops of Echinacea (PF) to boost immunity. To clear antibiotics from the system, use Coralroot (Spotted) (Peg).

Inner Cleansing Cactus (AK)
Bottlebrush (Aus B)
Australian Smoke Bush (Aus L)
Wild Potato Bush (Aus B)
Morning Glory (FES, Him A)
Red Carnation (PF)
White Hyacinth (PF)

Help For Specific Health Problems

Allergy Antidote

For hay fever, asthma and other allergic problems. Builds resistance to itching, watery eyes, runny nose and flu-type symptoms typical of an allergic reaction to grasses, pollens and so forth. Combats the breathing difficulties of asthma. Add 2 drops each of Sand Dollar (Pac) and Carrot (PF) for extra potency.

K9 (AK)
Lily (PF)
Grass Widow (Pac)
Eucalyptus (FES)
Lantana (PF)
Babies' Breath (PF)
Formulae 36 Immune booster (Him A)

Digestive Soother

For digestive upsets, nervous stomach, tension in the solar plexus, poor digestion, hyperacidity, ulcers and eating disorders. Calms the stomach, aids digestion, promotes enzyme activity and assimilation of nutrients. Add 2 drops each of California Pitcher Plant (FES) and Moss Rose (PF) for extra potency.

Paw Paw (Aus B)
Salvia (AK)
Chamomile (Dv, FES)
Curry Leaf (Him A)
Crowea (Aus B)
Orange Honeysuckle (Pac)

First Aid

For shock, trauma and accidents. Works on all levels – physical, mental and emotional – helping you to rebuild after shattering experiences. Clears grief, releases deeply held pain in the body after injury and trauma, restores the flow of energy and provides emotional stability in times of extreme stress.

Fireweed (Ask)
Waratah (Aus B)
Cowkicks (Aus L)
Arnica (FES)
Ashoka Flower and Tree (Him A)
Pear (Ma)
Nootka Rose (Pac)
Grape Hyacinth (Pac)

Clare's Floral Complexion Cream

To an aqueous cream base, which is available from most good health food stores, or Self Heal Cream (FES) add3 drops each of these essential aromatherapy oils:

Chamomile
Jasmine
Rose

Plus 2 drops of each of the following flower essences:

Billy Goat Plum (Aus B)
Lily (PF)
Aloe Vera (FES, AK)
Salvia (PF)
Sweet Annie (PF)

Headache and Migraine

For stress-related, tension-type headaches, migraines, and the neuralgia associated with menstruation. Add 2 drops each of Black-Eyed Susan and She Oak (Aus B) for extra potency.

Menzies Banksia (Aus L)
French Lavender (PF)
Mountain Devil (Aus B)

Curry Flower (PF)
Plantain (Pac)
Mussel (Pac)
Narcissus (PF)

Insomnia

For insomnia and disturbed sleep. An excellent tranquillizer bringing deep har-monizing sleep. Refreshes and recharges your whole being with vitality. Eases hyperactivity, excessive worry and fears in the subconscious, restlessness and nightmares.

Macrocarpa (Aus B)
Hibiscus (FO)
Valerian (Dv)
St John's Wort (FES)
Swallow Wort (Him A)
White Chestnut (Bach)

Jet Lag

For preventing and easing jet lag, typified by fatigue and feelings of disorienta-tion. Protects you during air travel and realigns your system on all levels to reduce sensations of disorientation.

Mulla Mulla (Aus B)
Sundew (Aus B)
Bush Iris (Aus B)
Thyme (GM)
Speedwell (Hb)

Premenstrual Relief

For premenstrual symptoms caused by hormonal imbalance. Eases over-emotional, agitated and irritable feelings, fluid retention and headaches. Aids absorption of iron, enhancing your strength and stamina during menstruation. Helps women to accept and accentuate their natural femininity. Add 2 drops of Cherokee Rose (PF) for extra potency. To tailor this mix for the menopause, add 2 drops each of Orange and Honeysuckle (Pac)

She Oak (Aus B)
Macrazamia (Aus L)
Mala Mijer (DAD
Pomegranate (FES)
Japanese Magnolia (PF)
Frangipani (FO)

Subtle Body Protection

Aura Protection and Repair Remedy
A combination that repairs and mends holes in the aura, strengthening, enhancing and protecting the auric field. Add 2 drops each of Vanilla (PF) and Pink Orchid (FO) for extra potency.
> White Yarrow (AK)
> Fringed Violet (Aus B)
> Angel of Protection Orchid (AK)

Subtle Body Harmonizer
A combination to clear blockages and discharge toxicity from the subtle bodies, bringing them all into correct alignment. Add 2 drops of Live Forever (GM) for extra potency.
> Lotus (AK, FES)
> Sweetgrass (Ask)
> Swamp Onion (Peg)

Chakra Balance
Helps to rebalance and restore smooth functioning to all the chakras. Add 2 drops of Lilac (GM) and Hydrangea (Green) (Peg) for extra potency.
> Lady's Slipper (Ask)
> Sweetgale (Ask)
> Lotus (Him A)
> Viridiflora (PF)
> Nootka Rose (Pac)

Note As a general rule of thumb, flowers that are the same colour as a certain chakra will benefit that particular energy centre (*see* Chapter Two for a list of the chakras and their associated colours). The effects will also spill over into those areas of the body linked with that chakra.

Meridian Rebalance
A potent remedy for clearing blockages in these energy channels, ensuring a smooth flow of *qi* and generally rebalancing the entire meridian system. Add 2 drops each of Gladiola and Trumpet Vine Nepal (Peg) for extra potency.
> Sitka Spruce Pollen (Ask)
> Silver Maple (GM)
> Northern Lady's Slipper (Ask)
> Crowea (Aus B)
> Clearing Blockages (DL)

Immunofluidium
Strengthens, activates and binds the immunofluidium, improving the flow of nourishment to the cells. Aids in building immunity against bacterial infection by activating and stimulating the white blood corpuscles to detect and destroy

viral and bacterial invaders. Add 2 drops each of Paw Paw (Aus B) and Pokeweed (Peg) for extra potency.

Manzanita (FES)

Bells of Ireland (Peg)

Addictions
Anti-Addiction Remedy
This is a basic mix for the addictive personality facing and dealing with the reasons behind addiction.

Releases patterns of abuse present in the general consciousness, strengthens the will to fight and break free of addictive habits, and negates the need for stimulants. Detoxifies the system on all levels, especially focusing on the nervous system. Cleanses the aura and rehabilitates the whole energy system, leaving it refreshed and sparkling. Offers overall support in addiction therapy.

Add 2 drops of Tundra Twayblade (Ask) for extra potency.

Blue China Orchid (Aus L)

Morning Glory (AK, FES, Haii)

Nirjara (Him E)

Rose Damaceria Bifera (Peg)

Forsythia (Pac)

Bush Iris (Aus B)

Withdrawal Remedy
This combination is for undoing the damage caused by heavy overuse of drugs. It repairs any deterioration in the nervous system, particularly that caused by morphine, counters 'spaced out' feelings, and encourages the letting go of habit patterns and lifestyles contributing to drug abuse, especially the tendency towards escapism. Mends holes in the aura resulting from drug abuse. Add 2 drops of Red Lily (Aus B) for extra potency.

The basic Anti-Addiction Remedy (above) can be tailored towards specific addictions by adding 2 drops each of any or all of the following essences:

Pennyroyal (AK, FES)

Sundew (Aus B)

Californian Poppy (FES)

Sagebush (FES)

Fringed Violet (Aus B)

Give Up Smoking
Assists the will to give up smoking, providing emotional support. Re-oxygenates, repairs and improves the condition of the lungs after the long-term effects of smoke inhalation. You may add Drum Stick (Him A) and Babies' Breath (PF) for any congestion and breathing difficulties.

Add 2 drops of each essence to the basic Anti-Addiction Remedy.
Blue China Orchid (Aus L)
Nicotiana/ Flowering Tobacco (FES)
Boronia + Bottlebrush (Aus B)

Kicking Caffeine

Clears the effects of caffeine from the nervous system, alleviating any deterioration due to long-term use of caffeine. Strengthens and detoxifies the overall energetic pattern of the liver. Revitalizes willpower when you are tempted to indulge.
Add 2 drops of each essence to the basic Anti-Addiction Remedy.
Yellow Ginger (Haii)
Hibiscus (FO)

Alcohol Overuse

Helps to bring clearer insight into and understanding of the problems that lead to alcohol abuse. Cleanses the blood, protects the liver and kidneys and strengthens and repairs the etheric body, which can be damaged by alcohol's loosening effect on the subtle bodies.

If you are only suffering from a typical hangover after drinking too much in one sitting, a good essence to take is Soberup (Him E).

Add 2 drops of each essence to the basic Anti-Addiction Remedy.
Almond (Ma)
Pennyroyal (FES)
Angelica (FES)
Boab (Aus B) for addictive family patterns passed on.

Note Do not use extra alcohol or brandy, use glycerine as a base.
(*see* Suppliers under Useful Addresses)

Fun Combinations

Sassy Mix

A fun combination to help us women feel sexy, sassy and full of fun.
Orchid Queen (FO)
Frangipani (FO)
Lehur (Haii)
Pink Orchid (FO)

Little Rascal Mix

Try this combination to help your little rascal to calm, slow down, be less restless, more centred, reasonable, and to be able to listen and be co-operative.
Grape blossom (Ma)
Banana blossom (Ma)
Strawberry blossom (Ma)
Lettuce blossom (Ma)

Man Mix
To aid a feeling of courage, inner strength and empowerment as a man.
>Sunflower (AK)
>Banana (AK)
>Strength (Him E)
>Tomato (Ma)

Hand-Picking Your Own Essences

An ideal remedy can be created from the flowers growing in your own garden, suggests Ian White of Australian Bush Flower Essences.

Before picking and preparing the flowers it is important to feel still and calm, so if possible practise some form of meditation.

When searching for flowers in the garden choose those in full bloom with an intense, vibrant colour. Rinse a bowl with salt water, fill it with spring water and float the flowers in the bowl for 2–3 hours in the sunshine. After this time, or when the blooms have become limp, lift them from the liquid with a twig and return them to the soil.

This is your flower essence, made from your immediate environment and will help you to be more in tune with your surroundings and encourage your own balance and healing.

To make the Mother Tincture use $^1/_2$ flower essence and $^1/_2$ brandy.

To make the Stock Essence use $^2/_3$ brandy and $^1/_3$ spring water, then add 7 drops of Mother Tincture to every 25ml.

To make Dosage Bottles use $^3/_4$ spring water and $^1/_4$ brandy, then add 7 drops of Stock Essence.

Take 7 drops of this dosage essence morning and evening for two weeks.

Flowers to the Rescue

Energy Medicine

Flower essences are unique in their ability to restore and enhance a sense of total wellbeing in mind, body and spirit.

Unlike most other remedies, flower essences act as catalysts to rebalance the body's vital energy. In doing so they provide the perfect antidote to stress-related upsets.

It is clear that stress in all its different guises disrupts and diminishes our natural life force. Feeling tired and depleted, for example, is a sure sign that the body's energies have been thrown out of kilter. Upsets at this level inevitably precede other kinds of niggling minor ills and may eventually lead to more serious conditions.

We may take a holiday to escape the stresses of life when we start to feel run-down. This temporarily recharges the batteries, but it will not get to the root of the problem. It is important that we redress the ingrained imbalance, which may originate and be linked to any shock or trauma that occurred many years ago.

Healers blessed with the ability to 'tap into' the body's energy may be able to bring all the systems back into balance. The problem with this is that we have to rely on someone else to rekindle our sense of wellbeing. The beauty of flower essences is that they have the power to evoke such changes. This means that you alone become responsible for inspiring your own happiness and good health.

To preserve an energetic equilibrium, we also have to become aware of those aspects of our personality and behaviour which are likely to upset the balance. Impatient people, for instance, who are easily irritated by the slowness or incompetence of others, merely agitate their own energy systems and always will – unless they find a way of tempering their impatience.

Many of these subtle remedies act on the mind, easing all kinds of emotional and mental turbulence. Feelings such as fear, guilt, anger, anxiety and irritability do not only detract from the pleasure of living; if left unchecked, they slowly and insidiously wear down the body's resistance to illness, leaving us vulnerable to all kinds of health problems. Negative, distracting emotions also cloud our vision making it difficult for us to see or understand our special role in life, so hindering any kind of spiritual development.

It should be stressed that flower essences are by no means cure-alls. They work best at nipping potential problems in the bud, so preventing illnesses from arising in the first place. However, these gentle remedies are also helpful at times when a more direct approach is required. Orthodox drugs, acting at the physical level, alleviate symptoms but do not give rise to a real sense of wellbeing. For example, tranquillizers may ease discomfort by distancing us from reality and dulling our reaction to stress, but they do not provide us with the tools we need for coping with and overcoming it.

For complete healing it is necessary to instil feelings of harmony and balance in mind, body and spirit. This is where flower essences come to the rescue.

The scale of remedies (*below*) shows the difference between the various forms of medicine available to us. The further up the scale you go, the more far-reaching are the benefits. Pharmaceutical drugs provoke profound physical changes, but they do not touch our emotional or spiritual wellbeing. In terms of our energy system, their effect can be likened to a sledgehammer, whose shattering impact can actually get in the way of complete healing.

In contrast, flower essences, and a new category, environmental and sound essences, act at the higher emotional, mental and spiritual levels before filtering into the body. When taken in conjunction with other forms of medicine, flower essences, environmental and sound essences enhance their benefits and at the same time clear away any unwanted side-effects provoked by the more physical or 'denser' types of medicine. These gentle remedies can be used successfully alongside prescribed drugs to speed recovery from accidents or operations and help you overcome all kinds of disease. They will also bring benefit to those who are trying to wean themselves off antidepressants, sleeping pills and other mood-elevating drugs.

How Do Flower Essences Work Their Wonders?

In many healing traditions, our natural disposition is believed to be one of perfect health and happiness. Unfortunately, all kinds of shock and stress conspire to shift us from this state of grace.

Given the right impetus, self-healing can be kicked into gear.

Flower essences act as catalysts in order to bring our energies back into balance so that we can begin to reach the potential for perfection which resides within our energetic blueprint. They have this capacity because they are able to vibrate at frequencies close to those of our own subtle energies. Vibrational flower essences are unique in their general effect of realigning and pulling the subtle

SCALE OF REMEDIES		
Classification	Remedy/Medicine	Mode of Action/Side Effects
Vibrational	Sound, light, Environmental and Flower Essences	Acting at the subtle, emotional/psychological and spiritual energy levels, filtering down to the physical – no toxic side-effects.
Vibrational	Gems	Acting at the physical and subtle levels occasionally heightening symptoms – cleansing effect.
Like with like	Homeopathy	Physical effect with reference to the emotional and psychological. Some side effects and heightening of symptoms before they clear.
Natural	Aromatherapy (essential oils)	Natural chemicals with gentle influence on physical system with emotional/psychological benefits.
Natural	Herbal medicine	Natural chemicals with gentle physical effects.
Synthetic	Pharmaceutical drugs	Basic physical level with toxic physical and subtle side-effects.

anatomy back into order so the self-healing process can begin. They also act in a very specific way, by travelling to the area or areas most in need of attention.

The ideal combination of flower essences should be matched to your individual energetic blueprint. This sets up a sympathetic resonance, a dynamic conversation which constantly reminds the body of how it really should be. It's like sounding a chord that brings all the notes into perfect harmony.

The Essence Pathway

Flower essences appear to follow a particular pathway through the subtle anatomy. After a few drops are swallowed, the essence is taken up by the bloodstream before moving directly to the meridians, the energy channels which feed the life force or *qi* into the body. The meridians form an energetic interface between the higher-frequency subtle bodies and the physical body. From here the essence's life force either enters the various chakras and subtle bodies or returns to the cells in the physical body.

Because of their ethereal nature, flower essences may at first be attracted to the subtle bodies. From here their beneficial vibrations may filter down into the physical body through the etheric body, chakras and the skin. However, a flower essence will also be instantly drawn to any place where vibrational imbalance exists. These areas act like a sponge, literally soaking up the essence's healing energy.

Rebalancing occurs as toxicity, in the form of disharmonious frequencies, is flushed from the system. Flower remedies are particularly potent in inducing changes in the chakras and subtle bodies, although some also directly influence the physical body. The ultimate therapeutic action depends at which energetic level the being is out of balance.

These remedies also enhance the connection between spirit, mind and body. They facilitate the flow of information from the Higher Self or inner voice, which always knows what is best for us, so we are far less likely to fall victim to emotional and physical problems in the first place. In other words, the remedies actually help to prevent the kind of problems that arise from ignoring what we instinctively know is right.

Reading The Signs: The Body Physical

For many people physical symptoms are the first sure sign that something is wrong. Seemingly minor problems such as headaches, stomach upsets or colds are the body's way of alerting you to the fact that you need to take steps to redress any imbalance. Such symptoms do not go away if they are ignored. They simply get worse and may spill into another system, giving rise to yet another source of physical discomfort.

To make it easier to recognize the source of your symptoms we must now look at the distinctive systems of the body. It is important to bear in mind, however, that all these systems are interconnected and that each exerts a profound influence over the others.

The Nervous System

The nervous system is rather like the body's telecommunication system because it is responsible for transmitting information around the body. It is composed of millions of tiny nerve cells called neurones which communicate with each other using weak electrical impulses. These cells are bundled together into fibres which spread, like branches, to form a vast and intricate network throughout the body.

The main branch runs from the brain, which masterminds the whole system, down through the spine. The brain assesses all the information coming into the body via the senses, then decides what action to take. For this reason the nervous system plays a vital role in enabling us to respond and adapt to ever-changing environmental conditions.

The nervous system is split into two parts, one we can control voluntarily (the voluntary system), and another which apparently functions below the level of consciousness (the autonomic system).

The Autonomic System

The autonomic system has received a great deal of attention in recent years because of its link with stress. It is divided into two branches, the 'activating' sympathetic part and the 'pacifying' parasympathetic part.

The sympathetic system comes into play when we need to handle emergencies or sudden changes. It gives rise to the so-called 'fight or flight' stress response characterized by a rush of energy, a racing heart and a feeling of alertness, changes caused by the secretion of the 'stress hormone', adrenaline.

Once the stress has passed, the parasympathetic system should take over to calm all the systems down, but thanks to the pressures of life today we often get stuck in sympathetic mode.

It now seems clear that our state of mind can influence the autonomic nervous system and that we can 'talk ourselves into' becoming more relaxed.

Being the most reactive of all the systems, the nervous system is the first place where emotional upset takes its toll. From here it goes on to affect any system that is particularly weak and vulnerable.

Signs of Nervous Upset

Increased heart rate; palpitations
Rapid breathing
Muscular tension
Sweating, feeling flushed
Disturbed digestion and a nervous 'knotted' stomach
Irritability and edginess
Restlessness
Insomnia; lying awake worrying
Aggressiveness
Cravings for alcohol or nicotine
Nervous habits such as nail-biting, foot-tapping or drumming
    repetitively with the fingers
Loss of appetite or overeating
Inability to relax
Feelings of being totally unable to cope – nervous breakdown

Case History: Insomnia

Rebecca, company director and self-confessed workaholic, was physically healthy but had suffered from insomnia for some time. She not only found it difficult to fall asleep, but also woke frequently during the night. By morning she was exhausted and felt she had not slept at all. She had also begun having slight premenstrual tension

Some of The Essences I Prescribed

• Star of Bethlehem (B) for long, slow shock, since it transpired that her drive to achieve stemmed from feeling unloved as a child. She had thus developed a strong desire to please and prove herself worthy of love.

- Five Corners (Aus B), for her low self-esteem which had led to her desire to prove herself.
- Pomegranate (FES), which helped her as a woman deprived of the nurturing needed for a positive self-image.
- A combination of Elm (B), Indian Pink (FES), Chamomile and Valerian (Dev, PF), to combat her feeling of being overwhelmed by the pressure of work and its debilitating effect on her nervous system, resulting in her sleeping problems.

Rebecca soon began to relax and found she could pace herself better at work. She reported feeling uplifted and more confident, and told me she had slipped into a regular sleeping pattern. The premenstrual tension also improved.

Now she began to wonder what her real purpose was in life.

I Prescribed
- Silver Princess (Aus B), to help her realize her inner direction and purpose.
- Zinnia (PVi), to keep her from taking life so seriously.
- Pink Seaweed (Pac), to help her take stock before rushing into anything new.
- Gruss an Aachen (PVi) and Fireweed Combo (ALK) to integrate the change and help her to move in a new direction

Case History: Anorexia Nervosa

Although women are more susceptible to anorexia than men, at the age of 25 John had the classic symptoms of this illness.

He is a highly sensitive, gentle person whose problems began in childhood. John's mother was distant while his father's domineering, military style of discipline frightened him. John grew up feeling inadequate and reproached himself for not fulfilling his parents' expectations. He withdrew from life and his emotions, entering a fantasy world and following intellectual pursuits. The feelings of anxiety and inadequacy stayed with him, upsetting his nervous system and digestion, leading to severe weight loss over a period of time due to the need to control events by consciously starving himself.

I Prescribed
- Chamomile (FES) and Hau (Haii), for calming and restoring the nervous system.
- Indian Pink (FES) and Star of Bethlehem and Pine (B), to clear the long, slow shock of his repressed childhood and the guilt and self-blame he took from his parents.

- Scarlet Monkeyflower (FES), to release his repressed anger and frustration with his parents.
- Neem (Him A), to help him to feel safe with his emotions.
- Paw Paw (Aus B) and Turquoise and Gold (AK), for anorexia and to facilitate absorption of vital nutrients.

While taking the remedies John lost the anorexic mindset and began to put on weight and felt happier and more able to be himself. He also began standing up to his father in a quiet but positive way.

The Immune System

Like an army the immune system defends the body from invaders such as viruses, bacteria and other potentially harmful organisms.

White cells, or leukocytes, act as soldiers and move freely around the body via the bloodstream to target the site of infection. The first battalion to arrive on the scene when something like a stomach bug enters the system is made up of granular leukocytes. These cells are armed with chemical weapons which immobilize and often destroy bacteria.

The rest of the army is broken down into two divisions of lymphocytes which are produced in the lymph glands and spleen. The T-lymphocytes are like the body's intelligence service, for they are concerned with recognizing foreign invaders. As well as viruses they regard implanted tissue as alien and prompt its rejection. The thymus gland, which orchestrates the functioning of the immune system, endows the T-cells with their discerning qualities.

If the T-cells verify an invasion, the immune system is switched to 'red alert'. Some of the T-cells possess deadly weapons which they then put to use.

B-lymphocytes are also brought into play. These cells make antibodies which act as straightjackets, immobilizing the invader until it can be attacked.

The B-cells have memories and can remember what type of antibody to make if it meets the same virus again. This means the invader can be dealt with more efficiently next time, and that any resulting symptoms will be mild. In the case of allergy, the B-cells start making a specific sort of antibody called IgE. During the scuffle between antibody and invader, inflammatory chemicals such as histamine are released which cause the typical allergic symptoms such as a runny nose, watery eyes, etc.

The way the immune system functions is complex and is still not fully understood. However, we know that if overworked or sabotaged it may fail to know the difference between an enemy and something innocuous – or even between an enemy and the body's own tissues. In autoimmune diseases such as rheumatoid arthritis and ME, it appears to turn on its own cells.

Shock, long-standing stress, a poor diet and/or environmental pollutants appear to act as immunosuppressants. Some researchers have found that certain negative emotions such as grief and feelings of despair are particularly effective at disarming the immune system. In contrast, unconditional love seems to strengthen its reserves.

Signs of Poor Immunity
- Frequent colds, sore throats, swollen glands
- Recurrent bacterial and/or viral infections
- Allergies
- Aching joints and muscles
- Depression, irritability, anxiety, emotional upset
- Lank, greasy hair
- Dull, blotchy skin
- Watery eyes
- Itchy, streaming nose
- Bleeding gums
- An increase in the amount of time it takes cuts and grazes to heal
- Low or fluctuating energy levels – making it necessary to rely on stimulants such as coffee
- Dull headaches
- General lack of vitality

Case History: Flu
Charlotte (a busy literary agent) had been laid low for a week with Asian flu, with the usual symptoms of fever, aching joints and a sore throat. Then the virus moved to her chest, giving rise to congestion and a debilitating cough. She was keen to avoid taking antibiotics, especially since the person who had passed the virus on to her had had the flu for eight weeks despite taking two courses of antibiotics.

I Prescribed
- Onion (PF) for clearing viruses.
- K9 (AK), a natural antibiotic.
- Formula 38 (Him A) to boost the immune system.
- Eucalyptus (FES) for the chesty cough.

Charlotte's recovery was speedy. Within a matter of days the flu symptoms and chestiness had cleared; she felt her healthy self again. Another good remedy is Coralroot (Spotted) (Peg), which helps to clear the effects of antibiotics from the system.

Case History: Herpes Virus

Aged 32, Helen had first caught herpes from her boyfriend; after they'd broken up it continued to flare up for about five days in every month, making her feel depressed, unclean and unable to contemplate a long-term relationship.

She had a history of susceptibility to viral infections, having contracted scarlet fever and whooping cough when she was three, then glandular fever in her late teens.

I Prescribed

- Thyme (PF) and Spinifex (Aus B) Marigold (PF), for fighting the herpes virus.
- Chamomile (FES) and Hau (Haii), for repairing and restoring the nervous system.
- Formula 38 (Him A) and K9 (AK), for boosting her immunity.
- Illyarrie (Aus L), to help her to realize she had the strength to cope.
- Billy Goat Plum (Aus B), for her feelings of revulsion associated with having herpes.

After taking the course of treatment, Helen noticed that the recurrences were becoming less frequent; then they ceased completely and have not come back for over two years.

Case History: ME

Angela was 40 and had for the last three years been suffering from ME, which was getting progressively worse. She was exhausted and ached all over. She was confined to bed most of the time as she was unable to walk or stand for more than a few moments.

Talking with her, I learned that as a child she had been pushed academically and told she was not clever enough to make the grade. She'd started taking drugs to evade reality, and had continued to use them heavily until her late thirties when she'd realized she needed professional help. However, the drugs had already taken a severe toll on her immune system and she had developed ME when at her lowest ebb, with no job, relationship or other form of support. She had been in and out of many relationships, all of them either unproductive or destructive.

I Prescribed

- Star of Bethlehem (B), for the long, slow shock of childhood and drug abuse.
- Morning Glory (AK, FES), to clear the toxic effects of drugs.
- Silverlace (PF), as an antiviral and immune booster.
- Comfrey (FES), to strengthen the nervous and muscular system.
- Dandelion (FES), to ease psychological tension stored in muscles.

- Dill (FES), to lift depression and to help her develop a healthier perspective on her emotional problems.

Angela reported that she was finding it easier to relax and felt less stressed. The burning aching in her body, especially in her legs, had eased and she was able to do simple (though previously impossible) daily tasks without getting exhausted.
Now was the time for a follow-on prescription.

I Prescribed
- Formula 38 (Aum A), to boost the immune system.
- Paw Paw (Aus B), to encourage assimilation of vital nutrients.
- Tomato (PVi), to help her throw off the disease.
- Zinnia (PVi), to lift her outlook on life and inspire humour.
- First Aid Remedy (Him A), as an all-round booster.

Slowly but surely Angela grew stronger, reporting increased energy levels and an ability to be mentally detached from her problems. She has also overcome her dependency on addictive, destructive relationships. She continued to feel better each day and is now leading a happy productive life.

Case History: Eczema
Charlie, aged 3, had developed very bad eczema (linked to an allergy to dairy products). In addition, his birth had been traumatic and he appeared to be shy, fearful and apprehensive.

I Prescribed
- Arnica (FES) and Pear Blossom (Ma), for traumatic birth.
- Mimulus (B) and Pineapple (Ma), for shyness and timidity.
- Sweet Chestnut (B), for anxiety.
- Aspen (B), for apprehension.
- Aloe Vera (FES Ak) and Salvia (PF), for his skin condition.
- Formula 38 (Him A), to boost the immune system.

A month later the eczema began to clear and Charlie appeared to be more confident and less fearful. Before the end of the second course his eczema had completely disappeared; there has been no recurrence.

The Lymphatic System

The lymphatic system is closely linked to the immune system because it plays a vital role in whisking away dead bacteria, disabled viruses and other debris from the tissues.
Lymph itself is a colourless, faintly opalescent fluid which bathes the body's

cells, furnishing them with nutrients and cleansing them of wastes and other impurities. In this respect it is rather like blood. Lymph, however, is not pumped around the body by the heart. It flows freely, relying on full, rhythmic breathing along with the contraction and relaxation of major muscles in the body for its circulation.

The network of lymphatic vessels is intimately connected with the main circulatory system. Blood seeps from its own vessels into those of the lymphatic system where it is cleansed and reconditioned before returning again to the veins and arteries.

Each organ has its own lymph supply, and the system itself has its own organs. The spleen, thymus, tonsils, adenoids, appendix and Peyer's patch are all part of this complex purification system. So too are bundles of sinus tissue called lymph nodes. The main ones are found under the arms, in the neck, behind the knees and in the groin. They can be felt as small lumps beneath the skin. Inside these nodes, lymphocyte cells are busy detoxifying wastes by engulfing or destroying them.

During an infection, the lymph nodes often swell and feel tender as battle gets underway within.

Eating food laden with fats, sugars, salt, additives and preservatives, as well as drinking alcohol and coffee, tends to 'pollute' the lymphatic system. The lymph fluid draws liquids from the tissues to dilute these toxins, which is what makes you look puffy and feel waterlogged when there is a problem with your lymphatic system.

Signs of Lymphatic Disorder
- Puffiness
- Bags under the eyes
- Skin blemishes
- Cellulite
- Congestion
- Swollen, tender lymph glands

Case History: Swollen Glands
Sarah, a 27-year-old public relations officer, was distressed by the presence of painful boils under her armpits. She had been prescribed a course of antibiotics which had not helped. Her lymphatic system was sluggish, she tended to gain weight easily, felt nauseous after eating and suffered from poor circulation.

I Prescribed
- Chamomile (AK, FES) and Hibiscus (FO), for emotional stress and nervous conditions affecting the stomach.

- K9 (AK), Formula 38 (Him A) and Gaillardia (PF) for boosting the immune system.
- Wild Potato Bush (Aus B) Yellow Ginger (Haii) and Vanilla Leaf (Pac), for clearing toxins from the blood and her whole system, reducing lymphatic swelling and clearing the skin.

During the first week Sarah came out in rash, which soon disappeared to be followed by a sore throat, which in turn cleared quickly along with the boils themselves. She felt wonderful.

Not long afterwards she went out drinking to celebrate her birthday. That night her whole arm swelled up and the lumps reappeared.

Sarah doubled her dosage and by morning both the swelling and the boils had gone.

The Respiratory System

Oxygen is the vital spark that kindles the physical energy necessary for powering life processes. Many ancient traditions teach that air, not food, is responsible for vitality, for it facilitates the flow of life force.

Breathing brings oxygen from the air into the lungs. Here the gas dissolves in the blood and is taken up by the complex iron-rich molecule, haemoglobin, present in the red cells or corpuscles.

In this form oxygen is distributed to every cell in the body. The byproduct of cell respiration, carbon dioxide, then combines with water in the red cells and is carried back to the lungs before being exhaled out into the atmosphere.

Full rhythmical breathing is best for the mind and body as it assures a continuous flow of oxygen to the cells and the swift removal of carbon dioxide. At rest, a typical man breathes around 8 litres of air a minute – a woman somewhat less. If deprived of oxygen for as little as three minutes, brain cells die and the heart struggles to keep beating.

Although breathing happens automatically, normal breathing patterns are easily disrupted. Sudden temperature changes such as stepping outdoors on a frosty day or into a very hot sauna make us gasp and temporarily hold our breath. Everyday stresses also play havoc with breathing patterns, although we tend not to notice. When anxious, fearful, angry or frustrated our breathing becomes rapid and shallow, a phenomenon known as hyperventilation.

Hyperventilation makes the heart pound, the head spin and the legs turn to jelly. Shallow breathing reduces the body's oxygen supply, leading to feelings of tiredness, lethargy and faintness as well as difficulty concentrating and frequent yawning.

Heavy air pollution also undermines our oxygen supply. Car exhaust fumes are rich in carbon monoxide, which competes with oxygen for haemoglobin in the blood. Other noxious chemicals include nitrogen oxides and hydrocarbons, which irritate the lungs and nasal passages – triggering asthma attacks, exacerbating chest troubles and increasing our vulnerability to chest infections and allergic rhinitis.

Signs of Respiratory Problems
- Shortness of breath
- Coughing
- Wheezing
- Frequent colds
- Hay fever and asthma
- Bronchitis
- Weakness and dizziness
- Anxiety
- Feelings of panic

Case History: Hay fever
Michael, a businessman in his late forties in a stress-charged profession, had been suffering from hay fever since he was 12 years old. Each year, during the second week of June, symptoms of itchy eyes, sneezing and a streaming nose would begin and continue until the end of July, signifying a typical allergy to grass pollens.

His normal treatment was to take antihistamines, although he had also unsuccessfully tried the inoculation method for several years.

I Prescribed
- Pink Fairy Orchid (Aus L), for feeling frenzied and overwhelmed by stress and the environment.
- Eucalyptus (FES) Lantana (PF), for allergic reactions and hay fever.
- Gaillardia (PF) and Formula 38 (Him A), to boost immunity.

Michael began taking the combination a few months before the start of the hay fever season. That year he was symptom-free. He has repeated this treatment for three years, and to date his hay fever has not recurred.

Case History: Sinusitis
Rosemary's sinus problems began at the age of 24, following an infection she appeared to pick up in a public swimming pool. As a child she had frequent chest infections; she had contracted tuberculosis when she was 20 and it had left her with a weakness in the chest area. She had great difficulty shaking off winter colds and was very sensitive to cold winds and dust.

I Prescribed
- Formula 43 Sinus/Cold (Him A), to clear the nasal passages and sinuses.

- Drum Stick (Him A), for lung and bronchial conditions.
- Eucalyptus (FES) and Babies' Breath (PF), to help breathing.
- Echinacea (Haii), to boost the immune system.
- Tomato (PVi), to ease the hold this condition had on her system.

Her sinus condition has cleared and she is now able to breathe more easily. She reports feeling better than she has done in over 20 years.

The Circulatory System

The circulatory system is closely linked to the respiratory system, as one of its main functions is to transport oxygen-laden blood from the lungs to the tissues and return it again, this time carrying carbon dioxide.

The heart is responsible for pumping an incredible five litres of blood around the body every minute. It starts beating when we are still in the womb, just a few weeks old, and continues to pulsate independently under the orchestration of its own inbuilt pacemaker for the rest of our lives.

The heart was once believed to be the seat of emotion – not surprisingly, perhaps, for feelings like anxiety, fear, anger, excitement and passion are felt here. Grief in particular seems to tear at the heart, hence the term 'brokenhearted'.

This vital pump forces blood along highly elastic vessels which spread through the body becoming increasingly fine as they reach the extremities. Tiny blood capillaries feeding the skin surface may be just one cell thick. Blood itself contains a variety of cells including the haemoglobin-rich red blood corpuscles and the white lymphocytes.

Along with oxygen, other nutrients absorbed from the digestive tract, hormones secreted by the glandular system and other chemicals are all circulated around the body in the blood.

As blood comes into close contact with every part of the body, its composition is a particularly good reflection of what is happening at the cellular level.

A tendency towards good or bad circulation tends to be inherited, but it can also be influenced by lifestyle. Tension held in the muscles interferes with the swift flow of blood to certain parts of the body. Such deprived regions tend to feel cold. It is interesting to note that people who have experienced a great deal of trauma in childhood often tend to have poor circulation.

Signs of Circulatory Upset
- Sluggish circulation
- Cold hands and feet
- Chilblains in winter
- Irregular heart beat
- Palpitations
- Dizziness and feeling faint

- Blurred vision
- Nosebleeds
- Constant fatigue

Case History: Circulatory Problems

Anne, who runs a small family business, was 52 when she was diagnosed as suffering from nervous angina. She had flu-like symptoms all the time and experienced pins and needles as well as pains down her left side. Every 70 days she would get night-time palpitations lasting for 10 minutes. Anne woke frequently during the night in a sweat, her pulse racing.

She was also suffering from water retention which caused her legs to swell, as well as cold hands and feet due to poor circulation.

She had been taking several angina tablets a day to open the arteries, as well as tranquillizers to soothe her nerves.

I Prescribed

- Rose Quartz and Ruby (Gem), for childhood sadness, as her parents had argued all the time and she had always been trying to keep the peace. Her very repressive father made her angry, but she would not express this feeling.
- Bleeding Heart (Peg), for regulating blood pressure and circulation.
- Yellow Ginger (Haii), Wild Potato Bush (Aus B) and Redwood (Peg), for cleansing the blood and strengthening the vessels.
- Saguaro (FES) to cleanse the lymphatic system and to ease fluid retention.

(*Please note*, although Gem Essences are not included in this edition they are available from AK, Him A, and Ask ranges.)

After the first course of treatment Anne's circulation had improved, she had not felt the need to take a tranquillizer for a month and her angina pains had lifted. Five days after finishing the essences she experienced some discomfort and was given a repeat prescription. She has now come off the tranquillizers completely and is down to taking just one angina tablet a day.

The Digestive System

The digestive system is responsible for extracting and absorbing essential nutrients from the foods we eat, as well as for disposing of wastes that would otherwise congest and clog up the system.

Digestion begins in the mouth, where food is pulverized by chewing and mixed with saliva which contains mild starch-digesting enzymes. It then passes to the stomach where digestion begins in earnest. Here food is mixed with a potent gastric juice rich in hydrochloric acid which creates an environment suitable for protein-digesting enzymes to carry out their task.

All kinds of emotional upset, from fear and frustration to anger and anxiety, upset the flow of gastric juice. While an oversecretion of acid gives rise to heartburn, undersecretion means food lingers in the stomach causing indigestion and feelings of heaviness.

On leaving the stomach, food passes into the small intestine, a long and convoluted tunnel where starches are broken down into sugars and digestion is completed. According to the traditions of Chinese medicine, emotions are processed in the digestive tract as well as foods. If sensations such as anger or fear are not properly dealt with, tension accumulates in this area giving rise to symptoms such as stomach knots and colicky pains.

Everything we absorb into the bloodstream through the intestinal walls is passed on to the liver, a remarkable organ which emulsifies fats and changes sugar into glycogen so it can be stored away until it is needed. The liver also detoxifies any undesirable chemicals such as alcohol and the food additives taken in with the vital nutrients. The liver functions best when we eat simply prepared, natural foods and keep regular eating and sleeping patterns; when overburdened with rich, fatty foods and impurities we feel nauseous and headachy, as if slightly hungover. From an emotional viewpoint, the liver is affected by angry outbursts more than anything else.

Foods that have not been broken down for nutrients then enter the large intestine or colon, where any water is reabsorbed and wastes are gathered for elimination. Eating plenty of fibre-rich vegetables and foods helps to speed digestion and prevent wastes from stagnating in the bowel.

Elimination is also carried out by two other organs in the body: the kidneys and the skin. The kidneys, like the liver, filter the blood to remove unwanted salts and noxious wastes. These are expelled in a diluted form as urine. The kidneys also play a vital role in maintaining the balance of body fluids by eliminating excess water and conserving it when in short supply.

Sweat glands in the skin secrete water that contains dissolved mineral salts and small quantities of other wastes through microscopic pores at the surface, helping to keep the body free of impurities. Wearing natural fibres such as cotton and wool allows the skin to breathe and perspire more freely than synthetics do.

Signs of Digestive Upset
- Indigestion/heartburn
- Bloating and wind
- Knots in the stomach
- Colicky cramps

- Diarrhoea
- Constipation
- Nutritional deficiencies
- Fluid retention
- Cystitis
- Blemished skin

Case History: Wind and Bloating

Susan was experiencing abdominal discomfort due to bloating, wind and constipation which had become worse during her divorce from a husband who was
both difficult and vindictive. During this period of intense emotional stress she
had also started to react to city pollution, suffering hay fever-type symptoms.

Her childhood was traumatic. Susan had been brought up during the Second
World War years by very strict parents who would not tolerate any show of
emotion. She had suffered from constipation as a child and was allergic to dairy
produce.

I Prescribed

For the past:
- Star of Bethlehem (B), for long, slow shock.
- Sweet Chestnut (B), for suppressed anxiety and not being able to
  express emotion.
- Mimulus (B), for timidity and fearfulness.
- Agrimony (B), for the British tendency to use a stiff upper lip as a
  protective mechanism.
- Vervain (B), for trying too hard to please and overexerting herself.

For the present:
- Chamomile (FES) and Crowea (Aus B), for stress that leads to a
  nervous stomach.
- Paw paw, Wild Potato Bush (Aus B) and Bamboo (PF), to cleanse the
  digestive system and ease wind, bloating and constipation.
- Eucalyptus (FES) to ease breathing and clear pollutants from the lungs.

Susan feels she has been able to clear the emotional upset of her childhood and
present life. The wind and bloating have subsided, the constipation has cleared
and her allergic reactions are less pronounced.

Case History: Gastric Ulcer

After three unsuccessful operations to treat an ulcer condition, Karen came to me
for help. The ulcer flared up roughly every three months, causing her to wake in
the night with severe pain under her ribcage. At these times she would feel cold,
shivery and headachy, as if in a state of shock.

She was found to be allergic to milk and dairy products generally.

Karen had also suffered long, slow shock as a child because her mother had never been there to nurture her and she was left to look after her younger brother most of the time. She had also been traumatized when her first child was stillborn. She had turned her fear and panic inward on herself.

I Prescribed
- Star of Bethlehem (B), for shock.
- Rock Rose (B), for fear and panic.
- Sweet Chestnut (B), for deep anguish and anxiety.
- Arnica (FES, AK), for suppressed shock which had turned inwards.
- Crowea (Aus B), for continuous worry linked to stomach ulcers.
- Bamboo (PF), to soothe the stomach and colon.
- Pennyroyal (FES), to protect her from negativity.

Karen's ulcer seems to have been calmed, for she has not experienced any repeat attacks and is now sleeping peacefully through the night.

The Endocrine and Reproductive Systems

The endocrine system describes the body's so-called 'ductless glands', namely the pineal, pituitary, thyroid, parathyroid, adrenal, pancreas and thymus glands. They all secrete hormones – chemical 'messengers' which play a vital role in controlling and coordinating important processes such as metabolism and growth. Our behaviour and emotions are influenced to a degree by the hormones circulating in our bloodstream. Each gland and its hormones has a specific job to do. While some enable us to cope with changes in our environment, others orchestrate the rhythms that regulate our sleep and fertility patterns.

The pituitary is the gland which ensures that all the other glands work together in harmony. In spite of its epithet 'master gland', it in turn falls under the influence of the hypothalamus, a region of the brain that detects and responds to emotional upset.

Stressful events, such as relationship problems and conflicts at work, can throw the entire endocrine system into turmoil. Is it any wonder that stress has such a disruptive effect on so many bodily processes?

Hormones produced by the pituitary gland also control the activities of the reproductive organs in both men and women. Although not officially part of the endocrine system, they too produce hormones. Along with the other glands they are also responsive to emotional upset. Reproductive problems such as irregular periods are often one of the first signs that the whole endocrine system is under stress.

Sex drive is thought to be regulated by the hormone testosterone, which is produced in males by the testes and in females in smaller quantities by the adrenal glands. Male fertility is fairly consistent, which may explain why men tend to be less susceptible to emotional highs and lows. Female fertility, in contrast, is a cyclical affair marked by distinct fluctuations in the two predominantly feminine hormones, oestrogen and progesterone.

Hormonal changes may precipitate or enhance all kinds of feelings from irritability and anger to sadness and insecurity, which is the reason why all women suffer from premenstrual mood changes. It is only when stress is added that these emotions can spiral out of control.

A woman's ability to conceive or sustain a pregnancy can also be affected by stress-induced emotions. In instances where there is no biological reason for infertility, negative attitudes and beliefs may underlie problems with conception. A woman who has, for instance, grown up believing that being a parent is incredibly difficult – a view probably passed on to her by her own parents – may subconsciously fear starting a family.

Pregnancy itself is a particularly emotional time, due to the hormonal upheavals that take place and because it raises all kinds of anxieties such as 'Will I love my baby?' and 'Am I ready to be a mother?' Emotional turbulence during this time may play a part in exacerbating symptoms such as morning sickness and feelings of exhaustion.

As the birth approaches it is natural to feel increasingly apprehensive and scared by the pain of labour, feelings that are sensed by the baby. Excessive fear at this time may encourage the baby to remain in a breech position. Interestingly, in India flowers are thought to bring about mental and emotional balance during birth. During the early stages of labour an Indian mother will bathe in water steeped with flowers.

Flower essences help to replace negative feelings such as fear and anxiety with a sense of excitement and anticipation.

Signs of Endocrine Upset
- Lack of sex drive or desire
- Premenstrual tension
- Absence of periods
- Irregular periods
- Period pains
- Infertility
- Mood swings in pregnancy
- Morning sickness
- Postnatal depression
- Menopausal problems
- Impotency in men

Case History: The Problems of Pregnancy

Mary had been married for eight years and although she was three months pregnant she had in the past experienced problems both conceiving and carrying a baby to full term. She had miscarried four years previously, had to have polyps removed from her uterus, then suffered another miscarriage two years later, in both instances at nine and a half weeks. She was very anxious about losing her baby, and her highly stressed job only made matters worse.

I Prescribed
- Star of Bethlehem (B), for past long, slow shock resulting from her parents' divorce when she was 14. It was very traumatic and set up a stress pattern which continued to affect her life.
- Hornbeam (B) for strength to cope.
- Chamomile (Dv, FES), to soothe the nerves and clear stress.
- Pomegranate (FES) and She Oak (Aus B), to stabilize the baby and the whole reproductive area.
- Pear Blossom (Ma), to boost self-healing and buffer both mother and baby from any future stress or shock.

This combination was taken as a four-month course of treatment.

At seven months Mary reported having had a trouble-free pregnancy and asked for more remedies for the last two months and for the birth itself.

I Prescribed
- A repeat of the Pomegranate (FES) and She Oak (Aus B).
- Cauliflower (PVi) to help the baby through the birth process.
- Vanilla(PF) to act as a protective shield for mother and baby.

The birth was trouble-free; both mother and baby are thriving.

Case History: Menopause
At 50, Jane began going through the menopause, suffering hot flushes and panic attacks. She had always suffered from premenstrual tension and depression around the time of her period. She was also finding her work as a counsellor highly stressful, as she tended to take her clients' emotional problems to heart.

I Prescribed
- She Oak (Aus B), Pomegranate (FES), Orange Honeysuckle (Pac) for the reproductive area and hormonal balance.
- Candysticks (Pac), for releasing pelvic tension and to boost energy levels.
- Correa (Aus L), for learning to accept her limitations in helping others.
- Pink Fairy Orchid (Aus L), to filter out the emotional stress of those around her.

Jane felt all her menopausal symptoms ease, especially the hot flushes, and she had ceased having panic attacks. She now feels more like her normal self again.

Case History: Premenstrual Tension

For some time Sophie had been experiencing severe premenstrual tension. She generally felt exhausted and overwhelmed by stress due primarily to her two young children: one was not sleeping through the night and the other was having mild learning difficulties.

I Prescribed

- Star of Bethlehem (B), for past long, slow shock caused by the fact that her mother had not been very nurturing.
- Vervain (B), for overexertion brought on by trying too hard to please and achieve.
- Chamomile (FES), for sleep loss due to the effects of stress on her nervous system.
- Pomegranate (FES), for rebalancing the reproductive area.
- She Oak (Aus B), for premenstrual hormonal imbalance and water retention.
- Noni (Haii), for awakening the maternal instincts of nurturing, caring and love so she could find it easier to cope with being a mother.
- Illyarrie (Aus L), for strength to overcome difficulties without feeling overwhelmed
- Leafless Orchid (Aus L), to find energy from within to keep working without becoming physically depleted.
- Russian Kolokoltchik (Aus L), to help conquer adverse conditions.
- First Aid Remedy (Him A), as an overall booster.

The month after Sophie started taking the prescription she did not have any premenstrual tension; the following month she experienced mild symptoms; since then she has been symptom-free and has felt much more balanced, with the energy to cope with a young family.

Endocrine Balance Using Australian Bush Essences

Pituitary: Yellow Cowslip Orchid
Pineal: Bush Iris
Hypothalamus: Bush Fuchsia
Thyroid: Old Man Banksia
Thymus: Illawarra Flame Tree
Pancreas: Peach-flowered Tea-tree
Adrenals: Macrocarpa
Ovaries: She Oak
Testes: Flannel Flower

The Skeletal and Muscular Systems

The bones, joints, muscles and ligaments provide the body with structure, strength and suppleness. They work together, enabling us to move with ease and comfort.

The spine is the linchpin of the skeletal system. It is made up of 24 drum-shaped vertebra separated by discs of fibrous tissue which act as shock absorbers. As babies our spines are relatively straight. Curves slowly develop as we spend more and more time upright.

Its S-shape endows the spine with remarkable resilience to physical impact. Sadly this does not prevent us getting backache brought on by poor posture and emotional tension. Those who suffer from bad backs often tend to bear the troubles of the world on their shoulders and feel overwhelmed by responsibilities. As the archetypal providers and supporters, married men with families are the classic example. Joints form the connections between two or more adjacent parts of the skeleton; they are held together by ligaments, tough elastic fibres which allow the joints to bend to allow movement and flexibility. Inflammation of the joints, as in the case of arthritis, is traditionally thought to be caused by wear and tear or disease. However, all kinds of inflammatory chemicals, such as those produced during an allergic reaction, contribute to certain forms of arthritis.

Muscles move the joints and bones. There are 620 we can move of our own accord, plus many more involuntary ones in the heart, blood vessels, intestines and so on that we cannot control.

Emotional tension is readily transmitted to the muscles. From early in life we often develop a habit of tensing certain muscles. Most people tend to raise their shoulders and tense the neck muscles when they feel threatened. We all develop our own ways of responding to stress. Repressed emotions, whether painful or pleasurable, are also stored in the muscles as tension, giving rise to a sort of 'muscular armour'. Such ingrained tensions not only limit our freedom of movement, they also stifle energy – which may explain why our natural vitality dwindles as we age.

Signs of upset
- Muscular aches
- Tension in the neck and shoulders
- Back aches and pains
- Slipped discs
- Stiff, sore joints
- Arthritis
- Rheumatism
- Poor posture

Case History: Hip Replacement
Juliet was 48 when she discovered she needed to have a hip replacement. As the day for the operation approached she became increasingly fearful and was unable to eat.

I Prescribed
- Indian Pink (FES), Hau (Haii) and Chamomile (FES, Ak), for stress affecting the nervous system and stomach.
- Star of Bethlehem (B), for shock brought on by any operation.
- Jasmine(PF) for healing the skeletal system.
- Russian Kolokoltchik (Aus L), for courage and strength.

The operation was very successful and Juliet's recovery amazed her doctor. After just four weeks she reported no pain, bruising or swelling and could walk without crutches. She continued with the remedies to consolidate the treatment, adding Ohai-ali'i (Haii) to help knit and strengthen the bones and Comfrey to help repair and rebuild muscle tissue. A month later she completely regained her mobility and could even run upstairs.

Case History: Arthritis
Margaret developed extremely painful arthritis in her hands and knees. She was taking the usual combination of anti-inflammatory agents, painkillers and paracetamol. At the same time she was exhausted and was not absorbing nutrients properly from her food.

I Prescribed
- Yarrow (PF), for the inflammation.
- Zinnia (PF), for arthritis.
- Gold (AL, Him A), to aid the assimilation of nutrients.
- K9 and Formula 38 (Him A), for autoimmune problems.
- Morning Glory (Him A, FES) to clear the toxic effects of the medication she had been taking.

Margaret charted her condition from December to mid-May. For the first 20 days the pain continued, but the next day it started to ease. Five days later it had disappeared and has not recurred since.

She now has more energy than before and, now able to kneel and squat without discomfort, she has resumed her passion for gardening.

The Mind – Thoughts and Emotions

Nobody understands exactly how the mind functions. Our thoughts, feelings and emotions ultimately depend on our outlook on life. This in turn is linked to our personality and shaped by upbringing and personal experiences.

For simplicity's sake the mind is regarded as the seat of consciousness, intelligence, thought, reasoning, memory, imagination, creativity, emotions and instinctive drives. These functions take place within the brain, the most complex and highly developed structure that exists.

The brain is composed of millions and millions of interconnecting nerve cells which pass snippets of information, in the form of chemical messages, from one to another.

Certain regions of the brain are associated with different functions. The most ancient reptilian region comprising the spinal cord, brain stem and midbrain controls our most basic survival and reproductive instincts. The next layer is the paleomammalian brain, also known as the limbic system. This is the control centre for emotions and states of mind such as fear, panic, pleasure and bliss. It is here that responses such as affection, sexual behaviour, altruistic impulses and even love originate. Bodily functions such as thirst, hunger, temperature and sexual drive are also regulated by this region.

The cerebral cortex is biologically the most recent region of the brain. It seems to have evolved once humans had overcome the basic function of survival and found time to sit around thinking, learning new skills, creating things and so forth. The cortex is where perception, memory, judgement and the intellect, something loosely defined as cognition, occurs.

The 'thinking' brain is responsible for mental activity. It is divided into two parts or hemispheres, the left and right, which deal with information in rather different ways. In modern Western society greater emphasis is placed on the logical, rational and analytical thinking which occurs in the left hemisphere. Recently we have begun to realize the importance of the right brain, which is concerned with creativity, inspiration and imagination. 'Whole brain thinking' is not only more effective, it also makes life seem richer.

Although the brain has a seemingly infinite capacity to store knowledge, in our information-orientated age there is a danger of mental overstimulation. By trying to make sense of it all, our minds become filled with swirling thoughts and an internal chatter which we cannot switch off.

When mentally exhausted we cannot think clearly or concentrate properly, we become forgetful and find it hard to make decisions. When the mind is in turmoil, thinking is distorted and so too is the way we act or behave.

The famous psychoanalyst R D Lang pointed out that mental turmoil may also arise when something we are told or seems to be fact is at odds with what we instinctively know or sense. Suspicions of being deceived and lied to can, he claimed, torment us to the point of insanity.

Similarly, powerful emotions like anger, fear and rage undermine our ability to think in a clear and rational manner. Emotions are part of our ancient inheritance and we probably share them in common with our distant ancestors. The psychologist Carl Jung referred to the 'collective unconscious' as being the hopes, fears and anxieties which all human beings hold in common.

It is natural and healthy for us to experience the whole gamut of emotions. However, certain ones such as anger and fear are seen as socially unacceptable, perhaps because they remind us of our primitive origins or just because they make us feel uncomfortable. We suppress them, learning from childhood that it is 'wrong' to lose our temper or break down in tears. Both Sigmund Freud and Carl Jung believed that repressed emotions do not go away; they stay in our psyche and crop up in our dreams. Without an outlet they become bottled up inside until the pressure becomes so intense that we may literally blow a fuse.

Negative emotions will not do us much harm if they are fleeting. However, if they become part of our behavioural response they slowly and insidiously wreak havoc on the system.

We inherit many behavioural patterns from our parents. As young children we copy the way they react to situations and handle their emotions. We also acquire perceptions about ourselves, others and the world in general from them. Their attitudes and opinions undoubtedly influence the way we think of and view life. It is believed that all experiences, even those we cannot consciously remember from childhood, are stored in the subconscious mind. From here they exert an influence on our behaviour and on the way we react to other people and situations in our lives.

This influence may be appropriate when we are growing up for it gives us a sense of structure and security. In later life, however, these inherited views and attitudes may no longer be helpful – can even be limiting – and their value to us has to be reassessed.

Thousands of years ago wise men realized we can only see things for what they really are when our minds are clear, still and free from cluttering thoughts. They developed meditative techniques for calming the mind and subduing the disruptive effects of our emotions. They also taught that, to be free of negative emotions, we have to find ways of turning seemingly negative situations into ones that can have a positive outcome. After all, what we think of as reality is really all in the mind.

Signs of Mental and Emotional Upset
- Confusion
- Inability to think clearly
- Persistent unwanted thoughts
- Forgetfulness
- Inability to make decisions

- Poor concentration
- Feelings of being overwhelmed by emotions of all kinds
- Emotional outbursts
- Mood swings
- Feelings of being on an emotional roller coaster, out of control

Case History: Stress

Elizabeth, a self-styled company director, had built her own business into a growing concern. Despite being extremely successful in her career, she always found herself in relationships with men in which she felt abused. These played havoc with her self-esteem and were a continual source of worry. She felt confused, overwhelmed and unable to sleep properly. Her tumultuous emotional life was beginning to affect her work. She could not concentrate or make decisions and was in danger of ruining her business.

I Prescribed

- Paw Paw (Aus B), for feeling overwhelmed and burdened by decisions.
- Scleranthus (B), to encourage decisiveness and belief in her own intuition.
- Stress/Tension (Him A), for general tension and nervous stress.
- Scarlet Monkeyflower (FES) and Relationship Combo (Aus B), for her difficulties with relationships.
- She Oak (Aus B), for bringing self-esteem by increasing sensuality and joy in femininity.
- Russian Kolokoltchik (Aus L), to help her conquer adverse conditions.

Elizabeth recovered her strength and her sense of being centred. She spent some time on her own and began to feel more positive about herself, realizing that she did not need the sort of destructive relationships in which she was always trying hard to please someone else, but never succeeding. Later she was drawn to a man who was gentle, kind yet strong in his own way, who treated her with the respect she desired and deserved. Her business and her new relationship continue to flourish.

Spiritual Harmony

Most people feel there must be more to us than merely mind and body. The dictionary defines spirit as the vital force, soul, the immortal part of us. It is not something that can be measured or analysed by science. Nonetheless, this elusive part of us has a profound influence on our behaviour, beliefs and the kind of relationships we form. The spirit is the real person and is unique to each one of us, whereas the soul is viewed as that essential spark of creation that is part of the universal soul from which we all originate. This is what gives us being and existence, connects us to all living things.

Spiritual harmony is best described as an awareness of, a knowing of who you are, why you are here and what your particular purpose is in life. This brings a tremendous feeling of wellbeing, an abundance of vital energy and a real sense of security and belonging or being 'at home' in the world. Spiritual harmony manifests when your personality or ego is in touch with and works together with the deeper aspect of yourself, your soul.

At the same time you are still aware of a kind of spirituality that is indefinable. This is the highest form of existence which usually lies just on the edge of your consciousness. The spirit and soul seem to give us a great deal of freedom, but luckily if we stray too far from our true path, warning signals are sent out – which we ignore to our cost.

It is interesting that we begin life full of energy and sparkle. As children we often have a clear picture of what we wish to do with our lives, too. We may speculate that during those early years the ego/personality is more in touch with or in tune with the inner spirit/soul. As adults many of us end up in relationships, jobs or environments which leave us feeling empty, unfulfilled and craving something to make our lives more meaningful. From the spiritual point of view, we are lost.

Over 60 years ago Dr Edward Bach understood that physical disease is the direct outcome of emotional upset, which arises from a conflict between the soul/spirit and the mind/ego. He wrote:

> Man has a soul which is his real self – it ever guides, protects and
> encourages us, leading us always for our utmost advantage. The
> soul knows what environment and what circumstances will best
> enable us to develop virtues which we lack and wipe out all that is
> wrong in us. So long as our souls and personalities are in harmony,
> all is joy and peace, happiness and health. When our personalities
> are led astray from the path laid down by the soul, either by our
> own worldly desires or by the persuasion of others, a conflict arises.
> This conflict brings disease ... which will never be eradicated
> except by spiritual and mental effort.

So we might view disease, whether physical, mental, emotional or spiritual, as the way our soul tries to attract our attention and make us realize that we are straying too far from our path, giving us the opportunity to take steps to regain our sense of inner harmony.

In difficult times, most people find themselves wondering why life seems so hard and full of suffering. One explanation is that we are here to learn certain lessons and can only do so by experience. Certain religions hold that the soul may incarnate over and over again into a succession of physical bodies to master lessons that can only be learned from a material existence. These lessons include how to give love without expecting anything in return and how to be compassionate.

The concept of reincarnation holds that life throws in our path a series of challenges that have to be met. As each situation arises we have to decide how we are going to deal with it. The choices we make constantly shape the rest of our lives. We create our own destiny. No two souls have ever walked an identical path; each chooses his or her own.

The notion of karma is part and parcel of a belief in reincarnation. What it basically suggests is that 'you reap what you sow'. In other words, what you have done and thought in the past are affecting you now. Similarly what you are doing and thinking now affects your future. We are creating our own good or bad karma all the time.

If you are going through a time of pain and suffering, you may be paying off some past transgressions. If you are one of those lucky people who seems to be in the right place at the right time, you may be reaping the benefit of past good deeds. It's a sort of universal justice system.

If someone wrongs you it is best to forgive him or her, knowing that in due course justice will be done, if not in this lifetime then in the next. Any feelings of resentment, hatred, ill will or contempt will tie you to the person for whom you feel such antipathy. Eventually you will have to undo those karmic ties.

Philosophers and sages contemplating the meaning of humanity throughout the ages have come to the conclusion that our reason for being is to achieve purity of spirit and matter. It was once said by Rama Teph, a Second Dynasty Nubian Pharaoh, that man's special purpose is to have his head in heaven but his feet firmly planted in the earth. To be a complete human being we must be both spirit and matter, beautifully combined together, each of us blending these two aspects in a unique way.

Sometimes we try so hard to find spiritual harmony that we literally get in our own way. The same problem occurs if we take this quest too seriously, over-complicating the whole process and missing the simplicity of it all. Life is best viewed as an adventure which enables the spirit to meet challenges, to rise above limitations, to grow in wisdom and vision. We don't need to take this spiritual quest too seriously – discovering our true nature can be fun. Life and this journey would be soulless without the essential element of humour. The art lies in taking life seriously in a non-serious way.

The beauty of succeeding is that it brings inner strength, a belief in your ability to achieve whatever you choose to do, a sense of purpose and a feeling of being in harmony with other people, with animals and the nature kingdom.

Signs of Disharmony
- Feeling ill at ease with yourself and life
- Lack of fulfilment

- Feeling empty, insecure, alone
- Feeling that your life is not as you would like it to be
- Feeling out of control; needing to manipulate life and control others
- Lack of flexibility and adaptability with the environment
- No sense of direction or purpose
- Feeling spiritually impoverished
- Feeling disconnected from nature

Case History: Shock

David was a wealthy businessman who suddenly lost all his money in a stock-market crash. He was shattered and traumatized. His life was falling apart, as money had given him his sense of security and he no longer saw any reason for living. His relationship with his wife began crumbling; he seemed paralysed, aimless, exhausted and at times suicidal. He turned to alcohol for comfort.

I Prescribed

- Emergency Essence (Aus B), for shock.
- Fringed Violet and Waratah (Aus B), for his black despair and suicidal feelings.
- Fireweed (Ask), to help him cope with and integrate the changes in his life.
- Gruss an Aachen (PVi), for intense challenge and fears associated with this evolutionary process, to calm, stabilize and offer him support to move forward.
- Shooting Star (Ask), to understand his purpose in life.
- Strength (Him E), to have a clearer image of himself and his role in the future.

David stopped using alcohol as an emotional crutch. He became positive and dynamic, which made him feel empowered. He realized that money did not bring him happiness and that his purpose in life was to initiate more ethical projects linked to saving the environment via the world he knew best, that of business and high finance. He was then headhunted for a highly-paid position to establish such ventures, enabling him to use money in a way that helped others. By his example he has instigated a change in consciousness and a realization in those he now works with that business can be both ethical and commercially viable.

CHAPTER EIGHT

Extra Advice For Practitioners

Practitioners of both complementary and orthodox medicine will find flower essences invaluable tools for helping others to help themselves. Like many natural remedies and therapies they are excellent for easing the ill effects of stress. Yet flower essences go further, highlighting the underlying patterns leading to emotional distress and its physical repercussions. They do so by cultivating self-awareness, helping others to see and understand the reasons why they are not feeling as well as they could be.

From the patient's or client's point of view it can be extremely beneficial to have someone with greater experience to help them become aware of their negative behavioural patterns and emotional responses, then guide them towards the most appropriate remedies.

As Dr Edward Bach pointed out over half a century ago:

> The physician of the future will have two great aims ... firstly to assist the patient to a knowledge of himself and to point out to him the fundamental mistakes he may be making; the deficiencies of his character which he should remedy, and the defects in his nature which must be eradicated and replaced by the corresponding virtues.
>
> Secondly to administer remedies to help his physical body gain strength and to assist the mind to become calm, widen its outlook and strive towards perfection, thus bringing peace and harmony to the whole personality. Such remedies exist in nature ...

These remedies are, of course, the flower essences for which he is famed.

Anyone prescribing these remedies needs to act as a finely tuned instrument, as a receptor, resonator and reflector for the patient. Clearly each practitioner will wish to evolve his or her own appropriate way of treating patients, and this will vary according to the actual needs of people coming for help. It is essential to be flexible, adaptable and creative in your approach to diagnosing and prescribing the flower essences. However, the following method can be used as a practical guide for those wishing to work with these remedies.

Building Up a Flower Essence Repertoire

Ideally you should aim to have about 100 remedies at your fingertips. In order to choose the most useful ones it is important to familiarize yourself with the major flower essence families listed in the Encyclopedia section of this book. Slowly read through them all, placing a tick beside those that reflect the sort of problems you most frequently come across.

If you specialize in treating certain kinds of symptoms, such as women's problems, it will be useful to look at the Ailment Chart (Chapter Five); this will tell you at a glance which are the most appropriate remedies for each type of condition.

Even when you have composed your repertoire it is important to keep abreast of new additions to the flower essence families.

Giving a Diagnostic Session

During the 20 years that I have been working with flower essences in a professional capacity, I have realized that straight discussion with the patient combined with a good working knowledge of the remedies does not always provide a clear enough picture of the more deep-seated problems involved. I have found that using a pendulum as a diagnostic tool helps me to be accurate in the selection of essences. The pendulum prevents the practitioner's opinions and ideas from impinging on the selection of essences, making the whole procedure far more objective.

Almost without exception everyone can become proficient at using a pendulum with a little practice.

Before you begin a diagnosis, arrange the stock bottles of flower essence in neat, orderly rows before you so they are easily accessible. Then ask the client to place one finger on each test bottle in turn. Gently lay one hand over the client's to create a link with him or her. Holding the pendulum in the other hand, you will find that it begins to move one way or the other, giving a distinct 'yes' or 'no' the instant you make contact with the patient.

Pick out each of the chosen remedies from the batch of stock bottles and put them to one side. These are the essences the client has selected for him- or herself with assistance from you, acting as a mirror for or extension of the patient.

It is quite acceptable to have diagnosed up to 15 different essences. The real art then lies in making sense of what they can tell you about your patient.

I have found that each remedy is either for the client's past, present or future condition.

- The past – childhood and other early traumas.
- The present – immediate emerging emotions as well as the client's psychological and physical state at the moment of treatment.
- The future – protection from and prevention of certain mental and emotional states which have their roots in the past and present, and which could easily manifest as major blockages later on.

To find out how many drops of each essence are needed, use the pendulum again. Count slowly from one to three; the pendulum will indicate a 'yes' when the correct number is reached. The number of drops required will also tell you to which life phase that particular essence applies:

- Essences for the past – 3 drops of each.
- Essences for the present – 2 drops of each.
- Essences for the future –1 drop of each.

With experience you will begin to see that one remedy naturally follows on from and connects with the others. In this way you will begin to build up a picture of your patient, using the past as a starting point, progressing to current problems and ending with future issues. It is in relating and making the connection between each particular remedy that your insight and intuition will come into play.

Case study

Emily was suffering from recurrent migraines and nervous stomach upsets. At the time she was working as a computer analyst in London and felt highly stressed.

During a diagnostic session the following essences were chosen for her:

- **Past**

  Star of Bethlehem (B), for long, slow shock. Emily suggested that this related to childhood. She was always trying very hard to prove herself in order to please her authoritarian father, but never felt up to the mark.
  Vervain (B), for overriding the stress pattern set up in childhood. She had become forceful, highly strung and prone to exhausting herself through over-effort.

- **Present**

  Indian Pink (FES), for stress from the environment.
  Chamomile (FES), for the effect of stress on the nervous system and stomach.
  Narcissus (PF), for stress resulting in migraine-type headaches.
  Illawarra Flame Tree (Aus B), to cultivate self-approval, confidence

and inner strength.

Environmental Stress Remedy (Him A), to protect against radiation given out by her computer and contributing to her headaches.

• **Future**

Chicory (B), for countering feelings of self-pity which could impair her improvement.

Occasionally the pendulum will keep swinging, telling you that 4 drops of a particular essence are needed. This suggests stress stemming from a past life, a possible trauma that is spilling over into this lifetime and creating a blockage. This will need to be addressed before complete healing can take place. Past-life traumas are often responsible for irrational fears that do not stem from childhood. A fear of water, for instance, could indicate that the person died by drowning in a previous existence.

The essence in the 4-drop position could also pertain to the birth experience. It can also sometimes suggest a past-life overspill or carryover. If it was traumatic there may be a reluctance to be here, which may manifest itself as daydreaming, escaping to a fantasy world. Someone who was born with the umbilical cord wrapped around their neck may have a problem swallowing, or may dislike having anything close-fitting around his neck (such as a tie or polo-neck shirt).

What to Say and What Not to Say

The whole reason for prescribing flower essences is to help patients become aware of their own stress patterns, enabling them to take back responsibility for their health and happiness. Handing back power to the individual is in fact the first stage of the self-healing process. It is therefore extremely important for you to inform and involve the client throughout the entire procedure.

You will need to give a brief description of what the essence is for, such as shock in the past. If the patient is relaxed and feels able to trust you, he or she will hopefully fill in the missing information by telling you the nature of the past trauma.

The Encyclopedia or Ailment Chart in this book can be used to discuss the descriptions of each essence with patients.

It is not a good idea to discuss issues such as reincarnation and past lives with clients during an initial consultation. If they already hold other beliefs they may feel uncomfortable with such concepts or react against them. Respect their views and you may find, in time, that they become more open-minded to these possibilities.

It is essential, however, that you give clients a brief description of the body's energy systems – the aura, chakras and subtle bodies, so they are able to understand how shock and stress affect the system (*see* Chapter Two).

Clients often ask me how long will it take to feel an effect and what to expect. I respond by letting them know that the remedies start to work at clearing the root of the problem at a very deep level and how soon they feel a change is dependent on how aware they are of their own processes. At times there can be a heightening of the emotional trauma or negative mental patterns from the past, but without the full impact of the original experiences, as it is cleared out of the system.

As remedies are excellent in speeding up the healing process it's good to reassure them that it take less time to clear the stress pattern than it did to create the situation in the first place.

In clearing the root of the problem the resulting physical manifestation is no longer being fed by the initial underlying cause.

Some of the qualities that develop when taking essences are:
- A growing awareness of the mind/body connection by feeling more in touch and caring towards their physical body.
- Reflective self-awareness, responsibility, moving out of victim mode into empowered choice.
- The ability to respond and benefit from challenges, greater courage, strength and endurance.
- Vitality enthusiasm and creativity enhanced.
- Harmonizes relationships and gives a sense of being on their path in life.

Combining Flower Essences With Other Therapies

Flower essences can be used in conjunction with both complementary and orthodox medicines because they are totally safe and free from any side effects. They are a perfect complement to all kinds of natural healing therapies, particularly aromatherapy and acupressure, enhancing their effectiveness in relieving symptoms and speeding the rate of recovery.

Flower Essences and Aromatherapy

Flower essences and essential oils work particularly well together. As both belong to the plant world, they have a special affinity for one another. While essential oils are only extracted from aromatic plants, flower essences can be made from those with little or no perfume, which greatly enhances the range of flora you can work with.

Even when essential oils and flower essences do come from the same plant you will notice that their properties may be different – although there may be overlaps. This is because their vibrational qualities are not identical. Generally speaking, the vibration of flower essences is higher and more ethereal than that of essential oils. While essential oils tend to work primarily at a physical level, they can also have some psychological benefits. Flower essences, in contrast, concentrate their influence mainly on our thoughts and emotions, benefits which filter into the physical body. This means that a practitioner using essential oils can draw on a flower essence to provide a particular vibration that cannot be found in any of the essential oils. The converse is just as true. Used in combination the benefits of each become more profound and far-reaching.

When selecting flower essences to complement essential oils, always opt for those whose qualities are most relevant for that particular person. Whether they come from the same or completely different flowers or plants is irrelevant. Add a drop or two of the chosen flower essence to a massage oil. This will bring to the blend a vibrational quality that complements that of the essential oil, making the treatment more complete. The Petite Fleur range of essences blend especially well with essential oils due to the way they are made.

Floral Acupressure

This is a budding form of therapy which is proving to be highly beneficial. Many find that improvements for all kinds of conditions occur faster and are more dramatic when appropriate flower essences are applied to certain acupuncture points on the skin.

Drs Vasudeva and Kadambii Barnao (Australian Living Flower Essences) and Drs Atul and Pupa Shah (Himalayan Aditi Flower Essences) have done pioneering work in this field. Their research is geared towards discovering which particular essences work best on key acupressure points. From their findings Drs Vasudeva and Kadambii Barnao have drawn up 'Floral Acu-maps' which can be obtained directly from the suppliers (see Useful Addresses).

I find that flower essences are particularly effective when used in combination with Shen Tao, thought by some to be the mother of acupuncture. This is a special kind of acupressure which differs from the traditional approach in that it accesses the extraordinary as well as the main meridians. The extraordinary meridians are seen as the reservoir, whereas the main meridians are seen as the rivers. They have a powerful influence on the whole subtle anatomy so the benefits they bring are emotional, mental and spiritual as well as physical. However, Shen Tao shares many key points with ordinary acupressure.

Useful Acupressure Points
The 'Hegu' or 'Hoku' acupoint is arguably the best pain-relieving point on the body. It is found on the back of the hand in the web between thumb and forefinger. In Shen Tao acupressure this point, known as 'Joining Valley', is also used for treating colds, constipation, laryngitis (sore throats) migraines and arthritis.

Good essences to use here are those that also have pain-relieving or relaxing qualities (see Ailment Chart, Chapter Five).

For headaches and other pains, Living Essences of Australia recommends either Dampiera (a mental and muscle relaxant) for dissolving rigidity in mind and body, or Menzies Banksia to help you to go with the pain rather than resist and so intensify it.

The 'Shenmen' acupoint on the ear is excellent for relieving stress and promoting relaxation. It can be found just inside the rim at the tip of the ear.

Suggested Living Essences of Australia:
- Pink Fairy Orchid – good for stress from environmental factors such as noise.
- Hybrid Pink Fairy (Cowslip) Orchid – helps ease stress caused by over-sensitivity to other people. Especially useful for easing premenstrual emotional and mental tension.
- Yellow Flag Flower – for when stress has taken all the sparkle out of life, making people dull and grim.
- Purple Flag Flower (Bush Iris) – releases stress which has been building up in the body. Acts as a valve for dispelling pressure.

In Shen Tao the 'Daling' point works wonders for calming the emotions. It can be found on the underside of your wrist, lying in the centre of the wrist crease. Use essences here that are appropriate for your particular emotional disturbance (see Ailment Chart).

For clearing the mind and lifting the spirit, one of the best points to work on is the 'Bai-hui' acupoint. Take a line from the top of each ear lobe and continue to the crown of the head. The Bai-hui point lies where these two lines meet.

Excellent essences to use here are Lotus (Him A) or Leafless Orchid (Aus L) to rebalance energy after excessive emotional or physical drain. Place a drop of either essence here every 15 minutes for an hour or so and you will find yourself revitalized.

In Shen Tao, working with the 'Shining Sea' point not only clears the mind but also helps to treat fluid retention, irregular periods and joint problems. It is found on the inner ankle directly behind the ankle bone.

Past Life and Soul Retrieval, Psychic Protection

Past-life and soul retrieval issues are usually treated by psychotherapy, hypnotherapy and shamanic healing practices.

Soul Retrieval

In the case of soul retrieval, shock, trauma, or long slow stress such as wounding, abuse or rejection will have a powerful effect on the psyche, or soul, resulting in unbalanced beliefs and behavioural patterns. These states are often accompanied by feelings of emptiness or incompletion or lack of self-worth, so when one works with energy or vibrational medicine, it is possible to reclaim these parts of us that have separated for their own protection. It is not uncommon for children who have experienced trauma in childhood to have little or no memory of those years. In the case of shamanic healing ancient universal healing practices have been synthesized and adapted in a form appropriate to contemporary life. These modalities have proved highly effective in dissolving the traumas of past events and in combination with precisely focused combination flower essences have proved even more effective.

Past Life

There are two ways of looking at this subject, symbolic and mythic, or a reality if one concedes that reincarnation is a possibility.

In the first case, the awareness of a troubling past-life memory, may be a genetic or cellular memory, or early forgotten trauma which has become locked deep within the psyche. For some people, a hypnotherapy session may be effective in releasing the toxic energy pattern. For others, shamanic journeying can be a transformative experience. Here the client works with the practitioner to re-experience, heal and gain understanding of the past event. It is sometimes surprising when they may have been the offending party in a relationship, for example, and have been repeating the same personality fault in their current life. Equally, if the client has been the victim this tendency is also continued in their existing relationships with people and events.

Again, the flower remedies offer a profound support for these processes, helping to identify and pinpoint the root cause of the underlying imbalance. Dissolving the negative vibrational resonances makes it easier for the stress pattern to be released during the treatment, allowing the full force of the soul to be integrated into the personality. The flower remedies will stabilize and anchor the reclaimed soul energy to be integrated into the whole being. In the case of past-life healing, the remedies help to dissolve ancient inherited karmic patterns leaving the being free from previous attachments and influences.

Remedies for Past-life Healing
The following range of flower essences are particularly appropriate for and support shamanic processes
From the Peter Aziz Shamanic Range and Andreas Korte Essences.

Past Life Orchid (AK) Assists us in opening the Akashic Records where hidden memories about our life experiences, past, present and future are stored. This essence can reveal deep-rooted causes for many emotional problems.

Release Cactus (AK) Helps us to release old negative patterns. It has a very deep effect as it reaches into the unconscious and even into our cellular awareness.

It removes blockages and helps us to regenerate.

Shadow Cactus (AK) Has a releasing effect on the solar plexus; we become conscious of our inner processes and are able to overcome them and then move on. We say goodbye to our shadow and we learn to accept death and to live in total awareness.

Thorne Apple (HUB) A very initiating essence that should be taken with very clear motivation. Helps movement between different planes of consciousness. Breaks limitations in the mind. Seeing beyond life and death.

Yellow Archangel (HUB) For understanding and accepting the balance between light and dark. Puts one in touch with hidden realms, and helps one accept all that may be found in these planes.

Psychotherapy

Flower remedies are a valuable tool which support psychotherapy and speed up the healing process. Reaching beyond the verbal level, flower remedies are often described as a form of liquid therapy.

Flower Essences and Orthodox Medicine

Many general practitioners realize that stress may be responsible for their patients' health problems, but feel powerless to help. While tranquillizers and other such drugs may help someone over a particularly bad patch, they do not provide the tools needed for dealing with stress. They tend to dull perception and subdue the stress response.

Tranquillizers also have less desirable side effects and tend to be addictive; coming off them suddenly can give rise to frightening withdrawal symptoms. Flower essences can safely be given to patients to help them cope with their particular source of stress. Many open-minded general practitioners are now adding flower essences such as Star of Bethlehem (B) for general shock to their prescription list.

As a flower essence practitioner you may frequently see patients who want to wean themselves off tranquillizers, antidepressants and any other mood-altering drugs but are worried about withdrawal symptoms. Flower essences can help to free them from their dependency, ease any side effects and clear the system of any imbalance that has been caused by long-term use of medicinal drugs.

Helping Yourself

As a practitioner it is easy to be affected by the problems of others. If steps are not taken to protect your own emotional wellbeing, you could start to feel energetically drained. With this in mind I have composed a special 'practitioner mix' for boosting energy levels and safeguarding against exhaustion.

Delph (AK)
Fringed Violet (Aus B)
Leafless Orchid (Aus L)
Lotus (AK, Him A)
Healing (Him E)

Use 2 drops of each essence.

New Developments in Flower Essence treatments

Flower Essences and Nutritional Support

Increasingly I have noticed with my clients a severe lack of nutritional assimilation and absorption generally. Stemming not only from emotional and stress-related issues but also from the immune system being under so much strain from having to cope with the barrage of pollutants with which its being faced.

The instances of intolerance have increased dramatically over the years not only to foods as well as the chemical sprays on food, but also to the chemical cocktail that we put on our skin.

Unfortunately, even if the food is organic the soil is basically deficient in the essential minerals/vitamins and trace elements due to the overworking of the land and lack of replenishment. These nutrients are of prime importance and are the elements that provide the vital sparks that ignite the correct functioning of our bodily systems as a whole.

This gap in the fulfilment of our fundamental needs became abundantly clear when testing for essences; the Australian Bush Paw Paw and Crowea would frequently be coupled together indicating both a lack of absorption and assimilation.

The need to create a solid foundation by replenishing the nutritional reserve in the body seemed an obvious next step by allowing the flower essences to act faster and more efficiently within the body's system as well as building up the deeply depleted reserves.

There is a large variety of vitamins and minerals on the market that make all sorts of wonderful claims, so why weren't my clients absorbing them? The answer became clear as it became apparent that the normal absorption of these tablets was only about 40 per cent. So I started my quest to find a liquid form of minerals/vitamins to do the job more efficiently, as a liquid would be more readily absorbed than tablets.

I came across an organic liquid mineral/vitamin with a unique delivery system that, when tested, acted really swiftly to replenish the area that normal tablets didn't seem to be able to reach. I noticed that this colloidal supplement called Maximol created a very rapid improvement in the absorption uptake as well as appearing to be suited energetically to work with the subtle energies of the flower essences. My conclusion was that Maximol significantly speeded up the essences' action in the body and therefore the self-healing process. Only a small, almost homeopathic, amount is needed a day to effect a result, and together with the correct flower essences, which address the root of the problem, they create a formidable team with which to obtain optimum health and wellbeing.

In the quest to address the incidents of chronic and autoimmune conditions that presented itself at my clinic, I've found that the addition of glyconutrients ('sugars' for short), in the field of 'Glycobiology' offers a wonderful opportunity to improve this situation. It has been discovered that eight essential sugar molecules are present in every cell of the human body. Whereas until now it was believed that carbohydrates/sugars are our fuel, and that protein/amino acids are our body's building blocks. It is now realized that the eight sugars are responsible for most of all the cellular communication in our bodies. Basically these eight sugars provide the software to run the countless programs that our bodies need. If the right sugars are produced, the body maintains its extraordinary ability to heal and regenerate itself. Conversely, without them the cell-to-cell communication breaks down resulting in the onset of many degenerative conditions that really should not have happened. The body also loses the ability to heal itself and begins to think there are problems where there are not. Here lies the cause of our auto-immune conditions – the body turns on itself. This is happening at an alarming rate.

Two of the eight essential sugars are found in the average diet. Until recently a healthy body was able to synthesize the remaining six from the basic two. Now the increasing toxic overload to which the body is subjected to, plus its daily exposure to free radicals, has seriously depleted our ability to produce these essential sugars for ourselves. As a result the body's defences begin to break down and chronic sickness, allergies and autoimmune disease appear.

There is a large body of information beginning to emerge about this new science of Glycobiology. I believe this to be important and essential. The product I offer to clients is from a natural plant source of eight of these glyconutrients. This is a broad spectrum and vital food supplement that I genuinely believe all of us should take. Almost everyone tested as needing these sugars has returned after three months feeling the benefits.

They appear to benefit sufferers from allergies, loss of energy, autoimmune conditions or any chronic sickness, or those who simply are not as vibrant and resilient as usual.

After three to five months some of the changes people are recounting are extraordinary. Guy Burgs, healer and meditation teacher has been using the sugars extensively in his healing practice with significant success, his mother was taken off HRT by her GP after only five weeks on the product. His diabetic sister-in-law showed reduced insulin requirements after only five days. My father, a natural sceptic, had only one functioning kidney working at 25 per cent, with dialysis being an almost inevitable next step. Five months ago, he was put on 1tsp of the glyconutrient powder per day. At his most recent checkup, his rather astounded French consultants informed him that his kidney was now fully functioning and likely to outlive him! As he had taken nothing else but the sugars it is clear that the body had healed itself!

Working in combination with flowers essences I have found them to be mutually supportive, significantly speeding up the healing process. By shifting old ingrained patterns from the body consciousness, the cells get the message of wholeness, the rest of the body listens, and acts appropriately to clear the roots of ill health. *Please see* Useful Addresses for Stockists.

Psychic Protection

From an ordinary reality perspective, what is termed psychic protection could be the need for protection in what is perceived to be a hostile environment, for example an office environment in which there is a very negative atmosphere with a lot of backbiting and undermining. Most people are instantly aware of this the minute they walk into a room. Realization is beginning to grow that the human body is not just a collection of solid systems and organs sealed within the skin, but a completely permeable organism, which the latest particle physics experts assure us is composed of pure energy, condensed and organized into different functions. This the ancient masters knew thousands of years ago as they were able to see energy. So this leaves us vulnerable to negative atmospheres or mental or emotional attack. We can also have our energy drained by certain people, this is of course generally completely unconscious. For example, how many of us have visited a hospital and come out completely drained?

There are many energy techniques to deal with this from; acupuncture, visualization and various forms of vibrational healing of which flower remedies have proved to be one of the most effective. This works as a preventative by infusing the auric field with protective vibrational energy, or as a healing after a problem by dispelling any negative influences from the system.

Remedies for Psychic Protection.

Angel of Protection Orchid (AK) Enhances communication with our guardian angels. This essence acts as a protective shield; it is particularly recommended for sensitive people exposed to hostile surroundings who therefore urgently need protection.

Aura Cleansing Cactus (AK) Cleanses and protects the aura, especially on the astral level. For people with a too porous energy field who have problems establishing boundaries between themselves and others. Helps to free the aura from foreign influences.

Crab Apple (B) Cleanses and purifies. Overthrows old negative patterns to help us develop new positive priorities. Use in situations in which we fear being contaminated by others.

Cuckoo Pint (HUB) Protects the spirit from invading entities, and quickly rebuilds vital energy when it has been lost. A great ally in soul retrieval.

Deadly Nightshade (HUB) Powerful third eye stimulant and psychic purge. Clears psychic interference. To be used as a single dose when required.

Larkspur (HUB) Strengthens and clears the aura, particularly the psychic gate. A good protection remedy it produces a vibration that casts out psychic parasites and external forces.

Lemon (AK) Cleansing and renewal. Removes old unwanted energies from the person.

Meditation: Stilling the Mind and Attuning to the Energy of the Flowers

In order to tune into the vibration of flowers and sense their subtle energies it's important to have some ability to still the mind in order to be able to receive the nuances that the flowers' message brings.

Meditation is practised in many philosophies, but to most of us it is associated with the Lord Buddha and has its roots in an ancient Brahmarual tradition born of Hinduism. In this tradition belief in rebirth, and its teachings (dharma) that Sansara (human suffering) can be transcended through individually working for liberation to the state beyond, known as Nirvana, is at the heart of this worldview.

Sacred texts and teachings were written which focused on understanding the mysteries of the universe, the interconnected continuum of life, man's relationship to the Divine, and of mediation as the discipline and concentration of the mind needed in order to achieve self-realization.

In Buddhism, 'attainment' through a form of sitting meditation is the bedrock of its philosophy. The Buddha, known as the awakened one, liberated himself through meditation, and it was his search for truth that led him to attain enlightenment. So when meditating one is tapping into an ancient and sacred lineage.

Gifted modern teachers such as Guy Burgs have benefited from this lineage and have been taught by significant living masters from Burma and Bali. He is known for his penetrating insight into the body/mind connection and its role in the disease process. Burgs purports that the first goal of meditation is to develop a harmonious and balanced mind by strengthening our mental capacity in preparation for higher concentration and meditation.

By working on developing awareness of the cellular and subtle anatomy systems and ensuring the base of the mind is strong, the body is able to provide support to shift stored dysfunctional energy that blocks accessing the high state of mindfulness. In this way a good foundation of energetic support is built in order to progress. Burgs talks of listening to the sound of the heart because it knows only truth and has a higher intelligence that can give the answer to all life's challenges, and suggests that through meditation, if you are able to quiet the mind, learn to listen and hear the silence of the heart you will find the answers already there.

When tuning into the subtle qualities of the flower essence it's helpful to have an experience of quieting the mind to be able to listen with the heart, as the flower's energy often connects with the chakra system, especially directly with the heart chakra, and communication begins from this point. This is beautifully illustrated by SSK in the plate section where she shows a colour impression of how she experiences the process of attunement and communication with orchids. This is how she receives the information and makes The Dancing Light Orchid Essences.

According to Burgs the following flower essences will facilitate the meditation processes.

Blue Dragon (Him E) Enhances single-mindedness. Pierces straight into the heart of any matter. Excellent for meditation.

Lotus (Him A) A spiritual elixir and aid to meditation. Calms the mind and improves concentration. Gently releases negative emotions, correcting imbalances. Aligns and balances the chakras by releasing, adding and directing energies to them. Clears the entire system of toxins. Balances, cleanses and strengthens the aura.

Red Lily (Aus B) The sacred lotus embodying Aboriginal spirituality. For daydreamers who are vacant and accident-prone. Balances spiritual and earthly aspects, enabling you to be grounded and practical while evolving spiritually.

White Nymph Waterlily (Aus L) For uncovering your deepest spiritual core. Brings tranquillity for reaching into the soul and using your Higher Self to integrate and respond to life from a universal rather than personal perspective. Helpful for spiritual practices such as meditation.

For meditation courses with Burgs *see* the resource list on page 401.

Proving the Essences Work

Some people argue that flower essences act as placebos, in other words that they make us feel better simply because we believe they are doing us good.

This does not explain, however, the numerous incidences in which flower essences have brought benefits to animals, babies and young children, who obviously do not know that what they are being given is 'supposed to' bring relief.

To test the placebo argument scientifically, Michael Weisglas PhD conducted a double-blind test on the Bach Flower Remedies in 1979. Neither he nor his subjects (who were suffering from depression) knew beforehand who had received and taken the remedies and who took the placebos. Results showed that those who were given the remedy mix reported experiencing a feeling of wellbeing, growth and self-understanding and acceptance, a better sense of humour and increased creativity, while those who took the placebo reported no significant change.

Dr Weisglas concluded that the effect of the remedies does not depend on the belief or faith of the user.

For at least 15 years I have conducted my own investigations into many flower essences. I have recently tested all the Bach remedies, the Orchids of the Amazon and most of the Californian remedies, as well as many others. During my teaching courses I typically give one particular anonymous remedy to ten people and ask each one to describe its properties. Without fail their descriptions of the essence, its qualities and place of action are accurate.

At their clinic in Delhi, Drs Atul and Pupa Shah (Aditi Himalayan Essences) combine flower essences with other natural therapies such as homeopathy, acupuncture, aromatherapy and crystal therapy. They claim great success in treating all kinds of problems including mental retardation, the problems of childhood, tumours, infertility and pregnancy problems, arthritis and any condition related to stress and tension such as irritable bowel syndrome, insomnia and hypertension. They have also found that flower essences work extremely well in conquering addictions. To prevent their own expectations from getting in the way of their assessments, the Shahs often ask other doctors to assess the improvements in their patients' conditions.

A Study on Radiation with Australian Bush Flower Electro Essence

Ian White, creator of Australian Bush Essences, concerned about the rising levels of radiation and the effect on mankind, has researched into finding solutions to this modern problem as well as other health concerns that are present in our society today. Electro, designed especially to target the increase in exposure to radioactivity and electromagnetic radiation is a unique combination essence developed by Ian in response to those particularly vulnerable to radiation. This combination has practical day-to-day implications, for instance whilst using mobile phones or working on computers.

It seems especially important to use it for our children when they are on their mobiles, chatting and texting, or on computers emailing their friends. Children, whilst they are still in the process of development are particularly affected by electromagnetic radiation.

In terms of large-scale exposure to radiation, one only needs to remember Chernobyl and the fact that 20 years on, the fallout from this disaster is continuing to affect millions of people as it spreads further throughout the food chain and water systems. Especially vulnerable were those countries in its direct path or in the vicinity of the winds that carried the fallout from that fateful day of nuclear power plant meltdown.

The republic of Belarus is one such place where the children are now heavily contaminated with high levels of accumulated radioactivity as a direct result of the Chernobyl accident. Australian Bush Flower Essences have been donating Electro Essence to the medical team in Belarus for The Radiation Rescue Program as part of their health rehabilitation programme. This specialist team of medical and health professionals take care of these children on a physical, emotional and psychological level, using many rehabilitation modalities. Recently the team has begun to utilize complementary therapies, and the medical team have discovered the treatment to be the most effective to date as it reduced the radiation levels by 25.3 per cent.

Then they tested Electro Essence on the same children and the results were amazing! The Electro reduced the radiation by 43 per cent in comparison with the control group which had only a 3.5 per cent reduction. These dramatic results were achieved after only two weeks on a dosage of 4 drops twice a day as opposed to the usual 7-drop dosage. Encouraged by these positive results the Belarus medical team are continuing to administer Electro to the children to find out just what the combination is capable of!

One of the ancillary effects of the Electro has been in treating the condition known as neurocirculatory dystonia syndrome. Its symptoms of fainting, headaches, heart palpitations, feeling as if the heart has stopped were very common when these children physically exerted themselves. However, There was a marked reduction in these symptoms when the children started to take Electro Essence, something that Ian attributed to the action of Waratah in Electro.

The other special ingredients in this combination are Mulla Mulla, which has the ability to address electromagnetic radiation, and Bush Fuchsia, which helps to protect and correct any imbalance that radiation causes. A further blend of Paw Paw, Fringed Violet and Crowea is included to help with blocking the absorption and storage of radiation in the body and helps to expel any already stored so as to keep the body's energy intact and the neurological systems functioning normally.

Generally Electro Essence is used to reduce electrical radiation emitted by meter boxes, overhead power lines, fluorescent lights and electrical equipment, especially televisions and mobile phones. It is useful in radiation therapy where it helps normal healthy cells withstand the radiation and recover after therapy. It has also been useful to negate earth radiation, found where ley lines cross and in houses where underground streams run.

Carrying a bottle of Electro offers protection from absorbing radiation from phones and computers for at least 6–9 months, at which point it then needs to be replaced with a fresh bottle. It is advisable to back this up with a 7-drop dosage at the end of the day, especially if the use has been excessive.

Women's Problems

The rising incidents of hormonal imbalance in women is another area of concern. It may be due to stress as well as being caused by the amount of hormones present in our drinking water due to the increased use of the pill.

These factors can upset a woman's delicate balance, and result in PMT, irregular periods, hot flushes, menopausal problems, weight gain and most worryingly infertility. Ian White has been working with the flower essence from She Oak and its benefit on the 25 per cent of infertility cases due to unknown causes. He has successfully addressed the infertility that stems from deep emotional causes, and he suggests, from his naturopathic stance, that dehydration of the uterus is the cause of infertility. He has discovered that She Oak is a tissue rehydrator which will correct the lack of hydration whilst simultaneously balancing the hormonal levels, regulating the cycle and the oestrogen/progesterone levels, which greatly enhances fertility and the ability to conceive. When working with She Oak, Ian and other flower essences practitioners had a 75 per cent success rate, and one Sydney doctor had a success rate of over 90 per cent!

She Oak is one of the ingredients of Woman Essence combination which is designed to harmonize hormonal imbalances, menstrual cramps, PMT, irregular menstruation, and weight gain and has proved to be very good at alleviating hot flushes and the general discomfort of menopause.

In hospitals in Brazil and Switzerland, She Oak and Woman Essence are being successfully used as an alternative to hormone replacement therapy without the increased risk of breast and cervical cancer.

Flower essences are so safe to use that it is one system of complementary medicine that can be given throughout pregnancy without fear of contraindications, in fact they are a tremendous support right from conception through to birth

She Oak is not the only Australian Bush Essence being used successfully in hospitals. Waratah Essence has had great success in Brazilian hospitals when used by cardiologists treating heart imbalances, ventricular failure and mitral valve insufficiency. It has also arrested the development of the condition of glaucoma, and in some cases it has even reversed it.

With kind permission of Ian White

Cancer Study Using Petite Fleur Range

According to Dr Judy Griffin who has taught in hospitals, hospices, and cancer support groups for the last 20 years, research with the Petite Fleur essences has provided some of the most powerful transformations with cancer, in particular Lilac flower essences, which she found released self-healing.

According to Judy's observations and deep understanding of the nature of the disease, cancer occurs on a subtle level, originating from a suppression of emotions and desires, when thought and feeling are suppressed in order to conform to the rules of society, and no alternative expression is substituted. When the emotions attempt to express themselves spontaneously, the intellect puts a block on them by a judgement call, this prevents dispersion of the natural expression of emotion which turns back in on itself. This negative energy collects in the chakras and expresses itself through an immune response, usually in an area of inherited or weakened immunity. As this energy becomes concentrated, abnormal tissue growth may occur forming tumours. However if the immune system is strong it will respond correctly by surrounding the area with an inflammatory response, attempting to protect it, so cutting off the negative energy feeding it.

The remedies appear to stimulate the electromagnetic charge that normally triggers the helper cells to replace killer cells, and produce new healthy tissue growth.

The success in reversing this situation lies in understanding the underlying suppression pattern and how it is expressed through the personality, this is where Petite Fleur Essences can help.

Suggestions for use from Judy in certain situations are as follows:

Blue Danube Aster To enhance antibody production and the power of encouragement.

Bouquet of Harmony Protection.

Christmas Cactus To reinforce strength and focus on what is right.

Dill To overcome the ego and fear of death.

French Lavender To appreciate every blessing and release the need for something very strong to 'kill' cancer.

Gaillardia To enhance macrophage bombardment of foreign matter, and determination.

Iberis Candytuft For self-healing and regeneration.

Indian Paintbrush For a success consciousness.

Lilac To release suppressed energy and let go of past hurts.

Old Blush Stamina.

Rose Campion For an inherited or predisposition for an illness.

Wandering Jew To overcome discouragement.

To any of these add from the following list for specific cancers.

Bone Cancer Crossandra, White Rose and Sunflower, then African Violet, Borage and Viridflora.

Brain and Neurological Cancer Stock, Echinacea, Verbena, then Iris, Azalea and Sweet Annie.

Breast Cancer Chamomile, Pansy, Zinnia and Lemongrass, then India Hawthorn, Crepe Myrtle, Wisteria.

Colon Cancer Garden Mum, Poppy, Periwinkle and Bougainvillea, then Black Mushroom, Dandelion and Rosemary.

Kidney/Prostrate Cancer Combine Marigold, Meadow Sage and Lilac, then Red Carnation, Pansy and Bachelor's Button.

Leukaemia (and bone marrow cancer) Jasmine, Dianthus, Red Malva, then Yarrow, Wandering Jew, and Anemone.

Liver Cancer Pink Geranium, Chamomile and Silver Moon, then Abate Anger, Bougainvillea and Wisteria. Add White Petunia for gallbladder.

Lung Cancer Babies' Breath, Spike Lavender and Thyme, then Poppy, Lantana and Morning Glory.

Lymphomas Soapwort, Salad Burnet and Tansy, then Lobelia, Cinnamon Basil and Curry.

Ovarian or Testicular Cancer Japanese Magnolia, Marigold, Ligustrum, then Self-Image, White Hyacinth and Bluebonnet.

Pancreatic Cancer Primrose, Moss Rose, Mexican Hat, then Mexican Bush Sage, Bouquet of Harmony and Yarrow.

Sarcomas from HIV: Silver Lace, Aquilegia Columbine, Lilac and Marigold.

Stomach Cancer Peppermint, Bamboo, Snapdragon, then Amaryllis, Lily and Magnolia.

Uterine Cancer Lilac, Marigold, Carrot and Ranunculus, then Madame Louise Levique, Marie Pavie, Marquis Bocella.

To help block metastasis and re-entry of cancerous cells Tansy, Lobelia and Snapdragon, then Dill, Yarrow and Wild Oats.

With kind permission of Dr Judy Griffin.

Another area of research involves observing the changes in the body's energy field after a patient has taken different essences. I asked Harry Oldfield to use his electro-scanning machine (which in effect photographs the aura) in an attempt to see what happened when certain flowers and their essences were introduced into my energy field. Looking at Figures 1 and 2 (*see* plate section) it seems clear that flower essences indeed have a measurable effect. This surely paves the way for further research into this field of investigation.

The Effect of Delph Essences on Brain Wave Patterns

Some fascinating research into the effect of essences on brain activity has been carried out on Andreas Korte Delph Essences by academic and medical doctors. The study was carried out by Dr Garcia (opto-crystallographic research) and Mr Haffelder (EEG research).

The EEG (electroencephalograph) monitors the brain's electrical activity by measuring the number of brain waves per second when someone is exposed to different stimuli. It is divided into to four frequency ranges:

The Waking state, BETA;

Relaxed concentration, ALPHA;

Full relaxation and dreams, THETA;

Deep Sleep state, DELTA.

In his Institute for Communication and Brain Research in Stuttgart, Gunter Haffelder has further developed the EEG measuring techniques for differentiating brain waves. He is able to analyse and order the frequencies recorded by the EEG into their individual vibration components and separate these vibrations more precisely by using spectrum analysis.

As a result, this is able to detect very subtle changes in brain wave vibration patterns, tracing them back to the original source of stimuli by using his unique Chromo-spectrum program to chart their course. The three-dimensional graphic representation depicts the interplay of the individual brain wave vibrations, divided by the right and left hemispheres, over a span of time.

Using this precise method, holding a bottle of Delph Essences in the hand was proved to be enough to change the individual brain wave patterns (*see* page 31 of plate section). This demonstrates that a change of consciousness can occur simply by holding a bottle of essence or flower remedy. This is something that highly-tuned individuals are already fully aware of but it refreshing to note that there are pioneers willing to explore, and find ways of recording these subtitles.

With kind permission of Andreas Korte

CHAPTER NINE

Conclusion

Medicine of the Future

It is time to realize that we must take responsibility for our own wellbeing. This is perhaps the hardest lesson to learn. How much easier it is to place the blame for our unhappiness and failing health onto something extraneous to ourselves.

In reality, how we feel is a reflection of the way we live our lives, how we think and act, and how we respond to other people and events. Anyone who is constantly anxious, irritable, frustrated or depressed should heed these signs and look inwards to discover the real source of his or her discomfort.

Flower essences enhance self-knowledge and understanding, helping us to take back responsibility for our own health, happiness and fulfilment. This is tremendously empowering. Knowing you are able to take care of yourself brings great rewards. As your confidence and inner strength flourish you will feel more in control of life and of your own destiny. Deep down you will experience a sense of safety and security that does not hinge upon anyone or anything else.

In the search for inner harmony we become aware that our own welfare is inextricably linked and interconnected to the wellbeing of everything else that exists in nature. Essentially what this means is that if we fail to respect and care for our home, the planet, and all living creatures, we in turn will suffer the consequences. Clearly, we can no longer afford to see ourselves as separate from everything around us.

As a race we seem to have forgotten this sense of duty and are threatening the very existence of life on earth. The World Conservation Centre in Cambridge, England, tells us that of the 270,000 species of flora inhabiting the earth, 41,000 are under threat. In Britain alone 27,000 flowering plants are struggling for survival, accounting for a staggering 10 per cent of the entire global population.

Survivors of certain indigenous peoples like the Native Americans and Australian Aborigines, who have a long tradition of living in harmony with the natural environment, regard the earth as a gift from the creator to be tended, nurtured and protected for future generations. Indeed, Native American peoples always think ahead for 'seven generations' to come before taking any action that may affect the course of nature. The wise men or spiritual leaders of such peoples are so alarmed at the way we are treating our home that they are finally breaking their silence and are now prepared to share their wisdom and knowledge with us.

The most dramatic instance of this occurred back in 1988, when Alan Ereira was in Colombia researching a documentary and chanced upon the Lost City of Taironas, as well as the descendants of those who had once inhabited this remarkable place – the Kogi. Breaking their 400 years of self-imposed isolation, the Kogi priests, or Mamas, asked him to film a message to give to the world, an urgent warning about the destruction of the planet: 'You are killing the earth and we must teach you how to stop.'

The Kogi live in the Sierra Nevada de Santa Marta, hidden away at the remote northern tip of Colombia. They call their home 'the heart of the world'. The Sierra could easily be described as a Garden of Eden. It is like the planet in miniature, boasting the whole spectrum of landscapes and climates. Its lush Caribbean coastline gives way to tropical rainforests, mountainous peaks and even desert in some areas. Every animal and every plant has its ecological niche in this equatorial zone.

Long ago the Sierra was inhabited by the Taironas – Indians who dressed in gold and lived in magnificent cities amid fields and orchards. They were all but annihilated by the Spanish conquistadors in the 16th century. Some survivors managed to flee up into the mountains where they settled and remained hidden from the world. The Kogi are directly descended from these people and are living proof that a harmonious existence with nature is neither fanciful, unrealistic or something that belongs to a bygone age. They are intelligent, sensitive people who dress in white; they walk barefoot to keep in touch with the earth. They see those of us in Western society as primitive and uncouth, calling us the ignorant 'Younger Brother'.

According to the Kogi story of creation, in the beginning was the mother. She is spirit, she is water, the life force that makes things alive – she is Aluna. The mother conceives all possibilities, everything that can be. Aluna gave birth to nine daughters or worlds, of which only one was capable of fertile growth, the earth. She then created humans to look after this world. But then 'Younger Brother' was created in the heart of the world. He was too dangerous to live among the Kogi, so he was given knowledge of machinery and sent far away across the sea. The Kogi believe that if Younger Brother returns to the heart of the world, then the whole world will die.

During the last 20 years the Kogi have witnessed what they regard as the return of Younger Brother. They have watched settlers move into the Sierra, forcing them to move higher and higher up into the mountains. They see the havoc these intruders are wreaking on the land by ripping down trees and digging up the earth, and this simply reconfirms their own beliefs.

As the elder brothers they see themselves as the caretakers or gardeners of the earth who are responsible for looking after nature. The philosophy of harmony underpins everything that they do. The Kogi Mamas, the priests, the enlightened ones, mentally work with Aluna to keep everything in balance, viewing themselves as guardians of the planet with a duty to keep humanity's spirituality alive. They believe that if we fail to be in harmony with ourselves we jeopardize not only our own health but also the harmony of the world. When this happens the life energy will become dangerous and uncontrolled. 'You will see new diseases appearing for which you have no medicine,' the Kogi tell us. They do not know about AIDS or BSE or the other diseases affecting people, animals and plants, but they know that new diseases have arisen because they are in touch with the deeper instincts of the world.

We do not have to have to look far afield to realize the truth in what the Kogi are saying. Throughout the world the indigenous countryside is slowly and insidiously changing. Fields and hedgerows, woodlands and forests are constantly being demolished to make way for new houses, roads and other 'developments'. We have allowed such changes to take place because of our desire for an increasingly materialistic society. We are now paying the price for our greed, as stress and pollution take their toll on our health.

We may feel that we are powerless to avert such global tragedy. However, just as we are capable of taking charge of our own wellbeing, so too can we take back responsibility for looking after the planet. Time and again it has been shown that when one person changes his or her perceptions and starts to see new solutions to personal and world problems, there is a knock-on effect, instigating a shift in the collective consciousness of the rest of humanity.

The Kogi do not see the death of the planet as an inevitability. They believe there are other options open to us. This is echoed by a Mayan elder priest, Apolinario – Achi Ijatz – fifth generation of the Kaqchikel lineage. As a time keeper of the sacred ancestral wisdom carried down by the Mayan elders since the Lemurian and Atlantean times, Apolinario recounts that the ancient Mayan prophecy predicts that as the 13th B'aqtun cycle draws to an end, a new cycle of great economic, social, political and spiritual change is occurring, with major climatic changes already being experienced. He emphasizes that if a rapid shift in our consciousness is translated into positive global action, the inevitability of the Mayan prophecy can be averted. The rediscovery of flower remedies has come at a time when it is most needed, as the future of the planet hangs precariously in the balance. Only by experiencing how they can help us to alter our perceptions and take back our own power will we really appreciate the value and importance of the world around us.

At the same time, flower essences appear to be offering us a way of finding inner balance by enhancing our wellbeing at a time when many other systems are failing us. In this respect they may truly be the medicine of the future.

USEFUL ADDRESSES

Consultations with Clare G Harvey
Centre for Complementary
and Integrated Medicine
14 Harley House
Brunswick Place
Upper Harley Street
London
+44 [0] 207 935 7848

Diploma Courses with Clare in Flower Essences
International Federation for
Vibrational Medicine
Middle Piccadilly Natural
Healing Centre
Holwell
Sherborne
Dorset DT9 5LW
+44 [0] 1963 250 750
info@vibrational
medicine.co.uk

Suppliers
UK
FlowerSense
19 London End
Beaconsfield
Bucks
HP9 2HN
+44 [0] 1494 671 775
Fax: 774
+44 [0] 1963 250 750
info@flowersense.co.uk
www.flowersense.co.uk
*Lines available: Australian
Bush, FES, Flowers of the
Orient, Aum Himalayan
Essence, Petite Fleur Essences,
Korte PHI, Masters Essences,
Soundwave Essences, 'Spirit of
Beauty' Skincare Range.
Also courses available.*

The Nutri Centre
7 Park Crescent
London W18 1PF
+44 [0] 207 436 5122
info@nutricentre.com
*Pacific, Australian Bush
Essences, Masters Essences
and Bach Healing Herbs*

Essence World
+44 [0] 1753 863214
helpme.now@essenceworld.com
*Findhorn, Gaia, Green Man,
Korte Phi, Sun Essences*

Suppliers Worldwide
France
Fleurs de Vie
Boite Postale 2
01170 CHEVRY
France
+33 4 50 426 232
www.fleurdevie.com

Spain
Milagra Flower Essences
Saladavicosa
E-11391 Facinas, Spain
+34 956 687 703

Italy
Spiritual Remedies
Via Settembrini 1
20124 Milano
Italia
+39 026 693950

Ireland
Clinic Support Centre
Unit 2
78 Walkintown Rd
Dublin 12
Ireland
+353 [0] 1 460 0203

USA
Flower Essence Pharmacy
6265 Barlow St
West Linn
Oregon OR 97068
USA
+1 503 650 6015/Fax: 6298
info@floweressences.com

Switzerland
Chruter-Drogerie Egger
Uiterstadt 28
CH -8202 Schaffhausen
Switzerland
+41 [0] 52 624 5030

Norway
Spiren a/s
Postboks 2527
N-7701 Steinkjer
Norway
+47 167 960

Japan
Masanobui Ogawa
A10S 8F, i-10-7 Higashi-
gotanda
Shinagawa-Ru
Tokyo 141-0022
Japan
+81 [0] 3 5447 7477
www.nature-essences.com

Producers
by country of origin of
essence

Australia
Australian Bush Essences
45 Booralie Rd
Terry Hills
NSW 2084 Australia
+61 2 9450 1388/Fax: 2866
info@ ausflowers.com.au
www.ausflowers.com.au

Australian Living Essences
Australian Flower Essences
Academy
Box 355
Scarborough
Perth
W. Australia 6019
+61 8 9443 5600/Fax: 5610
www.livingessences.com.au

USA
Alaskan Flower Essences
PO Box 1090
Victor, Montana 59875
+1 406 642 3670/Fax: 3672
afep@alaskanessences.com
www.alaskanessences.com

Dancing Light Orchid
Essences
[and Wild Divine]
823 Goldfinch Rd.
Fairbanks, Alaska, 99709
+1 907 455 8580
ssk@orchidessences.com
www.orchidessences.com

FES [Flower Essences
Society]
PO Box 459
Nevada City
CA 95959
USA
+1 530 265 9163
info@fesflowers.com
www.fesflowers.com

Master Essences
14618 Tyler Foote Rd
Nevada City
CA 95959
USA
+1 530 478 7655/Fax: 7652
mfe@mastersflower
essences.com
www.mastersessences.com

Petite Fleur Essences
8524 Whispering Creek Trail
Fort Worth
Texas 76134
USA

+1 817 293 5410/ Fax: 3213
+1 800 496 2125 (orders)
info@petitefl@aroma
healthtexas.com
www.aromahealthtexas.com

Desert Alchemy
PO Box 44189
Tucson, AZ 85733-4189
+1 520 325 1545/Fax 8405
Toll Free: (800) 736 3382
[USA & Canada]
info@desert-alchemy.com
www.desert-alchemy.com

Pegasus Products
PO Box 228
Boulder, CO 80306
USA
+1 303 667 3019/
+1 (800) 527 6104

Perelandra Inc.
Box 3603
Warrenton, VA 22186
USA
(800) 960 88806 [USA &
Canada]
+1 540 937 2153
www.perelandra-ltd.com

Star Peruvian Flower
Essences
130 W. Figueroa
Santa Barbara
CA 93101, USA
+1 805 962 7827/
Fax: 965 1619
www.starfloweressences.com

Gaia Hawaiian Essences
28 Glebelands Rd
Tiverton
Devon EX16 4EB
+44 (0) 1884 259 130
www.gaiaessences.com

Canada
Pacific Essences
PO Box 8317
Victoria BC V8W3R9
Canada

+1 250 384 5560
Fax 595 7700
info@pacificessences.com
www.pacificessences.com

United Kingdom
Bach/Healing Herbs –
The Flower Remedy
Programme
PO Box 65
Hereford
HR2 0UW
England
+44 [0] 1873 890 218
www.healingherbs.co.uk
*Healing Herbs remedies are
also available from most
healthfood stores and chemists
in the UK*

Bailey Essences
7/8 Nelson Road
Ilkley
West Yorks
LS29 8HH
England
+44 [0] 1943 432 012
Fax: 011
www.flowervr.com/
bailey.html

Sun Essences
Well Cottage
7 Church Road, Colby
Norwich
Norfolk
NR11 7AB
England
+44 [0] 1263 732 942
Fax: 251
enquiries@sunessence.co.uk
www.sunessence.co.uk

Sun Animal Essences
15 Connaught Road
Suffield Park
Cromer
Norfolk
NR27 0BZ
England
+44 [0] 1263 732 942
Helpline: 07000 785337

jane@sunessence.co.uk
www.sunessences
foranimals.com

Light Heart Essences
PO Box 35
Halesworth
Suffolk
IP19 0WL
England
+44 [0] 1986 785 216
info@lightheartessences.co.uk
www.lightheartessences.co.uk

Green Man Tree Essences
2 Kerswell Cottages
Exminster
Exeter
Devon
EX6 8AY
England
+44 [0] 1392 832 005
www.greenmantrees.
demon.co.uk

Habundia Flower Essences
Peter Aziz
PO Box 90
Totnes
Devon
TQ11 0YG
England
+44 [0] 1364 643 127

Soundwave Essences
Hertfield Cottage
Holwell
Sherborne
Dorset
DT9 5LM
England
+44 [0] 1963 232 04
soundwave@p-brune.
fsnet.co.uk

Purely Essences for Mother
& Baby
PO Box 227
Alton
GU34 9AN
England
+44 [0] 1892 724 244

info@purelyessences.com
www.purelyessences.com

Harebell Remedies
81 Main Street
St Johns Town of Dalry
Castle Douglas
Dumfries & Galloway
DG7 3UP
Scotland
+44 [0] 1644 430 607
ellie@harebellremedies.co.uk
*The essences are available by
mail order only.
SAE (or international reply
coupons) for catalogue appre-
ciated.*

Findhorn Flower Essences
Wellspring 31
The Park
Findhorn Bay
Findhorn, Forres
Morayshire
IV36 0TY
Scotland
+44 [0] 1309 690 729
Fax: 0933
www.findhornessences.com

France
Deva Laboratoire
BP 3
38880 Autrans
France
+33 [0] 4 76 953 587
Fax: 702
infofleur@lab.deva.com
www.lab-deva.com

Netherlands
Bloesem Remedies
Nederland
POSTBUS 6139
5960 AC HORST
+31 [0] 77 398
7826/Fax:7827
e-mail: info@bloesem-
remedies.com
www.bloesem-remedies.com

Amazon
Korte Phi
Rijksweg Zuid I
NL 5951
AM Belfeld
+31 [0] 77 475 4252
info@PHIessences.com
www.PHIessences.com

India
AUM Himalayan Essences
Himalayan Aditi Flower
Essences
Complementary Medicine
Research Centre
15(E) Jaybahrat Society
3rd Road
Khar West
Bombay 400 052
+91 22 648 6819
info@aumhimalaya.com
www.aumhimalaya.com

Himalayan Flower
Enhancers
PO BOX 43
Central Tilba
NSW 2546
Australia
+61 2 4473 7131
info@himalaya.com.au
www.himalaya.com.au

Flowers of The Orient
Middle Piccadilly
Holwell
Sherborne
Dorset DT9 5EL
+44 [0] 1963 250 750
clare@flowersense.co.uk
www.flowersense.co.uk

Retailers
UK Shops Supplying Bush
Essences and Master Mother
& Child Essences

Fresh & Wild
23 Ramillies Place
London
W1F 7LL

+44 [0] 207 025 6030
0800 917 5175
shop@freshandwild.com
Shops in Camden Town,
Clapham Junction, Notting
Hill, Soho, Stoke Newington
and Clifton (Bristol)

Revital Health
78 High street
Ruislip
Middlesex
0800 252 875
enquire@revital.com
Shops in London SW1 and
W1, Hounslow, Richmond,
Willesden, Beaconsfield,
Cambridge and Stratford-
upon-Avon.

Culpepers & Napiers
Bourton Bui Park
Bourton on the Water
Cheltenham
GL54 2HQ
+44 [0] 145 118 22681
mailorder@napiers.net
Shops in Edinburgh,
Glasgow, London, Salisbury,
Oxford, Chichester,
Cheltenham, Bristol, Bath
and Guildford.

Professional
Courses in Flower
Remedies
Australian Bush Workshop
Tours and Correspondance
Courses
Australian Bush Essences
45 Booralie Rd
Terry Hills
NSW 2084 Australia
+61 2 9450 1388/Fax: 2866
info@ausflowers.com.au
www.ausflowers.com.au

FlowerSense
19 London End
Beaconsfield
Bucks

HP9 2HN
Details on
www.flowersense.co.uk
+44 [0] 1494 671 775
Fax: 774
info@flowersense.co.uk

Living Essences of Australia
Box 355
Scarborough
Perth
W. Australia 6019
+61 8 9244 2073

The International Federation
for Vibrational Medicine
For two-year professional
course in International
flowers remedies
Courses are held at:
Middle Piccadilly Natural
Healing Centre
Holwell
Nr. Sherborne
Dorset
DT9 5LW
+44 [0] 1963 250 750
info@vibrational
medicine.co.uk

Sound of Light Workshops:
Soundwave Essences
Hertfield Cottage
Holwell
Sherborne
Dorset
DT9 5LM
+44 [0] 1963 23204
Soundwave@p-brune.
fsnet.co.uk
Also available at FlowerSense
*Sound of Light Treatments
available*: unique healing
modality, designed for cellular
repatterning.

Bach Healing Herbs – The
Flower Remedy Programme
PO Box 65
Hereford
HR2 0UW
England
+44 [0] 1873 890 218

Qualified IFVM
Flower Essence
Consultants and
Trainers
UK
Margaret Gallier
19 Maxwell Drive
Hazelmere
Bucks
HP15 7BX
+44 [0] 1494 717545
flowertalk2@hotmail.com

Dennis Smith
247 Glyn Road
Clapton
E5 0JD
cuinja@yahoo.co.uk

Jane Thrift
Duntish Lodge
Duntish
Dorchester
DT2 8SQ
07732 942 692 (mobile)
jane@1770.co.uk

Shelly Shiston
The Energy Centre
Orchard Oast
School House Lane
Horsmonden, Tonbridge
Kent TN12 8BN
07770 755 951 (mobile)
s.sishton@btopenworld.com

Beverly Downes
12b Earlswood Rd
Redhill
Surrey
RH1 6HE
07970 682 574 (mobile)
beverleydownes
@yahoo.co.uk

Sara Turner
Flowers 4 Health
95 Grange Rd
Ramsgate
Kent
CT11 9PB

07725 609 873 (mobile)
saraturner@msn.com

Yvonne Foster-Palmer
56 Sutton St
Flore
Northhampton
NN7 4LE
07803 562 248 (mobile)
yvonnefp@tiscali.co.uk

Pennie Telford
Tamarisk
North St
Westbourne
Emsworth
Hants
PO10 8SR
pennietelford@hotmail.com

Louise Larchbourne
11 The Springs
Witney
Oxon
OX28 4AS
+44 [0] 1993 200 602
louisej@fastmail.fm

Susie Black
Lulworth House
Bindon Rd
West Lulworth
Dorset
BH20 5RU
07973 273 625 (mobile)
lightning@ah-energy.
fslife.co.uk

Sharon Keenan
Homewood Chiropractic
Centre
30 Osborn Rd
Fareham
Hants
PO16 7DS
07899 095 279 (mobile)
sharonkeenanhere
@yahoo.co.uk
www.worldessences.com

Sian Pope
55 Woodacre
Port Marin

Portishead
BS20 7BS
07748 644 888 (mobile)
sianpope@netgates.co.uk

Laura MacKenzie
The Barn
Isle of Gigha
Argyll
Scotland
PA41 7AA
+44 [0] 1583 505 050
lauraongigha@yahoo.co.uk

Andrya Prescott
1 Deanery Place
Church Street
Godalming
Surrey
GU7 1ER
+44 [0] 1483 425 477
andrya@independent
midwife.com

Flor Taboada
Bradford on Avon
Wiltshire
+44 [0] 1225 868 554
flor_taboada@hotmail.com

Jacqui Meadows
Tyn-y-Celyn
Bwlchyddar
Llangedwyn
Powys
SY10 9LJ
+44 [0] 1691 648 784
info@crystal-union.com

David Corr
Corr Willbourn Research
and Development
Epsom
+44 [0] 1372 725 332
07941 061 795 (mobile)
david@corrwillbourn.com

Diane Green
Cedars
Old Church Rd
Lowers Ufford
Woodbridge
Suffolk

IP13 6DH
+44 [0] 1394 460 022
diane949@btinternet.com

Victoria Brudal
169 High street
Harham
Bristol
BS15
+44 [0] 1179 708 670
vicbru81@yahoo.co.uk

Shelagh Musoke
Orchard Cottage
2 Woodbridge Grove
Leatherhead
Surrey
KT22 7QJ
+44 [0] 1372 812 2281
shelagh.musoke
@btclick.com

Nora McDonnall
Tir Na Nog
Gratten St
Sligo
Ireland

Val Coutts
45 Springfield Gardens
Aberdeen
AB15 7RX
+44 [0] 1224 316 675

Rose Arnold
Longstone Cottage
Longstone Lane
Little Budworth
Cheshire
CW6 9ET
+44 [0] 1829 760 481
james@jamesarnold
photography.co.uk

Helen Ward
46 Barnfield Rd
Harpenden
Herts
AL5 5TQ
+44 [0] 1583 622 636
HelenFWard@aol.com

Tricia Mckinna
High Peak
Derbyshire
+44 [0] 1663 750 119
patricia.mckinna@virgin.net

Debbie Sellwood
PO Box 227
Alton
GU34 9AN
+44 [0] 1420 588 479
07940 821338 (mobile)
debbie_sellwood
@yahoo.co.uk

Isabel Appleby
19 Blendon Drive
Bexley
Kent
DA5 3AA
+44 [0] 208 304 2737
rayappleby@tiscali.co.uk

Mo Rawlins
Dilton Marsh
Wiltshire
+44 [0] 1373 859 469
mo@morawlins
freeserve.co.uk

Carolina Read
32 Craigwell Lane
Aldwich Grange
Bognor Regis
West Sussex
PO21 4AN
+44 [0] 1243 865 547
carolinaread@tiscali.co.uk

Anne Mari Clarke
61 Granville Road
Limpsfield
Oxted
Surrey
RH8 0BY
+44 [0] 1883 715 977

Gail Shaw
98 West Lane
Hayling Island
Hants
PO11 0EE
+44 [0] 1705 462 250

Meditation, Qi Gong and Messages from Water

Masaru Emoto
I.H.M. General Institute
East Side Blgs
IF, I-I-I-I Yanagibashi
Taito-ku
Tokyo 111-0052
Japan
+81 3 3863 0216
www.hado.net

Zhi-xing Wang
Chinese Heritage Institute
23 Penbridge Square
London W2 4DR
England
+44 [0] 208 771 6927
catherine@chineseheritage
institute.co.uk

Meditation by Guy Burgs
info: bookings
@justletgo.com
www. Justsitstill.com

Intuitive Clairvoyants

Peter Tadd
Foilnamuck,
Ballydehob
County Cork
Ireland
+353 [0] 2837540
chakra@indigo.ie

Laurence Harry
Canada USA
+1 250 729 7594
medium@laurence-harry.com
www.spiritual-medium.com

Kaitlyn Harvey
International Clairvoyant &
Spiritual life Coach
Birmingham
07738 706 226 (mobile)
lynn.365@virgin.net

Kirlian and Aura Photography

Harry Oldfield
The School of Electro-
Crystal Therapy
17 Long Drive
South Ruislip
Middlesex
HA4 0HL
England
+44 [0] 208 841 1716

Erik Pelham
Flower photographer and
Devic analyst
Cooks Farm
Tothill
Alford
Lincs
LN13 0NJ
+44 [0] 1507 450 382
Erik_pelham@yahoo.com

Professional Organizations

British Flower Vibrational
Essences Association
BFVEA,
London
WC1N 3XX
+44 [0] 1372 744426
Email: info@bfvea.com
www.bfvea.com

Resources

Ainsworth Homeopathic
Pharmacy
38 New Cavendish Street
London W1M 7LH
+44 [0] 207 935 5330

For supplies of blue dropper
bottles, glycerine,
Glyconutrients and
Maximol see FlowerSense
(address on page 396).

FURTHER READING

Edward Bach, *Heal Thyself* (C W Daniel Co. Ltd, 1931, reprint 1990)

Arther Bailey, *The Bailey Flower Essence Handbook*, (Arthur Bailey, 1997)

Vasudeva & Kadambii Barnao, *Australian Flower Essences for the 21st Century* (Living Essences,1997)

Julian & Martin Barnard, *The Healing Herbs of Edward Bach*, (Ashgrove Press 1988)

Julian Barnard, *A Guide to the Bach flower Remedies* (C W Daniel Co. Ltd, 1979; 1994)

David Bohm, *Wholeness and Implicate Order* (Routledge and Kegan Paul, 1980)

Barbara Ann Brennan, *Hands of Light* (Bantam New Age Books, 1988)

Barbara Ann Brennan, *Hands of Light* (Bantam New Age Books, 1988)

Jillie Collings, *The Ordinary Person's Guide to Extraordinary Health* (Aurum Press, 1993)

Deborah Craydon & Warren Bellows, *Floral Acupuncture* (The Crossing Press, 2005)

John & Farida Davidson, *Harmony of Science and Nature* (Holistic Research Company 1986–8)

Patricia Davis, *Subtle Aromatherapy* (C W Daniel Co. Ltd, 1991)

Lila Devi, *The Essential Flower Essence Handbook* (Hay House 1998)

Lila Devi, *Flower Essences for Animals* (Hay House, 2000)

Masaru Emoto, *Messages from Water 1&2* (Hado Kyoikusha Co Ltd, 2002)

Richard Gerber, MD, *Vibrational Medicine* (Bear and Co. 1993)

Kate Greenaway, *Language of Flowers* (F Warne, 1977)

Dr Judy Griffin, *Remember Me to the Roses* (Herbal Essence Publications, 1997)

Dr Judy Griffin, *Flowers that Heal* (Paraview Press, 2002)

Gurudas, *Flower Essences and Vibrational Healing* (Cassandra Press, 1996)

Clare G Harvey & Amanda Cochrane, *Healing Spirit of Plants* (Godsfield Press, 1999)

Clare G Harvey, *Flower Essences (Live Better Series)* (Duncan Baird Publishers, 2006)

Eliana Harvey & Mary Jane Oatley, *Acupressure* (Hodder and Stoughton, 1994)

Stephen W Hawkings, *A Brief History of Time* (Paul Banton Press, 1988; 1993)

Liz Hodgkinson, *Reincarnation – The Evidence* (Piatkus, 1989)

Steve Johnson, *The Essence of Healing* (Alaskan Flower Essence Project, 1996)

Anodea Judith, *Wheels of Light* (Llewellyn, 1987)

Patricia Kaminski & Richard Katz, *The Flower Essence Repertory*
(The Flower Essence Society, 1994)

Cynthia Athina Kemp Scherer, *The Alchemy of the Desert*, Second Edition
(Desert Alchemy, 1993)

Cynthia Athina Kemp Scherer, *The Art & Technique of Using Flower Essences*
(Desert Alchemy, 1993)

Andreas Korte, *Orchids, Gemstones and Their Healing Energies* (Bauer Berlag,
1993; Findhorn 1997)

Andreas Korte & Karin Huber, *Dolphins and Whales* (Gesundheit & Entwich-
lung, 1999)

Marion Leigh, *Findhorn Flower Essences* (Findhorn Press, 1997)

Jacob Liberman, *Light Medicine of the Future* (Bear & Co, 1991)

Lynne McTaggart, *The Field* (HarperCollins, 2002)

Sue Minter, *The Healing Garden* (Headline, 1993)

Dr Hiroshi Motoyama, *Theories of the Chakras* (Nati Book Network, 1981)

Masanobu Ogawa, *Flower Essences of the World* (Tokyo, 1999)

Harry Oldfield & Roger Coghill, *The Dark Side of the Brain*
(Element Books, 1988)

Sabina Pettitt, *Energy Medicine* (Pacific Essences 1993)

Drs Rupa & Atul Shar, *Aditi Himalaya Essences* (Aditi, 1993)

Machelle Small Wright, *Flower Essences* (Perelandra, 1988)

Smulkis & Fred Rubenfeld, *Starlight Elixers and Cosmic Vibrational healing*
(C W Daniel, 1992)

M Rudolf Steiner, *Cosmic Memory: Atlantis and Lemuria* (Harper & Row, 1981)

Titchiner, Monk, Potter & Staines, *New Vibrational Essences of Britain and
Ireland* (Waterlily Books 1997)

Dr Andrew Tresidder, *Lazy Persons guide to Emotional Healing* (Newleaf, 2000)

Gregory Vlamis, *Flowers to the Rescue* (Thorsons, 1986; 1994)

Ellie Web, *Harebell Remedies Handbook* (Harebell Remedies, 2001)

Nora Weeks, *The Medical Discoveries of Edward Bach Physician*
(C W Daniel Co. Ltd, 1940; 1983)

Ian White, *Australian Bush Flower Essences* (Findhorn Press 19991)

Ian White, *Australian Bush Flower Remedy Booklet* (Ian White, 1987)

Ian White, *Bush Flower Healing* (Bantam Books, 1999)

Ruth White, *Working with your Chakras* (Piatkus, 1993)

Bridge to Higher Consciousness (The Theosophical Publishing House, 1981)

'The Core Issue' – a web-based publication exploring specific healing issues
with flower essences

Index

Double Daffodil 125
Double Shirley Poppy 177
doubt 309
Douglas Aster 222
Douglas Fir 118
Down to Earth 154
Dragon Flower Cactus 235
Dream Machine 325
dreams 310
drug toxins (discharging) 298
Drum Stick 147–8
Dutchman's Breeches 235
Dwarf Fireweed 170
Dynamis Essence 73
dysfunctional pattern depro-
 gramming 309
dyslexia 298
dyspepsia (indigestion) 300
Dyssodia 191

E

Early Bloomer 265
Early Purple Orchid 131
ear problems 298
Earth Essence 288
Earth Mother Nurtures
 Environmental essence
 183
Earth Star Cactus 62
Easter Lily 200, 218–19
Easter Lily Cactus 235
Echinacea 137–8, 200, 253
Echium 61
Eclipse 232
Eclipse Spritz 285
Ecstasy 154–5
eczema 298, 352
Edelweiss 130
ego balance 310
Egypt, ancient 3
Elder 96, 103, 118, 130, 138
Elderflower 125
Elecampane 99
electrodynamic L-fields
 13–14
Electro Essence 73
Electro essence see Australian
 Bush Essences
electromagnetic pollution
 32–3, 275
electronic smog 32

electroscanning method
 (ESM), energy fields
 illumination 25
Elephant's Head 235
elimination 298
 see also digestive system
Elm 92
Emancipation 265
emergencies 310
Emergency Combination
 145
Emergency Cream 76
Emergency Essence 73–4
Emergency Mist 76
emotion(s) 306, 310
emotional body 23
emotional state, pre-
 cancerous 317–18
Emoto, Masaru 15–16
empathy 326
empowerment 326
emptiness 326
Enchanter's Nightshade 131
endocrine system 298, 360–1
 Australian Bush Essences
 363
 hormones 360, 361
 menopause 362–3
 pituitary 360
 pregnancy 361–2
 premenstrual tension 363
 problems, signs of 361
endurance 153, 310
energy 259, 298, 310–11
Energy Booster 334
energy fields/systems 12–25
 aura see aura
 capture methods 14–15
 chakras 17–21, 35, 154–5
 illumination 25
 subtle bodies 22–5
 TCM, Meridian system
 16–17
 water memory 15–16
energy imbalances 26–38
 illness and medication
 35–6
 inherited 36–8
 physical injury and 36
 pollution and see pollution
 shock-related 27–30
 social poisons and 33–5
 symptoms 27

Energy medicine 343–5
energy packets 12–13
The English Collection
 124–7
English Elm 119
Enhancement Spray 260
enlightenment 326
enthusiasm 311
environmental cleansing 298
Environmental Essences 289
environmental pollution 275
Environmental Protector
 334–5
Epipactis 62
Epstein Barr Virus 298
Ereira, Alan 394
Eros 100
escapism 311
Essence of the Edge
 Environmental Essence
 183
Essence pathway 345–6
Essence Skin Creams 64
essential oils 3
Eternal Youth 262
etheric body 22, 326
 shock effects 27, 29
 smoking effects 34
etheric envelope 24
etheric lining 22
Eucalyptus 119, 138
Europe 91–145
 Bach Flower Remedies see
 Bach Flower Remedies
 Bloesem Flower Essences of
 the Netherlands 142–5
 Deva Flower Elixirs see
 Deva Flower Elixirs
 Findhorn Flower Essences
 of Scotland 95–102
 Green Man Tree Essences
 117–23
 Habundia Flower Essences
 see Habundia Flower
 Essences
 Harebell Remedies see
 Harebell Remedies
 Light Heart Flower Essences
 see Light Heart Flower
 Essences
 Shamanic Essences 128–32
 Sun Essences 124–8
European Orchids 62

L

Labrador Tea 163, 178
Laburnum 120
Lace Flower 165
Ladies' Tresses 168
Lady Eubanksia 254
Lady's Mantle 97, 104, 125, 138
Lady's Slipper 163, 202
Lamb's Quarters 168, 178
language of flowers, history 6–8
Lani Ali'i 214
Lantana 250
Lapland Rosebay 170
Larch 93, 120
Larkspur 132, 202, 384
laryngitis 300
laughter (tonic) 314
Laurel 97, 130
Lavender 58, 104, 134, 202
Lavender Wand Penstemon 192
Lawson Cypress 120
laziness 314–15
Leafless Orchid 84
learning ability 315
Learning Skills 259
Le Language des Fleurs 8
Lemmon's Paintbrush 236
Lemon 60, 132, 135, 384
Lemon Grass 250
Lemuria 2–3
Leo Moon essence 158
Leopard Lily 236
Leo Sun essence 158
Let Go 156
Let Go and Trust 266
lethargy (mental) 315
Letting Go 111, 185–6
letting go 328
Lettuce 211, 273, 279
leukemia 390
Leyland Cypress 120
ley lines 33
Liard Hot Springs 290
Libra Moon essence 158
Libra Sun essence 158
Lichen Essence 75, 100
life
  learning lessons from 328
  rebuilding 330
Life Academy 77–86

Life Balance 116
Life Force 101
Life Force Cactus 63
Light Anchor 111–12
Light Being 101
Light Dancer 112
Lighten Up 172
Lighter Space 115
Light Hearted/Heart Light 184
Light Heart Flower Essences 108–17
  single essences 109–15
  therapeutic combinations 116–17
  'Truly Divine' combinations 115–16
  see also specific essences
Light Heart Space 116
Light Navigator 266
light quanta 12–13
Ligustrum 250
Lilac 104, 112, 120, 135, 170, 179, 192, 250, 389
Lily 250
Lily, Simon 117
Lily of the Valley 129, 138, 221
Lime 97, 120
Linden 135
Liquidambar 120
listening 315
  inner voice 328
Listening Heart 285
Little Flannel Flower 70
Little Rascal Mix 341–2
liver
  cancer 390
  disorders 300
Living Essences of Australia 77–86
  Australian Orchids 83–5
  Microvita Creams 85–6
  Russian Essences 85
  see also specific essences
Living Star Light 145
Living the Dream 112
Lobelia 255
Lobivia Cactus 236
Lombardy Poplar 120
loneliness 315
long-term Illness 300
loss/separation 320

Lotus 58, 135, 148, 153, 202, 385
  skin cream 64
Lotus flower
  ancient Egyptian use 3
  symbolism 7
Lotus Petals of the Heart 184
Louis Philippe 258
love
  ability to 315
  unconditional 332
  without end 88
Love Cactus 63
Love-Lies-Bleeding 202
Love Orchid 56
Loving Me, Loving You 112
Lucid Dreaming 184
Lucombe Oak 120
lung
  cancer 390
  imbalance 300
Lungwort 104, 125–6
lymphatic system 352–3
  disorder, signs of 353
  swollen glands 353–4
lymphomas 390

M

Machu Picchu, Andean Orchids 261–8
Macrocarpa 70
Macrozamia 80
Madame Alfred Carriere 258
Madame Louis Levique 258
Madia 202
Madonna Lily 129
Magenta Zeal Point Chakra 263
Maggie 258
Magic Healer 266
Magnolia 120, 250
Mai'a 214
Maidenhair Tree 60
Make Love 115
Malabar Nut flower 148
Mala Mujer 192
male balance 65, 315, 324
male empowerment 326
male inner strength 315
male power 259
male strength 266